# ADAM SMITH AND
# THE VIRTUES OF ENLIGHTENMENT

Charles Griswold has written the first comprehensive philosophical study of Smith's moral and political thought. Griswold sets Smith's work in the context of the continuing debate about the nature and survival of the Enlightenment, and also relates it to current discussions in moral philosophy.

Although Smith is often thought of today as an economist, he was in fact (as his great contemporaries Hume, Burke, Kant, and Hegel recognized) a seminal and insightful thinker whose work covers an immense territory including moral philosophy, political economy, rhetorical theory, aesthetics, and jurisprudence. Griswold explores such themes as the virtues, the emotions, ethical reasoning, impartiality, sympathy, the imagination, moral education, the rhetoric and methods of ethics, and skepticism. He demonstrates the relation between moral theory and political economy, and thus between the virtues and modern liberal and commercial institutions. Religious freedom, alienation, and political utopianism are also discussed.

Griswold argues that Smith is simultaneously a resourceful defender of the standpoint of ordinary life, a critic of the excesses of reformist theories, and an advocate of philosophy's reflective amelioration of human life. Throughout the book the author pays close attention to Smith's appropriation as well as criticism of classical philosophy, and to Smith's carefully balanced defense of a humane, enlightened, and decisively modern moral and political outlook.

This is a major historical and philosophical reassessment of a key figure in the Enlightenment that will be of particular interest to philosophers and political and legal theorists, as well as historians of ideas, economics, and political economy.

Charles L. Griswold, Jr., is Professor of Philosophy at Boston University. He has published in a variety of fields, including ancient philosophy, the Scottish Enlightenment, and German Idealism.

# MODERN EUROPEAN PHILOSOPHY

*General Editor*
Robert B. Pippin, University of Chicago

*Advisory Board*
Gary Gutting, University of Notre Dame
Rolf-Peter Horstmann, Humboldt University, Berlin
Mark Sacks, University of Essex

This series contains a range of high-quality books on philosophers, topics, and schools of thought prominent in the Kantian and post-Kantian European tradition. Nonsectarian in approach and methodology, it includes both introductory and more specialized treatments of these thinkers and topics. Authors are encouraged to interpret the boundaries of the modern European tradition in a broad way and in primarily philosophical rather than historical terms.

*Some Recent Titles:*

Frederick A. Olafson: *What Is a Human Being?*
Stanley Rosen: *The Mask of Enlightenment: Nietzsche's Zarathustra*
Robert C. Scharff: *Comte after Positivism*
F. C. T. Moore: *Bergson: Thinking Backwards*
Charles Larmore: *The Morals of Modernity*
Robert B. Pippin: *Idealism as Modernism*
Daniel W. Conway: *Nietzsche's Dangerous Game*
John P. McCormick: *Carl Schmitt's Critique of Liberalism*
Günter Zöller: *Fichte's Transcendental Philosophy*
Frederick A. Olafson: *Heidegger and the Ground of Ethics*
Warren Breckman: *Marx, the Young Hegelians, and the Origins of Radical Social Theory*

# ADAM SMITH AND THE VIRTUES OF ENLIGHTENMENT

CHARLES L. GRISWOLD, JR.

CAMBRIDGE
UNIVERSITY PRESS

PUBLISHED BY THE PRESS SYNDICATE OF THE UNIVERSITY OF CAMBRIDGE
The Pitt Building, Trumpington Street, Cambridge CB2 1RP, United Kingdom

CAMBRIDGE UNIVERSITY PRESS
The Edinburgh Building, Cambridge CB2 2RU, UK   http://www.cup.cam.ac.uk
40 West 20th Street, New York, NY 10011–4211, USA   http://www.cup.org
10 Stamford Road, Oakleigh, Melbourne 3166, Australia

First published 1999

Printed in the United States of America

Typeset in Baskerville 10.25/13 pt. in Penta/Aviion system [RF]

*A catalog record for this book is available from the British Library*

*Library of Congress Cataloging-in-Publication Data*
Griswold, Charles L., Jr. 1951–
Adam Smith and the virtues of enlightenment / Charles L. Griswold, Jr.
p.  cm. – (Modern European Philosophy)
Includes bibliographical references and index.
ISBN 0–521–62127–5. – ISBN 0–521–62891–1 (pbk.)
1. Smith, Adam, 1723–1790 – Ethics.   2. Ethics, Modern – 18th
century.   I. Title.   II. Series.
B1545.Z7G74   1998
192 – dc21          98–12845
                          CIP

ISBN 0–521–62127–5 hardback
ISBN 0–521–62891–1 paperback

To the Memory of my Father,
Charles L. Griswold, Sr.

The whole race is a poet that writes down
The eccentric propositions of its fate.
Wallace Stevens

# CONTENTS

# TEXTS AND ACKNOWLEDGMENTS

My references to Smith advert to the Glasgow edition of the given work. The texts and their abbreviations are as follows:

CAS    *Correspondence of Adam Smith.* Ed. E. C. Mossner and I. S. Ross. Indianapolis: Liberty Press, 1987.

EPS    *Essays on Philosophical Subjects.* Ed. W. P. D. Wightman and J. C. Bryce. Indianapolis: Liberty Press, 1982.

LJ    *Lectures on Jurisprudence.* Ed. R. L. Meek and D. D. Raphael. Indianapolis: Liberty Press, 1982. (2 sets, designated A or B)

LRBL    *Lectures on Rhetoric and Belles Lettres.* Ed. J. C. Bryce. Indianapolis: Liberty Press, 1985.

TMS    *The Theory of Moral Sentiments.* Ed. A. L. Macfie and D. D. Raphael. Indianapolis: Liberty Press, 1982.

WN    *An Inquiry into the Nature and Causes of the Wealth of Nations.* 2 vols. Ed. R. H. Campbell and A. S. Skinner. Indianapolis: Liberty Press, 1976.

When citing pagination of Smith's work I refer, unless otherwise noted, to *The Theory of Moral Sentiments.* For the sake of brevity I frequently omit "*TMS*" and simply supply the relevant citation.

The quotation from Wallace Stevens on the epigraph page to this volume is from "Men Made out of Words," in *The Collected Poems of Wallace Stevens* (New York: Knopf, 1989), p. 356. I have frequently supplied

xi

epigraphs at the beginning of chapters and sections. These are not necessarily meant to encapsulate the main point of the discussion in question. At times they offer a useful counterpoint or question to what I have to say, and in this and other ways are meant to enrich the discussion. Note that I have handled the familiar problem of gender and pronouns by using "he" and cognates for the most part, but I have occasionally reminded the reader, through the use of "she" and cognates, that the pronoun is generally to be heard in a gender-neutral sense. The alternatives are simply too distracting for the reader.

An earlier draft of parts of Chapter 1 and Chapter 4 (section 2) originally appeared as "Rhetoric and Ethics: Adam Smith on Theorizing about the Moral Sentiments," *Philosophy and Rhetoric* 24 (1991): 213–37. Section 1 of Chapter 4 draws on parts of my and D. Den Uyl's "Adam Smith on Friendship and Love," *Review of Metaphysics* 49 (1996): 609–37. As noted in that article, the discussion of love there principally originated with me, whereas the discussion of friendship (largely omitted from this book) originated with Den Uyl. Our collaboration led to many improvements throughout, and I am deeply grateful for it. Section 5 of Chapter 5 draws on my "Happiness, Tranquillity, and Philosophy," in *In Pursuit of Happiness*, ed. L. Rouner, Boston University Studies in Philosophy and Religion, no. 16 (Notre Dame, Ind.: University of Notre Dame Press, 1995): 13–37, reprinted (with significant emendations) in *Critical Review* 10 (1996): 1–32. A version of Chapter 7 (sec. 2) appeared in the *Journal of the History of Philosophy* 35 (1997): 395–419. Parts of Chapter 8 are drawn from "Nature and Philosophy: Adam Smith on Stoicism, Aesthetic Reconciliation, and Imagination," *Man and World* 29 (1996): 187–213. My thanks to editors and publishers of these journals and presses for permission to use previously published material.

I gratefully acknowledge grants and fellowships from the Earhart Foundation, the National Endowment for the Humanities, and the Woodrow Wilson International Center for Scholars that supported my work on this book. The Wilson Center provided me with a congenial "home" for over a year. The Center's excellent library staff and research assistants efficiently and cheerfully fulfilled my extensive requests for materials from the Library of Congress. Among the Center's hard-working research assistants I owe a particular debt of thanks to Benjamin Onu Arah.

Conversations and correspondence with Klaus Brinkmann, Charles Butterworth, Lawrence Cahoone, Harvey Cormier, Joseph Cropsey, Stephen Darwall, Edwin Delattre, Jorge Garcia, Ed Hundert, Drew Hyland,

Christine Korsgaard, Aryeh Kosman, David Lachterman, David Levy, Glenn Loury, Alasdair MacIntyre, Rudolf Makkreel, Jerry Muller, David F. Norton, Terry Pinkard, Robert Pippin, Henry Richardson, Christopher Ricks, Ian Ross, Lee Rouner, Jerry Schneewind, Roger Scruton, Allan Silverman, Wilfried Ver Eecke, and Stuart Warner have been very helpful to me in the course of my preparation of this book. Stanley Rosen patiently listened and skillfully queried on numerous occasions. He and others of these colleagues kindly commented on drafts of parts of the book as well. I am grateful to them all. D. D. Raphael commented critically and helpfully on the essay published in *Philosophy and Rhetoric*. William Galston offered an invaluable set of remarks on a paper that evolved into Chapter 2. Samuel Fleischacker generously commented in detail on various chapters and corresponded with me on things Smithean; I am grateful for his excellent suggestions. Donald Winch's detailed remarks on several chapters were of immense help. Douglas Den Uyl, Knud Haakonssen, and David Roochnik labored through various drafts, as well as queries from me about one topic or another, and I am forever in their debt. I thank the Press's anonymous referees for their useful queries and criticisms. I take full responsibility, of course, for whatever shortcomings this book may possess.

Terry Moore, executive editor at Cambridge University Press, patiently followed my progress on this project, lending encouragement and good counsel. I am much in his debt. I also thank Thornton Lockwood for preparing the Index, and Christie Lerch for her work as copy editor.

A draft of parts of Chapters 1 and 4 was delivered at an Eighteenth-Century Scottish Studies Society conference entitled "Glasgow and the Enlightenment." Drafts of parts of Chapter 2 were presented at a symposium sponsored by the American Philosophical Association (Eastern Division) and at a meeting of the International Hume Society. Drafts of section 2 of Chapter 7 were delivered as a Stranahan Lecture at Bowling Green State University, as a Bradley Lecture at Boston College, at Bryn Mawr College, at the Institut für die Wissenschaften von Menschen (Vienna), and at a joint annual meeting of the American Society for Eighteenth-Century Studies and the Eighteenth-Century Scottish Studies Society. Drafts of parts of Chapter 8 were delivered at Boston University, as part of a symposium (sponsored by the Boston University Center for Philosophy and History of Science in honor of Erazim Kohak) on the "Philosophies of Nature," as a Means Lecture at Trinity College (Hartford), and as an Olmsted Lecture at Yale University. I am grateful to these various audiences for their criticisms and comments.

A sabbatical leave from Boston University allowed me the time to pull the manuscript together. A semester at Yale University as Olmsted Visiting Professor was also helpful, and I thank Nori Thompson and Charlie Hill for their hospitality and good conversation during my stay in New Haven. I am grateful to the students in my Smith seminars at both Boston University and Yale for their excellent questions.

My greatest debt is to my family. Katie, Lisa, and Caroline Griswold encouraged my musings about Smith and patiently endured my absences at the office while I labored. Steven Griswold has been a constant companion in philosophical conversation and offered invaluable comments on the Introduction and Epilogue. Extended arguments with my father many years ago sparked a lifelong interest in the issues central to this book, and I owe much to his thoughtful provocations. A book is small recompense for such affection and friendship; let it be an expression of my gratitude.

# INTRODUCTION

Directly related to modern man's pride are his *irony* about himself, his awareness that he must live in a historicizing and twilight atmosphere, as it were, his fear that in the future he will be quite unable to preserve his youthful hopes and vigor. Here and there some go further, they become *cynical*, quite literally justifying the course of history, indeed the evolution of the world, for modern man's convenience according to the cynical axiom that everything was destined to be precisely what it now is. Men had to become what they now are and not something else, and against this "necessity" there can be no rebellion. The comfort afforded by this kind of cynicism is a refuge for those who cannot bear to live ironical lives.

Friedrich Nietzsche[1]

## 1. ENLIGHTENMENT'S SHADOWS

We find ourselves in a curious situation. Never in history have so many enjoyed so high a level of material prosperity, political and economic liberty, and peace and security. The benefits of the flourishing arts, sciences, and humanistic disciplines are within reach of an unprecedented

---

1 "History in the Service and Disservice of Life," trans. G. Brown, in *Unmodern Observations*, ed. W. Arrowsmith (New Haven: Yale University Press, 1990), p. 130.

number of people. We may praise the strict virtues of ancient Sparta or the high artistic and philosophical accomplishments of ancient Athens, but who among us would willingly return to either, or to any of the great medieval cities, let alone to a less distinguished polis? We are the children of the Enlightenment, and scarcely any of us would gladly claim a different patrimony. Life in premodern society strikes us as thoroughly undesirable. So widely shared is this conviction that in extraordinary numbers the peoples of the globe vote for it with their feet. The march of the liberal Enlightenment seems irresistible. It has all but destroyed its fraternal enemy, the illiberal Enlightenment fathered by Marx, and premodern cultures collapse under its advance with astonishing speed.[2]

And yet scarcely any of us still defend our patrimony without heavy qualifications. Criticism of the modern age and the Enlightenment from which it stems is a staple of our intellectual and spiritual lives, within academia and outside it. The "crisis" literature of the last century and a half remains a prominent part of contemporary rhetoric, especially among those who would seem to have least need for it. The period's greatest philosophers – Husserl, Heidegger, and Nietzsche among them – and legions of others have distinguished themselves in part by announcing and diagnosing our illness.[3] It may be that the future is always so opaque and the fear of loss so great that, given half a chance, the imagination will brood on the present with high anxiety. Yet our continuing failure of confidence, and our general despair about who we are in the midst of our plenty, cannot be dismissed with a psychological observation.

2 When I speak of "liberalism" I refer to the "classical liberalism" of the sort generally shared by the founders of the tradition rather than to the contemporary American credo currently contrasted with "conservatism." In using the term "liberal" to characterize a political regime, I refer to a regime whose institutions are structured so as to protect in reasonable measure the freedoms of religion, speech, assembly, accumulation and possession of property, and emigration (I do not mean the list to be a complete one). A "liberal regime" is thus one which holds that citizens are to be left relatively free to pursue their vision of the good life, within constraints of justice.

3 M. Horkheimer and T. Adorno, *Dialectic of Enlightenment*, certainly ranks as an important contribution to the genre, especially in its focus on the roles of technology, domination, objectification, and on the self-destruction of the Enlightenment. The historical context in which the book was written (namely, the horrors of the Second World War) helps make its point. The debate about what "enlightenment" comes down to is not new, of course; as James Schmidt reminds us, it is well represented in the eighteenth-century German context. See his introduction to the volume he edited, *What Is Enlightenment? Eighteenth-Century Answers and Twentieth-Century Questions* (Berkeley and Los Angeles: University of California Press, 1996), pp. 1–44.

We do find ourselves faced with unsettling questions, some especially characteristic of our period and others *quaestiones perennes* that now press with particular force. I began these introductory comments with the pronoun "we"; it is very often used in philosophy, especially in ethics, as it is in politics. But the question might immediately be put to my use of the word, whether parochialism does not lurk just beneath the surface. True, "we" enjoy a high level of material prosperity, liberty, and other treasured goods, but how many of our brethren toil in misery just outside the palace door? Is there a sense in which their misery is necessarily the price of our happiness?

Put the nasty suspicion underlying these questions another way: Might the seeds of our manifold troubles also, paradoxically, be the very same seeds that have yielded the fruits we enjoy? Might the world be structured in such a way that its flourishing is the natural cause of its decay, thanks to some relentless "invisible hand" that, like the divinities invoked by the ancient tragedians, transforms the good into the bad and even the bad into the good? Or, stated summarily with reference to several widely discussed contemporary developments, Might the apparent devolution of liberty into spontaneity, of pluralism into relativism, of knowledge into technology and thence into the self-vitiating mastery of nature, of science into a "worldview" produced by a given historical milieu, of culture into vulgarity, of reason into imagination and then into fantasy – in short, the devolution of the Enlightenment into what is widely termed "postmodernism" – itself be a natural consequence of the very premises of the Enlightenment?[4] And if this disturbing thought persuades, where to go from here?

The answer to this last question depends in part on how we analyze the virtues and vices of the Enlightenment. Accounts of the rise and fall of the modern Enlightenment usually place Bacon and Descartes at the birth and Nietzsche at the demise of the movement. One well-established camp offers a critique of the Enlightenment by holding that the period is to be understood as a fundamentally mistaken rejection of ancient and

---

4 J.-F. Lyotard remarks that at the core of "postmodernism" is a skepticism about the ability of philosophy to ground or "legitimate" itself, to provide what Lyotard calls a "metanarrative," or, in the current jargon, a "story" that explains and justifies the enterprise in question. Hence Lyotard's remark: "I define *postmodern* as incredulity toward meta-narratives. This incredulity is undoubtedly a product of progress in the sciences: but that progress in turn presupposes it." This is just to say that scientific progress is self-vitiating. *The Postmodern Condition: A Report on Knowledge*, trans. G. Bennington and B. Massumi (Minneapolis: University of Minnesota Press, 1989), pp. xxv and xxiv.

medieval philosophy. Partisans of this camp would have us secure the future by recovering the earlier phases of the Western tradition. Alasdair MacIntyre and Leo Strauss are among the best-known proponents of this approach, and we may think of them as oriented by the now traditional "quarrel between the ancients and the moderns." As the title of Mac-Intyre's *Whose Justice? Which Rationality?* intimates, however, some difficult questions await any effort to turn back.[5] Among those who in some sense wish to return to the Greeks, there is remarkable consensus that the political offspring of the Enlightenment are, at least in good part, worth preserving. (I refer to liberal institutions and political arrangements.) Enlightenment liberalism, however, is difficult to found on Aristotelian, let alone Platonic, moral theory. How can the older, virtue-centered tradition be made to mesh with modern political, jurisprudential, and economic practice?[6]

Another pressing difficulty with any return to the ancients is that, particularly in Aristotle, talk about human excellence or virtue seems tied to a teleological biology, and virtually no one today defends such a biology against the claims of modern science. Hence in MacIntyre, for example, the arguments in favor of an appropriation of classical "virtue" are explicitly severed from any moorings in a teleological biology.[7] This comes down to something like preserving Aristotle while replacing his notion of "nature" with that of "culture," and perhaps finally "history." Similar results arise given what is usually taken as the near impossibility of reviving anything like Platonic, Aristotelian, or indeed Stoic metaphysics. It then becomes doubtful that a modern revival of ancient

---

5 A. MacIntyre, *Whose Justice? Which Rationality?* (Notre Dame, Ind.: University of Notre Dame Press, 1988).

6 Consider MacIntyre's verdict: "Modern systematic politics, whether liberal, conservative, radical or socialist, simply has to be rejected from a standpoint that owes genuine allegiance to the tradition of the virtues; for modern politics itself expresses in its institutional forms a systematic rejection of that tradition." *After Virtue*, 2nd ed. (Notre Dame, Ind.: University of Notre Dame Press, 1984), pp. 254–5.

7 See *After Virtue*, p. 196 and context, and p. 148. Also B. Williams, *Ethics and the Limits of Philosophy* (Cambridge, Mass.: Harvard University Press, 1985), pp. 44, 120. For a fine discussion of the Enlightenment critique of teleology, see S. Salkever, *Finding the Mean: Theory and Practice in Aristotelian Political Philosophy* (Princeton: Princeton University Press, 1990), pp. 21–36. For general discussion of the difficulties of returning to the ancients, consider P. Simpson, "Contemporary Virtue Ethics and Aristotle," *Review of Metaphysics* 45 (1992): 503–24; Williams's remark that "in many substantial respects . . . no modern discussion [of ethics] can share the outlook of an ancient writer," *Ethics*, p. 49; S. Hampshire, *Two Theories of Morality* (Oxford: Oxford University Press, 1977), pp. 54–7; and J. Casey's remarks on pp. viii–ix of *Pagan Virtue* (Oxford: Clarendon Press, 1990).

thought can depend on any premodern (specifically, any pre-Humean or pre-Kantian) "metaphysics." This in turn suggests that ancient *philosophy* cannot be revived. A now classic criticism of such critiques of modernity maintains that they either accept much more of the ancients than can possibly be justified by contemporary standards or accept so little as to be, willy-nilly, exponents of a thoroughly anti-ancient modernism.[8] Any effort to revive the ancients begins to look like an exercise in nostalgia.

A second, equally well-established camp takes a different tack. In contrast to the critique of the Enlightenment that turns on a rivalry between ancients and moderns, more sweeping versions of the critique – such as those by Nietzsche, Heidegger, and Richard Rorty – see the Enlightenment as in some respects an extension of Platonism, with Christianity understood as carrying through the basic tenets of Platonism. The story is told variously, one thinker stressing the continuity of the theme of "self-empowerment" and the "revenge against time," another the dominion of "subjectivity" culminating in the eclipse of *Sein* (Being), and yet another the continuous variations on the theme of the mind as the "mirror of nature." These global criticisms of the Enlightenment come close to (and often explicitly affirm) a rejection of "philosophy" as such, at least insofar as the term denotes an effort to articulate "how things really are."[9] If the ancients and moderns are fundamentally one, if the Enlightenment is Platonism by other means, then the return to

8 C. Larmore argues that MacIntyre "is a pluralist, *malgré lui*," where "pluralism" entails the acknowledgment of "the existence of rationally irresolvable moral conflicts" so characteristic of modernity. *Patterns of Moral Complexity* (Cambridge: Cambridge University Press, 1987), pp. 39, 38. In their "Toward *Fin de siècle* Ethics: Some Trends," S. Darwall, A. Gibbard, and P. Railton note the self-reflexive problem faced by MacIntyre and Williams *qua* moral theorists and refer to them as "les théoriciens malgré eux." In *Moral Discourse and Practice*, ed. Darwall, Gibbard, and Railton (New York: Oxford University Press, 1997), p. 32. Similarly, in the course of a searching critique of Leo Strauss, S. Rosen remarks that Strauss's "conception of [the nature of] classical philosophy was inadequate because at bottom Nietzschean or modern, and therefore postmodern." *Hermeneutics as Politics* (Oxford: Oxford University Press, 1987), p. 123 (interpolation in the original).

9 At this writing, the latest major global critique of the Enlightenment is J. Gray, *Enlightenment's Wake: Politics and Culture at the Close of the Modern Age* (London: Routledge, 1995). In his preface Gray writes that the Enlightenment project "was self-undermining and is now exhausted" (p. viii). On pp. 151–2 Gray rejects MacIntyre's effort to return to a premodern tradition: "There can, in my view, be no rolling back the central project of modernity, which is the Enlightenment project, with all its consequences in terms of disenchantment and ultimate groundlessness. The modernist project of Enlightenment, though it broke with premodern, classical and medieval, thought at many points, was also continuous with it in its universalism and its foundationalist and representationalist rationalism" (p. 152).

the post-Socratic ancients is as pointless as satisfaction with modernity is unwarranted.

This sweeping critique of the Enlightenment faces its own quandaries. It undermines key Enlightenment moral and political notions, such as that of "natural rights," a phrase intimately tied to the political as well as philosophical defense of modern liberal regimes. Today the vocabulary of "rights" remains omnipresent but without the now strange-sounding qualification "natural."[10] How are we to retain (we again ask) the praiseworthy political fruits of the Enlightenment while rejecting the philosophical doctrines from which they grew? A formidable problem concerns the standpoint from which the obituary of the "Western tradition" is itself uttered. The problem is famously illustrated in Nietzsche. His announcements about the passing of the whole tradition since Plato struggle with the self-reflexive paradox generated by the fact that such announcements about the "death of philosophy" tend themselves to be articulated in the language of the very tradition being rejected.[11] Having cut out the ground from beneath their feet, global critics of modernity seem left with nothing to stand on. To change metaphors, we are told that we cannot go backward and cannot remain where we are, but the march forward seems to lead into darkness.

The two camps of critics are in sharp disagreement as to what the problem of the Enlightenment consists in exactly. We may safely say, however, that the learned and passionately stated obituaries of the modern age urged by both leave us with the pressing challenge of deciding what to do next, whether to rescue *some* version of premodern thought or whether to abandon the entire effort of justifying the assumptions and projects of an epoch. No matter which direction we take in the debate, we seem blocked by the inevitable difficulties. Correspondingly, the question of the foundations of Enlightenment liberalism (if talk

10 For a survey of the current debate about rights, see W. A. Galston, "Practical Philosophy and the Bill of Rights: Perspectives on Some Contemporary Issues," in *A Culture of Rights*, ed. M. Lacey and K. Haakonssen (Cambridge: Cambridge University Press, 1991), pp. 215–65. Cf. the dismissal of the notion of (natural) rights in R. Rorty, *Contingency, Irony, and Solidarity* (Cambridge: Cambridge University Press, 1989), p. 84, and in MacIntyre, *After Virtue*, p. 69.

11 The problem is discussed by MacIntyre in *Three Rival Versions of Moral Enquiry: Encyclopaedia, Genealogy, and Tradition* (Notre Dame, Ind.: University of Notre Dame Press, 1990), ch. 2 ("Genealogies and Subversions"). In *After Virtue* (p. 239) MacIntyre notes that although Nietzsche is the "ultimate antagonist of the Aristotelian tradition," it turns out "that in the end the Nietzschean stance is only one more facet of that very moral culture of which Nietzsche took himself to be an implacable critic." This is in effect another "malgré lui" objection (see n. 8 to the present chapter).

about "foundations" be accepted at all) is now wide open and is certainly the subject of vigorous debate. The net result is a widespread queasiness about the survival of our enlightened age. We sense that we have spent our moral and intellectual inheritance and lack the means to generate it anew.

An age of self-doubt has this advantage: it is fertile territory for philosophy. When the ground under our feet feels like terra firma, philosophy tends to degenerate into scholasticism; when it shakes, there follow not only a great deal of madness but also opportunities for true philosophical mania. Self-examination need not signal the ending of an epoch; it may, indeed, signal renewal. The owl of Minerva spreads its wings only at dusk, as Hegel remarked, but dusk is eventually followed by a new day that may provide nothing less than new light on the same ground.

We must make certain that we have mined that ground thoroughly before declaring it exhausted. Are there overlooked or misunderstood resources for self-criticism and justification in the Enlightenment itself, especially ones that also provide for the preservation of desirable aspects of ancient thought? If so, we should examine them with care. Adam Smith is one such resource.

## 2. ENLIGHTENMENT AND COUNTER-ENLIGHTENMENT IN THE WORK OF ADAM SMITH

It is Adam Smith's legacy, in part, that we now enjoy as well as question. He was a key figure in the Scottish Enlightenment and tied to the French and American Enlightenments. These Enlightenments are crucial chapters in the story of modernity. Smith's standing and influence were established early on. The publication of *The Theory of Moral Sentiments* in 1759 quickly made him famous, and not long afterward the work was translated (several times) into both French and German. It went through six editions in English during his lifetime. The book earned him high praise and respect from thinkers of the stature of Hume, Burke, and Kant. Smith's only other published book, *An Inquiry into the Nature and Causes of the Wealth of Nations* (first published in 1776), was similarly received and won the careful scrutiny of Bentham, Hegel, and Marx, among many others.[12] Gibbon paid tribute to Smith's work on the evo-

---

12 The six editions of *TMS* were published by Smith in 1759, 1761, 1767, 1774, 1781, and 1790, and editions of *WN* in 1776, 1778, 1784, 1786, and 1789. The number of editions

lution of society; Boswell, Adam Ferguson, William Robertson, John Millar, Lord Kames (Henry Home), Hugh Blair, Dugald Stewart, and Voltaire learned a great deal from him; the list of admirers could go on and on.[13] *The Wealth of Nations* clearly influenced thinkers in the American Founding and has served as a touchstone in scholarly discussions about the workings and defensibility of liberal economic arrangements ever since.[14] Scientists and philosophers of science have noted the contribution of Smith's work, as have sociologists.[15]

In spite of his influence and fame, Smith's fate has for some time resembled that of Epicurus. Epicurus became known as an "Epicurean," and so as an advocate of a hedonism at odds with his true teaching. Today Smith's name is widely known and ceremonially cited in support of certain economic and political programs, but his teachings are rarely studied with care by those enlisting him in their cause.

published during his lifetime indicates the popularity of the works. On the reception of *TMS*, see again the editors' Introduction, pp. 25–34. For this and other abbreviations of Smith's works used in my citations and notes, see "Texts and Acknowledgments" at the front of the present volume. For Bentham's response to Smith, see *CAS*, app. C (pp. 386–404). For further general discussion, see J. H. Hollander, "The Founder of a School," in J. M. Clark et al., *Adam Smith, 1776–1926* ([1928] rpt., New York: Kelley, 1966), pp. 22–52, and M. Palyi, "The Introduction of Adam Smith on the Continent," in ibid., pp. 180–233. For discussions of Smith's reception in Germany, France, the United States, Italy, Russia, India, Japan, and China, see the essays collected in H. Mizuta and C. Sugiyama, eds., *Adam Smith: International Perspectives* (New York: St. Martin's, 1993). On the relation between Smith and Hegel, see N. Waszek, *The Scottish Enlightenment and Hegel's Account of "Civil Society"* (Dordrecht: Kluwer, 1988).

13 See Smith's letter to Edward Gibbon of Dec. 10, 1788, *CAS*, p. 317 (as well as the editor's note); ch. 10 ("Smith and Gibbon") of C. R. Fay, *Adam Smith and the Scotland of His Day* (Cambridge: Cambridge University Press, 1956). Smith's influence appears in some unexpected quarters. For some indications of Smith's influence on Emerson, for example, see J. C. Gerber, "Emerson and the Political Economists," *New England Quarterly* 22 (1940): 336–57. On pp. 345–6 Gerber notes that Emerson's praise of *WN* as a "book of wisdom" suggests "that, on the whole, the Emerson, Emerson considered Adam Smith one of the great men of the ages, whose controlling principles are intuitively perceived." I. Ross comments that "Smith had his first success as a man of letters, and became famous as a contributor to the European Enlightenment, with the publication of his ethics lectures, new-cast as *TMS*, in 1759." *The Life of Adam Smith* (Oxford: Oxford University Press, 1995), p. xxi.

14 Thomas Jefferson praised Smith's *WN* highly in his letter to J. Norvell of June 14, 1807. See *Thomas Jefferson: Writings*, ed. M. D. Peterson (New York: Viking [Library of America], 1984), p. 1176.

15 T. H. Huxley's high opinion of Smith is cited in K. L. Brown, "Dating Adam Smith's Essay 'Of the External Senses,'" *Journal of the History of Ideas* 53 (1992), p. 337, n. 22. Cf. C. Darwin's reference to Smith in *The Descent of Man* (London: J. Murray, 1871), vol. 1, p. 81. See also A. Swingewood, "Origins of Sociology: The Case of the Scottish Enlightenment," *British Journal of Sociology* 21 (1970): 164–80.

He is seen solely as an economist, to the exclusion of his work in ethics, moral psychology, jurisprudence, rhetoric, and belles lettres, as well as political, economic, and intellectual history. Even worse, he is seen as an economist of a particular ideological bent. In short, he tends now to be known just as an advocate of crude laissez-faire capitalism and, to add insult to injury, of a capitalism inseparable from imperialism and colonialism.[16]

Given the breadth of Smith's work, his interest in political economy rather than economics alone, his insistent moral reservations about the unfettered operation of the free market, and his critique of imperialism, colonialism, and various forms of oppression – including slavery – these misinterpretations of Smith are striking.[17] Smith knew the Western philosophical tradition well. He was versed in ancient and modern languages, history, rhetorical theory, science, jurisprudence, religion, and literature, and his learning is evident throughout his work. It would be the envy of anyone claiming a liberal education. Above all, these familiar misinterpretations occlude the fact that Smith was first and foremost a philosopher, educated in philosophy by a great philosopher (Francis Hutcheson), close friend of one of the best philosophers in the history of Western thought (David Hume), and widely read and admired by philosophers. While in France he made the acquaintance of a number of the *philosophes*.

Many of the great themes of the Enlightenment, themes that inspire the modern age, are promulgated by Smith. To be sure, if one may speak of "the Enlightenment" in the singular at all, it is of a quarrelsome family. Critics of the movement were part and parcel of it from the start, and Smith himself may in some respects be counted among them. We may nonetheless say with confidence at the outset that when this period of several centuries is viewed from the general perspective I am adopting in

16  "Capitalism" is not a word that Smith uses, and in the body of the text when discussing his views I shall use expressions that are less encumbered with associations, less anachronistic, and more congenial to his own outlook.

17  These misconceptions are largely dead among the scholars who have studied Smith's work, and the last twenty years or so have witnessed a remarkable outpouring of work on Smith, including, increasingly, studies by philosophers. G. Harman remarks that he believes that *TMS* "is one of the great works of moral philosophy" and then goes on to note: "it is perplexing that Adam Smith's ethics should be so relatively unread as compared with Hume's ethics when there is so much of value in Smith." See "Moral Agent and Impartial Spectator," the Lindley Lecture, published by the Department of Philosophy, University of Kansas (1986), pp. 13–14. M. Nussbaum refers to *TMS* as "a central inspiration for the project" of her recent *Poetic Justice: The Literary Imagination and Public Life* (Boston: Beacon, 1995), p. xvi.

these introductory comments, Smith is a supporter of the Enlightenment.[18]

To begin with, Smith seeks to free us from war and faction. At least
since Hobbes, it has become axiomatic that disagreement, conflict, and
war are basic features of human political life that must orient any viable
political theory. In contrast to much of ancient political theory, the moderns often regard as fundamental the absence of agreed-upon norms for
the "good life." For the moderns, we begin with the potential for disharmony, not with the fact of consensus.[19] The primacy of conflict contributes to the special status of justice in much modern political theory,
including in Smith. Conflict is taken to be ultimately reflective of "nature," of the world we live in; its background story is cosmological, which
makes conflict an ineradicable feature of human life. The catastrophic
collapses of moral sensibility and the corresponding butchery in our own
century lend credence to this view of the world and render Smith's careful attention to moral sensibility all the more worthy of study.

Smith also takes it as his task to free us from repressive institutions,
especially religious institutions. What he polemically calls "superstition"
is frequently subjected to attack, and he provides a compelling analysis
of religion as a political problem – that is, of religious strife and oppression – that foreshadows James Madison's famous solution in the *Federalist Papers* to the problem of political faction. Smith's moral, political,
and economic doctrines are geared toward explaining how individuals
as well as nations can live together harmoniously in spite of the ever-
present potential for conflict. The regulation of religion by morality, and

18 Although Smith uses "enlighten" and its cognates in various senses, he does not use the
term "the Enlightenment" (though see his reported comment about the "more enlighten'd age" at *LRBL*, p. 146, also p. 111, and *TMS* II.ii.3.5). This ought not to prevent
us from understanding the important ways in which his thought forms part of the movement. Cf. Dugald Stewart's reference to *WN* as containing the "most profound and enlightened philosophy of the age." *Biographical Memoirs of Adam Smith, William Robertson,
Thomas Reid*, ed. W. Hamilton ([1858] rpt. New York: Kelley, 1966), p. 320. Cited
hereafter as *Memoirs*.

19 Of course the view that conflict is of crucial analytical importance has roots in "state of
nature" theories in Hobbes and Locke and is carried farther in Kant's discussion of
conflict in his essays on history, in Hegel's discussion of the master–slave dialectic in the
*Phenomenology of Spirit*, and in Marx's theory of the struggle between classes. For a sampling
of recent invocations of the same theme (at times put in terms of the deep disagreement
about notions of the human good), see C. Larmore, *Patterns of Moral Complexity*, pp. 38–
9; J. Rawls, *Political Liberalism* (New York: Columbia University Press, 1993), pp. xvi–xviii;
S. Darwall, *The British Moralists and the Internal "Ought": 1640–1740* (Cambridge: Cambridge University Press, 1995), p. 4; and R. A. Putnam, "Reciprocity and Virtue Ethics,"
*Ethics* 98 (1988), p. 381.

the conviction that the public realm is better off without state involvement in religious disputes, are pervasive themes in Smith.

Smith's advocacy of liberty of religious belief and practice accompanies scorn for theology and the associated disciplines of ontology, metaphysics, "pneumaticks" (the doctrine of the soul or spirit), and indeed
philosophy in some of its traditional guises. Long passages in *The Wealth
of Nations* and *The Theory of Moral Sentiments* ridicule and unmask institutionalized religion as well as academic philosophy. We are given to understand that all things, including human nature, can be comprehended
by the light of properly enlightened intelligence. "Science is the great
antidote to the poison of enthusiasm and superstition." Correspondingly, Smith advocates a state requirement that every person pass ex-
aminations in science before being permitted to "exercise any liberal
profession" (*WN* V.i.g.14). The new science of nature – that of Newton
– is, by contrast with the old philosophy, of real use to the improvement
of human life. The new science rejects teleological explanations and excludes religion as a trustworthy basis of such explanation. Moreover, it
also goes hand in glove with the famous "mastery of nature," a mastery
understood in both theoretical terms (such that "nature" is rendered
intelligible by human reason) and practical terms (such that physical
nature is material for the satisfaction of our wants).

The rhetoric of the Enlightenment pushes the paradigm of natural
science and of method farther: nothing is to be accepted at face value.
Unexamined beliefs are prejudices, traditions are dogmas until reviewed
by reason, and public life should be the arena of vigorous and open
debate. This attitude of criticism manifests a deep ethical commitment
to independence, self-sufficiency, and courage, and to freedom from the
shackles of custom, nature, and fortune. The point is elegantly articulated in Kant. True "maturity" or autarchy is autonomy; it is as self-
directed, self-legislating beings that we are fully human or free. Premodern thought is precritical, unfree, and in a sense immature.[20] The
path to enlightenment requires the courage of thorough self-

20 The first paragraph of Kant's 1784 "Was 1st Aufklärung" essay reads: "Enlightenment
  is man's release from his self-incurred tutelage. Tutelage is man's inability to make use
  of his understanding without direction from another. Self-incurred is this tutelage when
  its cause lies not in lack of reason but in lack of resolution and courage to use it without
  direction from another. *Sapere aude!* 'Have courage to use your own reason!' – that is the
  motto of enlightenment." "What Is Enlightenment," in Kant, *On History*, ed. L. W. Beck,
  trans. Beck, R. E. Anchor, and E. L. Fackenheim (Indianapolis: Bobbs-Merrill, 1963),
  p. 3.

examination, whether, as in Hume, by means of a "science of man" that is carefully based on experience, or, as in Kant, through a "transcendental" critique of the possibility of knowledge and morality, or, as in Hegel, by an elaborately dialectical account of the social and historical conditions that make human activity possible. Nothing is to be accepted simply because it has been accepted. Hence d'Alembert referred to the period as the "age of philosophy," and Thomas Paine entitled one of his books *The Age of Reason.*[21]

Freedom – achievable by all rather than just by a chosen few – is the great moral and political ideal.[22] It is accompanied by a commitment to a doctrine of the basic moral equality of human beings. To be "enlightened" is to understand the centrality of liberty in any moral or political scheme, and Smith is a partisan of what he calls "the obvious and simple system of natural liberty" (*WN* IV.ix.51), seeing it as part of his task to articulate the principles for the "establishment of perfect justice, of perfect liberty, and of perfect equality" (*WN* IV.ix.17). He is a moral egalitarian, and his Stoic doctrine of rule of the emotions by conscience or "the impartial spectator" certainly captures something of what is meant by "autonomy." Every modern ethical or political system seeks to persuade us by showing that it best captures principles such as liberty and equality. Even attempts to revive classical doctrines of virtue carry weight insofar as they succeed in integrating these modern principles into their framework. Slavery – accepted widely by philosophers and nonphilosophers alike until the modern period – is to be condemned, and Smith does condemn it. Like Hume, Smith points out that slavery was part of classical doctrines of virtue and of the social systems that appealed to those doctrines (the appeals were supported by, among other things, the view that labor is antithetical to the leisured exercise of excellence). Smith and Hume argued that modern market societies could abolish the conditions under which freedom is purchased at the price of slavery.[23]

21 Jean le Rond D'Alembert, "Le siècle de la philosophie," in *Essai sur les éléments de philosophie,* vol. 2 of d'Alembert, *Oeuvres philosophiques, historiques et littéraires,* ed. R. N. Schwab ([1759] Hildesheim: Olms, 1965), p. 9.
22 R. Pippin argues compellingly that the uniting theme of modernity is that of freedom, or in Kantian terms, autonomy. See his *Modernism as a Philosophical Problem* (Oxford: Blackwell Publisher, 1991), esp. p. 40.
23 See Hume, "Of the Populousness of Ancient Nations," in D. Hume, *Essays Moral, Political, and Literary,* rev. ed., ed. E. F. Miller (Indianapolis: Liberty, 1987), pp. 383–98, and Smith's comment on slavery and on Plato's *Laws* at *WN* III.ii.9. The words and deeds of a number of Enlightenment thinkers with respect to the moral status and enslavement

Smith's *Wealth of Nations* shows that modern commerce may liberate the common worker by developing a distinction between labor and service, work and subservience. The defense of commerce against the animadversions of the ancients – both pagan and Christian – is another Enlightenment theme espoused by Smith. Much of the moral thrust of Smith's political economy lies in its claim to better the lot of the ordinary person.

Smith articulates and defends a notion of "middling" moral virtue, even while acknowledging that in some respects it is inferior to the aristocratic excellence praised by the ancients. This more achievable notion of virtue is taken as reconciled with the pursuit of such fundamental goods as health, pleasure, "bettering of our condition," high reputation, and "worldly goods." It is available to nearly every decent adult and is more democratic and egalitarian than the ancient ideal. The defense of what Plato would have dismissed as "demotic virtue" is part of the enlightened moral outlook that grants ordinary people their place in the sun. Smith is a devoted and resourceful defender of the standpoint of ordinary life, and a central task of the present book is to analyze and evaluate that defense.[24] This moral vision, so characteristic of the Enlightenment, informs every aspect of his thought, including his analysis of the emotions, of the virtues, of the free market, and of jurisprudence. I shall argue that the centrality Smith gives to "sympathy" is itself reflective of his moral vision. The emphasis that his political philosophy places on the mean, on imperfection, and on the dangers of misplaced utopianism must also be understood in this light.

Because modern liberty demands moral virtue rather than wisdom, it is frequently built upon a doctrine of the moral emotions rather than on philosophical reason.[25] *The Theory of Moral Sentiments* is a book that

of Africans in particular leave much to be desired. By contrast, Smith is unimpeachable on that score (consider *TMS* V.2.9).

24  C. Taylor rightly remarks that the "affirmation of ordinary life" (the "life of production and the family") is one of the major themes of Christianity "which comes to receive new and unprecedented importance at the beginning of the modern era, and which has also become central to modern culture," being "one of the most powerful ideas in modern civilization." Other ideas include autonomy and the "importance of suffering." *Sources of the Self: The Making of the Modern Identity* (Cambridge, Mass.: Harvard University Press, 1989), pp. 14–15.

25  Descartes wrote that "there is nothing in which the defective nature of the sciences which we have received from the ancients appears more clearly than in what they have written on the passions." *The Passions of the Soul*, vol. 1 in *The Philosophical Works of Descartes*, ed. and trans. E. S. Haldane and G. R. T. Ross, (Cambridge: Cambridge University Press, 1972), art. I, p. 331. Not every modern treatment of the passions would make quite that

seeks to show that the "sentiments" (also termed "passions" or "emotions") can suffice for morality, virtue, liberty, and in general for a harmonious social order. We are creatures of the passions. Smith seeks to understand and justify the passions as a basis for decent ethical life. The passions are not exclusive of reason, but as a basis for human life they displace "theoretical" pursuits such as philosophy. The split between theory and practice is a pervasive theme in Smith, just as it is in the work of other key Enlightenment figures such as Kant. Virtue is not founded on philosophical knowledge; this anti-Platonic principle guides enlightened moral theory.

The operative metaphor in the term "Enlightenment" is of course an ancient one. Its most famous classical treatment is to be found at the beginning of Book VII of Plato's *Republic*.[26] There we learn that there is light both inside and outside the "cave" of political life. The sun's light could never illuminate the interior of the cave unless a great hole were punched through the roof. Why could that not be done, we wonder, since the cave is not an immutable product of nature but has been fashioned by human beings in a number of ways? Socrates calls it a "prison home" (517b2). As a prison, is it perhaps a structure that we have made? The fire that illuminates the cave is in one sense natural, of the same sort as the sun. But in another sense this fire is a product of artifice, stolen by Prometheus from the gods. It is lit, tended, kept in a particular spot, and used to project shadows shaped by "all sorts of artifacts" held like puppets. A road and a wall separate the puppet handlers from the rest of the cave; these too are human constructions. Yet few of the cave's residents can look directly at the source of the quasi-artificial light, and none seems to have his or her own fire. They are "prisoners," their necks and legs held by bonds or chains. It is easy to mistake this for a depiction of our natural condition. But chains do not grow on trees; they are fabricated and then placed on us. Socrates says that we are confined "from childhood" (514a5), but this is not to say that we are born enchained. The entire simile suggests that lack of enlightenment is the result of artifice, and therefore that it is an unnatural condition, one for which a historical account is appropriate.

charge, but certainly every major modern treatment of the passions – such as Smith's – takes itself as improving dramatically on the ancients. See his comment about recent progress in the "abstract science of human nature" at *TMS* VII.iii.2.5.

26 Throughout this book, I shall not distinguish between the views of Plato and Socrates and shall refer to the "Socrates" of Plato's dialogues only. Quotations from the *Republic* are from A. Bloom's translation (New York: Basic Books, 1968). Cited hereafter as *Rep.*

The architects of the modern Enlightenment inferred that what has been made can be unmade, if only we gather the necessary courage. They also suggested that once the chains have been broken there will be no need to leave the cave, for the prison can be transformed into a home. In his own way Smith agrees and offers us a striking and sustained redemption of ordinary, prephilosophical human life. Enlightenment does not require the hopelessly difficult ascent to the sun outside; fires lit in a cavern that is properly organized will suffice perfectly well. We might even be better off to liberate ourselves from the myth that there is light outside the cave, and thereby rid ourselves of zealots who claim to have ascended and returned full of "enlightenment" from that other world (cf. *Rep.* 516e–517a). Our destiny is in our entirely visible hands, waiting to be crafted by us.

As thus crafted or constructed, our liberation is not a return to nature or to some self-standing reality "outside" the cave whose pattern serves as a paradigm for harmonizing the soul. The artifactual or "poetic" character of the Platonic cave governs the modern view of enlightenment as sketched in the preceding paragraph, even as Platonic views about the content of true enlightenment are rejected. If freedom means independence and self-legislation in our theoretical, moral, and practical pursuits, then reason tends to have a constructive aspect rather than the passively apprehending or absorptive quality celebrated by Plato.[27] Surprisingly, the imagination often underlies, or at least works in close partnership with, Enlightenment doctrines of reason as constructive. The imagination turns out to be fundamental, not only to understanding the world but to practical reasoning as well. In Smith's terms, morality requires that we be able to see things from the other person's point of view. "Sympathy" is crucial to his moral system, just as it is a key term in our moral vocabulary. But, as he explains in a detailed and fascinating discussion, sympathy is also an act of the imagination. Emotions are themselves shaped by imagination. From sympathy (though not it alone) derive our "ideas" of the desirable and praiseworthy, and hence this or that particular sentiment. Since imagination turns out to be essential to the constitution of morality as well as to that of reason, we are creatures

27  D. Lachterman argues that the controlling theme of modernity is "the 'idea' of construction or, more broadly, the 'idea' of the *mind* as essentially the power of making, fashioning, crafting, producing, in short, the mind as first and last *poiétic* and only secondarily or subsidiarily *practical* and *theoretical*." In *The Ethics of Geometry: A Genealogy of Modernity* (New York: Routledge, 1989), p. 4. The Greek noun *poiesis* (related to the root of the English word "poet") can mean "making," "fabrication," "creation," "production."

of the imagination no less than of the passions. Here as elsewhere, Smith walks in the company of Hume and a large band of fellow travelers.

In the broad-gauged respects reviewed in the preceding paragraphs, Smith is unquestionably a partisan of the Enlightenment. It therefore comes as a shock to realize that he also confronts head-on many of the doubts we now have about the period. In crucial respects, he takes positions we associate with the denouement of the Enlightenment. Smith himself takes up problems that later critics of modernity insisted upon. To recall first an opening theme of this Introduction, he is acutely aware of the phenomenon of unintended consequences, of the importance of "moral luck," and in general of the roles that contingency and finitude play in human life. The "invisible hand" is the phrase most commonly associated with Smith. In Stoic language of the sort that he invoked, we are like actors in a play whose plot we do not understand and whose ending is not yet revealed to us but whose propensity for irony is well established.

Consider briefly several paradoxes embedded in the very conditions of our success. Smith's discussion of them prefigures contemporary critiques. Let us begin with the pursuit of wealth, a goal that *The Wealth of Nations* is designed to facilitate and promote. That book is undoubtedly the most famous and enduring Enlightenment contribution on the subject. It is obvious that the wealth we pursue has little to do with satisfying our basic needs; we are driven in good part by fears and wants fed by the imagination. Such has been the complaint of moralists in every age, and Smith is not only aware of the complaint but insists on its truth. He certainly understands that "consumption is the sole end and purpose of all production" (*WN* IV.viii.49) and that a successful commercial society would be what we now call "consumerist." It is one of his key teachings that the pursuit of wealth is made possible by what he calls the "deception" or "prejudices" of the imagination. Thanks to our self-deception, we associate wealth (as well as power) with happiness, or tranquillity. Neither the pursuit nor the possession of wealth actually produces tranquillity; on the contrary, both jeopardize it (*TMS* I.iii.2.1–3; IV.1.8–10). Smith describes this picture vividly, and it is bound to unsettle us: How can we affirm a social arrangement devoted to maximizing the "wealth of nations" when the pursuit of wealth is so deeply misguided? Smith seems to be arguing, just as we ourselves might, that the conditions of our material prosperity are tied to those of our spiritual poverty.

The problem is accentuated by the fact that the pursuit of wealth is often purchased at the cost, not just of high aristocratic virtue but of virtue altogether. Smith refers to this as the "corruption of the moral sentiments" and sees it as a natural danger in the commercial society he advocates (*TMS* I.iii.3). Greed, dishonesty, a willingness to exploit others, vanity; these are among the vices that both we and Smith associate with the promotion of our material well-being, or of what he calls "bettering our condition." He tackles head-on this ancient problem of the relation between wealth and virtue, and in Chapters 5 through 7 we will explore his analysis. The problem was in the air when he wrote, thanks in part to Rousseau's *Discourse on the Origin and Foundations of Inequality among Men*, which Smith knew.[28] As the continuing litany of complaints today about the moral decadence of materialistic Western cultures demonstrates, this problem is still with us.

The generation of wealth is inextricably connected with the division of labor. This key Smithean claim (*WN* I.i–ii) is now universally accepted, and in our chosen vocations we avidly pursue qualifications in some specialized area that will allow us to make ourselves useful and achieve distinction. Yet although our prosperity hinges on the division of labor, we sense that this gain comes at a cost. It seems to allow one group to exploit another – say, those specializing in management to exploit the workers who assemble widgets – but perhaps more importantly it may warp and stultify the mind and spirit of the specialist. Perhaps no philosopher, with the possible exception of Marx, has described these human costs of the division of labor more bluntly and harshly than has Smith. He laments the "gross ignorance and stupidity" that afflict the workers "in a civilized society" (*WN* V.i.f.61). A person who spends his life "performing a few simple operations" slowly "becomes as stupid and ignorant as it is possible for a human creature to become," incapable of "any rational conversation" as well as "of conceiving any generous, noble, or tender sentiment, and consequently of forming any just judgment concerning many even of the ordinary duties of private life." Hence expertise is "acquired at the expence of his intellectual, social, and martial virtues." This seems to be the lot of "the great body of the people" in "every improved and civilized society" (*WN* V.i.f.50).

Smith goes on to tell us that the "few" who have the "leisure and inclination" to philosophize can escape this dreadful debasement and reach extraordinary heights of intellectual refinement. But unless they happen

---

28 Smith read the essay in the original and both comments on and quotes from it in a letter to the *Edinburgh Review* (1756). Smith urges the *Review* to broaden its scope to include discussion of the *Encyclopédie* as well as works such as Rousseau's (see *EPS*, pp. 242–56).

to "be placed in some very particular situations" (i.e., hold political or economic power), they will "contribute very little to the good government or happiness of their society": that is, they will become university professors rather than philosopher-kings or queens. By contrast, "barbarous societies" produce individuals far more worthy of our approbation, but not philosophers (*WN* V.i.f.51). But the splendors of philosophy do not exist in a vacuum, and the dehumanization caused by the division of labor jeopardizes, as Smith next discusses, the foundations of a free society in which, presumably, philosophy might flourish: "in free countries, where the safety of government depends very much upon the favourable judgment which the people may form of its conduct, it must surely be of the highest importance that they should not be disposed to judge rashly or capriciously concerning it" (*WN* V.i.f.61). Wealth and liberty, wealth and virtue, commerce and human excellence, seem hopelessly at odds. Even liberty appears to undermine social cohesiveness, including the cohesiveness that is communicated through public education.

Consider the key example of religious liberty, to which I shall devote much attention in Chapter 7, in part by reconstructing his analysis of the matter as a reply to the classic argument of book X of Plato's *Laws* for a state-enforced civic religion. The peaceful proliferation of a multitude of religious sects is an accomplishment of which we are rightly proud. And yet we are troubled by several questions. First, the question of common purpose: If our religious convictions differ fundamentally, and if they express our deepest values and beliefs, what will bind us together in a common polity? Once religious liberty is instituted – not to mention the other liberties Smith argues for, such as those of commerce or trade, of deployment of labor and capital, of philosophical and political belief and expression, of assembly, and of movement – social fragmentation looms. The problem of social cohesiveness is among the most pressing now facing us, and some of the most influential philosophers of the moment have devoted considerable attention to it.[29] Smith is a neglected resource in the debate.

The Enlightenment scheme for religious liberty requires that religious teachings not claim political power enforced by the state, and the Enlightenment attack on superstition entails that natural phenomena are the province of science. Religion ought fundamentally to be a private

---

29 See, for example, the essays by C. Taylor and others collected in *Multiculturalism: Examining the Politics of Recognition*, ed. A. Gutmann (Princeton: Princeton University Press, 1994).

affair – a social, but certainly not a political, matter. Does all this not in turn dismember, or at least dilute, what is involved in a true religious teaching? Smith himself expresses the hope that liberty of religious belief will eventually lead to "that pure and rational religion, free from every mixture of absurdity, imposture, or fanaticism, such as wise men have in all ages of the world wished to see established" (*WN* V.i.g.8). True religion is the privatized religion of morality or conscience beloved of Enlightenment thinkers. We may wonder whether this is still religion at all, and therefore whether it will support the beneficial social consequences Smith hopes for it, especially that of reinforcing one's sense of moral duty as well as cementing ties of responsibility and concern for one's fellows. Does not "pure and rational religion," or what Kant called "religion within the limits of reason" or "the pure religion of reason," lead to the death of religion? If so, Smith's arguments for freedom of religion are just more fodder for MacIntyre's characterization of the modern age as that of "liberal individualism."[30] The specter of the invisible hand looms, and with it the possible self-undermining of the Enlightenment.

We may think of "sympathy" as that which holds us together. Smith's treatment of sympathy lies at the heart of his moral psychology and is among the best ever written, building upon and improving Hume's analysis. With the support of proper moral education, rearing, and institutions, Smith argues, we form the habit of understanding other people's situations accurately and of seeing things from their point of view.[31] And yet although sympathy may bind together, may it not also split apart? One may "understand" and "identify" with one group and therefore dismiss or detest some different group – Why should sympathy be universal? – and one person or group can always claim, with some conviction, that only others similarly situated could ever "understand." As long as sympathy is the basis for mutual understanding, we are open to the claim that we cannot possibly imagine the circumstances of the other without belonging to the other's circle, and that since we do not belong to it, mutual understanding is impossible. As I discuss in detail in Chapter 2, "identity politics" and consequent social fragmentation may be an

---

30  *After Virtue*, p. 195. Cf. the reference to "modern liberal, individualist politics" in MacIntyre, *Whose Justice? Which Rationality?* (Notre Dame, Ind.: University of Notre Dame Press, 1988), p. 335.

31  A. Sen remarks that Smith "provides a brilliant account of what it is like to place oneself in the position of another – an account from which modern welfare economists and social choice theorists have much to learn." See his "Adam Smith's Prudence," in *Theory and Reality in Development*, ed. S. Lall and F. Stewart (New York: St. Martin's, 1986), p. 30.

unintended result of a doctrine of sympathy, which was originally intended to produce social cohesiveness. Smith's analysis of sympathy,
imagination, and the emotions helps us to understand the possible internal instability of sympathy and what is required to avoid that instability.

Because of his own keen awareness of the ironies and shadows of the
Enlightenment, Smith is in a position to offer us valuable insights into
the reasons why liberal Enlightenment social and institutional arrangements and ideals are not altogether at odds with the tradition of the
virtues and of the communities based on virtues. His antidotes to the
problems sketched in the preceding paragraphs include, strikingly, commerce, religion, education, and other "mediating institutions" (as we
now call them). He has a great deal to say about virtue, including civic
virtue, and about how it can give ethical shape to our efforts to improve
our lot, as unphilosophical as those efforts may be. What one might call
the "mechanics" of freedom – liberal social and political arrangements
– can nourish, and in turn be sustained by, virtues such as honesty, moderation, prudence, and judgment. It is one of the chief tasks of this book
to explore and evaluate Smith's subtle and dialectical efforts to promote
the key themes of the Enlightenment in the face of his – and as it turns
out, our – own doubts. His efforts are informed by a deep understanding
of both the virtues and the vices of modernity, as well as of its classical
competitors.

We cannot grasp Smith's diagnosis of and therapy for the modern age
without devoting considerable attention to his analysis of the virtues (especially the virtue of justice) as well as to the theory of the emotions, of
the impartial spectator, and of sympathy. The problem of the relationship between selfishness and an impersonal or impartial point of view
demands our attention, as does that of the relation between virtue and
happiness. Therefore, these are central topics in the following pages. A
principal issue in several chapters concerns the relation for Smith between two models of morality, one founded on the virtues, another on
rules and law. These models have often been thought to work against
one another, for the morality of the virtues emphasizes character, judgment, and perception whereas the morality of rules emphasizes duty,
obligation, and conformity of action to principle. Smith attempts to combine them, with the first grounding the second.[32] He therefore places

---

32  Cf. O. O'Neill's point that in the past "Virtually everybody who wrote about what ought
    to be done also wrote about the sorts of lives it would be good to lead. Yet recently this
    has changed. Many philosophers writing in English in the last two decades apparently

great stress on judgment and context in ways that fit his theories of the "impartial spectator" and moral emotions. The old problem of how the moral theory and the political economy mesh also requires our attention. Smith thinks that the virtues of a free and commercial society are defensible because of, not despite, his general skepticism of state interference in economic and social matters, his anti-utopianism, and his doctrine of unintended consequences and the invisible hand. Although he refers to the ideal society of liberty and justice as a "utopia," his version of this ideal, we will find, is anti-utopian. My discussion of morality and political economy in Chapter 7 concludes with reflection on Smith's nuanced version of the "city in speech," a city in whose imitations we ourselves dwell.

Reconciliation with imperfection is a key aim of Smith's thought, and here as well as at other junctures we need to investigate his reconciliationist strategies. One may attempt to find tranquillity in contemplating oneself and the world from a detached, synoptic, external perspective. Although this is a natural step from the perspective of the "impartial spectator," Smith judges it a potentially destructive one. We will repeatedly reflect on this problem of the correct level of "spectatorship" or detachment, of the relative merits of "subjective" standpoints, because it too concerns Smith. The problem is an old one and continues to be debated vigorously in contemporary ethics. It is closely connected, too, with an issue that I have already touched on, namely, the meaning of "nature" and the question of whether it is possible to "live according to nature," as well as of nature's role in normative inquiry. Smith defines a decisive moment in the history of the idea of nature. Because Stoicism is a vehicle for his discussion of these issues, we will repeatedly explore his appropriation as well as his criticism of Stoic teachings.

### 3. PHILOSOPHY, RHETORIC, AND ENLIGHTENMENT

As my comments about Plato's simile of the cave suggest, an ancient debate about the true meaning of "enlightenment" may be seen as lying at the heart of Smith's enterprise. The debate partly concerns the mean-

assume that we must approach the moral life *either* through the categories of duty, obligation and right action, among which they think justice of prime importance, *or* through those of good character, hence of the virtues, and that these two approaches are not complementary but incompatible." "Duties and Virtues," in *Ethics*, ed. A. P. Griffiths, Royal Institute of Philosophy Supplements, no. 35 (Cambridge: Cambridge University Press, 1993), p. 108.

ing of philosophy and its relation to ordinary life. I have characterized Smith as a defender of ordinary life. One of the things that part of common life needs defending from is philosophy itself, in Smith's view, for philosophy – as understood by Plato, for example – may place the wrong demands on human life. Hence the meaning of "philosophy" and the relation between philosophy and ordinary life are also central themes of this book. I treat Smith as a philosopher who participates in a long conversation about these matters.

Smith often uses the term "philosophy" in senses that are perfectly familiar to us today, as when he speaks of "moral philosophy" – the topic of Part VII of *The Theory of Moral Sentiments* – or of "philosophy" as an academic discipline (*WN* V.i.f.25–33). "Philosophy" can here mean a comprehensive account of things taken as a whole, the speculative effort to provide an explanatory "system." He clearly understood that this distinctive discipline has divided and might further divide itself into minute areas of specialization, each labored by "a peculiar tribe or class of philosophers" (*WN* I.i.9). He also uses the term in at least two other senses that today are less familiar. On some occasions, he speaks of "natural philosophy." Sometimes it is difficult to ascertain whether he means only what we would now call "science" or wishes to include other branches of philosophical inquiry as well.[33] On other occasions, "philosophy" includes the ability to understand the structure of a thing or process in order to improve it: for instance, he speaks of a "philosopher" as thinking of a method for improving a machine used in an industry (*WN* I.i.9). When I raise the question of his notion of the relation between "philosophy" and ordinary life, I have in mind the more familiar meanings of the term and shall trust the context, or my explicit comment, to make it evident when the meaning shifts.

The ancient question about the nature and scope of philosophy is visible in the Enlightenment distinction between theology and natural or moral religion and in the Enlightenment polemic against theology. How well *argued*, in general, was the rejection of religious "enlightenment" in favor of humanistic and scientific "enlightenment"? An inspection of the "arguments" provided in the polemic is not reassuring; often they consist of mockery, dismissals, unmaskings, and vituperation.

---

33 E.g., see the beginning of the essay "Ancient Logics and Metaphysics" (*EPS*, p. 119). The ensuing discussion makes clear that "philosophy" there includes both "natural philosophy" and "metaphysics." Elsewhere Smith refers to the "Newtonian Philosophy," meaning Newtonian science ("History of Astronomy" IV.75, *EPS*, p. 103).

Smith contributes his fair share of these. It would be easy to infer that those prosecuting the attack simply did not believe in religion but instead in a different set of ideals and that they had, in the well-worn phrase, substituted a "faith in reason" for religious faith.[34] This is crudely stated but fits with my earlier observation that the Enlightenment view of reason as constructive is frequently articulated in terms of the imagination, which thus tends to underlie Enlightenment doctrines of reason and therewith the rationality of attacks on other modes of imagining the world. Today, "constructive reason" has evolved into "creativity," understood to be historically localized and, perhaps, inflected by race, class, and gender or simply by the contingencies of individual genius. Science, once the great paradigm of objective knowledge, edges toward being understood in terms of its sociology and aesthetics, each a way of accounting for its status as a human production. All of this ultimately implies that our arguments in favor of one notion of enlightenment amount merely to the expression of our particular persuasion: that is, the implication is that they would amount to rhetorical edification and polemic, and this undermines not only the rationality of our critique of the alternatives but also the rationality of our own stance.[35]

What I earlier characterized as the "global" critique of the Enlightenment points to just this result, and so to a significant constriction of the scope of "philosophy." Here again, Smith's position is complex, for even as he defends the modern Enlightenment and ordinary life, he also rejects the confident rationalism often associated with the period. I shall argue that Smith is a skeptic of a philosophically subtle sort, and that he discerns the productive work of the imagination in all aspects of human

---

34 E.g., see Hegel, *Faith and Knowledge*, trans. W. Cerf and H. S. Harris (Albany: State University of New York Press, 1977), pp. 55–6, 94; C. L. Becker, *The Heavenly City of the Eighteenth-Century Philosophers* (New Haven: Yale University Press, 1966), pp. 42–6. Also L. Strauss, *Philosophy and Law: Contributions to the Understanding of Maimonides and His Predecessors*, trans. E. Adler (Albany: State University of New York, Press, 1985), p. 30: "Thus the Enlightenment's mockery of the teachings of the [religious] tradition is not the successor of a prior refutation of these teachings; it does not bring to expression the amazement of unprejudiced men at the power of manifestly absurd prejudices; but it *is* the refutation. . . . Thus the importance of mockery for the Enlightenment's critique of religion is an indirect proof of the irrefutability of orthodoxy."

35 This seems to confirm H.-G. Gadamer's point that "*historicism, despite its critique of rationalism and of natural law philosophy, is based on the modern Enlightenment and unwittingly shares its prejudices.* And there is one prejudice of the Enlightenment that defines its essence: the fundamental prejudice of the Enlightenment is the prejudice against prejudice itself, which denies tradition its power." *Truth and Method*, 2nd rev. ed., trans. J. Weinsheimer and D. G. Marshall (New York: Continuum, 1994), p. 270. Emphasis in original.

life. Philosophy and science themselves are, on his Humean account, synthesizing and demiurgic activities of the imagination. The imagination's work is partly explained by him in terms of notions of the beautiful, proportional, harmonious. Surprisingly, he ascribes to the love of beauty a pervasive role in human life. Yet in spite of its apparently Platonic hue, Smith's strikingly aesthetic view of the world announces a deep break with classical philosophy, as we will see in the concluding chapter. Concerning the nature of "philosophy," its ability to grasp "the world," and the imagination, Smith may even seem to be a post-Enlightenment thinker.

The famous Platonic quarrel between philosophy and poetry remains with us, and viewed from the Platonic perspective, Smith has inclined to the side of the poets. From that perspective there may be some concern that once we incline to that path a slide into self-vitiating skepticism cannot be avoided. Smith provides a powerful and multilayered response to that Platonic suspicion. His lucidity about the fundamental problems of modernity makes his efforts to save the period from itself all the deeper and more intriguing. He attempts to synthesize views many now find unavoidable (such as the rejection of intuitionistic Platonism) with others we would gladly see defended (such as the superiority of liberal economic and political structures and the centrality of the virtues and "sympathy" to ethics). In the Epilogue, I shall assess the successes and shortcomings of Smith's ambitious project with the venerable history of the debate much in mind.

Some of the most interesting work in contemporary ethics concerns the limits of philosophical theory, and thus necessarily involves reflection on the nature of philosophy, its relation to ordinary life, and the sort of "justification" one could provide for an ethical persuasion or outlook.[36] One's commitments about these issues are embodied in how one "does" ethics. Such issues are close to Smith's heart, and the compelling manner in which he writes embodies his stand on them. In my study, Chapter 1 is devoted to the rhetoric of Smith's moral theory, and so to the problem

---

36 Darwall et al. comment that "debate has now extended even to the metaphilosophical level, as philosophers have asked with increasing force and urgency whether, or in what ways, theorizing is appropriate to morality." "Toward *Fin de siècle* Ethics," p. 32. Given Smith's close relationship with Hume, it ought not to surprise us that Smith had this sort of problem very much in mind. Smith would certainly approve of the related movement in contemporary ethics toward "more careful and empirically informed work on the nature or history or function of morality" commended in "Toward *Fin de siècle* Ethics" (p. 34).

of the relation between "form," "content," and audience. *The Theory of Moral Sentiments* is a methodologically self-conscious work, which both includes accounts of philosophical account giving and exhibits a well-thought-out position about what it means to do ethics. The rhetoric or method of Smith's book is tied to substantive theses about moral psychology and ethics, and in Chapters 2, 3, 5, and 6 I analyze them. Chapter 4 examines his skepticism, its ethical and theoretical motivations, and its consequences for his rhetoric.

My study emphasizes and assesses Smith relative to various figures in the history of philosophy, especially several classical figures and schools. Plato is especially prominent throughout because he so usefully differs from Smith, even where Smith shares with him a conception of the problem to be addressed. Although in many cases Smith himself invites us to compare and contrast, my primary motivation is to elicit the philosophically important features of his thought.

Let me be explicit. I have not sought to write a *Quellenforschung* or study of the influences on Smith, or a treatment of the quarrel between ancients and moderns, or an analysis of the relationship between Smith and another philosopher.[37] The present inquiry is not a study of "the Enlightenment." The Enlightenment is a vast canvas of extraordinary complexity. I am not claiming that all of its themes can be reduced to those of Adam Smith, or that Smith provides the magic key to unlocking the Enlightenment's mysteries, let alone that he somehow solves the many contemporary quandaries traceable to the period. Smith is a resource for our reflections on modernity, but that is not the same thing as a solution.

Although he does not use the term "the Enlightenment," I do believe that he encapsulates both Enlightenment claims and a profound appre-

---

37 Much valuable work remains to be done, such as a comprehensive discussion of Smith's relation to Hume that builds on K. Haakonssen's work. The step to Smith is a logical one for anyone working on Hume. Further philosophical study of Smith's relation to Hutcheson and other figures in the Scottish Enlightenment down through Reid would be very welcome, along the lines recently worked out by S. Darwall, for example. A comparative work on Smith and Rousseau holds tremendous interest. And we must hope for a full-scale philosophical treatment of Smith's relation to German Idealism, especially to Hegel, one that traces not only the fate of Smith's "political economy" but also the ways in which Smith's doctrines of imagination and freedom are transformed in Kant's theories of "spontaneity" and autonomy and in subsequent philosophies of "subjectivity." Such a treatment might fruitfully build on the wave of recent Hegel scholarship, such as that of R. Pippin and T. Pinkard. S. Fleischacker, *A Third Concept of Liberty: Judgment and Freedom in Kant and Adam Smith* (Princeton: Princeton University Press, in press) will make an important contribution.

ciation of the ironies and dissatisfactions associated with them and that, in his virtues and shortcomings, he is important to our understanding of modernity and of ourselves. I undertake this study of Adam Smith against the backdrop of the Enlightenment and indicate, where appropriate, connections with classical as well as current concerns. My primary aim is to understand and evaluate the principal themes in his rich and complex philosophy.

## 4. READING SMITH: INTERPRETIVE ASSUMPTIONS

In what follows I make a controversial methodological assumption more natural to the philosopher than the historian.[38] I accept an interpretive principle, commonly referred to as the "principle of charity," thanks to which I begin by assuming that in his published work Smith knew what he was doing and that he wrote exactly what he wanted to write. I take his work as a deliberate and self-conscious effort to state the truth about the topics of which he treats. This principle of interpretation may be understood as an attempt to grasp the author's meaning or intentions. A contrasting, more historically inclined approach might take Smith's utterances as in some sense determined by, or at least reflective of, his historical context *malgré lui*. It may be thought that appeal to authorial intention is an appeal to the author's state of mind and context – that is, that it is a fundamentally historical appeal. When referring to authorial intent, however, I mean to refer primarily to the supposition that the texts in question are unified products of design. I presuppose that a text is coherent and possesses a unified meaning unless shown otherwise. "Authorial intent" is not primarily a matter, in my view, of what was going through the author's mind as he or she wrote or of the causal factors that may have affected his or her thinking.

Hence when contemplating a puzzle, omission, or seeming inconsistency in or between Smith's texts, I first attempt an explanation that assumes that Smith intended the passage(s) in question to read precisely as written. In the vocabulary of a tradition that extends back to Plato, I am assuming that Smith's works, whether taken singly or collectively,

---

38 For some helpful commentary on the two perspectives, see the introduction to K. Haakonssen, *Natural Law and Moral Philosophy* (Cambridge: Cambridge University Press, 1996), esp. pp. 1–14.

possess organic unity. This is not to say that his works are miraculously detached from history. My principle of interpretation is not circular; it is falsifiable in specific cases and compatible with the observation that at a particular juncture Smith is uncritically echoing some social or historical tradition, or has made a mistake, or simply has not made up his mind. Although I shall argue that there are such junctures, my approach also opens up the possibility that what seems to be a mistake, or a historical reflex, or an ambiguity is in fact an interesting conceptual or argumentative move on Smith's part. We ought to explore the more promising alternative first and consider other explanations only if that alternative fails. To assume a principle that denies interpretive charity is irrevocably to close off from the beginning possible dimensions of the author's meaning and therefore to deprive ourselves of the full measure of what he or she has to teach. That, in turn, contravenes the purpose of reading the works of great thinkers.

There is a great deal to say about the philosophical assumptions underlying the principle of hermeneutical charity, and I refer the interested reader to a discussion of the matter I have provided elsewhere.[39] It is worth noting that Smith's own interpretive practice when reading other philosophers exhibits the principle of charity. In Part VII of *The Theory of Moral Sentiments*, when discussing the history of moral philosophy, he takes his predecessors at their word and tries to meet them head-on in a philosophical spirit. His theory of communication in the lectures on rhetoric, as well as the tenor of his interpretations of other philosophers, shows that he accepted the principle of authorial intention.

Another approach that contrasts with my own denies that authorial intention is a coherent notion, and thus denies that we are entitled to assume that the *corpus* or any of its individual parts speaks with a unified voice. On this view, as developed by Mikhail Bakhtin, for example, the emphasis is on the multiplicity of voices, "intertextuality," and the notion that in interpreting a work one cooperates in the production of its meaning.[40] Stated briefly, my objections to this approach are that it de-

39 In the introduction to *Self-knowledge in Plato's "Phaedrus"* ([1986] rpt. University Park: Pennsylvania State University Press, 1996), pp. 1–16.
40 For substantiation of the point about Smith's acceptance of the principle of authorial intentionality, see V. Brown, *Adam Smith's Discourse* (London: Routledge, 1994), ch. 1, sec. 2. In those and following pages, Brown espouses the Bakhtinian stance. As she notes, "One implication of this approach is that the issue of the coherence and consistency of Adam Smith's, *oeuvre* is something that has to wait upon the interpretation of the texts, and cannot be used as a prior assumption in reading the texts" (p. 20). Brown refers to

prives us of learning all that a truly fine work is capable of teaching us; that it is incapable of being discharged consistently in practice, since the interpreter inevitably makes assumptions about the unity of the text (or portions thereof), or of the period, or of other texts that form part of the "intertextuality"; that the fluidity of notions such as intertextuality invites undue arbitrariness of interpretation; that the Bakhtinian notion of "dialogism," in particular, impedes rather than encourages genuine dialogue; and finally that at a metaphilosophical level, dialogism cannot be articulated without making assumptions about the unity of meaning that contradict it. Denial of authorial intentionality impedes genuine efforts to understand one another's meaning, since the whole notion of "one another's meaning" is rejected and is replaced by the notion of "an interplay of voices." But a dialogue is not merely an interplay of voices; it is a mutual search for truth through a sustained effort to understand what each voice attempts to say. Dialogism is better termed "polyphonism" or "multivocity"; the denial of authorial intentionality undermines the possibility of dialogue. My approach by no means excludes the possibility that the author has written a text in which there are contending "voices"; indeed, I shall argue that Smith intended to do precisely that. The assumption of authorial intent – that is, of design and unity – allows us to search for the unified meaning of that feature of the book as well.

I conclude this discussion by mentioning several other of my interpretive assumptions. Both of Smith's published books went through many editions, sometimes with significant changes. There exists a debate as to whether or not the changes in the editions of the respective books represent substantive alterations. My own position is that in *The Theory of Moral Sentiments*, where the changes between editions are greater than in *The Wealth of Nations*, Smith's views did not fundamentally change from edition to edition.[41] There was, however, a great deal of expansion and elaboration, refining, and filling in of blank spots and ellipses.

It seems to be agreed that Smith's work originated in his university lectures in Glasgow.[42] This includes his reflections (now reprinted in

---

"intertextuality," "dialogism," and "an interplay of voices" (p. 21). See my review of her stimulating book in the *Times Literary Supplement*, July 14, 1995, p. 30.

41  For a different view, see L. Dickey, "Historicizing the 'Adam Smith Problem': Conceptual, Historiographical, and Textual Issues," *Journal of Modern History* 58 (1986): 579–609.

42  See Stewart, *Account of the Life and Writings of Adam Smith LL.D.*, in *Memoirs*, pp. 10, 66; D. D. Raphael, *Adam Smith* (Oxford: Oxford University Press, 1985), pp. 11–15. It is possible that Smith began to formulate some of his major themes (not just about rhetoric) in his Edinburgh lectures as well. On Smith's early conception of his basic project, see also note 57 in the present chapter.

*Essays on Philosophical Subjects*) on the histories of the sciences, and thus on the "aesthetics" of knowing. Smith is the sort of thinker who had, very early on, the fundamental outlines of his theories sketched out. Further, he must have thought that the sixth edition of *The Theory of Moral Sentiments* should prevail, as it contains important new sections and emendations. The fourth and fifth editions of *The Wealth of Nations* contain almost no changes by Smith.[43] Unless stated otherwise, I follow the Glasgow edition of both books and thus, in the case of *The Theory of Moral Sentiments*, the sixth edition, and the third in the case of *The Wealth of Nations*. These may safely be taken to represent Smith's idea of his most fully worked out treatments of the subjects.

Finally, I focus primarily on Smith's published work. Unpublished materials, including the student notes on rhetoric and jurisprudence, can be valuable aids to our understanding of the author. But those student notes did not receive Smith's imprimatur and unavoidably suffer from the inaccuracies of student note taking. Smith did not think most of his unpublished work worthy of publication and insisted that many manuscripts that he viewed in this light be destroyed upon his death. He was a careful writer, who went to some pains (to borrow a phrase that Dionysius of Halicarnassus applies to Plato) to "comb and curl" his works through several editions.[44] He had many opportunities to straighten out infelicities or errors in his formulations, and he did so. For these reasons, as well as out of fairness to his intentions, I have mostly confined my attention to the works he published or intended to publish.[45]

## 5. THE UNITY OF SMITH'S THOUGHT, AND THE PROJECTED *CORPUS*

My approach to reading Smith prompts me to assume, not only that the *The Theory of Moral Sentiments* and *The Wealth of Nations* individually possess

---

43 Concerning the third edition of *WN*, see Smith's letters to W. Strahan of May 22, 1783 (*CAS*, p. 266) and to T. Cadell, Dec. 7, 1782 (*CAS*, p. 263).

44 Dionysius of Halicarnassus, *On Literary Composition* ch. 25, ed. and trans. W. R. Roberts (London: Macmillan, 1910), pp. 264–5. As Smith himself put it (with reference to his revising *TMS* in preparation for the sixth edition), "I am a slow a very slow workman, who do and undo everything I write at least half a dozen of times before I can be tolerably pleased with it. . . ." Letter to T. Cadell, Mar. 15, 1788 (*CAS*, p. 311).

45 Consequently, although I devote a chapter to the topic of justice, I do not explore in much detail the historical application of "natural jurisprudence." That exploration has been successfully undertaken, in any event, in Haakonssen's work on Smith (see the Bibliography for references).

"organic unity" but that together they form a coherent whole. A hoary view in the history of Smith scholarship holds that the two books are substantively at odds with each other. Especially in Chapters 6 and 7, I show how this "Adam Smith problem" ought to be solved, even while granting that properly formulated, the problem cuts deep.

It is no doubt remarkable that *The Theory of Moral Sentiments* and *The Wealth of Nations* make no reference to each other, with the exception of the "Advertisement" prefixed to the sixth edition of the former work, where Smith does refer to his other book. He otherwise does not, in one published book, cite himself, or refer, or even – with certain exceptions – allude to his other published book.[46] This makes ethics appear to be independent from political economy, jurisprudence, and other inquiries. Smith gave no indication, however, that he thought that the two works were at odds with one another or that he had changed his mind about the fundamental tenets of his philosophy (as Kant and Heidegger, for example, did). A "change of mind" view would imply that Smith was more than a little unhinged, since he alternately revised his two books right up to the year of his death but gave no sign of recanting his views. Yet it cannot be denied that Smith forces the reader to do the labor of unification.[47] We must assess the *philosophical* significance of his striking silence about the connection between the two books, especially considering that throughout his work Smith frequently comments about "systems" and commends "systematic" thought. The problem of "system" points to the issue of the availability of philosophical completeness, as well as to the issue of the capacity of reason to grasp experience.

The relation between his two books is itself only a part of a still larger problem, namely that of the unity of Smith's entire projected *corpus*. He hoped to publish more than *The Theory of Moral Sentiments* and *The Wealth of Nations* and provided some indications of what the entire "system" would look like. My approach to the controversial issue of the *corpus* is governed by the interpretive assumptions specified earlier, which, in this instance, lead me – in confirmation of what I have claimed on behalf of these assumptions – to argue that the project of the *corpus* was incompletable in principle.[48] Because the *Lectures on Rhetoric and Belles Lettres*,

---

46 At *LJ*(B)12, Smith refers his students to *TMS*. In the context of oral lectures, that is, Smith made some effort to tie together his written work.

47 Smith did not provide us with an autobiography that, like Hume's "My Own Life," would give us insight into his view of the relationship among his writings.

48 See section 5 in Chapter 6. Consider D. Winch's statement that "Although we now have two sets of students' notes on the lectures on jurisprudence, there is a great deal of

the *Lectures on Jurisprudence,* and much of the material collected in *Essays on Philosophical Subjects* remained unpublished at his death, any reconstruction of the projected *corpus* must work with a web of published and (by Smith) unpublished documents, as well as with letters and student lecture notes. Shortly before his death, he ensured that sheafs of his unpublished writings were consigned to the flames.[49] That dramatic deed compounds the uncertainties inherent in the conjectural task of reconstruction.

What then would the projected *corpus* have looked like? My answer, stated schematically, is as follows (the evidence for this answer is offered subsequently). Smith divides philosophy as a whole into two main branches: moral philosophy, and what I shall term the "Philosophical History of the Liberal Sciences and Elegant Arts." Let us begin with the first of these. Moral philosophy consists of two branches: the theory of moral sentiments or ethics (treated in *The Theory of Moral Sentiments*), and the theory of "natural jurisprudence." The "ethics" side of this division is in turn divided into two areas, both treated in *The Theory of Moral Sentiments:* the virtues, and what I shall call moral psychology. The "natural jurisprudence" side of the division treats of the "natural rules of justice," the "foundation of the laws of all nations" without regard to convention, the "general principles of law and government," and the "science of a legislator." "Natural jurisprudence" seems to have two branches of its own: a theory of the principles of justice as such (missing from the *corpus*) and an account of the "different revolutions" of the principles or rules of justice "in different ages and periods of society."

disagreement about the nature of the missing element and whether Smith simply failed to complete it or found himself incapable of doing so for reasons that have nothing to do with the Great Reaper." "Adam Smith's 'Enduring Particular Result': A Political and Cosmopolitan Perspective," in *Wealth and Virtue,* ed. I. Hont and M. Ignatieff (Cambridge: Cambridge University Press, 1985), p. 255. S. Cremaschi argues that a deep "aporia" or "stalemate" in Smith's thinking prevented successful completion of the system. "Adam Smith: Skeptical Newtonianism, Disenchanted Republicanism, and the Birth of Social Science," in *Knowledge and Politics: Case Studies in the Relationship between Epistemology and Political Philosophy,* ed. M. Dascal and O. Gruengard (Boulder, Col.: Westview, 1989), pp. 100–1.

49 On Smith's wishes with respect to his unpublished manuscripts, see his letter to Hume of Apr. 16, 1773 (*CAS,* p. 168); J. Rae, *Life of Adam Smith* (Bristol, UK: Thoemmes, 1990), p. 434; and Stewart, *Memoirs,* pp. 73–4. Stewart claims (p. 74) that among the papers Smith ordered destroyed there "no doubt" were "the lectures on Rhetoric, which he read at Edinburgh in the year 1748, and of the lectures on Natural Religion and on Jurisprudence, which formed part of his course at Glasgow." See also Ross's discussion of the destruction of Smith's manuscripts in *The Life of Adam Smith,* pp. 404–5.

The latter, finally, has four parts: the treatment of justice (to which *Lectures on Jurisprudence* is directed), and the treatments in that work and in the *Wealth of Nations* of police, revenue, arms, and "whatever else is the object of law."

Smith did not complete the "Philosophical History of the Liberal Sciences and Elegant Arts" – the second main branch of "philosophy" as a whole. It would have included the sort of material contained in the *Lectures on Rhetoric and Belles Lettres* and the *Essays on Philosophical Subjects*. This "Philosophical History" would have focused on inquiry and theorizing, the "intellectual sentiments," rhetoric, language, and aesthetic appreciation. That is, it would have included the philosophy of art, as well as of science and of philosophical thought itself. In a moment I shall say more about the possible parts of this branch of the *corpus*.

Like any such schematic statement, this one does not capture the substantive interrelationships among the various branches and inevitably oversimplifies.[50] It does underline Smith's determination to produce a "system," in some sense of the term, and indicates that the division between the moral and intellectual sentiments is central.[51] By subordinating political economy to natural jurisprudence – and there are numerous references in *The Wealth of Nations* to justice – the schema also indicates that the study of the nature and causes of the wealth of nations is a subset of the larger enterprise of the study of government, law, and natural justice, not a replacement for that study. That larger enterprise is itself a branch of moral philosophy. Hence *The Wealth of Nations* must be understood in terms of a more extensive ethical project and conception.

The schema helps to bring out the differences between Smith's projected system and the types of systems he attributes to his predecessors.[52] There is no obvious place for metaphysics, epistemology, or theology in

50  It also does not exactly reproduce the division of Smith's lectures at Glasgow as reported by Millar, i.e., into natural theology, ethics (the substance of which became *TMS*), justice (Millar says that Smith followed Montesquieu's plan of "endeavouring to trace the gradual progress of jurisprudence"), and "expediency" or "the political institutions relating to commerce" (which "contained the substance" of *WN*). See Stewart, *Memoirs*, p. 12.

51  The apt term "intellectual sentiments" was coined by J. Cropsey in reference to Smith's work on the psychology of inquiry and understanding (much of it contained in *EPS* and *LRBL*). See Cropsey, *Polity and Economy: An Interpretation of the Principles of Adam Smith* ([1957] rpt. Westport, Conn.: Greenwood, 1977), p. 43, n. 3.

52  Smith claims that the ancients divided philosophy into logic, ethics, and physics, whereas the medievals added metaphysics, pneumatics, and ontology (*WN* V.i.f.26–9). He clearly prefers the ancient division but nonetheless alters it.

the projected system, even though Smith had examples of such inquiries before him in the work of Locke and Hume, among others. Further, Smith's *corpus* did not include, and would not have included, any pamphlets or tracts of a popular and political nature. As his treatment in *The Wealth of Nations* of the problem of the American colonies indicates, he did give advice on pressing issues of the day, but even there the advice is meant to illustrate the larger principles of the work, as is shown by the fact that he retained the relevant passages after the question of the American colonies had been settled.[53]

What is the basis for my reconstruction of Smith's projected *corpus*? The answer requires that we take further steps into the thickets of Smith's philosophy, piecing together what clues he left us. Toward the end of *The Theory of Moral Sentiments* (VII.iv.34) he remarks that "the two useful parts of moral philosophy, therefore, are Ethics and Jurisprudence: casuistry ought to be rejected altogether." Ethics includes, first, definitions and descriptions of the virtues, as well as exhortations to exercise these virtues (VII.iv.6). Second, it seems safe to infer that it includes what we would call "moral psychology," an analysis of the mechanisms that lead us to "praise" and to "blame" others' behavior as we do, for *The Theory of Moral Sentiments* is surely a work in "Ethics" and explicitly treats of both virtue and moral psychology.[54] Smith goes on to assert that hitherto we have lacked "a system of natural jurisprudence" of which systems of

---

53 In 1778 Smith's advice on the question was requested by A. Wedderburn, solicitor-general in Lord North's administration; Smith's memorandum is reproduced in appendix B in *CAS*, pp. 380–5. In the "Advertisement" to the third edition of *WN*, Smith calls attention to the shifting temporal framework denoted by phrases of his such as "the present state of things." By the third edition, that is, *WN* self-consciously preserves several temporally framed layers.

54 It might be objected that Smith does not explicitly say that moral psychology forms part of "Ethics"; that "the science which is properly called Ethics" (VII.iv.6) seems to consist, for Smith, in protreptic descriptions of the virtues; and hence that moral philosophy should be divided into ethics (the virtues), moral psychology, and natural jurisprudence. Although this is essentially a terminological issue, I would add that in *TMS* he treats of virtue and moral psychology but does not distinguish them until the end, thus suggesting that they are parts of a single inquiry distinct from jurisprudence; that the description of "ethics" here includes ascertaining "wherein consists the sentiment of the heart, upon which each particular virtue is founded, what sort of internal feeling or emotion it is which constitutes the essence" of virtues (VII.iv.3), this being a recognizable task of moral psychology; and that he does not use the term "moral psychology" or an equivalent. In the *WN* passage already cited (V.i.f.26–9) Smith writes of "ethics" and "moral philosophy" (plainly abstracting from jurisprudence) interchangeably. If a looser and stricter ("properly called") use of the term "ethics" be found helpful here, I do not object.

positive law are approximations. Earlier efforts have failed. Cicero's *De officiis* and Aristotle "in his Ethics" (presumably the *Nicomachean Ethics*) failed because they "treat of justice in the same general manner in which they treat of all the other virtues." Plato's *Laws* and Cicero's *De legibus* are unsatisfactory because they treat of "laws of police, not of justice." Grotius's *Of War and Peace* is a bit more adequate in articulating the normative "foundation of the laws of all nations" (*TMS* VII.iv.35–7). Smith may be taken to mean that Aristotle, at least, failed, not only in giving too general an account of justice but in treating all of the different virtues in the same manner. Smith's projected *corpus* implicitly claims originality and philosophical progress not only with respect to the relatively new science of "political economy" but also with respect to "natural jurisprudence." The ancients' treatment of justice was inadequate.[55]

Smith then concludes *The Theory of Moral Sentiments*, with this statement:

> I shall in another discourse endeavour to give an account of the general principles of law and government, and of the different revolutions they have undergone in the different ages and periods of society, not only in what concerns justice, but in what concerns police, revenue, and arms, and whatever else is the object of law. I shall not, therefore, at present enter into any further detail concerning the history of jurisprudence.

This statement appears to outline two distinct tasks for the "theory of jurisprudence," though unfortunately the force of the conjunction "and" uniting the first two clauses is not entirely clear. The first task seems to be an account of the "general principles of law and government." These principles seem to be equivalent to the "natural rules of justice" that constitute the "system of natural jurisprudence," which principles "ought to run through and be the foundation of the laws of all nations" (*TMS* VII.iv.37).[56] That the "philosophy of law" should be "treated of by itself, and without regard to the particular institutions of any one nation" is taken by him at the end of the book as the desider-

---

55 Smith is not alone in holding this view. Cf. J. Schneewind, "The Misfortunes of Virtue," *Ethics* 101 (1990), pp. 46–8, 58–60. Schneewind refers to Grotius's attack on Aristotle in *On the Law of War and Peace*, Prolegomena, sec. 43.

56 The last phrase quoted here is repeated by Smith. On natural jurisprudence, Smith remarks: "It might have been expected that these reasonings should have led [lawyers] to aim at establishing a system of what might properly be called natural jurisprudence, or a theory of the general principles which ought to run through and be the foundation of the laws of all nations" (VII.iv.37).

atum to be accomplished. Therefore it is not to be found in *The Theory of Moral Sentiments.*

The second task seems to consist in an account of the historical embodiment and evolution of laws. The quoted statement reads as if justice, police, revenue, and arms are all spheres within which the general principles of jurisprudence can be exhibited. In the "Advertisement" prefixed to the sixth edition of *The Theory of Moral Sentiments* he refers to this concluding statement and adds: "In the *Enquiry Concerning the Nature and Causes of the Wealth of Nations,* I have partly executed this promise; at least so far as concerns police, revenue, and arms. What remains, the theory of jurisprudence, which I have long projected, I have hitherto been hindered from executing, by the same occupations which had till now prevented me from revising the present work" (p. 3).[57] In other words, what remains to be written is the account of the historical evolution of justice and the "theory of [natural] jurisprudence" itself. Presumably the latter would treat directly of "the general principles of law and government," the first part of the dual task mentioned at the end of *The Theory of Moral Sentiments.*

The distinction between the two tasks of a natural jurisprudence seems again indicated in Smith's letter to the duc de la Rochefoucauld of November 1, 1785. Smith there says that in addition to revising *The Theory of Moral Sentiments* (the revisions incorporated into the sixth edition, published in the year of his death), he has "two other great works upon the anvil," one of which "is a sort of theory and History of Law and Government" (*CAS*, pp. 286–7). Once again, the force of the conjunction "and" is ambiguous. It is this "theory" – presumably the account of the "general principles" of natural jurisprudence – that seems to be missing, as distinguished from the "history," at least part of which is provided in *The Wealth of Nations.* Perhaps the draft of this "great work" was among the documents burned about the time of his death.

The "Advertisement" to the sixth edition of *The Theory of Moral Sentiments* implies that political economy, the task of *The Wealth of Na-*

57 As the Advertisement formed part of the sixth edition, published in the year of Smith's death, and as Smith had declared his intention to produce the system of natural jurisprudence in the first edition, it seems that he had the general shape of his system in mind more or less from the start of his publishing career – and probably earlier, given the origins of *TMS*, *WN*, and other writings in his lectures, and the early origin of some of the essays on language and on the "aesthetics" of inquiry (now collected in *EPS*). The projected treatment of natural jurisprudence is also mentioned in the "Fragment on Justice," evidently written before the first edition of *TMS* was published. (See app. A of the Macfie and Raphael edition of *TMS*, pp. 389 and 395.)

*tions*,[58] is a branch of a still more general science of "natural jurisprudence," a science that is the province of the legislator or statesman, properly conceived.[59] This inference is confirmed by the introduction to Book IV of *The Wealth of Nations*, even though to confine the scope of the book to "police, revenue, and arms" seems rather cramped, given that it also discusses topics such as education and public works and that it seems odd to think of political economy as a branch of jurisprudence. But it must be kept in mind that the genus is *natural* jurisprudence, understood as the articulation of the laws of natural justice that are the general principles of law and government.

The student notes of Smith's lectures on jurisprudence overlap with parts of *The Wealth of Nations*. The lectures frequently expand on points touched on in the book, including those concerning justice, police, revenue, and arms.[60] Some of the discussion of justice treats of laws as they have changed through "different revolutions . . . in the different ages and periods of society." These lectures fill out what the historical, or applied, part of Smith's missing "natural jurisprudence" might have looked like.[61] Hence that part of natural jurisprudence is in principle

---

58 At *WN* IV.ix.38 Smith glosses "Political Oeconomy" as the analysis "of the nature and causes of the wealth of nations"; given the title of the book, it seems clear that Smith took his study to constitute an inquiry into political economy, even though the title does not contain the term. He uses the term pejoratively to refer to mercantilist and agriculturalist doctrines, and may have refrained from using it in the title of his own book in order to avoid association with those doctrines as well as with James Steuart's book on the subject. For further discussion see D. Winch, "Adam Smith: Scottish Moral Philosopher as Political Economist," *Historical Journal* 35 (1992), pp. 97–101.

59 *WN* IV.ii.39: the "science of a legislator" is one whose "deliberations ought to be governed by general principles which are always the same," as distinguished from the "skill of that insidious and crafty animal, vulgarly called a statesman or politician." These unchanging "general principles" unquestionably echo the "general principles of law and government" of *TMS* VII.iv.37. Brown has argued that *WN* is not a work in "political economy" and that Smith's project in *WN* cannot be understood as part of the "science of a legislator." *Adam Smith's Discourse*, p. 130. This radical reinterpretation of the matter seems to me untenable. For some comments on Brown's general interpretation of Smith, see my review of the book, cited in note 40.

60 At *LJ*(B) 1 we read: "Jurisprudence is that science which inquires into the general principles which ought to be the foundation of the laws of all nations," and soon after, "The four great objects of law are Justice, Police, Revenue, and Arms. The object of Justice is the security from injury, and it is the foundation of civil government. The objects of Police are the cheapness of commodities, public security, and cleanliness. . . . Under this head we will consider the opulence of a state" (*LJ*(B) 5).

61 The view that the unpublished lectures on jurisprudence and the published work provide a coherent view of the basic dimensions (as well as many of the details) of natural jurisprudence as a whole is argued by K. Haakonssen in *The Science of a Legislator: The Natural Jurisprudence of David Hume and Adam Smith* (Cambridge: Cambridge University Press,

possible to work out. The lectures also give us brief discussions of social contract theory, "natural rights," various categories of "injury" (i.e., injustice) that can be done to a person, and the various forms of government (*LJ*(A) 12–23; (B) 5–18). There are brief discussions as to why contracts obligate (e.g., *LJ*(A) 56–60 et passim; (B) 176). There are occasional statements such as "There is no maxim more generally acknowledged than that the earth is the property of each generation" (*LJ*(A) 164). Taken together, these discussions may also illustrate or state some of the topics that would have been treated in the missing first branch of natural jurisprudence, namely an account of the "general principles of law and government" as such, but they do not seem equivalent to that treatment. (Recall that neither *TMS* nor *WN* is thought by Smith to provide the treatment in question.) We are therefore left wondering, not just about the specifics of the missing discussion of "the theory of jurisprudence" but even about its general structure.

As if this were not enough, there is another, also vexing, aspect to the *corpus* problem. The first of the "great works upon the anvil" referred to in the letter to Rochefoucauld is "a sort of Philosophical History of all the different branches of Literature, of Philosophy, Poetry and Eloquence." Playing on the suggestion of Smith's literary executors, Black and Hutton, I have denominated it the "Philosophical History of the Liberal Sciences and Elegant Arts."[62] The history is "philosophical" because, as the lectures on rhetoric and the essays show, it seeks not merely to report but critically to evaluate, as well as to connect the phenomena systematically.

It seems reasonably clear that the literature, poetry, and eloquence branches of this "great work" would have included thoroughly revised versions of the material in the student notes of Smith's lectures on rhet-

---

1981). If, as I am suggesting, one part of Smith's projected natural jurisprudence is effectively absent from the published and unpublished materials on the topic, perhaps because it could not be written, then the fit between these materials still leaves us with an interpretive and philosophical "system" issue of significance.

62 In the letter to Hume of Apr. 16, 1773, Smith writes: "As I have left the care of all my literary papers to you, I must tell you that except those which I carry along with me [i.e., the MS of *WN*] there are none worth the publishing, but a fragment of a great work which contains a history of the Astronomical Systems that were successively in fashion down to the time of Des Cartes. Whether that might not be published as a fragment of an intended juvenile work, I leave entirely to your judgment. . . . All the other loose papers . . . I desire may be destroyed without any examination" (*CAS*, p. 168). In their "advertisement" to *EPS*, Black and Hutton remark that the papers Smith left "appeared to be parts of a plan he [Smith] once had formed, for giving a connected history of the liberal sciences and elegant arts" (*EPS* p. 32).

oric and on belles lettres and also some of the essays published by his
literary executors (now in the *Essays on Philosophical Subjects*), such as the
discussions of imitation, the imitative arts, and of English and Italian
poetry.[63] The "philosophy" branch of this "great work" would probably
have included his "Considerations concerning the First Formation of
Languages" (published in 1761) and his contributions to the *Edinburgh
Review* (1755–6). This branch would certainly have included the three
key essays that are meant, as their full titles indicate, to "illustrate"
(Smith's verb) the "Principles which Lead and Direct Philosophical Enquiries."[64] That these three essays (on the history of astronomy, of logic,
and of metaphysics) have this same general title indicates that Smith
viewed them as segments of a single unified treatise, itself a segment of
the "Philosophical History of the Liberal Sciences and Elegant Arts."
Smith did not direct his friends to destroy these three manuscripts.

The "philosophy" branch of the projected "Philosophical History"
would also have included, presumably, a history of the discussion of the
"principles which lead and direct philosophical enquiries," not simply
of the disciplines that illustrate the principles. This would come down to
an account of the principles of "intellectual sentiments," of "theorizing," a type of "philosophy of mind." That account would have occupied
pride of place in Smith's system, since it would have shed so much light
on the very activity in which he was engaged throughout the entire *corpus*.
The question as to whether this Platonic-sounding dream of a "great
work" could be realized – or even whether the more modest task of a
philosophical history of the branches of philosophy that illustrate directing "principles" could be realized – parallels the challenge we have
just reviewed with respect to the other missing branch of Smith's intended system.

The incompleteness of his systematic project no doubt has some bear-

---

63  In his letter to A. Holt of Oct. 26, 1780, Smith refers to a "Work concerning the imitative
    arts" he had been drafting during the time following the first publication of *WN* in 1776,
    presumably "Of the Nature of that Imitation which Takes Place in what are Called the
    Imitative Arts" (*CAS*, p. 252).
64  The three essays (all in *EPS*) are entitled "The Principles which Lead and Direct Philo-
    sophical Enquiries; Illustrated by the History of Astronomy"; "The Principles which Lead
    and Direct Philosophical Enquiries; Illustrated by the History of Ancient Physics"; and
    "The Principles which Lead and Direct Philosophical Enquiries; Illustrated by the History
    of the Ancient Logics and Metaphysics." I add that there are several other manuscripts
    unpublished by Smith but preserved and published in *EPS*, such as "Of the External
    Senses," and that it is not clear where they would fit in the projected *corpus*. K. L. Brown
    argues that that essay would have directly supported the project of *TMS*. "Dating Adam
    Smith's Essay 'Of the External Senses.' "

ing on his fluctuating status in the philosophical canon. But that status also reflects something of his, as well as our own, views about philosophy and its relation to human life. That Smith has for a period had greater influence as a political economist than as a moral and social philosopher, and indeed that he should have been so poorly understood even as a political economist, itself signals well-known difficulties concerning the possible role of philosophy in public life. This old Platonic problem about how philosophers can engage the polis will be revisited repeatedly in the following pages.

# 1

# RHETORIC, METHOD, AND SYSTEM IN
## *THE THEORY OF MORAL SENTIMENTS*

> Of all the artificial relations formed between mankind, the most ca-
> pricious and variable is that of author and reader.
>
> Earl of Shaftesbury[1]

In comparison with other great works of moral philosophy, from the
Platonic dialogues to Kant's *Critique of Practical Reason*, Smith's *Theory of
Moral Sentiments* is stylistically distinctive. It is obvious at a glance that,
for example, the "geometrical" style of Spinoza's *Ethics* would for Smith
completely distort the subject matter. Smith's conception of ethics is
fundamentally different from Spinoza's and simply does not lend itself
to that kind of articulation. To overstate slightly: just as Spinoza's *Ethics*
is modeled on geometrical deduction, so Smith's book is modeled on
literary, indeed "dramatic," representation. In neither case is the rhetoric of theorizing merely window dressing. The distinctive rhetoric of
each is intrinsic to the argument.

Smith's extensive work on rhetoric dates back to his days in Edinburgh, a remarkable fact often forgotten by those who see him merely

---

1 Anthony Ashley Cooper, 3rd Earl of Shaftesbury, "Miscellaneous Reflections," in *Advice to
an Author*, in vol. 2 of *Characteristics of Men, Manners, Opinions, Times*, 2 vols., ed. J. M.
Robertson (Bristol, UK: Thoemmes, 1995), miscellany V, ch. 1, p. 296.

as an economist.[2] His early and abiding interest in rhetoric signals at the very least an awareness that what one wishes to say or write to others is shaped by the demands of the audience one envisions and by the constraints of the medium in question. But to leave the matter there would be to accord rhetoric a merely instrumental role in the communication of ideas. We have reason to believe that Smith understood that the subject matter itself may require expression of a certain sort if it is to be represented accurately. His work evinces a sophisticated awareness of the problem of the relationship between form, content, and audience.

The problem is an old one in the history of rhetoric, and he knew the discussions of rhetoric, composition, and style going back through Cicero to Aristotle and Plato. Smith would have known from Hume, too, that the interpretation of a text is linked to the manner in which the text is written, as well as to what the author wishes to convey.[3] Because both Hume and Berkeley wrote dialogues, Smith had before him contemporary examples of that form of philosophical writing. (Of course, there were numerous classical examples as well, including works by Cicero, Lucian, Augustine, and Boethius.) Shaftesbury's *Characteristics* included a great deal of highly sophisticated discussion (in the "Advice to an Author") about the problem of writing philosophy, including moral philosophy, in dialogue form. Moreover, a key tenet of the traditional "art" of rhetoric is that the good rhetorician must know when to remain silent (*Phaedrus* 272a).[4]

---

2 A colleague of Smith's at the University of Glasgow, John Millar, suggests that Smith thought that traditional logic and metaphysics were best replaced by the study of rhetoric (understood as the study of the communication of ideas through speech, especially through "literary compositions"). See Stewart, *Memoirs*, p. 11.

3 I refer to Hume's "Of Essay Writing" and "Of Simplicity and Refinement in Writing." Smith might also have known Hume's comments about Plutarch's use of the dialogue form in a note to "Of the Populousness of Ancient Nations"; see D. Hume, *Essays Moral, Political, and Literary*, p. 463, n. 278. Smith comments on the issue of esotericism in Platonic writing in section 3 of his essay "The History of the Ancient Logics and Metaphysics" (*EPS*, p. 122 n.).

4 For an excellent discussion of Smith's extensive knowledge of rhetoric, see I. Ross, "Adam Smith as Rhetorician," in *Man and Nature*, vol. 2, ed. R. L. Emerson, W. Kinsley, and W. Moser (Montreal: Canadian Society for Eighteenth-Century Studies, 1984), pp. 61–74. Q. Skinner's recent study shows just how important rhetoric was for Hobbes. Skinner comments that in Renaissance humanism the model for rationality and moral argument was heavily dialogical. *Reason and Rhetoric in the Philosophy of Hobbes* (Cambridge: Cambridge University Press, 1996), pp. 14–16. I am suggesting that Smith had not entirely made the shift to what Skinner calls the modern "monological style" of rationality (p. 16). Skinner also voices the hope that his work on Hobbes "may encourage others to reconsider the literary character of further works of early modern social and political philosophy. . . . The

In recent years the general issue of philosophical rhetoric has been the subject of extensive discussion. It is being pursued with vigor over the entire spectrum, from Greek philosophy (where Plato's use of the dialogue form has earned particular attention) to modern philosophy (where one thinks of the discussions of the form of Descartes', Hobbes', and Nietzsche's writings) to contemporary discussions of the ways in which rhetoric and argument influence each other.[5] A good deal of attention has also been devoted to the specific issue of writing about ethics.[6] Smith should be seen as an interlocutor in these broader discussions.

Smith's extreme care with the manner in which his work reached the public is well attested. He seems to have worried about student note taking at his lectures on the no doubt justified basis that students might

canon of leading treatises in the history of philosophy is at the same time a canon of major literary texts" (p. 14). I am obviously in agreement with this view. See also M. Prince, *Philosophical Dialogue in the British Enlightenment* (Cambridge: Cambridge University Press, 1996).

5 For the discussion with respect to Plato, see the introduction and chapter 6 of my *Self-knowledge in Plato's "Phaedrus,"* and *Platonic Writings, Platonic Readings*, ed. C. Griswold (New York: Routledge & Kegan Paul, 1988). On Descartes, see A. Kosman, "The Naive Narrator: Meditation in Descartes' *Meditations*," in *Essays on Descartes' Meditations*, ed. A. O. Rorty (Berkeley and Los Angeles: University of California Press, 1986), pp. 21–43, and B. Lang, "Descartes between Method and Style," in *The Anatomy of Philosophical Style* (Oxford: Blackwell Publisher, 1990), pp. 45–85; on Nietzsche, see A. Nehamas, *Nietzsche: Life as Literature* (Cambridge, Mass.: Harvard University Press, 1985). A. Baier prefaces her study of Hume by remarking: "Like Descartes in the *Meditations*, so Hume in his *Treatise* stages a thinker's dramatic development from inadequate and doubt-inviting approaches to more satisfactory reflections." *A Progress of Sentiments: Reflections on Hume's "Treatise"* (Cambridge, Mass.: Harvard University Press, 1991), p. vii. Her study illuminates the ways in which Hume is a dialectical and rhetorical writer.

6 For a start, see the essays in *Literature and the Question of Philosophy*, ed. A. J. Cascardi (Baltimore: Johns Hopkins University Press, 1987), particularly M. Nussbaum, " 'Finely Aware and Richly Responsible': Literature and the Moral Imagination" (pp. 167–91), and C. E. Larmore, *Patterns of Moral Complexity* (Cambridge: Cambridge University Press, 1987), esp. pp. 19–21. I suspect Smith would agree with B. Williams's comment: "There is no reason to say that [the theory of persuasion] is not a philosophical subject; the reason someone might have for saying so would probably be the false view that philosophy was cut off from substantive ethical issues. But it should remind us of how deeply impure philosophy is. . . . The ethical issues of objectivity, the questions of what truthfulness and an appropriate impartiality mean to us in our circumstances, remind us of that [philosophy's] impurity in another way: to think about those questions is also to think about a lot more than philosophy. It is to try to think seriously about a decent life in the modern world, and it is a platitude to say that it needs more than philosophy to do that." "Saint-Just's Illusion," in *Making Sense of Humanity* (Cambridge: Cambridge University Press, 1995), p. 148.

garble his words;[7] he did his best to ensure that nothing he had not judged publishable would survive his death; he was quite concerned about the publication of Hume's *Dialogues*;[8] and he took his work on ethics through six editions. He was a careful, self-conscious writer. Any connections between his rhetoric and the views he wished to communicate should be taken as deliberately crafted on his part.

From early on Smith evinced a deep interest in the evolution, typology, and classification of language, as well as the processes by which words come to be detached from their natural context and so acquire a "technical" philosophical or "metaphysical" meaning. His first publication was a review (for the 1755 *Edinburgh Review*, now reprinted in *EPS*) of Dr. Johnson's *Dictionary*, and in 1761 he published his "Considerations Concerning the first Formation of Languages, and the Different Genius of Original and Compounded Languages" (now reprinted in *LRBL*), an essay that was appended to *The Theory of Moral Sentiments* from the third edition on. Smith's reflections on how language communicates meaning and how rules of grammar originate were early, broad, and quite sophisticated. He himself was in command of several languages, modern and ancient, and his vast knowledge of the history of rhetoric and of literature was much admired.

Smith was acutely aware of the role of rhetoric in human life. As he is reported to have remarked to his students,

> If we should enquire into the principle in the human mind on which this disposition of trucking is founded, it is clearly the naturall inclination every one has to persuade. . . . Men always endeavour to persuade others to be of their opinion even when the matter is of no consequence to them. . . . And in this manner every one is practising oratory on others thro the whole of his life. (*LJ* (A) vi.56)

We are ever rhetoricians, as he also tells us in both of his published books (*TMS* VII.iv.25; *WN* I.ii.3).

How does Smith, master of rhetoric and student of language that he was, draw us into a view of ethics and persuade us of a certain self-understanding? In what respects is the rhetoric of his ethics distinctive?[9]

---

7  Raphael, *Adam Smith*, pp. 15–16. See also Bryce's introduction to the *LRBL*, p. 3.
8  For a discussion of the possible reasons for Smith's worries, see T. D. Campbell and I. Ross, "The Theory and Practice of the Wise and Virtuous Man: Reflections on Adam Smith's Response to Hume's Deathbed Wish," in *Studies in Eighteenth-Century Culture*, 11 (1982): 65–75.
9  In exploring the issue of the philosophical rationale for the rhetorical dimension of *TMS*, my main concern is not with how the analysis of rhetorical discourse set out in the *LRBL*

## 1. THE STARTING POINT OF ETHICAL INQUIRY

We may approach these questions by means of another. What is *The Theory of Moral Sentiments* about? One would expect some indication of the answer in an introduction to the work. Yet there is no introduction to *The Theory of Moral Sentiments* (in contrast to the "Introduction and Plan of the Work" Smith provided for *The Wealth of Nations*), and, even more strange, it is only in Part VII, the concluding section, that we learn what questions Smith sought to answer in the book.[10] These are note-worthy features of his rhetoric. Immediately after the title page and table of contents, the curtain goes up, as it were, and the play begins. These facts are of philosophical relevance, for they are connected to old and well-known problems concerning how one gets started in a philosophical work.[11] For Smith, an introduction to moral inquiry would start us at a stage of the argument more appropriate to the conclusion. The peculiar rhetorical features of the book reflect his understanding of the problem of making a start on the subject matter of ethics, as well as his under-standing of the solution – namely, to embed ethical theorizing properly in our ordinary moral self-understanding.

Consider the beginning of *The Theory of Moral Sentiments* – the title page. The strangeness of the book's title is a distinctive feature of Smith's presentation of the subject. What does he mean, first, by the definite article? Should we infer that he thinks that he has written *the* theory of moral sentiments – the definitive one – or rather, as Macfie and Raphael suggest in their edition, that he means to denote the subject treated?[12] In the title of the first section of Part VII, he refers to the requirements of "a" theory of moral sentiments, meaning by the indefinite article

might apply to *TMS*, and I have not sought to establish the characteristics of Smith's rhetoric by an examination of the text in light of the classical and neoclassical rhetorical traditions (though Smith knew them well). My concern is rather with his understanding of the demands on his rhetoric generated by the subject matter and audience.

10 Contrast this with Hume's procedure in section I of the *Enquiry Concerning the Principles of Morals* and in the introduction to the *Treatise*.

11 For some discussion of the general problem of beginnings, see my "Plato's Meta-philosophy: Why Plato Wrote Dialogues," in *Platonic Writings, Platonic Readings*, pp. 143–67. The problems include those of circularity (i.e., building into the beginning what one wishes to prove by the end) and of arbitrariness (i.e., taking as self-evident at the beginning that which is not).

12 See the editors' Introduction to *TMS*, pp. 14–15, and p. 397. By contrast to *TMS*, the title of *WN* begins with the indefinite article, as does Hume's *Treatise*, the *Essays* of Locke and Ferguson, and the *Inquiries* of Shaftesbury and Hutcheson, among many others. I note that I am focusing on the title page of the sixth edition of *TMS*.

"any." It would be difficult to counter the evidence that Macfie and Raphael offer to the effect that the title refers to the subject matter. Although this is not incompatible with Smith's believing that he has produced the best treatment of the subject matter to date, it leaves open the possibility of revision and makes no claim to finality. This is important, for it seems that Smith's general philosophical stance makes it unlikely that there could be such a thing as a final, definitive work in philosophy – *the* work in an area. Thus the title would seem to refer to a subject matter.

Yet there remains strain in the title; the book is not about "the theory of moral sentiments" in the sense of a preexisting body of literature, for *The Theory of Moral Sentiments* is neither a metatheory setting up the boundaries of the discipline nor is there any such well-defined, preexisting field to which it can claim to be making a contribution. In *The Theory of Moral Sentiments* Smith carves out his distinctive approach to ethical issues. Indeed, he seems to have invented the phrase "theory of moral sentiments." Even the use of the word "theory" in the title seems innovative, for it rarely occurs in the titles of major philosophical works in English prior to Smith.[13] The phrase "the theory of moral sentiments" – denoting either the subject matter or the title of the book – does not occur in the body of the book itself. So, even though the title refers to the subject matter, the book does not trumpet the subtlety or originality it implies. (Compare, say, the preface to the second edition of Kant's *Critique of Pure Reason* [esp. Bxxii–xxiii].) Smith thereby blurs the line between ordinary moral experience and the analysis of it offered by his philosophical theory.

The meaning of the term "theory" I shall discuss subsequently. That "sentiments" is in the plural reflects a substantive contention of Smith's that there is no single sentiment (such as benevolence) that alone is

---

13 According to the editors of our edition of *TMS*, L. de Pouilly's *Théorie des sentiments agréables* may have "suggested to Smith that a suitable name for the philosophy of morals, as he understood it, would be the theory of moral sentiments" (p. 14). This may or may not be so; "agreeable" (as Smith translated the "agréable" of de Pouilly's title) is a far cry from "moral." The editors note that Smith used the title "the Theory of moral Sentiments" in the manuscript fragment on justice that probably was written in the early 1750s; he had a distinct view of the matter very early on. Since he did not alter the main title through the six editions, we may assume that he maintained from beginning to end a constant view of the contours of his project. The title page did contain, in the fourth through the sixth edition, the subtitle "or An Essay towards an Analysis of the Principles by which Men naturally judge concerning the Conduct and Character, first of their Neighbours, and afterwards of themselves." It accentuates the question about the definitiveness of the main title.

"moral." Smith does not refer to the theory of *the* moral sentiments, as though there were a specifiable number of them. Nor does he think that there are certain sentiments that are always moral or immoral, for on his account they seem to have potential to become either (II.i.5.8). This is a theory about the processes by which sentiments can become moral. Smith obviously thinks he has produced a work in what he calls "moral philosophy" (see the title of Part VII of *TMS*), yet to approach moral philosophy as treating of the moral sentiments is to assume a very particular approach to that discipline. The book's title reflects a substantive position of Smith's about what it is that we discuss in reference to the foundation of morals, namely, *sentiments* – rather than, say, practical reason or divine law. Further, this is not a book whose primary focus is moral action; the sentiments point us in the direction of character, though not by any means to the exclusion of action.

The qualification of "sentiments" by "moral" implies that there exist nonmoral sentiments. Those referred to in my Introduction as "intellectual sentiments" fall into that category. They are not, therefore, the primary focus of *The Theory of Moral Sentiments*; they are discussed in the works constituting the "Philosophical History" branch of inquiry. As a description of what is discussed in the book, though, the title still puzzles, for Smith does analyze sentiments that do not seem particularly "moral," such as resentment and envy. Further, he uses the term "moral" in locutions such as "moral beauty" that strike us as meshing moral and aesthetic terms in a confusing manner. The line between moral and nonmoral sentiments is not *prima facie* clear, and Smith therefore begins to draw it near the beginning of the book in his discussion of the difference between moral and theoretical virtue.

Smith signed the first and second editions of *The Theory of Moral Sentiments* "Professor of Moral Philosophy in the University of Glasgow" (adding "formerly" in the sixth edition). This self-identification, though not consistently retained through the editions, poses a question that I shall return to about the sense in which this is an "academic" book, one intended for other scholars and best seen as forming part of an academic tradition.[14] The issue of Smith's identification with the academy has bear-

14  The first two editions were published while he was still at Glasgow University. At Smith's request, the reference to his professorship was dropped in the third edition, and remained absent in the fourth and fifth, although the third through fifth still put "LL.D." after his name, in spite of Smith's specific instructions (when the third edition was to be printed) that nothing be placed before or after his name. See his letter to W. Strahan (winter, 1766–7?) (*CAS*, p. 122). The title page of the third edition of *WN* refers to Smith

ing on the question of the relationship between the standpoints of philosophical theorists and ordinary moral actors. For example, in placing at the *end* of the book both his specification of the two questions to which *The Theory of Moral Sentiments* has been a response and his analysis of the history of moral philosophy, Smith chose an approach opposite to that which one would take if addressing an academic audience of peers or students.[15] As a result, the book does not look much like the now familiar philosophical work, and it often moves along, in a relatively "literary" way, by means of appeals to the experience and reflection of the thoughtful reader.

Smith is so intent on appealing directly to our everyday experience and reflection that in the body of the work he declines to mention names of philosophers, even where it would have been expected (say, Hume's name in *TMS* IV), thus avoiding the impression that he wishes to debate another philosopher rather than engage the reflective reader in consideration of a view that naturally suggests itself. Philosophers such as Hobbes, Mandeville, Shaftesbury, Locke, Rousseau, Hutcheson, Berkeley, and Hume are infrequently (or never) mentioned in the first six parts of the book; by contrast, playwrights, poets, contributors to the belles lettres, and historians are mentioned much more frequently. Hume, for example, is never named by Smith in the body of the text.[16] Prior to Part VII, there is virtually no explicit engagement in *The Theory of Moral Sentiments* with the thought of any philosopher.[17]

as "Formerly Professor of Moral Philosophy in the University of Glasgow" and cites his distinctions ("LL.D and F.R.S.") after his name. Although we do not know for sure that Smith wanted his original instructions followed in the sixth edition, it seems safe to assume that he did and that the publisher simply continued to act on his own. The title page of the sixth edition describes the author as "Adam Smith, LL.D. Fellow of the Royal Societies of London and Edinburgh; One of the Commissioners of his Majesty's Customs in Scotland; and formerly Professor of Moral Philosophy in the University of Glasgow."

15 It seems reasonably clear that in his Glasgow lectures, Smith *began* his discussion of ethics with a treatment of the history of the matter. See the note by Raphael and Macfie to the start of the beginning of Part VII of *TMS*, p. 265, and Raphael, *Adam Smith*, p. 14.

16 Smith is not unique in his decision to name so few of his sources and interlocutors; cf. MacIntyre's comment with reference to Hume in *Whose Justice? Which Rationality?*, p. 290. Although MacIntyre connects Hume's lack of acknowledgment of predecessors with allegiance to a "radically first-person [singular] point of view," I shall argue in a moment that Smith's allegiance is more to a first-person plural point of view. On occasion *TMS* reflects an ongoing discussion between Smith and other philosophers. It seems reasonably clear that in revising for the second edition of *TMS* Smith responded to criticisms of the first edition by Sir Gilbert Elliot and by Hume. (See the editors' Introduction to *TMS*, pp. 16–17, for the references to Smith's correspondence with Elliot and Hume.)

17 Smith does mention Voltaire, but at III.6.12 the reference is to *Mahomet* (cf. the

Correspondingly, Smith is strikingly parsimonious in his use of footnotes. In all of Parts I through VI, there is a grand total of nine footnotes. All but two supply the original Latin term or phrase, or a brief citation, or a brief citation and quotation of a relevant phrase or two. The two remaining notes, one in Part I and one in Part II, alone are of substantive import and amount to a separate and separated conversation, as it were.[18] Part VII ("Of Systems of Moral Philosophy"), in keeping with its more technical and academic character, contains eighteen notes; even so, all consist of brief references to authors or texts under discussion. On the relatively rare occasions when Smith wants directly to address his more academic audience in particular, he tends to do so in a footnote, outside the body of the text; as befits exceptions to the rule, in each case he responds to an objection of genuine significance. The problem of the relation between these notes and the text to which they are appended mirrors that of the relation between Smith's more removed philosophical reflections and his account of the phenomena.[19]

## 2. RHETORIC, THE PROTREPTIC ''WE,'' AND THE DANGERS OF THEORY

The truth, however, in questions about action is judged from what we do and how we live, since these are what control [the answers to such ques-

reference at III.2.35). Cicero is quoted at III.2.30, Epictetus at III.3.11; and so forth. There are references to "an author of very great and original genius" and the like (I.i.2.1; II.ii.1.5; II.ii.3.6; IV.1.2; IV.2.3). Rare exceptions include Smith's taking issue with Plato and Aristotle on the question of infanticide (V.2.15) and his reference to Aristotle on *megalopsuchia* (VI.iii.44). Smith entirely ignores the Bible and the Patristic writings, never even mentioning them; nor is Christ ever referred to (although an allusion may be found at III.6.13).

18 The first of the two substantive footnotes responds to a pointed objection put to Smith by an unnamed person about the connection between sympathy and pleasure, an objection that forces Smith to make a crucial distinction (note to I.iii.1.9). This is one of the few explicit acknowledgments in the book that it has a dialogical context, that it has been shaped by a conversation between Smith and other thinkers. The note has an academic air to it, though this is minimized somewhat by the suppression of the objector's name. (We know now that it was Hume.) The second footnote, by far the longest in the book, concerns the possibility that to ascribe our sense of fairness to resentment may strike "the greater part of people" as a debasement of that sense (note to II.i.5.6).

19 In *WN* Smith is also parsimonious in his use of footnotes, and indeed in any references to previous authors who have worked on the issues he treats. D. Winch attributes this to his desire to emphasize (through absence of citation) his distance from his mercantilist predecessors, in part because his attacks on them concerned rival conceptions of justice, not just economics. "Adam Smith: Scottish Moral Philosopher as Political Economist," pp. 97–101.

tions]. Hence we ought to examine what has been said by applying it to what we do and how we live; and if it harmonizes with what we do, we should accept it, but if it conflicts we should count it [mere] words.

Aristotle, *Nicomachean Ethics*[20]

The unusual narrative structure and characteristics of *The Theory of Moral Sentiments* show themselves in a number of other features. It seems reasonably well attested that much of the book originated primarily in Smith's Glasgow lectures. There are interesting traces of that lecture-hall origin in the published text. I refer not so much to the occasional use of "upon a former occasion" where "in chapter Y" would have been more appropriate[21] as to the strong sense of audience and ethical community evident throughout *The Theory of Moral Sentiments*, signaled by Smith's use of what I shall call the "protreptic 'we.' " The pronoun "we" first occurs in the second sentence of the work and is used numerous times after that. The pronoun is "protreptic" in that it is intended to persuade us to view things in a certain light, to refine the ways in which we judge and feel, and perhaps to encourage us to act in a certain manner. Smith uses the first-person plural pronoun both to adduce evidence – in the form of concrete observations about ethical situations and "our" reactions to them – for propositions in moral psychology and to pass ethical judgments on all kinds of issues.[22] *The Theory of Moral Sentiments* is a moralizing ethical theory.

According to Smith, a theory of moral sentiments is to treat of two questions. The first is:

> Wherein does virtue consist? Or what is the tone of temper, and tenour of conduct, which constitutes the excellent and praise-worthy character, the character which is the natural object of esteem, honour, and approbation?

This is what we might call the "virtue question," and he focuses on answers to it throughout, but in especially in Part VI.[23] He may be said,

---

20 Aristotle, *Nicomachean Ethics*, 1179a18–23; trans. T. Irwin (Indianapolis: Hackett, 1985). All citations advert to this translation, cited hereafter as *NE*.

21 As at *TMS* IV.2.9. The editors note there that "the word 'occasion' again shows the original lecture form of the material."

22 Smith's use of "we" also helps overcome the barrier presented by the written word, putting author and reader onto the same stage, as it were. For some interesting remarks (directed by Foucault to a comment of R. Rorty's) on the issue of what I am calling the "protreptic 'we,' " see the interview with Foucault in *The Foucault Reader*, ed. P. Rabinow (New York: Pantheon, 1984), pp. 384–86.

23 In a letter to T. Cadell of Mar. 31, 1789, Smith remarks that in preparing the sixth

with qualifications, to argue for an ethics of character, that is, an agent-centered ethics of virtue. The second question is:

> By what power or faculty in the mind is it, that this character, whatever it be, is recommended to us? Or in other words, how and by what means does it come to pass, that the mind prefers one tenour of conduct to another, denominates the one right and the other wrong; considers the one as the object of approbation, honour, and reward, and the other of blame, censure, and punishment? (VII.i.2)

This is a question about moral psychology, about the psychology of ethics, and Smith discusses it throughout. Discussions of virtue can affect our behavior by affecting our notions of right and wrong, whereas theories of moral psychology are alleged only to satisfy "philosophical curiosity" (VII.iii.intro.3); these latter are, as we might put it, merely academic. Insofar as in *The Theory of Moral Sentiments* Smith treats of virtue, the book is ethically protreptic. Just as Smith agrees with Aristotle that we cannot understand ethics from an external perspective and that ethics is not an exact, rule-bound science, so he seems to agree with Aristotle that lectures on ethics cannot be expected to make the vicious into good persons.[24] Such lectures can, however, reinforce ethical character (*NE* 1103b26–31).[25] "We" is in part an ideal construction, then – both a mirroring of an ethical community and a vehicle for normative suasion.

Smith carefully develops an account showing that we are "spectators" of each other, but spectators aware of being actors in the eyes of other spectators. We can talk philosophically about ethics only with people who can imaginatively enter into the particulars of another's situation and who are capable of rendering a judgment that is impartial. The activity of articulating the subject matter already implies a community. Since Smith writes as a Smithean, he cannot "prove" that his normative judg-

edition of *TMS* he is supplying a "new sixth part containing a practical system of Morality, under the title of the Character of Virtue" (*CAS*, p. 320).

24  I owe the phrase "external perspective" with reference to the ethical context to J. Lear, *Aristotle: The Desire to Understand* (Cambridge: Cambridge University Press, 1988), p. 158.

25  Ancient ethicists disagreed with one another about many issues, but did not (generally speaking) so much expect that ethical theory would "solve" these definitively as that it would make us better (and happier) human beings. By contrast, we today generally expect an ethical theory to solve problems and disagreements but do not entertain much hope for the capacity of ethical theory to make us ethical. See J. Annas's discussion in *The Morality of Happiness* (Oxford: Oxford University Press, 1993), p. 443. Smith affirms the ancient view on this issue, with a crucial (if partial) exception, namely with respect to matters of justice.

ments are "right" except by persuading other, sympathetic and presumably impartial persons to agree. (In the limit case this involves appeal to an "impartial spectator.") That is how moral actors ought to proceed (according to Smith) in the course of ethical reflection. The use of "we" reflects his views about the nature of moral theorizing, specifically the view that ethics is a social practice that assumes a context of mutual responsiveness, of responsibility to provide reasons that would persuade, of accountability (even if just, ultimately, to an idealized judge). The "theory" of moral sentiments must rest on ethical practice and, indeed, as protreptic, it *is* a form of ethical practice.

The book's rhetoric is yet more complex. Smith refers to "we agents," at times to "we spectators" (as at VII.iii.3.16; "First, we sympathize with the motives of the agent"). On occasion, "we spectators" also observe and judge other spectators who are looking at an actor's situation (as at VII.iii.3.9). "We" are here comparable to critics in the balcony of a theater, observing both the audience and the play. He also writes occasionally in the first-person singular. Sometimes his "I" means "me or you" *qua* ordinary agents or spectators.[26] Sometimes his "you" means "any one of us," though the pronoun naturally invites the reader to identify closely with the situation.[27] He infrequently speaks of a "we" of philosophers (as at II.ii.3.5; "In every part of the universe we observe means adjusted with the nicest artifice to the ends which they are intended to produce"). This "theoretical" level of the detached philosophical critic is most frequently referred to, however, by "I," as when he is making a technical point about the connection between sympathy and approbation in complex cases involving a spectator and two antagonistic actors (II.i.3.2, 3; "First, I say, that . . . ," "Secondly, I say, that . . ." ).[28] Only rarely does Smith break out of the framework of the

26  E.g., the repeated use of the pronoun "I" at I.i.4.5, III.1.6, and VII.iii.1.4 is impersonal, meaning something like "any one of us situated in this way." A different shade of meaning occurs at VI.ii.1.8, where he speaks less as a theorist than as a seasoned spectator of human life.

27  E.g., in the crucial passage at VII.iii.1.4 on sympathy and self-love, Smith examines cases in which "you" have lost your only son and "I" empathize with you.

28  In *WN*, the theorist, "I" is extremely common throughout, and this helps set the tone for the book. Far less frequently, "we" is used as referring to "we thinkers" (e.g., I.viii.23; II.ii.16). The authority of his voice is overwhelming here in comparison with *TMS*. The relevant "we" of theorists has yet to be forged by the book itself. This is connected with the fact that *WN*, far more than *TMS*, is a polemical work intended to destroy a whole way of thinking about political economy. (In his letter to A. Holt of Oct. 26, 1780, Smith refers to *WN* as "the very violent attack I had made upon the whole commercial system of Great Britain" [*CAS*, p. 251].) Occasionally in *WN* Smith speaks of "we" ordinary

story he is telling and address himself directly to the reader, as when he suddenly asks us: "Are you in earnest resolved never to barter your liberty for the lordly servitude of a court, but to live free, fearless, and independent?" His answer is strikingly passionate in its tone (I.iii.2.7), and the force of the passage is accentuated by the unexpectedness and rarity of the author's direct appeals to us. At times he uses these pronouns in their various inflections in close succession.[29]

What is the purpose of the interplay of perspectives implicit in Smith's use of these pronouns? It leads the reader to see, first, that there are no simple answers, that further questions and problems always arise in ethical reflection, both practical and theoretical. The conversational character of nearly every chapter conveys the importance of moderating our desire for a simple, systematic, univocal understanding of ethical life. The interplay of voices lets itself be guided by the subject matter, the particularities of the case, the story being recounted; it naturally suggests that closure is difficult to obtain honestly. His rhetoric embodies a virtue he finds lacking from much of moral philosophy, namely *sophrosyne*, or, in his approving gloss of Plato's term, "good temper, or sobriety and moderation of mind" (VII.ii.1.8). Second, as I have already stressed, he must build this explanation and protreptic from more or less common premises implicit in our ordinary self-understanding, there being (in his view) no Archimedean point. His supple use of pronouns contributes directly to this purpose.

We are helped in understanding Smith's views about how ethics should be approached by his detailed discussion in Part VII of his predecessors. Several patterns of criticism emerge there. First, we learn that moral philosophers have repeatedly distorted the phenomena by forcing them to fit into their system. For example, of Epicurus's view that virtue is prudence, Smith says: "By running up all the different virtues too to

---

economic actors, as in the famous passage about "our" discourse with the butcher, brewer, or baker (*WN* I.ii.2). He also appeals to us as prephilosophical actors when speaking of that which is "self-evident" (*WN* IV.viii.49), of the "obvious and simple system of natural liberty," or of the three duties of the sovereign as being "plain and intelligible to common understandings" (*WN* IV.ix.51). The frequent judgments in *WN* about justice (or the lack thereof, as at V.i.i.3) are meant to reflect the standpoint of the reflective moral actor. The interplay of voices so marked in *TMS* is not absent in *WN*.

29 So too at VII.iii.3.17 ("There is another system which attempts to account for the origin of our moral sentiments from sympathy, distinct from that which I have been endeavouring to establish"). At I.ii.5.1, I.iii.1.5, VI.iii.14. At I.i.1.13, I.ii.1.1, II.i.3.1, and II.i.4.2 ("if I may say so"), Smith speaks in his own voice in order to apologize for a certain turn of phrase.

this one species of propriety, Epicurus indulged in a propensity, which is natural to all men, but which philosophers in particular are apt to cultivate with a peculiar fondness, as the great means of displaying their ingenuity, the propensity to account for all appearances from as few principles as possible" (VII.ii.2.14). The partly aesthetic insistence on conceptual elegance or simplicity often makes philosophers' theories reductionistic. Similarly, Chrysippus is criticized for having "reduced their [the Stoics'] doctrines into a scholastic or technical system" (VII.ii.1.41) and Hutcheson for having reduced all the virtues to just one, benevolence (VII.ii.3.16). Mandeville and Hobbes wrongly insist that only self-love can explain the full range of the moral emotions, even though "sympathy" is simply not reducible to selfishness (VII.iii.1.4). But that is just to say that the theory has lost its grip on what it is supposed to be elucidating.[30]

Equally important, for present purposes, is Smith's attribution to Hobbes of a consequentialist, if not utilitarian, explanation of the sense in which virtue is good (VII.iii.1.1). That explanation may seem plausible to the spectator who takes the theoretical and impersonal point of view: "Human society, when we contemplate it in a certain abstract and philosophical light, appears like a great, an immense machine, whose regular and harmonious movements produce a thousand agreeable effects" (VII.iii.1.2). But as moral agents we do not promote virtue or condemn vice because of their relative social utility; the normal nonutilitarian view-from-within is discounted when a synoptic or "abstract" perspective is adopted. In addition to reductionism, Smith is objecting to a second mistake moral philosophers often make, that of confusing the perspectives of moral agents and of theorists in such a way as to make the former, or important aspects of the former, disappear. We will see that he criticizes the Stoics for committing this error. Ethical life cannot be rightly understood when what is indispensable to it – the subjective standpoint of the actor – is downplayed. This mistake can come about when reduction is pushed so far that the phenomena to be explained are trans-

---

30 Campbell notes that "Mandeville's position may not be compatible with ordinary moral experience, but to show this is not to provide a philosophical justification for that experience"; Smith did "not see the inadequacy of his own theory in this respect." T. D. Campbell, *Adam Smith's Science of Morals* (Totowa, N.J.: Rowman & Littlefield, 1971), p. 223. But the place of "ordinary moral experience" in philosophy, and thus the notion of a "philosophical justification," are precisely what is at issue, and I contend that Smith took a well-thought-out position on the matter. Smith may ultimately be mistaken in the position he took, but he did not fail to understand the fundamental problem.

formed into illusions. When Smith objects to Mandeville's "self-love" theory on the grounds that it ends up effacing the distinction between virtue and vice (VII.ii.4.6), he is in effect applying this second type of criticism.[31]

Smith understood himself as engaged throughout much of the book in a debate with Hume concerning just this question of appropriate perspective in ethics, and therefore of the legitimacy of constructing theories that discount the agent's point of view. The key issue emerges at the start of *The Theory of Moral Sentiments* (I.i.4.4), and in the section that is literally at the center of the book (Part IV, "Of the Effect of Utility upon the Sentiment of Approbation"), Smith alludes to Hume ("an ingenious and agreeable philosopher") as the author of views with which he strongly disagrees. This is striking in part because Hume himself evinced keen awareness of precisely the issue in question. Whether rightly or wrongly, Smith took himself as following through on some of Hume's best insights about this relation more consistently and subtly than Hume himself was able to do. Smith objects that the "ingeneous" philosopher's approach to approbation does not do justice to the phenomena, including the phenomenon of intellectual virtue. On the whole, in judging moral and intellectual virtue we behave like moral realists who focus primarily on the particular case rather than as consequentialists.[32] We "originally" praise a person or thing on account of the intrinsically good or beautiful qualities exhibited rather than considerations of utility. Smith thinks that Hume looks on the phenomena *too philosophically* or "abstractly," too much from a synoptic and impersonal perspective, when he ascribes the motive for all such activity to the end that reason posits in observing things comprehensively. That method of getting at what people "really" want is untenable, because it discards our experience of particulars that are the primary occasions for and objects of ethical judgment. Smith's method and rhetoric, by contrast, appeal continually to our experience in and of this or that situation, our sense of

---

31  At VII.ii.4.7 Smith alludes to Mandeville's assertion that ". . . the Moral Virtues are the Political Offspring which Flattery begot upon Pride."

32  See *TMS* I.i.4.4: "The utility of those qualities [of intellectual virtue], it may be thought, is what first recommends them to us; and, no doubt, the consideration of this, when we come to attend to it, gives them a new value. Originally, however, we approve of another man's judgment, not as something useful, but as right, as accurate, as agreeable to truth and reality: and it is evident we attribute those qualities to it for no other reason but because we find that it agrees with our own. Taste, in the same manner, is originally approved of, not as useful, but as just, as delicate, and as precisely suited to its object." For parallel comments in *WN* on the issue of utility, see I.ii.1 and IV.v.b.39.

what is important to our individual lives and to our roles in the human drama.

A third danger of moral philosophy is captured by one of Smith's objections to Hutcheson's theory of the "moral sense," namely "that it is strange that this sentiment, which Providence undoubtedly intended to be the governing principle of human nature, should hitherto have been so little taken notice of, as not to have got a name in any language." "Moral sense" is merely a philosopher's construction; hitherto it had been neither named nor perceived by ordinary moral actors (VII.iii.3.15). The pretense, of course, is that this new faculty incorporates and thereby explains the previously puzzling phenomena. Smith would consider it an advantage that his own account of sympathy does not require the invention of a new word or faculty and he is pointing to "a power which has always been taken notice of" (VII.iii.3.3). Correspondingly, in *The Theory of Moral Sentiments* he makes every effort to avoid creating a technical vocabulary and instead appropriates ordinary terms.[33]

This is not to say that he is entirely successful in so doing, as is most strikingly the case with the word "sympathy," perhaps the key term in his moral philosophy. In Smith's designedly stumbling prose: "sympathy, though its meaning was, perhaps, originally the same [as commiseration], may now, however, without much impropriety, be made use of to denote our fellow-feeling with any passion whatever" (I.i.1.5). His forcible expansion of the meaning of a familiar term points once again to the problem of the relationship between philosophy and ordinary life.[34] Philosophy cannot simply inhabit the everyday world and leave all as it

---

33 As I have presented them, the three sorts of mistakes Smith thinks were exhibited by his predecessors in moral philosophy parallel Nagel's specification of three courses available to an "objective" (or detached, impersonal) point of view when it is confronted by a recalcitrant element in a subjective (or individual, personal) point of view: "reduction, elimination, and annexation." An example of trying to "save the appearances" (Nagel's phrase) by the first means might be (Nagel notes) consequentialism; by the second means, an effort to "dismiss deontological requirements and other nonconsequentialist ethical intuitions as superstitious, selfish, or rule-bound"; by the third means, "metaphysical inventions" such as "will, the ego, the soul, or perhaps the command of God." T. Nagel, "Subjective and Objective," in *Mortal Questions* (Cambridge: Cambridge University Press, 1988), pp. 210–11.

34 The novelty of Smith's use of the term was noted by Thomas Reid in his lectures on Smith: "But Dr Smith makes his Sympathy to correspond not to what the person sympathized with really & actually suffers or enjoys but what he should or ought suffer or enjoy. . . . I conceive this meaning of the word Sympathy is altogether new & that if one had not a hypothes to serve by it he would never have dreamed that it is Sympathy that makes us blush for the impudence and rudeness of another." Quoted in J. C. Stewart-

was. This raises the question we encountered in examining the title of *The Theory of Moral Sentiments*: How can we meaningfully occupy the "subjective" standpoint of actors in ordinary life while offering a theory that necessarily requires us to take, to some degree, an impersonal or "objective" standpoint?

The features of Smith's rhetoric that we have been examining, and his criticisms of his predecessors, gravitate around his commitment to saving or preserving the point of view of the prephilosophical moral actor. Why does he make that commitment? He gives us part of his answer in a discussion of Mandeville's system in the concluding section of the book. We will return to the issue repeatedly in subsequent chapters, as also to the question as to how different points of view on human life ought be combined:

> A system of natural philosophy may appear very plausible, and be for a long time very generally received in the world, and yet have no foundation in nature, nor any sort of resemblance to the truth. . . . But it is otherwise with systems of moral philosophy, and an author who pretends to account for the origin of our moral sentiments, cannot deceive us so grossly, nor depart so very far from all resemblance to the truth. When a traveller gives an account of some distant country, he may impose upon our credulity the most groundless and absurd fictions as the most certain matters of fact. But when a person pretends to inform us of what passes in our neighbourhood, and of the affairs of the very parish which we live in, though here too, if we are so careless as not to examine things with our own eyes, he may deceive us in many respects, yet the greatest falsehoods which he imposes upon us must bear some resemblance to the truth, and must even have a considerable mixture of truth in them. (VII.ii.4.14)

When an author treats of moral philosophy "he proposes to explain the origin of our desires and affections, of our sentiments of approbation and disapprobation, he pretends to give an account, not only of the affairs of the very parish that we live in, but of our own domestic concerns" (VII.ii.4.14). A decently raised human being possesses a degree of moral, as distinguished from theoretical or scientific, self-knowledge. When we do ethics we are philosophizing on the basis of that self-knowledge and are attempting to give an account that preserves rather than violates it (*WN* V.i.f.26).

Smith's view that moral judgment is grounded in sentiments rather

Robertson and D. F. Norton, "Thomas Reid on Adam Smith's Theory of Morals," *Journal of the History of Ideas* 45 (1984), p. 314.

than reason and that moral philosophy is as much a descriptive as a constructive enterprise assumes a quasi-Aristotelian insistence on pre-theoretical moral knowledge.[35] Where Aristotle spoke of the *endoxa* (sound and reputable opinions) and the *phronimoi* (persons of sound judgment or practical wisdom), Smith speaks of natural sentiments and judgments of impartial spectators. Whereas Aristotle would probably wish to justify reliance on the *endoxa* by reference to the soul's capacity for understanding what is objectively true, Smith's position is, at the theo-retical level, considerably more skeptical. He must reconcile his appeal to the self-understanding of moral actors with his recognition that moral actors make mistakes, not just about means but about ends. (An analo-gous challenge arises with respect to Aristotle's reliance on *endoxa*.)[36] Smith must both appeal to ordinary experience *and* evaluate it.

He is selective in his examples, counterexamples, and appeals to com-mon opinion, and he has in mind a specific answer to the "What is virtue?" question, such that, for example, the "monkish virtues," as Hume scornfully called them, are treated as pseudovirtues.[37] Some such

---

35  Cf. J. Barnes, "Aristotle and the Methods of Ethics," *Revue Internationale de Philosophie* 34 (1980), p. 509: for Aristotle, "Human nature is so constituted that we possess a faculty for grasping truth – even if that faculty must be refined by experience. There is a gap between the premises that men have a natural aptitude for knowledge, and the conclu-sion that τὰ ἔνδοξα constitute a deep well of truth. But for Aristotle the gap is easily bridged: if nature does nothing in vain, and if we are naturally inclined towards truth, it follows that we do, for the most part, attain the truth. . . . We cannot infer that whatever a man believes, is true; nor even that whatever all men believe, is true." For discussion of Aristotle's "method of appearances," see M. Nussbaum, *The Fragility of Goodness* (Cam-bridge: Cambridge University Press, 1986), chs. 8–9. I take it that Smith could agree with some of this but that his skepticism (discussed in Chapter 4) would have deprived him of any "metaphysical" interpretation of "nature" or "truth." This does not mean that Smith is therefore subject to what Barnes calls "the conservative parochialism of Common Sense" (p. 510). On Aristotle's criticisms of a skeptical position, see A. A. Long, "Aristotle and the History of Greek Scepticism," in *Studies in Aristotle*, ed. D. J. O'Meara (Washing-ton, D.C.: Catholic University of America Press, 1981), pp. 79–106.

36  Consider J. Cooper's remarks: "Why however does Aristotle make philosophy answerable even in this limited way to the *endoxa*? In his extant works he never addresses this question squarely, but the obvious answer (and its obviousness may explain his failure clearly to articulate it) is that there is antecedent good reason to expect that some or all of what is reputably believed is true – whether it is reputable because someone with a reputation for wisdom believes it, or because it is embedded in our language itself, or is a common-place of everyday life. The structures of our language and the commonplaces of everyday life are cultural artifacts that were originated, shaped and reshaped by generations of human beings who, with their native intelligences, confronted and dealt with reality." "Review of M. Nussbaum, *The Fragility of Goodness: Luck and Ethics in Greek Tragedy and Philosophy*," *Philosophical Review* 97 (1988), p. 553.

37  *WN* V.i.f.30; *TMS* III.2.35, and Hume, *Enquiry Concerning the Principles of Morals*, cited from

selectivity must obtain if the discussion is to count as a *theory* rather than as just a description. As we shall see in Chapter 2, broad ethical and political concerns also mold the moral psychology, just as one would expect from a moral philosophy grounded in practical ethics. *The Theory of Moral Sentiments* is also a moral theory of moral sentiments. We are to "save the appearances" (to use the now common post-Aristotelian phrase) in terms that would be accepted by reflective moral actors. Yet it may be queried whether an approach of this sort must be either philosophically unambitious and uncritical or forced, by the admission that moral actors make mistakes, to smuggle into the qualifier "reflective" a great deal of philosophical straightening out of appearances.

To put the underlying question differently, Smith's broadly Aristotelian procedure of appealing to considered opinion means that the appeals cannot be "justified" in a way that will persuade everybody (say, those outside the bounds of the ethical "we"). Is the Smithean "we" unavoidably parochial as a result? Is it reducible, for example, to a community with which only Western children of the Enlightenment may be expected to sympathize? Similar questions have been raised about Aristotle's and Hume's appeals to communities; MacIntyre, for example, argues that Hume's context is well defined and local.[38] The questions push with particular force here because in spite of the analogies with Aristotle, Smith does not have at his disposal an Aristotelian notion of teleological "nature" that can serve as a standard. Although one of the best-known features of his moral philosophy is the "impartial spectator," Smith clearly passes various judgments that are not universally shared. (By his own admission, his judgment about infanticide is a case in point.) To what extent this philosophy of common life possesses the resources for genuine moral criticism can only be decided when we explore them. At this juncture, the aim is to elicit the distinctive features of Smith's rhetoric and method and to indicate how they are intertwined with his philosophy.[39]

*Enquiries Concerning Human Understanding and Concerning the Principles of Morals*, ed. L. A. Selby-Bigge, 3rd ed., rev. ed. P. H. Nidditch (Oxford: Clarendon Press, 1989), p. 270. (Hereafter, references to either *Enquiry* advert to this edition.)

38  MacIntyre, *After Virtue*, p. 231: "What Hume identifies as the standpoint of universal human nature turns out in fact to be that of the prejudices of the Hanoverian ruling elite."

39  Although my main focus is on *TMS*, I note that the dialectical style of parts of *WN* is also intended to be ethically protreptic in that it moves us to moderation, encourages judgment, values harmony, and makes balance central. *WN* is clearly meant to have a practical

## 3. RHETORIC, EXAMPLES, AND NARRATIVE

For arguments about actions and feelings are less credible than the facts;
hence any conflict between arguments and perceptible [facts] arouses contempt for the arguments, and moreover undermines the truth as well [as
the arguments].

Aristotle, *Nicomachean Ethics*

Smith draws us in partly by means of his remarkable use of examples.
We are asked over and over again to consider this or that situation and
this or that reaction to a situation and to draw the appropriate moral.
The examples are sometimes elaborated into little stories about a human
life. Smith is capable of elegant writing, and his stories are powerful (e.g.,
consider the sketch of the life of the "prudent man" on VI.i.8–11, of
the lover of wealth on IV.i.8, and the imagined dialogue between King
Pyrrhus and Cineas on III.3.31). These stories and character sketches
follow in the tradition of Theophrastus's *Characters*, a book Smith knew
and admired.[40] Literature also plays an important and variegated role in
*The Theory of Moral Sentiments*. Not only plays, novels, and poems but tragedies, in particular, intrigue Smith. Together they completely over-
shadow his relatively rare references to properly philosophical texts
(putting aside *TMS* VII). The notion that we are to understand literature
and drama as sources for moral theory and moral education is clearly
and strikingly evident in *The Wealth of Nations* as well (V.i.g.14–15).

So permeated with examples, stories, literary references and allusions,
and images is *The Theory of Moral Sentiments* that at times it presents the

effect; it is not written merely as an academic treatise but to persuade practicing politicians (see D. Stewart, *Memoirs*, pp. 55–6; cf. *WN* V.i.g.19). Smith states that political theory
can persuade and animate (*TMS* IV.1.11). At *WN* II.ii.67 he notes that ". . . this book
may come into the hands of many people who are not men of business. . . ." His vocabulary, including the polemics against businessmen as well as commentary on the dehumanization of the workers, is often more radical and inflammatory than anything one
finds in *TMS*, almost a call to arms. D. Winch cites Smith's comments on the American
Revolution as examples of didactic and rhetorical discourse. *Adam Smith's Politics* (Cambridge: Cambridge University Press, 1978), p. 171. For discussion of the rhetorical dimension of *WN*, see S. Copley and K. Sutherland, eds., *Adam Smith, "Wealth of Nations":
New Interdisciplinary Essays* (Manchester, UK: Manchester University Press, 1995).
40 Theophrastus was Aristotle's student and successor, and when Smith identifies himself as
accepting Aristotle's ethical teaching, he may have thought of that teaching as being
continuous with the sort of "painting" of ethical life presented by Theophrastus. For
Smith's admiring references, see *LRBL* i.193–7 (pp. 80–2).
The passage I quote at the beginning of this section is from *NE* 1172a34–b1.

character of a novel; narrative and analysis are interwoven throughout.[41] Smith's manner of writing seems calculated to convey the point that to understand and evaluate ethical situations properly our emotions should be engaged in the particulars of the context. One rationale for his use of examples is his theory that we arrive at moral judgments by considering the specifics of the situation. He remarks:

> When a philosopher goes to examine why humanity is approved of, or cruelty condemned, he does not always form to himself, in a very clear and distinct manner, the conception of any one particular action either of cruelty or of humanity, but is commonly contented with the vague and indeterminate idea which the general names of those qualities suggest to him. But it is in particular instances only that the propriety or impropriety, the merit or demerit of actions is very obvious and discernible. It is only when particular examples are given that we perceive distinctly either the concord or disagreement between our own affections and those of the agent, or feel a social gratitude arise towards him in the one case, or a sympathetic resentment in the other. When we consider virtue and vice in an abstract and general manner, the qualities by which they excite these several sentiments seem in a great measure to disappear, and the sentiments themselves become less obvious and discernible. (IV.2.2)

The use of examples and stories in *The Theory of Moral Sentiments* is as essential to the moral psychology as it is to the virtue theory.

In making moral judgments about another we are to put ourselves into that other's situation and thereby exercise imagination. Smith's constant invocations of examples and stories and his frequent allusions and references to plays (particularly tragedies) elicit the work of the moral imagination. As a writer on ethics, he strives to evoke in the reader, through the operations of "sympathy," an understanding of the situation

---

41 In a letter to Smith (Sept. 10, 1759), E. Burke says: "I own I am particularly pleased with those easy and happy illustrations from common Life and manners in which your work abounds more than any other that I know by far. . . . Besides so much powerful reasoning as your Book contains, there is so much elegant Painting of the manners and passions, that it is highly valuable even on that account" (*CAS*, pp. 46–7). In his review of the book in the *Annual Register* (1759), Burke again notes: "The illustrations are numerous and happy, and shew the author to be a man of uncommon observation. His language is easy and spirited, and puts things before you in the fullest light; it is rather painting than writing" (quoted in the editors' Introduction to *TMS*, p. 28). Cf. Hume's distinction between the approaches of the artist and the anatomist in the *Enquiry Concerning Human Understanding*, pp. 9–10, and similarly his letter to F. Hutcheson of Sept. 17, 1739, in *The Letters of David Hume*, 2 vols., ed. J. Y. T. Grieg (Oxford: Clarendon Press, 1932), vol. 1, pp. 32–3.

and motives in question.[42] In its narrative dimension, *The Theory of Moral Sentiments* focuses our attention on particulars and experience and attempts to get us to "see" things in a certain light rather than simply to argue us into accepting a philosophical position. This does not reflect the view that there is *no* room for moral justification, but rather (to anticipate) that such justification depends on our capacity to discern what is important or relevant in the given situation.[43]

In at least one further respect, *The Theory of Moral Sentiments* might be read as a story that unfolds in steps. Views that are propounded at the beginning may be refined substantially by the end, as would be natural in a literary dialogue or novel, so that later on the reader confronts unexpected questions about points advanced earlier in the book. This is another feature of the book's rhetoric. In Part I, "sympathy" is offered as an explanation of our ability to arrive at moral evaluations of each other's actions. At the end of Part I, it turns out that sympathy is also conducive to the "corruption of our moral sentiments." In Part II we

---

42 In his lectures on rhetoric Smith is, correspondingly, enthusiastic about what he calls "indirect narration," i.e., narration in which the motives of actors as well as the effects of the actor's actions on the sentiments of others are conveyed. He cites Thucydides as an outstanding practitioner of the genre. See *LRBL*, pp. 86–7, where Smith refers to "the Generall rule that when we mean to affect the reader deeply we must have recourse to the indirect method of description, relating the effects the transaction produced both on the actors and Spectators." For the reference to Thucydides, see *LRBL*, p. 96. He also remarks: "When the sentiment of the speaker is expressed in a neat, clear, plain and clever manner, and the passion or affection he is possessed of and intends, *by sympathy*, to communicate to his hearer, is plainly and cleverly hit off, then and then only the expression has all the force and beauty that language can give it" (*LRBL*, p. 25; see also p. 40). For further discussion see J. M. Hogan, "Historiography and Ethics in Adam Smith's Lectures on Rhetoric, 1762–1763," *Rhetorica* 2 (1984): 75–91.

43 Consider J. Dancy's discussion of justification and description in *Moral Reasons* (Oxford: Blackwell Publisher, 1994), p. 113: "To justify one's choice is to give the reasons one sees for making it, and to give those reasons is just to lay out how one sees the situation, starting in the right place and going on to display the various salient features in the right way; to do this is to fill in the moral horizon. In giving those reasons one is not *arguing* for one's way of seeing the situation." Rather, the "appeal consists in laying out that way as persuasively as one can. The persuasiveness here is the persuasiveness of narrative: an internal coherence in the account which compels assent. We succeed in our aim when our story sounds right. Moral justification is therefore not subsumptive in nature, but narrative." Dancy's metaphor of "shape" is also helpful: "a situation has a shape in the sense that its properties have a practically related profile," and this shape is articulated in "telling the story of the situation," something which can be done well or badly (p. 112). Smith would find much to agree with in this view of ethics and the articulation appropriate to it, while insisting on a place for moral rules, impartiality, ethical criticism, conversation, and argument, as will be discussed in Chapter 3, section 2 and in Chapter 5, section 2.

first learn that the moral sentiments furnish all that is needed for our sense of justice, but then it turns out that fortune deeply affects the ethical judgments rendered by the emotions, generating what Smith politely calls an "irregularity of sentiments," that is, irrationality of the moral emotions. Part III provides us with an account of "duty" that seems to compensate for the corruption and irrationality of the sentiments; the impartial spectator within the breast seems capable of correcting our judgment. But it turns out in Part III that duty is easily distorted into religious fanaticism. We are thus prepared for his reflections in Part IV on beauty, utility, the "invisible hand," and the place of philosophical justification in moral and political philosophy. Having given us the sense that for all its dangers, a suprapolitical view of human life is possible, he immediately proceeds in Part V to undermine the idea in his discussion of the "influence of custom and fashion upon the sentiments of moral approbation and disapprobation." He closes that part with a discussion of the problematic case of infanticide and then launches into a discussion of "the character of virtue" (Part VI), as though the problem of convention had never reared its ugly head. In the course of this part, many of the earlier themes – including those of philosophy, fanaticism, "low prudence," duty, and sympathy – are restated and rewoven.

Then comes the sudden shift to Part VII, in which we are finally told what questions we have been investigating and are provided with a view of the whole and its place in a larger philosophical conversation. Part VII provides us with a relatively detached perspective on the preceding discourse, and the movement from the first six parts to the seventh is roughly like that from the view within the spectacle to from without. Although Part VII is parasitic on the work of the preceding parts and is rightly placed at the end of the book, it also comments on them, puts them in perspective, frames them in a wider context – including the context of the *corpus* to which Part VII alone refers. From the standpoint of Part VII, we see that the first three parts, though presented as sequential steps of the narrative, are in fact a triptych. In the analysis and narrative they are separate, but in our moral lives propriety, merit, and duty overlap. In Part VII we are suddenly elevated to a plateau only episodically glimpsed earlier, and from that height we are permitted an overview of the still more expansive territory Smith hoped to cover.

A written philosophical work runs particular risks of encouraging an "academic" detachment from ordinary life and of reducing ethical debate to a merely theoretical, perhaps casuistical, enterprise. Yet the presence of Part VII also acknowledges that in setting out a theory of moral sentiments we cannot stay entirely within the horizon of the reflective moral actor. It bespeaks a need for sustained perspective on our work as a *theory* of a certain sort in which we seek to answer specific questions and are guided by some specific set of concerns and approach to the subject matter. Part VII in effect acknowledges that *The Theory of Moral Sentiments* indeed *is* a "theory," a theory among theories, as the first sentence of that part indicates. This acknowledgment implies detachment and perspective but not an ascent to some entirely external standpoint, such as those fortunate liberated souls in Plato's *Republic* experience.

Smith provides us no natural transition from the first six parts to the seventh, nothing like the "ascent" described by Plato. Nor does Part VII provide a natural transition back "down" to the level of ordinary experience, though appeals to the deep methodological assumption concerning the priority of ordinary experience are still made. I have suggested that Smith's methods of ethics reflect views about the nature of ethical theorizing as well as about the ethical intent of the moral philosopher. The structure of *The Theory of Moral Sentiments* suggests a discontinuity between the perspectives of reflective moral actor and the Smithean philosophical spectator. This discontinuity seems built into the conception of ethics we have begun to spell out. Moral philosophy is to preserve the integrity of the prephilosophical and indeed, as far as possible, articulate itself in the language of common life, yet it cannot lose its own character and aims as philosophy. Since this conception is itself controversial among philosophers, in taking it Smith must also teach moral philosophers why it is warranted and how to avoid the misuse of their own discipline. All of this makes for an exceedingly complex rhetorical project.

## 4. CRITICISM, GRAMMAR, AND THE THEATER

I only know myself as a human entity; the scene, so to speak, of thoughts and affections; and am sensible of a certain doubleness by which I can stand as remote from myself as from another. . . . When the play, it may be the tragedy, of life is over, the spectator goes his way. It was a kind of fiction, a work of the imagination only, so far as he was concerned.

Henry David Thoreau[44]

44 H. D. Thoreau, "Solitude," in *Walden*, in *The Portable Thoreau*, ed. C. Bode (New York: Penguin, 1981), p. 386.

How might we further characterize the stance that a Smithean moral philosopher ought to take in evaluating ethical life? Smith provides us with some clues when he distinguishes between approaching ethics in the spirit of a grammarian and of a critic. He suggests that we should recognize that all but one of the virtues admit at best of rules that are "loose, vague, and indeterminate," rules comparable "to those which critics lay down for the attainment of what is sublime and elegant in composition, and which present us rather with a general idea of the perfection we ought to aim at, than afford us any certain and infallible directions for acquiring it" (VII.iv.1).[45] This distinction between the perspectives of the grammarian and the critic is tied by Smith to the difference between justice and the other virtues: for "the rules of justice may be compared to the rules of grammar; the rules of the other virtues, to the rules which critics lay down for the attainment of what is sublime and elegant in composition" (III.6.11).

"All the ancient moralists" fall into the category of "critics" (VII.iv.3) – Aristotle and Cicero are named as examples – and "in treating of the rules of morality, in this manner, consists the science which is properly called Ethics" (VII.iv.6). Hence ethics is explicitly an inquiry that practices "criticism." Right ethical action and evaluation require sound judgment. By contrast, "all the casuists of the middle and latter ages of the christian church, as well as all those who in this and in the preceding century have treated of what is called natural jurisprudence" fall into the category of "grammarians" (VII.iv.7). They proceed as though justice were the paradigm of the virtues, and Smith is harshly condemnatory of their approach. Moral judgment is not, in general, like applying rules as one would in a legal context. The simile of the "critic" is explicitly used to describe *both* how ordinary spectators judge and how some moral philosophers approach their subject.

One task of the critic is to describe the spectacle he or she observes and to convey it as vividly as possible to others, who in turn will "see" the original through an act of imagination. Hence Smith emphasizes heavily the importance of rhetoric to "what is properly called Ethics."[46]

---

45  In the *LRBL* (pp. 25–7) Smith speaks critically of a complex system of rhetorical tropes built on distinctions of the "grammarians," yielding a "grammar" of rhetoric saturated with rules dictating how one should write and speak well. He has little patience with that approach and instead orients himself by the demands of the given effort at communication through sympathy.

46  In the *LRBL* Smith remarks that "if you'll attend to it all the Rules of Criticism and

It seems safe to assume that *The Theory of Moral Sentiments* is a work in "Ethics." The critic writes in order to educate us as to the rightness of a certain way of looking at, and of participating in, the drama. Criticism is an intrinsically pedagogic activity. Of course, the critic evaluates the performance; his or her activity is inescapably normative. Some standard as to what constitutes a good performance is indispensable. Smith mentions two standards that the critic may appeal to, the one a standard of "complete propriety and perfection" that no human being could achieve and the other "the idea of that degree of proximity or distance from this complete perfection, which the actions of the greater part of men commonly arrive at" (I.i.5.9). When, in one of his long footnotes, Smith claims that "the present inquiry [presumably the whole of *TMS*] is not concerning a matter of right, if I may say so, but concerning a matter of fact" (II.i.5.10), the "matter of fact" at issue concerns the standards that a human being, rather than God, would appeal to in judging other human beings. These standards may themselves be high or low, a distinction that is of repeated concern in this book (see VI.i.14–15 and VI.iii.23–5).

I think it fair to conclude that in *The Theory of Moral Sentiments* Smith regards himself as writing as a critic and thus as throwing in his lot with the ancient moralists. As judging critic, Smith describes, analyzes, assesses, evaluates, with an eye to persuading as well as informing. He works from within moral traditions – for a critic does not create the traditions being subjected to critique – but he is not therefore a mere recorder of conventions, any more than a fine critic would be.[47]

Although Smith does not specify what species of critic is the best model for doing ethics, and some passages imply that he has in mind a literary critic, *The Theory of Moral Sentiments* strongly suggests that the theater critic is the appropriate model. From the beginning, Smith compares human life to spectacles represented in plays, and the phenomenology of the book is oriented around a spectator–actor dichotomy (which we will explore in Chapter 2). The role he gives to the empathetic imagi-

---

morality when traced to their foundation, turn out to be some Principles of Common Sence which every one assents to" (p. 55).

47  In the preface to his *Pagan Virtue* (p. ix), Casey remarks in a spirit Smith would approve: "My enquiry into moral philosophy in some ways resembles an exercise in literary criticism. The literary critic rearranges and criticizes a literary tradition, and may even propose new and unexpected perspectives on the literary past, but he does not usually presume to invent a tradition *de novo*. In much the same way the moral philosopher cannot fruitfully assume that what he does stands outside history."

nation prepares us for those comparisons. (See the reference to the theater and the "prejudices of the imagination" at I.iii.2.2.) We also have
other evidence that Smith was keenly interested in the theater throughout much of his career as writer.[48] The terms "spectator" and "actor"
may derive from the theater. The title of Joseph Addison and Richard
Steele's famous periodical *The Spectator* itself alludes to the theater, as
Addison himself indicated.[49] The metaphor of the *theatrum mundi* is an
old, rich, and well-known one.[50] I shall return in later chapters to the

48  I refer to Stewart's comment on Smith's interest in the fine arts and the topic of imitation
    and Stewart's remark that "the history of the theatre, both in ancient and modern times"
    especially attracted Smith's attention. The theory of imitation, drama, and the theater
    "were a favourite topic of his conversation, and were intimately connected with his general principles of criticism," and in the "last years of his life, he sometimes amused
    himself, at a leisure hour, in supporting his theoretical conclusions on these subjects, by
    the facts which his subsequent studies and observations had suggested." Stewart says that
    the completed essay on the imitative arts would have included a section on the theater.
    *Memoirs*, pp. 49–50.
49  See D. Marshall's discussion of *The Spectator* in *The Figure of Theater: Shaftesbury, Defoe, Adam
    Smith, and George Eliot* (New York: Columbia University Press, 1986), pp. 9–11. Addison
    characterizes his readers as a "Fraternity of Spectators . . . in short, every one that considers the World as a Theatre, and desires to form a right Judgment of those who are
    Actors in it" (*Spectator* no. 10). Addison uses the phrase "impartial spectator" in *Spectator*
    no. 274. In no. 370 he says of himself: "so I, who am a SPECTATOR in the World, may
    perhaps sometimes make use of the Names of the Actors in the World." In J. Addison
    and R. Steele, *The Spectator*, 5 vols., ed. D. F. Bond (Oxford: Clarendon Press, 1965).
50  The metaphor is used by Smith's favorite Stoics. E.g., see Marcus Aurelius, *Meditations*
    10.27, 12.36, and Epictetus, *Encheiridion* 17 (where we are compared to actors in a play).
    It is also implicit in Plato's *Laws* 644d–e, 803c–804b; also *Phaedrus* 258b3 and context.
    Smith used the phrase "spectacle of human life" in the course of a long passage on
    Stoicism that was present in the first five editions of *TMS* (p. 59), and he also used there
    the metaphor of the theater (p. 58). At VII.ii.1.23 he again uses the "spectacle of human
    life" in the context of the Stoic view of life. Hume uses the example of a "man who
    enters the theatre" and observes both actors and spectators as a way of illustrating how
    sympathy is communicated in this "spectacle"; *Enquiry Concerning the Principles of Morals*,
    pp. 221, 251. See also E. R. Curtius, *European Literature and the Latin Middle Ages*, trans.
    W. R. Trask (New York: Harper & Row, 1953), ch. 7, sec. 5 ("Theatrical Metaphors"),
    and for some general reflections, J. A. Barish, *The Antitheatrical Prejudice* (Berkeley and
    Los Angeles: University of California Press, 1981), pp. 243–55. Marshall states that
    "Hutcheson . . . remarks in his *Inquiry Concerning Beauty, Order, Harmony, Design* (1725)
    that the world is a 'stupendous Theatre' adorned by God 'in a manner agreeable to the
    Spectators' "; and that there are other passages in which Hutcheson "moves easily, often
    without distinction, between considerations of 'Spectacles of Pity' on stage and in the
    world, between situations where people are spectators to the 'characters' of others and
    to the 'characters' in plays." Marshall, *The Figure of Theater*, p. 168. Smith refers (*TMS*
    V.2.10) to the Abbé Du Bos' *Réflexions critiques sur la poésie et sur la peinture* (1719), a book
    in reference to which Marshall notes: "For Du Bos, as for others in the eighteenth century, to talk about how people responded to the sentiments of others was to talk about
    representation and theatrical distance, while to talk about how people reacted to the

striking "theatricality" of the moral as well as commercial world as painted by Smith – a world in which vanity and role playing before strangers are crucial – for therein lies much of the rationale for my suggestion. The simile of the theater is helpful in characterizing what Smith thinks becomes visible from a detached philosophical point of view, namely, the phenomenon of irony (sometimes tragic, sometimes comic) that is echoed in his view of historical events as yielding unexpected outcomes, as though they were guided by an invisible hand.[51] The notion of a play also permits us to imagine a unified pattern in the seemingly unconnected sequences of events, and to talk about characters without talking about their "essence" – a valuable benefit of this picture for Smith. As moral actors we seek to interpret imaginatively and impartially the personae of our fellow actors, and as moral theorists we seek to do the same at a higher level of comprehensiveness, so as to include the play as a whole in our appraisal. The "life is theater" metaphor leads us to wonder whether our lives are in some peculiar sense like works of art, so that evaluating them, like evaluating a play, blurs the line between aesthetic and moral categories. (Smith uses the vocabulary of "moral beauty" and the like in *TMS*.)

Every drama critic is first a moral actor, not so much in that writing theater reviews is one way of performing in the theater but rather in that one judges morally, for Smith, in the persona of a reflective moral actor (or, as an actor who is an "impartial spectator").[52] The critic's objectivity

characters in a tragedy was to talk about the structure and experience of sympathy" (p. 169). E. Burke too used the metaphor of the theater frequently; consider P. Hindson and T. Gray, *Burke's Dramatic Theory of Politics* (Aldershot, UK: Avebury, 1988). Cf. also Stewart's reference to "the great theatre of the world" (*Memoirs*, p. 43). There is, then, ample context for my use of the theater metaphor in interpreting Smith. For still further references and discussion of the metaphor, see E. G. Hundert, *The Enlightenment's Fable: Bernard Mandeville and the Discovery of Society* (Cambridge: Cambridge University Press, 1994).

51 J. J. Spengler notes that the famous "invisible hand" was compared by Bernard Le Bovyer de Fontenelle (in a work Smith knew) to "that of the Engineer who, hidden in the pit of a French Theatre, operated 'the Machines of the Theatre' in motion on the stage." Spengler, "Smith versus Hobbes: Economy versus Polity," in *Adam Smith and the Wealth of Nations: 1776–1976, Bicentennial Essays*, ed. F. R. Glahe (Boulder: Colorado Associated University Press, 1978), p. 43. Cf. Hume's remark that "we are placed in this world, as in a great theatre, where the true springs and causes of every event are entirely concealed from us; nor have we either sufficient wisdom to foresee, or power to prevent those ills, with which we are continually threatened." *The Natural History of Religion*, ed. H. E. Root (Stanford: Stanford University Press, 1957), p. 28.

52 Smith uses the term "actor" instead of "agent" at VI.concl. 6; on p. 111 (in a section

is not that of an external spectator completely outside the theater (one looking in through the window, as it were). Smith's theorizing critic also sits in the theater but with a vantage point that allows observation both of the dramatis personae and the audience. Objectivity is achieved through relative, but not complete, detachment. Indeed, proper interpretation of the play also requires, whether one is a spectating agent in the audience or the trained critic in the balcony, proper engagement of the emotions; the critic is not objective or impartial by virtue of suppressing emotional response, or what Smith calls "sympathy."[53] The critic's impartiality also depends on an ability to refine, through careful reflection, his evaluative responses, as well as on a knowledge of the history of and literature about the genre.

Of course, writing could be a way of performing in the theater, and it is not un-Smithean to see Smith's books as intellectual dramas presented for an audience of spectators. Shaftesbury had characterized philosophical writing in these terms in his *Soliloquy, or Advice to an Author*, though he there criticizes those writers who "exhibit on the stage of the world" a type of "memoir" writing that should have remained private.[54] In *The Theory of Moral Sentiments* Smith comments on how various types of authors receive the applause, or lack thereof, generated by their productions (III.2.19–23). His elaborately staged rhetoric is meant to engage the attention of an unknowably large, international, and varied reading public. As noted, his own lectures on rhetoric discuss the necessity of an author's engaging the reader's "sympathy."

The theater metaphor fits with Smith's determination to theorize using rich and suggestive terms available in ordinary life. The vocabulary of the theater enables him to articulate his role as spectator viewing a peculiar "appearance," namely the appearance that is the "spectacle of human life," without falling into what he would regard as antiquated

---

withdrawn in ed. 2 of *TMS*); and in lecture 16 (p. 87) of the *LRBL* in a literary context. Nussbaum holds that Smith found in the "experience of readership a model of the attitudes and emotions of the judicious spectator" (*Poetic Justice*, p. 10). There are textual grounds for the point, but the theater model captures what Nussbaum finds valuable in the readership model and also incorporates other important aspects of Smith's philosophy absent from it. The two models are not mutually exclusive, in any case.

53 For an argument to the effect that the proper engaging of the emotions at a theatrical performance is requisite to the spectator's understanding of the play, see P. Woodruff, "Engaging Emotion in Theater: A Brechtian Model in Theater History," *Monist* 71 (1988): 235–57.

54 Shaftesbury, *Advice to an Author* in vol. I of *Characteristics*, pt. I, sec. I, pp. 108–9.

talk of essences, forms, or trans-human sources of knowledge. (This point is developed further in Chapter 4.) It also lets him articulate the distance that permits him to offer an analysis of the play, without pretending that he is somewhere outside the theater proposing a "view from nowhere" – the sort of standpointless standpoint that some philosophers seem to have claimed for themselves. Further, it helps us to characterize the "action" of *The Theory of Moral Sentiments*, a book in which the curtain just goes up, as it were, on a view of the moral sentiments, without the initial philosophical commentary on issues epistemological and metaphysical that one would expect from a philosophical theorist. The vocabulary of drama and criticism thus seems congruent with Smith's articulation of his own position as theorist, even though it may not be sufficient as a description of the theoretical standpoint.

This line of interpretation is supported by the fact that in his essays on the history of astronomy and the history of ancient physics, Smith uses the vocabulary in question. He speaks of the "theatre of nature" and of "philosophy" – by which he means "knowledge" broad enough to include what we think of as "science" – as a spectatorial endeavor that seeks to provide a comprehensive and coherent interpretation of the "spectacle" it observes.[55] Provoked to wonder by various aspects of the drama he or she observes, the philosopher's imagination develops a systematic explanation. This account of theorizing may be taken to apply to a book that Smith himself denominated a "theory," and *The Theory of Moral Sentiments* is carefully laced with terms (such as "surprise" and "wonder") that he uses in the "essays on philosophical subjects." We might say that the theorist-critic articulates in suitably systematic form the invisible theatrical machinery that manipulates the visible scenery.[56] Perhaps, then, we do not go far wrong in suggesting that this book is a "theory" in one Greek sense of the term, that is, a "viewing," a "looking

55 In the "History of Astronomy" Smith finds it fruitful to examine philosophies to see "how far each of them was fitted to sooth the imagination, and to render the theatre of nature a more coherent, and therefore a more magnificent spectacle, than otherwise it would have appeared to be. According as they have failed or succeeded in this, they have constantly failed or succeeded in gaining reputation and renown to their authors; and this will be found to be the clew that is most capable of conducting us through all the labyrinths of philosophical history" (II.12, *EPS*, p. 46). The theater metaphor is repeated at IV.13 (p. 62) and in the "History of Ancient Physics" 2 (*EPS*, p.107).

56 S. Cremaschi is nearly right when he remarks: "Smith states that theories are like 'imaginary machines,' or chains of ideas built by the imagination between two disjoined phenomena. The imaginary machine is supposed to link the observed phenomena while remaining out of sight behind the scenes of nature, like theatrical machinery." "Adam Smith: Skeptical Newtonianism," pp. 85–6.

at."[57] Since what we are observing is the drama of human life – that is, ourselves – perhaps Smith ought be understood as having writ large Hume's observation that the mind is a theater.[58]

Why would Smith have found this vision of the *theatrum mundi* compelling? Among other reasons, the flexibility of the metaphor would have commended it to him. A critic may well ask different questions about the "spectacle" – for example, how the play's effects are staged – and may wander backstage to examine the wheels and springs that invisibly produce many of the effects. He may ask about the cost of producing the show, of the scenery, of maintaining the theater, of the tickets. He may wonder how the levels of compensation of actors and technical crew affect their performance in their various parts; whether unionization is productive or not; what economic class or mix of classes the audience appears to derive from; and what history shows us about the relation of productions and their varying economic characteristics. In fact, he may wonder about the economic and social conditions that make the existence of trained critics possible (e.g., *WN* V.i.f.51, I.ii.4). The metaphor of the theater critic, in other words, may also extend fruitfully to the theorizing that goes on in *The Wealth of Nations*. Early in that treatise, Smith invokes the "spectator" – meaning, there, either a thoughtful observer or a theorist – in a discussion of mistaken views of the extent of the division of labor in businesses of varying sizes (I.i.2). Also, as we have noted, he relies on the metaphor of the theater and the philosophical spectator in his account of the "intellectual sentiments" and the creation of knowledge.[59]

## 5. METHOD, SYSTEM, AND CONVERSATION

But for the philosopher who pretends to be wholly taken up in considering his higher faculties, and examining the powers and principles of his un-

---

57 The Greek term *theoria* can mean being a spectator at the theater, as at *Crito* 52b4. See *A Greek-English Lexicon* (Oxford: Clarendon Press, 1985), compiled by H. D. Liddell, R. Scott, H. S. Jones, and R. Mckenzie, *s.v. theoria*.

58 "The mind is a kind of theater, where several perceptions successively make their appearance; pass, re-pass, glide away, and mingle in an infinite variety of postures and situations." Hume, *Treatise of Human Nature*, ed. L. A. Selby-Bigge; 2nd rev. ed., ed. P. H. Nidditch (Oxford: Clarendon Press, 1978), p. 253. (All further references to the *Treatise* are to this edition, cited hereafter as *T.*)

59 Perhaps the model of the "grammarian" would have been more suited to Smith's work on natural jurisprudence. Since he did not publish that work, we shall never know for certain.

derstanding, if in reality his philosophy be foreign to the matter professed, if it goes beside the mark and reaches nothing we can truly call our interest or concern, it must be somewhat worse than mere ignorance or idiotism. The most ingenious way of becoming foolish is by a system.

Shaftesbury[60]

To conclude my discussion of what it means, for Smith, to do ethics, I would like to comment further on the method of *The Theory of Moral Sentiments* and on the sense in which it is a "theory" and "system." As already noted, Smith himself is given to characterizing powerful explanatory theories in terms of their comprehensiveness, unity of explanation, ability to account for detail, elegance and simplicity, and the corresponding wonder and admiration that they provoke.[61] In the student notes of his lectures on rhetoric, he is reported as speaking of those as qualities of "Newtonian" rather than "Aristotelian" theorizing, and he stresses in the lectures on rhetoric that the former approach is considerably more satisfying than the latter. In his view the Newtonian method seeks to provide a minimal set of principles in light of which the varied phenomena can be explained, whereas the Aristotelian method is ad hoc and unsystematic.[62]

Interpreters of Smith infer that he thought of his system as Newtonian rather than Aristotelian in its mode of exposition. It is possible to reconstruct sections of *The Theory of Moral Sentiments* along roughly Newtonian lines, with sympathy, the imagination, the passions, and other concepts serving as "certain principles" that explain the workings of the moral sentiments. Smith stresses the importance of classification, of observation, of generalization through induction (see *TMS* VII.iii.2.6), so as to yield laws from which, as he says in *The Wealth of Nations* when discussing the history of efforts to systematize ethics, particular "maxims of pru-

---

60 "Advice to an Author," pt. III, sec. I, in *Characteristics*, vol. I, p. 189.
61 See *WN* V.i.f.25 and the "History of Ancient Physics," sec. 9, in *EPS*, pp. 112–14.
62 *LRBL*, pp. 145–6: in moral or natural philosophy we may "either like Aristotle go over the Different branches in the order they happen to cast up to us, giving a principle commonly a new one for every phaenomenon; or in the manner of Sir Isaac Newton we may lay down certain principles known or proved in the beginning, from whence we account for the severall Phenomena, connecting all together by the same Chain. – This Latter which we may call the Newtonian method is undoubtedly the most Philosophical, and in every science whether of Moralls or Naturall philosophy etc., is vastly more ingenious and for that reason more engaging than the other." Cf. Smith's remark that Newton proposed "so familiar a principle of connection, which completely removed all the difficulties the imagination had hitherto felt in attending to them [the movements of the Planets]," namely, gravity (IV.67, *EPS*, p. 98).

dence and morality . . . were all deducible, like effects from their natural causes" (*WN* V.i.f.25).[63] As the full title of that book indicates, he clearly aims to provide causal analysis in political economy, and the vocabulary of cause and effect is not absent from his moral philosophy.

Yet Smith never actually says in his published works that he himself sought to follow the Newtonian method. We have seen in the Introduction that the projected *corpus* would have formed a "system" in the sense of interconnected lines of investigation, but even there it is not easy to find a "Newtonian" scheme at work. Perhaps the *corpus* as a whole would have been closer to what Smith describes as the "Aristotelian" mode. *The Theory of Moral Sentiments* certainly does not look Newtonian, either in the sense exhibited by the *Principia* or in Smith's looser sense. *The Theory of Moral Sentiments* does not overtly "lay down certain principles known or proved in the beginning" and then proceed to connect the other salient features of the account with them. As I have noted, not even the two guiding questions of a theory of moral sentiments are distinguished until the end of the book. In keeping with what Smith thinks of as a convincing theoretical construction, he does use familiar terms (such as "sympathy"), though as also noted, he emends the meaning of the term precisely so that he can use it effectively in his theory. Further, it is not easy to specify what the analogous, familiar explanatory term is in *The Wealth of Nations*.

Even if one were to grant that Smith thought he had produced a moral system along Newtonian lines, we would have to account for the fact that he did not wear his Newtonianism on his sleeve. He leaves it to his readers to reconstruct his teaching as a Newtonian system, without offering a single published word of explicit encouragement to that effect.

---

63  The most determined effort to flesh out Smith's "Newtonian" method in *TMS* is probably Campbell, *Adam Smith's Science of Morals*. Campbell concludes, however, that *TMS* is a failure, judged by the standard of the Newtonian method itself (p. 236 and context). A parallel effort to see *WN* as Newtonian is S. T. Worland, "Mechanistic Analogy and Smith on Exchange," *Review of Social Economy* 34 (1976): 245–57. Worland too concludes that Smith failed fully to follow Newton's method. By contrast, Campbell suggests that the method of *WN* is nearer to the Aristotelian than the Newtonian method. *Adam Smith's Science of Morals*, p. 31. In a letter to Smith of Sept. 25, 1776, Thomas Pownall wrote: "When I first saw the plan and superstructure of your very ingenious and very learned Treatise on the Wealth of Nations, it gave me a compleat idea of that system . . . that might fix some first principles in the most important of sciences, the knowledge of the human community, and its operations. That might become *principia* to the knowledge of politick operations; as Mathematicks are to Mechanicks, Astronomy, and the other Sciences" (*CAS* p. 337). Pownall sustains the analogy in the succeeding paragraphs.

In some respects his procedure in *The Theory of Moral Sentiments* is, to borrow a term he is reported to have used in his lectures, closer to the "Socratic."[64] The book begins in the middle of a conversation, taking up a supposition held by unnamed persons, and then leads us one step at a time, by means of a complex rhetoric, down a path full of unexpected twists and turns, culminating in an anticipation of "another discourse" about a related topic. Smith's Socratic method is interwoven with the various rhetorical and pedagogic strategies that I have outlined, some properly Aristotelian, and is warranted by the subject matter and audience as he understands them. The sense of "Newtonian method" that Smith specifies in his lectures on rhetoric embodies dangers that he elsewhere identifies with the philosopher's potentially reductive and distorting "love of system." Although his use of a "Newtonian" method does not in itself betray Smith's evident skepticism about "metaphysical" explanations of phenomena (these being absent from all of his work), any effort to extract a rigorous system from *The Theory of Moral Sentiments* would seem to betray his allegiance to the standpoint of everyday life that informs, as I have been suggesting, the substance, and therefore the rhetoric, of his book.[65] We cannot spectate on morality in the way we can on nature, and thus the detachment suitable for a "Newtonian" view of nature is not in principle appropriate in moral philosophy.

That said, *The Theory of Moral Sentiments* is not, strictly speaking, a dialogue either, especially not anything like a Platonic dialogue, in spite of its Socratic, dramatic or literary, as well as dialectical character. Various voices are deployed but are not embodied in dramatis personae, especially not in a Socrates. Why did Smith not take the next step and write something closer to a true dialogue, one in which we are offered

---

64 In the *LRBL*, Smith tells us that through the "Socratic" method the audience is brought "by slow and imperceptible degrees to the thing to be proved," in contrast with the much harsher "Aristotelian method," according to which "we affirm the thing we are to prove, boldly at the Beginning, and when any point is controverted beginn by proving that very thing and so on." The former method is more useful when our audience is likely to resist our conclusion, the latter when the audience is likely to be friendly (pp. 146–7). In his illuminating discussion of the rhetoric of *WN*, J. R. Lindgren persuasively argues that *WN* too uses the "Socratic" method. *The Social Philosophy of Adam Smith* (The Hague: Nijhoff, 1973), p. 82, n. 13.

65 Recall Hume's point at the end of the appendix to the *Treatise* that "*the Newtonian* philosophy" is informed by "a modest scepticism to a certain degree, and a fair confession of ignorance in subjects, that exceed all human capacity" (*T* 639). These subjects would include all "metaphysical" questions that go beyond the appearances of objects to our senses.

opportunities of empathizing with specific interlocutors whose philosophical conversation unrolls in an identifiable context? Part of the answer may perhaps be found in Shaftesbury's sophisticated reflections on the Platonic dialogue; he argues that modern readers could not bear the sight of themselves in the "looking-glass" a true dialogue would provide.[66] I suspect that Smith thought it difficult to create an appropriate cast of literary characters with whom modern readers could identify and in whom they could see themselves.

He may also have wanted to avoid problems that a guiding figure such as Socrates would pose, and in neither of his published works is there any such philosopher, even in figurative guise. Socrates famously shows us how ordinary opinion is undermined when certain questions are put to it, and then how reflection on those questions necessarily leads to philosophical speculation that in turn reshapes, sometimes radically, the opinions with which we began. This reshaping may occur when a paradoxical conclusion is pressed (such as that virtue is knowledge), or when a comprehensive and synoptic standpoint (that of the philosopher outside the cave) is recommended as unqualifiedly the most desirable, or when we are left with a pressing question but no answers. None of these results is *prima facie* commendable from Smith's standpoint, and his writing is therefore dialectical and conversational but not dialogical. This is not to say that he fails to see how ordinary opinion might be undermined (or even on some occasions should be undermined), or to see that an impersonal and comprehensive standpoint is necessary (the "impartial spectator" being one such standpoint). It is to say, rather, that he understands the need to tend with care the main source of light we possess in moral philosophy, namely prephilosophical ethical life.

If *The Theory of Moral Sentiments* as a whole is a system, it might be best to understand the term not primarily in light of Smith's reported comments about Newton but rather with reference to Smith's "Of the Nature of that Imitation which Takes Place in What are Called the Imitative Arts," a posthumously published essay that apparently forms part of the projected "Philosophical History of the Liberal Sciences and Elegant Arts" (recall the discussion of the *corpus* in my Introduction). Smith describes the "perfect concord and correspondence" of the various instruments in a "well-composed concerto of instrumental Music," the

---

66 See Shaftesbury, *Advice to an Author*, in vol. I of *Characteristics*, pt. I, sec. III, pp. 134–5. Shaftesbury also refers there to the ancient dialogues as "mirror-writing."

"exact harmony" of the sounds, the "happy variety of measure," such that

> in the contemplation of that immense variety of agreeable and melodious sounds, arranged and digested, both in their coincidence and in their succession, into so complete and regular a system, the mind in reality enjoys not only a very great sensual, but a very high intellectual, pleasure, not unlike that which it derives from the contemplation of a great system in any other science. (II.30, *EPS*, pp. 204–5)[67]

This sort of system nicely describes the dynamic and flowing unity of *The Theory of Moral Sentiments*, even the intentionally surprising transitions, and is compatible with its "Socratic" and Aristotelian dimensions as well as with Smith's underlying view of how moral philosophy ought to develop its theories through attentive and creative reflection on the appearances.

---

67 In the paragraph preceding the lines quoted, Smith remarks: "Time and measure are to instrumental Music what order and method are to discourse. . . . By means of this order and method it [our aesthetic enjoyment] is, during the progress of the entertainment, equal to the effect of all that we remember, and of all that we foresee; and at the conclusion, to the combined and accumulated effect of all the different parts of which the whole was composed" (II.29, *EPS*, p. 204).

# 2

# SYMPATHY AND SELFISHNESS, IMAGINATION AND SELF

What we are supplying are really remarks on the natural history of human beings; we are not contributing curiosities however, but observations which no one has doubted, but which have escaped remark only because they are always before our eyes.

Ludwig Wittgenstein[1]

*The Theory of Moral Sentiments* is a theory of the "passions," "sentiments," or "emotions."[2] To what question, or questions, is this theory a response? Part VII informs us that any theory of moral sentiments proposes to answer two questions. The first is, in short: "Wherein does virtue consist?" The second concerns the means by which this or that "tone of temper, and tenour of conduct" come to recommend themselves to us as virtuous or not; that is, it concerns moral psychology. In this chapter and the next I shall focus on Smith's answer to the second question. I

---

1 *Philosophical Investigations* I.415, trans. G. E. M. Anscombe (New York: Macmillan, 1968), p. 125.
2 In *TMS* Smith generally uses the terms "sentiment," "passion," and "emotion" interchangeably, including in the first paragraph of the book. I have followed him in this practice except where doing so would conflict with modern usage of the terms and create confusion that the context does not dispel. In such cases, I select the term that best conveys the appropriate meaning.

begin with his account of sympathy, for that notion is central to his theory of moral sentiments. What exactly does he mean by "sympathy"? How are sympathy and selfishness to be distinguished? Why is sympathy central to ethics, on Smith's view?

In order to answer these questions, we need to understand his distinction between "agent" (or "actor") and "spectator," as well as the priority he gives to the latter. I shall explore a potential instability in his notion of sympathy: it may seem that, pressed in one direction, sympathy is possible only within narrowly defined social circles, for reasons that would make impossible the objective evaluation that ethics requires. After examining Smith's defense of sympathy against such objections, I conclude with discussion of the *pathos* entailed by the fundamentally "theatrical" relation between actor and spectator. We learn something about Smith's picture of the human condition from his insightful analysis of sympathy.

The issue of sympathy is of concern not only to Smith scholars but to a broader circle as well. Hume, Schopenhauer, Rousseau, Mandeville, Collingwood, Husserl, and Scheler (among others) also gave the notion their attention, and some recent work in ethics underlines the importance of "sympathy" to an account of morals.[3] The notion is of independent philosophical interest; some account must be given, just as Smith asserts at the beginning of his book, of the fact that we do enter into the situation of others and that our praise and blame of others often rests on our having entered into their situation appropriately. Morality demands that one be able to see a situation from the other person's

3 For example, see A. Goldman's APA Presidential Address, "Empathy, Mind, and Morals," *Proceedings and Addresses of the American Philosophical Association* 66 (1992): 17–41; the essays by A. Goldman, R. M. Gordon, and J. Deigh in the "Symposium on Empathy and Ethics," published in *Ethics* 105 (1995); J. Q. Wilson, *The Moral Sense* (New York: Free Press, 1993), ch. 2 ("Sympathy"); M. Johnson's *Moral Imagination* (Chicago: University of Chicago Press, 1993), pp. 199–203 ("Empathetic Imagination"); and A. J. Vetlesen, *Perception, Empathy, and Judgment: An Inquiry into the Preconditions of Moral Performance* (University Park: Pennsylvania State University Press, 1994). M. Scheler provides an interesting, if uneven, discussion of the problem of sympathy in part 1 of *The Nature of Sympathy*, trans. P. Heath (New Haven: Yale University Press, 1954). For an excellent discussion of the topic in connection with Husserl and Dilthey, see R. A. Makkreel, "How Is Empathy Related to Understanding?" in *Issues in Husserl's Ideas II*, ed. T. Nenon and L. Embree (Dordrecht: Kluwer, 1996), pp. 199–212. Also of interest is E. Stein, *On the Problem of Empathy*, trans. W. Stein (The Hague: Nijhoff, 1964). A large literature on sympathy exists in psychology and social science; see for example, L. Wispé, *The Psychology of Sympathy* (New York: Plenum, 1991), and N. Eisenberg and J. Strayer, eds., *Empathy and Its Development* (Cambridge: Cambridge University Press, 1990).

point of view. The notion of "sympathy" is also of particular contemporary interest. Some difficult problems in contemporary Western political cultures may be traceable to ambiguities in that notion, and I shall sketch these ambiguities in what follows.

## 1. PRELIMINARY ORIENTATION: SELFISHNESS, CONFLICT, AND SYMPATHY

The first sentence of *The Theory of Moral Sentiments* reads as follows:

> How selfish soever man may be supposed, there are evidently some principles in his nature, which interest him in the fortune of others, and render their happiness necessary to him, though he derives nothing from it except the pleasure of seeing it.

Let us put aside for now the objection that our deriving pleasure from a "selfless" interest in others renders that interest selfish, that is, the objection that there is no such thing as disinterested pleasure. Smith wishes to oppose the view that we empathize with others only when we think it to our advantage to do so – that is, that we treat others as means to our self-interest, narrowly understood. The term "selfish" denotes more than an undesirable trait of character, however; Smith is also assuming that because one person is able to "see" the situation of another, to enter into it, we are not "selfish" in the sense of being confined to our own selves. That is, selfishness is both an ethical issue and an epistemic one. Smith is working at both normative and analytical levels in using the term. From within a moral horizon, then, the issue of egoism arises: Do we ever really *care* about the welfare of another independently of what that caring might earn us? From within an epistemic horizon, the issue arises as to whether we are "selfish" in the sense that we cannot successfully get inside, or *understand*, the world of another. This general issue of harmonizing self and other is fundamental to both *The Theory of Moral Sentiments* and *The Wealth of Nations*. Both books are a response to the same fundamental problem, and insofar as there is a tension between sympathy and selfishness, it suffuses the *corpus* as a whole.

Like "selfishness," "sympathy" too has two meanings: "Pity and compassion are words appropriated to signify our fellow-feeling with the sorrow of others. Sympathy, though its meaning was, perhaps, originally the same, may now, however, without much impropriety, be made use of to denote our fellow-feeling with any passion whatever" (I.i.1.5).[4] In its narrow sense, sympathy is an emotion; in its broader, Smithean sense, it is also the means through which emotions are conveyed and understood. Smith occasionally slides back and forth between the narrow and broad meanings of the term, and so between what might in a Christian tradition be thought of as a laudable sentiment or virtue and a notion in moral psychology with bearing on epistemic issues.[5] When so doing, he slides back and forth between the two principal questions of any theory of moral sentiments.

Let us pause for a moment and examine Smith's procedure in setting up the problem to which "sympathy" is a response. Starting points in philosophy often embody a whole set of commitments and a general orientation. In a well-written book or *corpus*, the end is contained in the beginning. Smith is an excellent writer, and the opening lines of *The Theory of Moral Sentiments* set the stage well. He does not start with, say, the question about the nature of the good life, as Socrates might; or with reflections about the purposiveness of human life, as Aristotle does in the *Nicomachean Ethics;* or with a seemingly academic and technical problem of explaining "pure practical reason," as Kant does in the *Critique of Practical Reason. The Theory of Moral Sentiments* begins in the middle of a conversation, referring as it does, in the sentence that I quoted as I began this section, to a supposition entertained by an unnamed person or persons about human nature. In starting with this supposition, Smith shows us that he thinks it of such grave importance that the entire account must be oriented by it. His way of putting the point also shows us that there exists a fundamental disagreement about the question of selfishness.

Who holds the supposition Smith refers to and thinks it so necessary to oppose? The answer is, first, that *we* hold that supposition; we ordinary moral agents frequently attribute selfishness to each other. We observe it everywhere in the world; we see it in ourselves. It strikes us as a pervasive feature of human life. Second, it is a supposition, or at least a point of debate, in the philosophical tradition in light of which Smith is often working, namely, the modern natural law tradition from Grotius

---

4 Or again: "The word sympathy, in its most proper and primitive signification, denotes our fellow-feeling with the sufferings, not that with the enjoyments, of others" (I.iii.1.1).
5 For example, at II.ii.2.3 he speaks of the remorseful criminal's "hope for the consolation of sympathy in this his greatest and most dreadful distress." Here "sympathy" clearly means commiseration and understanding.

and Hobbes through Pufendorf to Hume.[6] In Part VII of the book Mandeville is explicitly identified as holding the "selfishness" theory, and Smith tends to conflate Hobbes and Mandeville (*TMS* VII.ii.4.6, VII.iii.1.1). As we noted in Chapter 1, Smith takes it that Mandeville's theory destroys the distinction between virtue and vice. How could it be, Smith asks, that so false and destructive a theory has imposed itself on so many (VII.ii.4.14)? The answer is that it "bordered upon the truth"; human beings are indeed vain and the passions often vicious to some degree. But human beings are not always vain, and their passions are not always vicious. In order to spell this out, Smith there launches into discussion of theories of moral psychology, starting with the self-love theories, which he attributes explicitly to Hobbes, Pufendorf, and Mandeville (VII.iii.1.1). And this leads him in Part VII to a spirited defense of the thesis that "sympathy" cannot be understood as "selfish." In that defense, the sense of the term "selfish" has shifted from the area of the virtues and vices to moral psychology.

Why is the problem of selfishness so pressing? If the supposition at issue is as widespread as I have just indicated, that fact alone might well motivate a moral philosopher to choose it as the starting point. But I would suggest that Smith is assuming a background picture in the context of which selfishness becomes particularly prominent. For many modern political philosophers the salient political problem is war or conflict, and war (including religious war) is connected at a deep level with selfishness in both of the senses just discussed.[7] It has been argued persuasively that this view of the primacy of conflict is the starting point of modern natural law theory.[8] It is as though these modern thinkers hold that the picture of the unwinding cosmos presented in the great myth in Plato's *Statesman*, in parts of Thucydides, and also by rhetoricians such as the Callicles of Plato's *Gorgias* better captures political reality than does the picture of fundamental harmony and agreement seemingly assumed by Aristotle's *Nicomachean Ethics*. The polis being long dead, the initial

---

6 For a detailed discussion of the twists and turns of the modern natural law tradition, see Haakonssen, *Natural Law and Moral Philosophy*.

7 Cf. *WN* IV.iii.c.9: "The violence and injustice of the rulers of mankind is an ancient evil, for which, I am afraid, the nature of human affairs can scarce admit of a remedy."

8 I refer to J. Schneewind, "Modern Moral Philosophy: From Beginning to End?" in *Philosophical Imagination and Cultural Memory*, ed. P. Cook (Durham, N.C.: Duke University Press, 1993), pp. 83–103, and Schneewind, "The Misfortunes of Virtue." The primacy of war to Smith's political economy is also noted by P. Minowitz in his *Profits, Priests, and Princes: Adam Smith's Emancipation of Economics from Politics and Religion* (Stanford: Stanford University Press, 1993), pp. 94–97.

problem is not that of specifying what the good life is but rather of specifying how peace and stability may come about in large, commercial, and to some extent free societies. For Smith this means that the view that we are ruled by selfishness, understood as a vice of character, and the view that we are selfish in the sense that we are not able to understand the situation of other (perhaps quite different) human beings, must both be taken up at the outset.

The proposition that war or conflict is the backdrop of any viable moral and political philosophy helps us to see why Smith thought it necessary to set out a new theory of justice that sharply distinguished, in a way and to a degree that Aristotle did not, between justice and the other virtues. In a passage relevant to my discussion here, Smith remarks that men, "though naturally sympathetic, feel so little for another, with whom they have no particular connexion, in comparison of what they feel for themselves" that without a constraining sense of justice they would "like wild beasts" be at all times ready to attack one another. Without justice, "a man would enter an assembly of men as he enters a den of lions" (II.ii.3.4). Reasons such as these help explain why *The Theory of Moral Sentiments* begins as it does and where it does – in mid-conversation and with the problem of selfishness. Sympathy is the foundation of the entire book, because selfishness is key to the conflictual and dissolving nature of human life as it shows itself to us.

Let us pause once again and notice a quite different feature of Smith's starting point. He clearly wishes to focus, not on the relation between any two persons but on that between what he calls the "agent" (or "actor") and the "spectator." This approach to stating the fundamentals of the problem, of organizing the basics of his presentation, determines the course of his exposition. His "phenomenology" or description proceeds by the presentation of examples, each example embodying the relation between agent and spectator.[9] The first paragraph mentions one person selflessly taking an interest in the good (or perhaps bad) fortune of others; the second paragraph mentions a "we" who observes the painful experience that some agent undergoes without itself undergoing those experiences; the third paragraph describes uninvolved persons observing someone who is about to be struck, or a tightrope walker, or the painful physical condition of beggars on the street; the fourth paragraph men-

---

9 Recall the comment at IV.2.2 to the effect that the philosopher who inquires into virtue and vice is left with abstractions and "vague and indeterminate" ideas unless particular examples are considered.

tions an audience (now called the "spectator") observing the trials and tribulations of characters on the stage or in literature. The examples go on and on, and by steps the key poles are established. It is almost always a matter of a "bystander" (as Smith puts it in the fourth paragraph) and a person undergoing some experience or other. We are not presented, for the most part, with the relation between two bystanders or between two actors.[10] His phenomenology is therefore selective. The phenomena of bystanders observing each other, or of agents acting on each other, do not capture the relation Smith seems to think fundamental. The basic human relation on which this book turns is thus asymmetrical. Further, the bystander *looks* rather than touches or feels or smells or hears; *The Theory of Moral Sentiments* offers us an "impartial spectator" rather than an "impartial auditor" theory of moral evaluation. Thus the contrast from the start is between one person who is *doing* something (or to whom something is being done) and another who is *watching*. The space between doing and seeing is bridged in part by means of the imagination's creative and "sympathetic" work.

The spectator turns out to be the measure, and I shall discuss subsequently how the asymmetrical relation of actor and spectator becomes lexical insofar as judgments of value and truth are concerned. The old Platonic superiority of *theoria* is to that extent preserved here. Thanks to their appropriately tailored rhetoric, the first four paragraphs of the book already put us in mind to accept both the asymmetry and this ranking. Smith's privileging of the standpoint of the spectator is reflected in his use of examples, pronouns, and the first-person plural; *The Theory of Moral Sentiments* is largely written from the standpoint of the spectator, and the reader naturally identifies with that standpoint. The applause comes from the side of the audience (and the critics). Smith's presentation of the problem of the relation between actor and spectator places us, as readers, in the position of silent spectators and thus recapitulates his fundamental actor/spectator model.[11] He portrays, and in his portraying enacts, the theatricality of the moral sentiments. As spectators, he shows us, we "act out" in imagination the role of the actor, we sim-

10 A rare example of a spectator judging a spectator occurs at *TMS* VII.iii.3.9 (see also VII.iii.3.14), but even here the distinction is "between the observer and the person observed," and the observed spectator plays the role of an actor.

11 The association between sympathy and theatricality is not unique to Smith. See D. Marshall, *The Surprising Effects of Sympathy: Marivaux, Diderot, Rousseau, and Mary Shelley* (Chicago: University of Chicago Press, 1988). For an interesting sociological approach to the theatricality of ordinary life, see E. Goffman, *The Presentation of Self in Everyday Life* (New York: Anchor, 1959).

ulate to ourselves the drama before us (e.g., see II.i.5.3). This simulation is crucial to our mutual understanding as well as to our self-understanding, and so, Smith wants to argue, to ethical appraisal. Moral understanding is fundamentally a sort of practical rather than theoretical knowledge.

We have been reflecting on the way in which Smith starts off his moral philosophy. As he notes, the term "sympathy" is normally understood as "commiseration" and therefore is oriented toward the suffering of others; hence his use of it points to suffering as our natural condition. Compassion is a virtue at home not in aristocratic schemes (such as those of Plato and Aristotle) but in the Christian tradition. "Sympathy" resonates with love of humankind, goodwill, willingness to ease the suffering of others. It thus resonates with our common human lot, not with the extraordinary achievements of the philosophical *aristoi*. As a careful writer, Smith would have understood perfectly that in his somewhat forced emendation of the term, as well as in his sliding back and forth between its narrow and broad senses, the reader would feel the moral force of a received virtue. Smith's focus on "sympathy" is both at home in and formative of what one might broadly call the moral framework of the Enlightenment. He aims to vindicate the standpoint and virtues of ordinary life and to alleviate our common human constitution or estate both ethically and materially, thereby promoting peace, happiness, and the betterment of our condition.

## 2. SYMPATHY, SEPARATENESS, SELF-LOVE, AND SPECTATORIAL IMAGINATION

Totus mundus agit histrionem.[12]

With these preparatory comments in mind, let us return to the beginning of the book. In order to specify the sense in which we are unselfish social beings, Smith indicates the respects in which we are separate. First, we are physically separate: "we have no immediate experience of what other men feel" (I.i.1.2). Other things being equal, we have an immediate experience of ourselves, of our pleasures and pains, that we lack of others' pleasures and pains. In Part VI of *The Theory of Moral Sentiments*, devoted to "the character of virtue," we find a section heading referring

---

12 The sense of this motto from the Globe Theater (London, 1599) is captured by Jaques in Shakespeare's *As You Like It* 2.7.139–43: "All the world's a stage / And all the men and women merely players; / They have their exits and their entrances, / And one man in his time plays many parts, / His acts being seven ages."

to the "individual." At the beginning of the first chapters in this section
(a chapter entitled "Of the Order in which Individuals are recommended by Nature to our Care and Attention"), Smith invokes one of
his favorite Stoic observations:

> Every man, as the Stoics used to say, is first and principally recommended
> to his own care; and every man is certainly, in every respect, fitter and
> abler to take care of himself than of any other person. Every man feels his
> own pleasures and his own pains more sensibly than those of other people.
> The former are the original sensations; the latter the reflected or sympa-
> thetic images of those sensations. The former may be said to be the sub-
> stance; the latter the shadow. (VI.ii.1.1; cf. II.ii.2.1)

The brute facticity of our own sensations of pleasure and pain, in combination with our inability literally to feel each other's sensations, separate us fundamentally. Our embodiment removes us, perhaps even
conceals us from each other at the start; the body seems to mask the
self. Our embodied selves are separate; one person's feelings can no
more be experienced immediately by another than physical pleasures
can be.

Indeed, so Smith will argue, we even demand of each other that our
pleasures and pains, as well as some of our passions, be concealed. The
self learns to conceal the body. For, just as we are not able literally to
experience each other's bodily states, we demand from each other that
expression of extremes of bodily pain and pleasure be masked. Smith
argues that the passions that "take their origin from the body" are always
thought fit to be controlled; temperance is everywhere praiseworthy
(I.ii.1). Agents or actors must learn to "act" (in both senses of the term);
they must dissemble if they are to earn the approbation of spectators.
This holds also of certain nonbodily passions.

We could not demand anything from each other, though, unless we
were somehow aware of each other as subjects of experiences like our
own, and Smith thinks we are naturally so aware. Sociality is not a philosophical construct, something that is not there until philosophers figure
out a theory proving its existence. It is presupposed by a whole range of
ordinary beliefs, actions, and emotions. We do feel with others, in many
different ways and on all sorts of occasions, and others do accept that
feeling-with. We recognize in others experiences like our own, or like
those that we might imagine ourselves undergoing. Conversely, we recognize in ourselves experiences that others have undergone or that we
imagine they have undergone.

The feeling-with Smith calls "sympathy." In this wide sense of the term, "sympathy" articulates our fundamental understanding of others as "beings like us." The possibility of sympathy in the narrow sense of the term (commiseration) thus rests on sympathy in the wider sense, for the former assumes that we are able to enter into the world of another person. Because one can sympathize with almost any passion, it must be possible to "sympathize" with someone and *not* approve of them, not even be "sympathetic" in the narrow sense of the term. Sympathy does not preclude a spectator's fellow feeling with an actor's selfish passions. Indeed, Smith's theory of sympathy allows that one could "sympathize" with an agent's selfish passions, recognize that one's own passions would under similar circumstances resemble those of the agent (a recognition that would require one to "sympathize" with oneself), and then condemn both the agent and (hypothetically, as it were) oneself for having inappropriately self-centered passions. In sum, sympathy is not to be equated with approval; that would destroy the possibility of ethical evaluation and entail that disapproval amounts to no more than the inability of a spectator to empathize with an actor.

In Smith's redefinition of the term, "sympathy" is not a specific passion or virtue or judgment, although sympathy and the passions shape each other in subtle and interesting ways.[13] Hence his is an ethics of sympathy, but not simply of love or compassion. Sympathy is not simply a vehicle for *moral* emotions; Smith provides examples of people sympathizing with the joy that the wealthy seem to take in their riches.[14] Sympathy can be distorted and distorting; it is natural to human beings but must also be cultivated and refined. Sympathy articulates the fundamental fact of our already being "in" each other's world, but of course vanity can distort this. Sympathy is an act of the imagination, but not every act of imagination is an instance of sympathy. For example, in the "History of Astronomy" essay Smith speaks of philosophical systems as "mere inventions of the imagination" (IV.76, *EPS*, p. 105), and in *The Theory of Moral Sentiments* he uses phrases such as "idea of the imagination" (I.ii.1.8).

Precisely how the imagination functions in sympathy (and I shall use the word in Smith's broader sense unless I indicate otherwise) is a matter

13 This point is important given that a plank of the generally discredited "Adam Smith problem" consists in the mistaken identification of sympathy with benevolence.

14 Smith remarks that "Every body is eager to look at him [the man of rank and distinction], and to conceive, at least by sympathy, that joy and exultation with which his circumstances naturally inspire him" (I.iii.2.1).

of some delicacy and brings us to another problem. Smith writes, in the second paragraph of *The Theory of Moral Sentiments*, that our senses can never carry us beyond our own situation. Only through imagination can we "form any conception" of, say, sensations of pain that our brother undergoes. Then "by the imagination we place ourselves in his situation, we conceive ourselves enduring all the same torments, we enter as it were into his body, and become in some measure the same person with him, and thence form some idea of his sensations, and even feel something which, though weaker in degree, is not altogether unlike them" (I.i.1.2). The imagination does not simply join us to others; it gets us "inside" their experience. It joins us to their world, to their motivations, to the circumstances to which they are responding. We thus understand emotions as tied to objects or situations; we naturally take them as relational or intentional.

All of this holds whether we are observing actors on the stage or individuals in everyday life. Smith almost immediately introduces examples from the arts (I.i.1.4) to illustrate our responsiveness to the situations of others and implies that our sympathizing with imagined characters is the same process or experience as our sympathizing with "real" people in everyday life. This is one reason why drama and literature not only provide Smith with examples that nicely illustrate the workings of the imagination but on his account are also essential to moral education. Precisely because sympathy is essential to the formation of ethical judgment, drama and literature become necessary to the formation of the moral imagination and thus to ethics. Smith elsewhere provides us with reason to characterize his use of examples as an effort to communicate by means of sympathy.

Imagination, the means by which we change places (I.i.1.3) with another, only allows us to form *some* idea of the other's sensations or emotions, as is indicated in the passage just quoted. The idea that one person forms of the sensations or emotions that another is experiencing is always less lively than those sensations or emotions are to their possessor. As Smith puts it, "Mankind, though naturally sympathetic, *never* conceive, for what has befallen another, that degree of passion which naturally animates the person principally concerned" (I.i.4.7; my emphasis). Our fundamental separateness, then, is not obliterated through the imagination. The point is not just that one person (let us, following Smith in the fourth paragraph of *TMS*, call him or her the "spectator") does not feel the passions of the person principally concerned (the "actor" or "agent") to the same degree that the latter does.[15] In the literal sense, the spectator does not feel the actor's feelings; he or she imagines being in the actor's *situation* and responds accordingly. Smith writes: "sympathy, therefore, does not arise so much from the view of the passion, as from that of the situation which excites it" (I.i.1.10). The qualification is significant, for spectators must also imagine or understand the actor's response to a specific situation in order to evaluate the appropriateness of that response. The actor's character – if you like, the actor's "story" – must also be grasped, in some cases.

Smith's insistence on the priority of entering into another person's situation, rather than simply of entering into another person's feelings, is important. First, it allows a measure of objectivity. If we were unable to see the situation except from the standpoint of the person affected or identified completely with the agent's emotions, no independent evaluation would be possible. Our ability to see the situation helps to explain how we can sympathize but not approve.

Second, the primary orientation of sympathy to the actor's situation demands a measure of understanding – at times sophisticated understanding. For the situations that give rise to a passion can be complex and multilayered; more than one actor may be involved (as is typically the case in situations where claims about justice or injustice are being made), and the facts of the matter may be complex. This is especially the case when we have a "divided sympathy" and seek to evaluate the merit of claims about unfair treatment (I.ii.4.1). Smith presents us with a spectrum of sympathy, ranging from the "contagion" view described in the third paragraph of *The Theory of Moral Sentiments* (e.g., that we instinctively shrink back when we see a blow about to land on someone else's leg), to the "divided sympathy" cases in which elaborate assessment may be required, to the cases in which we do not actually stop to represent to ourselves the other's situation (say, because we just lack the time) but nonetheless express ourselves as we would have had we really

---

15 Smith usually contrasts the spectator with the "person principally concerned" (that is, either the person being acted upon, or the "agent"), but at VI.concl.6, he also uses the term "actor" (as at *LRBL*, p. 87). L. W. Beck notes that "Each of us is an agent, but there are no spectators without actors, no actors without spectators. 'Agent' is an ontological term, 'actor' and 'spectator' are perspectival and histrionic terms. . . . Calling an agent an 'actor' raises the question 'Actor for what spectator?' " *The Actor and the Spectator* (New Haven: Yale University Press, 1977), p. 34. Smith seems to want to combine the agent and the actor, for insofar as we are conscious of ourselves as moral beings, we view ourselves through the eyes of a spectator.

stopped to sympathize (I.i.3.4). The spectator's moral perceptions cannot simply be understood on a model of intuition or immediate apprehension; clearly, a blending of deliberation, understanding, and insight often goes into the spectator's perception.

In some cases, we "feel with" the other and identify with the other's emotions; this is close to what we often term "empathy" and amounts to re-creating in oneself a sort of "analogous feeling" to that experienced by the actor.[16] In other cases, the spectator's emotions have the emotions and experiences of others as their objects; we may feel resentment at, or compassion for, the anger or grief of another. In still other cases, we "feel with" the other in that we acknowledge the actor's feelings as understandable, even though we actually feel nothing ourselves when sympathizing with the actor.

Smith's notion of sympathy is thus a supple one. In no case of sympathy, though, do we simply identify with the other. If I am grieving on "your account," as Smith puts it (VII.iii.i.4), my grief will no doubt be less wrenching to me than would be my grief over my own loss of the same sort. Sympathy does not dissolve the sense of separateness of either party, as Smith tells us explicitly.[17] And he thinks this appropriate, not only because it reflects our fundamental separateness as subjects but because it also permits the spectator "emotional space" in which to comfort and assist the actor. Given the actor's desire for the fellow feeling of the spectator, it leads the actor to try to adjust his responses to a level that the spectator can sympathize with. This in turn is both practice in self-control and helpful in alleviating the grief in question (I.iii.1.13). And, to repeat, it permits a measure of detachment essential to ethical judgment.

Third, tying sympathy to situation allows Smith to explain cases in which the spectator sympathizes with the actor even though the actor does not in fact feel the emotions that the spectator thinks he

---

16 Smith himself uses the verb "identify" when speaking of the actor's attempt to see himself through the eyes of, and to adopt the sentiments of, the impartial spectator (III.3.25, 28). Following his lead, I shall use the verb repeatedly.

17 "What they [the actors] feel, will, indeed, always be, in some respects, different from what he [the spectator] feels, and compassion can never be exactly the same with original sorrow; because the secret consciousness that the change of situations, from which the sympathetic sentiment arises, is but imaginary, not only lowers it in degree, but, in some measure, varies it in kind, and gives it a quite different modification" (I.i.4.7). Cf. J. Deigh's point: "it is distinctive of empathy that it entails imaginative participation in the other's life without forgetting oneself." "Empathy and Universalizability," *Ethics* 105 (1995), p. 759.

does.[18] For example, we may sympathize with the insane, with infants, and – significantly for other aspects of *The Theory of Moral Sentiments* – with the dead.[19] Imagine being in the last of these conditions, in a cold grave, "a prey to corruption and the reptiles of the earth," soon to be forgotten. The idea that death is a terrible misfortune arises "from putting ourselves in their situation [that of the dead], and from our lodging, if I may be allowed to say so, our own living souls in their inanimated bodies, and thence conceiving what would be our emotions in this case" (I.i.1.13). If we were confined to feeling other people's feelings, then in the case of the dead we would be unable to feel anything (and we would not feel for the insane or infants in the same manner in which they presumably feel). Thus far, we are not, on Smith's account, worried about our own death, though we are portrayed as identifying through imagination with the situation of the dead and asking how we would feel in that situation – how it would be to be dead. Yet Smith does not simply portray us as grieving on account of the dead either; it is not so much that we feel for their loss of their lives as that we find their situation miserable.

"Sympathizing with the dead" is obviously a common yet complex act. The life of the dead, as we picture it, is on Smith's account a figment of our imagination (I.i.1.13). Thus we here seem to be sympathizing with a fictional entity of our own imagining. The immobility of the dead person is not a figment of our imagination, but our picture both of the fate of the lifeless body and of the "dreary and endless melancholy" that seems the lot of the dead is fanciful. Identification with the dead is an illusion, for the dead feel nothing of the misery we attribute to them. Sympathy seems capable of entering into a situation and of grasping an actor's response to that situation, even when the description of the situation and of the actor are largely of its own making. It is for this reason that in the extreme case of sympathizing with the dead, sympathy seems "selfish," in the sense that we are grieving in light of what we imagine we would feel were we in that situation. Smith later also refers to our "sympathy" with the dead as "illusive" (II.i.2.5, II.i.5.11). This "illusive sympathy" is not to be understood as "selfish" in the sense that we care

18 Conversely, as we shall see, it allows the actor to imagine what a spectator would judge, even when there is no real-life spectator in the situation.
19 With respect to sympathizing with the insane, he remarks: "The compassion of the spectator must arise altogether from the consideration of what he himself would feel if he was reduced to the same unhappy situation, and, what perhaps is impossible, was at the same time able to regard it with his present reason and judgment" (*TMS* I.i.1.11).

only for our own welfare; in fact, Smith speaks of "illusive [deceptive] sympathy" in the context of our resentment at the mortal harm done to another. But precisely because the object of the imagination has no reality in this case, sympathy is in a sense deceptive, and the experience of "changing places" with the dead is illusory.

This "illusion of the imagination" thanks to which we sympathize with the deceased leads us to fear our own death. The fear of death thus springs from what one might call the "projective imagination." Here the mechanism of sympathy produces a selfish outlook, in the sense that one becomes preoccupied with one's own fate. And this "selfishness" is in a crucial sense a good thing, for the dread of death is "the great restraint upon the injustice of mankind" and "guards and protects the society." An illusion of the imagination is key both with respect to our desire to punish injustice and to refrain from doing it. This unintended result is a typically Smithean example of the "invisible hand" at work. The result is both good and bad, for, as Smith himself says, the fear of death is also destructive to the happiness of the individual (I.i.I.13).

Sympathizing with the living (including with the living who are grieving on account of the death of a third person) would seem to come to more than imagining *oneself* in their situation; otherwise sympathy would collapse into self-centered projection. Obviously, there are disanalogies between the "illusion" of the imagination generated by sympathy with the dead and the sense in which we sympathetically imagine the situation of living selves. Among other things, sympathy with the living can be a two-way process.

Yet Smith's own preliminary formulations of the issue, as well as the "sympathizing with the dead" example, prompt the following question: Is every sympathetic identification of spectator with actor an illusion, in that the spectator simply projects his or her own feelings into the situation and then attributes them to the actor? Given our fundamental separateness from one another, could not what Smith says of our sympathy with the dead be applied to our sympathy with the living? It might generally be claimed that our response to another's situation "arises altogether from our joining to the change which has been produced upon them, our own consciousness of that change, from our putting ourselves in their situation, and from lodging . . . our own living souls" in their situations, and "thence conceiving what would be our emotions in this case" (I.i.I.13). The illusion would seem unavoidable when the situation is one that the spectator could not possibly experience. Let us listen again to another of Smith's preliminary formulations:

As we have no immediate experience of what other men feel, we can form
no idea of the manner in which they are affected, *but by conceiving what we
ourselves should feel in the like situation.* . . . Neither can that faculty [of imag-
ination] help us to this any other way, than by representing to us what
would be our own [sensations], if we were in his case. It is the impressions
of our own senses only, not those of his, which our imaginations copy.
(I.i.1.2; emphasis added)

Formulations such as these are meant to show that we are not by nature
"selfish," in the sense of being incapable of entering into the situations
of others or of caring about them. Yet the process does seem, so to speak,
"self-centered." This introduces a perplexing ambiguity into the whole
idea of sympathy.

One could drive the point home by arguing that sympathy is fundamentally "illusive" in yet another respect – namely, in regard to the
impartial spectator. Smith discusses the impartial spectator in Part III,
"of Duty," and it is essential to his whole theory of duty and of autonomy that actors be able to judge themselves in light of how an impartial spectator would see them, no matter how actual spectators judge.
Smith refers to this imagined spectator as the "higher tribunal," or
the "man within the breast, the great judge and arbiter" of our conduct (III.2.32). Evidently we imagine, through "illusive sympathy," a
nonexistent spectator, then imagine what we would look like from the
standpoint of this imagined fiction, thereby sympathizing with ourselves from an external standpoint, so to speak. Our sympathizing with
ourselves is not itself an act of "illusive" sympathy, but it is exercised
from a standpoint created by "illusive" sympathy. Yet the impartial
spectator is meant to counter "selfishness" in the ordinary moral sense
of the term (Smith speaks a great deal in Part III of conscience overawing our vanity), but that seems deeply "self-centered." Smith intends this self-reflecting process to provide critical perspective and
detachment from oneself, but ultimately it seems to rest on a projection of self.

Or so one might object. Smith certainly denies that sympathy need
be "selfish" in a perspective-destroying sense. Sympathy is not a matter
simply of imagining what *we* would feel were we in the other's situation. Hence he ultimately denies that sympathy is "selfish" even in this
mild sense of "self-centered." Consider his example, this time offered
in the concluding pages of the book, of a man sympathizing with a
woman's pain in childbirth. The surrounding passage is worth quoting
at length:

Sympathy, however, cannot, in any sense, be regarded as a selfish principle. When I sympathize with your sorrow or your indignation, it may be pretended, indeed, that my emotion is founded in self-love, because it arises from bringing your case home to myself, from putting myself in your situation, and thence conceiving what I should feel in the like circumstances. But though sympathy is very properly said to arise from an imaginary change of situations with the person principally concerned, yet this imaginary change is not supposed to happen to me in my own person and character, but in that of the person with whom I sympathize. When I condole with you for the loss of your only son, in order to enter into your grief I do not consider what I, a person of such a character and profession, should suffer, if I had a son, and if that son was unfortunately to die: but I consider what I should suffer if I was really you, and I not only change circumstances with you, but I change persons and characters. My grief, therefore, is entirely upon your account, and not in the least upon my own. It is not, therefore, in the least selfish. . . . A man may sympathize with a woman in child-bed; though it is impossible that he should conceive himself as suffering her pains in his own proper person and character. (VII.iii.i.4)

The object of this passage is to establish that sympathy is not "selfish" or a function of "self-love" (Smith here uses the terms interchangeably). This comes down to explaining why there is a distinction between, say, a spectator's grief on his own account and his grief on the actor's account. The argument assumes that the distinction between grieving for one's own sake and for another's sake is given in ordinary experience. He seems right in that assumption. Consider a case in which a spectator has lost a son and, upon hearing of the actor's loss of a son, is reminded of his own loss and falls into grief. Clearly he mourns on his own account, not on the actor's account. Smith's commitment to "saving the phenomena" of ordinary life requires him to preserve this important distinction, and he does so by insisting that sympathy cannot be a selfish principle. That is, it cannot merely amount to a spectator's projection of his own feelings into the actor's situation, in ignorance of the actor's presence in and response to that situation. If sympathy were selfish, Smith wants to ask, how could it be the case that you do sympathize with people whose situation you could not in principle experience yourself?[20]

---

20 Hume seeks to counter the self-love view by taking exactly the opposite of Smith's tack: "No force of imagination can convert us into another person, and make us fancy, that we, being that person, reap benefit from those valuable qualities, which belong to him. Or if it did, no celerity of imagination could immediately transport us back, into ourselves, and make us love and esteem the person, as different from us. . . . All suspicion, therefore,

Let us review. We seem pulled in different directions on the issue of whether or not sympathy can escape the charge of being selfish. Smith began the book with the problem ("selfish" being the second word in the book proper). There it was a question of whether or not we naturally take an interest in the fortunes of others, of whether or not we identify with their happiness or misery, regardless of the immediate advantage to us of doing so. Let us call that opening notion of selfishness "sense (1)" of the term. The second paragraph of the book initiated the explanation of how it is possible for us to identify with others, and Smith mentions the "imagination" for the first time. In the third paragraph the process is referred to as one of "changing places"; in the fourth paragraph the distinction between "spectator" and "the person principally concerned" arises, and we hear of an "analogous emotion" arising in them; and in the fifth paragraph Smith introduces "sympathy" as the key explanatory term. The narrative evolves until, at the end of the book (in the passage just quoted at length), we reach the more nuanced sense of selfishness. Let us call that "sense (2)" of the term. In sense (2), "selfishness" would prevent us from entering into another's situation and person and would deny us transcendence of ourselves. Smith rejects the reduction of sympathy to selfishness in sense (2), arguing that we rightly take ourselves to be capable of genuinely stepping outside the circle of our own selves and our own experiences.

Is there not something paradoxical about Smith's insistence at the end of the book on the opposition between sympathy and sense (2) selfishness? Presumably one could refrain from treating others selfishly in sense (1) of the term even if sympathy were selfish or "egoistic" in sense (2). That is, I could care about others, be interested in their fortunes, and have their happiness matter to me, even if my sympathy with them could in principle come only to my imagining how *I* would feel in their situation rather than how *they* actually feel. Further, since he himself insists at the beginning of the book that "we have no immediate experience of what other men feel," how could I sympathize with you *except* by imagining how I would feel were I in your situation? If Smith is right in insisting that sympathy be entirely nonselfish, he would seem to have raised the bar impossibly high, thus dooming us to what he would insist is selfishness.

These are meaningful questions for Smith. He is attempting to found

of selfish regards, is here totally excluded." *Enquiry Concerning the Principles of Morals*, p. 234.

an ethics of virtue on fellow feeling, and this move is open to the Kantian objection that sympathy tends to be partial and so quite unreliable as a foundation for objective moral judgment. In Kant's terms, Smith's ethics is at heart "empirical" and not appropriately principled.[21] It would seem to follow that it is incapable of genuine universality and so of escaping the charge of selfishness. The difficulty is one that pertains also to contemporary efforts to articulate an ethics based on "care" or "compassion." Smith's emphasis on impartiality and self-command would seem to signal his awareness of this danger of egoism; one might go so far as to say that they signal his Kantian twist to his Humean sympathy theory. His skepticism (to be discussed in Chapter 4) prevents him from proposing an extrahuman or *a priori* "foundation" for ethics, yet he does not think the result is egoism in any ethically dangerous sense.

Smith must therefore deny (1) that sympathizing with another requires that the spectator have had an experience *analogous* to that of the actor, and (2) that the spectator's experience forms the *basis* of his understanding of the actor's experience. Otherwise, understanding another – on the relatively few occasions when the experiences of actor and spectator match each other – would come down to remembering how *I* acted or reacted in the situation. But my action or reaction may be idiosyncratic, and in any case is not yours. Say that I have a high tolerance for pain and therefore reacted with little emotion when I broke my leg while skiing. I would have little sympathy, presumably, for another's emotional reaction to his breaking his leg while skiing; I did not react that way, so why should I not judge his reaction cowardly? Reasoning of *that* "unsympathetic" kind seems selfish in our second sense of the term. Conversely, if sympathizing were bounded by such conditions, then a spectator could not sympathize in cases in which he or she has no similar experience to imagine from, so to speak. On this view, the circle of our sympathy would be quite narrow.

21  See Immanuel Kant, *Grounding for the Metaphysics of Morals*, trans. J. W. Ellington, 3rd ed. (Indianapolis: Hackett, 1993), p. 46, n. 30, where Kant lumps the "principle of sympathy" together with Hutcheson's moral sense theory. In the first chapter (Remark II) of the Analytic of the *Critique of Practical Reason* Kant presents ethical theory based on "moral feeling" (Hutcheson is cited) as one whose practical material grounds are subjective and "internal," an approach to ethical theory that is dismissed as empirical. Trans. L. W. Beck, 3rd ed. (New York: Macmillan 1993), p. 41. Kant nonetheless had genuine respect for Smith's moral philosophy, and there are unquestionably Kantian themes in Smith's work. See S. Fleischacker, "Philosophy in Moral Practice: Kant and Adam Smith," *Kant-Studien* 82 (1991): 249–69, and K. Haakonssen, "Kantian Themes in Smith," in ch. 4 of *Natural Law and Moral Philosophy*, pp. 148–53.

Yet there is a certain commonsensical foundation for the "actual-experience" limitation on sympathy, and so for the view that sympathy cannot be entirely selfless. It seems plausible to claim that if I have had an experience similar to yours – say, that of losing an only son – I can in principle understand your similarly caused grief at a deeper level than can someone who has not had such an experience. It could further be claimed that no one is ever entitled to pass judgment on another person whose experiences he or she has not shared. How could one judge a woman's response to childbirth, or the plight of a South African black person struggling under apartheid, or a victim's response to some terrible misfortune, or a starving person's hunger, or the religious response of an eighth-century-B.C. Greek to nature, without having been in the same situation? And conversely, for an agent to agree to have been "understood" and judged by a spectator who lacks the appropriately similar experience may seem like a surrender of "identity."

One can envision a Smithean "politics" of sympathy that would be the opposite of that suggested by *The Theory of Moral Sentiments* (in which case we would have, contrary to Smith's best intentions, an example of the subverting "invisible hand" at work). Given the apparent epistemic limitations of any act of sympathy, it might seem that fellow feeling, and so mutual understanding, are possible only within shared-experience groups, only between people who can identify with each other by means of what they take to be a common and definitive set of experiences.[22] In Smithean terms, this would come down to a privileging of the standpoint of the actor over that of the spectator, and so the triumph of selfishness in both of the senses we have been entertaining. The shift of emphasis might be seen as a shift from the value of "sincerity" (insofar as that entails a willingness to demonstrate one's accountability to others) to that of "authenticity."[23] One can see that the result of substituting an

22 Smith does allow that sympathy can flow along boundaries defined by groups, some (such as the family) less arbitrary than others (such as one country). E.g., in the discussion of the family at *TMS* VI.ii.1.7, he remarks: "What is called affection, is in reality nothing but habitual sympathy."

23 These terms are borrowed from L. Trilling, *Sincerity and Authenticity* (Cambridge, Mass.: Harvard University Press, 1971). Trilling understands "sincerity" as requiring "a rhetoric of avowal, the demonstration of single-minded innocence through attitude and posture, exactly the role-playing in which Rousseau had found the essence of personal, ultimately of social, corruption" (p. 70). I take it that Smith would see "authenticity" as linked to exhibitionism and, in the extreme case, to the "fanaticism" that comes from a misheard "voice of conscience." Smith would be fascinated, I think, with the ways in which authenticity itself has come to be something sympathized with, even a thing of fashion and a commodity of sorts.

expressivist for a spectatorial model of social interaction might be a culture of exhibitionism and narcissism. Attempts to communicate one's perspective outside one's boundaries would look more like the collision of bodies than a communion of selves. This in turn would suggest that one experience group could not evaluate another from a moral point of view, since by definition they would be incapable of sympathy with, of entering into the situation of, one another.

If this were the result of the difficulty of separating sympathy from selfishness, then the whole notion of sympathy would be dialectically unstable, and Smith's entire moral philosophy would be self-undermining in an ironic manner. Smith's doctrine of sympathy would be an instance of the internal instability of the Enlightenment (recall my review of that point in the Introduction). Let me therefore digress to develop further the issue of the potential of sympathy for self-subversion and then explain, in sections 4 and 5, why Smith thinks he can successfully rebut these reproaches to sympathy.

### 3. DIGRESSION: SYMPATHY, AUTHENTICITY, AND SOCIAL FRAGMENTATION

Many have noted that the dissolution of community and the corresponding rise of differentiation or separateness seem to be defining characteristics of contemporary Western cultural life. This fragmentation seems related to the problem of "selfishness" with which Smith begins *The Theory of Moral Sentiments*. I suggested that the large-scale background for the problem of selfishness is a vision of life as prone to conflict, dissolution, and war. In contemporary Western society this tendency manifests itself in fragmentation of a particular sort. One could produce many examples of individuals or groups who demand what one might call recognition of their special identity. A special identity is held to embody a moral status worthy of respect and strong enough to constitute a salient feature of those thus identified.

Correspondingly, claims to recognition are frequently accompanied by accounts of the special "culture" exhibited by the individuals in question. What makes this self-delineation seem paradoxical is the equally widespread insistence that it is impossible for those who are not members to "understand" the group in question. Recognition is demanded from outsiders, but understanding is denied to them. Thus, if you are not, say, deaf, then I as a deaf person may well deny that you have any "right" to evaluate my world; you cannot in principle enter into it, for you are not one of us. This general view of things – of mutually excluding groups demanding equal recognition from one another – is now so thoroughly embedded in culture, including academic culture, that it has given rise to new ways of expressing moral authority. One frequently hears people declare, with passion: "Speaking as an X, I can assure you that Y," where X is the name of the relevant group and Y stands for some description or evaluation of X's situation or beliefs. An auditor not in group X cannot speak with any authority about that group but must defer immediately. The moral authority embodied in statements preceded by "Speaking as an X " stems in part from an epistemic thesis to the effect that the point of view shared by all members of X is not accessible, or at least not sufficiently accessible, to non-X persons.

The fault lines along which differences are taken to be relevant are, on the whole, representative of experiences rather than interests. One might say that there is a "shared experience" criterion at work in the claims to differentiation. You can be one of us if you have had experiences like ours, and to have had them you must be very similar to us in relevant respects. But there is more at work than the deployment of a criterion of that sort. For the moral force of the claim to recognition, and not just to difference, arises also from the view that the shared experience has had something to do with a history of suffering and sacrifice. As already noted, Smith's own use of the word "sympathy" already inclines us to see the sufferings rather than joys of others as the primary object of our attention. From the very beginning of the book (consider again the examples in the first three paragraphs of misery, torture, suffering, horror) to the examples at the end of the book of the loss of a son and the woman in childbirth (VII.iii.1.4), this tendency is reinforced.

Let us finish tracing the path from sympathy to social fragmentation. For we must note that *undeserved* suffering, such that compassion is due, is crucial to the picture. Think of the image of "the Vietnam veteran," for example, in popular American mythology. By contrast, we would think it comic for, say, members of a Billionaires' Club to preface professions of suffering with the remark "Speaking as a billionaire, I can tell you that. . . ." We have no compassion for a group that has much to rejoice in. In a famous passage Smith points out that we have "sympathy" with persons of rank and fortune and want to be like them, but this is a matter more of vanity than of compassion (I.iii.2.2). Nor would we be inclined to recognize a group of Nazi concentration camp guards who made claims upon our compassion by virtue of having a unique shared experience and of having suffered much during and after the war. We would be likely to think that their shared experience was morally reprehensible and that their suffering was justified.

The fragmentation, if not balkanization, of social groups may thus be drawn along the lines of shared and undeserved pain and is associated frequently with the sense of victimization. Naturally, group X's shared experience of unmerited victimization generates a particularly insistent demand for recognition and compassion. Smith explains that the agent demands our sympathy more when he suffers than when he rejoices and that the sympathetic pain we spectators feel is more "lively and distinct" a perception than our sympathy with pleasure (I.iii.1.3). When we do enter into the agent's pain and see it as having been caused without justification, we experience real resentment at those responsible for inflicting the harm. Thus the politics of compassion and of resentment seem to be flip sides of the coin. And resentment is, on Smith's account, the "unsocial" passion that underlies our sense of justice. As we have noted, Smith thinks our resentment against injustice so powerful that we frequently experience it (via "illusive sympathy") even when those suffering the injustice do not (II.i.2.5).

In some contemporary Westernized societies of the type Smith would label "civilized," victimization is often construed broadly under the rubrics of race, gender, and class and is then defined more narrowly in keeping with the "shared experience" criterion, each subgroup claiming to have lived and suffered in a distinctive manner that is hardly intelligible to those not similarly privileged but that is in each case worthy of compassion and recognition. The inaccessibility to the spectators' sympathy of the actor's pain seems, ironically, also prepared by Smith's emphasis on our basic separateness and his argument to the effect that "though our sympathy with sorrow is often a more pungent sensation than our sympathy with joy, it always falls much more short of the violence of what is naturally felt by the person principally concerned" (I.iii.1.8). From the actor's standpoint, the spectator has no right to judge. The actor holds that one must "pathei mathos" (learn through suffering), in the old phrase of the Greek dramatists, and is resentful of an outsider who fails to recognize him *and* of one who claims to understand him. Obviously this stance, in turn, risks degenerating into narcissism and into the complete denial that one group can be the measure of another. Self-knowledge risks being reduced to mere expression of self. Correspondingly, this stance seems to lead to the destruction of any notion of community except as the arena within which war is waged for recognition (and for the political and economic benefits that follow from recognition). That arena comes to be dominated by rhetorical, and then of course legal, struggles. The politics of compassion seems inseparable not only from the politics of resentment but from the politics of the court – in the sense of "court of law." There is once again an eerie anticipation of this in Smith's argument that justice is founded on the emotion of resentment.

Charles Taylor has written that "a fragmented society is one whose members find it harder and harder to identify with their political society as a community."[24] One might add that a fragmented society is also one in which society cannot identify with its members or groups of members. But thus to continue Taylor's thought is to rely heavily on the notion of "identification." How is that notion to be understood? Few hesitate in providing the answer: it is to be understood in terms of compassion or sympathy. A fragmented society is one in which the "bonds of sympathy" (in Taylor's words) are weakened, one in which the ties of compassion have broken down.[25] The vocabulary of sympathy or compassion comes naturally to us in this context, perhaps in part because of Smith's influence. The question I am raising in these digressive comments is whether the notion of sympathy is intrinsically unstable in a way that makes intelligible the decline of sympathy – which one would have thought the glue holding community together – into group or individual narcissism. If so, then the problem is not insufficient sympathy in public life; it is the centrality of an intrinsically unstable notion (sympathy) to public life.

Smith has several strategies at his command for responding to the collapse of sympathy into selfishness that I have sketched in this digression. In particular, he can call into question the relevance of the "actual experience" criterion, the notion that the appropriate sympathy due to the actor on account of his or her suffering is to be determined by the actor rather than the spectator, and the epistemic privileging of the standpoint of the actor. Let me develop these responses in steps.

## 4. FROM LOVE TO DEATH: SYMPATHY'S REACH AND THE IDEAL UNITY

Smith plainly thinks that in order to sympathize with others we need not be bound by the actual-experience condition. Part of his evidence is also an appeal to ordinary experience. That fellow feeling is taken to occur

---

24 In *The Ethics of Authenticity* (Cambridge, Mass.: Harvard University Press, 1991), p. 117.
25 Ibid., p. 113.

by both spectator and actor on all sorts of occasions when the spectator and actor have not shared the same (or the same kind of) experience just seems to be widely accepted. We do allow for the power of imagination to permit a "change of situations." Part of the evidence for the proposition that we must be able to put ourselves in others' shoes and see their situation from their point of view lies in the fact that persons whose experiences are not of the same sort *do* find occasion for "mutual sympathy" that both parties take as genuine. I may have no son, let alone an only son, let alone an only son who died, yet I may in fact sympathize under such conditions and the sympathy is sometimes accepted by the actor. For this to occur, I must be imagining what it would be like "if I were really you."

Even among persons who claim to have had the "same" experiences, their actual experiences are not *identical*, if only because they are always parts of different biographies, always "of the same sort." It would seem to follow that, where imagination bridges the experiences of two persons, the spectator's sympathy is not "selfish" as long as it takes cognizance of the differences between the spectator and actor. For where their experiences are not identical, or even of the same sort, the spectator cannot honestly reconstruct the actor's situation on analogy with his own, or at least not solely by analogy. Indeed, to "substitute" (to use a term from drama) one's experiences for another's, as an actor on the stage does for a character when trying to get inside that character's emotional life, has as its goal the accurate representation of *that character*. It thus assumes a difference between arbitrary reconstruction and true interpretation. One has to know what experiences to substitute, how, and when. A spectator can sympathize erroneously.

Yet given both that the spectator cannot feel the actor's feelings or sensations (and never does so in the same degree), and that the spectator cannot in the end escape from the fact that *he* (or she) would still be the one imagining the feeling of the actor, does it make sense to insist on the distinction between my imagining how I would feel in your situation and my imagining how you feel in your situation? I think the answer affirmative, if it is properly qualified.

Surely individuals often respond to the same situation differently, as my example of varying tolerance to pain indicates. Failing to see that someone else's biography has developed in a way different from that in which my life might develop in similar circumstances might be termed "selfish." I cannot grieve on "your account" until I know what *your* situation is. Even where the two biographies overlap such that my reaction to the imagined prospect of an event taking place in my life is similar to your reaction to the event having taken place in yours, there is a difference between my sharing in the reaction because I imagine it taking place in *my* life and sharing in it because I enter into *your* life. Again, the first reaction might be characterized as "selfish"; it is to substitute my story for yours. It is consistent with this judgment that in the course of understanding your story I might imagine how I would have reacted or have reacted under similar conditions. And it is unavoidable that in imaginatively grasping how you have reacted, *I* must do the imaginative grasping. But, crucially, this does not preclude the "changing places" that Smith depicts and consequently does not in itself jeopardize Smith's argument that sympathy need not collapse into selfishness.

With this in mind, the various scenes of sympathy and selfishness may be arranged in the following spectrum:

a. Sympathizing in cases where the object of our sympathy is not in fact "there." Smith provides us with four examples in the last half of the first chapter of the book, the most striking of which is that of our "sympathizing" with the dead. In this case, the situation of the dead is not reproducible in imagination, and we have no idea, or no accurate idea, of their emotions or situation. As noted earlier, Smith refers to this as "illusive sympathy." We thus have no basis for identifying their situation correctly; we must simply imagine, in the sense of "conjure up," that which we enter into. Sympathy here must mean imagining what we would feel if we were in the situation we have ourselves re-created on the basis of physical cues (such as the corpse of the deceased) and our own passions. In this instance, sympathy would be "selfish" in our second sense of the term. It might also be selfish in the first sense; when Smith first discusses the issue, he slides quickly from an explanation of our grief over the death of another to our fearing our own demise (and thus into sense (1) of the term).

b. Sympathizing with someone's physical condition and sensations that cannot literally be shared with us. Smith's example is that of a spectator sympathizing with the pain felt by the man on the rack (I.i.1.2). We form some conception of what the agent feels by placing "ourselves in his situation" and conceiving "ourselves enduring all the same torments." This appears to remain "selfish" in our sense (2); nonetheless, the spectator's imagination is not simply fabricating that which is sympathized with, since the living agent is in some sense there before his eyes. This does not appear to be selfish in sense (1).

c. Sympathizing in cases where the actor is not primarily experiencing physical pain or pleasure but rather an emotion "derived from the imagination" (such as grief, or joy, or anxiety, or fear). The example here is of the spectator sympathizing with a person who has lost a son (VII.iii.i.4). The spectator does not consider what he would feel if he were in the same situation as the actor; rather, he considers what he would feel if he *were* the actor. He and the actor "change persons and characters." This does not seem selfish in either sense (1) or (2).

d. At the other end of the spectrum, we have a situation into which the spectator's imagination cannot enter. In some respects it resembles case (a), except that this time there is supposed to be real sympathy between two living persons, so to speak. However, both persons are actors. Neither is a spectator of the other; neither is "outside" the other in the relevant sense. Smith's example is that of (romantic) love between two persons. Their worlds are thoroughly intertwined, but spectators cannot sympathize with the actors' mutual sympathy: "Our imagination not having run in the same channel with that of the lover, we cannot enter into the eagerness of his emotions" (I.ii.2.1). Thus lovers strike spectators as in some measure "ridiculous." Spectators do not really understand the lovers' mutual affection; they cannot imagine or sympathize with them. Smith does not say of these lovers that they "sympathize" with each other, for sympathy, properly speaking, requires a distance and impenetrability, so to speak, of one by the other. (I shall comment further on love and sympathy in Chapter 4.)

From an ethical perspective, what is the ideal attainable point on this spectrum? It would seem to be case (c). In spite of questions I have myself put to Smith, he does seem able to defend (c) as a genuine example of nonselfish sympathy. Yet even there we may be left, at the end of the day, with a significant gray area with respect to the question of whether a spectator has ever *really* understood the experiences of an actor, ever really escaped the circle of selfishness. The question may seem ineluctably ambiguous, precisely because the spectator cannot literally feel the actor's sensations or emotions and because the identification is normally not total.[26] I see no reason why Smith would have to deny that ambiguity. He often writes as though sympathy between persons is an ongoing process of adjustment, a continual search for equilibrium. The consensus (or "mutual sympathy") reached at any point between two or

---

26 This is the conclusion reached by Haakonssen, *The Science of a Legislator*, p. 48.

more persons could be characterized from a Smithean standpoint as a fiction or story with this or that history of accommodations and claims to understanding, claims that need not be illusory but that come to be trustworthy only after standing up to repeated challenge in various contexts. It is a process with analogies in the economic sphere, not only with respect to the search for equilibrium in supply and demand (as expressed by price) but more generally with respect to the importantly rhetorical dimension of selling and buying (*TMS* VII.iv.25; *WN* I.ii.2). Persuasion in the political sphere too is seen by Smith as a search for mutual sympathy. It is evident that in a sympathy-based moral and political theory, fellowship among citizens and classes of citizens will hinge on their willingness to sympathize with each other appropriately, a willingness that can be shaped by institutions. Correspondingly, Smith is concerned in *The Theory of Moral Sentiments* and *The Wealth of Nations* with the problem of the "corruption" of the moral sentiments that might interfere with (among things) appropriate fellow feeling.

To review an earlier objection, though, the decision in favor of (c) as the ideal attainable point on the spectrum could be disputed on grounds we have already examined. From the beginning of the book, the asymmetry between actor and spectator emerges, as well as the privileging of the standpoint of the latter. Yet in spite of the implications of Smith's choice of examples, it may appear that an actor rather than the spectator might play the role of judge: "Every faculty in one man is the measure by which he judges of the like faculty in another. I judge of your sight by my sight, of your ear by my ear, of your reason by my reason, of your resentment by my resentment, of your love by my love. I neither have, nor can have, any other way of judging about them" (I.i.3.10). This "I" might seem to be that of the actor – say, of the sufferer described in my digressive comments. That on Smith's view this is not so begins to emerge explicitly in the fourth chapter of Part I of his book on ethics, where he discusses the process of mutual adjustment between the actor and the spectator. There is a difference in their respective adjustments; whereas the spectator's sympathy makes him look at the actor's situation, the spectator's passion does not undergo any great modification. The actor's passion, on the other hand, is reduced to a "reflected passion," and his whole view of himself changes substantially when he views himself through the eyes of the spectator.

This asymmetry has normative consequences: in viewing himself through the eyes of the spectator, the agent sees his situation in a "candid and impartial light" (I.i.4.8). (This is the first use of the term "impartial" in the book.) There is no suggestion that the spectator has come to view himself in an impartial light. Indeed, insofar as the spectator has come to view the actor or himself in an impartial light, it is by *spectating* more accurately; and this is precisely what the actor too is doing – spectating, not acting. The standpoint of the spectator constitutes, when it is properly sympathetic and informed, impartiality. This soon develops in what in one sense is a central and often repeated thesis of the book: ". . . if we consider all the different passions of human nature, we shall find that they are regarded as decent, or indecent, just in proportion as mankind are more or less disposed to sympathize with them" (I.ii.intro.2). Since there is no difference between how the passions of actors are "regarded" by impartial "mankind" and how they *are* (so far as their moral attributes are concerned), the standpoint of the impartial spectator is ethically definitive.[27] To repeat, Smith proposes an impartial spectator, not an impartial actor, account of moral judgment. Sentiments are moral or virtuous when approved by the impartial spectator, and therefore the "theory of moral sentiments" is a theory of the spectator's approval of the emotions.

As already noted, the superiority of spectator to actor embodies a superiority of looking to doing and in this sense retains a residue of Platonism. Smith's privileging of the spectator is not simply a result of a "theory," in some descriptive or scientific sense, but also a result of a moral and even political conviction on Smith's part that human life will be better if we accept his construal of the spectator–actor relation. The theory of the moral sentiments seems driven in this decisive respect by moral sentiments. The skillful and subtle rhetoric of *The Theory of Moral Sentiments* is geared in part toward reinforcing the ability of the imagination to carry us into the situations of others and makes sympathy seem a natural feature of human life. This is a protreptically rhetorical book and an effort in moral education.

This is not the final word in Smith's crucial defense of the privileged status of the spectator, however.

## 5. SPECTATORSHIP, MIRRORING, AND DUALITY OF SELF

It may seem that the theory of sympathy is meant to explain how an actor gets "out" of his or her own self and "into" another self, as though

27 For reiterations of the point, see also III.5.5, VII.ii.I.49, VII.iii.2.7.

selves were separately constituted as isolated monads to begin with, as though the theory were intended to solve a Cartesian problem of other minds. That is quite the opposite of Smith's view. His view is, rather, that we always see ourselves through the eyes of others and are mirrors to each other.[28] We are not transparent to our own consciousness; indeed, without the mediation of the other, we have no determinate moral selves "there" waiting to be made transparent. Smith performs a thought experiment: he asks us to suppose that "a human creature could grow up to manhood in some solitary place, without any communication with his own species." What sort of creature would result?

> To a man who from his birth was a stranger to society, the objects of his passions, the external bodies which either pleased or hurt him, would occupy his whole attention. The passions themselves, the desires or aversions, the joys or sorrows, which those objects excited, though of all things the most immediately present to him, could scarce ever be the objects of his thoughts. The idea of them could never interest him so much as to call upon his attentive consideration. (III.1.4)[29]

Because no passion becomes the object of reflection, no passion arouses a new passion. We acquire what have been called "second-order desires" as a result of forming positive or negative judgments about our "first-order desires."[30] We then act to change our desires, motives, "passions." This would be impossible outside of society; we do not have a moral self outside of the human community. Presumably this is why he uses the

28 The mirror metaphor is Smith's (III.1.3). For classical uses of it, see Aristotle, *NE* 1166a30–3, *Eudemian Ethics* 1245a28 ff., *Magna Moralia* 1213a10–27; and Plato's *Phaedrus* 255d5–6 and *Alcibiades* 1 132d–133c. Cf. Hume, *Treatise*, p. 365.

29 The passage continues: "The consideration of his joy could in him excite no new joy, nor that of his sorrow any new sorrow, though the consideration of the causes of those passions might often excite both. Bring him into society, and all his own passions will immediately become the causes of new passions. He will observe that mankind approve of some of them, and are disgusted by others. He will be elevated in the one case, and cast down in the other; his desires and aversions, his joys and sorrows, will now often become the causes of new aversions, new joys and new sorrows: they will now, therefore, interest him deeply, and often call upon his most attentive consideration."

30 I refer to H. G. Frankfurt's well-known article "Freedom of the Will and the Concept of a Person," *Journal of Philosophy* 68 (1971): 5–20. Frankfurt remarks: "Many animals appear to have the capacity for what I shall call 'first-order desires' or 'desires of the first order,' which are simply desires to do or not to do one thing or another. No animal other than man, however, appears to have the capacity for reflective self-evaluation that is manifested in the formation of second-order desires." These last are desires to "want to have (or not to have) certain desires and motives" (p. 7).

striking and almost oxymoronic phrase "human creature" in the passage just quoted, a "creature" being less than fully human.

Smith does not wish to suggest that human beings ever were in the position of the "human creature . . . in some solitary place" and so has no wish to explain in a genetic sense how we became the creatures we are. He takes it that such has occurred and argues that the capacity to develop new passions is an observable feature and that its existence presupposes society. Nor does he attack the logical paradox implicit in the question as to how an actor recognizes another person as the sort of being who can recognize that actor in the requisite manner. The process seems to assume the individual's cognition of himself as at least potentially a being recognizable as a human, accountable self, yet that is, at the same time, the end to be arrived at.

Smith's scheme thus far suggests that we cannot be a human individual without that connectedness resulting from recognition of one another as spectators, a relation that, paradoxically, provides detachment from immediate sensation and apprehension of the external causes of those sensations. Our individual selves are not things that are just "there," pre-given and waiting to be discovered. We have no "immediate" apprehension, no recognition through our own devices alone, of our pleasures and pains, our passions and sentiments, as being appropriate or inappropriate, graceful or unbecoming. Characterizations or evaluations of sensations and passions arise only in communities of members of a species of a certain sort. However naturally they may arise, such characterizations of ourselves are social artifacts. By means of them we humanize ourselves. For to "be in society" means, Smith says, to imagine ourselves as seen through the eyes of others. We cannot "be ourselves" as moral agents without imagining how we are seen by others. The asocial "creature" not only lacks a sense of "personal beauty and deformity"; it also lacks any sense of moral beauty and moral deformity. Not even the beauty or deformity of one's "own face" (III.1.3–5), let alone that of one's soul, is visible to an individual in a Rousseauean state of nature. Our natural state is, so to speak, in society.[31] Spectatorship is the condition for the possibility of agency. This helps to explain why spectatorship is normatively prior.

---

31 Smith's rejection of social contract theory is related to this point; like Hume, he argues that there never could be such a thing as a "state of nature," or some determinate presocial state on the basis of which we could meaningfully choose a conception of justice. See LJ(A)iv.19, v.114–16; LJ(B)15–18.

When we tell a story about another's situation and person we have imaginatively grasped, we take ourselves to be in the same world as that other. It does not follow that on this account we entirely live outside our bodies. Our pleasures, pains, emotions, are still ours in a sense inaccessible to others. Smith's account of sociality does not destroy any notion of the "inner life." Your emotions, however mediated by your apprehension of how they are apprehended by others, are still *your* emotions. The narrative of a life is a narrative about this rather than that life, yours rather than his or hers. Yet sympathy is key to our self-conception; on Smith's account, the logic of self-knowledge is an extension of the logic of our understanding of others.[32] This process can extend to the point where an actor who views himself as reflected in an *imagined* spectator rather than in an *actual* spectator becomes morally self-governed in such a way as to be quite at odds with the community. This is a story Smith tells in Part III of the book, and I shall return to it shortly.

The privileged position of the spectator in this account is ultimately grounded in Smith's depiction of the natural sociability of human beings and so of our natural dependence on others for our self-conception. In sum, we are aware of ourselves through being aware that others are aware of us; the dependence on the spectator is built in (or "natural," as Smith says). We evaluate ourselves as we imagine that others evaluate us. As just noted, the story does not end there – we also learn to free ourselves of mistaken views that actual spectators hold – but it would seem to start there. To see oneself as a human self is to see oneself being seen, but in a certain way – as being praised or blamed – and so by other beings of a certain kind – those who can accord praise and blame. When we judge others, we do so as spectators of their conduct, and vice versa. The standpoint of the spectator is privileged in its connection to evaluation, and in Smith's account this privileging of the spectator is internalized in the actor: we cannot see and judge ourselves except by looking at ourselves from the outside; that is what it means to take an evaluative per-

---

32 Cf. Beck's useful remark: "I learn to communicate about my feelings in very much the same way I learn to detect from their communication what the feelings of others are and what feelings they are ascribing to me. . . . There are two wholes having a common part, namely the situation. . . . Both my self-knowledge and knowledge of another actor are synecdochic. I feel my emotions and I do not feel another's, but I learn what they are, what they are called, how they are appropriately expressed by watching other people respond to what I believe is the same public world having the same emotion-provoking features, listening to what they say, and speaking the same language." *The Actor and the Spectator*, pp. 64–5.

spective on ourselves or others.[33] Moral self-consciousness requires that I "divide myself, as it were, in two persons" (III.1.6).[34] The internalized or idealized judge is still a spectator. The imagination preserves the privileged position of this spectator – the stand-in for "the public." The theatrical relation is thus internalized; we become our own public.

Consequently, the actor has no exclusive epistemic access to his or her own emotions, none that dispenses with the spectator – with the public, with the community, with "mankind." The claim to that privileged access cannot even be stated except through the mediating presence of the spectator or other (language itself being a public phenomenon). Smith is also showing that any claim on the actor's part to be the measure by which the appropriate expression of pain or the appropriate level of compassion by the spectator are gauged cannot be sustained at the theoretical level. The measure is, once again, public in principle, and the standpoint of the spectator alone provides the requisite perspective. This is Smith's bottom-line reply to any move to privilege the standpoint of the actor.

Of course this philosophical reply is not necessarily decisive in terms of the formation of the moral sentiments, for in a culture of sympathy people may still insist on misconceiving the nature of sympathy. We sometimes abandon the perspective of the spectator; selfishness and narcissism are always a temptation. Our selfish passions can make us ethically ignorant and our society fragmented, and sympathy can, ironically, be degraded and used against itself in the ways described earlier. This is why moral education, and through it the right formation of the imagination and of sympathy, are essential. Self-command over our selfish emotions, which requires that we understand the connection between ordering ourselves well and viewing ourselves from the outside, is naturally encouraged by the pleasure we take in mutual sympathy.[35] Our

33 "We can never survey our own sentiments and motives, we can never form any judgment concerning them; unless we remove ourselves, as it were, from our own natural station, and endeavour to view them as at a certain distance from us. But we can do this in no other way than by endeavouring to view them with the eyes of other people, or as other people are likely to view them" (*TMS* III.1.2).

34 This theme was well established by Smith's time. For example, see Shaftesbury's gloss on the Delphic inscription: "Recognize yourself; which was as much as to say, divide yourself, or be two. For if the division were rightly made, all within would of course . . . be rightly understood and prudently managed." Pt. I, sec. II of *Advice to an Author*, in vol. I of *Characteristics*, p. 113.

35 "Respect for what are, or for what ought to be, or for what upon a certain condition would be, the sentiments of other people, is the sole principle which, upon most occa-

other passions, as well as the communication of emotion and understanding that is sympathy, not to mention the impossibility of conceiving
oneself to be both human and a "creature" in the "solitary place," also
pull us toward sociality and away from selfishness in both sense (1) and
(2) of the term. His doctrine of pleasure and pain (discussed in Chapter
3) helps to explain why the judgments of others and moral rules tend
to "stick," even when the actor's self-interest (narrowly understood) suggests that it is to his or her advantage to violate the norm.

## 6. THE *PATHOS* OF SOLITUDE AND THE BEAUTY OF SYMPATHY

If someone should try to strip away the costumes and makeup from the
actors performing a play on the stage and to display them to the spectators
in their own natural appearance, wouldn't he ruin the whole play?
Wouldn't all the spectators be right to throw rocks at such a madman and
drive him out of the theater? . . . This deception, this disguise, is the very
thing that holds the attention of the spectators. Now the whole life of
mortal men, what is it but a sort of play . . . ?

Desiderius Erasmus[36]

I conclude this discussion by returning to the issue of sympathy as a
response to the problems of selfishness, of lack of caring or compassion,
and of fragmentation and dissolution of community. It is important to
grasp the implications of the issue for Smith's picture of the human lot.
The centrality of sympathy in our lives can be understood in light both
of what sympathy seeks to escape and what it seeks to provide. *Pathos* is
intrinsic to the human condition. For we have no persona without an
audience to observe us having a persona and without our being aware
that we are being observed. We are not ourselves without the mask that
sociality imposes, but that mask both reveals and conceals. Without a
mask, we cannot be actors either to ourselves or others, and do not exist
as human or moral selves. In this sense human life is fundamentally
theatrical. It is not simply that we cannot be known as we really are; it is
that we *are not* unless we are known by the spectator. That which is pri-
mordially concealed from society is subhuman, like the pleasures and

sions, overawes all those mutinous and turbulent passions into that tone and temper
which the impartial spectator can enter into and sympathize with" (VI.concl.2).
36 *The Praise of Folly*, trans. C. H. Miller (New Haven: Yale University Press, 1979), pp.
43–4.

pains and passions of that unfortunate creature in the solitary place. The suspicion that we do *not* have a "self" hidden in there seems the ultimate terror. At bottom we may suspect that we are nothing, that we have no "substance" and are just a "shadow" (the terms Smith uses at VI.ii.1.1) or the figments of a collective "illusive imagination," that we are, so to speak, intrinsically ghostlike until brought to life by the imaginations of spectators.

The *pathos* in this situation goes deep: for with a mask, we are partially concealed from both others and ourselves.[37] The mask that is worn by a human being naturally suggests a distinction between inner and outer self; the difficulty is that we cannot, on this account, have the inner without the outer. Our longing for sympathy is a longing to take the mask off, to be known as we are. We all long to be like lovers, united with another, for the "chief part of human happiness arises from the consciousness of being beloved" (I.ii.5.1). As Smith tells it, part of maturation involves recognizing that the mask can never come off and that, by and large, it should not come off, since others cannot enter into your world with the degree of passion that you do (if one may thus phrase it). Our desire for the love of others must and should remain unrequited in part. Self-command, including command over the yearning to be known by spectators, is therefore a leading virtue for Smith.

At the end of the book, Smith remarks that we want desperately to be believed, and it is a step in this direction to have persuaded others to sympathize with us and to follow us in our estimation of ourselves. Smith thinks that language may itself be founded on this desire.[38] In political contexts, especially, this comes down to persuading others to let us lead

37 As Marshall puts it, in Smith's scheme there is a "theatrical distance" between a self and itself as well as other selves (*The Figure of Theater*, p. 180). Marshall emphasizes the "radical separateness, isolation, and solitude of people" that he thinks the theatrical view of life entails (p. 170). I am presently emphasizing that in Smith's account, actor and audience are already deeply linked. Rousseau's criticisms of the theater in (among other places) the *Letter to M. d'Alembert on the Theater* focused on the externalization of self, the distance between persons, and the possibilities for detachment and indifference on the part of spectators and actors that could be attributed to the theater and theatrical social relationships. Smith, by contrast, sees virtues in detachment and possibilities for community in the sympathetic adjustment of spectator and actor to one another.

38 "The desire of being believed, the desire of persuading, of leading and directing other people, seems to be one of the strongest of all our natural desires. It is, perhaps, the instinct upon which is founded the faculty of speech, the characteristical faculty of human nature. . . . Great ambition, the desire of real superiority, of leading and directing, seems to be altogether peculiar to man, and speech is the great instrument of ambition, of real superiority, of leading and directing the judgments and conduct of other people" (*TMS* VII.iv.25).

them. As we will see, motivation in the economic sphere has a connected source. To be beloved is not just to be believed but to be believed in – to have standing, to be recognized. Conversely, complete exclusion from the human community leaves us little to fall back on. Unpersuasive, not believed in, and unloved, we are left with a mask but without the conviction that there is anybody on either side of it; that is, we are left with the "darkness of solitude" (III.3.39).[39] Smith silently excludes the possibility that the soul's apprehension of God or a Form of the Good might realize a "higher self" that supersedes the desperate need for sympathy. He has also excluded the possibility that we are to be understood as "incomplete" or "lacking" or "images" relative to some higher being; rather, we are incomplete relative to each other. Consequently, his scheme is not teleological in a Platonic or Aristotelian sense. Nor is it meant to accommodate a Romantic "individualism" to the effect that we each have within us a true or authentic self to be realized and shaped by the individual's choices. The impartial spectator "within" may offer solace, to be sure, but as a peculiar exercise of sympathy with self, it recapitulates the structure implicit in the sympathy between actor and spectator.

No thinker as dialectical as Smith could leave it at that. The principle that the good can be an unintended outcome of the bad is central to his account from the beginning. Sympathy not only allows us to escape the pain of selfishness (in the sense of unbridgeable separateness) but also, in so doing, responds to the disinterested pleasure that arises from the apprehension of concord. The issue of disinterested pleasure arises in the first sentence of the book and then is promptly taken up in chapter II ("Of the Pleasure of Mutual Sympathy"). This pleasure is what one might call aesthetic, because it consists in the apprehension of harmony, symmetry, and peace between self and other.[40] Key terms such as

---

39 On II.ii.2.3 Smith sketches the remorse – "of all the sentiments which can enter the human breast the most dreadful" – felt by the "violator of the more sacred laws of justice," in particular the criminal's exclusion from all fellow feeling with other humans. He "dares no longer look society in the face, but imagines himself as it were rejected, and thrown out from the affections of all mankind. He cannot hope for the consolation of sympathy. . . ." The violator longs for solitude but in fact could not bear it and is driven by the "horror of solitude" back to society, "loaded with shame and distracted with fear."

40 Smith contrasts remorse (see the preceding footnote) with the sentiment felt by the virtuous person as he reflects on his meritorious conduct: "His mind, at the thought of it, is filled with cheerfulness, serenity, and composure. He is in friendship and harmony with all mankind, and looks upon his fellow-creatures with confidence and benevolent satisfaction, secure that he has rendered himself worthy of their most favourable regards" (II.ii.2.4). Early on in the book Smith speaks of the actor's wish that the emotions of

"propriety" already signal the extent to which Smith's ethics is, so to speak, aestheticized. The pull of sympathy in our lives testifies, in short, to our love of beauty. Beauty is a pervasive theme in *The Theory of Moral Sentiments* and is explicitly discussed in Part IV (where both of the two chapter headings refer to beauty). The beauty of sympathy is its promise of wholeness and transcendence of self.

The themes of disinterested pleasure and beauty point back to Plato (through that great modern Platonist, Shaftesbury) as well as forward to Kant's notion of "Zweckmäßigkeit ohne Zweck" (purposiveness without purpose). At this juncture I am underlining what one might call the beauty of sympathy. Right after describing our "desire of being believed," Smith remarks that the "great pleasure of conversation and society, besides, arises from a certain correspondence of sentiments and opinions, from a certain harmony of minds, which like so many musical instruments coincide and keep time with one another" (VII.iv.28). The longing for symmetry is the other face of our fear of measurelessness. The one is a longing to be part of a whole, the other a fear of being part of nothing. This interdependence of opposites is a fine example of what Smith refers to as the "oeconomy of nature" (II.i.5.10), and it underlies not just our daily "changing of places in fancy" but the exchanges Smith seeks to describe in his political economy.

spectators "beat time" with his own, thus consoling the actor, and of the actor's need to "flatten" his emotion so as "to reduce it to harmony and concord" with the emotions of the spectator. That concord (as determined by the spectator) is the right "pitch" of the emotions and constitutes "propriety." The correspondence of the actor's and the spectator's sentiments, while not a "unison," "is sufficient for the harmony of society" (I.i.4.7).

# 3

## THE PASSIONS, PLEASURE, AND
## THE IMPARTIAL SPECTATOR

Thus I contend with fancy and opinion, and search the mint and foundery of imagination. For here the appetites and desires are fabricated; hence they derive their privilege and currency.

Earl of Shaftesbury[1]

Smith's theory of moral sentiments makes emotion so central to human life that at first glance we may seem to be little more than creatures of the emotions. Smith distinguishes between emotions whose origin is in the body and those whose origin lies in "a particular turn or habit of the imagination" (I.ii.2.1). Given the great influence of those passions that originate in the imagination, not to mention the role that imagination plays in sympathy, we might also say with some accuracy that the imagination is the "mint and foundery" in which we are given shape. How are emotions, imagination, and understanding connected? How do the passions, or emotions, become "moral," and how do they become corrupted? In this chapter, I continue examination of Smith's view of these matters, as well as of the closely related topics of pleasure and pain, the love of virtue, and the impartial spectator.

1 "Advice to an Author," Pt. III, sec. II, in vol. I of *Characteristics of Men, Manners, Opinions, Times*, p. 207.

## 1. THE PASSIONS, IMAGINATION, AND THE CORRUPTION OF PLEASURE

### The Passions and Imagination

Smith's view of the imagination, which emphasizes its creative capacity, both borrows from and extends Hume's treatment of the subject.[2] The category of the "passions which take their origin from the body" (or, in my shorthand, the "bodily passions") is a time-honored one; the second general category, that of the "passions derived from the imagination" (or what I call the "passions of the imagination") is somewhat startling, for here the imagination has replaced what an earlier tradition (extending as far as Descartes, though with a change of meaning) would have referred to as the "soul."[3] Phenomenologically, the key to the distinction between the two kinds of passions seems to be, in Smith's account, that bodily passions are taken to be expressions or consequences of bodily affections or physical states (such as an empty stomach or an open wound), whereas this is not the case, at least at the level of ordinary experience, with states of mind – such as fear and hope – that depend on the work of the imagination.[4] Further, the passions of the imagination are more easily sympathized with by others than are passions of the body.

The relationship of imagination to the passions is key to whatever self-directedness human beings can attain.[5] Although the passions introduce

---

2 For helpful discussion of this point see D. D. Raphael, " 'The True Old Humean Philosophy' and Its Influence on Adam Smith," in *David Hume: Bicentenary Papers*, ed. G. P. Morice (Edinburgh: Edinburgh University Press, 1977), pp. 23–38. Raphael concludes that "both Hume and Smith again had much to say that is enlightening about the work of the imagination in moral judgement, and on that particular topic Smith was, I think, even more perceptive than Hume" (p. 37). See also M. J. Ferreira, "Hume and Imagination: Sympathy and 'The Other,' " *International Philosophical Quarterly* 34 (1994): 39–57, and my remarks about the imagination in Chapter 8.

3 I refer especially to Descartes's *Passions of the Soul*. Intellectual sentiments and virtue are discussed by Smith but in a nonmoral context. I shall return to these issues in Chapter 4 (sec. 1).

4 I do not see that Smith would be particularly bothered by the idea that "states of mind" are physically embodied and inseparable from states of the body or that he would find fault with the effort to specify the material (say, neurophysiological) conditions for the exercise of passions and mind. The phenomenological point holds at the level of ordinary experience, and it is within that horizon that the distinction between the two categories of passion presents itself.

5 By misunderstanding the potential for self-motion implicit in the notion of an emotion "derived" from the imagination, J. Cropsey is led to the view that for Smith all action originates in emotion. Cropsey infers that Smith cannot account for moral judgment and

an ineliminable element of passivity into the self, passions can also be formed and directed by the imagination, and the imagination can itself be educated and directed. Smith does not explicitly connect morality with "autonomy" – not a word he uses – or with the notion of a freely legislating "will" – a word he rarely uses. His theory, nonetheless, insists on a place for agency or self-determination. By means of the imagination's capacity to reflect on self from the standpoint of the spectator, and to identify with that standpoint, one can direct one's actions and shape one's character. That one type of passions is guided by an "idea" of the imagination already indicates that for Smith the emotions are in some way cognitive; beliefs are part and parcel of emotions, and beliefs may be true or false, adequate or inadequate. Smith could therefore speak of erroneous or inadequate emotions; indeed the whole notion of rational criticism of an actor's emotions from the standpoint of a spectator is supported by this interpretation of the emotions (a point to which we will return in this chapter and in Chapter 5), and he certainly speaks of our emending such emotions in order to more closely approximate the standards of virtuous character and action.

Does Smith hold that there is a natural limit to passions? Clearly the imagination leads us to transgress physical limits – say, the capacity of the stomach to absorb food, or the amount of calories required by the body for it to function. Most of our bodily passions are elaborated or expanded upon by the imagination: the two kinds of passion interact. Indeed, Smith argues that we cannot understand human life – and so the forces driving commerce – without understanding how the passions are expanded by the imagination, and so the sense in which the imagination is a "social" phenomenon. The prominent role he gives to the imagination, in his account of the passions, seems to entail that "human nature" is, at least in its specific passions, malleable. The proper degree of its passions is not determined by appeal to nature but by the judgments of the impartial spectator.

Smith does not say so explicitly, but his typology of passions is intended to be exhaustive. This differs, of course, from the proposition that there is a finite stock of specific passions in each category, or even of modalities of specific passions (such as fear). The passions are not per se good or evil; this is to be emphasized especially with respect to the bodily passions. We do not properly praise or blame the passions as such,

---

motivation and is, therefore, "involved in an inconsistency" of the most serious kind. *Polity and Economy*, p. 17.

but the expression of them. All the passions are equally natural; Smith does not divide them into the natural and the artificial. Moreover, he does not here rank the passions – according to their level of rationality, for example. He denies that the bodily passions are lower because shared with "the brutes," since we also share with animals nonbrutish passions, such as gratitude (I.ii.1.3). We do not emerge from this section of the book with a hierarchical view of the self.

As we have seen, the various emotions are communicated in different ways. Some (such as grief and joy) spread almost infectiously – this reminds us of Hume's notion of sympathy – some only after deliberation (such as a spectator's concurrence with one person's resentment of another). The bodily passions are communicated with more difficulty than those of the imagination, and as a consequence we generally demand greater restraint with respect to the former than the latter. As we noted in Chapter 2, our access to another person's world – the scene of another's emotions, "story," perspective – is through the imagination. Our imaginative sympathy with another person's physical pains and pleasures is bound to fall far short of what he or she feels. A sheer physical condition, a state of being, can be pictured by the imagination but does not transport the spectator into it; the "drama" surrounding that condition can be relived, so to speak, in the spectator's imagination. To paraphrase Smith, we do not grow hungry simply by imagining the situation of a hungry person; we may, however, become terrified when we bring home to ourselves someone else's terrifying situation. The sympathetic imagination is not solely representational or reproductive. It is also narrative, always seeking to flow into and fill up another situation and to draw things together into a coherent story, thus bringing the spectator out of himself and onto the larger stage. It is other seeking and poetic. And this helps further to explain why Smith refers to plays and literature so frequently in *The Theory of Moral Sentiments*, starting in the fourth paragraph of the book. Literature can exemplify something of the essential nature of the sympathetic understanding or imagination that is at the heart of sociability as well as of moral evaluation.

The bodily passions are hunger, thirst, sexual desire, and other "appetites" or feelings (such as certain kinds of pleasure and pain). As already mentioned, our fundamental physical separateness severely limits our ability to sympathize with the expression of such feelings; consequently we understand command of those emotions to consist in the virtue of temperance, a command we expect in a far greater degree than the actor's experience of those same emotions would otherwise suggest to him or her. Smith mentions in passing that the virtue of prudence consists in conducting one's life as health and fortune prescribe, that is, so as to satisfy the bodily passions over time in a way that an impartial spectator could approve. In Part VI of the book, added in the sixth and last edition, Smith again discusses the question of prudence and refers to "security" as its "principal object" (VI.i.6). That is not its only object, and Smith's further specifications make it reasonably clear that prudence is a virtue primarily involving the selfish passions. The selfish passions (which I shall define shortly) and the bodily passions are bound to overlap, for one object of concern for self is concern for one's own life and health. This is not to say that prudence and morality are at odds with one another. Rather, Smith is distinguishing between types of passions and appropriate domains of various virtues as determined by the impartial spectator.

Smith divides the passions of the imagination into three types: the "unsocial," the "social," and the "selfish." His discussion implies that this tripartite division is exhaustive. The unsocial passions are, above all, those of hatred, anger, and resentment. These are "unsocial" because they "drive men from one another" or assume that they have thus been driven (I.ii.3.5). They are disagreeable to both the person who experiences them and to the spectator. Consequently the spectator generally expects them to be well controlled, at least until all sides of the situation have been examined. The actor's anger or resentment is painful and therefore difficult to sympathize with. But if, after surveying their purported causes, the spectator agrees with them, the spectator expects the actor to express them at an appropriate level (not to express them sufficiently may also be cause for blame). Surprisingly, justice is founded on the unsocial passions; consequently these passions are "necessary parts of the character of human nature" and are useful both to the individual and to society (I.ii.3.4). The spectator most admires justified expression of resentment or anger when it is done with magnanimity, "guarded and qualified" so as not to extinguish a sense of humanity (I.ii.3.8). This is another case in which the passions may overlap (the unsocial passion of resentment and the social passion of humanity).[6]

6 Several of the points Smith makes about anger or resentment, including the crucial distinction between resentment on account of harm received or pain undergone and resentment that is moral because approved by the impartial spectator as warranted and just, are anticipated in Bishop Butler's *Fifteen Sermons* (nos. 8–9). Butler distinguishes between "sudden anger" and "settled anger" (the latter being "deliberate anger or resentment") and also connects deliberate anger with "fellow feeling," as Smith connects moral re-

Although the unsocial passions require from the spectator a divided sympathy, the social passions elicit a "redoubled sympathy" that renders these passions particularly agreeable and becoming. These passions or affections include generosity, humanity, kindness, compassion, mutual friendship and esteem. So agreeable to the spectator are they that "we have always . . . the strongest disposition to sympathize with the benevolent affections" (I.ii.4.1). Even when an actor shows too much benevolence, we do not regard him with aversion and philosophize instead about the sorry state of a world that requires a restriction on good intentions (I.ii.4.3).

The selfish passions, finally, hold a "middle place" between the other two, for they are never so odious as the one or graceful as the other. These passions include grief and joy "conceived upon account of our own private good or bad fortune" (I.ii.5.1). These passions seem not reducible to pleasure or pain in a physical, private, sense; the selfish passions are not passions of the body even though there is overlap. Perhaps in this context the term "selfish" would better be understood as meaning "centered on self." We should note that even with respect to these passions, spectators are prepared to sympathize in some cases, particularly with great (and justified) sorrow and small (and justified) joy. Smith does not indicate here just how far we are motivated by the selfish passions. Presumably the selfish passions are at the core of the "desire to better one's own condition," whose importance he underlines in both *The Theory of Moral Sentiments* and *The Wealth of Nations*. Smith writes provocatively:

> Every man is, no doubt, by nature, first and principally recommended to his own care; and as he is fitter to take care of himself than of any other person, it is fit and right that it should be so. Every man, therefore, is much more deeply interested in whatever immediately concerns himself, than in what concerns any other man: and to hear, perhaps, of the death of another person, with whom we have no particular connexion, will give us less concern, will spoil our stomach, or break our rest much less than a very insignificant disaster which has befallen ourselves. (II.ii.2.1)

"Selfishness" so understood is not per se a vice; in fact, it seems to be the basis for the virtue of prudence.

However, an impartial spectator could not go along with an actor's

---

sentment with sympathy. The quoted phrases from sermon 8 (pars. 7–8) will be found in J. Butler, *Sermons*, ed. W. E. Gladstone ([1726] Oxford: Clarendon Press, 1896), pp. 140–1.

expression of the selfish passions if that expression justifiably arouses the unsocial passions of spectators. That is, when concern with one's own welfare leads the actor to ruin his neighbor, he has acted unjustly, and by definition the impartial spectator is moved to sympathetic anger against the actor. At the same time, the impartial spectator can go along with the actor's effort "to pursue with more earnest assiduity, his own happiness than that of any other person" (II.ii.2.1). Smith's impartial spectator may think it morally acceptable that a person should be concerned first for himself and his immediate circle, and secondarily for a wider circle that includes friends and aquaintances, and only last, and less avidly, for his fellow citizens or for humanity as such (VI.ii.1.1–4). The selfish and restrictively directed social passions may express themselves without bringing into play injustice or moral fault.

It is striking that Smith says nothing about the desire for self-preservation as such, either with reference to the passions of the body or to those of the imagination. His explanation of the fear of death suggests that this fear is, if anything, a passion of the imagination, presumably of the selfish sort.[7] This in turn opens the door to an explanation of the fact – or what Smith takes to be a fact – that individuals are sometimes willing to sacrifice themselves for moral and religious reasons. Here is one of the key points on which Smith's theory differs from Hobbes'. At least on one long-standing reading, in the *Leviathan* Hobbes privileges the passion for self-preservation, or more accurately the fear of violent death, above all others. Smith would regard that as a mistake.[8] The fear of death, fueled by the imagined picture of what follows death, he argues, can be overcome by a love of fame or of what is praiseworthy (a love that also originates in the imagination).

## Pleasure and Pain

> When the original passions of the person principally concerned are in perfect concord with the sympathetic emotions of the spectator, they necessarily appear to this last just and proper, and suitable to their objects; and, on the contrary, when, upon bringing the case home to himself, he finds that they do not coincide with what he feels, they necessarily appear

---

7 "Fear, however, is a passion derived altogether from the imagination, which represents, with an uncertainty and fluctuation that increases our anxiety, not what we really feel, but what we may hereafter possibly suffer" (I.ii.1.9).
8 See D. Levy, "Adam Smith's 'Natural Law' and Contractual Society," *Journal of the History of Ideas* 39 (1978): 665–74.

to him unjust and improper, and unsuitable to the causes which excite
them.

Adam Smith, *TMS* I.i.3.1

Why do actor and spectator seek harmony with each other's emotions?
Smith asserts that mutual concord of the emotions or sentiments, "mutual sympathy," is pleasurable to both actor and spectator. He presents
this as a brute fact about human nature; as actors, we just do find that
the sympathy of others enlivens our joy and alleviates our grief (I.i.2.2).
Pleasure seems to move us, without our knowing it or actively seeking it,
to find "sympathy" with others. In a certain sense, the pleasure of sympathy gives rise to the spectator's moral approbation of the actor: "what
is agreeable to our moral faculties is fit, and right, and proper to be
done; the contrary wrong, unfit, and improper. The sentiments which
they approve of, are graceful and becoming: the contrary, ungraceful
and unbecoming. The very words, right, wrong, fit, improper, graceful,
unbecoming, mean only what pleases or displeases those faculties"
(III.5.5). The "agreeable" is that which gives our "moral faculties" pleasure, and they are exercised through sympathy. In Smith's explanation
of the moral sentiments, pleasure and pain have great influence.[9] Indeed, the word "pleasure" occurs in the very first sentence of *The Theory
of Moral Sentiments* and in the title of the second chapter ("Of the Pleasure of Mutual Sympathy").

The theory that agreeable sympathy founds the sentiment of approbation is open to the objection, which was in fact made to Smith by
Hume, that sympathy with an actor's pain or grief entails a *painful* fellow
feeling on the part of the spectator and cannot therefore be pleasurable.[10] Although Smith agrees that sympathy may communicate pain as

9 Here as elsewhere, Hume is not far in the background. Consider *T* 574: "The chief
spring or actuating principle of the human mind is pleasure or pain. . . ."; "We have
already observ'd, that moral distinctions depend entirely on certain peculiar sentiments
of pain and pleasure."

10 See Hume's letter to Smith of July 28, 1759 (*CAS*, pp. 42–4). As Hume says, if we sympathized with pain as we do with pleasure, "an Hospital would be a more entertaining
Place than a Ball." Particularly good on the challenge posed by Hume's question is E.
Heath, "The Commerce of Sympathy: Adam Smith on the Emergence of Morals," *Journal
of the History of Philosophy* 33 (1995): 447–66. Heath usefully notes that "When sympathy
does not arise via natural associations, the prospective pleasure of sympathy furnishes a
motive for examining the situation in one's imagination. This motive may cause one to
change one's representation of the facts, pay closer attention to these facts, or to assume
the values and preferences of the actor whose conduct is under consideration (I.i.4.2)"
(p. 460).

well as pleasure, depending on the kinds of passions at play in the given situation, he adds that the emotion in the spectator that arises from "observing the perfect coincidence" between the spectator's (possibly disagreeable) sympathetic emotion and the emotion of the actor is always pleasurable or agreeable (I.iii.1.9). This second-order pleasure, if one may so call it, provides both actor and spectator with a motive (not necessarily the only one) for attempting to understand one another, for reaching "mutual sympathy." The pleasure we take in mutual sympathy is understood by Smith aesthetically, as a disinterested attraction to harmony, concordance, system, and balance. It is not "mere pleasure." Thus even the ordinary interchanges of daily life testify to a measure of self-transcendence. This Platonic theme is crucial to Smith's account (granting that he ultimately puts it to anti-Platonic purposes). That beauty moves us shows that we are not narrowly "selfish" and that our quite ordinary desire for the pleasure of harmony transcends narrow calculations of prudence.

One might object that the role of pleasure upsets the asymmetry between actor and spectator, for the spectator, no less than the actor, is drawn to harmony by the intrinsic pleasure it promises. However, Smith builds into the notion of the actor a greater need for approval or applause that is not felt, at least in the same degree, by the spectator. The theatrical model is again helpful here. It is the actor who finds it necessary to do the work of obtaining the applause of the spectator, for on this model it is the actor who, in the relevant context and moment, is engaged in action and is therefore subject to moral evaluation.[11] The spectator experiences no such intense longing or need for relief. The actor experiences, further, pleasure or pain within the object-level situation; the spectator does not, or at least not in the same degree. The actor's emotions are engaged; the action and its context "affect in a particular manner" the actor more intimately than the spectator (I.i.4.5). The actor's emotions are related to a real situation; the spectator's sympathetic emotions are accompanied by "the secret consciousness that the change of situations . . . is but imaginary" (I.i.4.7). The actor has more at stake than does the spectator and has more "invested" in the situation. Hence the actor has to work harder to earn the sym-

---

11 The "person principally concerned [the actor] is sensible of this [that the spectator cannot feel the actor's emotions with the same degree of intensity], and at the same time passionately desires a more complete sympathy. He longs for that relief which nothing can afford him but the entire concord of the affections of the spectators with his own" (I.i.4.7).

pathetic approbation of the spectator than will the spectator in regard to the actor. Smith is assuming that the spectator does not normally have a passion for spectating or for imagining the situations of others to so great an extent that the "secret consciousness" is obliterated. In other words, our natural separateness contributes fruitfully to the spectator's detachment and normally checks any inclination to identify completely with the actor. Presumably the pleasure of concordance of sentiment will feel different to each, thus preserving the asymmetry.

It seems clear that the actor's longing for the pleasure of sympathy is accompanied by a keen desire to avoid the pain of solitude, whereas the spectator is led by the imagination's natural proclivity to enter into the situations of others and by the disinterested pleasure it takes in a harmony of sentiments. This helps to explain why the psychic pleasure that comes from mutual sympathy is a midwife of the virtues. The difference in the kind of effort required to achieve mutual sympathy constitutes the foundation for two kinds of virtues, which we may call "actor virtues" and "spectator virtues." The former generally require that one tone down one's emotions, and this is more difficult or painful than the achievement of the latter, which generally require that one heighten one's emotions. In the spectator's willingness to enter into the actor's sentiments lie the "amiable" virtues, those of "candid condescension and indulgent humanity," whereas in the actor's willingness to bring down his emotions to a level with which the spectator can sympathize lie the "great, the awful, and respectable, the virtues of self-denial, of self-government," virtues related to the command of the passions (I.i.5.1).

Smith admits that second-order pleasure can in some degree affect first-order pleasure or pain, such that the actor's distress, for example, is alleviated by sympathy and his joy enlivened by it (I.i.2.2). Just how far mutual concord is possible and desired depends on the kind of pleasure and pain involved as well as the mix of the two. First, we are inclined to sympathize more readily with pleasurable (or agreeable) sentiments than with painful ones, and the actor desires sympathy more intensely with his painful than with his pleasurable sentiments. Both inclinations arise out of a natural preference for pleasure over pain. "Joy is a pleasant emotion, and we gladly abandon ourselves to it upon the slightest occasion. We readily, therefore, sympathize with it in others, whenever we are not prejudiced by envy. But grief is painful, and the mind, even when it is our own misfortune, naturally resists and recoils from it" (I.ii.5.3). When we are convinced of the appropriateness of the actor's emotions, our sympathy tends to be "very strong and very sincere" (I.ii.5.4). But if an actor's sorrows are occasioned by a stubbed toe or a nagging wife, Smith says, we may even make fun of him. As spectators, we will say that the actor's sorrow is "out of proportion"; the pain is not worth our entering into.

Further, the spectator's sympathetic emotions are much more likely to approximate the actor's pleasurable than his painful emotions. The spectator is naturally inclined to indulge in agreeable emotions to the full extent appropriate but is disinclined to do so with painful emotions. When the spectator does share in the actor's painful emotion, the shared feeling is never as intense for the spectator as it is for the actor. Smith thinks that this is part of nature's benevolent scheme of things.[12]

Pain, whether of body or of mind, is "a more pungent sensation than pleasure" (I.iii.1.3). This simple observation is fundamental to Smith's moral psychology and his theory of the virtues, and it is tied to the prominence, for Smith, of the problems of war, faction, and conflict. For actors, the "pungency" of pain makes it more important to avoid pain than to enjoy pleasure. And although, as spectators, we praise moderation in the pursuit of pleasure, we bestow higher praise on the control of expressions of pain. We find that we can go along entirely with the high, perhaps even heroic degree of sorrow that an agent's self-command leads him to exhibit; we approve entirely of that degree of sorrow and, indeed, are surprised by it in light of our awareness of the effort it took. The actor's self-command under these conditions (and Smith refers here to Socrates' self-control the day of his death) demands our admiration. We weep for Socrates' fate, and perhaps take a certain pleasure in these emotions of the heart, but had Socrates wept uncontrollably on that day we would think much the less of him (I.iii.1.14). Actor virtues as well as spectator virtues should, of course, be combined in the same person, but as Smith's language indicates, they do not warrant the same degree of approbation. Actor virtues are more difficult, and thus in *The Theory of Moral Sentiments* Smith devotes more attention and praise to them than to spectator virtues, as his discussions of the Stoic sage indicates.

We respond to the pleasures and pains of the body differently than we do to those of the psyche. Since we cannot literally feel or readily imagine each other's physical pleasures or pains, we find it difficult to sympathize with those of others, and in any case our fellow feeling with

---

12 "Nature, it seems, when she loaded us with our own sorrows, thought that they were enough, and therefore did not command us to take any further share in those of others, than what was necessary to prompt us to relieve them" (I.iii.1.12).

them is always quite disproportionate to that which is experienced by the actor (I.ii.1.5). Consequently we generally expect others to moderate their expression of physical pleasure, and especially their expression of physical pain: "the little sympathy which we feel with bodily pain is the foundation of the propriety of constancy and patience in enduring it" (I.ii.1.12). Pleasures or pains of the psyche – those that, as Smith puts it, arise from the imagination, can be more easily shared: "my imagination is more ductile, and more readily assumes, if I may say so, the shape and configuration of the imaginations of those with whom I am familiar" (I.ii.1.6). Correspondingly, literary tragedies concern themselves with physical pleasure and pain as an occasion for exploration of nonphysical emotions and passions of agreeable and disagreeable nature. Indeed, Smith argues that physical pain is more easily tolerated than nonphysical pain, at least in that the former is sooner forgotten than is the latter. We will readily forget a dreadful toothache and be scarcely able to recall just how painful it was, but the pain of an insult may goad us for a long time.

Smith comments that "the causes of pain and pleasure, whatever they are, or however they operate, seem to be the objects, which, in all animals, immediately excite those two passions of gratitude and resentment" (II.iii.1.1) – the passions so closely connected, on his account, to the virtues of benevolence and justice. As pleasure and pain inflect the passions in varying ways and degrees, so the spectator's willingness to sympathize with them, and approve or disapprove of them, varies.[13] What counts as hitting the mean thus depends in part on the pleasure or pain felt by the spectator, and this may coincide with the actor's experience. Indeed, Smith goes on to say in this passage that "the passions the spectator is most disposed to sympathize with" – that is, the passions the spectator finds most agreeable and judges to be highest in point of propriety – are just those "of which the immediate feeling or sensation is more or less agreeable to the person principally concerned." Thus friendship is pleasurable to the actor and also for the spectator to sympathize with, whereas hatred is painful to each. Pleasure and virtue, pain and vice, thus seem coordinated on this scheme, but the relationship between the terms in each of the pairs should not be reduced to a causal one.

13 "In some passions the excess is less disagreeable than the defect; and in such passions the point of propriety seems to stand high, or nearer to the excess than to the defect. In other passions, the defect is less disagreeable than the excess; and in such passions the point of propriety seems to stand low, or nearer to the defect than to the excess" (VI.iii.14).

Finally, Smith distinguishes between pleasurable and painful responses in theoretical and in practical matters. Disagreements in theoretical discussions, he claims, do not particularly touch us. The pleasurable emotion of admiration for someone's intellectual prowess does not really affect us – that is, does not move us to *moral* approbation or disapprobation. By contrast, when the passions are engaged, sympathy enters, and the pleasurable and painful emotions are considerably more intense and important. Theoretical issues are heavily dependent on the work of the intellectual imagination and are provoked to a certain kind of pain (that of wonder, puzzlement, lack of tranquillity) by mystery or incoherence. We find a distinct pleasure or satisfaction in grasping an elegant and systematic synthesis or solution to an *aporia* (difficulty, perplexity) or in agreeing with and admiring someone else's theories. But in these matters, *moral* passions are not engaged, because the imagination has not been called upon to function "sympathetically." There is no need to change places with the other in order to grasp either the subject matter or what our interlocutor is arguing about it. The pleasure of theorizing guides the theoretical virtues, but generally seems not, on Smith's account, either to lead to action or to require moral passion.

## The Corruption of Pleasure: Epicurean Themes

> Sweet it is, when on the great sea the winds are buffeting the waters, to gaze from the land on another's great struggles; not because it is pleasure or joy that anyone should be distressed, but because it is sweet to perceive from what misfortune you yourself are free.
>
> Lucretius[14]

Smith finds a place in his own virtue theory for Epicurus's doctrine of prudence. Although he does not comment on whether Epicurean hedonism might play a role in his own moral psychology, Smith's emphasis on pleasure and pain suggests that in this regard too he has drawn on Epicurus. Perhaps for reasons of prudence Smith did not emphasize the point. Smith's linking of happiness to tranquillity, and that to enjoyment (III.3.30), underlines the Epicurean background of his view. Epicurus's system, Smith claims, is "altogether inconsistent" with his own (VII.ii.2.13), but the reason given lies in Epicurus's consequentialism and in Smith's insistence that moral approval stems primarily from sympathy rather than from the calculation of utility. That is, Epicurus made

14 *De rerum natura*, 2.1–4, trans. C. Bailey (Oxford: Clarendon Press, 1947), vol. 1, p. 237.

the philosopher's mistake of forcing practice into the mold of theory. Yet Smith also comments: "In ease of body, therefore, and in security or tranquillity of mind, consisted, according to Epicurus, the most perfect state of human nature, the most complete happiness which man was capable of enjoying" (VII.ii.2.7). Would Smith disagree?[15] When he comes to describe the virtue of ordinary prudence, a primary virtue in his entire picture of a flourishing commercial society, he characterizes it as "Epicurean" (VI.i.15).

As Smith plausibly construes Epicurus, virtue is defined relative to its utility to the agent's desire for mental tranquillity and thus pleasure. This might be accused, on Smithean grounds (though Smith does not make this accusation), of turning the "selfish" passions into the sole source of motivation, just as it reduces all of the virtues to prudence. A question for Smith is whether or not he can separate pleasure and the selfish emotions convincingly. His doctrine of pleasure through mutual sympathy seems delicately balanced; one could argue that by tying pleasure to sympathy it ensures that the spectator is not motivated primarily by desire for his own pleasure. One could also argue that since Smith privileges the standpoint of the spectator and since in the final analysis the spectator seems motivated (even if unconsciously) by desire for the pleasure that he or she will take in sympathy, the doctrine ultimately is Epicurean.

Smith was obviously quite aware of this problem, as our examination (Chapter 2) of the relationship between sympathy and selfishness indicated. It is not accidental, then, that after praising Epicurus's argument to the effect that virtue and self-interest are mutually supportive, Smith turns immediately to Bernard Mandeville's self-love theory. This is the pivot of Smith's entire discussion of his predecessors and leads up to another effort to distinguish between self-interest and sympathy. But just as he can separate self-love from sympathy while affirming that the spectator is necessarily present in any act of "changing places," so too he can insist that the spectator's pleasure in mutual sympathy is not the pleasure of self-love. What gives the spectator pleasure, Smith claims, is the *mutuality* of the concord of sympathy; the spectator is experiencing a disinterested pleasure taken in the harmony of sentiments. This is different from taking pleasure in one's own private good or in one's having

---

15 At I.iii.1.7 Smith asks in his own voice: "What can be added to the happiness of the man who is in health, who is out of debt, and has a clear conscience?" For Smith, mental tranquillity and a clear conscience are inseparable.

successfully persuaded the other to see things one's own way. It exhibits our love of beauty, and Smith frequently articulates the pleasure of concord in musical metaphors.

The major role Smith's account gives to pleasure and pain underlines a characteristic feature of his theory, namely, that it often seeks to build that which is admirable in human life – say, the virtue of justice – on the seemingly base foundation of that which is common, reliable, constant, and relatively undemanding. This strategy is so striking that at one point he finds it necessary to respond to the accusation that in founding the "laudable" principle of justice on the "odious" passion of resentment he is debasing the former. His long response in a footnote argues that it is part of the wisdom of nature not to demand that things crucial to human survival depend on the "uncertain determinations of our reason," for "so weak and imperfect a creature as man" is better served by the passions, pleasure, and pain (II.i.5.7–10). It is part of his philanthropic purpose, a purpose shaped by the ever present possibility of war and dissolution, to improve the human condition by founding virtue on passion. From one perspective, as he is aware, this seems a debasement of humankind. From another perspective – his own – it is an act of genuine care, an effort to better our condition in practice and not just in theory. Smith connects the pleasure we take in mutual sympathy with an apprehension of the inherent beauty of that concord or harmony, and this too contributes to a defense of ordinary life. In this respect Smith's moral psychology forms part and parcel of his allegiance to the great moral project of the Enlightenment.

Yet, can the "Epicurean" doctrine of pleasure and pain avoid decaying, in the context of this moral project, into a relatively low hedonism? If the "laudable" is based on the psychology of the "odious," might not the former be dragged down – not so much sullied by association but simply reduced – to the level of the latter? Smith himself insists on this question, for he discusses three forms in which such corruption occurs.

First, because spectators sympathize more perfectly with joy than with sorrow, and because nearly all of us associate wealth with the former rather than the latter, we are naturally led to accumulate wealth and "parade" it. We experience an intense desire to pursue and show off our wealth as well as to conceal our poverty. What makes wealth so attractive, Smith claims, is not that it procures physical pleasure or necessary material goods but that it procures the psychic pleasure of being "attended to," and sympathized with, on account of the possessor's presumed happiness and joy. We are here in the grip of vanity, and that is founded on our belief that we are the object of approving sympathy (I.iii.2.1). The process is circular: the wealthy (or powerful) person is the object of approbation and sympathy because spectators suppose him to be happy, which happiness in turn derives in large part from his awareness that spectators sympathize with him. The pleasure of vulgarized sympathy leads to the nearly universal toils of emulation. Hence arise our passionate and unceasing efforts to better our condition – itself a major theme of *The Wealth of Nations*. This problem of vanity (or self-love) and of deep misorientation about the true nature of the ends of human life (and especially of happiness) is a species of corruption.

Second, because of the intensity of our desire for attention and approbation, we may take the short-cut to riches and power: "to attain to this envied situation, the candidates for fortune too frequently abandon the paths of virtue" (I.iii.3.8). This has, of course, been the complaint of moralists of all ages, and Smith passionately expresses it in his own voice (I.iii.2.7).

Third, the sheer painfulness of acknowledging to ourselves our own vices makes it difficult to throw off "the mysterious veil of self-delusion" (III.4.4). This makes us partial in judging our own case: "This self-deceit, this fatal weakness of mankind, is the source of half the disorders of human life" (III.4.6). Mutual sympathy is, to be sure, pleasurable, but being worthy of it could require the pain of honesty with oneself that most of us would rather avoid. Thus the vices of vanity and pride, too, give us a pleasure (or at least a means of avoiding pain) that displaces moral self-knowledge as defined by the standpoint of the impartial spectator.

In these respects, the very mechanisms that lead to virtue also seem to lead us away from it. "Sympathy" may foster, rather than counter, selfishness and self-love; the pleasure of mutual sympathy seems transformed into the pleasure of mutually reinforcing vanity. We are again confronted by the paradoxical prospect that the very system that is meant to improve us undermines itself. This supports the oft-repeated lament about modernity's degeneration into a culture of low and vulgar hedonism. It is a danger that Smith himself recognizes and analyzes in detail.

How then might the passions give birth to virtue rather than vice? Smith's complex answer combines further analysis of moral psychology with an understanding of the nature and the role of both moral education and social institutions. To begin with the moral psychology: he attempts to show that we are naturally inclined to view ourselves in the light in which others see us or would see us if they were well informed.

This is meant to help explain how we acquire the habit of seeing ourselves through the eyes of the *impartial* spectator. If there were no such proclivity on which moral education and social institutions could build, then the pleasure of mutual sympathy *simpliciter* will prevail, and while out natural desire for sympathy might normally force us to check our most outrageous indulgence in self-delusive egoism, since spectators would not go along with *that*, it would not necessarily force mutual sympathy to rise above mutual flattery. Let us turn next to the pleasures of virtue, and to the impartial spectator.

## 2. THE IMPARTIAL SPECTATOR AND THE LOVE OF VIRTUE

> But, though a wise man feels little pleasure from praise where he knows there is no praise-worthiness, he often feels the highest in doing what he knows to be praise-worthy, though he knows equally well that no praise is ever to be bestowed upon it.
>
> Adam Smith, *TMS* III.2.7

The spectatorial perspective is at the core of Smith's system of the moral emotions, for without it the emotions would seem to be a rather unstable, subjective, and variable basis for morality. In and of themselves, they seem to lack principle, a firm notion of "what is right" as distinguished from what is taken at the moment to be right. We have examined the distinction between seeing and doing, and the priority of the former, as well as the differing ways in which pleasure and pain may affect the actor and spectator. In Chapter 2 (section 2) I noted that understanding and deliberation are required of the spectator, especially in the case of a "divided sympathy." The requirement that the agent see and evaluate himself from the standpoint of a spectator who does not feel the actor's emotions to the same degree as the actor does, and who examines primarily the situation, entails a measure of detachment from self on the actor's part. Since the agent's (dis)approbation of self or other must be reached from the standpoint of a spectator, moral judgments cannot be simply expressions of our own emotions. Smith's theory of moral sentiments is not "emotivist" in a narrow sense of the term.[16] As a "theory

---

16 E.g., it does not fit MacIntyre's definition of emotivism (*After Virtue*, pp. 11–12): "Emotivism is the doctrine that all evaluative judgments and more specifically all moral judgments are *nothing but* expressions of preference, expressions of attitude or feeling, insofar as they are moral or evaluative in character." MacIntyre attributes three other charac-

of moral sentiments," it is a sophisticated emotivism, according to which the emotions that the judgment of an informed and judicious spectator finds warranted (or appropriate, suitable, fitting) are moral. Perhaps this is so unusual a version of emotivism that the term is better avoided in this context.

Let us turn, first, to what Smith calls the "real love of virtue" (III.2.7), and thus to the distinction between praise and praiseworthiness. We will then be in a position to discuss the crucial notion of the "impartial spectator."

## The Love of Virtue

> He knows perfectly what he has done; but, perhaps, scarce any man can know perfectly what he himself is capable of doing.
>
> Adam Smith, *TMS* III.2.15

Do we have a natural incentive to be virtuous? For Smith this question is tied to the question of whether we have a natural love of praiseworthiness rather than of mere praise – that is, whether we have a natural propensity to view ourselves through the eyes of the impartial spectator. If the answer is affirmative, then we have (on his account) a means to overcome the pull of vanity and self-love. If the answer is negative, then we are primarily creatures of custom, and although Smith may have explained how agents view themselves through the eyes of spectators, he has not explained how agents become *moral* beings.

Smith's answer is affirmative, and he thus has an important place in his moral system for the notions of "duty" and conscience. This gives his broadly Aristotelian ethics of virtue an interestingly Kantian twist.

teristics to emotivism: (1) it makes for interminable debate, because it holds that there is "*no* valid justification for any claims that objective and impersonal moral standards exist and hence that there are no such standards" (p. 19). (2) Its social context is such as to exhibit the "obliteration of any genuine distinction between manipulative and non-manipulative social relations" (p. 23). Emotivism cannot supply a basis for distinguishing between treating persons as means and as ends, and it reduces moral reason entirely to persuasion. (3) The emotivist self is "lacking any necessary social identity," it is "criterionless" (p. 33), and so at home in the Enlightenment social order, where ends are given and only means are rationally assessed. None of these three characteristics is entailed by Smith's version of emotivism, and he would certainly not think any of the three desirable. Hence if Smith's version succeeds, his theory is not liable to the "emotivism" criticisms MacIntyre levels against the Enlightenment. I grant, however, that according to one sense of "objective," Smith's theory drops "objective" moral standards; I shall explore this in Chapter 4.

Smith's argument is not that norms of praise- and blameworthiness necessarily govern each person's moral self-consciousness but that the fundamental structures and psychology of moral judgment provide us with
a means of distinguishing between the two and also with a natural inclination to do so. It is an inclination to be realized through moral education, such that the impartial spectator's practical reason becomes our
own, becomes (as it were) our second nature. Our awareness of the
"voice" of conscience is not a "fact of reason," to borrow Kant's
phrase,[17] or some innate "moral sense" but rather an acquired form of
moral self-awareness.

The argument unfolds out of the account of spectatorship, and then
spectatorship on self. Just as we learn in childhood not only to view and
judge others but also to view and judge ourselves through the eyes of
others, so too do we wish to be praised for what we find praiseworthy in
them and to avoid being blamed for what we find blameworthy in them.
Smith's account is oriented, as always, from within the standpoint of the
ordinary moral agent and the agent's moral development.

In judging others, we evaluate the propriety and merit of their intentions and conduct relative to, among other things, the context and relevant facts. When praise or blame is given, Smith claims, it is believed
to be given on account of the virtues or vices we have decided the person
(or his actions) possess. This is a sense in which moral judgment is "ab-
solutist" or nonrelative. We do not believe that the person whom we
have praised is praiseworthy because we have praised him. Rather, we
take ourselves to have praised him because, after due consideration, we
believe him praiseworthy in respect of specific qualities of character or
actions. Just as we would like to think ourselves adequate judges of others, so we would like to think ourselves adequately judged. The logic
implicit in praising others, that is, suggests to the actor the distinction
between praise and praiseworthiness.

---

17 The phrase will be found in the first chapter of the Analytic of the *Critique of Practical
Reason* (p. 31). *TMS* III.3.4 does, admittedly, sound Kantian: our "strongest impulses of
self-love" are (Smith says) checked by "reason, principle, conscience, the inhabitant of
the breast, the man within, the great judge and arbiter of our conduct. It is he who,
whenever we are about to act so as to affect the happiness of others, calls to us, with a
voice capable of astonishing the most presumptuous of our passions, that we are but one
of the multitude, in no respect better than any other in it; and that when we prefer
ourselves so shamefully and so blindly to others, we become the proper objects of resentment, abhorrence, and execration. It is from him only that we learn the real littleness
of ourselves, and of whatever relates to ourselves, and the natural misrepresentations of
self-love can be corrected only by the eye of this impartial spectator."

The distinction is pressed home for another reason, namely, that we are not always adequately judged. Most painfully, we are sometimes blamed when we are not blameworthy. (Smith recalls here his point that pain is a "more pungent sensation than the opposite and correspondent pleasure"; III.2.15.) Spectators sometimes have inadequate information about the facts or are ill motivated toward us. The social "mirror" often reflects badly. This elementary and familiar experience teaches the difference between blame and blameworthiness and thus between the view that ordinary spectators take of us and that which a well-informed and impartial spectator would take. We also find through experience that we at times receive praise that we secretly know to be unmerited and, Smith claims, that just as "unmerited reproach . . . is frequently capable of mortifying very severely even men of more than ordinary constancy" (III.2.11), so too "the most sincere praise can give little pleasure when it cannot be considered as some sort of proof of praise-worthiness" (III.2.4).

Smith argues that our moral lives include a significant role for conscience as well as remorse and guilt. He relies on the combination of the following facts: we view ourselves through the eyes of others; we learn to distinguish between praise and blame actually given and that which ought to be given; we praise and blame others, and thus ourselves, with respect to qualities we take to be praise- or blameworthy; we thus become capable of viewing ourselves through the eyes of an "ideal" other (an impartial spectator). Remorse and guilt arise when we know ourselves to be blameworthy, whether or not we are actually blamed. This knowledge is attained by observing ourselves through the mediation of the impartial spectator pictured in our imagination. Here again we see how thoroughly we are, as moral beings, shaped by the imagination. The impartial spectator seems to gaze down upon the guilty one, reminding him of his faults, filling him with dread that his misdeeds might be found out, and making him feel painful guilt at the recognition that he is in fact detestable.[18] He cannot live with himself, unless he is a quite corrupt human being. Smith vividly depicts the inner life of the criminal who

---

18 Smith writes: "though he could be assured that no man was ever to know it, and could even bring himself to believe that there was no God to revenge it, he would still feel enough of both these sentiments to embitter the whole of his life. . . . These natural pangs of an affrighted conscience are the daemons, the avenging furies, which, in this life, haunt the guilty, which allow them neither quiet nor repose" and drive even the most hard-hearted to seek exculpation through confession or punishment (III.2.9).

sympathizes with those who abhor him (II.ii.2.3). Smith's evocative descriptions of the agent's moral consciousness are remarkable.

The self-approbation that derives from knowing oneself to be praiseworthy is a natural outgrowth of the process by which, through sympathy, we approve of others. Were this process impossible, we would be fit only for the "affectation of virtue" and the "concealment of vice," rather than for the "real love of virtue" and the "real abhorrence of vice," and would therefore wish merely to *appear* to be fit for society (III.2.7). The love of virtue is not the love of the approval of some other person, called the "impartial spectator," but of an aspect of ourselves with which we "sympathize." At this level it is a question of the self's relation to itself. As we become habituated to observing ourselves from the impartial point of view, our emotions are themselves shaped so as to diminish the motivation to act from self-love alone, and our loves are consistent with our love of virtue; for we *are* impartial spectators of ourselves. The love of virtue is an outgrowth of sympathy.

This does not mean that indifference to praise is a requirement of the love of the praiseworthy. Smith's view is, as always, balanced. He holds that those "splenetic philosophers" who attribute all of our motivations to love of praise are not credible; they are in effect the self-love theorists (III.2.27). But he also agrees that no one can *completely* ignore unmerited reproach or the absence of merited praise, and indeed that this is a good thing, for it prevents us from altogether disregarding the sentiments and judgments of our fellows. Conscience, which is the internalized "impartial and well-informed spectator," "the man within the breast, the great judge and arbiter" of our conduct, is like "the demigods of the poets, though partly of immortal, yet partly too of mortal extraction" (III.2.32). Thus the "demigod within" can be "astonished and confounded by the vehemence and clamour of the man without." We are composite beings, and our imaginations sympathetically entertain both the opinions of actual spectators and those of the impartial spectator. The latter can "over-awe" the former, but not so far as to suppress its clamor entirely. Smith's phenomenology of inner struggle is remarkably well articulated, and powerfully supported by observations of moral exemplars. (For instance, he reminds us that people are willing to sacrifice their lives to achieve a moral good because they understand their own true worth and perhaps imagine the fame that a future and more enlightened humanity will bestow; III.2.5.)

The pleasures of social approbation, then, are not absolute. They dominate us if we are vain and subject to self-love. The extent of vanity, of course, varies from person to person, and over a person's lifetime; Smith's point is simply that to exist in society we must learn self-command to some extent and that we have strong motivation to learn it to a considerable degree. Education and right ordering of institutions are certainly crucial to checking self-love and containing the disorders it creates. Moreover, self-approbation is pleasurable and the lack of it intensely painful. Warranted self-approbation yields the greatest pleasure of all, namely tranquillity (III.2.3, III.3.30, 33), whereas this is not easily secured, and perhaps is positively threatened, when we take account solely of the views of "the indulgent and partial spectator" (III.3.41) and the partial counsels of self-love.

Clearly, though, moral struggle is our lot. The "delusions of self-love" press in upon us: "so partial are the views of mankind with regard to the propriety of their own conduct, both at the time of action and after it," that this "self-deceit, this fatal weakness of mankind, is the source of half the disorders of human life" (III.4.5–7). Vanity is "the foundation of the most ridiculous and contemptible vices" (III.2.4) and arises from an "illusion of the imagination" (III.2.4); Smith also refers to this as "self-delusion" (III.4.6,4). Moral blindness is thus a major theme in Smith's vivid depiction of moral experience. Such passages about inner moral life are almost short stories in themselves and exhibit a touch worthy of Jane Austen. Self-delusion is of course a complicated notion. Smith uses it because it fits with his view that conscience is a function of the actor's own projective and sympathetic imagination and thus is fundamentally a matter of the self's relation to self; because it fits with his notion that in viewing ourselves we have divided ourselves into two, one part of ourselves being capable of deluding the other; and finally because it fits with his view that acting in accordance with self-love generates remorse or guilt, which the agent may try to ignore or keep down. Self-deluded persons tend to exhibit equivocal behavior, thanks to the conflict among their emotions, and self-delusion is illustrated by Smith's descriptions of persons who desperately try to block out the wrong they have done or the good they have failed to pursue or the lies they are living. By contrast, a person who views himself in the mirror of the impartial spectator's gaze is by definition not self-deluded; he is divided from self but not against self; his happiness as actor and his self-approbation as impartial spectator of self coincide perfectly (VI.iii.50). (We will return to happiness and virtue in Chapter 5.)

## The Impartial Spectator

For the excellent person judges each sort of thing correctly, and in each case what is true appears to him. For each state [of character] has its own special [view of] what is fine and pleasant, and presumably the excellent person is far superior because he sees what is true in each case, being a sort of standard and measure of what is fine and pleasant.

Aristotle, *Nicomachean Ethics*[19]

Smith's doctrine of impartiality grows out of this analysis of spectatorship, and that out of his phenomenology of sympathy. The background description of ordinary life, the agent–spectator distinction, and the privileging of the standpoint of the spectator are essential to keep in mind if his notion of the impartial spectator is to make much sense.

Insofar as we empathize too closely with the actor, we cease to be fair spectators and become partial to the actor. Insofar as we do not sympathize enough with the actor, experiencing our own emotions undirected by the other's, we cease to be fair spectators of the actor and show partiality to self. The quasi detachment from the insistent demands of one's own and the other's emotions is an important element in impartiality. The term "impartiality" is introduced at the end of the paragraph in which Smith describes the imaginary change of positions effected by spectator and actor through sympathy and discusses the "reflected passion" conceived of by the actor when viewing his own passions in the "candid and impartial light" of the relatively detached spectator. The word "spectator" is introduced earlier, in the fourth paragraph of the book, where it is used synonymously with "by-stander." Not until the end of Section I of Part I, some twenty pages later, does the term "impartial spectator" crop up (I.i.5.4). Soon after this Smith speaks of "the cool and impartial spectator" (I.ii.3.8) and of the "indifferent person" (III.4.2) and "indifferent spectator" (I.ii.4.1; III.4.4; VI.iii.5). These formulations emphasize that the spectator is the personification of the public, of a point of view that abstracts in a relevant way from that of the agent. At this stage of the story, the impartial spectator is not an idealized fiction but any person who takes this stance with respect to others.

A spectator is impartial just by virtue, first, of those traits of detached yet sympathetic *engagement* discussed earlier. Smith goes on to compare the spectator to both a judge and a critic. (In Chapter 5 I shall consider

19 *NE* 1113a29–33; interpolations in Irwin's translation.

the metaphor of the judge and the place of moral rules in impartial evaluation.) We have discussed the critic in Chapter 1. The critic may invoke a higher or a lower standard of judgment, that is, a standard of "complete propriety and perfection" or a standard that "the greater part of men commonly arrive at" (I.i.5.9–10). The impartial spectator has a critical perspective and estimates the degree of approbation due. This spectating critic is not a philosopher; he or she does not deliberate about first principles, or (at least initially) speculate about the utility of this or that action or character in the context of a general system of morality or nature. The object of evaluation is a particular – this or that performance or person, this or that situation, as "sympathetically" judged in light of a reasonable standard (extrapolated from thoughtful observations) governing how individuals may be expected to behave or respond in just this or that sort of situation.

The spectator-critic's evaluation of the particular matter in question is that of an "indifferent" or "cool" observer, in that the spectator does not have the same emotional "investment" in the situation that the "sufferer" or agent does and thus can be relatively detached and critical. "The passions," Smith says quoting Malebranche, "all justify themselves, and seem reasonable and proportioned to their objects, as long as we continue to feel them" (III.4.3). But the impartial spectator is not therefore unemotional. As argued in Chapter 1, the critic can evaluate the play well only by being appropriately engaged in it. The critic who fails to detest Iago or to esteem Othello (Smith's examples at I.ii.3.2), or who is "indifferent" (in the sense of inappropriately cool) to them emotionally is not impartial but uninformed. Smith speaks of the impartial spectator as having feelings or sentiments (e.g., I.ii.3.8; III.3.25; VII.ii.1.49). "Indifference" is better understood as "disinterestedness": not as the lack of any emotional connection with the world but the ability, in a specific situation, to judge it without any prejudice generated either by one's own private emotions of the moment or by any narrow desire to "better one's condition" through manipulation of the situation. Consequently, the impartial spectator lacks only those emotions (such as envy and excessive self-love) that interfere with good judgment, or at least is not subject to the degrees of those emotions that bias or distort judgment.[20]

20 A. Piper argues that "to be impartial is to treat competing preferences and interests on their own merits and without being biased by one's own," this being a "metaethical requirement" that in turn requires that we know "what these interests are and for what

On Smith's theory, the emotions are not like prisoners who must be disciplined and isolated from civilized society by a stern and impartial judge. The emotions are essential to morality. As we have seen at length in Chapter 2, through sympathy the emotions communicate evaluations as well as information to other agents. Crucially, the sentiments are "cognitive," in the sense that judgments form part of them (although the actor is not always reflective about those judgments), and Smith therefore speaks of emotions as judging (VII.iv.33) as well as being judged.[21] The emotion of resentment, for example, embodies the judgment that someone's action has caused unwarranted harm. Even when not adjudicated by the impartial spectator, emotions are evaluative, discerning worth (or lack thereof) in their objects. The emotions are not mere "feels" and may be improved or degraded through habit, reflection, and imagination.

Yet, this does not capture a crucial aspect of their role in Smith's ethics: emotions not only embody judgments; they guide judgment, by informing it as to what matters and what does not. Of course they sometimes mislead us. But if they fail to guide us normally and regularly, then moral criticism and deliberation are effectively blindfolded, unable to pick out the factors in a particular situation that carry ethical weight. The eyes of the emotions help us to understand what is worth caring about and what, in a specific situation, is relevant. Naturally, the emotions also motivate us, in different ways and with different intensities. Without their motivational force, we would be immobilized; we would not *care*, and that lack of moral feeling and sensitivity would itself be a blameworthy deficiency in one's character. In sum, although the sentiments are moral only insofar as they are such as an impartial spectator would feel, for Smith the sentiments or emotions are indispensable to moral apprehension. This entails that the line between feeling and re-

they are competing." That knowledge, Piper argues, in turn requires both "modal imagination" (the ability to imagine deep interests and preferences that the agent and others may not have and may never have had) as well as "empathic imaginative involvement" with others. "Impartiality, Compassion, and Modal Imagination," *Ethics* 101 (1991), pp. 746–7. This is entirely congenial with Smith's view of the impartial spectator.

21  Smith's view of the emotions is what A. Gibbard calls "judgmentalism" or (following R. Solomon) "emotional cognitivism." Gibbard distinguishes between strong versions (according to which emotions are cognitive judgments) and weak ones (according to which emotions consist of cognitive judgments in part). Gibbard, *Wise Choices, Apt Feelings* (Cambridge, Mass.: Harvard University Press, 1990), p. 129 and note. Given what Smith says, and not finding the "strong" version entirely intelligible, I attribute the "weak" version to Smith.

flection, moral perception and evaluation, cannot always be cleanly drawn.[22]

A certain degree of detachment and perspective is built into spectatorship. But impartiality and spectatorship cannot be identical for the simple reason that there are partial spectators. Spectators may be "partial" in being poorly informed about the facts of the case, or in being attached to the case in a way that necessarily biases their perspective, or in failing to enter into the situation "sympathetically." A drama critic who has a financial stake in the success of a play would be a "partial" spectator and judge of it; so too would one who misunderstood the details of the plot, or one who for personal reasons was jealous of the producer, or again, one who for personal reasons could not engage emotionally in the drama in the appropriate way. This is spectator partiality. It may result from well-intentioned error, but more commonly, one surmises, it results from the spectator's own absorption in self and lack of attentive care for the actor.

Its mirror image is actor partiality. "Self-love" that produces partiality toward oneself is a species of selfishness that manifests itself in distorted moral evaluation. (Smith speaks at III.4.12 of the actor's "too partial views which self-love might otherwise suggest" and at VII.ii.1.40 of the "private, partial, and selfish passions.") The distortion consists in a failure to acknowledge one's vices or shortcomings or moral failures, or in caring too much for oneself in comparison with others, or in thinking overly well of one's virtues or achievements ("we are all naturally disposed to over-rate the excellencies of our own characters"; III.2.34). The pleasure of self-congratulation and the pain of honesty with oneself tend to lead the actor to "self-delusion" (III.4.4). Thus the gravest source of partiality in both the spectator and the actor is, for Smith as for Kant, self-love – our omnipresent theme in *The Theory of Moral Sentiments*.

The "abstract and ideal spectator" (III.3.38) or impartial spectator, is a logical development, entertained at times solely in our imagination, of traits of actual spectators. In one passage Smith compares the process by which we learn to exercise balanced moral judgment to that by which we learn to make correct visual judgments. He has Berkeley's *New Theory of Vision* in mind, a book of which he thought highly. The basic idea is that just as I cannot gauge the correct proportions of objects of different sizes and at varying distances except by "transporting myself, at least in fancy, to a different station, from whence I can survey both at nearly

22 In Chapter 5, I shall say more about judgment, moral rules, and moral perception.

equal distances," so too I cannot accurately evaluate the magnitude of my passions in comparison with another's except by viewing them "neither from our own place nor yet from his, neither with our own eyes nor yet with his, but from the place and with the eyes of a third person, who has no particular connexion with either, and who judges with impartiality between us" (III.3.3). The "natural misrepresentations of self-love can be corrected only by the eye of this impartial spectator" (III.3.4; cf. III.5.5). Smith claims that, as in cases of sensory perception, so too in moral judgment we learn to acquire perspective by "habit and experience," not by philosophy. He once refers directly to the standpoint of the impartial spectator as that of "reason" (III.3.5) and of the "reasonable man" (II.i.2.3), but reasonableness or impartiality should not be confused with philosophical rationality. The "reasonable man" is the person of reflective and informed imagination and appropriately engaged emotions, suitably detached from the actor so as to allow perspective. The agent should, Smith says, "act so as that the impartial spectator may enter into the principles of his conduct" and thus "humble the arrogance of his self-love" (II.ii.2.1). The impartial spectator, and thus the moral imagination, give us at least part of what Kantian moral reason is meant to provide – and for Smith, all we really need for moral life – without any of the problematic claims about the transcendental status of reason, the reduction of emotions to "incentives" or "inclinations," the meshing of "maxims" with the *a priori* machinery of the categorical imperative, or claims about the mysterious noumenal status of freedom.

The meaning of "impartiality" is brought out by a contrast with the partiality of self-love engendered by emotion. Even though impartiality is not itself passionless reason, it is a rational trait in multiple senses; it involves looking at self or other from a general point of view (i.e., from one defined by the spectator rather than just the actor), acquiring and grasping relevant information, understanding the situation, and abstracting from one's emotions that distort a fair apprehension and sympathy. Impartiality does not require our acting or choosing as though we had no knowledge of ourselves that distinguishes us from others; it does not require a Rawlsian veil of ignorance.[23] There is a place in

23 In *A Theory of Justice* (Cambridge, Mass.: Harvard University Press, 1980), Rawls suggests that the impartial spectator theory of the sort outlined by Hume and Smith need not, in itself, be at odds with his own theory, but this seems to be so only because "The impartial spectator definition makes no assumptions from which the principles of right and justice may be derived. It is designed instead to single out certain central features characteristic of moral discussion, the fact that we try to appeal to our considered judgments after

Smith's account for a weak sort of universalizability, namely, through "general rules," but that is not understood as a decision procedure, as I will point out subsequently. There is also a place in this scheme for a notion of reversability of roles. When speaking of the internalization of the actor–spectator relationship – the result of our dividing ourselves into two persons (III.1.6) – something like this role reversal has taken place, for the agent is called upon to put his own sentiments into perspective by viewing himself from the outside. The spectator's sympathetic projection of self into the actor's situation also amounts to a kind of "role reversal" or changing of positions. Hence to be impartial is to be prepared to act against that which we might unreflectively feel to be in our own private interest, unless on independent examination that interest is justifiable.

One might infer that to be impartial is to act on the basis of non–self-regarding sentiments. But one of the advantages of Smith's doctrine is that it quite explicitly does *not* require us to take a completely universal (Smith would say Stoic) moral standpoint. Impartiality does not require that as agents we treat ourselves as mere parts of the moral universe on an exact moral par with each of the other such parts. This would be to take the stance of what Smith calls "universal benevolence," and from that standpoint one's own interests or that of one's "own particular order or society" should always be "sacrificed to the greater interest of the

conscientious reflection, and the like" (p. 185). By contrast, "The contractarian definition is more ambitious: it attempts to provide a deductive basis for the principles that account for these judgments." After setting out a utilitarian version of the spectator theory, Rawls remarks: "We can understand the point of the [impartial spectator] definition once we see that its parts are designed to give free scope to the operation of fellow feeling. In the original position, by contrast, the parties are mutually disinterested rather than sympathetic; but lacking knowledge of their natural assets or social situation, they are forced to view their arrangements in a general way. In the one case perfect knowledge and sympathetic identification result in a correct estimate of the net sum of satisfaction; in the other, mutual disinterestedness subject to a veil of ignorance leads to the two principles of justice" (p. 187). And "From the standpoint of justice as fairness there is no reason why the persons in the original position would agree to the approvals of an impartial sympathetic spectator as the standard of justice. This agreement has all the drawbacks of the classical principle of utility to which it is equivalent" (p. 188). But Smith's theory is not utilitarian, and as I have stressed, is a running critique of Hume's view of the role of utility in moral evaluation. For discussion of the un-Smithean view of the impartial spectator presented by Rawls, see D. D. Raphael, "The Impartial Spectator," in *Essays on Adam Smith*, ed. A. S. Skinner and T. Wilson (Oxford: Clarendon Press, 1975), pp. 96–7. Smith's impartial spectator theory does have some interesting parallels with Rawls's notion of "constructivism" as developed in lecture 3 of *Political Liberalism* (New York: Columbia University Press, 1993).

state or sovereignty, of which it is only a subordinate part" (VI.ii.3.3). The happiness of the whole is the goal of the "sympathy which we feel with the misery and resentment of those other innocent and sensible beings" (VI.ii.3.1). Why is this not a proper extension of the doctrine of the impartial spectator? Smith's answer is that "the administration of the great system of the universe, however, the care of the universal happiness of all rational and sensible beings, is the business of God and not of man" (VI.ii.3.6). All of the Stoic "sophisms" and "paradoxes" arose from one fundamental mistake, namely, holding that nature ought ideally be coordinated with philosophical reason and that we ought to look at ourselves "from the point of view of the universe." Correspondingly, as we have seen, Smith rejects the idea of a "rational morality" of the sort he sees espoused by philosophers from the Stoics to Hutcheson. These philosophers have adopted the wrong level of spectatorship.[24]

This objection to an impersonal outlook is supported by Smith's rigorous adherence to the standpoint of ordinary moral life and his resistance to its reorientation by philosophical moral theories, let alone by those – like the Stoic – which make demands on us that are inappropriate to our natural concern for ourselves and those in our own circle (as well as our concern for others). Smith's notion of impartiality does not generate the paradoxes of impersonality to which Kantian and utilitarian schemes are subject, in part because it sees the emotions as constitutive of moral value. Emotions are not *replaced* by some other criterion when viewed impartially, though they may certainly be criticized and modified. Smith never requires the impartial spectator to stop caring about the sentiments and thus about local and particular attachments. Much hinges on adopting the right level of spectatorship. (Smith's differences with the Stoics on this issue are discussed further in Chapter 8.)

Smith adds: "To man is allotted a much humbler department, but one much more suitable to the weakness of his powers, and to the narrowness of his comprehension; the care of his own happiness, of that of his family, his friends, his country" (VI.ii.3.6). Neglect of even the smallest duties in the areas under our immediate supervision is not excused

---

24 "From the point of view of the universe" is Henry Sidgwick's phrase (he is characterizing his own, utilitarian, position), and "rational morality" is a phrase B. Williams uses in his discussion of Sidgwick. Williams's discussion contains remarkable parallels to Smith's critique of the Stoics. (Smith reads the Stoics, and Hutcheson, in a way that gives them common features with what became known as utilitarianism.) For both quotations see Williams, "The Point of View of the Universe: Sidgwick and the Ambitions of Ethics," in Williams, *Making Sense of Humanity*, pp. 161, 159.

by "sublime speculation" about the happiness of the whole. A moral theory that demands that we be impartial in a way that abstracts completely from our own happiness, or that of our particular context, and focuses simply on the general good also requires a knowledge of that general good that as finite beings we lack and, paradoxically, leads us to ignore the moral obligations that fall within our particular sphere. And what magnitude ought those humble obligations to have? That magnitude will be judged, once again, by an impartial look at our particular situations, informed by our emotional attachments sympathetically grasped and evaluated. "I shall only observe at present, that the point of propriety, the degree of any passion which the impartial spectator approves of, is differently situated in different passions" (VI.iii.14). Smith does not speak of "impartial reason"; his view concerns impartial spectatorship.

Smith's impartial spectator corrects the "misrepresentations of self-love" but also judges that we properly owe our own children and communities greater care and support than we do the children and communities of other people. Our natural sentiments and mutual dependencies are not features of our moral lives that a well-informed, candid, and ideal spectator would seek to reform radically. That is, an impartial judge will approve of our partiality toward those who properly fall within our narrow circles of sympathy. In defending the standpoint of ordinary life, Smith rejects moral theory that imposes demands we cannot meet and that requires guilt we ought not to bear. For him such a "universal benevolence" theory would be a variant of (perhaps a secularization of) a religious teaching that makes morality subservient to the life to come rather than happiness in this life and that thereby defines this life as a vale of tears. Such is the teaching of the "whining and melancholy moralists" who "are perpetually reproaching us with our happiness, while so many of our brethren are in misery," and Smith will have none of it (III.3.9). The virtues of enlightenment rescue the individual's chance for happiness here and now from the rigoristic demands of fanatical moralities.

The impartial spectator must be well informed, but this is not to say "wise" or omniscient. Smith's idea is that when impartial we are indeed well informed about the matter at hand but perhaps not perfectly or completely informed even about it. This theory does not demand something from the moral agent that is in principle unobtainable. Smith remarks at one point that even the impartial spectator is subject to the "irregularity of sentiment" thanks to which our judgment of the merit of an intention or action reflects an assessment of consequences that are determined by chance (II.iii.2.1). Impartiality does not require abstraction from this human proclivity for taking unforeseen or unforeseeable consequences into account in assessing the moral worth of an intention or action. The impartial spectator will also have ethical and possibly religious commitments; the specific situation, the specific kind of virtue or vice at stake, will determine which of these it is appropriate for the impartial spectator to bracket, if any. For example, in judging whether a competing nonviolent religious sect should be allowed to open shop in town, the impartial spectator will consider the issue of justice and will not seek to prevent this development, but he will simultaneously warn all those of concern to him to avoid that sect and its teachings. The impartial spectator does not forget his own conception of the good life but understands when a virtue (especially justice) calls for restraining his demand that others act in accordance with his conception.

With rare exceptions, Smith always refers to the "impartial spectator" in the singular, thus suggesting that in any particular case all such spectators will agree in their judgment.[25] One can imagine cases in which they would approach the matter at hand from different perspectives. But as impartial, they will surely consider all the relevant facts, engage properly in the actor's situation, be free of distortions caused by their own passions, and thus will arrive at the same conclusion about the passion or habit or conduct or character in question.[26] Hence the impartial spectator is an idealization of the moral demand for social unity, though it is not itself a function of any given social consensus. The demand is

25 One exception is at III.2.3, but the grammar of the sentence (given that the subject is "we") would make the singular awkward and thus the statement does not constitute a clear-cut exception to the rule. The same applies to III.3.42. Samuel Fleischacker has suggested to me that the singular in Smith's locution underlines Smith's conception of the impartial spectator as an *individual*; this explanation fits well with my interpretation. By contrast, Campbell argues that "to talk of *the* impartial spectator is simply a shorthand way of referring to the normal reaction of a member of a particular social group, or of a whole society, when he is in the position of observing the conduct of his fellows." This reduces the theory to a "sociological concept," however. *Adam Smith's Science of Morals*, p. 145. A related question is whether the impartial spectator is "gendered." I am in agreement with H. Clark's argument that it is not. See his "Women and Humanity in Scottish Enlightenment Social Thought: The Case of Adam Smith," *Historical Reflections* 19 (1993): 335–61. His footnotes refer to much of the quite extensive literature on the question of gender in Smith's writings. See also S. Justman, *The Autonomous Male of Adam Smith* (Norman: University of Oklahoma Press, 1993), and my review of his book in the *Journal of the History of Philosophy* 35 (1997): 629–32.
26 Smith usually speaks of the impartial spectator judging conduct or an emotion, but at III.2.3 he says that the impartial spectator may also judge one's character.

generally realized in the particulars; the impartial spectator normally judges this passion, or conduct, or habit. Yet there is no reason one could not spectate impartially on the virtues and vices of political or economic systems, and in *The Wealth of Nations* Smith speaks of impartiality in the conduct of those systems as well as of the great importance of our evaluating them in an informed and fair manner. Were philosophy needed for that evaluation, though, emendations of Smith's theory of the impartial spectator would be necessary.

I have emphasized that the impartial spectator is a refinement of the ordinary exchange of moral life. That exchange is, on Smith's account, characterized at least in part by sympathy; the impartial spectator exemplifies sympathetic understanding at its best, a stance of caring for the other, of caring to understand the truth of the matter and the reasons for which the people in question have acted as they have. This sympathetic care is at the core of morality and sociability; it holds us mutually responsible to each other, drawing us together in the exercise of responsiveness and perceptive judgment. It is the core of a reasonable and moral community. The impartial spectator has normative force in part because it *defines* the moral point of view already latent in ordinary life.[27] And its moral force is most valuable when self-love is most dangerous to social harmony. It is therefore striking that the first use of the term "impartial spectator" in *The Theory of Moral Sentiments* occurs in the context of the need to restrain "the insolence and brutality of anger" and to exhibit a "noble and generous resentment" (I.i.5.4).

The verb "define" must be given its full weight here. The "precise and distinct measure" of virtue is to be found in the "sympathetic feelings of the impartial and well-informed spectator." "The very words, right, wrong, fit, improper, graceful, unbecoming, mean only what pleases or displeases those [moral] faculties," and by definition the impartial spectator exercises the moral faculties in the proper manner. Whatever this impartial spectator takes to be morally good or not is such

---

27 Cf. R. Firth's point: "Most of us, indeed, can be said to have a conception of an ideal observer only in the sense that the characteristics of such a person are implicit in the procedures by which we compare and evaluate moral judges, and it seems doubtful, therefore, than an ideal observer can be said to lack any of the determinable properties of human beings." "Ethical Absolutism and the Ideal Observer," *Philosophy and Phenomenological Research* 12 (1951-2), p. 344. As already noted, Smith would add that the impartial spectator cannot possess properties human beings can never have, such as the "omniscience" Firth claims to be essential. This and other Smithean criticisms of Firth's construal of the impartial spectator are presented in Raphael, "The Impartial Spectator," pp. 95–6, as well as Campbell, *Adam Smith's Science of Morals*, ch. 6.

(III.5.5). Thus to say that X is better than Y is to say, as one commentator puts it, "If anyone were, in respect of X and Y, fully informed and vividly imaginative, impartial, in a calm frame of mind, and otherwise normal, he would prefer X to Y."[28] The impartial spectator is not a heuristic procedure, one way among others of checking the accuracy of our view of things; Smith has and can have no well-defined moral test or procedure to offer here. We judge well by *becoming* impartial spectators. The impartial spectator does not look off to principles of impartiality, as though to a Platonic Form. The standards for impartial spectatorship are not ultimately independent of the impartial spectator, and the impartial spectator is not an "image" of some moral "original."

This is one reason Smith does not proffer a moral theory that articulates any such "original" or "form" of morality. Rather, the impartial spectator is constitutive of the moral outlook.[29] The responses of the impartial spectator are defining: they determine that certain passions and actions are moral, these being "rendered" (VII.iii.2.7) worthy of approbation or the contrary by his or her reflective sentiments. The impartial spectator is the "natural and original measure" of virtue (VII.ii.3.21). Thus in looking to the impartial spectator as the measure, in attempting to "identify" with and become the impartial spectator, we adopt as moral agents a standpoint that is definitive of the moral determination in question, not one from which a further search for spectator-independent standards is conducted. Were the standards entirely independent of the impartial spectator, we would be on to the next question, namely, By virtue of what is that something right?

If the impartial spectator *is* the "measure," then how can the impartial spectator "make use of two different standards" when evaluating an action (I.i.5.9–10)? The answer is that the impartial spectator *ultimately* defines the standards, but only after a process of reflection on and refinement of what is given. This is just what Smith says in referring to

---

28 J. D. Bailiff, "Some Comments on the 'Ideal Observer,'" *Philosophy and Phenomenological Research* 24 (1963–4), p. 423. Cf. Bailiff's intriguing suggestion that we understand "impartiality" in accordance with C. Perelman's theory of argumentation.

29 This distinction between heuristic and constitutive versions of the impartial spectator is drawn by M. Nussbaum in *Love's Knowledge: Essays on Philosophy and Literature* (Oxford: Oxford University Press, 1990), pp. 344–5, and I am indebted to her insightful discussion. She remarks that Smith has "built into the account of the spectator the most essential features of our moral humanity" and that "the spectator's responses are themselves constitutive of what is and is not morally appropriate" (p. 345), the contrast being to a view in which "moral appropriateness and propriety in passion exist independently" of the ideal judge (p. 344).

these standards as "the slow, gradual, and progressive work of the great demigod within the breast"; in shaping them, the wise and virtuous person "imitates the work of a divine artist" (VI.iii.25). Since spectators' moral sentiments are woven into the world – into practices, traditions, and institutions, for example – and since the impartial spectator is a reflective refinement of the exchanges of ordinary moral life, moral evaluation typically begins with established rules and standards. The impartial spectator's judgments culminate a process of often complex reasoning that determines the relevant relations of "propriety." These judgments do not amount to writing on a blank slate, so to speak, or to stipulating moral value out of the blue. The impartial spectator may work up several different standards of evaluation and then judge that one or the other is appropriate in the context. His or her determination and use of these standards is definitive; there is in principle no higher court of appeal above the impartial spectator.

The characterization of the impartial spectator as "constitutive" ultimately makes a metaphysical point. The idea is to contrast the notion that the impartial spectator is the source of value with the view that moral evaluation mirrors an independent order of moral facts. This in turn raises a significant issue broached in the next chapter and pursued further in Chapter 8, namely, the constructed or projected nature of value. From Smith's spectating standpoint in the philosophical critic's balcony of the *theatrum mundi*, the (so to speak) non-natural nature of moral standards is inseparable from the fact that all of morality, and indeed all of the human "world," is a complex whole that we communally impose on ourselves. Yet Smith also holds that this "poietic" character of the "world" is not generally visible to either actors or spectators. As a result, morals are ordinarily thought to possess a reality and authority that is external to us. The standpoints of philosopher and ordinary moral agent are not the same, however skillfully Smith intertwines them in the passages we have been examining.

# 4

# PHILOSOPHY AND SKEPTICISM

In that case, Diotima, who *are* the people who love wisdom, if they are
neither wise nor ignorant?

Socrates[1]

Smith's account of the passions does not mention the love of wisdom.
The "intellectual sentiments" of wonder, surprise, and admiration are
the basis for our praising the "intellectual virtues" (I.i.4.3). But these
emotions are spectatorial and not especially strong. They do not seem
to have a place in any of the three categories of passion we examined in
Chapter 3. By characterizing the intellectual sentiments as "spectatorial"
I mean to underline the relative detachment they entail; whether the
spectator is the philosopher-scientist observing the great "theatre of nature" ("History of Astronomy," III.1, *EPS*, p. 48) or the person admiring
the philosopher-scientist's acumen, "theoretical" knowing seems pro-
pelled not by a desire to live out our lives with greater perfection but by
a desire to restore a certain tranquillity to the nonsympathetic imagination. Consequently Smith's theory of the passions provides no explicit

---

1 Plato, *Symposium* 204a8–9, trans. A. Nehamas and P. Woodruff (Indianapolis: Hackett,
1989).

147

place for philosophy, in the etymological and edifying Platonic sense of the term.

To be sure, in its natural proclivity to enter into and understand the situation of another, to take interest in and weave together the other's story, the sympathetic imagination resembles the urge to comprehensiveness and unity tied to eros in Plato's *Symposium* and *Phaedrus*. But of course for Plato, eros also binds together mortal and divine, providing a "ladder" ascending from the ordinary (such as another's physical beauty) to the extraordinary (such as of the Forms). The highest of these steps is philosophy; in gathering together and ordering the passions of the soul in a unifying and perfecting vision of the divine, philosophy overcomes the division between theory and practice. No such account is possible for Smith, and his seeming omission from the doctrine of the passions in *The Theory of Moral Sentiments* of anything like this love of wisdom reveals his purpose. Before we turn to his virtue theory, we must pause to consider the restrictions he places on the scope of philosophy and also examine the related issue of his skepticism. Consideration of the first issue is best approached through a discussion of Smith's views about friendship and love.

## 1. LOVE AND PHILOSOPHY IN THE *THEATRUM MUNDI*

A philosopher is company to a philosopher only; the member of a club, to his own little knot of companions.

Adam Smith, *TMS* I.ii.2.6

The centrality of "sympathy" to *The Theory of Moral Sentiments* points to the centrality of love in the book. As remarked in Chapter 2, although Smith delineates a somewhat unusual, technical sense of "sympathy" ("fellow-feeling" for *any* emotion), his use of the term sometimes slips into the more ordinary sense of "compassion" or affectionate fellow feeling. This no doubt intentional equivocation helps to suffuse the book with these themes, so that without much exaggeration, one could say that *The Theory of Moral Sentiments* is generally about love: our need for love and sympathy, love as friendship, self-love, the love of praise and praiseworthiness, the love of beauty.[2] Even in *The Wealth of Nations*, our

---

2 For example, Smith says in his own voice: "the chief part of human happiness arises from a consciousness of being beloved" (I.ii.5.2). The key role of love in Smith's moral theory did not escape Thomas Reid, whose lecture notes on Smith show him to have remarked,

loves are thought to be very important in explaining our behavior.[3] Smith is unusual among modern moral philosophers in according a central place to love in this broad sense (which includes friendship), although of course Christianity made love a central theme in reflection on ethical life, and Hutcheson made benevolence the key virtue in his ethical system.

As we have seen, at the beginning of the section of *The Theory of Moral Sentiments* on the social passions, Smith runs together "generosity, humanity, kindness, compassion, mutual friendship and esteem, all the social and benevolent affections" (I.ii.4.1) and argues that these passions are rendered agreeable to the "indifferent spectator" by a "redoubled sympathy." Next he turns to the emotion of love and praises it too as agreeable to the spectator. His example of love is quite specific, namely, love among family members. Of such love, Smith is thoroughly approving. For we spectators can sympathize with it entirely, and it is the paradigm, it seems, of social cooperation, of the social passions at their best. At one point Smith observes that where love, friendship, and the like motivate people to assist one another, society flourishes and is happy; there the "agreeable bands of love and affection" are "drawn to one common centre of mutual good offices" (II.ii.3.1).

Earlier in the book, however, Smith provides us with another discussion of love. As we have noted, the degree to which the spectator can sympathize with the actor forms one distinction between the bodily passions and the imagination. Smith implies that the spectator cannot much sympathize with "the most furious of all the passions" that unites the two sexes (I.ii.1.1–2), for it is a bodily passion. As Smith prepares himself in the next chapter for the long discussion of the passions derived from the imagination, he speaks of love as the bridge between the two categories of passions, perhaps because physical love, or lust, may be "the foundation of [romantic] love" (I.ii.2.1–2). And his argument is surprising, for he claims that romantic love between the sexes too is virtually

in explaining the teaching of *TMS*, "Sympathy seems to me to be inseparably connected with Love Affection and Esteem. I cannot possibly love a Man without being pleased with every good that befals him and uneasy at his misfortune[.] If you ask me why I take so much concern in his good or bad fortune it is because I love him." In Stewart-Robertson and Norton,"Thomas Reid on Adam Smith's Theory of Morals," p. 313.

3 At *WN* V.i.b.2, for example, Smith speaks of the great importance to human life of our "love of present ease and enjoyment" and at III.ii.10, of our "love to domineer" and the role that this plays in the phenomenon of slavery. Of course sexual desire and procreation have significant economic consequences that are discussed at various junctures throughout the book.

closed to the spectator: "Our imagination not having run in the same channel with that of the lover, we cannot enter into the eagerness of his emotions." If our "friend" is in love, we cannot change places with him; we cannot appreciate his passion, for it seems to everyone but our friend "entirely disproportioned to the value of the object." Our friend's love for another person, in short, strikes us as laughable and "ridiculous," for we cannot sympathize with it. Hence "though a lover may be a good company to his mistress, he is so to nobody else" (I.ii.2.1). We can, to be sure, enter into the lovely hopes for eternal friendship entertained by the lover, or the lover's anxieties and distress, but not his or her love proper.

Thus tragedies about love treat only the "secondary passions" that arise from the situation (I.ii.2.2–5). We infer that love itself is better treated in comedies, precisely because to spectators it is ridiculous on account of its extravagant disproportion to its object. Of course, lovers *qua* lovers do not see the disproportion. The reason is that, in Smith's portrayal of both erotic and romantic love, both persons are agents. Neither is a spectator of the other; neither is "outside" the other in the relevant sense.[4] The worlds of the lovers so thoroughly meld together that they live each other's lives. Consequently, they lose perspective on each other. Perhaps we may simply say that the lovers have extended "sympathy" so far as almost to transcend it. Sympathy has become synonymous in this instance with absolute approval and affirmation.[5]

Smith concludes this discussion by returning to the issue of friendship and explains that for such reasons we must exercise reserve in talking of our friends, studies, or professions – in short, of any of the things we truly love and cherish. I began this section by quoting Smith's remark that "A philosopher is company to a philosopher only; the member of a club, to his own little knot of companions" (I.ii.2.6). This remark echoes the earlier point to the effect that a lover is good company only to his mistress. On the one hand, then, love of humankind and sympathy

---

4 Nussbaum, in *Love's Knowledge*, makes a somewhat similar point about love and spectatorship in Smith (p. 344).
5 Love thus understood is what classical writers thought of as perfect friendship. One is also reminded of Montaigne's description, in "Of Friendship," of his relationship with La Boétie. The two were so self-enclosed that Montaigne liked to cite the phrase attributed to Aristotle, "O my friends, there is no friend," to indicate how much beyond the ordinary was his relationship as well as the extent to which two had become one. In M. Pakaluk, ed., *Other Selves: Philosophers on Friendship* (Indianapolis: Hackett, 1991), p. 194.

resonate throughout the book. On the other hand, early on in the book, lust and both love and loving friendship of the nonfamilial sort are characterized as closed off to the spectator and as generally ridiculous or laughable. The love of wisdom, in particular, seems intelligible to only a small knot of similarly minded lovers. It remains, at least potentially, outside the social web, inaccessible to sympathy, perhaps even antisocial.

Romantic love may be blissful to the lover and the beloved insofar as it fuses them into one, just as Aristophanes describes in his comic speech in Plato's *Symposium*. Smith sees the Socratic sense of love (eros) as a potentially dangerous extension of the Aristophanic. It promises a harmony of soul and of transcendence it cannot deliver, while encouraging a number of deleterious consequences. When actors are deeply in love with others like them or with elegant schemes for political perfection or with God, they risk becoming "fanatics." No spectator can influence them; all nonlovers seem to be mere objects to be manipulated as they see fit. The lovers see no reason to moderate their passion, for they are not in a relation of sympathy with spectators. In his discussion of duty, for example, Smith recalls Voltaire's tragedy *Mahomet*, a story in which two young persons who are very fond of one another mistakenly think that God, whom they love with all their hearts, requires them to kill a man they have esteemed greatly (III.6.12). Smith takes this play as a brilliant reductio ad absurdum of passionate love.

Analogously, Smith speaks of a "love of system" (IV.I.11) and provides what might be called a political aesthetics. The lover of system, seduced by "the supposed beauty of his own ideal plan of government," destroys liberty and everyone who opposes him. Religious and political fanatics claim objectivity and perspective, but Smith replies: "To them, it may be said, that such a spectator [the "real, revered, and impartial spectator"] scarce exists any where in the universe. Even to the great Judge of the universe, they impute all their own prejudices, and often view that Divine Being as animated by all their own vindictive and implacable passions" (III.3.43). Love that cancels the need for sympathy of a spectator is inherently dangerous politically, for it privileges the perspective of the actor over that of the spectator and thereby loses perspective altogether. Love is once again "disproportioned to the value of its object." Love defined from the standpoint of the actor tends to be selfish, unsympathetic, and destructive of social concord. Asocial spectating degenerates into narcissism, the flip side of voyeurism. These lovers have no proper self-approbation because they no longer view themselves through the eyes of the impartial spectator; self-approbation and spectatorship ought on Smith's account be inseparable. We are back to the problem of "selfishness" discussed in Chapter 2.

The collapse of the love of wisdom, in particular, into self-love seems linked, strikingly, with the close connection between the love of wisdom and the love of beauty. Recall Smith's repeated criticisms, in Part VII of *The Theory of Moral Sentiments*, of the reductionistic systematizing impulses of the philosophers. Over and over again, we learn that philosophers are, in effect, lovers of system. Lovers of wisdom may share the view that "human society, when we contemplate it in a certain abstract and philosophical light, appears like a great, an immense machine, whose regular and harmonious movements produce a thousand agreeable effects" (VII.iii.1.2). This machine is "beautiful and noble"; just like the lover who is entranced by the beloved's beauty, so the lover of wisdom becomes dangerously entranced by the beauty – in the sense of elegance, symmetry, order, and utility – of a conceptual scheme or of a complex whole. Insofar as the "sentiment of approbation arises from the perception of this beauty of utility [itself frequently the property of a system]," Smith says, "it has no reference of any kind to the sentiments of others" (IV.2.12). The love of systematic beauty abstracts from sympathy, thus disengaging us from particulars and from spectating agents.[6]

In the case of what Smith refers to as a "political view" of the admirable machine that is human society, our love of beauty encourages a revealing mistake in our account of the grounds of approbation and disapprobation. We do not normally praise or blame on the basis of a purely philosophical view of the matter, nor should we. The love of wisdom risks corrupting the ordinary actor's sympathetic grasp of the particulars of a situation by forcing the actor to abstract from them. Love of this type, including the love of wisdom, not only shuts itself off from the understanding of nonlovers; it fails to understand both itself and those uninvolved spectators sympathetically. Every little knot of loving companions seems, then, to be a potentially dangerous cabal, both shutting out and shut off from the ordinary interchange of actors and spectators.

In sum, in physical lust the actors shut themselves off from the sympathetic understanding of spectators; in romantic love the actors cease

---

6 In his comments about political fanaticism and the love of the beauty of system, Smith may well have had the French Revolution in mind, as is noted by Macfie and Raphael in their introduction to *TMS* (p. 18).

to be spectators of one another; in zealous religious love of God, the actors identify themselves with their beloved and lose perspective on their own selves; in philosophical love, the actors lose perspective on self and others. In each case, love and spectatorship, or in different terms, the attachment of love and the detachment of vision, drift away from each other. This whole spectrum of love is therefore hostile, on Smith's account, to healthy or "respectable" love – that is, to love that incorporates spectating.

As a consequence there is also in the end a profound distance between Smith's view of friendship and classical, especially Aristotelian and Platonic, views based on doctrines of self-perfection. The noblest friendships of the classical variety (especially the Platonic) lack the social perspective Smith demands, as does (for the same reasons) the erotic love of wisdom itself.[7] The intensity and single-mindedness characteristic of philosophic eros in the *Symposium* also describe the attitude of classical friends toward each other. The eros that drives each individual toward the good (including truth itself) is the basis for the *philia* (friendship) they share. Since their passion for the good or truth is intense, their friendship is proportionately so. In the *Phaedrus* Socrates portrays philosophical friendship as the outcome of the lovers' romantic involvement with one another, a love affair that perfects them through philosophical *anamnesis* (recollection) even as it renders them unintelligible to the nonlovers or spectators (256b–e; 249c–e). This erotic love is characterized as divine madness, a true friendship of virtue. From Smith's standpoint, this is altogether too dangerous, too distorting, too susceptible to human madness and loss of perspective.[8] On Aristotle's classic account, a friend is a second self (*NE* 1166a30–3), that is, all friendships are modes of friendship with oneself. On Smith's account, this risks collapsing into self-love and thus self-delusion. That is, the classical ideal of love has here divided into self-interest or self-love, on the one hand, and friendship or sociality on the other.

As portrayed by classical philosophers such as Plato and Aristotle, true

---

7 Were this a discussion of classical friendship, I would draw distinctions between Plato and Aristotle here, calling attention to passages such as *NE* 9.7 on love toward one's works, 8.9 on community as the essence of friendship, and of course the issue of the self-sufficiency of the wise described in 10.7.

8 As if in confirmation of Smith's worries, the famous account of eros in the *Symposium* is delivered by a priestess (Diotima), referred to as an initiation into mysteries and cast as a narrative about a beloved's induction into mysterious secrets barely intelligible even to Socrates, who is Diotima's student.

friends do not adopt the social perspective because to a large extent their friendship is measured by the degree to which they distance themselves from the gaze of the spectator. For this reason classical friends, like lovers, may first appear ridiculous, then dangerous. But unlike the situation with lovers, there are no public social institutions, such as marriage, by means of which classical friends may be opened to and measured by the spectator's view. Or even if such institutions are created – perhaps the Academy is one such place – the problem of the political role of the love of wisdom, in particular, remains. Smith ends up, then, separating self-love from self-approbation, erotic love from friendship of virtue, and finally friendships of virtue from philosophy. When Smith refers to "men of virtue," he does not mean philosophers. He has in mind what Aristotle would have called "gentlemen," persons of outstanding moral virtue for whom theoretical matters are of comparatively little consequence. Smith rehearses the charge that Marcus Aurelius neglected the Roman empire in favor of philosophical speculation; Smith implies that this would be a damaging accusation, for "the most sublime speculation of the contemplative philosopher can scarce compensate the neglect of the smallest active duty" (VI.ii.3.6).

Potentially dangerous kinds of love, then, risk blinding moral spectatorship on self or other. They close off perspective, detachment, or what one might call – keeping in mind both the literal Greek sense of *theoria* as "looking at" or "viewing" and the double sense of "reflection" – "reflective theoria." On Smith's account, love and "reflective theoria" must always be combined if love is to be healthy; or more precisely, the actor must always in principle be visible through sympathy to other onlookers. Although it preserves the classical (especially the Platonic) emphasis on the primacy of vision, this account is nevertheless deeply antiphilosophical, from that ancient standpoint, in that it closes off the highest sort of *theoria*, namely, the passionate contemplation of things that are forever outside of all society – the Forms or self-contemplating God. These highest objects of love are not like mirrors, and contemplation of them is not a way of seeing oneself reflected, or of viewing oneself. As Plato especially stresses, the highest form of love consists in the soul's complete absorption in an intelligible object that does not itself return the soul's gaze, in nonreflective "theoria." Philosophy escapes the *theatrum mundi*. Smith's way of connecting spectatorship and love, by contrast, makes this undesirable. In the end he keeps self-approbation from straying too far from the social, or the theoretical virtue from overawing the practical. Divine madness is not liberated from moderation.

For reasons of humanity, Smith reins in the urge to transcendence so that it stays within the circle of sympathy, within the dialectic of recognition. At least from the Platonic perspective, the lack of escape to the solitude of noetic contemplation constitutes the ultimate *pathos* of the human condition. For Smith, the realization that the *theatrum mundi* is home means liberation from the darkness of fanaticism and conflict; for Plato, it means confinement to the cave, however many fires may dissipate the shadows, and however elegantly and synoptically "philosophical" one may be in one's removed balcony up on the side of the structure. Smith limits the erotic love of wisdom in order to safeguard love and friendship, and this is intrinsic to his effort to alleviate the human estate and to propagate the virtues of enlightenment rightly understood. The intended result is moderation political and ethical. Smith's skepticism of traditional Platonic views of philosophy has an ethical motivation, then; but it also has other motivations, in tune with a sense of "philosophy" that differs from the Platonic. What more might be said about the character of Smith's skepticism?

## 2. SMITH AND SKEPTICISM

And again, just as it is not impossible for the man who has ascended to a high place by a ladder to overturn the ladder with his foot after his ascent, so also it is not unlikely that the Sceptic after he has arrived at the demonstration of his thesis by means of the argument proving the non-existence of proof, as it were by a step-ladder, should then abolish this very argument.

Sextus Empiricus[9]

Smith's "history of moral philosophy" in Part VII of *The Theory of Moral Sentiments* contains some remarkable omissions.[10] The discussion is strikingly selective, both in terms of topics and of philosophers mentioned. Thematically, Smith almost entirely omits Plato's metaphysics, even though the theory of Forms is intimately connected, in the *Republic*, with the ethics. A similar pattern occurs with the treatment of Aristotle and the Stoics. Smith refers to the *Nicomachean Ethics* with approval but in

9 *Against the Logicians (Adversus mathematicos)* VIII 481, in vol. 2 of *Sextus Empiricus*, trans. R. G. Bury (Cambridge, Mass.: Harvard University Press, 1968). (This four-volume edition of Sextus is used throughout.)
10 He refers to Part VII as "concerning the History of moral Philosophy" in a letter to T. Cadell, Mar. 15, 1788 (*CAS*, pp. 310–11).

fact calls upon only a small segment of that book. In general, he shows scarcely any interest here in the epistemological and metaphysical views of his predecessors. He proceeds as though ethics were a discipline that has been undertaken in isolation from these other fields. That this is, to say the least, a selective approach to the history of moral philosophy cannot have escaped his attention.[11] Moreover, he himself proceeds as though the isolation is warranted: *The Theory of Moral Sentiments* is not part of an articulated metaphysical or epistemological system, and Smith did not publish a book on metaphysics or epistemology (though it is possible that some form of theorizing about such topics – in particular, about sense perception – might have been included in the projected *corpus*).

Perhaps the most striking omission in Part VII concerns the skeptics. Indeed, Smith does not explicitly discuss skepticism in any of his writings, and, to the best of my knowledge, he is not reported as mentioning the term in any of his lectures on any subject or in his correspondence. He does use the term "sceptical" in one crucial passage, to be examined shortly. Yet skepticism and issues concerning skeptical ethics were alive and well in his time, thanks in good part to Bayle, Montaigne, Shaftesbury, Berkeley, and above all Hume (whose work provoked Beattie, Kames, Oswald, and Reid, among others, to much discussion about the subject).[12] Schneewind notes that "Pyrrhonic skepticism was a major con-

---

11  Smith discusses aspects of Plato's and Aristotle's metaphysics in "The Principles which Lead and Direct Philosophical Enquiries; illustrated by the History of the Ancient Logics and Metaphysics," in *EPS*. When Smith comments on metaphysics, it is to criticize (p. 125). See also his "Considerations Concerning the First Formation of Languages" (also entitled "A Dissertation on the Origin of Languages"), in *LRBL*, esp. pp. 214, 219, 221; and *LRBL*, pp. 10–11, on the mistaken "metaphysical" use of propositions.

12  On the reintroduction of skepticism at the dawn of the Enlightenment, see R. Popkin, "The Revival of Greek Scepticism in the Sixteenth Century," in Popkin, *The History of Scepticism from Erasmus to Spinoza* (Berkeley and Los Angeles: University of California Press, 1979), pp. 18–41; C. B. Schmitt, "The Rediscovery of Ancient Skepticism in Modern Times," in *The Skeptical Tradition*, ed. M. Burnyeat (Berkeley and Los Angeles: University of California Press, 1983), pp. 225–51; and M. A. Stewart, "The Stoic Legacy in the Early Scottish Enlightenment," in *Atoms, Pneuma, and Tranquillity: Epicurean and Stoic Themes in European Thought*, ed. M. J. Osler (Cambridge: Cambridge University Press, 1991), pp. 273: "In Scottish thought in the eighteenth century we find something of a reenactment of the ancient debates between Stoics and Skeptics." Hume is a key figure in the reenactment. On p. 288 Stewart remarks: "The seventeenth century, then, far from rejecting the ancients as Bacon had seemed to recommend, restored to the public curriculum the three schools of thought [Stoic, Epicurean, Skeptic] which had competed against Aristotelianism in the ancient world." Smith possessed Sextus Empiricus's writings as well as Montaigne's *Essays*.

cern for philosophy in the seventeenth century and not least for moral philosophy."[13] The intellectual atmosphere in which Smith wrote was saturated with the topic of skepticism. As in the related case of his decision not to mention, in *The Theory of Moral Sentiments*, the name of Hume – the great skeptic to whom Smith elsewhere refers as "by far the most illustrious philosopher and historian of the present age" (*WN* V.i.g.3), a man who obviously commanded Smith's attention, friendship, and respect – his silence about skepticism is best interpreted as deliberate.

Indications of the influence of skepticism on Smith's philosophy are not difficult to find, even if the word and its cognates are almost entirely absent. To begin with, his account restricts the role that reason plays in ethical evaluation. Reason can formulate general rules of morality and deliberate about means to an end. In both respects, reason permeates moral reflection, but it does not provide us with "the first perceptions of right and wrong."[14] Smith writes:

> Reason may show that this object [any particular object] is the means of obtaining some other which is naturally either pleasing or displeasing, and in this manner may render it either agreeable or disagreeable for the sake of something else. But nothing can be agreeable or disagreeable for its own sake, which is not rendered such by immediate sense and feeling. If virtue, therefore, in every particular instance, necessarily pleases for its own sake, and if vice as certainly displeases the mind, it cannot be reason, but immediate sense and feeling, which, in this manner, reconciles us to the one, and alienates us from the other. (VII.iii.2.7)

Passages such as this require careful interpretation in their context, for as we have seen in discussing sympathy and the "impartial spectator," it would be misleading to characterize Smith's moral theory as simply noncognitivist or emotivist. Nonetheless, it should be granted at the outset that he rejects ethical rationalism understood as the doctrine that moral qualities are apprehended through reason alone.

A moral theory could restrict the role that reason plays in moral judgment but still be objectivist, in the sense of holding that moral values exist independently of our means of apprehending them. Smith, however, associates ethical rationalism with moral realism (VII.iii.2.1–9), and

---

13 J. B. Schneewind, "Natural Law, Skepticism, and Methods of Ethics," *Journal of the History of Ideas* 52 (1991), p. 294.
14 VII.iii.2.7. Smith also remarks: "The general maxims of morality are formed, like all other general maxims, from experience and induction" (VII.iii.2.6).

in light of the history of moral philosophy the association is not unnatural. Reason is easily seen as grasping objective, mind-independent "moral facts," and the emotions or sentiments as expressing "subjective" dispositions. Judged according to that outlook, Smith's account of morality in terms of the emotions is subjectivist, in the sense that the meaning of moral terms is determined by what pleases or displeases the impartial spectator and not by some altogether external standard or state of affairs. It is clear that for Smith, not only do we know no answers to questions about what "really" is good or bad independent of the *considered* responses of "our" emotions, but also that moral qualities are "rendered" such by the reflective moral sentiments. To overstate the point for the sake of clarity, morality is not a mirror of the world but a result of our responses to the world. It does not follow that moral judgment is merely "relative" to the individual or even to culture in any sense that blocks meaningful adjudication of competing judgments, let alone that reason and reflection have no important role to play in moral judgment.[15] Like the ancient skeptics but unlike other classical moral philosophers, to be sure, Smith does not argue that most people are ethically confused in a way that, for the most part, a *philosophical* theory could or should clear up (say, by providing knowledge of the Good and the Beautiful by which they order their lives).[16] But the alternative to such knowledge is not irrationalism; it is understanding and reflection conceived of as part of the resources of prephilosophical human life.

At the beginning of *The Theory of Moral Sentiments* Smith tells us that debates in philosophy, and similar subjects, are of little practical value (I.i.4.5). When he turns to the moral psychology question at the end of the book, he makes an additional observation: "the question concerning the nature of virtue necessarily has some influence upon our notions of right and wrong in many particular cases. That concerning the principle of approbation can possibly have no such effect. To examine from what contrivance or mechanism within, those different notions or sentiments arise, is a mere matter of philosophical curiosity" (VII.iii.intro.3). The

---

15 Smith is not a moral skeptic in the sense defined by M. Singer, for whom the various moral skeptics "agree in maintaining, in one way or another, that there can be no such thing as a good reason for a moral judgment, that there are no valid moral arguments, that morality has no rational basis, and that the difference between right and wrong is merely a matter of taste, opinion, or convention." Quoted in D. F. Norton, *David Hume: Common-Sense Moralist, Sceptical Metaphysician* (Princeton: Princeton University Press, 1982), p. 12, n. 26.

16 On the point about the ancient schools, see J. Annas, *The Morality of Happiness* (Oxford: Oxford University Press, 1993), pp. 359–60.

virtue question is, then, also a "practical" one; it affects our notions of right and wrong and might be expected to influence our behavior. The moral psychology question, by contrast, is supposed to be a purely theoretical one.

Smith sets limits to reason in other contexts as well. In his narration in *The Wealth of Nations* of great historical developments, such as the emergence of freedom of religion, he makes it clear that the "feeble efforts of human reason" played a limited role (V.i.g.24). Of course, his famous notion of the "invisible hand" expresses, among other things, the extent to which the world is subject to unforeseeable ironies. Smith details the counterproductive nature of state efforts to intervene heavily in the economy according to some master plan (*WN* IV.ix.51). As will be discussed in detail in Chapter 7, in thus emphasizing the epistemic limitations of the state, so to speak, he affirms the importance of the individual's liberty to choose and decide about how to dispose of his or her labor. In *The Theory of Moral Sentiments* he criticizes the "man of system" who tries to implement an abstract philosophical scheme for social organization and improvement and treats others as pieces on a chessboard. This is not only unjust, Smith argues, but unworkable (*TMS* VI.ii.2.17). His writings on the history of science and philosophy, to which I return in a moment, also attest to a broadly skeptical view. Further, he expresses a Voltairean contempt for theology and for theologically inspired metaphysics and ontology (*WN* V.i.f.28–9).

It therefore is no surprise that interpreters of Smith have referred to his thought as being "skeptical" in one respect or another.[17] Indeed, Schneewind has not only described important modern instances of a type of Pyrrhonist skepticism in ethics, but has also suggested that Smith continues in the same vein.[18] The precise meaning of such terms, and the

17 E.g., see D. Winch's discussion of the "sceptical qualities" of Smith's thinking, "which unite him with Hume in eschewing large-scale extrapolation into an unknowable future." *Riches and Poverty* (Cambridge: Cambridge University Press, 1996), p. 123. Also Haakonssen, *The Science of a Legislator*, p. 81, and his "What Might Properly Be Called Natural Jurisprudence?" in *The Origins and Nature of the Scottish Enlightenment*, ed. R. H. Campbell and A. S. Skinner (Edinburgh: Donald, 1982), p. 221.

18 See Schneewind, "Natural Law, Skepticism, and Methods of Ethics." He argues that for Hume, as for Shaftesbury and Hutcheson, "there is no source of rightness in action other than a motive which receives the felt approval of our moral faculty" (p. 299) and that this may be seen as a "skeptic's method of ethics" in the Pyrrhonist tradition. He also refers to this as a " 'constitutive' method of ethics" (p. 298). Schneewind thinks that *TMS* "offers a complex version of the skeptical method" (p. 299, n. 34) and argues that Kant does as well. I am offering an interpretation of Smith's complex version of the method. Schneewind does not here claim that the thinkers he interprets as following the

relation of Smithean skepticism to the skeptical tradition, are complex issues. The interpretation of both ancient and Humean skepticism is a matter of controversy, and the interpretation of ancient skepticism by modern writers on the subject is also a complicated matter.[19] For present purposes we may rely on plausible construals of those positions in order to illuminate an interpretation of Smith. My discussion of the role of skepticism in Smith's thought may be taken as a reconstruction of the general frame of his philosophy. It is not an "argument from silence," nor simply an argument about his silence – though it is that derivatively – but an interpretation of what he does say.

I have mentioned several indications of the influence of skepticism on Smith's work. When the moral system as a whole is considered, another aspect of his skepticism becomes evident. In good Pyrrhonist form, Smith is holding that morality is best understood within the confines of the "appearances" (that is, the phenomena) as they show themselves to ordinary agents. As we have seen, morality is grounded in reflective moral sentiments, these being communicated or grasped through sympathy. As was said at the conclusion of Chapter 3, the impartial spectator is ultimately constitutive of morality.[20] The implications of the theory of moral sentiments are clear: value is something we determine for ourselves, without recourse to philosophically mysterious entities lodged outside of the this-worldly phenomena of human life. Recall Smith's remark "But nothing can be agreeable or disagreeable for its own sake, which is not rendered such by immediate sense and feeling" (VII.iii.2.7) and his point that

> there is no appeal from the eye with regard to the beauty of colours, nor from the ear with regard to the harmony of sounds, nor from the taste with regard to the agreeableness of flavours. . . . The very essence of each of those qualities consists in its being fitted to please the sense to which it is addressed. It belongs to our moral faculties, in the same manner to

skeptical method characterized themselves in just such terms. I have already intimated that Smith does not explicitly characterize himself as a skeptic.

19  Hume's interpretation of ancient skepticism (and hence the manner in which he sees his own position as related to it) is distorted. See Norton, *Hume*, pp. 266–7, and M. Frede, "The Sceptic's Two Kinds of Assent," in *Philosophy in History*, ed. R. Rorty, J. B. Schneewind, and Q. Skinner (Cambridge: Cambridge University Press, 1990), p. 277. Beyond distinguishing between the "dogmatic" and the "nondogmatic" skeptic, I shall not compare the positions of the classical skeptics, because so fine-grained an analysis of classical skepticism is unnecessary for present purposes.

20  Smith's view as here described is consonant with Schneewind's description of the skeptical method; see p. 300 of "Natural Law, Skepticism, and Methods of Ethics."

determine when the ear ought to be soothed, when the eye ought to be indulged, when the taste ought to be gratified, when and how far every other principle of our nature ought either to be indulged or restrained. What is agreeable to our moral faculties, is fit, and right, and proper to be done; the contrary wrong, unfit, and improper. The sentiments which they approve of, are graceful and becoming: the contrary, ungraceful and unbecoming. The very words, right, wrong, fit, improper, graceful, unbecoming, mean only what pleases or displeases those faculties. (III.5.5)

This is just to say that ultimately morality must be understood as arising "from us," not as established by nature or the divine.[21] For given the limits of reason, those nonhuman or suprahuman sources are impenetrable by us, as far as an account of value goes. We are therefore left with the one remaining, in principle intelligible, source. Just as morals pertain to "what passes in our neighbourhood" and "the affairs of the very parish which we live in" (VII.ii.4.14), so too any intelligible understanding of the source of value must attend to one we can know, namely, ourselves. The orientation by the "appearances" or "phenomena" shapes not only Smith's virtue theory but also his moral psychology and hence its view that value is in some sense of our making.

Further, he holds that intellectual systems are to be analogously understood, as his writings on the history of philosophy and science (reproduced in *EPS*) show. As he puts it in a passage to be discussed shortly, he takes himself as having analyzed "all philosophical systems as mere inventions of the imagination." Not just our confinement to the ap-

---

21 Cf. Hume, "The Sceptic," in *Essays Moral, Political, and Literary*, p. 162: "If we can depend upon any principle, which we learn from philosophy, this, I think, may be considered as certain and undoubted, that there is nothing, in itself, valuable or despicable, desirable or hateful, beautiful or deformed; but that these attributes arise from the particular constitution and fabric of human sentiment and affection" (also p. 166, "Objects have absolutely no worth or value in themselves"). See also Hume's argument in the *Treatise* that the viciousness of an action or character "lies in yourself, not in the object. So that when you pronounce any action or character to be vicious, you mean nothing, but that from the constitution of your nature you have a feeling or sentiment of blame from the contemplation of it. Vice and virtue, therefore, may be compar'd to sounds, colours, heat and cold, which, according to modern philosophy, are not qualities in objects, but perceptions in the mind" (*T* 468–9). In the first appendix to the *Enquiry Concerning the Principles of Morals* he says that aesthetic and moral taste "has a productive faculty, and gilding or staining all natural objects with the colours, borrowed from internal sentiment, raises in a manner a new creation" (p. 294). However, the analogy between color and moral qualities (and so between color perception and the apprehension of value) does not, in spite of Smith's reference to color at III.5.5, figure prominently in his characterizations of the manner in which value is dependent on us. In Chapter 5 I say more about the role of "perception" in Smith's theory.

pearances but their being "rendered" or shaped by us are the obverse of the restricted role of philosophical reason. Correspondingly, Smith (like Hume) gives a large role to the imagination. The imagination is key to explaining this "rendering," and its importance in Smith's account follows from the skeptical framework.

The features of Smith's rhetoric that so aptly express his moral psychology and virtue theory dovetail with his skepticism. His appeal to experience and ordinary life, his multivocal use of the protreptic "we," his understanding of moral philosophy as "criticism," his use of the metaphor of the theater, the structure of *The Theory of Moral Sentiments* (including the discontinuity between Part VII and the preceding parts), and his avoidance of classical metaphysical and epistemological vocabulary and issues fit well with a skeptical view. These features mesh with Smith's insistence on the importance of virtue, judgment, context and particular, and his argument (to be explored in Chapter 5) that general rules arise out of experience. In expressing the view that ethical theory must be worked up from "within," from an "internal" perspective on life, rather than being derived from *a priori* first principles, these features of Smith's rhetoric fit nicely with the sort of skepticism under discussion.[22]

My reconstruction of his metaphilosophical stance helps us to see why his own essays on reason took the form of *histories* of astronomy, physics, and logic, meant to "illustrate" the "Principles which Lead and Direct Philosophical Enquiries." By extension, it also helps us to see why one branch of the missing *corpus* was to be (in my phrase) a "Philosophical History of the Liberal Sciences and Elegant Arts." Rather than setting out a metaphysics or ontology, a skeptic of this kind would describe the history of successes and failures of others who conducted philosophical inquiries. The skeptic would rely on a narrative about the attractiveness of certain types of explanations in terms of the operation of the "intellectual sentiments" and the imagination, as these sentiments of curiosity, surprise, wonder, astonishment, and the like seek to create a unified story accounting for the varied phenomena in question. Issues of rhetoric, aesthetics, and the expectations of inquirers would come to the fore, and do come to the fore in Smith's surviving essays on the matter. A skeptic of this kind would likely be attracted to the study of language

---

22 Annas notes that Sextus Empiricus frequently presents himself "as being on the side of *bios* or 'Life,' against the philosophers' abstractions." *Morality of Happiness*, p. 354.

as the medium within which the intelligible "appearances" arise. A study of the evolution and uses of language might shed light on how "metaphysical" talk arose in such a natural way and would seek an account of linguistic meaning that does not depend on "Platonic" assumptions. Especially given Smith's interest in rhetoric, such a study might also help to explain how norms shape and are shaped by the sentiments and sympathy, how (also in circular fashion) they arise out of as well as embed themselves in collective life. Smith was unmistakably attracted by the prospect of such a "linguistic turn," which may help to explain why he attached to *The Theory of Moral Sentiments* (starting with the third edition) an early essay entitled "A Dissertation on the Origin of Languages."[23]

At this stage a distinction ought to be underlined. The part of the "Philosophical History" we have does not amount to an argument in favor of the view that "objective reality" or the essential structure of things is *unknowable*. Smith nowhere supplies an argument of that sort. What he has sought to provide in his essays on the history of science and philosophy, as well as in his moral philosophy, political economy, and (if students' notes can be trusted) his jurisprudence and rhetorical theory are plausible positive accounts of human activity that simply drop classical metaphysical, theological, and connected epistemological issues. This suggests another sense in which Smith's skepticism is in the tradition of Pyrrhonist thought: he proceeds in the manner of a nondogmatic skeptic who avoids providing theories as to whether reality can or cannot be known, or as to whether moral judgments *really* reflect the timeless essence of perfected "human nature."[24] A skeptic of this kind does not

23 The essay was first published in 1761 and is now reproduced in *LRBL*. Smith's discussion of the evolution of language makes clear that linguistic forms are "invented" (a favorite verb in the essay) through a process that is shaped by contingencies (such as the meshing of different languages due to historical circumstance and the invention of writing), unforeseen consequences (invisible-hand effects), and principles of psychology. The essay is a sort of conjectural or natural history of the formation of speech and thought, thanks to which the creation of "metaphysics" can be both understood and seen as a compelling illusion. A similar point is made in his essay on the history of ancient logic and metaphysics (*EPS*, p. 125). For a good discussion of Smith's view of language and inquiry, see Lindgren, *The Social Philosophy of Adam Smith*, ch. 1 ("Inquiry"). Lindgren remarks that for Smith "the way in which things and people are or may be related to one another, independently of our conventional schemes, does not fall within the range of human knowledge" (p. 6).

24 Cf. Hume's statement at the end of the appendix to the *Treatise:* "As long as we confine our speculations to *the appearances* of objects to our senses, without entering into disquisitions concerning their real nature and operations, we are safe from all difficulties, and

have a "philosophical position" on these matters; he or she seeks to "suspend judgment" on the entire controversy. In practice this skeptic is guided by various nonphilosophical sources, including natural impulses, laws, customs, knowledge of the arts, and feelings, by how things "appear." Nonetheless, even within these constraints the skeptic could claim to have conceptions about things.[25] For example, Sextus talks about things appearing to reason and about objects of thought as appearances. When engaging in philosophical argument with a realist, this kind of skeptic may even adopt the linguistic practices of his opponent and argue ad hominem, but without affirming these practices as his own.[26] Sextus tells us that the skeptic does not doubt the appearances so much as (dogmatic) *logoi* that have been given of the appearances (*PH* I 19). This leaves open the possibility that a skeptic can (as the word indicates) inquire about the appearances, putting together explanations in terms that are familiar and satisfy the imagination.[27]

By contrast, a different kind of skeptic, the negative or dogmatic skeptic, has a position – say, that nothing in morals can be known objectively – that he or she defends as being the case. This is simply one philosophical position among others. This negative or dogmatic position would be compatible with holding that in the realm of nonmoral facts (as studied by the natural sciences, for example) we may possess "positive" knowledge about how things "really" are.

I am suggesting that with respect to the issue of the philosophical argument about classical metaphysical and theological issues, Smith's skepticism is best interpreted as an elaboration of the sort of nondogmatic skepticism described by Sextus Empiricus rather than as negative or dogmatic skepticism. In that it is skeptical across the board, Smith's

---

can never be embarrass'd by any question" (*T* 638). On my interpretation, Smith is adopting this Humean stance while adding that the same holds true of any appearances to our emotions or intellect and that "disquisitions" should be taken to mean "philosophical analyses."

25 At least, Sextus Empiricus does so in *Outlines of Pyrrhonism* II.10. (Cited hereafter as *PH*.) On the "various non-philosophical sources," see *PH* I.23–4, 145–63, 231. See also M. Burnyeat, "Can the Skeptic Live his Skepticism?", in *The Skeptical Tradition*, pp. 127–8, for references. Cf. Sextus's distinction between two senses of "dogma," as referring to the nonevident, and in an everyday sense as approval of something, at *PH* I 13; the skeptic can have the latter but not the former.

26 See Frede, "The Skeptic's Two Kinds of Assent," in Rorty et al., eds., *Philosophy in History*, pp. 255–78, esp. p. 258, for a description of this point and more generally of the two kinds of skepticism.

27 See Sextus's comments about skepticism and the "methodic" school of medicine. *PH* I 236–41.

skepticism again resembles that of Sextus.[28] Smith's account of theorizing in science, philosophy, and ethics is of a piece and appeals throughout to the "sentiments" and to the imagination. He is not so much "antifoundationalist" (in the current jargon) as he is self-consciously nonfoundationalist. He proceeds as though he has simply suspended judgment about classical philosophical disputes of the sort just described. Hence in *The Theory of Moral Sentiments* he presents us with a view of the matter that makes appeal, through constant use of examples literary and other, to "our" sensibilities and singles out various principles (such as "sympathy") that explain the operations of the moral sentiments. His skepticism concerns the limits of reason and makes place for, rather than undermines the possibility of, a positive philosophy within those limits.

A significant difference between Pyrrhonist and Smithean skepticism must now be noted. Smith does not hold that as moral actors we normally treat morality as a skeptic would. Rather, we act as though commonsense moral realism were valid, that is, as though moral qualities exist objectively in the nature of things, are external to us and claim authority over us. As he says in the passages I quoted, virtue is taken to please "for its own sake." Smith does not say whether people act as though a moderated form of ethical rationalism (understood as the view that ethical qualities are grasped by reason, perhaps in conjunction with emotion) were also sound, but nothing in his account prevents it, and his analysis of ethical reasoning and judgment supports a species of moderated ethical rationalism. In practice, then, we are not moral skeptics.[29]

Smith's statements about the limited practical import of philosophy are sufficiently general to include his own philosophical framework, which therefore in its impact is supposed to be limited to the realm of theory. In this respect, his skepticism is of the Humean rather than Pyrrhonist variety, for, as in Hume, the argument implies that skeptical theorizing ought not to budge our everyday beliefs.[30] Indeed, the remarks

---

28 I am not saying that Smith's strategy is the same as that of Sextus; e.g., Part VII of *TMS* does not present us with arguments from conflicting appearances, or "equipollence" arguments. And, as we will see, Smith rejects Sextus's view that one ought to *live* as a skeptic (and so that one ought to live without assenting to anything that goes beyond the appearances).

29 Shaftesbury discussed the distinction between moral and epistemological skepticisms and also claimed that one could be a skeptic on all matters of philosophical speculation and yet be entirely religious and moral. (See Norton's discussion in *Hume*, pp. 241–2.)

30 See Hume, *Enquiry Concerning Human Understanding*, pp. 159–60, and *T* 183, 264–74. On living "undogmatically," see Sextus, *PH* I 23, 226, 231; II 246, 254, 258; III 235; also the distinction between two senses of "dogma" at I.13. It is possible that Sextus had

about the moral sentiments that Hume puts into the mouth of the skeptic sound in several respects rather like Smith's own views.[31] Smith does not think that moral agents should judge with the consciousness that "objective" values in fact originate in the emotions (as Smith's moral psychology itself teaches), as though moral agents should live with skeptical inner detachment from their own values.

Combining Smith's view of the "realism" that moral qualities are taken to possess in ordinary moral life, his view that theoretical debates about such things as moral psychology lack motivating purchase on agents, and his view of the centrality of imaginative sympathy to moral life, we may infer that he would agree with the classic *apraxia* argument against skepticism – the argument that the doctrine cannot in practice

room for something like nondogmatic belief. For a powerful argument to the effect that Sextus did not mean to assert that the skeptic lives without *any* beliefs, see Frede's "The Skeptic's Beliefs," in Frede, *Essays in Ancient Philosophy* (Minneapolis: University of Minnesota Press, 1987), pp. 179–200. On this view, the skeptic's assertion that we can act without beliefs is a move in the dialectic with the dogmatist (cf. *PH* I 20) and assumes a dogmatic sense of "belief." The skeptic finds it desirable and possible to live without beliefs about how things "really" are and suspends judgment about attempts of reason to uncover this reality behind the appearances (cf. *PH* I 215). The skeptic nevertheless has beliefs about how things are (and they appear to him as being this or that way). This in turn assumes that ordinary beliefs need not be, or need not explicitly rely on, theoretical or philosophical doctrines about "reality." As Frede notes, that assumption may differentiate the manner in which skeptics and "ordinary" persons hold beliefs. The distinction lies in their respective "attitudes" toward their beliefs, the skeptic's being less dogmatic. "The Skeptic's Beliefs," p. 199. This interpretation of the skeptic complicates the contrast with Smith, but ultimately Smith would deny that as ordinary moral agents we can or should live holding moral beliefs toward which we take some special, nondogmatic, skeptically detached attitude.

31 I refer to Hume, "The Sceptic," in *Essays Moral, Political, and Literary*, pp. 169 ff., on the limited practical scope of philosophy. On p. 166 (n. 3) Hume remarks: "Were I not afraid of appearing too philosophical, I should remind my reader of that famous doctrine, supposed to be fully proved in modern times, 'That tastes and colours, and all other sensible qualities, lie not in the bodies, but merely in the senses.' The case is the same with beauty and deformity, virtue and vice. This doctrine, however, takes off no more from the reality of the latter qualities, than from that of the former; nor need it give any umbrage either to critics or moralists. Though colours were allowed to lie only in the eye, would dyers or painters ever be less regarded or esteemed? There is a sufficient uniformity in the senses and feelings of mankind, to make all these qualities the objects of art and reasoning, and to have the greatest influence on life and manners. And as it is certain, that the discovery above-mentioned in natural philosophy, makes no alteration on action and conduct; why should a like discovery in moral philosophy make an alteration?" Moreover, Hume puts into the mouth of the skeptic a complaint about the tendency of philosophers to force their "favourite principle" to account for the phenomena (p. 159), a charge that Smith makes against various philosophers, as we saw in Chapter 1.

be lived or acted upon.[32] We do not live the life of a skeptic, for we do not live without "dogmatic" belief. But beliefs are primarily the products of our reflective "sentiments," not our philosophical reason, and thus are neither likely to be dislodged by attacks on philosophical reason nor guided by such reason. We do not live by philosophical theory (whether skeptical or not) alone. Hence the Smithean theorist views others and himself through the eyes of a detached philosophical spectator but does not live through those eyes; his theorizing self is detached from his active self.[33]

Presumably Smith does not believe that his discussion will transform us into skeptics even on the level of theorizing. In his discussion of the relationship between theory and practice early in the book, Smith declares that "we approve of another man's judgment [about "the subjects of science and taste"] not as something useful, but as right, as accurate, as agreeable to truth and reality: and it is evident we attribute those qualities to it for no other reason but because we find that it agrees with our own." That is, although *in fact* another person's judgment appeals to us because it fits with our own disposition and persuasively addresses our "intellectual sentiments" of surprise, wonder, and admiration, we talk *as though* the appeal rested on the correspondence between a judgment and reality, without our being continually aware that this is just an "as though" (I.i.4.4).[34] Appraising "theory" is in principle no more and

32 The *apraxia* argument holds that no one can actually live as a skeptic; skepticism is not a doctrine that can be embodied in practice. Sextus responds to this argument by stating that "in arguing thus they do not comprehend that the Sceptic does not conduct his life according to philosophical theory (for so far as regards this he is inactive), but as regards the non-philosophic regulation of life he is capable of desiring some things and avoiding others," and then goes on to illustrate with the skeptic's response to a tyrant's orders. The skeptic is not reduced to "inactivity" or to becoming "like a vegetable." See *Against the Ethicists:* 162–6. J. Annas notes that ancient moral skepticism is "profoundly subversive of everyday life"; the skeptic claims that the agent "becomes the uncommitted spectator of his own actions and his own impulses." "Doing without Objective Values: Ancient and Modern Strategies," in *The Norms of Nature,* ed. M. Schofield and G. Striker (Cambridge: Cambridge University Press, 1986), p. 22. Smith would agree that *this* kind of spectatorship is subversive and therefore to be avoided on ethical grounds.

33 Up to a point, Smith's view fits Annas's description of modern moral skepticism in which "there is not felt to be any conflict between accepting arguments that render one skeptical about morality, and yet acting on firmly held moral beliefs." In "Doing without Objective Values," p. 26. As we will see, though, Smith is doubtful that a separation of theory and practice can be antiseptic.

34 As to the meaning of "reality," and more broadly of the kind of ethical realism that Smith is dropping as a *theoretical* doctrine, see P. Butchvarov, *Skepticism in Ethics* (Bloomington: Indiana University Press, 1989), p. 3: "Very roughly, I shall mean by unqualified realism with respect to x the view that (1) x exists and has certain properties, a nature,

no less "objective" a matter than appraising moral judgments. On Smith's account, the basis of our agreement with convictions and opinions of another, and that of our agreement about moral matters, are in this respect analogous (I.i.3.2).[35] Similarly, he does not expect that by and large we will suspend belief, even in the course of our theoretical endeavors; rather, we will see our beliefs as rationally grounded in mind-independent "reality." At the end of the day we will not be detached from our theoretical beliefs, except in those moments when we compel ourselves to think philosophically and without blinkers.

A remarkable passage in his discussion of philosophy and science makes just this point and, not coincidentally, mentions skepticism. The passage occurs on the last page of the essay on the history of astronomy (which is to be found in the posthumously published *Essays on Philosophical Subjects*). Referring to Newton, Smith suggests that the more satisfying to the intellectual imagination a proposed system is, the more likely we are to take the system as describing how things are objectively, independent of the human mind:

> And even we, while we have been endeavouring to represent all philosophical systems as mere inventions of the imagination, to connect together the otherwise disjointed and discordant phaenomena of nature, have insensibly been drawn in, to make use of language expressing the connecting principles of this one [Newton's system], as if they were the

and (2) that its existence and nature are independent of our awareness of it, (3) of the manner in which we think of (conceptualize) it, and (4) of the manner in which we speak of it." At least in seeing objective morality through the lens of a moral psychology according to which morality is originated by us, and in seeing that psychology as a second-order explanatory doctrine, Smith's theory has affinities with S. Blackburn's Humean "quasi realism" view, a summary of which may be found in Blackburn, "Errors in the Phenomenology of Value," reprinted in *Morality and the Good Life*, ed. T. Carson and P. Moser (Oxford: Oxford University Press, 1997), pp. 324–37. But as I shall suggest, Smith would share the "unease" about the "tension between the subjective source which projectivism gives to morality, and the objective 'feel' that a properly working morality has" (Blackburn, p. 327). What Smith's version of "projectivism" (if that is the right term) comes down to, i.e., how the moral psychology actually works, might not be accepted by Blackburn at any number of junctures. And talk of "projection" would, for Smith, have to be carefully modulated so as not to suppress the roles of receptivity and responsiveness, as my discussion of sympathy in Chapter 2 of the present volume suggests.

35 As Smith summarizes his thesis: "Every faculty in one man is the measure by which he judges of the like faculty in another. I judge of your sight by my sight, of your ear by my ear, of your reason by my reason, of your resentment by my resentment, of your love by my love. I neither have, nor can have, any other way of judging about them" (I.i.3.10). In the chapter immediately following this remark, the relevant analogy between the basis for theoretical and practical concordance is further developed.

real chains which Nature makes use of to bind together her several operations.

Indeed, "the most *sceptical* cannot avoid feeling this," he remarks here.[36] Since *The Theory of Moral Sentiments* is an example of Smithean theorizing, presumably he expects it to be treated on the whole as an attempt to represent how things really are, though when spectating upon his creation with detachment, he will see it as one of many "inventions of the imagination." Had he completed his "Philosophical History of all the different branches of Literature, of Philosophy, Poetry and Eloquence," the same description applied here to astronomy would have been extended to philosophy itself. In sum, he may be seen as assuming a double skepticism (one on the level of theory, the other on the level of practice), each of which usually is "insulated"[37] from our natural belief in the correspondence of judgments with "reality."

To this line of interpretation of Smith as a nondogmatic skeptic it may be objected that in offering positive theories he is far from being agnostic, since in setting them out he is making pronouncements about how things "really are." For example, in *The Theory of Moral Sentiments* (VII.iii.2.9) he declares that Hutcheson has decisively refuted the view that moral distinctions arise primarily from reason. Hence Smith has not (the objection continues) suspended judgment about whether or not these distinctions arise from reason; the entire book presents an account of their arising primarily from emotion. In response I note, to begin with, that Smith merely refers us here to Hutcheson's arguments without presenting them himself and rhetorically dismisses any disagreement on the subject as "superstitious attachment to certain forms of expression" or as showing ignorance of Hutcheson's writings. More persuasively, Smith's skepticism is in part an intellectual stance toward certain kinds of metaphysical arguments, in particular, those about "reality" and "substances" such as "Forms" and God, rather than toward arguments about

---

36 "The History of Astronomy," IV.76, in *EPS*, p. 105 (emphasis added). Haakonssen refers to this passage as a "very Humean piece of teasing, double-edged scepticism." *The Science of a Legislator*, p. 81. See also J. R. Lindgren, "Adam Smith's Theory of Inquiry," *Journal of Political Economy* 77 (1969), esp. pp. 900–1. Had Smith completed and published the branch of the *corpus* of which these essays would have formed part, we might possess more detailed and explicit reflections on the skepticism issue. For reasons given farther on in this chapter, though, Smith might have decided to avoid difficulties inherent in setting out a skeptical theory as his own.

37 The term is taken from M. Burnyeat, "The Sceptic in His Place and Time," in *Philosophy in History*, p. 225.

points of moral psychology. The skepticism is not contradicted by his providing a "positive" philosophy that moves within the appearances or phenomena of the *theatrum mundi* and makes judgments about better and worse explanations of the phenomena. He grants, as already mentioned, that as ordinary moral actors – and he frequently writes in that voice – we do not speak or act as skeptics. As already noted, he also grants that as philosophers and scientists we frequently do not speak or act as skeptics, and he sometimes writes in *The Theory of Moral Sentiments* in an old-fashioned philosophical voice (as in some of his invocations of "nature," for example).

One might also object that Smith nowhere denominates his position "skeptical" (putting aside the one use of the term "skeptical" that I have mentioned). In response, I reiterate that the plausibility of my reconstruction of his basic framework rests primarily on its fit with his work. But further, if Smith was a nondogmatic skeptic with respect to philosophizing, there was good reason for him to have avoided arguing straightforwardly for the objective truth of nondogmatic skepticism. To do so would have risked contradicting the view in question. That is, I suggest that Smith grasped the obvious self-referential problem – one long discussed in the history of philosophy, starting with Plato's *Theaetetus*, then taken up at the start of Sextus's *Outlines of Pyrrhonism* (I 14–15 in a chapter entitled "Does the Skeptic Dogmatize?") and also sketched by Hume – inherent in a skeptic's assertion that skepticism is "true."[38] For such an assertion would seem to belie the skeptic's view that no statements about the "truth" of philosophical doctrines can be sustained in face of arguments to the contrary. This is a time-honored and obvious counterattack on skepticism, and the battles between skeptics and their opponents were at Smith's fingertips. His general silence about the unsoundness of dogmatic views and the soundness of the skeptical alternative can be understood as a preemptive answer to the ancient charge of inconsistency. His reticence is an intelligible move in a longstanding dialectic.[39] Especially after Moore and Wittgenstein, the puzzles

---

38 Hume, *T* 186–7. R. J. Fogelin glosses Hume's argument as follows: "skeptical arguments are self-refuting, but this only puts us on a treadmill, since setting aside our skepticism and returning to the canons of reason inevitably puts us on the road to yet another skeptical impasse." "The Tendency of Hume's Skepticism," in Burnyeat, *The Skeptical Tradition*, p. 402.

39 It is worth recalling Sextus's remark at *PH* II 258–9 that a dogmatist who attempts to refute a skeptic is actually strengthening the skeptic's suspension of judgment about these endlessly debated issues.

attending any effort to philosophize one's way back to the plain, natural (as Smith's would say), everyday world are well known, but the essential problem goes back to ancient skepticism.[40]

Finally, one might object that it is implausible to attribute this kind of skepticism to Smith because there are no substantial modern precedents for it. Putting aside the response that Smith is capable of thinking through his own position, I have already cited testimony to the effect that skepticism was much in evidence during the modern period preceding Smith, including a "skeptic's method of ethics" in the Pyrrhonist tradition. This is the *type* of method I am attributing to Smith. Further, on at least one plausible interpretation, Hume's skepticism is quite close to Smith's. It would be perfectly natural for Smith to have read Hume as a "mitigated skeptic" and then to have decided to carry that stance to its logical conclusion.[41] I suggest that Smith's work *enacts* skepticism and in this respect may be seen as carrying out Hume's program by both continuing and developing it. Consistent with this enactment, Smith drops Hume's discussions of epistemology and metaphysics and so the entire schema of impressions, ideas, and the rest. The projected *corpus* would perhaps have treated these as part of a "philosophical history" of an unsupportable project, though, as noted, the *corpus* might also have contained essays on some aspects of epistemology, and certainly essays on aspects of the philosophy of language.

We may also consider that having been persuaded of the force of the attacks on the classical metaphysical and theological tradition undertaken by Hume and others, Smith had a choice to make. He could reiterate arguments of the type proposed by Hume in the first book of the *Treatise* and risk either the charge of self-refutation or of rehashing what had already been demonstrated. Or he could get on with the positive work of construing the "appearances" in a coherent, constructive, and persuasive way. Smith chose the latter. And this is a powerful argumentative strategy. For if Smith can successfully *enact* skepticism so under-

---

40 For some discussion of the issue, see T. Clarke, "The Legacy of Skepticism," *Journal of Philosophy* 69 (1972): 754–69. Clarke concludes: "Skepticism frees us from antiquated problems, including itself, offering us a new, challenging problem. In his practice Moore was, in one sense, the compleat philosopher: outside the circle of the plain does not lie what we wished and presumed. Skepticism leaves us the problem of the plain, of its structure, the character and source of its relative 'non-objectivity,' and one major tool for unlocking its secrets, the plain skeptical possibilities" (p. 769).

41 I refer to D. F. Norton's construal of Hume's "mitigated" skepticism, in "How a Sceptic May Live Scepticism," in *Faith, Scepticism, and Personal Identity*, ed. J. J. MacIntosh and H. A. Meynell (Calgary: University of Calgary Press, 1994), pp. 119–39.

stood, if he can in *deed* show the "truth" or fruitfulness of his stance, then the motivation behind classical philosophical inquiry into theological and metaphysical subjects is badly undermined.[42]

This skeptical account of the appearances is still a *philosophy* of ordinary life, but in a different sense of "philosophy" than the one we associate with Plato (or indeed Kant, who has a still different conception of "objectivity" and philosophy).[43] Smith's skepticism is of a "second-order" sort, in the sense that it is directed to debate about such things as the "Platonic" objective reality of moral qualities.[44] It leaves us with the extensive positive project, as philosophers, that is Smith's (the full intended dimensions of which I set out in section 5 of the Introduction), while relieving us of trying to answer classic Socratic "What is it" questions in the manner that Socrates demanded. It does entail that, with respect to the issue of the objectivity of moral qualities, the truth of the ordinary "Platonic" view is indemonstrable, when judged by the standards of the skeptical theory.

But from this skeptical theoretical standpoint, moral qualities remain objective and real in a sense that counts: we rely on them, they govern the lives of individuals and communities, they are woven into traditions and practices and character, they are the basis of decent and civilized life, they matter profoundly. They can be deliberated about and queried and improved, as is shown by Smith's impartial spectator theory, virtue theory, and political economy. We can and do talk meaningfully about the "truth" of moral propositions, about being ignorant or understanding of them. Moral qualities are not mere tastes, matters "relative" to the individual. From a theoretical standpoint, we may be said in some sense to originate them, for they are not read in the book of nature or

42 Smith's skepticism would have to be reconciled with his Stoicism, of course, given the traditional antipathy between the two schools. For now I note that some of Smith's favorite Stoics, such as Marcus Aurelius, evince a strongly antiphilosophical prejudice (e.g., *Meditations* 2.13). As already noted, Smith ignores Stoic metaphysics and epistemology and concentrates instead on themes in Stoic ethics. Cf. Frede's comment in "The Skeptic's Beliefs," p. 199, about the skeptical Stoic.

43 The type of skepticism I have attributed to Smith has nothing to do with a Cartesian skepticism about the existence of the material world. From Smith's standpoint, that kind of skepticism would itself be a "dogmatic" philosophical construction.

44 Similarly, J. L. Mackie refers to his own moral skepticism as a "second order view, a view about the status of moral values and the nature of moral valuing, about where and how they fit into the world," Mackie's second-order thesis being that "morality is not to be discovered but to be made." *Ethics: Inventing Right and Wrong* (New York: Penguin, 1977), pp. 16, 106. For the Platonic Forms as paradigms of "what objective values would have to be," see p. 40.

handed to us by God – and here Smith's Humean view of the imagination becomes especially important, as we will discuss in Chapter 8. But moral qualities are not therefore created by isolated individuals, not made out of whole cloth. We recall that one never undertakes moral life as that "creature" in "some solitary place" but rather as a member of a community whose moral norms are external to any individual (e.g., at the levels of law, institutions, and traditions).

Neither from Smith's theoretical perspective nor from that of ordinary life, then, are moral qualities fantasies or illusions or made up. They are not mere expressions of the emotions, and it usually requires cognition and understanding to grasp them. Moral qualities, and the practices of reasoning and action organized around them, have objective reality and substance, even as, in the course of ordinary life, we Platonize those qualities in viewing them (and the individuals who exhibit them) with the conviction that their authority and dignity are surpassing.[45] Seen from a *philosophical* standpoint as an exaggeration of the objectivity and reality that moral qualities can be known to possess, this ordinary Platonic sentiment may perhaps be termed an error, or, perhaps better, a philosophically unwarranted commitment. But it is not an error, from that same standpoint, to hold that moral qualities may be objective and real, or that they are informed by features of the world external to any one of us. Indeed, one consequence of Smith's skepticism is that it would unburden us of hopeless philosophical debates about ultimate metaphysical "realities" and return us to the more promising inquiries available within the *theatrum mundi*. And these will include inquiries – philosophical, scientific, literary – into how world and self are involved with one another.

## 3. RHETORIC AND THE SEPARATION OF THEORY AND PRACTICE

Though you despise that picture, or that poem, or even that system of philosophy, which I admire, there is little danger of our quarrelling upon that account. Neither of us can reasonably be much interested about them. They ought all of them to be matters of great indifference to us both.

Adam Smith, *TMS* I.i.4.5

45  Which is not to say that for Smith we generally do, or should, respond to this conviction with the type of Platonic philosophizing I discussed in section 1 of this chapter.

I have argued that Smith's rhetoric has an ethical intent, and this might also be said, by extension, of the skepticism that frames it.[46] My discussion in section 1 of this chapter of the motivation behind Smith's determination to keep philosophy within the *theatrum mundi* and the spheres of sympathy and spectators, to keep love from straying into dangerous madness and fanaticism, culminated in the observation that the intended effect is moderation, both political and ethical. Smith is plausibly understood as enacting, by means of his skepticism, a humane ethical outlook. This ultimately comes to a vision of the dignity of ordinary life, of what I am calling the virtues of enlightenment, over against the traditional claims of the philosophers as well as otherworldly religious sects. Smith's skepticism keeps our attention focused on matters that count and about which there can be fruitful understanding and action.

His skeptical framework, then, is part of a broadly enlightened ethical vision of the self-sufficiency, dignity, and indeed liberty of the human being. That liberty is not simply defined negatively as freedom from the moral authority of a divine being. His skepticism suggests that we have within ourselves sources of moral guidance, such as our moral emotions and imagination, that allow us to direct our lives and live together. This "us" potentially includes all human beings, for no high philosophical reason is ordinarily required for the task. One of Smith's purposes is to teach philosophers how to discharge their métier ethically, and he does this largely by example, by keeping attention focused on the context, by resisting easy condemnations of common life, by exemplifying and analyzing good judgment and ethical criticism, and by denying that one ought to live according to undecidable metaphysics and theology.

Smith's views about philosophy and skepticism may have the beneficial ethical effects he certainly wishes to see promulgated. But it does not follow that he would want those views themselves propagated in their entirety among nonphilosophers. Were his skepticism and attendant theses to become public credo, they would risk corrupting ordinary life and the realism that is its spirit. As moral agents we ought not to live with the consciousness that "appearances" are *only* that, even though our philosophy tells us that that is how things stand, and it would make a difference which outlook we took on the appearances.[47] To *live* as a

---

46 I note that Sextus Empiricus too tells us that the skeptic is a philanthropist whose aim is therapeutic or medicinal. Sextus says at one point that the skeptic applies different kinds of rhetoric as the case demands. At times the skeptic attacks the dogmatist's "self-conceit" and in other cases uses milder sorts of "persuasion," with the result that the skeptic sometimes uses arguments that, out of context, appear unpersuasive. *PH* III 280–1.

47 Mackie writes: "If there were something in the fabric of the world that validated certain

skeptic would require a radical, across-the-board reformation of ordinary experience, and Smith's philosophy mitigates against any such reformation.[48] This raises the question of whether, on this point, Smith's moral psychology and supporting philosophical outlook push against his own ethical purpose. The method and structure of much of *The Theory of Moral Sentiments* tend to obscure this question, precisely in intertwining so effectively the strands of the theory of moral sentiments. Smith's insistence that pure philosophy can only be a matter of intellectual "curiosity" also tends to obscure the question. Before we turn to his virtue theory, this concern about a tension between his theory and ethical purpose requires further comment. (I shall return to the question in the Epilogue as well.)

In Part I of *The Theory of Moral Sentiments* Smith distinguishes between two kinds of judgments of propriety, and there makes clear that judgments about moral virtues are taken to be personal in a way that judg-

kinds of concern, then it would be possible to acquire these merely by finding something out, by letting one's thinking be controlled by how things were. But in the world in which objective values have been annihilated the acquiring of some new subjective concern means the development of something new on the emotive side by the person who acquires it, something that eighteenth-century writers would put under the head of passion or sentiment." *Ethics*, p. 22. Farther on, Mackie reiterates that the belief in (Platonic) objectivity "has been incorporated in the basic, conventional, meanings of moral terms" (p. 35); were it abandoned, "a decay of subjective concern and sense of purpose" might result (p. 34). For an excellent discussion see B. Williams, "Ethics and the Fabric of the World," in Williams, *Making Sense of Humanity*, ch. 14. Since Mackie's view is that "morality is not to be discovered but to be made" (Mackie, *Ethics*, p. 106), Williams concludes that "Mackie's theory, and any like it, leaves a real problem of what should happen when we know it to be true" (p. 180). Cf. also S. Lovibond's illuminating *Realism and Imagination in Ethics* (Minneapolis: University of Minnesota Press, 1983), esp. pp. 144–6.

48 This is why Smith could not endorse Mackie's concluding aspiration: "My hope is that concrete moral issues can be argued out without appeal to any mythical objective values or requirements or obligations or transcendental necessities. . . ." Mackie, *Ethics*, p. 199. For Smith, this hope of the philosopher to correct a profound "error" that is part of the "fabric of the world" – such as the certainty that morals possess a kind of objectivity – is itself a profound, if predictable, error. Mackie is aware of the point: "In so far as the objectification of moral values and obligations is not only a natural but also a useful fiction, it might be thought dangerous, and in any case unnecessary, to expose it as a fiction. This is disputable" (p. 239). Smith would also probably point out that insofar as Mackie engages in object-level ethical theorizing, he (predictably) proceeds in as "realist" a fashion as the average erring ordinary moral actor does. (This kind of criticism of Mackie is made by Blackburn in "Errors in the Phenomenology of Value," pp. 324–5.) Shortly after the passage just quoted, Mackie notes that for moral reasons we cannot simply rest on received tradition and practices; new and better ethical principles and practices must be sought. Smith would agree, and his work in ethics and political economy aims to improve human life; it is not a "conservative" endorsement of the status quo. The delicate problem, then, is to correct without altogether subverting.

ments about intellectual virtues are not.[49] To question my virtue is to call me into question; to doubt my philosophy is not, so Smith wants to hold, to doubt something that goes to the core of who I am. This is connected with his distrust, discussed in the first section of this chapter, of Platonic eros.

The insulation of theoretical and moral matters from each other cannot be as antiseptic as Smith sometimes suggests, and his characterizations of them as such are self-consciously overstated. That differences in ideas about speculative matters have occasioned bitter controversies is a matter of long-standing record, and Smith himself notes an example of it when discussing the ire that Hobbes' theories provoked, as well as Hobbes' hope that his theories would have the salutary practical effect of promoting peace (VII.iii.2.2–3). The worries about the pernicious effects of Mandeville's views concerning the sources of moral approbation reveal the permeability of the boundaries between discourses on virtue and on moral psychology (VII.ii.4.12–14). Smith recounts other battles about the work of Racine, Voltaire, Pope, and Gray. He remarks on the contrast between bitter "literary factions" and the equanimity of mathematicians and scientists (III.2.19–23). Just after the only reference in *The Theory of Moral Sentiments* to the "invisible hand," he talks about the "love of system" and "regard to the beauty of order, of art and contrivance" that may animate the "patriot" to exercise "public spirit" (IV.i.11). Speculative works can indeed motivate us to action, even though they do not engage our sympathy. Were this not the case, his warnings about the actions of philosophical utopians or "men of system" would be moot.[50] *The Wealth of Nations* – a "speculative work," by Smith's own admission (*WN* V.iii.68) – has certainly had a huge practical (political and moral) effect, just as Smith intended. And, importantly for our purposes, he also discerns significant ethical dangers inherent in the universalistic philosophical standpoint of the Stoics and seeks to show

49 One kind of judgment of impropriety concerns the sentiments (emotions) of another on an occasion when "the objects which excite them [the emotions of another] are considered without any peculiar relation, either to ourselves or to the person whose sentiments we judge of"; the second kind pertains when "they [the objects or matters in question] are considered as peculiarly affecting one or other of us" (I.i.4.1). The spectator's disagreement with the actor's emotions on the former occasion need not become personal; continued friendship is possible.

50 Stewart speculates that Smith did not delineate a new constitution because he worried about inflaming "the passions of the multitude." *Memoirs*, p. 56. And yet, as we noted in Chapter 1, the *WN* in effect called for a radical reformation of the contemporary political economy, on the grounds of efficiency as well as justice.

how the standpoint of the impartial spectator differs from that of the Stoic sage. (I shall explore that crucial topic in Chapter 5, section 5, and Chapter 8, section 2.)

Smith's occasional overstating of the separation between practical and theoretical matters is protreptic in intent. He encourages us to proceed as though the gap between philosophical speculation and moral practice, theory and action, or analysis and rhetoric is greater than it is in fact. The discussion thus far helps to provide a rationale for this move, namely, his wish to avoid the danger of the subversion of moral practice by philosophers. He also provides a reason for nonphilosophers to avoid involving themselves in complex philosophical disputes. Since these matters are not supposed to make any practical difference, there is no point in waging half-comprehending battles over them, any more than there was a point in waging wars over theological curiosities. Even though from the first sentence of the book he has sought to persuade us of his sympathy view of moral psychology and thereby sought to encourage a lived *ethical* outlook, it serves his own purpose to deny any practical import to the abstract philosophical discussion of the very matters with which he concludes the book.

If the boundaries between practice and speculation, or sympathy and philosophy, are in fact permeable, then Smith's "double" skepticism itself may pose the sort of danger to healthy moral sentiments that critics of skepticism have always feared. Although we may not be able to live as skeptics, the doctrine may nonetheless sap our devotion to moral norms by depriving them of the authority, and appearance of mind independence and immutability, that they naturally seem to possess. This danger presents Smith with the unusually complex challenge of articulating a fundamentally skeptical framework – part of which is supposed to consist in a sustained allegiance to ordinary experience – without endangering the integrity of ethical life, while also protreptically persuading us of enlightened virtues and addressing both philosophical and nonphilosophical readers. Smith is not writing just for the likes of Hutcheson, Hume, and Burke, and he is obviously aware of the gulf between them and ordinary readers, as is indicated by his many statements in *The Theory of Moral Sentiments* distinguishing between "the wise and virtuous man" (VI.ii.25) and the "multitude" (VI.iii.27) or "great mob of mankind" (I.iii.3.2). My point is not that Smith is an esotericist who has secret teachings hidden between the lines or that his work is an interplay of multiple and conflicting "voices" over which he has little control, but that he has chosen to present his thought in a rhetorically complex way because he is a thinker whose philosophical agenda is multifaceted and sophisticated. The agenda includes a creatively developed Humean view of the imagination's constructive and unifying power, as well as of the ultimate source of morals in the activity of the self (or better, the interconnected activities of selves). We should therefore stress the normative tone of Smith's remark, quoted in the epigraph to this section, about aesthetic, literary, and philosophical matters: they "*ought* all of them to be matters of great indifference to us both" (*TMS* I.i.4.5, emphasis added). But they sometimes *are* matters of the greatest importance to all concerned.

# 5

# THE THEORY OF VIRTUE

The man of the most perfect virtue, the man whom we naturally love and revere the most, is he who joins, to the most perfect command of his own original and selfish feelings, the most exquisite sensibility both to the original and sympathetic feelings of others. The man who, to all the soft, the amiable, and the gentle virtues, joins all the great, the awful, and the respectable, must surely be the natural and proper object of our highest love and admiration.

Adam Smith, *TMS* III.3.35

Virtue occupies Smith's attention throughout the *The Theory of Moral Sentiments* and is the chief topic of an entire section (Part VI). Virtue is the "natural object of esteem, honour, and approbation"; it is that on which moral evaluation focuses (VII.i.2). "Virtue is excellence, something uncommonly great and beautiful" (I.i.5.6), and that excellence concerns primarily the perfection of self, though we also speak of virtuous or vicious action or conduct. Morality is to be understood primarily in terms of an ethics of character. In the course of an approving summary of Aristotle's ethical theory, Smith writes: "When we denominate a character generous or charitable, or virtuous in any respect, we mean to signify that the disposition expressed by each of those appellations is the usual and customary disposition of the person" (VII.ii.1.13). This, in turn, means that Smith must place significant weight on excellence of character, on the right "pitch" or "tenor" of the emotions, and on judgment. Smith is unusual, among modern moral philosophers, in according judgment so important a role.[1]

So persuaded is he that morality should be approached in terms of virtue that he seeks to show that the major competing moral philosophies can also be understood as attempts to answer the question "Wherein does virtue consist?" (VII.i.1, 2). He is well aware that his own answer, and indeed his conviction that he has formulated the right question, reflect his appropriation of ancient virtue theory. While Plato and Aristotle in particular are selectively but firmly endorsed, the Stoics too come in for detailed assessment.

The other question that any analysis "of the principles of morals" must answer concerns what I have termed "moral psychology." What leads us to view an action or character as right or wrong, or as possessing or lacking virtue?[2] Here Smith discusses at length the theories of sympathy, the emotions, pleasure and pain, and the impartial spectator, all of which we examined in preceding chapters. He sets out three kinds of answers to the "What is virtue?" question, and three to the question in moral psychology about the source of moral value:

| *Virtue* | *Moral Psychology* |
|---|---|
| propriety (various ancients, Smith) | self-love (Hobbes, Mandeville) |
| prudence (Epicurus) | reason (Cudworth) |
| benevolence (Hutcheson) | sentiments (a)  moral sense (Hutcheson) |
| | (b.i)  based on utility (Hume) |
| | (b.ii) based on sympathy (Smith) |

---

1 Larmore notes that "One of the few moral philosophers in modern times to have acknowledged the importance of judgment in moral experience was Adam Smith in *The Theory of Moral Sentiments*." *Patterns of Moral Complexity*, p. 17. If Baier's interpretation of Hume is accepted, then Hume too ranks with Smith in placing great emphasis on judgment: "Reason in its new guise [accorded it by Hume] is the power of judgment, along with the aids we judge helpful for judgment." *A Progress of Sentiments*, p. 282.

2 Smith's formulation of this question runs: "by what power or faculty in the mind is it, that this character, whatever it be, is recommended to us? Or in other words, how and by what means does it come to pass, that the mind prefers one tenour of conduct to another, denominates the one right and the other wrong; considers the one as the object of approbation, honour, and reward, and the other of blame, censure, and punishment?" (VII.i.2). The phrase "principles of morals" is used at VII.i.2.

Smith takes himself as a propriety theorist with respect to the virtue question and a sentiments theorist with respect to the moral psychology question. Only modern theorists are named as proponents of the relevant moral psychologies. Smith remarks that even in Ralph Cudworth's time "the abstract science of human nature was but in its infancy" (VII.iii.2.5), implying that progress in moral psychology is recent. It would therefore appear that the ancients had a better approach to understanding the good life for the human being, whereas the moderns are superior in their grasp of how we determine virtue and vice. Roughly speaking, Smith sees himself as synthesizing an ancient view about the nature of virtue with a modern approach to the problem of the source of moral value. Consequently the moral psychology (especially the notions of sympathy and the impartial spectator) and the virtue theory must be understood in light of each other. He also takes himself as contributing to the philosophical analysis and development of each of the elements of this synthesis.

The purpose of this chapter is to analyze Smith's conception of virtue and the particular virtues and thus to discuss a number of closely related issues, such as the distinction between "high" and ordinary virtue; the relation of duty to virtue, as well as of moral rules to judgment; the character of ethical evaluation; our propensity to vice and the "corruption of the moral sentiments"; moral ideals and moral education; and the nature and place of happiness. The virtue theory is the moral foundation of Smith's political economy, political theory, and "natural jurisprudence." Hence the virtue theory is closely tied to his doctrine of liberty as well as to his views about the pursuit of wealth.[3] However "ancient" the virtue theory may in some respects be, Smith combines it with a modern view of the social and political institutions appropriate to virtue. Smith's analysis of the specific virtues, especially of justice, departs significantly from classical theory. He is writing in and for a world that the ancients imagined only in rough outline, while selectively appropriating their ethical views and methods.

## 1. VIRTUOUS EMOTIONS

Smith's answer to the question "What is virtue?" is that virtue consists in the "proper government and direction of all our affections," and not

3 I explore these connections in Chapters 6 and 7.

simply in the agent's government of any one type of passion (whether
of the selfish, social, or unsocial variety). "Virtue consists in propriety"
(VII.ii.intro.1); that is, it consists in the appropriate "pitch" of the given
emotion. As Smith says in approvingly summarizing the account of virtue
in book IV of Plato's *Republic*, the virtuous person's emotions are molded
in such a way that each "performs its proper office with that precise
degree of strength and vigour which belongs to it" (VII.ii.1.11). Alternatively, adapting the Aristotelian terminology that he thinks fairly close
to his own and invokes in various places, virtue is the "habit of medi-
ocrity according to right reason." An emotion hits the mean when it lies
in the "middle" between excess and defect, this being pretty much
Smith's notion "concerning the propriety and impropriety of conduct"
(VII.ii.1.12; cf. *NE* 1106b36–1107a2). As noted earlier, Smith explains at
length that the "mean" differs depending on the type of passion at issue
(I.ii.intro.2; VI.iii.14–18). The moral rules pertaining to each type of
emotion differ correspondingly. Aristotle tells us that the mean is relative
"to us" ("pros hemas"; *NE* 1107a1), and in a sense Smith agrees. "Or-
thos logos" (right reason) is determined by the impartial spectator. That
which is "right" and "good" is defined relative to the responses and
judgments of a person whose dispositions and knowledge of the situation
are of an appropriate sort. Any passion or emotion can be virtuous or
vicious depending on its character, the situation, and its "temper" or
"pitch," as measured by the virtuous person.[4]

Smith distinguishes between two "aspects" under which the spectator
may evaluate a motive, action, or character, although in common life we
"constantly" shift back and forth between these aspects. The first aspect
is "propriety." Propriety and its contrary lie in the "suitableness or un-
suitableness, in the proportion or disproportion which the [agent's] affection seems to bear to the cause or object which excites it" (I.i.3.6).
The second aspect concerns "merit" or "demerit," which lie in "the
beneficial or hurtful nature of the effects which the affection aims at, or
tends to produce," that is, "the qualities by which it is entitled to reward,

4 Recall *NE* 1113a25–b2; the *spoudaios* (excellent, virtuous person) judges everything rightly,
and what seems to him to be the case is the case; he is the "measure" (*metron*) of the
noble and pleasant. This is rather similar to Smith's notion of the impartial spectator as
the "measure" (discussed in Chapter 3, section 2 of the present work). Aristotle does not
of course speak of an "impartial spectator," and his ethics does not have a clear-cut role
for impartiality or the taking of a "general point of view." However troubling for modern
readers this may be, and however complex the issues, it is clear that Aristotle's ethics is
not a form of ethical egoism that sanctions selfishness, precludes altruism and care for
others, or ignores the value of seeing things from another's point of view.

or is deserving of punishment" (I.i.3.7). Roughly speaking, then, our
judgments of virtue and vice normally evaluate the reasonableness of a
sentiment or action (1) relative to the cause or object that prompts it,
and (2) relative to the consequences engendered by the agent.

"Propriety" is a term that blends the ethical and aesthetic. Smith's
use of it helps to explain his proclivity for terms such as "moral beauty"
and in general his running together of moral and aesthetic vocabulary.
He speaks of "propriety" synonymously with "gracefulness," "proportion," "suitableness," "decency," and of course these are notions closely
tied to those of "harmony" and "symmetry," a fact underlined by his
striking fondness for musical metaphors (such as "pitch") to express the
proportion in question. The notion of propriety is a very old one. It
seems roughly equivalent to what Cicero called, in a text Smith certainly
knew, *decorum*, for which the Greek is, Cicero adds, *prepon* (*De officiis*
1.27).[5] At the heart of *decorum* are the ideas of self-control, temperance,
and moderation in all things. On Cicero's account, *decorum* is so thoroughly interwoven with virtue that in its most general sense propriety is
simply that which is suitable and in harmony with human nature; in the
more specific contexts of particular virtues, it is that which is appropriate
for a praiseworthy person to do in the circumstances. Cicero illustrates
this by mentioning the propriety at which poets aim, namely the harmony between characters in their dramas and the words and deeds of
these characters (*De officiis* 1.28).

Since in Part VII Smith defines virtue altogether as propriety, it seems
strange that propriety is cast early on in the book as only one of the
aspects in question. But in fact the second aspect, merit, is also built up
from considerations of propriety.[6] The sense of merit is "a compounded

---

5 Plato's *Statesman* (283d–285c) contains a well-known discussion of measure and distinguishes between mathematical and qualitative measurement. The latter measures relative
to the "fitting" (*prepon*), the "opportune" (*kairon*), the "necessary" (*deon*), and all that
tends toward the "middle" (*meson*). This kind of measurement ascertains what exceeds
and falls short of the mean (*metron*), and in "saving" the mean produces all that is good
and beautiful (284b1–2). How is the moment of the *prepon* to be determined? The Eleatic
Stranger refers us to a mysterious standard of "the precise itself" (*auto takribes*; 284d2)
but says nothing more about it. Aristotle's doctrine of the "mean" (*meson*) is closely connected to the same nexus of ideas; for him, it is the task of *phronesis* (practical wisdom)
to measure propriety. Since for Smith the "right" proportion is to be determined by the
impartial spectator, we understand why the metaphor of the "critic" (discussed in Ch. 1
of the present volume) so naturally fits with Smith's notion of virtue and why Smith's
scheme creates a significant place for the notion of judgment.
6 As is argued by Haakonssen, *The Science of a Legislator*, p. 64. Smith uses the language of
"propriety" in defining merit (e.g., II.i.4.1, 2, 4).

sentiment, and to be made up of two distinct emotions; a direct sympathy with the sentiments of the agent, and an indirect sympathy with the gratitude of those who receive the benefit of his actions" (II.1.4.2). (The sense of demerit functions in an analogous way.) Smith comes close to saying that "direct sympathy" comes to a judgment of the propriety of the actor's motive, and "indirect sympathy" to an evaluation of the appropriateness of the response of the person acted upon. When we think the motives of the agent to be mean, for example, we are not disposed to enter into the gratitude of the beneficiary, for the agent seems not to deserve gratitude. When we approve the agent's motives, we do not sympathize with the distress of the person acted upon (II.1.3.1).

Just as in the case of propriety, where we may sympathetically enter into the situation of the agent and determine through "illusive sympathy" what the agent would or should have felt, so too in cases of merit we may as spectators determine that the agent deserves reward or punishment, even if the person "acted upon" (II.i.4.1) is not, or is no longer, capable of responding to the actor. When we view the agent and the person acted upon as forming part of an ethical whole, their responses will be "sympathetically" evaluated with respect to one another. (Presumably this is why Smith speaks of our sympathy with the recipient of the action as "indirect," that is, as mediated by our understanding of the intentions of the agent.) The principles of sympathy, then, underlie judgments of merit or desert as well as of propriety.

Smith begins *The Theory of Moral Sentiments* with a discussion of propriety, because that is the foundation of the account, and then in Part II turns to merit. Part III concerns duty, that is, our application to ourselves, rather than to others, of judgments of propriety and merit. Although propriety logically grounds the scheme, these three parts should be understood as panels of a triptych, which in ordinary life are folded one over the other. Our moral lives are "constantly" conducted under all three aspects, at least once we have reached moral maturity. This is an astute analysis. It embodies Smith's commitment to preserving the complexity of ordinary moral life and requires a significant place for judgment in moral life, including with respect to deciding how much weight should be given to each type of moral consideration (propriety, merit, and duty).

We have noted that virtue is divided for Smith into the intellectual and moral, the theoretical and the practical (I.i.4.4). The moral virtues follow, first, the division of the passions into those derived from the body and those derived from the imagination. Virtues of the "bodily" passions include self-control, temperance, and modesty. The passions of the imagination, as we saw, are divided into three categories – the unsocial, social, and selfish. The virtues of the "unsocial" passions (passions such as anger, hatred, resentment, envy, and malice) tend to require a particularly high level of self-command and share with some of the virtues of the "selfish" passions the title of "the great, the awful and respectable, the virtues of self-denial" (I.i.5.1; cf. VI.iii.17). Smith's chief example of the virtue of an "unsocial" passion is – strange though it may seem at first – justice. The virtues of the "social" passions include benevolence, humanity, friendship and love; Smith refers to these as "amiable" virtues. The last category is that of the "selfish" passions, and they are properly expressed in such virtues as prudence, industry, frugality, moderation, and self-control. When considered as the virtues of a "private and peaceable life," these have a "sober lustre" (VI.iii.13). Magnanimity seems to be a virtue related to both the unsocial and selfish passions (I.ii.3.8, VI.iii.6, 33), and a high form of prudence combines various virtues (VI.i.15). Further on in this chapter, I shall discuss several of the virtues, and in Chapter 6 I shall turn to justice.

## 2. JUDGMENT, RULES, AND MORAL CRITICISM

Actions and emotions are to be judged with respect to their propriety or merit (the latter itself a compounded form of propriety). Propriety is a kind of fittingness – but fittingness to what? The answer is guided by whether one is determining propriety or merit; we have reviewed Smith's general answer to the "fitting to what?" question for each of the two. Clearly, judgments of fittingness in a specific case depend on a proper grasp and weighing of the particulars involved, on right perception of the context, and on appropriate sympathy and discerning emotional response. Judgment as to propriety also involves appeal to a general standard; we often say that such and such is right because it fits a standard, thus offering a different sort of reason for our judgment. In this section we will consider the place of general standards or rules (and so of duty) in Smith's virtue ethics, as well as the way in which the sense of duty can degenerate into fanaticism or "erroneous conscience." We will then briefly examine how Smithean "moral criticism" would assess two social practices (slavery and infanticide).

### Moral Rules and Judgment: After Virtue?

Smith uses the term "general rules" in two ways. In some contexts, he has in mind inductive generalizations about moral psychology or behavior that are not meant to serve as guides for moral action, though they may surely be relevant to ethical deliberation.[7] By contrast, action-guiding rules range from principles of politeness to indispensable principles of justice, all developed out of moral experience and encapsulating accumulated wisdom. Smith's first use of the term "general rules" illustrates this second, moral sense; he makes a point about sympathy by imagining a situation in which we learn, in the course of a busy day, of someone's misfortune but do not have the time or inclination to "picture out in our imagination" what they are going through (I.i.3.4). On the basis of past experiences of others' misfortunes, we have developed a "general rule" to the effect that it is proper to express sympathy in this situation, for we know that if we stopped to reflect and to enter into the particulars, we would actually feel the appropriate commiseration. In acting in accordance with such a rule, we correct our present indifference toward the actor's misfortunes with the proper expression of sympathy. In this manner rules may supply perspective, for they may represent the settled convictions of reasonable spectators. If we are decent, we have made these rules our own.[8]

Moral rules are arrived at through the observation of particulars. Smith insists on this point: morality is not "originally" a matter of applying a rule, but of approving (or disapproving), through spectatorial sympathy, of an actor or his actions in a particular context. To be sure, at first we receive rules from others in the course of our upbringing.[9]

---

7 E.g. III.2.13: "The person who is deliberately guilty of a disgraceful action, we may lay it down, I believe, as a general rule, can seldom have much sense of the disgrace; and the person who is habitually guilty of it, can scarce ever have any." For another instance, see VI.iii.14.

8 E.g., III.4.7: "Our continual observations upon the conduct of others, insensibly lead us to form to ourselves certain general rules concerning what is fit and proper either to be done or to be avoided. Some of their actions shock all our natural sentiments. We hear every body about us express the like detestation against them. . . . We thus naturally lay down to ourselves a general rule. . . ." Since we learn to judge others by watching how others judge us, and vice versa, a strict separation between individual and group formation of rules does not make much sense here. Cf. VI.ii.1.7, where the general rule is a sort of reasonable expectation.

9 Hence Smith's use of the first-person plural in his key formulations of the point: "They [general rules] are ultimately founded upon experience of what, in particular instances, our moral faculties, our natural sense of merit and propriety, approve, or disapprove of. We do not originally approve or condemn particular actions; because, upon examination, they appear to be agreeable or inconsistent with a certain rule. The general rule, on the contrary, is formed, by finding from experience, that all actions of a certain kind, or circumstanced in a certain manner, are approved or disapproved of" (III.4.8). Also III.4.7 and VII.iii.2.6: "The general maxims of morality are formed, like all other general maxims,

The rules have histories and are continually modified and reinterpreted over time; they are not reinvented wholesale by each and every person, but are grounded in our perceptions of the noble and base. Why are moral rules necessary? An ideal judge or "archetype of perfection" (VI.iii.25) would perfectly evaluate each case and would not need rules to direct or correct his or her judgments. The "perfectly virtuous" ideal spectator would, by definition, be impartial, not compromised by any faults of character. Imperfect agents, however, are often moved and biased by strong passions when they are about to act.[10] Still worse, we may at the moment talk ourselves into thinking that we *have* viewed things impartially; as Smith says, quoting Malebranche, "the passions . . , all justify themselves, and seem reasonable and proportioned to their objects, as long as we continue to feel them" (III.4.3). Unless we are perfectly wise, we seem to be left at the mercy not just of self-love but of "self-deceit."

Moral rules counter this tendency to moral corruption, since once we have acquired a reasonable respect for them and the habit of following them, they provide a readily available moral standard for judging ourselves and others, as well as a motivation to act as duty requires (the sense of duty being defined as "regard to those general rules of conduct").[11] These "general rules" or "general maxims and ideas" stand in for the impartial spectator to such a large extent that most of us "regulate the greater part of our moral judgments" by them (VII.iii.2.6). With their help we may do our duty tolerably well.[12] The actor often

from experience and induction. We observe in a great variety of particular cases what pleases or displeases our moral faculties, what these approve or disapprove of, and, by induction from this experience, we establish those general rules."

10 "We cannot even for that moment divest ourselves entirely of the heat and keenness with which our peculiar situation inspires us, nor consider what we are about to do with the complete impartiality of an equitable judge" (III.4.3).

11 "The coarse clay of which the bulk of mankind are formed, cannot be wrought up to such perfection [of the perfectly virtuous]. There is scarce any man, however, who by discipline, education, and example, may not be so impressed with a regard to general rules, as to act upon almost every occasion with tolerable decency, and through the whole of his life to avoid any considerable degree of blame" (III.5.1).

12 Smith comments on Cicero's distinction between perfect virtue and happiness, on the one hand, and the realm of *officia* on the other (though Smith prefers Seneca's term, "convenientia"). The latter category, Smith says, contains "those imperfect, but attainable virtues," and so "proprieties, fitnesses, decent and becoming actions," that is, the sum of Stoic "practical morality" (VII.ii.1.42). For Cicero, the duties he is examining belong to a world that is not populated by paragons of wisdom (*De officiis* 3.4). So too for Smith, the realm of "propriety" is, insofar as it is governed primarily by moral rules rather than by the judgments of the impartial spectator, the realm of virtue for the

learns to value general rules the hard way – in retrospect and with regret about his moral blindness. Spectators who do not sympathize with the agent's "selfish" emotions do their best to insist that the rules be followed, that the agent neither make an exception for himself nor rationalize a selfish course of action. In these ways, we are motivated to adopt general rules. Once they are "universally acknowledged and established, by the concurring sentiments of mankind, we frequently appeal to them as to the standards of judgment, in debating concerning the degree of praise or blame that is due to certain actions of a complicated and dubious nature." The rules take on a life of their own. They are always present as valuable, often guiding, elements in the moral universe.

Earlier in this chapter we focused on virtue and on character, judgment, and moral perception. A significant change of emphasis to a deontological ethics of duty and rule following seems to have taken place. The two seem to push against each other. Whereas deontological and utilitarian theories have roles for the virtues in their schemes – for example, the virtues may be understood as the habit of following the relevant rules or of maximizing intrinsic values – virtue theories typically give pride of place not to rules but to judgment by persons of a certain character. In virtue theories, doing one's duty is understood to mean acting in accordance with the judgments of a virtuous person. The virtuous person may develop expectations, which can be articulated as general rules or maxims of acceptable conduct (for example, the rule that one ought to be honest may be derived from the notion that honesty is a virtue). His life is principled. He feels ashamed when he fails to live up to these expectations, and he disapproves of others who fail. These shortcomings are viewed as failures of character if they are repeated frequently enough, and as failures of judgment if intermittent.

How do moral rules function within an ethics of sympathy? This needs to be fleshed out further. Smith is surely right that moral rules are givens in the moral landscape and that their role does demand explanation. If the phenomena are to be explained, then there is no point in insisting upon an extreme particularism, as though it is only a matter of moral perception and judgment of each case solely in its own terms.

We might start by noting that, as derivative from moral judgments, moral rules are open to revision. Smith insists that moralists err when they take such rules as the "ultimate foundations" for morality, as

nonwise. Moral rules help to solve the problem of how the imperfectly virtuous are to live together.

though moral judgment were simply analogous to juridical reasoning that consists of applying lawlike rules to specific cases, through a process of subsumption. The impartial spectator remains the ultimate court of appeal as to the soundness of the rule or maxim. The "original judgments of mankind with regard to right and wrong" are not "formed like the decisions of a court of judicatory" (III.4.11). It seems clear from Smith's discussion that we will often find ourselves trying to justify a rule in light of experience and reflecting on its applicability to a particular situation. Moral reasoning therefore consists, in good measure, of a conversation in which moral perceptions and rules are adjusted in light of each other. The value of general rules does not obviate the need for the exercise of judgment by a person of virtuous character.

Smith distinguishes between two kinds of moral rules. One kind resembles the rules of grammar; they are precise and determine with exactitude our obligations. These rules of justice are of this sort, and jurisprudence prescribes them for judges (VII.iv.8). These rules are chiefly concerned with defining what conduct is prohibited and with the punishments for transgression; in short, with obligations that may be exacted by force. It must follow that in many such cases there is no "mean" for judgment to hit and that the rules are absolute. Such moral rules are essential in the case of justice, and so to the governance of the "unsocial" passions. Without "tolerable observance" of the rules of justice, human society "would crumble into nothing" (III.5.2; III.3.6). The importance of "grammatical" rules is in proportion to their role in the avoidance of conflict, war, and asociality. Roughly speaking, judgment by appeal to such rules generally has a deductive character; given an accurate description of the action and of the rule(s) under which it is to be considered, the conclusion follows about its rightness or wrongness. It is not inaccurate to say that the rules may be applied to the case. Yet judgment is still required here, for there are no rules for applying rules, and we must still discern the relevant features of the case as well as the relevant rule(s) under which it falls.

Necessary as they are, the place in the moral universe for rules of this sort is strictly limited. The profoundly misguided attempt to create similar "rules for the conduct of a good man" is at the heart of casuistry (VII.iv.8; cf. VII.iv.34). In fact "it belongs to feeling and sentiment only to judge" of moral virtues other than justice (VII.iv.33). The rules for the exercise of nonjuridical moral virtues are, in Smith's often-repeated phrase, "loose, vague, and indeterminate" and may be compared to "those which critics lay down for the attainment of what is sublime and

elegant in composition, and which present us rather with a general idea
of the perfection we ought to aim at, than afford us any certain and
infallible directions for acquiring it" (VII.iv.1). It is the province of "the
science which is properly called Ethics" to spell out these general "precepts" or "ideas" and thus help to "inflame our natural love of virtue"
as well as "to correct and to ascertain our natural sentiments with regard
to the propriety of conduct" (VII.iv.6). They have a protreptic and pedagogic role.[13] These rules amount to general descriptions of the virtues,
a "picture" of them (VII.iv.4) and of "the ordinary way of acting to
which each virtue would prompt us." It is impossible to depict all the
modifications of the moral passions with precision. Moral rules are "maxims," resembling rules of thumb – general guidelines and patterns that
embody norms, rather than precise directives from which we may somehow deduce what ought to be done.

Thus when Smith speaks of the impartial spectator as a "judge," we
should not automatically imagine that he means a judge in a court of
law; in the case of most of the virtues, this judge is a *phronimos* (person
of practical wisdom), and the rules being applied are not like laws of
jurisprudence. Indeed, most moral rules are not, strictly speaking, being
*applied* at all; rather, in light of general maxims, an evaluation of the
specific context is undertaken and a decision reached. Smith goes so far
as to say that in the case of virtues other than justice, we should not be
directed so much by the rule as by "a certain idea of propriety," or the
"end and foundation of the rule" (III.6.10). It is up to the "great judge
and arbiter of our conduct" to determine, in all areas where the rules
are loose, vague, and indeterminate (which is to say most areas of human
life) what is virtuous and what not (VI.ii.1.22). Defensible rules encapsulate norms such as a person of good character would approve. This
means that there is no single procedure, method, or formula of moral
justification or reason giving, even though we can specify the general
structure of reason giving in terms of propriety and its two branches.

As Smith describes them, some of these rules of thumb state commendable principles in a general way ("one should always love one's
parents"); others are more like "precepts" or terse distillations of moral
experience ("a good friend never betrays you"). They help focus atten-

---

13 They may help us to improve the "imperfect ideas which we might otherwise have entertained of these virtues [prudence, magnanimity, beneficence]," just as general principles of good writing may help us to move from grammatically correct composition to
expression that is elegant and sublime (III.6.11). Note the comparison between moral
criticism and literary criticism.

tion on what matters ethically in this or that context. Reciprocally, we could not make much use of either kind without the proper contextual knowledge and feel for the situation, and this in turn both requires and guides emotion, imagination, and one's grasp of the relevant particulars. The process is circular, and it is the task of moral education to help us trace this circle by helping us to become ethically sympathetic and sensitive persons who can move back and forth between maxims and context, tuning our emotions in this way.[14] In deliberation, examples play a guiding, not just an illustrative, role. When these paradigms are well chosen, they help to adapt the more general maxim or precept and the situation to each other. In using them, we reenact the movement of reflection by which rules are both discovered through reflection on experience and in turn "applied" to experience.[15] Moral reflection and criticism may helpfully be thought of in terms of the model of conversation. The conversation attempts to clarify what is important to the evaluation of the situation and to arrive at persuasive reasons favoring a judgment about the matter. The give-and-take process requires the emotions and the engagement of the imagination, and so the stitching together of the relevant factors into a coherent "account," as well as the presenting of this account by someone to someone. The rhetorical features of Smith's own writing, which we examined in Chapter 1, are reiterated in this process of ethical evaluation.

Aristotle remarks that the degree to which blame is due in a situation is a matter of "perception"; the judgment (*krisis*) lies with the percep-

---

14 Smith's nonjuridical moral rules are similar to what B. Herman calls "rules of moral salience." *The Practice of Moral Judgment* (Cambridge, Mass.: Harvard University Press, 1993), ch. 4. Herman takes these "rules" to "constitute the structure of moral sensitivity" (p. 78) and holds that they do not themselves generate duties (p. 79). They "provide the substantive core in a moral upbringing" (p. 82) and affect the content of "moral perception" in that they "represent the moral understanding that in part defines a 'moral community' " (p. 83). They are "preprocedural moral rules" (p. 86). One difference between my Smith and her Kant is that on her account all rules of moral salience are subject to adjudication by the categorical imperative or the basic conceptions associated with the Kantian moral law (p. 92), whereas on my Smithean account there is no further appeal beyond the virtuous person (the impartial spectator). Smith has a great deal to say about the "structure of moral sensitivity" and so, in effect, about questions of moral salience, not just with reference to "moral rules" but also to the emotions, whereas Herman's Kant cannot (by her admission) work without these rules, even though Kant in fact says little about them (p. 93).

15 S. Fleischacker insightfully remarks, in discussing Smith's notion of ethical reasoning: "Smith implies that determinant and reflective judgment necessarily belong together, a point in the theory of judgment that Kant himself never properly explored" ("Philosophy in Moral Practice: Kant and Adam Smith," p. 267).

tion (*aisthesis*; *NE* 1109b23). Smith would agree, as long as the terms are appropriately defined. He uses the vocabulary of perception in a moral context (e.g., III.3.2–3) and notes that although relevant moral differences and distinctions among "circumstance, character, and situation" are often "undefinable," they are not therefore "imperceptible" (VI.ii.1.22). It would be tempting to infer (as many have in discussing Aristotle) that "perception" should be understood as immediate apprehension or intuition, especially in light of Smith's remark that "it belongs to feeling and sentiment only to judge" of moral virtues other than justice (VII.iv.33). This would be a mistake, for even quite simple cases of moral perception or feeling involve, for Smith, reflection and interpretation. The idea of perception is built into his metaphor of the "spectator," but this does not mean that spectating is just an "either you see it or you don't" matter; otherwise the argument for the priority of spectator to actor would carry little weight. Smith's rejection of Hutcheson's theory of moral sense, and with it of any notion that we have a special mental faculty for seeing moral values, further shows that Smith's theory is not intuitionist.

The detachment implicit in moral perception constitutes a "critical" stance. Smith argues that in this respect visual and moral perception are analogous. Just as, in the one case, perspective is necessary in order to gauge the true size of the objects in an "immense landscape" that you see through your window, so in taking the true measure of an ethical landscape, perspective and correction of natural bias are required (III.3.2, 3). Reflection and imagination are indispensable if moral vision is to bring the landscape into focus and to let us accurately "see" its features.

Further, in sympathizing we do not necessarily "identify" immediately with the situation of the other and certainly do not approve or disapprove automatically; often, some degree of interpretation is required. Indeed, an interpretation of the situation, or a judgment, is already embedded in our emotion, as we have discussed. Even where, as in Smith's examples at the beginning of the book, an emotion is communicated immediately, the imagination rushes in to fill gaps with an account or story that contextualizes the particulars under evaluation. The imagination assembles the background assumptions and narrative within which someone's emotion or action or expression strike the observer as noble or base, graceful or offensive.

The notion of propriety requires comparison, matching up, consideration of proportionality: Was this response that you exhibited fitting to the cause that provoked it or the object to which it is directed? In some cases, this is a very complicated matter, and we do not perceive the answer without a great deal of reflection. And again, unless we are perfectly virtuous, general moral rules form part of our moral consciousness, as does a conversation that brings them and the case at hand together. The "eye of the mind" (III.3.2) perceives with them in mind. The point is not that we are never hit with a perception of moral beauty, or that we are never pushed unreflectively by an emotion. Rather, the point is that when we perceive morally we are not simply intuiting in some immediate, extrarational way.

We have distinguished between two types of general rules, the juridical and the looser, indeterminate principles. Which of them is relevant varies with the nature of the passion in question.[16] Even among the nonjuridical virtues, the role of rules varies. Some passions and virtues are more susceptible than others to precision; the general duties of gratitude, for example, can be more exactly specified than those relevant to friendship. Thus judgment is also required in order to determine whether the rules of "grammar" or "criticism" are more suitable in the context and when too much precision is being demanded of a rule that seeks to specify what a virtue requires of us. Judgment will be needed to determine when insistence on a virtue has gone too far or not far enough.[17] In some cases we are more praiseworthy when we do *not* act from a rule (although we still act in accordance with it), since the action ought to flow from the sentiment in question (III.6.4–8). The "cold sense of duty" that acts entirely from a rule (such as the rule that parents ought to care for their children) may indeed be blameworthy (III.6.4). On other occasions, it is more admirable to act dutifully from a rule, where punishment is required but is imposed only "with reluctance" (III.6.5). Determining whether it is nobler to act in accordance with or from a rule once again requires reflection and judgment, as well as evaluation of the particulars, and the context – all in a manner that befits a person of virtuous character.

16 For example, with respect to the selfish passions it is best to be animated by the object of our self-interest rather than by a rule; in the case of the unsocial passions, e.g., justified resentment, it is best to act from the general rule rather than from the passion of vengeance; with respect to the social passions, it is virtually required that we act not from the rule but from the appropriate affection (e.g., paternal love).

17 For example, we cannot "ascertain by rules the exact point at which, in every case, a delicate sense of justice begins to run into a frivolous and weak scrupulosity of conscience" (VII.iv.33), but ascertain we nonetheless must.

## Erroneous Conscience and Fanaticism

> Of all the corrupters of moral sentiments, therefore, faction and fanaticism
> have always been by far the greatest.
>
> Adam Smith, *TMS* III.3.43

The appropriate exercise of judgment in the light of rules is subject to various dangers, as the dialectical rhythm of Smith's exposition shows. In the first two parts of *The Theory of Moral Sentiments*, morality is closely tied to praise and blame, and so to a social morality that provides incentives to virtue. But then we learn that "corruption of the moral sentiments" may result from these very incentives. The stern internalized voice of an impartial judge is required as an antidote, and Part III is devoted to "duty." There Smith links morality to conscience, remorse, and guilt – internal sources of judgment. Guilt and remorse are like the Furies, and conscience resembles the demigods depicted by the poets (III.2.9, 32). Conscience is the voice of the impartial spectator addressing the agent and motivates us to do that which is praiseworthy and avoid that which is blameworthy. But then it turns out that the impartial spectator is not always at hand, in the heat of the moment; moral rules are also needed to correct distortions of judgment and to support impartiality. This remedy creates a further danger of its own, however.

Before "the age of artificial reasoning and philosophy" explicated these rules for us, religion made them holy through the natural workings of sympathy and the emotions. Smith sketches, in effect, a psychological anthropology of religion (III.5.4) intended to explain why moral rules are so often backed, in our imaginations, by the authority of the divine. Our motivation for believing in the divine has various sources, and in the end people commonly regard basic moral principles as divinely sanctioned. We may appeal from the "tribunal" of actual spectators to that of the impartial spectator and thence, faced with continuing resistance from actual spectators, to the "still higher tribunal, to that of the all-seeing Judge of the world" (III.2.33). Thus "religion enforces the natural sense of duty" (III.5.13). Smith has in mind not religion as theological doctrine but a "natural religion" composed of beliefs about God, the soul, and the afterlife.

Unfortunately, when supported by conscience, a belief in divine sanction, and a model of divinely provided "juridical" rules defining duty, the passion for moral rectitude easily degenerates into "erroneous conscience," or "fanaticism" (III.6.12). The very mechanism that affords us a supposedly normative and objective standpoint – religion – also supplies an incentive for the corruption of norms. The rules ossify into a formula or method for moral assessment. The fanatic's vanity leads to an exaltation of a precise system of duties supposedly derived from God (which in turn leads to casuistry), a system that is then asserted to be obligatory for all.[18] It is precisely in the appeal to an imagined impartial spectator as judge of our (and others') true worth, in the face of the judgments of actual spectators, that vanity becomes most tempting, and most dangerous. The motivation for abandoning common sense and our own capacity for judgment in exercising our duty derives in part from our deep desire to be praiseworthy and avoid guilt; it is in this sense easier, and more in keeping with our self-love, to abandon ourselves to an imagined directive from above. This corruption of the moral sentiments is vanity in the guise of selfless purity of soul. Only if the agent could, when adopting the standpoint of an impartial spectator, justify his total abandonment to divine authority would the agent have shown that he was not acting from self-deceived vanity. Yet, Smith holds, the standpoint of the virtuous person is and ought to be final, even when evaluating the degree to which religious duty ought to govern us.

Because of the danger of self-delusion, not to mention the need to interpret the commands of the divine, it is not enough simply to cite the divine as authority. Further, the importance of distinguishing among spheres of life appropriately regulated by different kinds of moral rules and of paying attention to the imprecision built into the moral phenomena entitle us to reject the absolutizing of all moral rules. Purity of soul and conscience, understood as requiring utter submission to strict rules of divine authority, is on this account a species of hypocrisy; one "acts" the part of the selfless enlightened soul but thereby betrays a conceit that dispenses with the need for spectatorship on self, judgment, a sense of proportion, and moral sensitivity to the human consequences of one's actions. It is moral blindness masked as enlightenment.[19]

Hence Smith ends the long discussion of duty in *The Theory of Moral*

---

18 "False notions of religion are almost the only causes which can occasion any very gross perversion of our natural sentiments in this way" (III.6.12; he says "almost" because political ideals can have a similar influence).

19 Although Smith's critique of the transformation of duty into fanaticism is the flip side of his insistence on the centrality of judgment to morality, it has a social context, namely that of a revealed religion and its institutional structures. Smith provides a short history of some Christian practices in order to explain the context in which the natural desire to be in the right was exploited (VII.iv.16–18).

*Sentiments* with this sentence: "No action can properly be called virtuous, which is not accompanied with the sentiment of self-approbation" (III.6.13). We have seen that self-approbation ought to be won through self-governance in accordance with the perspective of the impartial spectator. In Kantian terms, Smith ultimately affirms the moral priority of human freedom and autonomy to any religious doctrine of duty, and does so in part out of a fear of the possible effects of self-love. But he accomplishes this while asserting the primacy of virtues rather than rules, the importance of rules to the exercise of virtue, the indispensable role of judgment, and the natural function of religion in helping us to adhere to the rules we have laid upon ourselves. Smith's acute sense of the dangers of corruption inherent in the interplay among social morality, conscience, rules, religion, and the impartial spectator commends his account. He captures in this interplay something of the genuine polyphonic complexity of moral life, especially (given the roles of revealed religion and conscience) as that complexity manifests itself in the modern age. For that reason, his account makes all the more pressing the problem of how moral criticism is to be sustained in a balanced way.

What will check the transformation of good conscience into erroneous conscience or fanaticism? First, of course, moral education; the habit of deliberating with appropriate appeal to general rules, and so with an understanding that they are *general*, ought to be ingrained in the character of a virtuous person. Smith has written a book on the moral emotions, and he clearly envisions a developmental process that enables us to shape ourselves so that our passions are rightly attuned and have the right "pitch." Conversation with self and others on the great stage of human life is part and parcel of this education. Hence the habit of engaging in reasonable persuasion, of exercising thoughtful rhetoric, humanizes. Of course other factors will matter, including proper social institutions that encourage the evolution of conscience but not religious fanaticism. In Book V of *The Wealth of Nations* he argues that the separation of church and state, along with other liberal political and social arrangements, supports the goal of balance and moderation.

## Moral Criticism

I have already indicated above that the relationship between the perception of particulars and the appeal to moral rules is circular. There are other circles here as well, and because one of them might be thought quite damaging to Smith's view of ethics, we ought first to confront it before turning to discuss briefly how the kind of moral criticism we have been examining might work in specific cases.

*Conversation.* The fact that the "impartial spectator" is rooted in Smith's phenomenology of actor and spectator suggests that the form of reason giving that an impartial spectator employs has a conversational structure, as one might expect of a notion of moral reason giving built on sympathy between an actor and a spectator who occupy a species of "theatrical" relation to each other. This process of achieving impartiality through conversation is other-directed and responsive to an audience. It is a kind of ethical practice and engagement. Smith's view is that moral reason is fundamentally social and (in the best sense) rhetorical, even when it is internalized in the agent. To adopt the standpoint of the impartial spectator is implicitly to hold that one's judgments ought to persuade others. Understood in terms of notions such as harmony, persuasion, and agreement, universality is part of Smith's notion of impartiality.

All of this may seem unacceptably circular. We give reasons to people who can receive them, who in turn are the same people who would give the same kind of reasons to us. As we noted in Chapter 1, however, Smith's view of ethics involves no altogether external standpoint; one must already be in the ethical sphere even to have the proper detachment from it.[20] The circularity implied is not vicious, however, because of the suppleness and porousness of the notion of "conversation" itself. It allows for a range of considerations, from factual error to the inconsistency or insufficiency of one's interlocutor (recall Smith's criticisms of his predecessors) to the shamefulness of one's opponent's stand. Perhaps the most powerful resource at Smith's disposal, as a practitioner of this ethical conversation, is his impressive ability to "save the appearances" (in the phrase of a commentator on Aristotle) through sensitive attention to the detail of ordinary, prephilosophical life and also to unify it

---

20 Smith's standpoint is thus congenial to that which J. McDowell attributes to Aristotle: "If a person conceives her practical situation in terms provided for her by a specific ethical outlook, that will present her with certain apparent reasons for acting. On a better understanding of Aristotle's picture, the only standpoint at which she can address the question whether those reasons are genuine is one that she occupies precisely because she has a specific ethical outlook. That is a standpoint from which those seeming requirements are in view as such, not a foundational standpoint at which she might try to reconstruct the demandingness of those requirements from scratch, out of materials from an independent description of nature." There is "no reason to succumb to the fantasy of an external validation." *Mind and World* (Cambridge, Mass.: Harvard University Press, 1994), pp. 80, 82.

systematically without distorting reduction. At the most general level his own presentation establishes its reasonableness by reminding us, and helping us to refine, the self-understanding we already possess of "our neighbourhood, and of the affairs of the very parish which we live in" (VII.ii.4.14). In some respects that self-understanding is paradoxical, as we have seen in the immediately preceding sections, and few moral philosophers are better than Smith is at eliciting paradox without losing their grip on the phenomena.

As philosophers we might find all this quite persuasive, as far as it goes, but remain convinced that anything short of an "absolute" standpoint is "mere rhetoric." We may demand that conversation become a Socratic dialogue that drives "upward" to first principles, seeking to leave all else in the dust. Smith is skeptical of any such philosophical skepticism, and much of his conversation in the book consists in efforts to show why *that* demand for more is misplaced. If Smith is right that ordinary moral life can persuasively claim to possess the resources for moral criticism then the broad circularity of ethical reflection is not self-undermining.

Two examples of objectionable social practices will help us understand the resources available to Smithean moral criticism.

*Slavery and Infanticide as Test Cases.*

> There is not a negro from the coast of Africa who does not . . . possess a degree of magnanimity which the soul of his sordid master is too often scarce capable of conceiving. Fortune never exerted more cruelly her empire over mankind, then when she subjected those nations of heroes to the refuse of the jails of Europe, to wretches who possess the virtues neither of the countries which they come from, nor of those which they go to, and whose levity, brutality, and baseness, so justly expose them to the contempt of the vanquished.
>
> Adam Smith, *TMS* V.2.9

Smith was well known as a critic of slavery and esteemed by abolitionists of the time.[21] He attacks slavery on multiple fronts simultaneously. To

---

21 See D. B. Davis, *The Problem of Slavery in the Age of Revolution: 1770–1823* (Ithaca: Cornell University Press, 1975), p. 347. Montesquieu too provided a battery of arguments against slavery, some calculated to expose the hidden "partiality of the defenders of slavery." See Davis, *The Problem of Slavery in Western Culture* (Ithaca: Cornell University Press, 1967), p. 408. Smith was criticized for his views, including the statement quoted at the beginning of this section. See A. Lee, *An Essay in Vindication of the Continental Colonies of America, from A Censure of Mr. Adam Smith, in his Theory of Moral Sentiments; with some Reflections on Slavery in general* (London, 1764).

begin with, slavery is unprofitable relative to free labor; enslaving others is thus inconsistent with the self-interest of the enslavers themselves, as well as with the economic progress of society over time. Slaves are more expensive than free labor; the work a slave does is of poorer quality, since it is "squeezed out of him by violence only," and riches built on slavery increase class antagonism, since slave owning is at odds with the welfare of the poor freemen. In short, the institution is unprofitable to all concerned (*WN* III.ii.9; I.viii.41; IV.ix.47). Smith could have added that slave societies require expensive policing mechanisms and generate much inconsistency in the law (because of the incoherent views of slaves as both persons and possessions). Arguments from economic efficiency do not resolve the question of justice, but they do block justifications by reference to the alleged utility of the institution for the majority, and given the history of the debate, this is a constructive point.

Further, Smith argues that people overlook their own economic interest when they enslave others because, to put it bluntly, they enjoy dominating others.[22] The institution thus exhibits and encourages corruption of character; it stems from a particularly damaging kind of vanity or desire to be admired. It also degrades the character of the enslaved, encouraging servility and many other vices. The master may deny all this; here Smith attempts to show that the denial depends on rationalizations stemming from the master's "self-deceit," or defective self-knowledge. For example, an enslaver might maintain that his and the slave's positions are proportionate to his inherent virtue and the slave's inherent vice. As in so many other instances, Smith argues that any such "justification" is entirely *partial*. The stirring denunciation of the enslavers quoted at the beginning of this section helps to shock us out of any complacent assumptions we may make on this score.

Smith thinks that human beings are by nature roughly equal in their moral and intellectual abilities. Almost all differences can be explained, he holds, by reference to social conditions and education.[23] This is a complex matter, of course, but it is another arena where Smith enters

---

22 "The pride of man makes him love to domineer, and nothing mortifies him so much as to be obliged to condescend to persuade his inferiors." *WN* III.ii.10. See also *LJ*(A), iii.114, on "this love of domination and tyrannizing" and the statement at iii.117 that "Slavery therefore has been universall in the beginnings of society, and the love of dominion and authority over others will probably make it perpetuall."

23 See *WN* I.ii.4: "The difference between the most dissimilar characters, between a philosopher and a common street porter, for example, seems to arise not so much from nature, as from habit, custom, and education." See also *LJ*(A), vi.47–8.

the debate against slavery. He attacks Aristotelian arguments that some human beings are by nature slaves and therefore legitimate tools of others, and he also attacks justifications of slavery that appeal solely to received convention or tradition – for example, by showing that the institution has not been received elsewhere or could be changed.

Even if the social or economic utility in slavery were demonstrated, we have also seen that Smith will not permit arguments from utility to trump moral arguments based on sympathy and the moral sentiments. The process of ethical evaluation we have been examining comes into play here; one examines the relevant particulars in light of general rules (such as "Do not treat others unjustly"). Smith seeks to show that an impartial spectator who looks at the situation sympathetically, and therefore also from the standpoint of the slaves, will feel the appropriate resentment against the masters and benevolence toward the slaves and will therefore pronounce their enslavement unjust. An understanding (perhaps provided us through well-crafted literature and historical reports) of the particular contexts – say, the capture and transportation of human beings on slave ships or the violent splitting up of families – will form an important piece of the argument. So too will general propositions or "rules" to the effect that it is unjust to deprive a person of the fruits of his or her labor.[24]

A patronizing master might respond by holding that his slaves are perfectly content with their lot. But it is important to recall that in passing moral judgment we imaginatively consider not just the emotions of the actor but their appropriateness relative to the situation. Thus it would be of little account that a given group of slaves seemed "happy," for we can still experience the resentment they ought to be experiencing (and would experience, had they not been misshapen by their situation), just as we can feel for the madman who himself feels nothing (I.i.1.11).

At least part of Smith's attack would consist in forcing a self-satisfied slave owner into a dialectical examination of his own premises and actions that would reveal underlying vanity, partiality to self, false beliefs, or inconsistency with other accepted views (e.g., that might does not

---

24 See *WN* I.x.c.12: "The property which every man has in his own labour, as it is the original foundation of all other property, so it is the most sacred and inviolable. The patrimony of a poor man lies in the strength and dexterity of his hands; and to hinder him from employing this strength and dexterity in what manner he thinks proper without injury to his neighbour, is a plain violation of this most sacred property." What holds for the "poor man" holds *a fortiori* for the slave.

make right). Smith's strategy in matters of moral evaluation is in this sense, as one commentator has noted, strongly Socratic.[25] Smith does not simply invoke abstract principles – say, a doctrine of natural rights – even though it follows from his own theory of justice that depriving a person of liberty is a greater harm than depriving another of his property (say, a master of his slave). Nor does he simply study the records of history or report moral judgments of his time (the morality of slavery being much controverted at the time). His Socratic strategy allows for this but also for a great deal more.

If a slave owner were insensible to all appeals of humanity, uncomprehending of demonstrations of his errors about the alleged utility of the system, and indifferent to the reduction of justice to the exercise of brute force, then he would fall outside the sphere of ethical conversation. In such a case, neither Smith's nor anyone else's arguments will reach him. If there is truth to the "intuitionism" or "immediacy" view of moral "perception," it is here. Imagine that after going through all of the considerations just described, an "indifferent spectator" is presented with the spectacle of husband and wife and children being violently and permanently separated and sold into slavery. Imagine that this spectator truly is "indifferent," feeling nothing, and is still unable to understand why this horrible event merits his condemnation. Here we would declare: "He just doesn't see it," and discussion would come to an end.

Let me turn briefly now to the example of infanticide, in order to bring out another point about the kind of moral criticism Smith proffers. He touches on this example several times, but especially in one passage in *The Theory of Moral Sentiments*. At the end of Part V, "Of Custom," as if to compel the question of the extent to which convention is open to ethical criticism, he cites the example to show that dreadful customs may arise for broadly "economic" reasons. As he notes in *The Wealth of Nations*, in "miserably poor" nations people are sometimes reduced to abandoning infants, the old, and the sick, so as to avoid dying themselves, and this led to a systematized practice, as in China and ancient Rome, of collecting and exposing unwanted infants (*WN* intro.4, I.viii.24; *LJ* (A) iii.80). After the economic conditions that led to this practice

---

25  Haakonssen, *The Science of a Legislator*, pp. 56, 66. In chapter 6, Haakonssen ably examines the way in which Smith's philosophy allows critical evaluation of a number of other social phenomena, from polygamy to international relations.

changed, custom still "authorized" them. The "imaginations of men" having been habituated to the practice, moral blindness on the issue became the norm, even among the greatest philosophers of the past. Plato and Aristotle are named. Although Smith judges the original practice in specific contexts to be understandable and "excusable," he also pronounces it a "barbarity." Economic need does not mitigate moral blame. His moral judgment is based in part on sympathy, and he briefly conjures up for us the terrible situation of the helpless victim (*TMS* V.2.15).

Thus great philosophical ability does not necessarily protect its possessor from shocking moral blindness. Unlike impartial spectatorship, philosophy – even at the level of Plato and Aristotle – may instead provide conceptual tools for rationalizing a barbaric practice. Implicit in this passage is a pointed moral critique of philosophy. The greatest philosophers have some monumental moral blind spots, and on Smith's account this reflects the inability of theoretical reason alone to grasp that which is of moral value. Smith also means to suggest that when philosophers persuade themselves that excellence of character can be reduced to acuteness and comprehensiveness of mind, they succumb to an entirely human propensity to vanity. To recognize all this is to grant Smith another resource for moral discussion, since it focuses attention on practice, sympathy, and virtuous character.

Further discussion of the "content" of Smith's ethics must depend largely on the examination of specific virtues, to which we now turn.

## 3. EXCELLENCES OF CHARACTER: SELF-COMMAND, PRUDENCE, AND BENEVOLENCE

The man who acts according to the rules of perfect prudence, of strict justice, and of proper benevolence, may be said to be perfectly virtuous.
Adam Smith, *TMS* VII.iii.1

Much of Smith's ethical theory consists in discussion of specific virtues and of the characters who embody them. The cardinal virtues for Smith are self-command, prudence, benevolence, and justice. We will examine these here, reserving justice for the next chapter. Although Smith provides no complete list of the virtues, some candidates are certainly excluded, most obviously those he associates with the "futile mortifications of the monastery."

## Self-Command

Self-command, Smith tells us, "is not only itself a great virtue, but from it all the other virtues seem to derive their principal lustre" (VI.iii.11). Why is this so? Self-command must permeate all of the virtues, since all of them require that self-love be checked to the degree judged appropriate by the spectator (VI.iii.1). The actor is generally called upon to view himself from a less biased standpoint than his own, and to control the passions correspondingly. As we have seen, the degree to which a passion ought to be moderated depends in part on the kind of passion that is in question. In general, the more self-command required of the agent, the more approbation and self-approbation are warranted (III.3.26). This principle follows directly from the spectator-oriented ethical theory. While self-command is a component of every virtue, it is not a sufficient condition for virtue entire; one could possess great command over one's fear of death, thus being (in the appropriate context) courageous, while also being unjust (VI.iii.12; VI.concl.7). There is strain in denominating self-command a virtue. Since we do praise self-command as a distinct trait of character, Smith is entitled to single it out as a virtue. Yet, since it is an admirable feature of all the virtues, it is bound to overlap with other virtues such as prudence.

## Prudence

A chief virtue of the "selfish" passions, one that is recommended to us by the pursuit of our own happiness, is prudence. It is of critical importance to Smith's scheme of the virtues. He distinguishes among several kinds of prudence; let us call one "ordinary" and another "high" or "noble" prudence. The former is closely associated by him with frugality, industry, discipline, thrift, economy, virtues that are normally the prerequisites for the successful pursuit of the crucial drive to "better our condition" of which he speaks in both his books.[26] "Prudence" is a bridge between the two books because it is both a moral and an economic virtue.[27] Bettering one's own condition, as we have seen, is mo-

26 At I.ii.1.4 prudence is said to restrain the bodily passions within the bounds prescribed by health and fortune while temperance commands bodily appetites with "grace" and "propriety." This sort of prudence seems lower than what I am calling "ordinary" prudence because it is concerned with bodily passions rather than with those of the imagination.

27 In *WN* Smith refers to prudence at I.x.b.20, II.ii.28, II.ii.36, II.iv.2, V.i.a.14, and V.i.f.25

tivated not so much by basic needs as by the desire to become the proper object of respect on account of one's "credit and rank in the society" (VI.i.3). The virtue of prudence consists in the combination of "superior reason and understanding" (about the consequences of our actions and the advantages they might bring us) and self-command over our appetite for present gratification (IV.2.6). The impartial spectator goes along with the agent's postponement of pleasure, since to the observer, the agent's present and future pleasures carry equal weight, and since the spectator admires the self-command it takes for an agent to see it in that light (IV.2.8). This does not mean that ordinary prudence is reducible simply to "prudential considerations," for to act solely from them is to lack the full character that makes prudence a virtue. Those who are "prudent" in the sense of possessing skill in prudential considerations rather than an ingrained sense of propriety do not have their passions under control and frequently succumb to anger, lust, and the corresponding vices (VI.concl.4, 5).

High prudence is exhibited by "the great general, . . . the great statesman, . . . the great legislator" and "necessarily supposes the utmost perfection of all the intellectual and of all the moral virtues." Consequently it comes close to constituting the "character of the Academical or Peripatetic sage, as the inferior prudence does that of the Epicurean" (VI.i.15). This sense of prudence amounts to Platonic *sophia* (VII.ii.1.6), that is, to self-command over all of the emotions to the appropriate degree and in the right manner.

Smith is one of the last philosophers in the Western tradition for whom prudence remains a virtue, a morally praiseworthy disposition of character, whereas for Kant and most of his successors prudence is mere *Klugheit*, or cleverness.[28] That Smith should think it a virtue confirms his unwillingness to banish self-regarding motives and actions from the realm of the praiseworthy, that is, to collapse self-interest into self-love, on the one hand, and impartiality into impersonalism on the other hand. In understanding even ordinary prudence to be a virtue, Smith implicitly denies that bettering our condition is intrinsically vile or contemptible. His resistance to the reduction of self-interest to self-love, and of virtue to benevolence, gives his theory of prudence a classical flavor. And yet,

---

and to associated virtues at I.x.b.38 ("a long life of industry, frugality, and attention") and III.iv.3 ("habits . . . of order, oeconomy and attention"). In *WN* "prudence" does tend to be confined by its economic context and therefore comes closer to meaning skill in advancing one's interests (as at II.ii.86) than it does in *TMS*.

28 See Kant, *Grounding for the Metaphysics of Morals*, p. 26.

the content he gives ordinary prudence removes it significantly from Aristotelian *phronesis* (prudence, practical wisdom), in two respects. First, Smithean prudence is tied to a notion of self-approbation rather than self-perfection, and, in at least one of its manifestations, to relatively low or quotidian ends or objects, such as social standing and worldly advancement. Second, ordinary prudence requires judgment and a sense of "propriety" but not any wisdom that extends beyond one's own local situation. Thus it requires a modicum of "intellectual virtue," but only that.[29]

In a manner reminiscent of Theophrastus, Smith paints a wonderful portrait of this "sedate and deliberate virtue" (VI.concl.6), thereby explaining the virtue by means of a character who exhibits it. The object of prudence is, first, security, and then the goods of fortune and reputation accumulated over time. The prudent man is cautious, frugal, parsimonious, polite, decent, capable of friendship, not particularly passionate, reliable. He is not interested in putting on a public show, is sincere but reserved, and dependable. He will do his public duty when called upon but essentially minds his own business. That is, he is disposed to be an apolitical citizen. He sacrifices present enjoyment for future enjoyment, lives within his means, and gradually works himself into a position of gentle retirement and relaxation. He is parsimonious but not a miserly penny pincher (III.6.6). He attains "secure tranquillity" (VI.i.12–13). He exhibits in steady fashion the "gentler exertions of self-command" (VI.iii.13), for he has lived "in the great school of self-command, in the bustle and business of the world" (III.3.25). He warrants our confidence, esteem, and goodwill. The prudent man earns both the "cold esteem" as well as the "entire approbation of the impartial spectator" (VI.i.11, 14). There is nothing in him an impartial observer could object to, and much to praise.

As Smith paints this character, it is clear that the prudent man is also just, in that he does not cheat, steal, or harm others, has no ambition to dominate them and none to prostrate himself before the great or powerful, and does not engage in rash enterprises that end up harming people (VI.i.12). He perseveres in a reasonable life. This certainly includes his caring for those in his charge – his family, for example, or, as appropriate, members of any civic association to which he belongs. He

---

29 For an excellent discussion of this point, the Aristotelian texts, and in general of Smith's notion of prudence, see D. J. Den Uyl, *The Virtue of Prudence* (New York: Lang, 1991), p. 62 and ch. 5.

is entirely trustworthy; you can leave your children and bank account in his hands, and they will be safeguarded until you return. Smith says nothing about his being religious or belonging to a church.

The "prudent man" in effect represents Smith's picture of a superior but achievable type of human being that a liberal and commercial society would do well to foster (e.g., *WN* II.iii.16; IV.vii.c.61; IV.ix.13).[30] That prudence earns only "cold esteem" suggests that a society made up of prudent persons would warrant the same honor – neither warm admiration nor condemnation, at least in regard to that virtue, but esteem nonetheless. But the prudent man is not *Homo economicus* – a mere bundle of grasping passions for self-advancement come what may – or a disgustingly vulgar and corrupt person. Today, when we condemn "consumerism" and the types of individuals that we imagine populate a commercial society, we are thinking of vain, not prudent, persons. Nor is prudence primarily an economic virtue, focused on skill in the accumulation of wealth. A prudent person is not a mere monad in a society of strangers, intent just on improving his or her material lot, and a society of prudent persons is not a formula for social anomie. The prudent person has moral ties to others, including those of benevolence and justice, and exhibits other virtues as well.

By contrast, the person of "high" or "noble" prudence is of unambiguous moral worth. Because he unites "the most perfect wisdom combined with the most perfect virtue," a nobly prudent person could not but command our highest admiration. This ideal is presumably out of our reach. An achievable simulacrum of noble prudence or wisdom is a more complicated matter and represents a third type of prudence located somewhere between the other two: "every impartial spectator" admires "the real merit of those spirited, magnanimous, and high-minded persons," but as long as they are successful in their great projects, is also blind to "not only the great imprudence, but frequently the great injustice of their enterprises" as well as their "excessive self-estimation and presumption" (VI.iii.30). Their self-command is accompanied by unqualified self-approbation and is what Descartes described as *générosité*. They exhibit a strange blend of self-command and immoderation, of admirable ambition and questionable willingness to take great risks. Smith names them: the "splendid characters, the men who have performed the most illustrious actions, who have brought about the greatest revolutions, both in the situations and opinions of mankind; the

30 For a similar view see Winch, *Riches and Poverty*, p. 105.

most successful warriors, the greatest statesmen and legislators, the eloquent founders and leaders of the most numerous and most successful
sects and parties" (Socrates being among them; VI.iii.28). Smith's evaluation of them is rightly ambivalent, for such "splendid characters" are
both necessary and dangerous.

Smith's discussion of high prudence grows out of his analysis of what
he calls the "virtues of self-command," in particular command over fear,
anger, and resentment. Those who command these passions greatly diminish their fear of death, and whether or not they are virtuous (Socrates
is again named, VI.iii.5), we admire them for it: "The command of fear,
the command of anger, are always great and noble powers" (VI.iii.12).
We would lack heroes and defenders were this self-command impossible.
War and faction are "the best schools" for acquiring this kind of character. And yet much of it is not praiseworthy, for those who are insensible
to these emotions become too hard and insensible to the distress of
others. Such a person appears to be supremely virtuous, but is not; for
he no longer feels what he should; he simply does not feel enough. And
thus his character is not shaped by "the great demi-god within the
breast" so much as it is unidimensional and insufficiently examined
(VI.iii.18–20). The step from there to hardened fanaticism or over-
weening ambition is uncomfortably short.

Hence the proper aspiration to high prudence is a delicate matter. If
Smith, as a humanized Socrates, were prudent in this relatively high or
noble sense, intending to bring about "the greatest revolutions, both in
the situations and opinions of mankind" (for example, by reforming the
entire economic system of Great Britain), how would he conduct himself
as a public philosopher? What public face would his *générosité* assume? I
take it that the answer is exhibited in the rhetoric and content of his
published books and shall return to the question in Chapter 7 as well as
the Epilogue. We also find more of the answer, however, in his remarks
about benevolence.

## Benevolence

As the virtue of what he terms the "social passions" and other-regarding
conduct, "benevolence" (or "beneficence" – Smith goes back and forth
between the terms) may in a broad sense stand for social cooperation,
the great desideratum of so much of his moral theory. (For the "social"
passions, see Chapter 3, section 1.) His emphasis on goodwill, friendship,
love, harmony, sociality, conversation, ordinary human sympathy (in a

nontechnical sense), and all of the "agreeable passions" testifies to his desire to see benevolence written into our daily lives. But he also holds that as a distinct virtue of the "social passions" it is best expressed locally, within our relevant circles of sympathy. As we saw in our examination of impartiality in Chapter 3, the "universal happiness of all rational and sensible beings" ought not be our ethical goal; we lack the knowledge to aim for it well, in pursuing it we would ignore those spheres effectively under our purview, and our passions are not made for so lofty a love (VI.ii.3.6). Two striking features of Smith's discussion of benevolence are his refusal to reduce all of moral goodness to it and his insistence that it be expressed in its proper spheres. Those spheres are dictated in part by our emotions, including our "selfish" emotions, as well as by the natural propensity of sympathy to entertain that which is closer and more familiar first. Benevolence allows for warranted partiality toward members of our own circle, and is thus closely tied to a view of the contexts in which our moral identities and view of the good life are developed.

Thus nature inclines us first to care for our individual selves, then for our family – immediate family first, then extended family, and among the immediate family the children first, then our parents, then our friends, acquaintances, our country. Humanity *qua* humanity is last on the list. These define our circles of belonging and carry with them a variety of moral obligations, or, in Ciceronian language, duties of "office." We are subject to obligations of justice to all humanity but not of benevolence to humanity as such. Smith's portrait of benevolence chimes with his picture of the relatively apolitical character of the prudent person. Indeed, the first proper object of benevolence, namely, one's own self, seems to amount to a species of prudence. More broadly understood, benevolence requires the exercise of judgment, for there will be competing loyalties in some cases, and indeed judgment will be required to determine in some cases whether we are to act with benevolence or prudence.

In one of his best-known and most compelling passages, Smith describes the degeneration of the public-minded spirit of a great person into the "spirit of system," or political fanaticism, motivated not by base self-interest but by a perception of the "imaginary beauty" of an "ideal system" for government. This "intoxicated" person of high prudence imagines that he can manipulate his fellow citizens "with as much ease as the hand arranges the different pieces upon a chess-board." This is dangerous "arrogance" masked as selfless and benevolent public service. Thus some of Smith's best lessons about high prudence are offered in the course of his discussion of great benevolence. He hopes to show us that the ambitions of the great dangerously combine self-approbation with a vision of a beautiful social order. The secret to long-lasting and morally defensible success therefore lies in a combination of ambitious vision, suitable moderation, religious adherence to principles of justice, and a keen awareness that individuals and their contexts ought to be the beneficiaries of our efforts rather than the instruments of our ideals. This is by no means a formula for quietism. In times of faction and disorder, a wise patriot may think it necessary to change fundamentally the constitution of the nation, but deciding when and how to do so "requires, perhaps, the highest effort of political wisdom to determine." Finding the mean between a "dangerous spirit of innovation" and quietist conservatism is surely a task for high prudence. Smith's example is Solon, who established not the best regime but the best the people could bear (VI.ii.2.12, 16).

Smith's views on benevolence have bearing on one of the most famous passages in *The Wealth of Nations*. It runs as follows: "It is not from the benevolence of the butcher, the brewer, or the baker, that we expect our dinner, but from their regard to their own interest. We address ourselves, not to their humanity but to their self-love, and never talk to them of our own necessities but of their advantages" (I.ii.2). That is, we address ourselves to the prudence, not the benevolence, of the shopkeeper in our daily exchanges; and presumably they address themselves to ours. Contrary to a common reading of these lines, they are not an encomium to greed or depraved selfishness but a morally acceptable statement of a fact that may hold in any instance of exchange (whether in a "capitalist" or barter economy). Smith's examples are well chosen; he refers to ordinary working people who supply our necessities and who themselves toil to supply their own. Appeals to your benevolence *qua* business person are normally not appropriate when I seek to feed myself. In normal exchanges with us, the shopkeeper acts virtuously, that is, in accordance with ordinary prudence and justice; the sphere of the shopkeeper's benevolence ought not to extend indiscriminately to all those who want the goods he sells, though on occasion it may extend to some. Smith follows the statement quoted with a reference to the "beggar" who also chooses to avoid taking charity if possible. Yet the shopkeeper may owe the beggar charity; as always, judgment is required, and nothing Smith says precludes its benevolent exercise under these circumstances.

Smith's examples evoke the picture of a town, in which sellers and buyers know one another, but his point does not require such mutual knowledge. He is writing about a context in which economic relations will largely be conducted among strangers, and his picture of the virtues holds that these economic relations are not debased simply because they are not premised on benevolence. Economic relations in a commercial society, especially, do not take place between a "little knot of companions" (to recall Smith's term; I.ii.2.6), and Smith has no patience with any "organic" political model that would collapse the circles of sympathy into one. Prudence, and within its proper spheres benevolence, are civic virtues. What Smith calls the "assembly of strangers" (*TMS* I.i.4.9), that is, modern society, does not necessarily destroy virtue; it may encourage it, as long as it is supported by justice.

## 4. MORAL EDUCATION

> In free countries, where the safety of government depends very much upon the favourable judgment which the people may form of its conduct, it must surely be of the highest importance that they should not be disposed to judge rashly or capriciously concerning it.
>
> Adam Smith, *WN* V.i.f.61

I have repeatedly stressed the value of moral education for Smith. He did not write, or intend to write, an essay or book on education, and no chapter or part of *The Theory of Moral Sentiments* is solely devoted to it. There is no Smithean analogue to, say, Rousseau's *Emile*. But moral education is a continuous theme not only in *The Theory of Moral Sentiments*, in connection with individual virtue and judgment, but also in *The Wealth of Nations*, where it is addressed in connection with civic virtue and self-government. Like religion and justice, moral education is one of the bridges between the two books.

We have examined at some length Smith's moral psychology and the process by which we become responsible moral agents. Our growth into impartial spectators takes place by degrees and has much to do with the way in which approval and disapprobation, pleasure and pain, and emulation are structured. In familiar Aristotelian fashion, it is a matter of the formation of character through a process that includes words as well as deeds, instruction as well as actions (cf. *NE* 1114a9–13). As we saw in Chapter 2, Smith harbors no illusions about the existence of a preformed self, a miniature adult within the child, whose freedom or inborn virtue need only be released in order for it to gain moral autonomy. The "human creature" in "some solitary place" has no moral self (IV.2.12);

that self arises through social interaction. The "mirroring" process of sympathy is a necessary condition for the development of moral self-consciousness and character.

The "exercise and practice" requisite to establish the habits of virtue, and thus moral agency, are acquired over time (III.3.36). The goal is to develop persons who habitually "identify" themselves (to use Smith's verb) with the impartial spectator and who thus act virtuously. As we have seen, this involves an agent's learning self-command with a view to satisfying the expectations of a spectator. That is, the actor's natural need, as a child, for the spectator's approval must be developed, since it is essential that the standpoint of the spectator be privileged over that of the actor. The spectator's expectations will certainly be formulated as general rules, and these will be learned as time goes by, for there are "different shades and gradations of weakness and self-command."[31] It is a matter of "constant practice" and "habit" to learn to view oneself from the spectator's standpoint; moral agency is acquired by degrees (III.3.22, 25). Only through practice do we learn to feel what it is appropriate to feel and, correspondingly, what it is appropriate to praise and blame, what a good and what a "harm" truly is. In this fashion we learn to judge which emotions are fitting and praiseworthy. Since the "harmony and concord" between agent and spectator is key here, we may also say that moral education consists in learning to appreciate moral beauty.

What Smith repeatedly refers to as the "great school of self-command" begins at home. Here the model for the spectator normally is, and ought to be, the parent, whose love supplies the context in which the requisite care, attention to detail, knowledge of the child, responsiveness, and sympathy can be counted on. The parent shows by example, as well as precept, that self-command makes one not only lovable but able to love; thanks to sympathy, the process by which one comes to have perspective and proper concern for one's self is inseparable from that by which one has the same for others.[32] The child's earliest friendships, those with his siblings, as well as later friendships with playmates and extended family, are necessary to the instruction in self-command.

31 Even "the most vulgar education teaches us to act, upon all important occasions, with some sort of impartiality between ourselves and others, and even the ordinary commerce of the world is capable of adjusting our active principles to some degree of propriety" (III.3.7).
32 "Our sensibility to the feelings of others, so far from being inconsistent with the manhood of self-command, is the very principle upon which that manhood is founded" (III.3.34).

Where one's parents might "understand," perhaps a bit too much, one's friends may not, and this can be salutary.

Smith is insistent that the education of young boys and girls not be conducted at distant boarding schools.[33] He does not refer to what we call "home education" but to the notion that the primary context for moral education is the home and the family; during the day only, let the children be sent out, he says, to school. The circles of sympathy and care bring with them various duties – love, in the case of the family; friendship, in the case of a wider circle; fidelity, in the case of discharging the obligations of one's office (e.g., as a soldier, teacher, or citizen). Moral personality would be stunted were one somehow limited to just one of these spheres, and Smith assumes that we normally do and ought to expand our moral selves by means of these various attachments. This has the important political implication that these circles of sympathy should be nourished, and that the moral individual should, ideally, be able to expand his horizon so as to encompass several of them.[34]

Moral education does not consist in self-command that focuses simply on suppressing the "selfish" passions and instilling "self-discipline," and the virtues we must acquire are not to be reduced to one. The virtuous person feels the right things at the right times in the right way. Although the "untaught and undisciplined feelings" (III.3.28) need constant tutoring, the ultimate aim is propriety and proportion, not extirpation of emotions. One discerns in the background a critique of an excessively religious moral education that would treat certain emotions as though they were enemies within.

The spectator also adjusts his or her emotions in light of the actor's situation, and the parent must show by example and in deed how this is to be done. The mutuality of sympathy, with all of the time and attention it requires, is nourished by the bond between child and parent; this is

33 "Domestic education is the institution of nature; public education, the contrivance of man. It is surely unnecessary to say, which is likely to be the wisest" (*TMS* VI.ii.1.10).

34 Smith rightly worries about the deformation of the moral sentiments that occurs when a person is educated solely by the "school of self-command" imposed by war or, alternatively, by "the mild sunshine of undisturbed tranquillity, in the calm retirement of undissipated and philosophical leisure." In one case we will become too hardened to the gentle virtues of humanity. In the other case we will become too soft, too easily given to empathetic words for the downtrodden, and yet also irresolute and easily disheartened by really demanding battles (III.3.37). If our emotions are not "sufficiently blunted and hardened by early education and proper exercise," we will be unable to discharge our duty and endure what is difficult (VI.iii.19). Neither the soldier nor the philosophy professor easily qualifies as "the man of the most perfect virtue" referred to in the epigraph to this chapter.

the basis for mutual respect that, Smith says in addressing the reader directly, imposes restraints upon the child's conduct as well as "your own" (VI.ii.1.10). Given the importance of imitation or "emulation" in the development of the agent's love of virtue – that is, the love of that which is praiseworthy as distinguished from praised – it will matter that the agent be surrounded by persons worthy of being emulated. Moral exemplars (the equivalent of Aristotle's morally excellent person) of necessity must play a leading role in Smith's notion of moral education. The agent will often be guided, in moral situations, by the question "How would this person of virtue, X, act in this situation?"

Underlying Smith's picture of the well-formed person is a view of a harmony or beauty, including the graceful "fittedness" of moral virtues to self and to each other. The ideal is a harmony of emotions, words, and deeds, a wholeness of self, and so a unity of the virtues. A life in accordance with moral beauty has, like a good narrative, internal unity and proportion, and its resulting grace commands our admiration and compels our emulation.[35] Inspired by this paradigm, we yearn for a correspondence of our own emotions with those of the impartial spectator that makes harmony possible and, if we achieve it, are rewarded with both happiness and self-approbation. To switch metaphors, perception of perfected moral character is of "musical" unity, of polyphony orchestrated and composed into a complex whole. This "aesthetic" view of a perfected and integrated self guides Smith's drawing of the moral sentiments and their virtues.

The ability to distinguish between the praised and the praiseworthy, as well as the blamed and blameworthy, will grow out of the agent's desire for praise and aversion to blame, or even the agent's desire to appear worthy of praise and not blame. This is why Smith comments that "the great secret of education is to direct vanity to proper objects." If the desire for esteem and admiration can be focused on objects that are the proper objects of those sentiments, then vanity, or even the love of glory, can lead to real virtue (VI.iii.46). Complete identification with the

---

35 In every person the idea of a high standard of virtue is "gradually formed from his observations upon the character and conduct both of himself and of other people" through the "slow, gradual, and progressive work" of conscience. Developing this standard and then measuring up to it is a lifelong process of moral self-improvement. The more one loves the "divine beauty" of the "archetype of perfection" and tries to "assimilate his own character" to it, the more one imitates "the work of a divine artist." The better one accomplishes formation of self, the more clearly one sees details in which one is still imperfect, whether from "want of attention, from want of judgment," "both in words and actions, both in conduct and conversation" (VI.iii.25).

impartial spectator or "man within the breast" is a rare achievement. We have seen that moral rules compensate for the difficulty we have in identifying sufficiently with the standpoint of virtue and that "there is scarce any man . . . who by discipline, education, and example, may not be so impressed with a regard to general rules as to act upon almost every occasion with tolerable decency" (III.5.1). When we are in the habit of evaluating ourselves impartially, by viewing ourselves through the eyes of the impartial spectator or in light of general rules, we are prepared to act with tolerable decency when spectators are not present and when they are present but are partial and corrupt. Internalization of impartial spectatorship is crucial for moral agency. Thus a key aim of moral education is the development of a sense of conscience and duty. That is why a decent person must be able to feel remorse and guilt.

Adherence to moral rules should not replace judgment, as we have seen, and a moral education will teach the observer how to judge. To that end, we must learn how to sympathize properly, and therefore how to think imaginatively about another's and our own situation. The imagination must be trained rightly. Judgment about the ethical course of action to be followed in a given situation requires imagination, since we must represent to ourselves possible courses of action, consider the intended effects of our choice on others and thus view the situation from their standpoint, and indeed review our own motivations from the standpoint of an impartial spectator.[36]

Smith always resists easy descriptions of what this might entail. At an elementary but crucial level, it will be a matter of extending the imagination so that the real situation of the other becomes visible to the spectator. In some cases, moral imagination is needed to carry us beyond the conventional reification of others and so the unethical practices to which those others are subjected. Our examination of slavery illustrates the point and also why literary and rhetorical evocations of the slave's situation and emotions – such as Smith's moving description of the "negro from the coast of Africa" – can help the spectator to grasp the slave's humanity. Through cultivation of sympathy, partiality may be countered, and we learn to share in a common human world and in its improve-

---

36 As Larmore puts it in *Patterns of Moral Complexity* (p. 12): "Moral imagination is the ability to elaborate and appraise different courses of action that are only schematically determined by the given content of moral rules, in order to learn what in a particular situation is indeed the morally best thing to do. It expresses therefore a far more active and thoughtful interest in the moral life than does the observance of fully determinate moral rules."

ment. In general, Smith's use of examples, stories, and anecdotes illustrates that moral education must be grounded in experience and hence be dependent on a suitable circle of experience and suppleness of reflection. A keen sense of duty supplemented by a tutored moral imagination, an alert conscience, and good judgment are essential to the development of the sense of justice, without which, as Smith insists, society collapses into conflict.

Especially in cases where merit and demerit are at stake, right judgment is a complex process. The intellectual ability to assimilate and sift through the relevant information is also required, and therefore a level of intellectual excellence is necessary for moral virtue. At a minimum it involves grasping the situation at hand; responding with the right emotions; understanding accurately the emotions of the agent; entertaining as necessary a conversation in which the multiple factors are assessed and weighed; and, of course, doing all of this with respect to ourselves, if we are the agent to be evaluated. The moral actor ought to be receptive to persuasion as well as capable of offering it. Cultivation of the mind is thus a moral task.

Smith's continual references to literature, especially tragedies, are surely meant to help us to grasp how so difficult an achievement as moral education is to be attained. For study of literature teaches us how ethically complex human situations can be, how to stretch the moral imagination so as to size up the relevant factors, how to carry on a conversation about the competing claims of the dramatis personae. The emotions have a cognitive dimension, as we saw, and can be evaluated relative to the situations in which they occur, as well as in accordance with general rules or maxims. Learning how to judge and how to feel are, though distinguishable, inseparable.[37] Tragedies can educate the moral emotions in another manner too, by teaching us that luck, unforeseen consequences, and tragic irony permeate moral life, and how to respond to this fact. They teach us how to feel about the feelings of others, and so how we ought to feel. Thus moral education should teach

---

37 Cf. Hume's statement, in the *Enquiry Concerning the Principles of Morals*, that although moral judgment is ultimately founded on "some internal sense or feeling, which nature has made universal in the whole species," it is also true that "in many orders of beauty . . . it is requisite to employ much reasoning, in order to feel the proper sentiment; and a false relish may frequently be corrected by argument and reflection. There are just grounds to conclude, that moral beauty partakes much of this latter species, and demands the assistance of our intellectual faculties, in order to give it a suitable influence on the human mind" (p. 173).

us the difference between "moral sentiment" and sentimentalism or easy empathy. Sentimentalism would on Smith's account be a preference for the easy and undisciplined emotions that mask themselves as serious feeling. The sentimental person is really feeling sympathy for himself, endorsing his own emotion without carrying it through, indulging in the pleasure of feeling it.[38] This kind of self-interest is not to be confused with genuine sympathy.[39]

In this light it is useful to note which works of literature Smith praises most highly. When discussing "erroneous conscience," that is, vanity and fanaticism, he lauds Voltaire's *Mahomet* as "perhaps the most instructive spectacle that was ever introduced upon any theatre" (III.6.12), on the grounds that it teaches us so effectively the horrible consequences of religious fanaticism. It is essential that moral education explain what it means to misconceive the nature of duty and rules, as well as represent through the study of literature and history the destructive consequences of that misconception. Racine's *Phèdre* is "the finest tragedy, perhaps, that is extant in any language" (III.2.19), presumably because it depicts so movingly the phenomenon of remorse, thus showing us how the voice of the internalized impartial spectator cannot be entirely extirpated. Voltaire's *L'orphelin de la chine* is cited as a "beautiful tragedy" because it so effectively makes visible to us different shades of "circumstance, character, and situation" that no "casuistic rules" could ever define (VI.ii.1.22). The play shows us that the sentiment of love can become twisted in a ruler's single-minded ambition and then educated by the moral example set by the sentiments of true love as well as by the firm-

---

38  I am grateful to Roger Scruton for suggesting to me this formulation of the problem of sentimentality. See also his "Emotion, Practical Knowledge, and Common Culture," in *Explaining Emotions*, ed. A. O. Rorty (Berkeley and Los Angeles: University of California Press, 1980), pp. 519–36.

39  Smith criticizes the schools of moral philosophers who attempt to correct our self-love in the wrong manner. One school consists of those "whining and melancholy moralists" who always reproach us for our happiness while others are in misery; the other school is that of the Stoics, who attempt to diminish our "sensibility" to ourselves rather than increase our feeling for others (III.3.7–11). We have seen that this second school is partly right, but only partly. The extreme of "stoical apathy" is to be rejected, and thus "the poets and romance writers, who best paint the refinements and delicacies of love and friendship, and of all other private and domestic affections, Racine and Voltaire; Richardson, Maurivaux [Marivaux], and Riccoboni; are, in such cases, much better instructors than Zeno, Chrysippus, or Epictetus" (III.3.14). Smith means this as a criticism of philosophy as moral educator; the poets and literary writers provide us with a more balanced and sensible moral education than the philosopher's reductive insistence on a moral life according to reason.

ness of character of the ruler's intended victims. Smith's choice of high literature is telling, for it points to a conviction that the distortion of sound judgment and sympathy (whether by casuistry, religion, or crude ambition) poses a particular danger to moral education.[40]

## 5. VIRTUE, THE PURSUIT OF HAPPINESS, AND THE TRANQUILLITY OF THE STOIC SAGE

For who is content is happy. But as soon as any new uneasiness comes in, this Happiness is disturb'd, and we are set afresh on work in the pursuit of Happiness.

John Locke[41]

Smith's works are full of comments about happiness, and indeed happiness is mentioned in the first sentence of *The Theory of Moral Sentiments*. What does he mean by "happiness," and how is it related to virtue? Ancient ethical theories typically connected happiness with virtue (or excellence of character), virtue with reflection, and at some level, reflection with philosophy. We cannot be truly happy unless we rightly assess the conditions of our happiness. The model theory, Aristotle's, defines happiness as the activity of the soul in accordance with virtue. Kant's position is the antithesis of Aristotle's, in that it denies any necessary connection between the two (even while holding that the *summum bonum* is the synthesis of virtue and happiness) and views the content of happiness as a matter of empirical psychology. Smith's position is multifaceted, as always, and is connected to a broader reconciliationist enterprise. What does he mean by happiness? He takes his bearings by the sense

---

40 Moral education has institutional and social prerequisites, some of which are discussed in *WN*. It is not simply a matter of sufficient funding for public education but of structuring institutions so that they properly shape moral sentiments. Smith notes in *WN* that "the understandings of the greater part of men are necessarily formed by their ordinary employments. The man whose whole life is spent in performing a few simple operations, of which the effects too are, perhaps, always the same, or very nearly the same, has no occasion to exert his understanding, or to exercise his invention in finding out expedients for removing difficulties which never occur. . . . The torpor of his mind renders him, not only incapable of relishing or bearing a part in any rational conversation, but of conceiving any generous, noble, or tender sentiment, and consequently of forming any just judgment concerning many even of the ordinary duties of private life" (V.i.f.50). These words, with their emphasis on judgment, sentiment, and imagination ("invention"), resonate with my discussion of moral education and are closely linked to the argument of *TMS*.

41 *An Essay Concerning Human Understanding*, ed. P. H. Nidditch (Oxford: Clarendon, 1990), II.xxi.59 (p. 273).

in which we can speak of a person as *generally* "happy," as happy over the long term. We do speak of happiness in quite different senses, as when remarking "that was the happiest moment of my life" or "that was pure bliss." Aristotle remarks that "one swallow does not make a spring, nor does one day; nor, similarly, does one day or a short time make us blessed [*makarion*] and happy [*eudaimon*]" (*NE* I.vii.1098a18–20). Kant too, for all of his differences with Aristotle, speaks of "happiness" in this long-range sense.[42] Smith implicitly distinguishes happiness from joy, ecstasy, romantic transcending bliss, and the like. Happiness, in the sense at issue, is not a mood.

Further, Smith regularly understands happiness in terms of tranquillity, that is, repose and rest. This understanding runs consistently from the moral philosophy to the discussions of intellectual virtue in the *Essays on Philosophical Subjects*.[43] Tranquillity is "the principle and foundation of all real and satisfactory enjoyment" (III.3.31). Smith has good grounds for this approach; phenomenologically speaking, happiness (in the sense of the term that can be predicated of a person over time, of a person's life) does seem more like rest than motion, and this in two senses. First, it consists in one's being at rest in the sense of lacking significant discord; it is peaceful, at a deep level. Second, happiness is more like coming to a stop than like a process of moving toward a goal. Happiness resembles an end state, a completion or fulfillment, rather than a condition of lacking and overcoming of lack.[44] When you say of yourself "I have lived happily" or "I am deeply happy," you mean, among other things, that you do not experience significant internal discord and that fundamentally you occupy a spiritual place from which you do not desire to move. You are not, at a deep level, anxious; basically, you are properly oriented, and your fundamental stance toward the world is complete, at rest. Happiness is rather like a state of peacefulness, being in control, inner harmony, calm, rest – as opposed to a state of war, desiring that which is out of one's control to obtain, internal discord, disturbance, motion, perturbation.

One might assume that felt tranquillity is real tranquillity, thereby eliminating both the possibility of a person's being mistaken about being

---

42 See the *Grounding*, p. 27.
43 E.g., "History of Astronomy" IV.13, *EPS*, p. 61: ". . . the repose and tranquillity of the imagination is the ultimate end of philosophy. . . ."
44 Compare Rousseau's remarks about happiness in the fifth *Promenade*, in *The Reveries of the Solitary Walker*, trans. C. Butterworth (New York: New York University Press, 1979), pp. 68–9.

happy and with it the distinction between contentment and happiness, tranquilization and tranquillity. But an account of happiness must preserve the possibility of self-deception or failure of self-knowledge, and Smith's does so. We require *something* like an objectivist view of the sort Aristotle articulates, that is, a view according to which virtue is both a necessary condition of happiness and is understood as excellence of self. The tranquillity view of happiness tends to be associated with *apatheia* – passionlessness, a leveling out of the emotions, detachment or indifference. This is precisely because of the close association of tranquillity with rest, peacefulness, and the other qualities already spoken of and the contrary association of emotions and attachment with perturbance, discord, motion. Yet to live a life of tranquillity so understood rightly strikes Smith as barren, dry, uninspired, as forsaking much that is of value in human life. To eliminate psychic motion altogether, rather than to *moderate* it as appropriate, and then to call the resulting tranquillity "happiness" seems to purchase happiness at the price of human fulfillment, serenity at the price of our humanity. Why should we accept a notion of happiness that demands so high a price? Epictetus tells us: "Never say about anything, 'I have lost it,' but only 'I have given it back.' Is your child dead? It has been given back. Is your wife dead? She has been given back."[45] Epicurus is said to have claimed that the wise man could be happy (retain *ataraxia*, tranquillity) even on the rack.[46] This is precisely the sort of reasoning that both fascinates and repels Smith.

The background against which Smith's view is set may be found in Hobbes. In the *Leviathan*, we read:

> *Continual success* in obtaining those things which a man from time to time desireth, that is to say, continual prospering, is that men call FELICITY; I mean the felicity of this life. For there is no such thing as perpetual tranquillity of mind, while we live here; because life itself is but motion, and can never be without desire, nor without fear, no more than without sense.[47]

45 *Encheiridion* 11, in vol. 2 of *Discourses*, 2 vols., trans. W. A. Oldfather (Cambridge, Mass.: Harvard University Press), p. 491. Epictetus recommends (par. 26) that a man react to the death of his child or wife just as he would to another man's loss of his child or wife.

46 See Diogenes Laertius, *Lives* 10.118. Cf. Epictetus, *Discourses* IV.iv.36–7, on the association of happiness with tranquillity, *apatheia*, and having one's affairs under control.

47 *Leviathan*, ed. E. Curley (Indianapolis: Hackett, 1994), ch. VI.58, pp. 34–5. Further on in the book Hobbes takes up the same theme. After declaring that there is no such thing as a *summum bonum*, contrary to the "books of the old moral Philosophers," he states: "Felicity is a continual progress of the desire, from one object to another, the attaining of the former being still but the way to the latter. . . . And therefore the voluntary actions

Life is, in other words, ceaselessly driven by desire, anxiety, and fear, especially the fear of violent death. Human life is fundamentally disturbance and disquiet. We move from one object of desire to another, one contentment to the next, in a restless search for the stability that stems from security, that is, an equality of power with other people. If life were like this, in motion and anxious, then we surely would not call it happy; we would not possess what Hobbes calls "perpetual tranquillity of mind," that is, general cessation of spiritual motion. Hobbes seems right in associating contentment with the movement from one satisfaction to the the next; it seems intrinsically unstable even though it seeks stability. The essential contrast in Hobbes' picture, then, is between "felicity" – or what we might, taking our cue from his own words, better call repeated "contentment" – and tranquillity over time. Felicity is inseparably interwoven with anxiety, whereas tranquillity is not.

Another general feature of happiness captured by tranquillity, and implicit in the quotations from Hobbes, is that the enemy of tranquillity is anxiety, and this at two levels. The first is anxiety about this or that event – for example, the anxiety you have about your stock portfolio losing value. The second is a general anxiety about things being out of kilter, not stable, not holding, potentially dissolving. When Hobbes talks about people's ongoing fear that their competitors might gain more power, enough power to be threatening, he is getting at the second level, though he remains within the sphere of the political. Perhaps it is something like the dread that we are at risk not from the power of another person but in the sense that the foundations on which we built our life are not yet finished, or may crumble, or never were well laid. Perhaps (one thinks silently to oneself) my life has been a waste, amounted to nothing: What have I become? What will become of me? Was this a praiseworthy life? In Chapter 2 we noted the *pathos* intrinsic to Smith's picture of the self, and in Chapter 3 we noted his remarkable depiction of inner moral struggle, guilt, remorse, and the sense of moral unworthiness. At least in one place he muses about "the most melancholy of all reflections" – the idea that we live in a "fatherless world" (VI.ii.3.2). When doubts such as these eat away the soul, anxiety (or *tarache*) in our second sense of the term has won out over happiness.

and inclinations of all men tend, not only to the procuring, but also to the assuring of a contented life. . . . I put for a general inclination of all mankind, a perpetual and restless desire of power after power, that ceaseth only in death." *Leviathan*, ch. XI.1, 2, pp. 57–8. For a similar contrast between "uneasiness" and "happiness" see Locke, *Essay* II.xxi.42–6.

Hobbes's parallel distinctions between felicity (repeated but short-lived contentment) and tranquillity, motion and rest, desiring and completion, and his identification of true happiness with tranquillity, seem to be accepted by both Locke and Smith. (See the quotation from Locke at the beginning of this section.) The confusion of happiness with contentment is, nevertheless, widespread. The often belated recognition that the two are distinct is perhaps not as widespread, but it is the sort of stuff of which the wisdom of the elders is made. Smith plausibly argues that the confusion is systematic, and this helps him to explain why it is that people strive so mightily for goods that will not, in fact, bring them happiness (in the sense of long-term tranquillity). Reformulating Hobbes' point about our eagerness for "continual prospering," Smith sees us (in both *TMS* and *WN*) as naturally bent on "bettering our condition" by accumulating the goods of fortune – external goods – as well as wealth, reputation, and power. The "desire of bettering our condition . . . comes with us from the womb, and never leaves us till we go into the grave." Between birth and death one is never "so perfectly and completely satisfied with his condition, as to be without any wish of alteration or improvement," and "augmentation of fortune is the means by which the great part of men propose and wish to better their condition" (*WN* II.iii.28). As we noted in Chapter 3 (section 1), in *The Theory of Moral Sentiments* Smith argues that not "passions of the body," not "physical" needs, but the drive to be the object of approbation underlies this never-ending effort to better ourselves. In that approbation, we think, lies happiness.[48] A man who imagines himself in the condition of the rich "thinks if he had attained all these [good things], he would sit still contentedly, and be quiet, enjoying himself in the thought of the happiness and tranquillity of his situation. He is enchanted with the distant idea of this felicity" (IV.I.8).

In Smith's account, this remarkable phenomenon is aesthetic at two levels. First, we yearn for the harmony or beauty of a correspondence of sentiments with spectators that we (rightly) imagine is the good fortune of the wealthy and powerful. Second, the spectators' approval of the wealthy and powerful is "disinterested" (I.iii.3.2), a function of the spectators' appreciation of the beauty of countless "trinkets of frivolous util-

---

48 "When we consider the condition of the great, in those delusive colours in which the imagination is apt to paint it, it seems to be almost the abstract idea of a perfect and happy state. It is the very state which, in all our waking dreams and idle reveries, we had sketched out to ourselves as the final object of all our desires" (I.iii.2.2, 1; cf. III.1.7).

ity" possessed by the rich and powerful. We are drawn, not by any sense of the purposes to which these goods (from watches to clothes to carriages to houses) may be put but, rather, by their intrinsic fineness, and this attraction of the beautiful "is often the secret motive of the most serious and more important pursuits of both private and public life" (IV.1.7, 6). Both levels of aesthetic appreciation are the work of the imagination, yet the association of happiness with that seemingly beautiful life is fallacious. Smith refers to that association as a "deception" produced by our imagination and thus as imposed (his verb) on us by nature (IV.1.10).

The immediate result of this deception is that, except in those rare moments when we view beauty in an "abstract and philosophical light" (IV.1.9), we are plunged into the world of unceasing work, of "bettering our condition," and therefore of unhappiness.[49] Bettering our condition leaves us "constantly dissatisfied" (VI.iii.51). Human life is naturally restless, driven not only by fear (as Hobbes suggested) but also by longing for beauty.[50] The comic irony of this general picture of human life is unmistakable. It is crucial to see that *The Wealth of Nations*, and so the world of wealth getting it promotes, is painted *within* this frame. Here we have a fundamental part of the framework within which human life in modernity, as conceived in Smith's Enlightenment project, is to be understood.

Smith is not claiming that the life of nonphilosophers is unalterably lived in "deception" about happiness. Through sympathy, imagination, experience, and our detachment as spectators, it is possible to come to understand where a large-scale mistake in our understanding of happiness has occurred. Tragedies are once again sources for moral instruc-

---

49 Smith writes : "If we consider the real satisfaction which all these things are capable of affording, by itself and separated from the beauty of that arrangement which is fitted to promote it, it will always appear in the highest degree contemptible and trifling. But we rarely view it in this abstract and philosophical light. We naturally confound it in our imagination with the order, the regular and harmonious movement of the system, the machine or oeconomy by means of which it is produced. The pleasures of wealth and greatness, when considered in this complex view, strike the imagination as something grand and beautiful and noble, of which the attainment is well worth all the toil and anxiety which we are so apt to bestow upon it" (IV.i.9). The "we" in the first sentence is that of the theorist or philosopher; the "we" in the second and third sentences that of ordinary moral actors.

50 In a parallel way, intellectual life is driven by a restless search for conceptual harmony, coherence, elegance, and thus tranquillity. The goads to inquiry are the sentiments of surprise and wonder; Smith makes it clear that these and the accompanying states of dissatisfaction are unpleasant. "History of Astronomy," I.5–6, II.6–10 (*EPS*, pp. 35–6, 40–4.)

tion in that they can show us the "learning through suffering" that supplies the evidence in question even to those initially governed by great hubris. Smith himself sometimes narrates similar stories.[51] The evidence he offers to the effect that we make profound mistakes about happiness is drawn in part from experience. How might the ordinary person understand the "deception" for what it is?

In one of Smith's vignettes, the unhappy social climber gains self-knowledge in recognizing that happiness is tranquillity.[52] With that recognition, he regrets how he spent his life. The phenomena of regret and shame also supply evidence that we naturally connect happiness with some objective state of affairs. When one's state of mind is at odds with the relevant facts of one's life, as in Smith's example, one is likely to feel regret or shame. Suppose you earned your feelings of tranquillity by means of some immoral but secret act. Your condition of life and mind is such that you may seem to be happy; spectators think you are happy; but if the facts were known to others you would be ashamed. Even if the facts are not known, *you* know, somewhere in your soul, that you do not deserve to be happy, and so are not happy. You are not what you say you are. A sense of guilt and an anxiety about being found out bubble underneath the surface of your life. This is not an uncommon experience, and Smith depicts it vividly. It buttresses the case for a distinction between happiness and contentment. In this way Smith could grant Kant's distinction between happiness and the worthiness to be happy, except that Smith would see the former as contentment, and the latter (when

51 Cf. III.3.31, where having agreed with the Stoics that "Happiness consists in tranquillity and enjoyment," Smith reconstructs a dialogue between King Pyrrhus and Cineas about true and false happiness. Smith counsels that you "examine the records of history, recollect what has happened within the circle of your own experience, consider with attention what has been the conduct of almost all the greatly unfortunate, either in private or public life, whom you may have either read of, or hear of, or remember; and you will find that the misfortunes of by far the greater part of them have arisen from their not knowing when they were well, when it was proper for them to sit still and to be contented."

52 At what point does a person see that he has sacrificed "a real tranquillity that is at all times in his power"? It tends to be in old age, once he has attained wealth and power, as he lies "in the last dregs of life, his body wasted with toil and diseases, his mind galled and ruffled by the memory of a thousand injuries and disappointments which he imagines he has met with from the injustice of his enemies, or from the perfidy and ingratitude of his friends, that he begins at last to find that wealth and greatness are mere trinkets of frivolous utility, no more adapted for procuring ease of body or tranquillity of mind than the tweezer-cases of the lover of toys" (IV.1.8). Then he sees the difference between contentment and real tranquillity.

accompanied by tranquillity) as happiness.[53] Usually, though, for most of us, the moral self-knowledge gained in this fashion does not seem powerful enough to overawe our love of beauty and gnawing urge to better our lot.

In sum, happiness rightly understood provides a sense of reflective integration over time.[54] This is the Aristotelian dimension of Smith's discussion of the matter, except that Smith wants to understand "reflective integration" by means of the notion of the "impartial spectator." Happiness as tranquillity in this long-lasting, structural sense is compatible with anxiety and lack of contentment in the everyday sense. At the same time, it is not reducible to what Hobbes calls "felicity." It is not so much equanimity as it is equipoise, balance, coherence and settledness in one's basic stance. The fittingness of one's basic stance is evident through reflection and, affectively, by the feeling that one would change nothing fundamental in one's life, in spite of what has happened. One has lived and would live in this manner; at that structural or second-order level, one is at rest, and tranquillity is, correspondingly, a sort of rest, of peacefulness. By contrast, the anxious person determined to "better his condition" tends to be fundamentally anxious, off-balance, never settled. (The life of the philosopher presents its own problems with respect to tranquillity, as we will see in Chapter 8.)

On this view of real but not rigidly Stoic happiness, one can and indeed must have all kinds of emotions, attachments, commitments. These may well be turbulent at times. The moral emotions are essential to the happy life. Fortune will affect the course of things at this level. At the second-order level, however, one can be tranquil in the midst of first-order-level perturbance, though not every perturbance. One can be peaceful but engaged. According to this view, virtue is productive of as well as required by real tranquillity. Yet morality is not *supremely* valuable, for luck and external goods also have an essential role to play in that which is supremely valuable, namely true happiness.

Smith does not want us to infer that the perpetually dissatisfied effort to better our condition is devoid of virtue. The "deception" of the imagination does not necessarily lead to the "corruption" of the moral sentiments; *that* inference ranks among the fallacies of traditional moral

---

53 For Kant's distinction see the *Critique of Practical Reason*, p. 136: "morals is not really the doctrine of how to make ourselves happy but of how we are to be *worthy* of happiness."
54 For some helpful discussion of the temporal dimension of this integration, see Rémi Brague, *Aristote et la question du monde* (Paris: PUF, 1988), pp. 479–81.

philosophy Smith seeks to question. Through moral education, habitu-
ation in moral rules, and a reasonable arrangement of social institutions
and life, most people can shape their passions so as both to pursue their
betterment *and* be virtuous in the sense of just, industrious, self-
disciplined, prudent, and benevolent. The prudent person possesses at
the end of his life "secure tranquillity" in a sense that includes satisfaction
with one's rank and economic circumstances (VI.i.12). As already mentioned in the discussion of that virtue, prudence would be a worthwhile attainment in a society of persons bent on bettering their condition.

   In the kind of twist so typical of his thinking, Smith explicitly argues
that the fact that most individuals are *not* perfectly happy contributes to
the "happiness of mankind, as well as of all rational beings." The deception of the imagination underlying the drive to better our condition,
vulgarly understood, creates "progress" or "civilization," that is, productive labor, which may increase the wealth of nations. This may in turn
lead to the various social, political, and scientific improvements we prize.
It is in this context of our deception by our own imaginations that Smith
makes the one reference, in *The Theory of Moral Sentiments*, to the "invisible hand," the principle thanks to which the efforts of individuals to
better their condition leads to the quite unintended distribution of their
wealth and goods to others, thus advancing the interest of society
(IV.i.10). We can be decent without being truly happy (and this does
not mean that there is no such thing as real happiness or that happiness
is entirely subjective and unprincipled). We can have moral virtue without fulfillment or perfection of self and without abandoning such ideas
altogether. And from one perspective, it is good that things are arranged
thus.

   Smith plays "high" and "low" notions of happiness and virtue off
against one another. His use of the figure of the Stoic is dialectical. What
is in one sense the "highest" level – the Stoic sage who desires only "the
greatest possible happiness of all rational and sensible beings" and the
"discharge of his own duty" (VII.ii.1.21) – constitutes a breathtakingly
high standard. This level is contrasted in Stoic doctrine with the realm
of "imperfect virtues" or "proprieties, fitnesses, decent and becoming
actions," that is, of "attainable virtues" in the area of what is in itself
"indifferent" (VII.ii.1.42). One could argue that in rough form this Stoic
distinction between high and low virtue is reproduced in the difference
between *The Theory of Moral Sentiments* and *The Wealth of Nations* – with the
high realm of virtue, on the one hand, and the low realm of the pursuit
of wealth and associated virtues of prudence and "negative" justice on

the other. But that would be far too simple. For the "high" is not simply ideal; aiming at "universal happiness" is not in fact required of us by the impartial spectator; *apatheia* is positively undesirable; and the general Stoic insulation of virtue and happiness from fortune is achieved at too high a price. Stoicism is incompatible with genuine happiness or tranquillity. The impartial spectator would not approve of the Stoic sage without qualification.[55] Correspondingly, the worldly realm (which includes the "indifferents" – the external goods of fortune, in effect – and the virtues connected with their peaceful pursuit) is partially revalued. That realm does have worth.

Both the transient satisfactions of the imperfect *theatrum mundi* and the tranquillity of the detached Stoic sage may be distinguished from a non-Stoic but still high standard of virtuous character that would be approved of enthusiastically by the impartial spectator (VI.iii.25). This standard would be the "prudent" person, in the high sense of the term (VI.i.15), or the perfectly just person (VI.ii.intro.2), or the Platonically just soul (VII.ii.1.10, 11). This standard, which a "wise and virtuous" person does and ought to try to meet, serves as the measure against which the lower virtues can be ranked and derives its own plausibility in part from the ultimate undesirability of the Stoic view. Virtues such as ordinary prudence represent the highest moral standing that a life of bettering one's condition, as normally understood, can attain, and it earns our "cold esteem." This is a life structured by general moral rules.

Viewed in this dialectical way, reflection on the Stoic sage actually returns philosophers to this world, not uncritically but rather with a hard-won appreciation of the virtues of this world's imperfections.[56] These include the virtues conducive to what Smith will call the "system of natural liberty." Smith thus moderates the philosopher's ambition to transform the world and reconciles philosophy to a "spectacle" that is, seemingly, unhappily constituted. The "truth" of the opposition be-

---

55 In one passage Smith remarks that the beggar "who suns himself by the side of the highway" possesses not just the security but the peace of mind that kings are fighting for (IV.1.10). But at that extreme, tranquillity becomes unappealing; the indolent and detached beggar may feel safe but could not be the paragon of virtue we would wish to emulate.

56 Thus V. Brown's stimulating analysis of the interplay in Smith between the Stoic's notion of high virtue and of *officia*, or low virtue, is incomplete at best, overlooking both the extent of the limitations of the former and the significant if partial vindication of the latter. Smith's overall scheme is not so much "operating within a discursive space mapped out by Stoic moral philosophy," as calling it into question in reworking it. Cf. *Adam Smith's Discourse*, pp. 85–95.

tween the Stoic sage's tranquillity and the ordinary and lowly pursuit of happiness redeems the mean between them. Reconciliation does not mean acquiescence or quietism. It is wisdom about the kind of ethical wholeness and "identification" one ought to expect from public life under conditions of modern freedom and justice.

# 6

# JUSTICE

Clearly, no one has a higher claim on our reverence than the man who possesses the instinct and the strength for justice. . . . In fact, the will to be just is not enough; and man's worst miseries are the result of justice that lacks discernment. This is why the general welfare demands above all else that the seeds of judgment be sown as widely as possible so as to distinguish between fanatic and judge, and to recognize the difference between the blind desire to be judge and the ability to judge. But how can we possibly develop such discernment?

Friedrich Nietzsche[1]

Justice differs from the other virtues in a number of respects. It seems preeminently a social or political virtue, bearing on the relations required for the very existence of community in a way that other virtues do not. Unlike the other virtues, justice may rightly be exacted from us by force. The principles or rules that define justice are ordinarily taken as enforceable whereas the rules of benevolence are not. The rules specifying what actions justice requires or prohibits are more precise than those of the other virtues; as we have seen, Smith compares them to the rules of grammar. Further, justice is distinct in that it is primarily a "neg-

---

1 "History in the Service and Disservice of Life," pp. 113–14.

ative virtue" (II.ii.1.9), defined in terms of abstention from wrongdoing. Whereas Smith insists on the distinctness of justice, he also holds that justice is a virtue or excellence of character, though not an admirable disposition of self in quite the same sense as the other virtues. Justice is not restricted to the "basic institutions of society."[2]

Smith's effort to combine a virtue ethics inspired by the ancients with a modern jurisprudential framework of commutative justice and rights is as intriguing as it is controversial.[3] Virtues as well as rights, excellences of character as well as "juridical" moral rules, have their roots in his moral psychology, and he views them as indispensable to a flourishing liberal commercial polity. The sense of justice, and therewith the whole jurisprudential structure built on it, is itself founded in a sense of resentment at injury done to others such as would be approved by an impartial spectator. Because Smith largely leaves distributive justice up to private benevolence (for reasons we will explore in section 4), the proper sense of compassion and, thus, the education of imagination and "sympathy" are crucial. The emphasis on commutative justice makes benevolence more, not less, important.[4]

We tend somewhat vaguely to think of distributive justice as a duty the state or sovereign is alone charged with, one that goes beyond commu-

---

2 The quoted phrase is the one Rawls uses in defining the scope of his conception of justice as "social justice." *Theory of Justice*, pp. 4, 7.

3 Cf. J. G. A. Pocock, "Cambridge Paradigms and Scotch Philosophers: A Study of the Relations between the Civic Humanist and the Civil Jurisprudential Interpretation of Eighteenth-Century Social Thought," in Hont and Ignatieff, *Wealth and Virtue*, pp. 235–52, esp. pp. 249–52. Pocock comments on the prominent but still unsolved problem of reconciling civic humanism and civil jurisprudence, especially in the context of Smith's thought. More than one commentator has found Smith's attempted synthesis impossible and therefore that Smith's "Aristotelian" virtue-ethics talk is "vestigial" relative to his modern jurisprudential talk. For the "vestige" term and view see Cropsey, *Polity and Economy*, pp. x, 79. See also P. Minowitz, *Profits, Priests, and Princes* (Stanford: Stanford University Press, 1993), p. 133 (he calls these "danglers" as well), and V. Brown, *Adam Smith's Discourse*, p. 212. On p. 94 of *Polity and Economy* Cropsey refers to Smith's acknowledgments of the defects of commercial society as "tokens of his [Smith's] regret," and on p. 92 to Smith, "curious ambivalence" on the issue. I shall argue in this and the next chapter that there is no ambivalence here; Smith is setting the argument out in a dialectical and balanced manner.

4 In this connection see M. Nussbaum's comments on Smith, distributive justice, and compassion in "Compassion: The Basic Social Emotion," in *Social Philosophy and Policy* 13 (1996): 27–58. Smith is, however, skeptical about how far we can depend on compassion to produce beneficence outside our circles of sympathy (e.g., VI.ii.1.21), as I noted in Chapter 5. Were compassion exercised "locally" but in a sustained manner, in part through the kind of institutions Smith praises (e.g., religious sects), it might nonetheless have a significant social impact.

tative or rectificatory justice because it entails allotment of such things as rights, opportunities, advantages, offices, entitlements, duties, taxes, even risks, in accordance with need or desert. This may include the forcible redistribution of goods held in private insofar as they, like these other items, are in some respect the result of society's cooperative endeavor. Often the goal is to rectify an inequality or unfavorable condition some person or group experiences due to no fault of its own but traceable somehow to the basic structure of the society's institutions or communal traditions and practices. When we think today about market societies, the problems of distribution and inequality strike us as particularly pressing. We have in mind issues of the fair distribution of wealth and opportunities, as well as issues of equality of opportunity and a decent standard of life, of disparities in class and power, and of the role of fortune or luck in determining people's chances to better their condition. These issues struck Smith too as morally pressing, and *The Wealth of Nations* is full of comments about justice.[5] On what grounds, then, does he recommend commutative justice as the controlling model?[6]

Our now familiar issue of the relation between philosophy and ordinary life is also germane to the analysis of justice. Judgments about justice are, according to Smith, subject to a beneficial "irregularity" or irrationality concerning the role of fortune or luck, and he argues that philosophers ought not to straighten out this quirk in the moral sentiments. Smith took himself, though, to be engaged in a task that none of his predecessors, ancient or modern, had completed successfully: the articulation of a philosophical theory of "natural jurisprudence," or of the "rules of natural justice" (VII.iv.36, 37). As I noted in the Introduction, he consigned his manuscripts on the subject to the flames shortly before his death. Could he have completed the hoped-for system of justice? I conclude this chapter by offering an answer.

5  Rawls notes that the "allocative conception of justice" assimilates "justice to the benevolence of the impartial spectator and the latter in turn to the most efficient design of institutions to promote the greatest balance of satisfaction." *Theory of Justice*, pp. 88–9. Rawls's misinterpretation of Smith's notion of the impartial spectator to one side, Smith would agree that this allocative conception of justice is to be rejected, as he would with Rawls's criticisms of "distribution according to virtue" and with the point that "the idea of rewarding desert is impracticable." *Theory of Justice*, pp. 311–12. Smith is thoroughly attuned to problems of practicality, including the ones Rawls sketches here.
6  Controlling but not exclusive: even in *TMS*, as when he declares that "mere justice is, *upon most occasions*, but a negative virtue" (II.ii.1.9; emphasis added), the door is left open for something more "positive," a point to which I return later in this chapter.

## 1. NOBLE RESENTMENT AND COMMUTATIVE JUSTICE

The word "justice" has several, historically shifting, senses. This makes confusion about the topic easy right from the start. In the course of his discussion of Plato in Part VII of *The Theory of Moral Sentiments*, Smith helpfully distinguishes between several meanings of the term (VII.ii.1.10). The first sense amounts to commutative justice, and concerns specifications of the sorts of injury or harm that can be done to another's person, property, or reputation, as well as specifications of punishment and redress of those injuries. Roughly speaking, to be "just" is to abstain from actions that violate rules or laws that define injury. This is the sense whose basis Smith claims to analyze in this book, and in characterizing someone as "just" we too seem often to have in mind the sort of person who religiously avoids inflicting harm so understood.

He claims that his notion coincides with what Aristotle meant by commutative justice (VII.ii.1.10), but that is not quite accurate, for the corresponding part of justice in Aristotle's scheme is the *diorthotikon dikaion* (*NE* 1131a1 and context), that is, corrective justice that rectifies inequalities in voluntary or involuntary exchanges between individuals. Smith's commutative justice seems a bit broader than Aristotle's, since it specifies wrongs and punishments in any area in which force may be used to compel obedience, and this may include groups as well as individuals. Thus businesses that have monopolies that in turn preclude other individuals or groups from entering the market may be commutatively unjust. A sovereign who is not impartial among nonfanatical religions, or who does not administer justice in a regular and impartial manner, or who does not obey the law is commutatively unjust. A sentinel who falls asleep at his post is also unjust in the commutative sense (II.ii.3.11). In addition, notions of "fair play" and liberty are central to commutative justice for Smith.

He also specifies a second, broader sense of justice. According to it, we do justice to someone when we positively "exert ourselves to serve him and to place him in that situation in which the impartial spectator would be pleased to see him." Smith thinks this is what some thinkers, such as Grotius, call distributive justice. It need not be discharged by the sovereign or state. Smith understands this "distributive justice" as "proper beneficence," as the exercise of charity, generosity, liberality, and the other social virtues, and this more or less folds it into his discussion of benevolence in Part VI. This sense of "justice" covers what can be morally required of people in their dealings with others.[7]

In a third and most extensive sense of the term, we are unjust when we do not value a thing or person with the degree of esteem that an impartial spectator would accord to it or him. In this sense one may do injustice to a poem or to the objects of our self-interest or do injustice in any instance in which we have failed to exercise a particular virtue. Justice is here the perfectly harmonious functioning of the soul under the guidance of reason, what Smith calls "perfect propriety of conduct," such that each action and passion may be called virtuous. He notes that this is evidently what Plato meant by "justice" – Smith apparently has in mind book IV of the *Republic*. This is justice in the sense of a full-fledged, comprehensive virtue of character. Smith clearly does not think of justice in this sense as *political* justice, the failure in which can be punished by the state. The "Platonically" just individual would seem to have the "character of the perfectly innocent and just man" and would exercise both distributive and commutative justice without fault.[8]

The topic of justice first arises in the course of Smith's analysis of merit (and so that which is deserving of reward) and demerit (and so that which is deserving of punishment). As we saw in Chapter 5, merit and demerit are types of approbation or disapprobation of motives and actions distinct from judgments of propriety and impropriety and are tied to the "beneficial or hurtful effects which the affection proposes or tends to produce." That is, merit and demerit consist in good or ill desert. Moral praise and blame are prompted by certain emotions; in this case, gratitude (which prompts us to reward) and resentment (which prompts us to punish), mediated by sympathy with the persons acting and acted upon, as felt from the perspective of the "reasonable man"

7  *TMS* VII.ii.1.10. For a discussion of the background of Smith's views on distributive justice in Grotius, Pufendorf, and Locke, see I. Hont and M. Ignatieff, "Needs and Justice in the *Wealth of Nations*," in Hont and Ignatieff, *Wealth and Virtue*, part 4. Smith notes that Aristotle's sense of distributive justice is different from his in that it "consists in the proper distribution of rewards from the public stock of a community," i.e., in the allocation of public goods to specifiable individuals who can be seen to merit them. Smith does not think distributive justice in Aristotle's sense to be the task of the state, since it would amount to distribution of public goods (or the forced redistribution of private goods) according to the moral virtue of the recipients. We shall examine Smith's reservations about distributive justice further in section 4.

8  The character of the perfectly just person is almost always "accompanied with many other virtues, with great feeling for other people, with great humanity and great benevolence" (VI.ii.intro.2). Presumably the contrary holds for the unjust person.

(II.i.2.3).[9] These passions belong to those "derived from the imagination." Thus Smith's theory of justice grows organically out of the psychology of sympathetic imagination we have examined at length in the preceding chapters.

Thus, he argues, if a Nero were, in his diseased mind and corrupted soul, to hatch destructive plots that, if carried into practice, would hurt others but that he is absolutely incapable of carrying out because, say, he is totally isolated on a distant island and is permanently powerless, we would consider him with pity and contempt but not necessarily with resentment. We would want not to punish him so much as to revile him. In some circumstances we might even laugh at him. But were he plotting as emperor, the issue of demerit would become salient, and our resentment, anger, and indignation would be called forth, as would our desire to punish him for conducting himself destructively in office, especially if his plans issued in actions. (See II.i.5.6 for Smith's reference to Nero.) The response of the moral sentiments should depend on the relevant but contingent features of the situation being evaluated.

Resentment, then, is "never properly called forth but by actions which tend to do real and positive hurt to some particular persons" (II.ii.1.4). Each part of this statement is important to Smith's account, for it serves as the basis for drawing a crucial distinction between justice and benevolence and for narrowing the relevant sense of justice to the commutative. Let us focus on the criterion of "real and positive hurt." How is that to be understood?

The notion of "illusive [illusory or deceptive] sympathy" is primary here, for as spectators we are called upon, in the case where the greatest possible harm has unjustifiably been done to another person – the taking of his life – to place ourselves in the position of the deceased and to imagine the anger and resentment that this person would feel. The harm that "in our fancy" (imagination) the deceased has undergone calls forth, under the right conditions, "sympathetic tears" and "sympathetic indignation" and hence our powerful desire to punish the perpetrator (II.i.2.5; II.i.5.6). This is simply an extension of Smith's discussion, at the end of the first chapter of *The Theory of Moral Sentiments*, of our sympathy with the dead, which depends on an "illusion of the imagi-

9 The sense of merit is a "compounded sentiment" consisting of approval of the sentiments of the agent and of the gratitude of the beneficiaries of his actions, whether or not the beneficiaries actually feel the gratitude they ought. Smith speaks here of our acting the part, in our imaginations, of the actor in a scene of benevolence or justice and reaching our various judgments accordingly (II.i.5.2, 3).

nation" that involves putting "our own living souls in their inanimated bodies, and thence conceiving what would be our emotions in this case." This is the illusion that leads us to dread death, an illusion that is "the great restraint upon the injustice of mankind" (I.i.1.13). In other words, the sense of commutative justice is an extension of the prephilosophical imagination's sympathy, thanks to which we may govern ourselves and live in tolerable harmony. This is so remarkable a feature of the phenomenon that at several junctures Smith feels compelled to step back and comment from a detached philosophical perspective on its meaning.

What, then, is the hierarchy of harms to which a person may be subjected? Since "death is the greatest evil which one man can inflict upon another" and "excites the highest degree of resentment," murder is the greatest of crimes against an individual. There next follows harm to one's person – first one's body, then extensions of self, such as one's reputation. Then comes property, the deprivation of which is a greater harm than disappointment of an expectation; then various breaches of contract (II.ii.2.2).[10] This hierarchy of wrongs reflects levels of resentment felt by the impartial spectator, whose role Smith is here assuming. Because "we" (the pronoun is common in these pages) feel this emotion in these respects, we are moved to punish the doer of harm as well as forcibly to compel adherence to precise rules that prohibit the harm. These rules are the principles of justice. By contrast, failure of an agent to exercise proper beneficence does "no real positive evil." It may disappoint, hurt, anger, and even lead to condemnation of the agent, but it does not warrant *resentment* and hence the use of punitive force. Therefore beneficence may not be legally compelled nor its absence punished by force. We are under a "perfect and complete obligation" to perform the duties of justice but not any of the other virtues. Beneficence is "always free" in this jurisprudential sense, wheras justice is not "left to the freedom of our own wills" (II.ii.1.5). On the basis of his analysis of moral psychology, Smith is articulating an ethical view about the responses of a person of good character to different types of unmerited injury. His view of the matter is entirely plausible, especially in modern, nonheroic culture.

The dividing line between duties of beneficence and justice is not always clear; an obvious case concerns the duties of parents toward their children. Smith acknowledges that in such cases, the sovereign may

---

10 For a detailed analysis of Smith's jurisprudence, especially of the *Lectures on Jurisprudence*, see Haakonssen, *The Science of a Legislator*, chs. 5–7.

"command mutual good offices to a certain degree," but "of all the duties of a law-giver, however, this, perhaps, is that which it requires the greatest delicacy and reserve to execute with propriety and judgment." We are not surprised by the emphasis on judgment or by Smith's presumption in favor of the notion that relations of beneficence are free. To go too far in extorting beneficence is "destructive of all liberty, security, and justice" (II.ii.1.8).

Notice that justice is tied closely to *actions*; this grows out of the starting point in resentment for harm done. An action causes harm in a sense in which a mere intention, or emotion, or thought of an action generally does not. (There is a problem here, however, that we will discuss shortly.) Notice too that at this founding and basic level, the actions are directed by individuals toward or against other individuals. This is reinforced by the insistence that the proper object of our gratitude or resentment must be capable, not just of intentionally causing but also of feeling the sensations of pleasure and pain (II.iii.1.6). Of course, the *administration* of (commutative) justice is obviously a political and jurisprudential matter, and its fairness can be evaluated. But Smith's account makes it clear that the original and primary context of our passions and sympathetic imagination concerns individuals. They are the fundamental moral units; it is the harms and benefits to them that weigh most heavily in the sympathetic imagination.

Having laid the foundations in his discussion of merit, the passions of gratitude and resentment and their connection with reward and punishment, and of the difference between hurt feelings and "real positive evil," Smith is prepared to define "justice" as the obligatory regard for principles of conduct whose violation causes, in the judgment of an impartial spectator, real harm and arouses warranted resentment as well as a demand for proportionate punishment (II.ii.1.4, 5). Justice and retaliation are inseparable (II.ii.1.10). Smith has thus explained several of the differences between justice and the other virtues: the sense of obligation that accompanies it, its "negative" character, and its particular connection with harm and pain. Not just the urgency but the exactitude of the rules governing justice seem connected with the fact that the marked "pungency" or sharpness of pain (I.iii.1.3) allows us to detect differences between kinds and amounts of pain with relative precision.[11]

---

11 Admittedly the connection between the "pungency" of pain and the precision of the general rules of justice is somewhat obscure. As Haakonssen notes, Smith does not spell out the connection. *The Science of a Legislator*, p. 86. I suspect the full answer would identify

The close connection between injustice, specific actions, and external goods such as property brings it into a public and visible arena that facilitates estimation by spectators of just how much wrong has been done, how much the agent should be punished, and how much must be restored to the sufferer in order to balance the scales. By contrast, if I have failed to show someone the proper degree of friendship, how is a spectator to discern with any distinctness how much justified harm has been caused and what punishment the state ought to inflict? Expert discernment in such matters is better left to finely sensitive novelists than to jurists whose decisions are enforced by police powers.

Since the impartial spectator's resentment is aroused by specific actions directed at specific individuals and causing specific injury, judgments about the actor's injustice are not in the first instance judgments about the actor's character, life plan, scheme of virtues, or happiness. Hence Smith's use of the term "fair play" here; the actor may "in the race for wealth, and honours, and preferments," run "as hard as he can, and strain every nerve and every muscle, in order to outstrip all his competitors," and the spectators may well think the entire competition to be silly and driven by some "deception" of the imagination. But impartial spectators will not *resent* the actor's playing of the game unless he "should justle, or throw down any of them [his competitors]," for that violates "fair play." In the spectator's judgment about *merit*, the "right" and the "good" are distinct. The spectator has no reason to grant the actor's partiality or selfish bias in favor of himself (II.ii.2.1). This fair play conception of justice requires neither equality of outcome in the game nor equality of starting points (e.g., skill at playing the game), as Smith's qualified reconciliation with the fact of a social hierarchy of wealth and power indicates.

Being commutatively just "does no real positive good" and may sometimes be fulfilled by "sitting still and doing nothing" (II.ii.1.9); it also is deserving of "very little positive merit." The just person may therefore seem to be a moral blank slate, a rights bearer devoid of virtue. One

a nexus of different ideas. Part of the explanation may lie in the urgency the spectator feels to respond to pain. To take a relatively straightforward example, the sight of a child being beaten requires of the decent spectator a swift and certain response whose proportionality to the crime must be precisely fixed on the spot. An equality between the pain endured and the pain inflicted as punishment on the perpetrator seems a necessity (both emotive and prudential) of the spectator's response, and this equality must generally be stated precisely (just this much punishment for just that crime). By contrast, however much and however easily the spectator may participate in a child's joy in, say, a new toy, the spectator presumably and rightly feels no urgency to further that joy right away and to just such and such a degree.

might infer that the virtue consists simply in obeying rules, and also, because these define what one ought not to do, that justice is only a quasi virtue. On that interpretation there would seem to be no connection between commutative justice, understood as a political phenomenon, and justice as a disposition of self, as a virtue of character. Consequently there may seem to be little connection between political justice and any of the other virtues.[12] The problem here is one at the heart of contemporary discussions about the relationship between civic and individual virtue, especially in the context of a liberal society.

The divorce between political justice and just character cannot be complete, for the just person is not *simply* someone who consistently follows rules that prohibit doing harm to others. Rather, the just person is governed by a reverence for rules of justice and a determined resolve never to be guilty of hurting others without just cause. Smith's language in this regard is striking. He speaks over and over again of the just person's "conscientious," "sacred," and "religious" respect for the "sacred" rules of justice.[13] Even when sitting still and causing no harm throughout his life, the just person demonstrates a "habitual reverence" for the principles of justice. This constitutes a "positive" character trait. Not only does the existence of society depend on a tolerable observation of these basic principles (III.3.6, III.5.2); society "cannot subsist among those who are at all times ready to hurt and injure one another" (II.ii.3.3). The just person not only abstains from hurting others; he is not ever *ready* to hurt others without warrant, and this is a fixed disposition of character.

Smith's remarkable language about the just person's "religious" regard for the rules of justice is complemented by an equally remarkable passage in which he discusses the unfortunate case in which a just person has unintentionally harmed an innocent person. Just as the holy ground consecrated to a god in a pagan religion is never to be trespassed upon, so

> the happiness of every innocent man is, in the same manner, rendered holy, consecrated, and hedged round against the approach of every other man; not to be wantonly trod upon, not even to be, in any respect, igno-

---

12  This is more or less what V. Brown concludes in *Adam Smith's Discourse;* the moral system of *TMS* "excluded the development of a political personality, and accorded a lower moral status to the public as opposed to the private virtues" (pp. 211–12). I find this only partially true, at best.

13  See VI.ii.intro.2, VI.iii.11; VII.iv.8, 9; III.5.2, III.6.10; II.ii.1.10, II.ii.2.2, 3; VII.ii.intro.2; *WN* I.x.c.12. This vocabulary is remarkable in an author whose views about religion are so skeptical.

rantly and involuntarily violated, without requiring some expiation, some atonement in proportion to the greatness of such undesigned violation. (II.iii.3.4)

The rules of justice are sacred because what they protect – the human individual – is as sacred as is the domain of a god. This ringing declaration of the sanctity of the individual is at the heart of Smith's moral philosophy and political economy.[14] Thus the concern requisite for warranted resentment is not primarily the thought of the welfare of society but rather "the general fellow feeling which we have with every man merely because he is our fellow-creature" (II.ii.3.10). That respect is part of the character of the just person. So deeply rooted in us is this respect that even a person whose character is corrupt will likely feel, after harming another person, its effects.[15] Smith provides us with a vivid depiction of the remorse, shame, horror, and inner dissolution that attends the unjust person who is torn between an inability to face society and an inability to endure "the horror of solitude." These passages are among the most poetic and affecting in *The Theory of Moral Sentiments*. Remorse, "of all the sentiments which can enter the human breast the most dreadful," is composed of shame at our past conduct, grief for its effects, pity for those who suffered by it, and terror at the prospect of the punishment inflicted by the resentment of "all rational creatures" (II.ii.2.3–4).

What motivates a person to do injustice? On Smith's account, there are many answers to this question. There is no single, well-defined character type who is unjust. Self-love characterizes all vice, not just injustice. Smith's understanding of that point is arguably a strength of his account.[16] As we have seen, the character type of the commutatively just

---

14 Consider Smith's pronouncement in *WN* that "the property which every man has in his own labour, as it is the original foundation of all other property, so it is the most sacred and inviolable." To deprive a "poor man" from deploying his strength and ability in whatever manner he thinks best, as long as he does no injury to his neighbour, "is a plain violation of this most sacred property" and an "encroachment upon the just liberty" of the individual (I.x.c.12). Although Smith shows in *WN* that public measures and individuals do so encroach – sometimes intentionally and sometimes not – a virtuous person will certainly protest them. Smith himself does protest them by publishing *WN*.

15 On the resonance with Kant's notion of the moral law as a "fact of reason," see Chapter 3, n. 17.

16 Consider B. Williams's criticism of Aristotle in chapter 6 ("Justice as a Virtue") of *Moral Luck* (Cambridge: Cambridge University Press, 1988), especially concerning the question of *pleonexia* (greediness, the desire to have more than one's share) as *the* motive for injustice (*NE* 1129b1–11, 1130a14–24).

person is better defined, for it includes an ingrained respect for others simply as human beings. Even so, it remains the case that commutative justice is peculiarly "negative"; it consists in religiously *abstaining* from doing harm to others. One could be "just" in this real but limited way and still be underdetermined, so to speak, as a character type. This helps to explain why Smith does not provide us with a full-fledged character sketch of the commutatively just person.[17] And this certainly fits with his view of a large commercial society structured in accordance with modern ideas of liberty and rights, for such a society is bound by principles of justice and harbors a great variety of character types.

Smith is working, in sum, with the intuitive idea that justice is fundamentally tied to our (the spectator's or bystander's) resentment at the infliction of what we judge to be unwarranted harm (that is, injury). The "negative" character of justice stems from this original picture, as does the idea that to do justice is to balance the scales. Smith resists revising these intuitions and instead explains their underlying basis in moral psychology (the theory of sympathy, pleasure and pain, and the passions) as well as the principles of jurisprudence that accord with them (a jurisprudence of rights, as determined or specified by impartial spectators in the given historical context). He offers arguments in favor of the utility of this view, properly understood, and explains the shortcomings of alternative views. His view dovetails with his defense of the standpoint of ordinary life and is appropriate to his egalitarian outlook. But the standpoint of ordinary life is not without its own imperfections, and this poses an interesting challenge to a theory of the moral sentiments.

---

17  Smith writes: "A sacred and religious regard not to hurt or disturb in any respect the happiness of our neighbour, even in those cases where no law can properly protect him, constitutes the character of the perfectly innocent and just man; a character which, when carried to a certain delicacy of attention, is always highly respectable and even venerable for its own sake, and can scarce ever fail to be accompanied with many other virtues, with great feeling for other people, with great humanity and great benevolence. It is a character sufficiently understood, and requires no further explanation" (VI.ii.intro.2). This is the character of a person who is commutatively just without fail, and its being already well understood also helps to explain why Smith did not describe the just character in Part VI of *TMS* (entitled "Of the Character of Virtue – Consisting of Three Sections"). This character overlaps with that of the person of high prudence, who exhibits "a sacred regard to the rules of justice" (VI.i.15), and even with that of the person of "ordinary" prudence, who "respects with an almost religious scrupulosity, all the established decorums and ceremonials of society," is "an exact observer of decency," minds his own business, and would not inflict harm on others (VI.i.10). Yet the "narrowly" just person may not be prudent and is in that and other respects distinct.

## 2. THE "IRREGULARITY" OF THE MORAL
## SENTIMENTS, AND MORAL LUCK

Smith's discussion of merit and justice leads into a remarkable analysis of an "irregularity of sentiment, which every body feels, which scarce any body is sufficiently aware of, and which nobody is willing to acknowledge" (II.iii.intro.6). This irregularity consists in the fact – or Smith plausibly argues that it is a fact – that ordinary moral spectators judge merit and demerit not solely in accordance with the actor's intentions (including the intended consequences of the action) but also to a large extent in light of the contingent and unforeseeable consequences. This is an "irregularity," or better an irrationality, because it is "self-evident" to reflection that actors cannot be held responsible for the unforeseeable consequences of their deeds, since these are wholly under the control of "the empire of fortune," or luck.[18] Luck also affects excellence of character. Reason tells us that the moral value of the deed lies solely in the agent's intentions or will. Yet we seldom judge in accordance with this "rule"; the moral sentiments follow a different logic, thanks to which the "unintended and unforeseen consequences" (II.ii.intro.4, 5) of our actions do bear, sometimes heavily, on our judgments of the agent's merit and demerit. This irrationality deeply affects the way in which we feel resentment, reach judgments about harm and injustice, and accord punishment. It affects how spectators judge whether a person's actions (and indeed life) are admirable and how agents judge the value of their own lives. Smith wants to acknowledge, explain, and then persuade us to see the good in this.

The explanation of the "irregularity" hinges once again on the key roles of pleasure and pain in forming gratitude and resentment in the spectator. As already noted, for something to be the proper object of gratitude and resentment, it must be the cause of pleasure or pain; capable of feeling them (otherwise inanimate objects as well as people could become the legitimate objects of moral praise or blame); and capable of producing them from "design" – indeed a design that is approved of, in the case of praise, and disapproved of in the case of blame (II.iii.1.6). We note again the "cognitivist" (and arguably un-Humean) view of the emotions here. The next step is to recognize that pleasure and pain are more keenly felt when caused by actions and their conse-

---

18 I take it that by "fortune" Smith means not that which is uncaused but that which is unforeseen or unintended by us.

quences than when caused by mere intentions. In particular, if an agent's intentions fail to produce their effects, the agent's merit or demerit strike those affected, and even the impartial spectator, as imperfect or incomplete (II.iii.2.2). Smith repeatedly illustrates the point with examples from everyday life.

The architect whose plans are badly executed is mortified, even though the plans were excellent. He does not receive the degree of approbation he ought to, because "his" building is imperfect. In general "the merit of talents and abilities which some accident has hindered from producing their effects, seems in some measure imperfect." You may in principle be a first-class general, capable of saving the nation and fully prepared to do so, but as things turned out, never be in a position to act. Even in your own eyes, to be deprived of the chance to exhibit your character in action diminishes the "lustre" of your character (II.iii.2.3). And that bad luck will affect your assessment of the success of your whole life, the worth of all of the time and effort you invested in becoming a military officer of the first rank, even the exact degree to which you possess the qualities you believe yourself to possess. For if you have no chance to display these virtues in action, can you, or spectators, be certain that you possess them?[19] And if you had been able to act, with success, your character would have been shaped by that fact, as well by the choices subsequently available to you, not to mention by your and the spectators' assessment of you. It is but a very short step from here to a notion of "constitutive luck," that is, to the notion that our characters are to some extent the product of luck. Since the development of moral character depends heavily on a process of moral education, moral agency will be unevenly distributed, at times simply because of luck. "Fortune," Smith remarks, "governs the world" (II.iii.3.1).

Analogously, vicious intentions that happen not to be fulfilled are not resented or punished as much as those that are fulfilled, even though the "real demerit is undoubtedly the same in both cases, since his [the agent's] intentions were equally criminal" (II.iii.2.4). And where fortune leads to harmful consequences that were not intended, our sense of the demerit of the intentions is, irrationally, affected by the degree of pain that they cause. Thus we punish agents in spite of the small degree of

19 Samuel Fleischacker has pointed out to me that if one had no chance to act on one's virtues and is frustrated by that, the confidence with which one believes oneself to be, for example, courageous might diminish, making one more reluctant to desire to be courageous and thus more doubtful that one actually is courageous, even *in potentia*. Having little occasion to display the virtues, one's possession of them might well decline.

responsibility they may really bear for the effects of their actions. The influence of fortune on our sentiments is so pervasive that we sometimes find our self-approbation deeply affected by our having been causally responsible for doing some harm for which we are in no respect legally or morally responsible. The regret we feel permeates our lives. We take it, and the surrounding events, to be part of the fabric of our being, and we try hard to make reparations, hopelessly ineffective as any reparations may be. In this and other respects we are deeply shaped by luck.[20]

As a result of this "irregularity," though "absurd and unaccountable," it is a "necessary rule of justice, therefore, that men in this life are liable to punishments for their actions only, not for their designs and intentions" (II.iii.3.2). This is the beginning of Smith's justification of the "irregularity," and, not surprisingly, he focuses first on the issue of harm, pain, and resentment. Were the moral passions not sensible in this fashion to pain, we would feel resentment against the intention to harm someone with the intensity that we do against a harmful act and its consequences. The result would be a nightmare in which "every court of judicature would become a real inquisition" (II.iii.3.2). The distinction between the private self and the public realm would be erased. Every bad wish, view, or design would be as severely dealt with as would their attempted or effected execution and, whenever imagined, would be liable to criminal prosecution. We ought not to live in accordance with an ideal of pure rational agency. It is in accordance with "cool reason" that "human actions derive their whole merit or demerit" from "sentiments, designs, affections." But a morality in accordance with reason would extend the notion of harm and the reach of just punishment so far as to produce an "inquisition." It is in this context that Smith makes the comparison, already noted, between the consecrated precinct of a god and the inviolable happiness of the individual.

Further, our tendency to be more grateful for beneficial actions than for beneficial intentions leads us to exert ourselves mightily to change the external circumstances of ourselves and our fellows, that is, to master fortune insofar as possible. When we are asked about our lives "What have you done?" and answer that we have strained every muscle to improve the world but have failed, through lack of opportunity, we do not want to be told: "We esteem you, and love you; but we owe you nothing,"

20 *TMS* II.iii.3.4, 5. This should be compared with what Williams calls, in *Moral Luck* (p. 27), "agent-regret." Just as Smith here refers us to Oedipus, so too does Williams in his discussion (p. 30, n. 2).

because ours has merely been a "latent virtue." This is not a response most of us can bear with equanimity. We desire to have accomplished things worthy of esteem. Smith comments here that "man was made for action," thus denying implicitly that we are made primarily for philosophical speculation (II.iii.3.3).

The irregularity of the moral sentiments stems from and in turn shapes the agent's and the spectator's experience of harm, pain, pleasure, and the passions. In Chapter 2 we examined Smith's privileging of the standpoint of the spectator or the public and his argument that his doing so might lead to unjustified encroachment upon the agent's point of view on himself. We now see that Smith's privileging of the spectator leads to just the opposite, namely a tight restriction on the proper reach of the law and a religious determination to leave the rest of spiritual life free for its proper moral development. Smith might argue that were the standpoint of the actor privileged, the line separating the public from the private, action from motive, would blur dangerously – for then the intention or "sentiment of the heart" might become, as reason demands, the more important object of judicial scrutiny, because the actor might claim a privileged perspective on his or her own motives and would expect purity of intention from himself as well as others. It would be rather like a republic of lovers who enter into each other's worlds completely, demand a wholesomeness of intention, and bitterly resent any departure from that standard. As we saw in the discussion of love (Chapter 4), such "sympathy" between lovers is so complete that the boundaries separating them collapse; they live in each other's imaginations and find as much pain or pleasure in them as spectators find in actions and their consequences. Smith's reference to the Inquisition is meant to evoke a particular instance of this phenomenon.

In sum, an effort to shape human life in accordance with the dictates of "cool reason" would demand a radical reconstruction of moral life. One reason for Smith's fascination with Stoicism is the fact that in their denial that chance or fortune influence moral life the Stoics embody a quite logical response to the problem of moral luck.[21] For Smith this standpoint extinguishes, paradoxically, the source of moral value – the

---

21 "Human life the Stoics appear to have considered as a game of great skill," namely the skill of securing the "propriety of our own conduct" entirely within the sphere of our wills and outside the sphere of "what is vulgarly understood to be chance" (VII.ii.1.24). Thus for the Stoics "happiness was either altogether, or at least in a great measure, independent of fortune" (VII.ii.28). In Chapter 8 I discuss Smith's response to Stoicism at greater length.

244                                    JUSTICE

sentiments, sympathy, the primacy of particulars, the chance-filled formation of character, the weight of consequences of actions not under
our control. It is not just that liberty would be endangered if our moral
lives were restructured in accordance with the demands of purely rational moral agency. Ethical life itself would be undermined by the effort.
And yet, those demands and the standpoint they embody are very often
attractive to philosophers.

## 3. JUSTICE AND PHILOSOPHY

> Do you come to a philosopher as to a *cunning man*, to learn something by
> magic and witchcraft, beyond what can be known by common prudence
> and discretion?
>
> David Hume[22]

Smith is resolute in working up his account of justice in his usual manner, from appeal to what "we" perceive to be the case in ordinary experience, from examples, and from his moral psychology. The result is
a view of justice that plainly does not appeal to any notion of divine
origin or to a utilitarian analysis and justification, or to any Platonic
notion of the rule of knowledge, or to any version of a social contract
theory. Smith's "ordinary experience" approach blocks all of these philosophical moves and relieves him of trying to imagine, say, how rational
agents or abstract persons behind a veil of ignorance would conceive of
justice. As we have seen, his "impartial spectator" does not work that
way. His approach is consistent with his own skeptical framework.

As we have also seen, however, on some occasions ordinary experience
is irrational and seems to warrant emendation by the philosopher. We
have been discussing one case in which philosophy ought to restrain its
benevolent intentions. Toward the beginning of his discussion, after
showing that judgments of demerit stem from the spectator's "sympathetic indignation" at the harm intended by the agent, Smith provides
us with a long footnote, the longest in *The Theory of Moral Sentiments*. It
begins: "To ascribe in this manner our natural sense of the ill desert of
human actions to a sympathy with the resentment of the sufferer, may
seem, to the greater part of people, to be a degradation of that sentiment" (II.i.5.7). The fact that this long reflection is placed in a footnote,
in academic form, at the bottom of the page for the attention of aca-

---

22 "The Sceptic," in *Essays Moral, Political, and Literary*, p. 161.

demic readers and that it culminates in a technical point about the sense in which "sympathy" operates in cases of merit and demerit suggests that the observation about the possible reception of this point of Smith's theory is directed primarily to philosophers. Why do philosophers need to understand that what appears in Smith's analysis of justice to be a deflationary move is actually a revelation of what he here calls the admirable "oeconomy of nature"? The answer, I believe, is that philosophers need not only to understand the truth about the foundations of the virtues but also not to despise that truth. They must find reconciliation with ordinary life. Smith declares here that "we are not at present examining upon what principles a perfect being would approve of the punishment of bad actions; but upon what principles so weak and imperfect a creature as man actually and in fact approves of it" (II.i.5.10). The "irregularity" of the moral sentiments, which is essential to a flourishing ethical life, is an affront to reason. As philosophers we need to be taught how to reconcile ourselves to imperfection, so that we understand the virtues of enlightenment.

Smith is explicitly arguing that we must resist attempting to make ordinary life rational and impervious to luck. Hence one chapter heading here is "Of the utility of this constitution of Nature," which introduces several pages of reflection on teleological and mechanistic analysis. Another chapter is entitled "Of the final cause of this Irregularity of Sentiments" (II.iii.3), a phrase whose academic, Scholastic terminology is rare in Smith's book. It is in this chapter that Smith justifies, to us as philosophers, the focusing of our resentment and gratitude on actions rather than intentions, and congratulates the "wisdom of Nature" in so structuring things that the "happiness of every innocent man" is as a precinct of an ancient god. Smith's justification is multifaceted. He appeals to us as moral agents, rousing our resentment at the prospect of a "most insolent and barbarous tyranny" that would result were mere intentions to be punished (II.iii.3.3). He appeals to us as theorists in asking us to contemplate the utility, and thus the beauty, of a world in which the "low" (resentment) is transfigured into the "high" (justice), human imperfection into the cause of its own transcendence. We should admire a world in which rightly ordered sentiments may produce results that "the slow and uncertain determinations of our reason" (II.i.5.10) cannot reliably bring about. He reminds us not to mistake, in our explanation of the origin of justice, the efficient for the final cause, and thus not to confuse theoretical or systematic coherence with moral justification (II.ii.3.5, 6). We infer that, day to day, we do not need philosophy in order to be just. Rather, in order for justice to prevail we need to keep the properly educated sentiments of resentment and gratitude from being radically reconstructed by philosophy.

It is as a consequence of this view that there is no natural step from conflicts about justice, and so all the divided sympathies and resentments that we feel, to philosophy (though of course there is a natural step to the reasonings of the impartial spectator). Disputes common in matters where justice is at stake seem to cry out for discussion of first principles, for a method for resolving disagreements. In Plato's *Republic*, Glaucon and Adeimantus put the problem of selfishness in the starkest possible terms, asking why we ought to be just even when doing so violates the counsels of prudence. Socrates' answer leads to a definition of justice in book IV – dutifully summarized and endorsed by Smith – as well as to questions about the connection between justice and knowledge, demotic and political justice, and finally between civic life and the necessity, disruptive to both philosophy and civic life, of the revolutionary rule of philosophy based ultimately on the philosopher's vision of the Good. In his various comments on Plato's views, Smith avoids this gradual Socratic ascent to philosophical first principles. *The Theory of Moral Sentiments* provides no obvious bridge between its own description or story about justice and its philosophical, high-altitude reflections on the utility of this constitution of things. No ordinary actor or impartial spectator, on Smith's account, seems particularly worried about the "irregularity" of the moral sentiments, at least not enough to philosophize about it. Smith does not object, for he is wary of the destructive effect philosophy might have on common life.

In order to drive home this point, Smith associates himself with none other than Plato. He praises Plato's "divine maxim" that rulers are made for the state, not the state for the rulers who would reform it (VI.ii.2.18 and *Crito* 51c), and declares that the Greek philosopher's definition of justice coincides perfectly with his own (VII.ii.1.10, 11). It seems plausible that Smith has Plato much in mind in these discussions of justice and is determined to preempt the authority of the philosopher traditionally taken to be the most radical *philosophe* of them all. In thus quoting Plato, Smith aligns himself with Socrates and his readers with Crito. Crito is in need of Socrates' therapeutic rhetoric, for he is proposing that he assist Socrates in breaking out of the jail where Socrates is awaiting execution. Crito is no philosopher, and Socrates' arguments against his proposal could scarcely be called decisive. Smith knew, of course, that elsewhere Socrates' picture of the inviolability of local law is quite different. Hence in quoting selectively, Smith uses Plato against himself. So as not to miss the full dimension of the irony, let us note that we are here presented with a skeptic quoting a radical philosophical communist in order to support a modern commercial and liberal society. In discussing the irrationality of the moral sentiments, Smith confirms our worst suspicions about human life so that we may then recognize that we ought not to seek perfect isomorphism between human life and the truth. We came to a similar conclusion in our consideration of happiness in Chapter 5.

Smith's protreptic rhetoric applies to philosophers as well as to non-philosophers, and the problem of the relation between the two is at the heart of his rhetorical strategy. Smith's motivation with regard to the philosophers is at least to some degree ethical, for he implicitly warns that the regularizing of human life in accordance with the rule of knowledge would, just as depicted in *The Republic*, alter it radically. And that, in turn, would lead to dissolution and the "most insolent and barbarous tyranny," perhaps such as that described at the end of book VIII of *The Republic*. This means that *The Theory of Moral Sentiments* is at one level anti-utopian, antireformist, and antiphilosophical, insofar as it both suppresses a natural ascent from opinion to philosophy and the natural descent from philosophy back to the cave of politics. It has replaced the entire drama of the Platonic "cave" – the drama of liberating ascent and blinding descent – with the less edifying but more humane view that the cave may be remade into home. And in doing this, Smith as philosopher enlightens the cave.

The agent who feels regret for wrongs (resulting from his actions) that he is not, strictly speaking, responsible for may summon all his "magnanimity and firmness of soul" in an attempt to keep his true moral worth squarely in mind. Smith comments revealingly on the "fallacious sense of guilt" that "constitutes the whole distress of Oedipus and Jocasta upon the Greek . . . theatre." Some of the finest scenes in ancient and modern drama are premised upon what is in a sense an absurd confusion between guilt and involuntary error (II.iii.3.5). Should observation of that absurdity warrant our dismissing the drama as a poor comedy and our adopting the stance of the debunking cynic, or our rewriting the play so that the tragedy is resolved philosophically, perhaps with a calm Socratic dialogue about the meaning of "responsibility"? Smith wishes to avoid both courses. As philosophers we are in the theater ourselves and ought to engage in the "spectacle of human life" on its own terms. At the same time, when we observe the "fallacious" emotions of ordinary actors – including our own – from a synoptic and systematic perspective, we recognize that they are not always to be straightened out, because, thanks to the "wisdom of nature," the drama does not, when taken as a whole, necessarily have a tragic ending. It is therefore *more* philosophical – in the sense of wiser, exhibitive of greater self-knowledge, and more conducive to human good – to resist the restructuring of ordinary life by philosophy. The "irregularity" or irrationality of the moral sentiments is finally not a moral failing; the effort to extirpate it would be. As I have maintained throughout this study, Smith's decision to distance ordinary life and philosophy itself embodies a philosophical and moral position. It is a question of doing justice to human life.

But this is still not the end of the story, for Smith's description of the human drama is hardly neutral. "Ordinary life" is not an unchanging and self-explanatory datum in the universe. In setting out his hierarchy of harms, Smith implicitly asks us to agree that piety and justice are different from each other in such a way that we do not resent accusations about the falsity or perverseness of an agent's religious views as much as we do accusations of other harms. This may well be the enlightened view of the matter. Yet one could easily imagine a setting in which the mere presence of a religious view incompatible with one's own – let alone a loudly established presence – would cause a person profound pain and provoke indignant resentment. One might well be moved to punish the "infidels" harshly on the grounds that they are persuaded of views repulsive to any civilized person. Just as we no longer hesitate to enter a precinct once sacred to a heathen god, to recall again Smith's own analogy, so we might not hesitate to stamp down the infidels who dwell in any such precinct, precisely because of our resentment at the harm we feel their presence causes. Smith objects that such things as religious differences and the failure of others to sympathize with and endorse one's own faith may hurt but they do not cause the kind of harm that in an impartial spectator provokes resentment and the desire to punish. To deny this is to start down the path to twisted resentments, "fanaticism," and eventually the "inquisition."

Smith's reply may be charged with begging the question. Has he not simply *assumed* a view of the natural or healthy functioning of the moral sentiments, and so of resentment, without offering any argument to the effect that the "fanatic's" construal of "harm" is corrupt? This is finally a question about the thrust of both the virtue theory and the moral psychology. As I suggested in the Introduction, Enlightenment "arguments" against religion often seem, on inspection, to be polemical denunciations rather than careful philosophical refutations.

Smith does have resources at his command for replying to this charge of begging the question. First, as we noted in Chapter 5, he can draw on the same resources available to him in other disputes (such as the arguments about slavery and infanticide). These include the demand that we pay close, sympathetic attention to the contested phenomena. (Recall his fondness for tragedies that insightfully and movingly explore the ethical and psychological consequences of fanaticism.) The effort is, in part, to show that supposed purity of religious motivation inflicts unacceptable harm and masks vanity or some other blameworthy passion. Second (as we will see in Chapter 7) Smith has at his disposal an argument about the dangerous social and political effects of state-supported religion. Part of the argument is that religion undermines its own claims when it uses the police powers of the state to institute its dogma. If true, this is a compelling critique.

Third, Smith can reply that his view about what constitutes "real positive evil" is not viciously circular, because the moral psychology is not fitted to one and only one set of virtues. He deploys the same moral psychology when discussing the quite different conception of the virtues held by native Americans or residents of distant centuries and places. The theory of "natural jurisprudence," which is based on the impartial spectator theory, is supple enough to explain many different historical schemes of justice.[23]

But if one wants a "proof" generated from outside any broad ethical scheme, then one wants something Smith cannot provide, as was explained in the last two chapters. Moral criticism must take a more piecemeal approach, and in the present instance this must include a dialectical response: Why, he would ask, is a proof that stands outside any ethical frame required? What would such a proof look like? Since you are demanding such a demonstration from me, can you provide one supporting *your* view of the matter? The conversation would unfold from there.

## 4. DISTRIBUTIVE JUSTICE

No society can surely be flourishing and happy, of which the far greater part of the members are poor and miserable. It is but equity, besides, that they who feed, cloath and lodge the whole body of the people, should

---

23 Just how would have been explained in detail in missing parts of Smith's *corpus*. Once again, I refer the reader to Haakonssen's *Science of a Legislator* for discussion.

have such a share of the produce of their own labour as to be themselves
tolerably well fed, cloathed and lodged.

Adam Smith, *The Wealth of Nations*[24]


Smith's decision to focus on commutative justice and for the most part
to assimilate distributive justice to beneficence does not proceed out of
indifference to the lot of the less fortunate or from blindness to any
claims of equity. He is committed to the view that human beings ought
to enjoy a decent standard of living. His spirited defense of commutative
justice in *The Wealth of Nations*, his outrage against legal and political
arrangements that deny people their liberty to dispose of their labor as
they think best, and his obvious commitment to a scheme of political
economy that will benefit the poor testify to his moral outlook.[25] Yet in
spite of the statement quoted at the beginning of this section, he does
not advocate an ongoing scheme for state redistribution of goods on
grounds that its recipients are owed a decent standard of living, equality
of opportunity, or equity.

The explanation is multilayered. To begin with, Smith is assuming that
principles of justice must be capable of precise specification. They cannot
resemble, as we have seen, the rules specifying the duties of friendship,
for these are "loose, vague, and indeterminate," and it is difficult to say
with precision what would constitute their violation. Because the state
brings its enormous police powers to bear in enforcing rules of justice,
these rules must be specifiable, explicable, and precise. I take Smith to
hold that beyond the rules of commutative justice we cannot meet these
criteria. The effort to specify the rules of distributive justice would on
his view terminate in casuistry, and in practice such rules could not be
enforceable in a fair, consistent, non-arbitrary way. He repeatedly insists
on "the exact administration of justice" (*WN* IV.ix.51; V.i.b.1; V.i.c.2);

---

24  *WN* I.viii.36. Marx picks up on this passage (and blends it with others as well as with his
own views) when he remarks: "Since . . . according to Smith a society is not happy in
which the majority suffers, and since the wealthiest state of society leads to suffering for
the majority, while the economic system (in general, a society of private interests) leads
to this wealthiest state, it follows that social *misery* is the goal of the economy." First of
the "Economic and Philosophical Manuscripts" (1844), in *Karl Marx: Early Writings*, ed.
and trans. T. B. Bottomore (New York: McGraw-Hill, 1964), p. 74.

25  Consider *WN* IV.viii.30: "To hurt in any degree the interest of any one order of citizens,
for no other purpose but to promote that of some other, is evidently contrary to that
justice and equality of treatment which the sovereign owes to all the different orders of
his subjects." Cf. the reference at *WN* IV.ix.3. to "the liberal plan of equality, liberty, and
justice."

this duty is one of the three he ascribes to the sovereign. Distributive justice is not a promising candidate for exact administration. Determining equity hinges in part on specifying who is to take responsibility (and to what degree) for the situation to be redressed. Determining what is beyond a person's control is, of course, a controversial matter. Especially given the role of luck in human life, it is hard to sort out the mix of fortune, individual responsibility, and social responsibility that constitutes a person's opportunities. Smith himself emphasizes the formative role that the family, properly structured (e.g., so as to exclude polygamy), plays in the moral education of the individual. Because different families will discharge their responsibilities differently, the opportunities of individuals are bound to vary. What is the individual owed in compensation for any deficiencies in upbringing? Outside the sphere of commutative justice, Smith largely suspends judgment about that mix, so far as state intervention is concerned. In general, individuals cannot be indemnified by the state against bad consequences arising from factors outside their control. Smith's decision not to set out a theory of free will suggests that he thinks there is generally no means of determining precisely what we are responsible for and what not. His political skepticism links up here with his more comprehensive skepticism.

Smith does not deny that harm can be done in a manner that, ideally, warrants redress beyond what commutative justice can offer. He understands, as his historical accounts of the genesis of various schemes of justice indicate, that even if the playing field is level, the players come to it with varying degrees of skill and advantage.[26] And he begins *The Wealth of Nations* by denying that differences in ability between a porter and a philosopher (that is his example) are natural, ascribing them primarily to the effects of the division of labor, education, and the like. He advocates dismantling any commutatively unjust legal strictures that preclude the porter from becoming a philosopher, or vice versa (*WN* IV.ii.40). But he thinks that there is no equitable way, on the whole, to specify within a jurisprudential framework how goods are to be (re)distributed so as to remove the inequality of the "opportunities" of individual players. This is *a fortiori* so in a complex commercial society, for there the relationship between an individual and his or her oppor-

---

26 His clearheaded realism is evident in many passages, e.g., *WN* V.i.b.12: "Civil government, so far as it is instituted for the security of property, is in reality instituted for the defense of the rich against the poor, or of those who have some property against those who have none at all."

tunities, as well as between the individual and social or political arrangements, is bound to be enormously tangled.

Smith's comment in *The Theory of Moral Sentiments* to the effect that
distributive justice is to be assimilated to beneficence helps to focus the
issue further (*TMS* VII.ii.1.10). The obligations of beneficence are no
less real for being imprecise, but imprecise they are, for apart from an
assessment of the specifics of the situation, they are vague generalities.
Does the beggar – say, the one Smith mentions in the famous passage
about the butcher, brewer, and baker – have a defensible demand on
our benevolence? That may well be a delicate matter. Consider how
much more complex it would be for a state bureaucrat to ascertain the
truth of the matter and the remedies due. Smith frequently emphasizes
that the legislator lacks sufficient knowledge to direct individuals in their
decisions about employing labor. It is not only unjust of the state to
control the individual's distribution of his efforts; it is folly for good
epistemic reasons as well. Generally speaking, individuals are far better
positioned than the state to assess their own actual and potential abilities,
risks, and the particulars of local opportunities. This point is made in
both *The Theory of Moral Sentiments* (VI.ii.1.1) and *The Wealth of Nations.*[27]
It applies to the state's effort to redistribute goods to the deserving;
assessing in a consistent manner who the deserving are and just what
they are due lies beyond the ken of the legislator or statesman.

Smith is generally and rightly skeptical both of the abilities and the
motivations of the legislator or statesman, except the most philosophical
of these, and he does not expect the philosophers to rule (*WN* V.i.f.51).
Ever the clearheaded realist, he fully expects those with power to lean
toward their own self-interest, even when they assume the mantle of public benefactor.[28] As he puts it, the authority needed to direct the affairs

27  E.g., as to what type of labor is more likely to yield value, Smith comments: "Each indi-
    vidual, it is evident, can, in his local situation, judge much better than any statesman or
    lawgiver can do for him. The statesman, who should attempt to direct private people in
    what manner they ought to employ their capitals, would not only load himself with a
    most unnecessary attention, but assume an authority which could safely be trusted, not
    only to no single person, but to no council or senate whatever, and which would nowhere
    be so dangerous as in the hands of a man who had folly and presumption enough to
    fancy himself fit to exercise it" (*WN* IV.ii.10). See also *WN* II.iii.36: "It is the highest
    impertinence and presumption, therefore, in kings and ministers, to pretend to watch
    over the oeconomy of private people." And *WN* IV.v.b.16: "But the law ought always to
    trust people with the care of their own interest, as in their local situations they must
    generally be able to judge better of it than the legislator can do." See also the references
    to the limits of "human wisdom" at *WN* I.ii.1; IV.vii.b.21; IV.vii.c.80; and III.iv.17.
28  In his own voice he declares: "I have no great faith in political arithmetick" (*WN*

of private individuals could not "safely be trusted" to any single person or council or senate "whatever," let alone to someone presumptuous enough to think that he could exercise the authority wisely (*WN* IV.ii.9). Smith doubts that there exists a "remedy" for the "violence and injustice of the rulers of mankind."[29] He speaks of a "legislator" who is "guided by general principles which are always the same" – and who thus sounds rather like a Platonic philosopher-king – but contrasts him with "that insidious and crafty animal, vulgarly called a statesman or politician"; it is clear that the latter run the world (*WN* IV.ii.39). His comments about the partiality of merchants and businesspeople toward their own interests could not be more condemnatory; indeed he views them as almost always engaging in a "conspiracy against the publick" (e.g., *WN* I.x.c.27; IV.iii.c.10). The legislature seems dominated by the "clamorous importunity of partial interests" (*WN* IV.ii.44), and this is typical of the public sphere for Smith. In the next chapter we shall examine Smith's analysis of the deplorable behavior of institutionalized religion under conditions of monopoly.

When states are charged with the delicate task of redistributing wealth so as to correct inequities and of equalizing, not just the playing field but the ability of the players to compete on an equal footing, there are grave dangers of abuse of the power requisite to so large a task, including those of self-promotion and self-perpetuation by the self-interested and unwise class of politicians. A scheme for distributive justice risks becoming what we would call an "unfunded mandate," or at least a mandate whose extent and duration seem impossible to specify in advance. Smith's skeptical comments about the conceits of the "man of system" (e.g., *TMS* VI.ii.2.15–17) mesh well with the stance of *The Wealth of Nations* here.[30] Incorrectly handled, distributive justice risks generating warranted resentment and therefore both social instability and the devolution of sympathy into an actor-centered, rather than spectator-centered, public ethics. It risks transforming the state from an impartial umpire into a selectively benevolent parent. And as always, unforeseen and negative consequences may be generated by the noblest of impulses.

I have hedged my formulations of this issue, for Smith does propose

<hr/>

IV.v.b.30) and "I have never known much good done by those who affected to trade for the publick good" (*WN* IV.ii.9).

29 *WN* IV.iii.c.9. Cf. V.i.g.19 and the reference to "management and persuasion" as the "easiest and the safest instruments of government."

30 Consider Hume's comments about distributive justice in the *Enquiry Concerning the Principles of Morals*, pp. 192–4. Smith must have known those comments.

some schemes for equity, compulsory education being a very important one.[31] These also include proportionally higher taxes on luxury vehicles, so that the "indolence and vanity of the rich is made to contribute in a very easy manner to the relief of the poor" (*WN* V.i.d.5; cf. V.i.d.13), a measure he backs up by observations that it is not "unreasonable" for the rich to contribute proportionally more than do the poor to public expenditures (*WN* V.ii.e.6) and by strenuous objections to taxation that supports "inequality of the worst kind" (that in which the poor bear a heavier burden than the rich; *WN*V.ii.e.16–19). Although the motivation for such measures from grounds of humanity is undeniable, he does not actually say that the poor are *owed* publicly funded education as a matter of justice but that public utility demands they be subjected to it – as long, of course, as the means chosen are carefully thought through so as to prevent the evils that always accompany the creation of state-enforced standards (e.g., the creation of administrators of those standards, in this case teachers, whose income is assured). By contrast, when discussing the question of whether the government ought to redistribute food in case of a famine – for example, by ordering corn dealers to sell their food stock at what the government considers to be a reasonable price – Smith objects on grounds of both efficiency and justice. The "unlimited, un-restrained freedom of the corn trade" is in fact the best preventative against famines, and corn traders also deserve to charge more during times of dearth in order to recoup profits they lost during normal times (*WN* IV.v.b.7, 8).[32]

Smith has to a large extent shifted the problem of caring for the "laboring poor" to the market and to that extent avoids the traditional problem as to the moral bearing that the genesis of inequality (e.g., the problem of the "original" division of the land) should have on the re-distribution of goods. He takes it for granted that numerous inequalities, many unjustified according to the standards of commutative justice, have developed over time. The "natural system of perfect liberty and justice" (*WN* IV.vii.c.44), whose establishment he advocates, is intended to put an end to unjust inequalities. However, the view that the market, under conditions of liberty and commutative justice, should be largely entrusted

---

31  For discussion of other examples, see N. Rosenberg, "Some Institutional Aspects of the *Wealth of Nations*," *Journal of Political Economy* 68 (1960): 361–74.
32  For discussion of Smith and the corn laws, see Winch, *Riches and Poverty*, pp. 205–9. I am much in agreement with Winch's remarks in this book about Smith's view of distributive justice (pp. 97–103).

with alleviating inequalities, and so the condition of the poor, makes at least two large empirical assumptions.

The first is that, under these conditions, people's resentment at ancient harms will fade and therewith demands for rectification. The impartial spectator's imagination is definitive of what constitutes a harm in need of rectification, and presumably the moral imagination is not expected to entertain forever a long chain of harms stretching back through time and across changing circumstances. Will imperfect spectators too let the past go? Second, will the free market (and so a system of liberty and justice) in fact improve the condition of the poor, and do so much more effectively than mercantilist schemes? Of course, Smith is arguing for an affirmative answer.[33] Were he mistaken about this distributive result of the operation of the "invisible hand" (*TMS* IV.i.10), then it would seem fair to say that his stance on the question of distributive justice is jeopardized on its own grounds.

It is inevitable that at some historical junctures, the condition of the laboring poor will *not* improve even under the "system of natural liberty" (*WN* IV.ix.51). Judging whether or not the *system* is to be rejected altogether is necessarily complex, for two reasons. First, as Smith himself points out, any liberal and commercial society will only approximate, but never match, the "Utopia" of a "system of natural liberty" (*WN* IV.ii.43). Thus it can always be claimed that a society's failings under present conditions result from failure to implement the system adequately. Second, Smith presents us in Book III of *The Wealth of Nations* with a theory of the "natural progress of opulence" through gradual stages (those of agriculture, manufacturing, and foreign trade). He is not proposing that a free society can be pumped into any historical context whatever, like a magic vaccine into the body politic, with beneficial results. Thanks to various historical contingencies, it is possible for a society to skip stages in its development by, say, building up its manufacturing capacity before its agriculture is sufficiently productive. But that will introduce various strains, and these indict, not the system of natural liberty, but the way in

---

33 We read at *WN* IV.ix.17, for instance: "it can never be the interest of the unproductive class to oppress the other two classes [the "cultivators" and the "proprietors"]. . . . The establishment of perfect justice, of perfect liberty, and of perfect equality, is the very simple secret which most effectually secures the highest degree of prosperity to all the three classes." It does not follow that one could not have a degree of prosperity without freedom. See D. Forbes, "Sceptical Whiggism, Commerce and Liberty," in *Essays on Adam Smith*, ed. A. S. Skinner and T. Wilson (Oxford: Oxford University Press, 1975), p. 201.

which it has been grafted onto a particular society at a particular historical juncture.

One's affirmation of a particular theory of political economy must be informed by an appreciation of its virtues relative to the competition, and these must be understood at least in part through historical analysis. Smith's argument in *The Wealth of Nations* is indirectly supported by his argument against alternatives, such as mercantilist and physiocratic views. He would certainly push the defender of premodern polities to justify both the system of slavery on which they were usually built and their general poverty. (Cf. Smith's comment at *WN* III.ii.9 on the "city in speech" of Plato's *Laws.*) The defense of his own view of the *best practicable* society is, once again, multifaceted, dialectical, a blend of empirical and philosophical reasoning. It is backed up by appeals to justice as well as to wise judgment.

## 5. NATURAL JURISPRUDENCE: UNFINISHED BUSINESS

I conclude by returning briefly to the question, addressed in the Introduction, as to why Smith never finished writing the part of the system of "natural jurisprudence" that would have articulated the "general principles of law and government" as distinct from "the different revolutions they have undergone in the different ages and periods of society." This part of the projected *corpus* would seem to amount to an account of the "natural rules of justice" or principles that "ought to run through and be the foundation of the laws of all nations" (*TMS* VII.iv.37), that is of the "general principles which are always the same" (*WN* IV.ii.39). Presumably these would be the normative principles of commutative justice as such. The meaning of the term "nature" is always complicated in ethical discussions, and I shall examine it in Chapter 8. At this juncture, we may safely assume that such principles are "natural" at least in that they arise from the impartial spectator's "sense of justice" (VII.iv.36). What counts as normatively natural is here determined by the impartial spectator's judgment. Therefore one might argue that the "general principles which ought to run through and be the foundation of the laws of all nations" just amount to the moral psychology of *The Theory of Moral Sentiments.* Smith's view about the origin of moral rules (which we examined in Chapter 5), as well as his repeated conjoining of the "theory" of natural jurisprudence to the "history" of law and government, may suggest that any further account of the principles of natural jurisprudence will have to be extracted from a narrative about the "different revolutions they have undergone in the different ages and periods of society." The first difficulty with this line of interpretation, however, is that even after finishing the sixth edition of *The Theory of Moral Sentiments* Smith explicitly stated that the core of "natural jurisprudence" remained to be written, and nothing we have in his published or unpublished works (including the student lecture notes) comes anywhere close to articulating "general principles which are always the same." (By Smith's admission, *TMS* does not.) Second, if the missing work amounted to a discussion of the "general principles" as yielded by the study of history, the problem is obvious: How can history yield general normative principles that are always the same? Is not the process either circular or inherently impossible? *Qua* system, the principles of natural jurisprudence would have to be complete. But as dependent on the experiential or historical, the system would have to be open-ended. Even the exact mix between the systematic and the open-ended would vary, perhaps, from one period to the next, such that we could not as theoreticians state the ideal "formula" for combining the two. Thus the philosopher must rely on the historians, rhetoricians, and literary authors for information about the context. They, in turn, cannot begin to formulate in a satisfactory fashion the principles suggested by the context, or the principles they assume in interpreting the context, or even why there is a need for formulating principles at all. Although we may speak of a "dialectical tension" or the like between principles and practice, this at best establishes meta-level consistency without solving the problem of circularity inherent in this approach to the systematic "conceptual foundations" project Smith evidently envisioned.[34]

I infer that at the level of his projected systematic project Smith faced an *aporia* from which he could not free himself. Perhaps attempts to work out the *aporia* were among the unpublished manuscripts burned at his

34 I am grateful to Knud Haakonssen for suggesting to me some of the formulations used in this paragraph. Similar questions arise with respect to a crucial part of Smith's other missing body of work that I have titled the "Philosophical History of the Liberal and Elegant Arts." How could he "illustrate" the "Principles which Lead and Direct Philosophical Enquiries" unless he already knew those principles? But what would a theory of the intellectual sentiments look like, over and above something comparable to a theory of the moral sentiments? Given the central role of the imagination in the three surviving essays, the missing account would presumably have included a treatment of the "principles" of this very faculty, i.e., of the imagination as such. Since any such account would itself be the product of the imagination – for the imagination is inventive or productive in its thinking, as we will see in Chapter 8 – the account seems circular or impossible.

urgent request. Given his skeptical stance, Smith could not fulfill his aspiration for a final and comprehensive philosophical system articulating the "general principles of law and government." To pursue questions about first principles is to seek a standpoint external to the human spectacle, and he thinks that that is unavailable. His own philosophical framework suggests that the "general principles" *are* the (moral and intellectual) sentiments – these being the "same" insofar as human nature remains the same through time – and that any further account of the general principles could only show how they are "illustrated" or embodied in time.

Yet Smith could not find that resolution entirely satisfying, partly for reasons we have just reviewed. He himself provided a further explanation as to why anything short of the envisioned *corpus* would be unsatisfying, namely the imagination's desire to unify through system and to provide a synoptic and "Newtonian" *logos* stretching between first principles and historical contingency. (In Chapter 8, I will return to the theme of the imagination.) The "beauty of a systematical arrangement" (*WN*V.i.f.25) is irresistible. The desire to grasp this beauty is paradigmatically philosophical. A system responds to our demand for comprehensiveness, and that to a certain commitment to give the phenomena their due. As philosophers we strive to do justice to questions that arise when we reflect on our experience – questions such as those concerning the normative principles of the true "science of a statesman or legislator" (Smith's phrase at *WN* IV.intro) – and we quite naturally imagine that justice will be done only through comprehensive system. As we have seen, Smith writes Platonic eros out of his philosophy, but it reappears in his plans for the written system. His own dream of a comprehensive and systematic account stretching from first principles to historical particularity testifies to the continuing power of the Platonic aspiration.

When Smith compelled his friends to burn his unpublished manuscripts, and therewith whatever he had written about the missing branch of natural jurisprudence, he consigned to the heat and light his hopes for an account of ahistorical, self-standing first principles. At the end of the day, he still found himself torn between two conceptions of enlightenment. The story of his anxiety to ensure that his unpublished manuscripts be thrown into the fire seems ultimately an allegory about the disharmony between reason's limits and our desire to transgress them.[35]

---

35 Kant remarked that "human reason has a natural tendency to transgress" its limits and must be reined in, and Smith would agree. *Critique of Pure Reason*, trans. N. K. Smith (New York: St. Martin's, 1965), A642 = B670.

# 7

## THE MORAL SENTIMENTS AND
## *THE WEALTH OF NATIONS*

The ancient politicians forever spoke of morals and of virtue; ours speak only of commerce and of money.

Jean-Jacques Rousseau[1]

*An Inquiry into the Nature and Causes of the Wealth of Nations* has among its chief aims to promote the just and effective pursuit of wealth. Smith's book is undoubtedly the most famous and enduring Enlightenment contribution to the subject. The Enlightenment, in turn, is closely tied to the liberation of the desire for wealth, and so to commerce and the free market which are, Smith persuasively argues, the most effective means to the satisfaction of that desire. This is no sooner said than ethical controversy surrounds the entire project. Is not the pursuit of wealth, especially when organized on a mass scale and sanctioned by law and custom, profoundly corrosive of virtue, good character, and community? Does not the creation of wealth require the exploitation of the workers, indeed their spiritual impoverishment, as they toil in the production lines for depressed wages while the rich reap profits from their stupefy-

1 The quotation is from part II of J. J. Rousseau's *Discourse on the Sciences and Arts*; trans. V. Gourevitch, in *Rousseau: The Discourses and Other Early Political Writings* (Cambridge: Cambridge University Press, 1997), p. 18.

ing labor? Consider too the vulgarity of the "consumerist" cultures of societies that have succeeded, thanks to the very sorts of social and economic mechanisms advocated by Smith, in becoming wealthy. The various liberties these societies enjoy, such as liberties of speech and religious belief, themselves slip (some would say) ineluctably and predictably into chatter and religion-of-your-choice sentimentality. The moral reproach to the project of *The Wealth of Nations* is ancient, going back through millennia of Christian and Greek thought, and it is contemporary too, heard in one form or another in enthusiastic denunciations of "Western materialism" (now worldwide materialism), as well as in Western hand wringing about the dissipation and lawlessness of the young.

Adam Smith himself insisted upon the moral and human problems inherent in the project he was advocating. In a crude and now discredited critique, some of his readers characterized his seeming ambivalence as the "Adam Smith problem," a problem supposedly reflected in Smith's published *corpus*. Admittedly, Smith leaves it to the reader's imagination to discover how *The Wealth of Nations* and *The Theory of Moral Sentiments* form a coherent whole. At first sight the books do seem rather different from one another in substance, style, and purpose. But the "Adam Smith problem" depended on a misunderstanding of the terms "sympathy" and "self-interest," according to which the first was taken to mean "benevolence" and the other "selfishness." The "problem" then seemed to be that the book on ethics praised virtue whereas the book on political economy built a large edifice on vice. Smith's famous remark to the effect that in procuring our dinner we address ourselves not to the humanity or benevolence of the butcher, brewer, or baker but to their self-love (*WN* I.ii.2) seemed to underline the point and to encapsulate everything that is both necessary to and morally repulsive about market economies.

In the preceding chapters we have already seen that this interpretation of Smith is a mistake. But this does not resolve the more interesting philosophical issues, many raised by Smith himself concerning the moral status of political economy. Recall from my reconstruction (presented in the Introduction) of his projected *corpus* that *The Wealth of Nations* is concerned with a branch of the science of "natural jurisprudence," and that natural jurisprudence, in turn, is a branch of moral philosophy. *The Wealth of Nations* is a "moral" work, then – but in what respect?² And how do virtue and commerce, moral education and modern liberties, support one another, especially given Smith's own questions and qualifications about commercial society and the project of wealth getting?

I would agree that *The Wealth of Nations* is "the greatest working-man's tract ever written."³ In the book's first chapter we learn that the division of labor increases productivity and thus improves the material well-being of the laborer to the point that "the very meanest person in a civilized country" is better off than "an African king" (I.i.11).⁴ The increase of productivity under conditions of commutative justice is fundamental to Smith's whole scheme for increasing the wealth of the poorest members of society. Yet his famous example here of the pin factory points forward to a problem fully developed later in Book V to the effect that specialized and repetitive labor destroys the laborer's mind and moral personality. Pins are trivialities, used primarily, one imagines, in the production of such things as fashionable clothes. For so absurdly superficial an end are the minds of the laborers degraded. Having confronted us with this observation, how does Smith propose to counter that degradation?

Smith forces the reader to put commercial liberal society into question even as he elucidates it and argues for its virtues. Just as in *The Theory of Moral Sentiments*, the rhetoric of the book is complex. *The Wealth of Nations* is thick with paradox and irony. Once again, we must understand that here, too, Smith's rhetoric has the same ethical as well as intellectual purpose, and the same stubborn resistance to the distorting imposition of system. In both rhetoric and argument, *The Wealth of Nations* forms part and parcel of his reconciliationist enterprise. Smith characterizes the scheme of things that his ideas would (if implemented) bring about as a "Utopia" (*WN* IV.ii.43; V.iii.68). The reader is meant to understand and thus accept, I shall argue, the imperfection inherent even in this utopia.

---

2 My view of *WN* as part of Smith's moral project runs counter to that of V. Brown in *Adam Smith's Discourse*. She argues that *WN* assumes the "autonomy of the conception of progress . . . an autonomy that makes economic progress a self-regulating and independent process" (p. 160). *WN* is "amoral monologism," a univocal text devoid of the "discourse of conscience" and marked by "no tension between nature and reason" (p. 195), a "basically amoral discourse" (p. 218). The desire to better our condition "is accepted as something entirely natural" without any of the moral disapproval attending the term in *TMS* (p. 215). I am arguing against all of these claims.

3 I quote from K. Haakonssen, *s.v.* "Adam Smith," in *The Routledge Encyclopedia of Philosophy*, ed. E. Craig (London: Routledge, in press).

4 For a similar example see J. Locke, *Second Treatise of Government* 5.41.

I begin (in section 1) with discussion of the notions of "bettering our condition," the "corruption of our moral sentiments," and the free market. I turn next to the way in which religious liberty and institutionalized religion are meant to support virtue. I give detailed attention to this issue because it may serve as a paradigm, in both its strengths and weaknesses, of the "solution" to the problem of liberty and virtue (section 2). The "subject" of political economy and its connection with the view of the self in *The Theory of Moral Sentiments*, the roles of civic institutions and state intervention, and the problems of dehumanization and alienation are discussed in section 3. I conclude with a general discussion of Smith's "politics of imperfection," and of the difference between political moderation and quietism or resignation (section 4).[5] The matter of philosophy's political engagement will once again occupy us.

## 1. THE "CORRUPTION" OF THE MORAL
## SENTIMENTS AND THE "DECEPTION" OF
## THE IMAGINATION

The great mob of mankind are the admirers and worshippers, and, what may seem more extraordinary, most frequently the disinterested admirers and worshippers, of wealth and greatness.

Adam Smith, *TMS* I.iii.3.2

*The Theory of Moral Sentiments* makes the drive to better our own condition fundamental to human life. That drive is analyzed within the framework of "sympathy" and of our yearning for the approbation of our fellows. As we have seen, in the discussion of happiness (Chapter 5, section 5), Smith also argued that it is governed by a "deception" of the imagination. The deception consists in the belief that by attaining all of those good things we strive for we will be happy and tranquil. In fact, however, this pursuit of happiness condemns us to a life of toil, anxiety, and transient satisfaction. It "rouses and keeps in continual motion the industry of mankind" (IV.1.10), pushing us far beyond anything like the satisfaction of basic "needs" and thus requires such things as the invention of the arts and the division of labor. (In addition to the passages already cited, see the discussion in *LJ*(A) vi.12–20.) *The Wealth of Nations* insists even more strongly that "the desire of bettering our condition" is one

5 The quoted phrase is K. Haakonssen's. See his "Jurisprudence and Politics in Adam Smith," in *Traditions of Liberalism*, ed. K. Haakonssen (St. Leonards, Australia: Centre for Independent Studies, 1988), p. 112.

that "comes with us from the womb, and never leaves us till we go into the grave."[6] Smith argues that properly channeled (e.g., within the constraints of justice and of efficient administration of law), the "uniform, constant, and uninterrupted effort of every man to better his condition" is the principle from which both national and private wealth are derived (*WN* II.iii.31). These statements, and others like them, clearly resonate with the remarks on self-betterment in *The Theory of Moral Sentiments* (IV.1.10).

We therefore have every warrant for bringing the point about deception to bear on *The Wealth of Nations*, even though Smith does not there stress that betterment, so understood, is founded on a deception.[7] And when we do, the entire argument of the book for a free (nonmercantilist) commercial society is cast in a revealing light. In both of his books Smith is recommending a society devoted to the improvement of the human lot but governed by a systematic self-deception about its own ends. Such a society is therefore inclined to private, though not necessarily public, unhappiness. The failure of the pursuit of happiness on the part of the great mass of individuals in modern commercial society is known to the philosopher at the outset. They are assumed to be, for the most part, in the grip of the imagination, held by the psychological equivalent of an invisible hand; they work themselves to exhaustion and rarely understand why. Paradoxically, labor in turn frees society from nature's grip. Through "uninterrupted effort" over time, the humanly wrought common world is transformed into an approximation of the system of natural liberty. We are made by the imagination to work, to transform the world and ourselves, and so to engage in a species of *poiesis*, namely, "production."

This life of "bettering our condition," understood in the "vulgar" sense, is not without its satisfactions, if it is joined with "middling virtue," as we saw in our consideration of the "prudent man." It should be reiterated that "bettering our condition" is not to be assimilated to greed and that it is receptive to virtue – but not to "high" virtue. Smith's

6 Smith continues: "In the whole interval which separates those two moments, there is scarce perhaps a single instant in which any man is so perfectly and completely satisfied with his situation, as to be without any wish of alteration or improvement, of any kind. An augmentation of fortune is the means by which the greater part of men propose and wish to better their condition. It is the means the most vulgar and the most obvious" (*WN* II.iii.28). "Vulgar" certainly reiterates the qualified disapprobation in *TMS* of the ordinary desire to better our condition.

7 In addition to the reasons presented here, I refer the reader to the discussion of my principles of interpretation in the Introduction.

impartial spectator approves of such striving, though he perhaps accords it only "cold esteem" (*TMS* VI.i.14). It may, of course, degenerate into greed and injustice, and indeed Smith implicitly claims that the dynamics of the *public* sphere are especially conducive to corruption. *The Wealth of Nations* is a clear-eyed and moderate defense of a "mean," or middle way, between a utopia in which citizens better their own condition by means of the attainment of self-perfection and high virtue and an immoral and factionalized society in which individuals strive for preeminence without constraint. As we will see, that "mean" is itself termed "utopia" by Smith. Reading *The Theory of Moral Sentiments* together with *The Wealth of Nations*, as their joint references to "bettering our condition" obviously invite us to do, is essential to evaluating the moral frame of *The Wealth of Nations* and thus the claims that Smith is willing to make on behalf of a free commercial society.

Precisely because such a society is, at best, one of middling virtue and deception, and because it is so closely linked with the "sympathetic" drive for approbation based on wealth and power, decay and degeneration are continual dangers for it. One of the great strengths of Smith's account is that he insists on facing this problem. He is under no illusion that the free market will automatically and infallibly generate a wise and virtuous society, even in attenuated senses of those terms. As Smith emphasizes in various passages in *The Wealth of Nations*, self-interest constantly pushes against justice: for example, those engaged in the business of "bettering themselves" naturally conspire against the public good in seeking to narrow the competition by means of monopolies (*WN* I.xi.p.10; I.x.c.27). This is a kind of corruption, since it is, at the least, an indifference to the violation of the liberties of others. *The Wealth of Nations* inveighs against that corruption as well as the whole mercantilist economic system built on it. Shortly after setting out the "prejudices of the imagination" that fuel our pursuit of wealth and power, Smith provides a chapter whose title reads, in part: "the corruption of our moral sentiments, which is occasioned by this disposition to admire the rich and the great" (I.iii.3). The chapter generalizes the point just made: especially in the "superior stations of life," the "candidates for fortune frequently abandon the paths of virtue" (*TMS* I.iii.3.8). Although the prejudices or deceptions of the imagination do not necessarily degenerate into moral corruption, they can. How will they be prevented from doing so?[8]

---

8 S. Justman comments: "As a defender of commerce, Adam Smith had to face the question of how men could preserve their autonomy and moral standing in spite of the corruption

The answer is neither universal philosophical education (though philosophy has a role to play here) nor universal enlightenment about the true nature of happiness. Political liberation is not contingent upon spiritual emancipation. Moral education must play its part, and, as I have already intimated, it will not be sustainable without appropriate political and social institutions and arrangements. One would expect this of a "virtue theorist." The *Wealth of Nations* helps us to understand what kind of institutions and arrangements further restraint. This is not to be confused with a wholesale revival of "classical humanism." Smith has a completely unblinkered, unedifying view of routine politics, and this view is central to his argument. He presents the public sphere as often driven by corrupted and corrupting "self-interest." The history of bloody religious wars in Europe could only have reinforced this cold view of what "politics" amounts to in reality. A breakdown of sympathy – analogous to that which we examined in Chapter 2, the subversion of the standpoint of the spectator into that of the actor – is a danger in the public life of all but the simplest societies, with the result that individuals and groups see themselves as beholden only to their own standards. Surprisingly, Smith thinks that commerce should be included among the properly structured institutions and practices that help to sustain the moral character of citizens.

Taken together, then, *The Theory of Moral Sentiments* and *The Wealth of Nations* form complementary parts of a larger whole in which moral philosophy, political economy, social science, and history support an unsentimental vision of the decent and productive life of the nonphilosopher. Smith seeks to detoxify the pursuit of wealth and to provide a limited defense of its virtues against Greek as well as Christian accusations that it necessarily destroys moderation (e.g., *Rep.* 555c–d), that it destroys martial spirit and thus jeopardizes liberty, or that it invariably leads to pettiness, softness, possessiveness, and morally unacceptable inequalities.[9] The accusations range from the view that the activities related to the acquisition and consumption of wealth are necessarily degrading and base to the view that as an entirely this-worldly matter such activities distract us from preparing ourselves for the next life. Aristotle held that

---

of and yearning for false goods – in eighteenth-century terms, the vanity and luxury – that prevail in commercial society." *The Autonomous Male of Adam Smith*, p. 149.

9 For further discussion of the "classical" view that Smith is rejecting and Smith's alternative, see C. J. Berry's excellent piece "Adam Smith and the Virtues of Commerce," in *Virtue*, vol. 34 of *Nomos*, ed. J. W. Chapman and W. A. Galston (New York: New York University Press, 1992), pp. 69–88.

the acquisition of goods is acceptable, or "by nature," only as a means to self-sufficiency, and he criticized profit-seeking commerce on the grounds that it serves excess gratification and the accumulation of wealth without limit (*Pol.* 1257a1–1258a18). Aristotle quotes Solon to the effect that wealth, and implicitly the desire for it, knows no boundary but replies that there is such a limit, namely that defined by the good life (*Pol.* 1256b30–9). Commerce unregulated by a vision of the good or virtuous life destroys the character of the citizens, of its rulers, and the public character or virtue of the polis. Degeneracy and degeneration are then inevitable. That is, from this ancient standpoint, the "deception" of the imagination *is* "corruption" at a deep level and leads to the other problems Smith himself discusses in both his books. Smith's response, correspondingly, ought be worth considering, in part because he himself insists on the presence of "deception," denies that deleterious consequences necessarily follow from it, and argues that the ancient cure for the deception has its own destructive consequences.

Corruption does not consist in the excesses of wealth getting alone. As was mentioned in Chapter 5, Smith judges that the greatest corruptors of the moral sentiments are faction and fanaticism, especially of the religious variety: "False notions of religion are almost the only causes which can occasion any very gross perversion of our natural sentiments" (III.6.12; III.3.43). This extreme form of corruption is not, of course, particular to commercial society, but it is, according to Smith, most effectively countered by the principles of liberty and of justice characteristic of that society. Remarkably, the same principles may also sustain those virtues that religion can provide. What is the argument for these provocative claims?

## 2. RELIGION AND THE VIRTUES OF LIBERTY

> The good temper and moderation of contending factions seems to be the
> most essential circumstance in the publick morals of a free people.
>
> Adam Smith, *WN* V.i.f.40

We might begin by reminding ourselves that the architects of what one might call "classical" or "Enlightenment" liberalism saw themselves as committed to refuting the claims to political sovereignty by organized religion.[10] The arguments against the legitimacy of a state-supported re-

---

10 The list of thinkers in the "classical liberal" tradition simply reads as the roster of key Enlightenment figures: Bayle, Hobbes, Locke, Spinoza, Hume, Smith, Voltaire, Kant, to

ligion and, in the extreme case, of a religious monopoly are so integral a part of Enlightenment efforts to put politics on a stable and just foundation as to constitute one of the controlling themes of the period. Liberal politics requires religious toleration, or better, liberty of religious belief. And this in turn implies that religious institutions must be privatized, as it were, and that just politics must be secularized. Legitimate rule is to lie in the consent of the ruled rather than in the laws of God as interpreted by his ministers on earth. Differences in religious outlook are to be settled, as Thomas Jefferson tells us, by persuasion, not by force, and persuasion is a private matter. The state has no role to play except (to simplify somewhat) that of preventing the use of force by the parties involved. As Jefferson strikingly puts it, "The legitimate powers of government extend to such acts only as are injurious to others. But it does me no injury for my neighbour to say there are twenty gods, or no god. It neither picks my pocket nor breaks my leg. . . . Reason and persuasion are the only practicable instruments [against error in religion]."[11]

The issue of religion is useful for prying open the commitments of liberalism. First, religion is an issue that has been discussed continuously since Plato. The rich history of the debate provides us with well-explored arguments. Second, the religion issue continues to function in contemporary discussions of liberalism as a sort of touchstone of the cogency of liberalism.[12] The issue acquires that status in part because it cuts to the core of the problem of justification of political rule, raising the question of what counts as a "rational" justification in politics, and so of whether liberal arguments against religiously based justifications for rule are

name a few. Consider the role that religious freedom plays in Kant's "What Is Enlightenment?" essay, for example. I reiterate that in speaking of "liberalism" I refer to the "classical liberalism" of the sort roughly shared by the founders of the tradition rather than to the contemporary American credo currently contrasted with "conservatism" (so too with my use here of the term "liberal"). (See my comment in note 2 to the Introduction.)

11 *Notes on the State of Virginia*, query 17, in *Thomas Jefferson: Writings*, pp. 285–6. In the "Bill for Establishing Religious Freedom," Jefferson writes: "our civil rights have no dependance on our religious opinions, any more than our opinions in physics or geometry . . . the opinions of men are not the object of civil government, nor under its jurisdiction." *Writings*, pp. 346–7.

12 To take just one example: consider the use to which T. Nagel puts the issue in "Moral Conflict and Political Legitimacy," *Philosophy and Public Affairs* 16 (1987): 215–40, at p. 225. For a recent, non-Smithean discussion of various argumentative strategies concerning the religion–politics issue, see R. Audi, "The Separation of Church and State and the Obligations of Citizenship," *Philosophy and Public Affairs* 18 (1989): 259–96.

ultimately more than rhetorical, as some thinkers have charged. The differences between religious and nonreligious outlooks may be so profound as to call into question the possibility of public rationality and dialogue that seems crucial in arguments for liberal regimes. Third, there exists a relevant empirical history concerning the role of religion in public life, and in any discussion of the best practicable regime that history will play a leading role. Finally, the religion issue can serve as a convenient lever for eliciting the assumptions that political theorists make about moral psychology in setting out conceptions of the just regime.

## Smith's Reply to, and Appropriation of, the Platonic Tradition

The *locus classicus* of arguments for state-supported religion – at the limit, for a civic religion that is granted a monopoly – is book X of Plato's *Laws*. For the sake of convenience we may refer to this type of antiliberal argument as falling within the "Platonic tradition."[13] The religious tenets that the Athenian Stranger sets out are not those of conventional Greek religion. They purport to rest on philosophical argumentation about the nature of the soul and the cosmos. For present purposes I can largely bypass those arguments and set out the basics of the general scheme for a civic religion in the *Laws*. The Athenian Stranger argues that a stable and relatively free society requires a shared moral outlook – a shared doctrine of the virtues, in effect.[14] The Stranger indicates at 744d that the "greatest illness" of a city is "civil war"; the first duty of

13 The phrase is an imprecise one, of course, and I do not mean to overlook the great differences between the theological views expressed in the *Laws*, in the many branches of Christian thought, and in what Smith calls "natural religion"; nor do I pretend that later contributors to the tradition credited the *Laws* as their inspiration. My point is simply that with respect to several broad principles bearing on the ethical and political function of religion, Plato and some of his Christian successors share common ground, in partial contrast with Smith. See, for example, the argument in "Libertas," an 1888 encyclical of Pope Leo XIII, where the basic Platonic argument about the relationship between religion, virtue, and community is made; then inferences drawn about the error of separating church and state, about the ethical and conceptual poverty of "liberalism," and the like.

14 At 701d the Stranger remarks: "We said that the lawgiver must in laying down his laws aim at three things, namely that the city for which he legislates be free, that it be a friend to itself, and that it possess intelligence." The degree of political liberty (including freedom of speech) permissible is to be measured by several demands, including those of survival, the rule of law, and the flourishing of personal excellence among those capable of such excellence. I am using T. Pangle's translation of the *Laws* (New York: Basic Books, 1980).

the sovereign is to secure the conditions under which the rule of law can take place and the citizens can be free from unjustified injury. Peace and liberty require a shared notion of the good life.

What is the shared moral outlook in the *Laws*? It will be based on an understanding of what an excellent human being is (707d). And that understanding is to be woven into the fabric of the ordinary beliefs of the community by raising citizens to view themselves as part of a larger, intelligently ordered whole. In the language of a later tradition, this view is theistic. We are not to think that the good or the just is whatever our individual passions dictate; rather, we are to believe that these norms are embedded in the nature of the whole, or cosmos. Like the Athenian Stranger, Smith sees our excessive partiality toward ourselves (the "misrepresentations of self-love") as a major source of the disorders of human life.[15] A similar theme runs through Shaftesbury, Hutcheson, and Kant. The Stranger's theism of book X is meant to lead us to look at ourselves impartially, from the standpoint of the good of the whole. He argues that injustice arises from one's effort to get more than one's share, more than is fair (906c), and correlates with a failure to take an impartial view of what is right in light of the whole (903c). It suffices for the Stranger's proposals that this theistic theology be *believed* to be true, even if proving its truth philosophically lies beyond our abilities. Fundamentally, the Stranger's argument is ethically motivated; to overstate somewhat, for him religion is an extension of the requirements of morality and communal life.[16] In its intended ethical and political focus, it is a predecessor of what Smith will call "pure and rational religion."

On the Stranger's view, religious liberty and civil peace are incompatible, and it is the duty of the statesman to secure the latter. The motivation is not mere control or power over the citizens; indeed, one of the views rejected here is that might makes right. The Stranger assumes that moral and religious beliefs can ameliorate our behavior, just as unhealthy or false beliefs corrupt.[17] Indeed, his view is that the shared moral norms

---

15 *TMS* III.4.3–12. The Athenian Stranger strikingly remarks: "The truth is that the excessive friendship for oneself is the cause of all of each man's wrongdoings on every occasion. Everyone who cares for something is blind when it comes to the thing cared for, and hence is a poor judge of what is just and good and noble, because he believes he should always honor his own more than the truth. . . . So every human being should flee excessive self-love" (731e–732b).

16 Smith comments, for example, that the "first duty" religion should require is "to fulfil all the obligations of morality" (*TMS* III.5.13).

17 This is an assumption to which Smith would assent; *TMS* III.5.4; III.5.12–13; III.6.1. At *Laws* 889e we are told that the atheist is a materialist who holds that the gods "exist by

become most effective when articulated in religious terms, for those terms supply an accessible framework as well as incentives for virtuous behavior (cf. III.5.6).[18] In Plato's scheme, these incentives also include severe civil penalties for the public promulgation of either a private religion or of impiety of several other kinds.[19] The infamous "Nocturnal Council" (909a), for example, is charged with talking well-intentioned atheists out of their views. (The persuasion is to take place for at least five years, in the "moderation tank.") Publicly expressed atheism is to be suppressed, not because individual atheists cannot be moral but because a society of atheists would lack the beliefs that sustain virtuous behavior.[20]

art – not by nature but by certain legal conventions, and these differ from one place to another, depending on how each group agreed among themselves when they laid down their laws." There are no just things by nature, according to the atheist; the just is the powerful; and by the public promulgation of such views "civil strife is instigated" (890a). Hence atheists should be suppressed in the interests of peace and justice. At 907d the Stranger sets out the various punishments for the various kinds of impiety. At 904d–905c the Stranger refers to Hades and an unspecified place where the just are rewarded and insists that no one can escape the justice of the gods. The Stranger does not dwell in great detail on punishments and rewards in the afterlife.

18 This thought has, by now, a long history. Locke wrote that "The philosophers, indeed, shewed the beauty of virtue: they set her off so as drew men's eyes and approbation to her; but leaving her unendowed, very few were willing to espouse her." Thanks to Christianity, "virtue now is visibly the most enriching purchase, and by much the best bargain"; and "Upon this foundation, and upon this only, morality stands firm, and may defy all competition." *The Reasonableness of Christianity*, ed. I. T. Ramsey (Stanford: Stanford University Press, 1958), p. 70, par. 245. The gulf between Locke's conception of rational agency and Smith's "internal conception" of the same is nicely spelled out in J. Dunn, "From Applied Theology to Social Analysis: The Break between John Locke and the Scottish Enlightenment," in Hont and Ignatieff, *Wealth and Virtue*, pp. 119–35. Dunn concludes that "the development of a purely internal conception of rational agency has left human individuals impressively disenchanted and undeceived. But it has also left them increasingly on their own and devoid of rational direction in social or political action, prisoners in games of self-destruction to which, on these terms, there may well be no rational solutions" (p. 134). The general thought here is one to which I shall return in the Epilogue.

19 The other kinds of impiety include out and out atheism; the view that the gods do not care for human beings; and the view that the gods can be bribed. The Stranger is particularly concerned with persons who either do not believe in gods or believe that the gods are appeasable or careless, who use religion as a mask for private gain, and who "entice the souls of many of the living while pretending to entice the souls of the dead" (909b). Smith's concern with fraudulent religion shows at *TMS* III.5.13, where he argues that we are right to have greater confidence in people "deeply impressed with religious sentiments," as long as those sentiments are not corrupted, e.g., by efforts to bribe or bargain with the Deity.

20 The Stranger addresses the issue of moral atheists at *Laws* 908b–c. For a similar suspicion of a society of atheists, see J. Locke, *A Letter Concerning Toleration*, ed. P. Romanell (Indi-

It might be objected that we have no solid evidence that Smith knew book X of the *Laws*, even though he knew and refers to the dialogue as a whole.[21] Putting aside the reply that Smith's argument could parallel another's argument without his knowing it, he did in fact have the debate and in some respects a similar point of view before him, as put forward by that great modern Platonist, the earl of Shaftesbury. I refer to Shaftesbury's *Inquiry Concerning Virtue or Merit*, whose controlling theme is none other than the relationship between religion and virtue. Shaftesbury ends up arguing that belief in theism (which he defines as the doctrine that "everything is governed, ordered, or regulated for the best, by a designing principle or mind, necessarily good and permanent") is socially beneficial.[22] Shaftesbury understood virtue in connection with affections (emotions) or actions that advance the public good, and vice primarily as a deficiency of such affections or as an excess of "self-affections." Excessive partiality toward oneself is again the root of evil, and it is to be countered in part by a "theistical belief" in the "superintendency of a supreme Being, a witness and spectator of human Life" (*Inquiry* bk. I, pt. III. sec. III, p. 268). As indicated earlier, Smith argues that religion

anapolis: Bobbs-Merrill, 1985), p. 52, and also F. Hutcheson, *A System of Moral Philosophy* (1755; rpt. New York: Kelley, 1968), bk. III, chap. 9: "As to direct Atheism, or denial of a moral providence, or of the obligations of the moral or social virtues, these indeed directly tend to hurt the state in its most important interests: and the persons who directly publish such tenets cannot well pretend any obligation in conscience to do so. The magistrate may therefore justly restrain them by force." Hutcheson goes on to argue that "as to various forms of external worship and the different schemes of religion," it would be "the greatest folly and cruelty" to attempt to persecute them (pp. 313–14). Cf. bk. I, ch. 10: " 'Tis a needless inquiry whether a society of *Atheists* could subsist? or whether their state would be better or worse than that of men possessed with some wicked superstition? True religion plainly increases the happiness of both individuals and of societies. Remove all religion, and you remove some of the strongest bonds, some of the noblest motives, to fidelity and vigour in all social offices" (p. 219). Ed Hundert points out to me that the problem of a society of atheists was placed on the modern philosophical agenda by P. Bayle, *Miscellaneous thoughts on the Comet* (1680), the text to which Hutcheson is probably alluding.

21 In paragraph 9 of his "History of Ancient Physics" essay, Smith refers to the origins of "theism" in pre-Platonic philosophy as well as in Plato's *Timaeus*, the key theistic idea being that the world is a "complete machine" or a "coherent system, governed by general laws" set down by some intelligent being. In *EPS*, pp. 113–14. In par. 11, Smith suggests that the Stoics here seem "as in most other things, to have altered and refined upon the doctrine of Plato" (p. 116). The reference to Plato's *Laws* at *TMS* VII.iv.37 is to the whole dialogue, thus suggesting that Smith had at least paged through it.

22 *Inquiry* bk. I, pt. 1, sec. II, in vol. I of *Characteristics of Men, Manners, Opinions, Times*, p. 240. It does not follow that Shaftesbury thought atheists to be immoral. For discussion see D. Den Uyl, "Shaftesbury and the Modern Problem of Virtue," *Social Philosophy and Policy Journal*, 15(1998): 275–316.

can help us to control our passions and our natural partiality toward ourselves; knowing that one is being watched by a just Supreme Being contributes to this restraining effect (*TMS* III.5.12). As we saw in Chapter 5, Smith argues that self-command is the key to the virtues and is tied to our ability to see ourselves as part of an ordered whole (*TMS* VII.ii.1.20). As Shaftesbury also puts it,

> He who, as a sound theist, believes a reigning mind sovereign in Nature, and ruling all things with the highest perfection of goodness, as well as of wisdom and power, must necessarily believe virtue to be naturally good and advantageous. For what could more strongly imply an unjust ordinance, a blot and imperfection in the general constitution of things, than to suppose virtue the natural ill, and vice the natural good of any creature?[23]

Properly ordered religion supports virtue and community. Again, Smith explicitly endorses this proposition.[24]

In both the *Laws* and the *Republic* (book II), the controlling perspective from which the religion issue is approached is political and pedagogic. This is the perspective from which Smith approaches the matter in Book V of *The Wealth of Nations*. He is concerned to integrate religion with moral education and civic peace. The general section of which his discussion forms a part (ch. 1, pt. III) is entitled "Of the Expence of Publick Works and Publick Institutions"; the discussion itself occurs in article III, which is entitled "Of the Expence of the Institutions for the

---

23 *Inquiry* bk. I, pt. III. sec. III, p. 277. Shaftesbury remarks in ibid., sec. II, pp. 264–5: "Nothing can more highly contribute to the fixing of right apprehensions, and a sound judgment or sense of right and wrong, than to believe a God who is ever and on all accounts represented such as to be actually a true model and example of the most exact justice and highest goodness and worth. Such a view of divine providence and bounty extended to all, and expressed in a constant good affection toward the whole, must of necessity engage us, within our compass and sphere, to act by a like principle and affection." Virtue is "no other than the love of order and beauty in society"; belief that the very order of the world is just, beautiful, harmonious and proportioned will enliven that sense of virtue (ibid., p. 279). Shaftesbury makes it clear that whether or not this theism is objectively true, it is highly advantageous to the cause of virtue. It should be noted that Shaftesbury's dislike of both institutionalized religion and of what J. Viner (following A. C. Fraser) calls "theological utilitarianism" ran deep. For the quoted phrase, see J. Viner, *The Role of Providence in the Social Order* (Princeton: Princeton University Press, 1972), p. 70.

24 E.g., "religion enforces the natural sense of duty" (*TMS* III.5.13) and "religion affords such strong motives to the practice of virtue, and guards us by such powerful restraints from the temptations of vice, that many have been led to suppose, that religious principles were the sole laudable motives of action" (*TMS* III.6.1; see also III.5.3–4).

Instruction of People of all Ages." Smith believes that morality and religion are learned affairs although they are founded on human nature.
The formation of right character and the appropriation of sound rules
of conduct are heavily affected by institutional context.

Let me turn to this section of *The Wealth of Nations*, for it is here that
Smith proposes his non-Platonic solution to Platonic worries. He leads
up to the analysis of institutionalized religion with a discussion of education. Correspondingly, questions of theology are remote from his discussion. At the same time, he does not think that religion is an opiate;
he sees it as having a constructive role to play in character formation.
For example, he thinks that the worker who finds himself thrown into a
large urban context feels unaccountable to others. Anonymous and sunk
in obscurity, the worker neglects himself and turns to "every sort of low
profligacy and vice." By becoming a member of a small religious sect,
however, he becomes responsible to others and so to himself (*WN*
V.i.g.12). Religion is thus helpful in countering this source of corruption
in commercial society. Smith's concern with religion is motivated in part
by a concern for the moral education of the community, that is, for civic
virtue. Properly controlled religion is only one aspect of moral education; in these pages Smith also speaks of state-imposed requirements for
education in science and philosophy and about the civic role of the arts.
Even when ideal conditions prevail and religions compete with one another, a role for the state remains.[25] But the contribution of religion to
moral education is complicated by several potential dangers.

In the paragraphs immediately leading up to article III, Smith observes that the better educated a people, the less susceptible they are to
the "delusions of enthusiasm and superstition, which, among ignorant
nations, frequently occasion the most dreadful disorders."[26] This is particularly important in free societies, where "faction and sedition" can
ultimately be countered only by the people themselves.[27] These state-

25  In a nonideal situation, an established church may be the next-best solution, and Smith
    praises one such arrangement (*WN* V.i.g.41). The distinction between ideal and nonideal
    helps to resolve the seeming contradiction here that is insisted upon by C. G. Leathers
    and J. P. Raines in "Adam Smith on Competitive Religious Markets," *History of Political
    Economy* 24 (1992): 499–513.
26  *WN* V.i.f.61. Concerning the meaning of the terms, see Hume's "Of Superstition and
    Enthusiasm," in *Essays Moral, Political, and Literary*, pp. 73–9. For the complex history of
    the terms, see S. Tucker, *Enthusiasm: A Study in Semantic Change* (Cambridge: Cambridge
    University Press, 1972). Smith does not himself clearly distinguish between superstition,
    enthusiasm, and fanaticism.
27  "An instructed and intelligent people besides are always more decent and orderly than

ments might be taken to suggest that Smith thinks religious belief incompatible with a free society. This is not the case, however. Rather, he thinks that religious belief becomes dangerous "fanaticism" in the context of improper institutional arrangements. Let us see how he develops the argument.

The discussion of education leads Smith to a prolonged analysis of the Roman Catholic Church of the early Middle Ages, whose history he uses as a test case. He focuses first on the incentives of the Catholic clergy to expand the sphere of their influence.[28] The incentives arise because many of the inferior clergy derive much of their subsistence from voluntary donations. This point leads Smith to a long and, in this context, revealing quotation from Hume's *History of England*. In essence, Hume there argues that organized religion is an unmitigated evil and that the best way to control it, and so secure civil peace, is for the sovereign to "bribe their [the priests'] indolence" by subsidizing their livelihood. Establishing a church will keep priests lazy and unenthusiastic (*WN* V.i.g.3–6), whereas competition encourages "enthusiasm" and exacerbates the danger of faction. In quoting this passage, Smith effectively asks whether popular religion is a good thing and whether there are effective means of controlling it.[29]

Smith agrees with Hume that assuring priests an income would tend to render them less active and, conversely, that forcing them to compete for disciples (thus forcing sects to recruit actively) keeps religious zeal alive. And Smith agrees with Hume that there is a tension between civic peace and the authority of the sovereign, on the one hand, and organized religion on the other. I have already quoted Smith's comment that political liberty depends on the ability of the citizens to resist the "delusions of enthusiasm and superstition." He goes to some lengths to argue that the interests of an established church are never the same as

an ignorant and stupid one. . . . They are more disposed to examine, and more capable of seeing through, the interested complaints of faction and sedition, and they are, upon that account, less apt to be misled into any wanton or unnecessary opposition to the measures of government" (*WN* V.i.f.61).

28 "In the church of Rome, the industry and zeal of the inferior clergy is kept more alive by the powerful motive of self-interest, than perhaps in any established protestant church" (*WN* V.i.g.2).

29 Smith seems to be assuming here that fanaticism is a danger when the religion in question is monotheistic. For some discussion (which Smith must have known) of toleration in polytheistic religions and the tendency to intolerance in the monotheistic, see Hume, *The Natural History of Religion*, section IX. However, Smith's talk about the impartiality of the sovereign with respect to different religions (*WN* V.i.g.16) implies that the religions in question may include non-Christian religions.

those of the sovereign.[30] A monopoly by one church led to the "grossest delusions of superstition," which were so effectively supported by the self-interest of many individuals as to be "out of all danger from any assault of human reason" (*WN* V.i.g.24). Nevertheless, Smith disagrees with two aspects of Hume's argument. Organized religion is only partly an evil, namely when it leads to fanaticism, and in fact plays a constructive role in building community; and establishing a church will have an effect contrary to that which Hume envisions, for it will lead to war rather than peace. Granting a church a monopoly corrupts both religion and politics. Let me focus, first, on the latter argument concerning the relationship between state subsidies and religious warfare.

Smith begins by answering Hume's *History* with some history of his own. State support of religion was rarely if ever granted with the intention Hume recommends. Religions that ally themselves with the winning party in a political struggle soon request that the civil magistrate grant them a monopoly, subdue other sects, and provide a subsidy. The sovereign, having benefited from the sect's help during the struggles, is hard pressed to resist the request. Once a sect is established, it persecutes its rivals (with state support). Indeed, the very lassitude of the now subsidized ruling sect forces it to control its flock, not by actively recruiting their loyalty but by eliminating the opposition. The sect's lassitude, as well as the effort to persecute, in turn fans the flames of "enthusiasm" and of war. Neither of these are the effects hoped for by the church or sovereign.[31] Smith argues at length that in establishing a church, the sovereign is actually jeopardizing his own security. It is typical of Smith's analysis of politics to point out the importance of the unintended consequences of a given policy.

Preliberal politics, that is, in which force is used to bind together the polis into a coherent moral whole, does not create community; it destroys it. Indeed, it corrupts the character of all concerned. The persecuted turn either to fanaticism or to violence, and the persecutors hypocritically pretend to a piety they have long since stopped feeling and stoop

---

30  *WN* V.i.g.17. Indeed, "it may be laid down as a certain maxim, that, all other things being supposed equal, the richer the church, the poorer must necessarily be, either the sovereign on the one hand, or the people on the other" (*WN* V.i.g.41).

31  As Smith says of the churchmen who requested state support, "They were weary, besides, of humouring the people, and of depending upon their caprice for a subsistence. In making this demand [for state support] therefore they consulted their own ease and comfort, without troubling themselves about the effect which it might have in future times upon the influence and authority of their order" (*WN* V.i.g.7).

to violence that destroys the virtues of forgiveness and love they profess. The administration of justice ceases to be, in Smith's key term, "impartial" (used at *WN* V.i.g.8); or again, to borrow a term from *The Theory of Moral Sentiments*, the persecutors become "vain." By contrast, Smith claims that liberal political arrangements allow for real community, based on voluntary participation and genuine "care." Therein lies a key element of his critique of the Platonic tradition. I shall return to it later in this section.

How, then, are religious fanaticism and strife to be controlled? Smith's moral psychology eliminates two possibilities, namely, (1) that social conditions can be structured in such a manner that religion ceases to be a felt need, and (2) that the threat of temporal punishments will succeed in quelling religious fervor. As Smith strikingly puts it, "the authority of religion is superior to every other authority. The fears which it suggests conquer all other fears" (*WN* V.i.g.17). Not even a standing army can control it, since the soldiers themselves are susceptible to the appeals of the common religion. The Platonic tradition is again mistaken in this matter. And this brings us to the first step in Smith's "liberal" solution to the problem, namely a "free market" of religions.

We must distinguish between the genesis of any such liberal structure and the analysis as to why (given certain views about moral psychology and lessons drawn from the history of the subject at hand) liberalism solves the problem of religious war. As to the former, Smith is clear that religious war is principally brought about – if it is brought about – not by the designs of philosophers or the exhortations of statesmen but by "the natural course of things," which gradually weakens the authority of established religion to the point that the civil magistrate can not only cease to support it but can take an "impartial" standpoint amongst competing religions.[32] As to the latter, Smith tells us, first, that if the state did not support any one sect more than the next, it would have "dealt equally and impartially with all the different sects, and have allowed every man to chuse his own priest and his own religion as he thought proper"

---

32  Smith remarks that in the medieval period the Roman Catholic Church "may be considered as the most formidable combination that ever was formed against the authority and security of civil government, as well as against the liberty, reason, and happiness of mankind, which can flourish only where civil government is able to protect them.... Had this constitution been attacked by no other enemies but the feeble efforts of human reason, it must have endured forever" (*WN* V.i.g.24). For a helpful discussion of the history of intolerance in Christianity, see G. G. Stroumsa, "Le radicalisme religieux du premier christianisme: Contexte et implications," in E. Patlagean and A. Le Boulluec, eds. *Les retours aux écritures: Fondamentalismes présents et passés* (Louvain: Peeters, 1993), pp. 357–82.

(*WN* V.i.g.8). As a consequence, there would have arisen "a great multitude of religious sects." As predicted by Hume, each religious teacher would vigorously pursue new converts. Given that disagreement in religion is natural, we can expect a multitude of sects to arise.

In short, Smith seems to think that once the state has taken an impartial stance toward religions, the natural impetus will be toward fragmentation of institutionalized religion into many sects (*WN* V.i.g.9).[33] One reason for this is that, according to Smith, many of the truth claims in religious teachings are not "verifiable" in even a generous sense of the term. Much of religious doctrine is not subject to meaningful debate; this is a consequence of the epistemology of religious belief, on Smith's view. (See *WN* V.i.f.29 on ontology, metaphysics, and "pneumaticks.") The persuasiveness of such claims is bound up with the personal history, psychological makeup, and economic background of the auditors and with the rhetorical powers and the force of personal example of the leaders. In the language of *The Theory of Moral Sentiments*, it is difficult for "impartial spectators" who are not similarly situated with an actor to sympathize with his religious beliefs. "Sympathy" requires an act of imagination; indeed, Smith takes religious pictures of the world to be exercises of imagination.[34] Thus to sympathize with, and perhaps agree with, others' religious views is imaginatively to enter into others' picture of the soul, God, the afterlife, and other beliefs. The variations in the religious pictures of the world that people have imagined are endless. This is not to deny that large numbers of people can come to agreement about a detailed set of religious tenets. But they will more easily do so insofar as they are similarly situated and develop significant bonds of friendship and community of outlook. In *The Theory of Moral Sentiments* (VI.ii.1–3) he indicates that our circle of affection (or "sympathy") is generally small. A local church, affiliated though it may be with a far-flung religion, may supply the relevant community.

He assumes, second, that the society in which a multiplicity of religious sects – and with it the possibility of religious freedom – arises will be a reasonably large one that includes distinctions of wealth and power as well as the circulation of differing moral views.[35] And this is why he

---

33 As is also noted by J. Z. Muller in *Adam Smith in His Time and Ours* (Princeton: Princeton University Press, 1993), p. 157. Muller does not pursue very far the question as to *why* the fragmentation occurs or why it leads to political moderation.

34 This is, of course, also a Platonic view of the conventional religion promulgated (on his account) by poets.

35 Smith seems to assume that in hunter or nomadic cultures, as well as early agricultural

says, later in the discussion, that in small republics a pure "free market" solution did not work (*WN* V.i.g.36). Like Hume before him and James Madison after him, Smith seems to think that political liberty is better protected in a large rather than a small nation.[36]

But why should differentiation into a multiplicity of competing religious sects lead to restraint and abjuration of violent means in pursuing converts? Here Smith says:

> The teachers of each sect, seeing themselves surrounded on all sides with more adversaries than friends, would be obliged to learn that candour and moderation which is so seldom to be found among the teachers of those great sects, whose tenets being supported by the civil magistrate, are held in veneration by almost all the inhabitants of extensive kingdoms and empires, and who therefore see nothing round them but followers, disciples, and humble admirers.

But because every other sect would be doing the same, the efforts of the one would be matched by the efforts of the other. In a free market, that is, religious sects will control each other, each serving as a check on the other. Further, where there is a multiplicity of sects, even the unruly will be insufficiently powerful seriously "to disturb the publick tranquillity" (*WN* V.i.g.8). Should the sects coalesce into one or a few great sects that act in concert or with discipline, however, a reversion to preliberal politics is nearly inevitable.

Smith is arguing that a liberal political arrangement will lead to the formation of the virtues of public moderation and honesty (and indeed he cites liberal Pennsylvania as evidence that "philosophical good tem-

societies, religion is not a political issue, either because disagreement about religious tenets does not arise, or because theology has not been invented. I note that the "city in speech" of book X of the *Laws* is tiny, but for the Athenian Stranger it is big enough to make the issue of religion a political problem.

36 In a small republic the community of "sympathy" (in Smith's sense) may be too small for the splintering of groups to occur; it may also be relatively easy, in practical terms, to form a majority faction and suppress political liberty. See Hume, "Idea of a Perfect Commonwealth," in *Essays Moral, Political, and Literary*, pp. 527–8. James Madison's famous solution in *Federalist* no. 10 to the problem of faction seems modeled on the solution he provides elsewhere to the problem of religious faction: "In a free government the security for civil rights must be the same as that for religious rights. It consists in the one case in the multiplicity of interests, and in the other in the multiplicity of sects. The degree of security in both cases will depend on the number of interests and sects; and this may be presumed to depend on the extent of country and number of people comprehended under the same government." *The Federalist Papers*, ed. C. Rossiter (New York: New American Library, 1961) no. 51, p. 324.

per and moderation" is the result of such a regime).[37] Paradoxically, this does not mean that religions will become less energetic and vigorous – Smith's immediately preceding argument seeks to establish the contrary. Rather, the point is that zealous advocacy of a religious view will go hand in hand with restraint in the means chosen to pursue recruitment to the sect. That is, sects under these conditions will both pursue religion more vigorously *and* accept their status as "privatized." Smith is proposing a counterintuitive coordination of political moderation and religious enthusiasm, and this is a crucial part of his thesis.

Thus Smith claims that under perfect conditions of competition the tenets of the sects might come to resemble each other in their common rejection of fanaticism and superstition.[38] That is, the result would be the "religion of morality" so beloved of Enlightenment thinkers. Smith does not, I think, mean here that all sects will agree on all major tenets of religious doctrine. Rather, he means that whatever their doctrines, they will be free from willingness to commit violence ("fanaticism"), from dishonesty ("imposture"), and from superstition ("absurdity") and will praise basic virtues such as benevolence, moderation, justice, and humility.[39] These are in effect the ethical and political benefits that the scheme of Book X of the *Laws* sought to achieve, but here they are achieved through multiplicity of and competition among religions rather than through state enforcement of a religious monopoly.

At the same time, Smith's view implies that as a religion of morality takes hold, theological disputes will come to seem uninteresting. Thus

---

37 A similar expectation was suggested by Thomas Jefferson. See his letter to T. Cooper of Nov. 2, 1822, in *Writings*, pp. 1464–5. Cf. Voltaire's statement that "If there were only one religion in England, there would be danger of tyranny; if there were two, they would cut each other's throats; but there are thirty, and they live happily together in peace." In the sixth of the *Philosophical Letters*, trans. E. Dilworth (New York: Macmillan, 1961), p. 26.

38 "The teachers of each little sect, finding themselves almost alone, would be obliged to respect those of almost every other sect, and the concessions which they would mutually find it both convenient and agreeable to make to one another, might in time probably reduce the doctrine of the greater part of them to that pure and rational religion, free from every mixture of absurdity, imposture, or fanaticism, such as wise men have in all ages of the world wished to see established" (*WN* V.i.g.8).

39 Similarly, Spinoza states, in chapter XIV of the *Theologico-Political Treatise*, "I shall now make bold to enumerate the dogmas of the oecumenical creed, or the basic beliefs which Scripture as a whole aims to convey. These . . . must all reduce to the following: that there exists a supreme being who loves justice and charity." And: "worship of God and obedience to him consists solely in justice and charity (or love) toward one's neighbor." Quoted in D. Den Uyl, "Power, Politics, and Religion in Spinoza's Political Thought," *Jewish Political Studies Review* 7 (1995), p. 88.

"pure and rational religion" would seem to be distinguishable from theological metaphysics. The latter line of inquiry Smith thinks an otiose, distracting, and potentially dangerous fabrication of the imaginations of insufficiently occupied Schoolmen and university professors. I shall return to this distinction later in this section.[40]

Yet the analysis so far as to *why*, under conditions of free competition, moderation would result seems quite unconvincing. The question is particularly pressing because Smith is clear in *The Theory of Moral Sentiments* that shame and love of fame can overcome the fear of death (I.iii.2.10; VI.iii.7) and so that the threat of death is insufficient to restrain religious enthusiasm. Smith's "free-market" solution to the problem of religious strife cannot be a merely prudential one, as though various sects will refrain from violence simply because they think it advantageous to their present bargaining position to do so. The "commodity" here has a qualitatively different grip on the imagination than do other sorts of goods exchanged in the market. Why would a free-market solution not result in the war of all against all? Smith himself points out that prudential reasons are insufficient restraints on passions such as anger (VI.concl.3,4). We need to understand better why Smith thinks that consumers of religion will support nonviolent, nonhypocritical, and nonsuperstitious religion under conditions where religious liberty obtains.

Specifically, Smith's solution of this problem runs somewhat as follows: what restrains teachers of religion are neither threats from the state nor threats of violence from other sects but competition for disciples. But further, potential disciples expect, under ideal conditions, to benefit in certain respects from adherence to a religion and will penalize those religions that fail to deliver. Smith holds that religious "teachers" (to use his word) who fail to learn honesty and moderation will, under conditions of competition and religious diversity, find themselves preaching to empty pews. Where choice among sects is an option, the consumers of religion will tend to patronize sects that are vigorous but nonviolent in pursuing converts. The key thus lies in the psychology of fanaticism and moderation. How does this psychology function?

40 *WN* V.i.f.27–30. For an excellent discussion of the relation in Smith between theology and "natural religion," see Haakonssen, *The Science of a Legislator*, pp. 74–7. For a recent discussion of Smith's views of religion, see R. A. Kleer, "Final Causes in Adam Smith, *Theory of Moral Sentiments*," *Journal of the History of Philosophy* 33 (1995): 275–300. Nothing in Smith's scheme assumes atheism, however, contrary to Minowitz's argument in *Profits, Priests, and Princes*. I shall return in Chapter 8 to the question of the religious dimension of Smith's thought.

## The Psychology of Moderation and Fanaticism

Smith has argued that the causes of violence in connection with religion are (1) the perception by the dominant religion that assistance from the state (in the form of police powers) is available to increase the size of its fold, with all of the corresponding temporal benefits, and (2) feelings of resentment on the part of the persecuted religions. Under liberal political arrangements, the cycle of persecution and state involvement in religion slows or halts. Of course, it is possible that religions might still advocate persecution of other sects. But in *The Theory of Moral Sentiments* Smith seems to think that, all other things being equal, what people desire from religion is not power over others but comfort in the face of death, community as a context for the development of virtues, and assurance that there exists a standard of right (an "impartial spectator") over and above the judgments of the moment. Theologies that call for the extermination of other sects will, Smith seems to suggest, lose much of their compelling force when adherents can choose whatever religion they think answers the just mentioned wants, as long as religion is not serving as a proxy for political or economic power. And as more and more potential consumers judge the worth of religions on the basis of their ability to provide the properly religious benefits just mentioned, religions that sanction violence as a means to temporal power will attract fewer adherents, thus being more easily controlled. That is, as institutional incentives for warping self-interest into vain greed decline, theological doctrines that sanctify warped self-interest lose appeal. In the language of *The Theory of Moral Sentiments*, "general rules" arise to the effect that violence inspired by religious difference ought not to be sanctioned. Hence Smith's hope is that eventually religions in a liberal society will become "pure and rational," that is, "natural" or "moral" religions responding to genuine needs. Pure and rational religion performs the tasks that religion ought by nature to perform.

With respect to the issue of "dishonesty" ("imposture") or hypocrisy, I have said enough to indicate why Smith thinks that in free societies hypocrisy in religion will decrease. I add that the competition among religions contributes directly to this result in that each sect is intent, as Smith implies, on recruiting from the next; and this is effectively accomplished by exposing a religious teacher's hypocrisy. Adherents expect their leaders to exhibit the rigorous morals their leaders profess. Because a leader's vanity can also be quickly exposed, and because adherents presumably have minimal need to sympathize with a leader who is explicitly vain (rather than outwardly pious and dedicated), the incentives for vanity that operate so powerfully in state religions are here removed. Smith discusses in some detail the tendency of austere systems of morality especially to characterize the religious sects among the poor, who, for reasons he also discusses, demand that their leaders display unusual rigor in their morals.[41] This is not to say that the leaders of vigorous sects will lack bombast and rhetoric, or "coarse and rustick eloquence" (*WN* V.i.g.29) – on the contrary. Smith's point is that as they are allowed to advocate their views they will focus more on the arts of persuasion and the integrity of their personal dedication than on the arts of war. By contrast, there seems to be a connection here between hypocrisy and a propensity to advocate violence, for, as *The Theory of Moral Sentiments* suggests, both have roots in vanity, though not just in vanity.

With respect to the issue of superstition, Smith's story has another chapter to unfold. Clearly he believes that superstition is a major root of religious fanaticism, that is, of the claims of religious views to authority over political life, and he notes that the susceptibility of people to superstition will make it difficult to establish in law a separation between church and state (*WN* V.i.g.8).[42] He goes on to argue that as "science is the great antidote to the poison of enthusiasm and superstition," the state should require the study of science and philosophy "among all people of middling or more than middling rank and fortune" (*WN* V.i.g.14). This suggestion is startling in the mouth of a theorist supposedly dedicated to laissez-faire in all areas. But Smith is concerned with institutional structures that support a free society, and he takes education to be one of them. Presumably, when fortified with a strong dose of science and philosophy people will be less tempted to explain puzzling

---

41 *WN* V.i.g.10–11. The rich can afford a liberal and loose system of morals, and tend not to disapprove so strongly of "the vices of levity" that are apt "to arise from great prosperity." By contrast, the poor can ill afford even short flirtation with such vices; their situation renders even a week's dissipation ruinous. Thus as new sects arose to challenge the Catholic clergy in the sixteenth and seventeenth centuries, the "common people" contrasted the "strict regularity of their [the new sects'] conduct with the disorderly lives of the greater part of their own [Catholic] clergy" and espoused the former (V.i.g.29, 38). This theme of esteem and respect is present throughout the treatment of religion in *WN*; the last sentence of V.i.g. refers to a clergyman's "sanctity of character which can alone enable him to perform those duties [of his function] with proper weight and authority" in the eyes of the "common people."

42 Cf. *TMS* VI.iii.27: "The frequent, and often wonderful, success of the most ignorant quacks and imposters, both civil and religious, sufficiently demonstrate [*sic*] how easily the multitude are imposed upon by the most extravagant and groundless pretensions." See also *WN* IV.v.b.40.

natural phenomena in religious terms.[43] This in turn has beneficial political consequences. Science will disarm any claims of religious leaders to be somehow superhuman or superior to the rest of us by virtue of some natural hierarchy. That is, science demystifies superstition and thereby has a positive ethical and social role to play.

Science plays this role by helping to free religion and politics from each other. The need for this additional measure indicates that Smith does not think that merely separating church and state, permitting liberty of religious belief, and encouraging a flourishing free market of religions will adequately control superstition and fanaticism. Liberal education is also required (and it in turn will be subject to conditions of competition, as outlined in article ii of Book V of the *WN*). As always in Smith, social and political institutions are interdependent. Indeed, he also argues that in order to counter the "unsocial and disagreeably rigorous" tendency of sects that develops under conditions of religious liberty, the state should encourage "dramatic representations and exhibitions" of all kinds (to include drama, painting, poetry, music, dancing), so as to dissipate "that melancholy and gloomy humour which is almost always the nurse of popular superstition and enthusiasm." Such "diversions" have always been "the objects of dread and hatred, to all the fanatical promoters of those popular frenzies." Smith seems particularly interested in encouraging comedies in which the "artifices" of religious leaders can be exposed to "publick ridicule" (*WN* V.i.g.15).[44] It is not merely a question of mockery but of expanding the spectators' imaginations and capacity for sympathy, lest they be confined to an artificially narrow view of duty.

As already indicated, Smith takes *theology* to be a misguided effort to make conceptual or philosophical sense of what properly belongs to the imagination and the sentiments to judge. By contrast, *religion* arises pre-reflectively (*TMS* III.5.4). This is a critical distinction. What is the source of the religious impulse? Recall that toward the beginning of *The Theory*

43 For such, on his view, is the origin of superstition, as is indicated *inter alia* in paragraph 9 of the "History of Ancient Physics," in *EPS*, pp. 112–13. Interestingly, Smith does not tell us what sort of "philosophy" it is that he recommends as an antidote to fanaticism. It might be natural to take the term loosely, as synonymous with "science," but it might mean more – say, something along the lines of a "public philosophy" or elaboration of the arguments for toleration and reason in the public sphere. I discuss the issue further in the Epilogue.

44 As mentioned in Chapter 5, Smith heaps praise on Voltaire's *Mahomet* (*TMS* III.6.12). As a drama that educates the moral imagination and teaches how "conscience" can become fanatical, it would be a good candidate for one of the public "dramatic representations."

*of Moral Sentiments* Smith speaks of the "illusion of the imagination" that permits us to "sympathize" with the dead and to picture ourselves as living on after our own dissolution.[45] Religion may provide comfort in the face of death. Moreover, when faced with the injustice of this world, we naturally hope for an afterlife in which things will be set straight (see *TMS* III.2.12, III.5.10, 11; III.2.33). Smith also conjectures that notions of supernatural beings also originate in an effort to explain the forces of nature. Our imagination attributes intentionality to those forces and transforms them into entities capable of praising and blaming and of being praised and blamed. Hence the idea of immortality, which, when connected with a notion of merit and demerit, and of God, gives rise to a set of moral rules defining the virtues and regulating behavior. We take the moral rules to be derived from God's will and imagine that God – by definition much more powerful and wise than we are – enforces those rules. Moral rules become customary, embedded in the fabric of life, and institutions arise around them. Natural religion stands in a reciprocal relationship with morality and the sentiments.[46]

Thus anxiety, not just about death but about the next life, as well as the need to place confidence in an impartial spectator as guarantor of the rightness or wrongness of moral judgments, motivates natural religion.[47] Shared religious practices also provide a sense of belonging, and Smith thinks that sense to be very important given our fundamentally "social" nature. As we view ourselves through the eyes of others, their approval provides us with an initial source, not just of morality but also

45 From this illusion "arises one of the most important principles in human nature, the dread of death, the great poison to the happiness, but the great restraint upon the injustice of mankind, which, while it afflicts and mortifies the individual, guards and protects the society" (I.i.1.13).

46 Cropsey comments: "It is to be distinctly observed that the moral effect of religion is produced not exclusively or principally through any anticipation of reward or punishment to be visited upon the immortal soul but through the mutual supervision that prevails in small religious communities as small communities, and not as religions. In this we see the full force of secularism in full presence of religion." *Polity and Economy*, p. 82. This misses the full force of Smith's counterintuitive argument, for it is just when sects do operate as religions that their beneficial moral effect may be provided and the conditions under which this is supposed to occur are none other than those of political moderation and liberty.

47 E. Heath intriguingly suggests that the process by which "pure and rational religion" emerges from a competition of religions is analogous to that by which "the impartial (moral) point of view" emerges through the "interaction of individuals" and their "sympathetic imagination." "The Commerce of Sympathy: Adam Smith on the Emergence of Morals," p. 450. The challenge would be to flesh the analogy out in terms of sympathy, given the tremendous divergence between the religious views the believers actually hold.

of a sense of community.[48] We can thus explain Smith's crucial statements that "the authority of religion is superior to every other authority. The fears which it suggests conquer all other fears" (thus rendering the threats of the civil sovereign relatively ineffectual; WN V.i.g.17). Religious fears concern the afterlife, the judgment of an all-powerful being, and of exclusion from the community. These are more powerful than the fear of death.

As we saw in Chapter 5 (section 2), appeals to a divine impartial spectator can easily be confused, in the actor's mind, with the "delusions of self-love" (TMS III.4.7). The prospective leader of a religious sect imagines a detailed system of rules and duties, supposedly derived from God, intended to better our weak human nature, and he refuses to tolerate any deviation from them. This leads to the "very gross perversion of our natural sentiments" already referred to (TMS III.6.12). Fanatics wish to control others, to dictate their life plans, in accordance with some strict regimen and from the standpoint of a position of supposed superiority. The fanatic is shocked and affronted by a refusal to join the cause and naturally conceives of the disbeliever as vicious. He demands not only behavior but also conviction.[49]

But why do people follow the fanatic? For Smith, it must be that they "sympathize" with the fanatic's claims.[50] The unusual self-command, the rigor of the self-imposed regimen, impress us. But there is more to it than this. People also go along with the fanatic because (issues of prudence and self-interest to one side) they then share in the sense of superiority and find themselves "confirmed" (to use Smith's word) in their view of themselves. (Cf. the argument about "emulation" at TMS III.2.3.) They take themselves to possess the moral worth they thought they discerned in the religious leader. Smith remarks, in the context of our desire to better our own condition, that "It is the vanity, not the ease, or the pleasure, which interests us [in the rich and powerful]. But vanity is always founded upon the belief of our being the object of at-

---

48 "What reward is proper for promoting the practice of truth, justice, and humanity? The confidence, the esteem, and love of those we live with. Humanity does not desire to be great, but to be beloved" (TMS III.5.8).

49 The ability of religious fanaticism, in particular, to overawe our other fears (especially the fear of death) seems to distinguish it from nonreligious political fanaticism. In the case of the political fanatic, the problem is not one of erring conscience but of immoderation born of love of system and vanity.

50 Smith acknowledges that there is "something respectable in the character and behaviour of one who is thus betrayed into vice, by a wrong sense of duty, or by what is called an erroneous conscience" (TMS III.6.12).

tention and approbation" (*TMS* I.iii.2.1). So too with the admiration for religious sects and the desire to belong. Not all participation in religious sects is, of course, founded on vanity for Smith. Only sects claiming a moral superiority so great as to warrant both a rigorous and detailed system of duties and of efforts to compel adherence by nonbelievers attract the vain who long for an exclusive claim to perfection.

Moreover, and this is a significant point, since such sects promise punishments for nonadherents and rewards for adherents, it is likely that they will attract especially by virtue of promising that justice will be done. As we have discussed, Smith takes justice to be based on the sentiment of resentment. It thus seems likely that fanatical religious sects will find fertile ground among people who harbor a particularly acute sense of resentment, and the suppression of one religion by another seems, in Smith's analysis, to cause the hatred in question. The more closely religion is tied to the allocation of worldly goods by means of political power, the more likely it is that religion will be mixed with resentment on the part of those who take themselves to be unfairly excluded or cheated by that allocation.

Correspondingly, under conditions of political liberty, when the state is impartial among competing religions, that source of resentment is obviated and with it a powerful motive for sympathizing with fanatical or persecutory religious sects. Although vanity may encourage sympathy with a given religious leader, other things being equal even the vain will abandon a leader who is exposed as corrupt or hypocritical, and in a free market of religions the chances of vanity being exposed are relatively good. Some sects may nevertheless resort to violence to secure their ends; bereft of support from the state and unsupported by other sects, however, the damage will be limited – or so Smith's argument implies.

As already noted, once liberal politics has been established, Smith would expect there to arise "general rules" to the effect that moderation is a praiseworthy quality. To repeat, people will come to expect even religious leaders to praise moderation and to condemn religious violence and the fanaticism that encourages it. Adherents will by and large demand that religions deliver the promised spiritual goods – a moral teaching and the personal example of the leader(s). The *nomoi* (customs, laws) will tend to support toleration and peace even when fanaticism arises.

## Concluding Questions about Smith's Proposal

To summarize, Smith agrees with the Platonic tradition that religion is and ought to be a permanent natural feature of the human landscape and that when properly structured it is essential to sustaining community based on a shared notion of the virtues. Religious beliefs can influence our behavior and can restrain our natural partiality toward ourselves. But Smith thinks that the Platonic scheme for incorporating religion into civic life destroys community by conducing to vices such as fanaticism, hypocrisy, and superstition. The Platonic scheme undermines both good government and religion, and thus serves as a classic illustration of good intentions yielding undesirable results. That scheme illustrates how reason or speculation ought not to guide practice. Smith therefore proposes a liberal political arrangement which should – given assumptions about moral psychology – encourage the development of many religious sects that, though often fervent in their spiritual appeals, will generally be moderate in their demands for political monopoly. A moderate religion may perhaps be termed a "civic religion," or what Smith calls "pure and rational religion," and it replaces the detailed theology provided by the Platonic tradition as the unifying dogma. Smith thinks that a single, shared theological doctrine is unnecessary for bringing about the results aimed at by the Platonic tradition itself. Correspondingly, he thinks a plurality of religious communities preferable to a single community; within the limits of a shared doctrine of political moderation, the practices that sustain the virtues are better pursued locally. Political liberty and diversity of religious belief are the true means to peaceful and genuine community.[51] The larger whole of which these communities are parts will not be a community in the same sense, nor need it be. Smith is surely in agreement with Aristotle's criticism, at the beginning of the *Politics*, to the effect that Plato erred in seeing only a numerical difference between different kinds of unity throughout the polis.

Further, Smith's argument for liberal policies with respect to religion and his adaptation of the language of the market to the realm of politics do not commit him to the view that society is simply a "collection of strangers" structured so as to encourage the individualistic *pleonexia* (greediness) of its constituents.[52] As I have argued, a purpose of his

---

51 G. M. Anderson argues that for Smith free markets of religions "produce changes in individuals that facilitate their participation in the contractual order of the market economy." See "Mr. Smith and the Preachers: The Economics of Religion in the *Wealth of Nations*," *Journal of Political Economy* 96 (1988), p. 1074. He also remarks that "An economy based on capitalist individualism was best served by religious movements that emerged from free markets themselves" (p. 1086). Anderson's argument reminds us that in speaking of choosing among various religions Smith is assuming a social context in which people are not once and for all born into a given social group that defines itself in terms of a particular religion.

52 The quoted phrase is that of MacIntyre, in *After Virtue*, p. 251. For a helpful critique of

scheme is to counter "individualism" in *that* sense. His moral psychology holds that we are thoroughly "social," interdependent, and communal beings whose good can be achieved only in concert and through sustained friendships. He argues that the structure and dynamics of an extended and liberal commercial republic are congenial to genuine cooperation and friendship.[53]

For Smith the state ought to be "neutral" between competing tolerant religions only in the sense of remaining impartial (though not with respect to all of the social conditions that support toleration). But this does not require abandonment of a conception of the "good person" or of virtue or of community. Smith's arguments for freedom of religion do not entail that the public sphere is amoral. He argues that when the state does *not* establish a particular religion, then impartiality, and the virtues of justice, moderation, and prudence, are better secured and the vices of intolerance, violence, and hypocrisy are more effectively prevented from emerging or surviving. We might go still farther and recall that Smith is a eudaimonist with a reasonably well-defined notion of happiness as tranquillity and of the virtues internal to this *summum bonum*. To oversimplify, his view is not that (within broad limits) any conception of the human good is as defensible as the next but that the chance of people's living out productive and respectable lives, however mistaken their view of real happiness may be, is greater within liberal political and economic structures than in a nonliberal society, and that stipulation by political means of citizens' deepest values is neither feasible nor just. In these ways, the state's impartiality is a deeply moral stance. Procedural neutrality on the part of the state is also espoused by Smith in light of an understanding (formed by observation of history and analysis of moral psychology) of how conceptions of the human good work out. For Smith, as for the Platonic tradition, the "human good" and the virtues remain central to politics. But politics (in the broad sense of the term) must also be given full consideration in theories of how the human good and the virtues may come to be practiced.[54]

MacIntyre's proposed antithesis between liberal individualism and the virtue tradition, see part 3 of J. Paul and F. Miller, "Communitarian and Liberal Theories of the Good," *Review of Metaphysics* 43 (1990): pp. 807–16.

53  For an interesting discussion of Smith's views of friendship, especially his theory that the impersonal market relations typical of modern commercial society create a place for personal relations of affection free from the calculative exchanges of the market, see A. Silver, " 'Two Different Sorts of Commerce': Friendship and Strangership in Civil Society," in *Public and Private in Thought and Practice*, ed. J. Weintraub and K. Kumar (Chicago: University of Chicago Press, 1997), pp. 43–74.

54  Thus Smith would reject the dichotomy Cropsey attempts to force on him: "The real

Smith's scheme is not without substantive commitments of its own with respect to truth in religion. A scheme for the political neutrality of religion cannot claim to be theologically or metaphysically neutral. The commitments entailed by his solution to the political problem of religion are visible at a number of junctures.[55] His assumption that individuals should be allowed to choose which religion to follow might itself be anathema to revealed religion, for from the standpoint of the latter there may be no meaningful "choice" between the word of God and false prophets. From the standpoint of the Platonic tradition, or at least from that of those who criticize the modern Enlightenment, has not Smith argued in a circle? For it might be replied to Smith's reply to the Platonic tradition that Smith's own argument in favor of liberty of religious belief simply spells out, and in turn supports, his assumptions about the nature of religion.

As suggested in our earlier discussion of the problem of circularity (Chapter 5), Smith's response would be first a dialectical one, that is, an insistence on the internal defects of both the Platonic tradition and the position of those who criticize the modern Enlightenment, and an insistence that he can better accomplish much of what the Platonic tradition aimed at, at least insofar as the political sphere is concerned. We have now seen how this argument unfolds. I expect Smith would argue that the debate is at least to some extent an empirical one and would point, as he does when citing the "publick tranquillity" of Pennsylvania, to the positive consequences for the honesty and even enthusiasm of religious belief that in fact have obtained when a free market of religions is implemented. He would certainly do his best to unmask the true motives behind much of institutional religion, as well as to point out the contradictions between its rhetoric and its practical effects.

Further, Smith might argue that the philosophical commitments un-

choice after all is said, had been between society somehow based upon the principle of virtue and society based upon some substitute for virtue, such as commerce." *Polity and Economy*, p. 93.

55  I have referred to his assumptions about the epistemology of religious belief, that is, his skepticism about theology, his suspension of discussion about it, and his distinction between it and natural religion; to the notion that proper religion is that which supports morality, and the corresponding ideal of "pure and rational religion"; to his view that religious pictures of the world are fundamentally exercises of the imagination; to his use of the term "superstition" and his assumption that philosophy and science are better equipped to explain what superstition dimly conceives; to his use of the term "fanaticism" to designate religions that are prepared to use political force to coerce nonbelievers; and to his views about the psychology of fanaticism and moderation. The list of virtues Smith thinks his scheme supports are not, and could not be, all-inclusive; he joins Hume in mocking the "monkish virtues" (*TMS* III.2.35).

derlying his own views are minimally restrictive, given their political consequences, for precisely in the context of a "system of natural liberty," *any* religion except an intolerant one is permitted. The exclusion of intolerance is, to be sure, an exclusion of some religious views but permissive with respect to a vast number and variety of others. These first two strategies, consistently and thoroughly carried out, are powerful.

But, next, since these commitments are finally skeptical (or so I have interpreted Smith), he does not have a head-on philosophical *argument* to show that theological views are false. He could argue that, at best, certain of these views are no stronger than many of their competitors, that we have no means of deciding which is "true," that the debates are fruitless, the language involved hopelessly ambiguous, and in general that the issues at stake (such as the immortality of the "soul" and the nature of God) so far transcend the "appearances" as to preclude anything like knowledge. It is consistent with this general skeptical strategy that Smith's attack on religious truth claims (like his attack on ontology, metaphysics, and "pneumaticks") often takes the form of mockery or polemic (e.g., *WN* V.i.f.28, 29). All of this will seem to the religious believer to beg the question of the truth of the theological view under consideration. But as we have just seen in detail, Smith can *also* offer an ethical and political argument that his scheme leads in practice to better religion and politics, supports virtues such as moderation and justice, and helps to secure social harmony and peace.

The example of religion seems to be one in which liberal practice speaks for its own virtues, even though at the theoretical level the arguments about the truth or falsehood of religion may be equipollent and are, in any case, highly complex. Smith is obviously not advocating that liberal culture be shaped by philosophical inquiries into theology but hoping that such inquiries, like ancient Scholastic battles, will become irrelevant in moral life and also, if possible, in theoretical inquiry as well. Thus, for the ordinary moral actor, there will be belief but no *aporia* about which religion is "best" in the sense of "truest." And this will bring us, in Chapter 8 as well as the Epilogue, to another problem. Smith does not, and cannot, hold that ordinary actors simultaneously believe in a religion and suspend judgment about the truth of their belief. They do not believe as a skeptic would. As members of a given community, they are not conscious of their "personal" beliefs as the constructs of this or that historical circumstance, as one outcome among many others (these others being clearly available in the marketplace of religions). Yet as just noted, Smith is also suggesting that, at least under ideal conditions, the faithful in one religion will not receive competing claims to truth as calling their own into question. This seems to come close to abandoning the whole notion of truth in the sphere of religion. He seems to assume that believers will act as though they are Smithean skeptics even while taking themselves to be thoroughly committed to the truth of a particular view. It is not clear that even the fabled invisible hand could orchestrate for long so complex a spectacle.

Another problem looms as well. Smith does not spell out precisely how broadly toleration is to be understood. For example, he nowhere denies that individual atheists can be moral;[56] unlike Plato, Shaftesbury, and Hutcheson, he does not explicitly address the question of whether communities of atheists can be moral or indeed be at liberty to pursue their lives. And this is, I think, because, given his assumptions about human nature, he does not think that atheism will ever be more than a marginal phenomenon in society. Yet some two hundred years after Smith's death, we may wonder whether implementation of his scheme for religious liberty might not lead, as some argue it has led in the United States, to the gradual demise of "enthusiastic" religion altogether. We might wonder whether Smith has not helped to put religion on the road to gradual extinction. Perhaps enthusiastic religion requires, as Nietzsche suggested, the motive of resentment and that motive can be fueled by political repression of religion or by a mingling of politics and economics with religion. When Smith praises the "philosophical good temper and moderation" (a phrase he underlines by repeating it in successive sentences at *WN* V.i.g.8) that has resulted from religious freedom in Pennsylvania, it is difficult not to imagine a plurality of competing religions, all of which are denuded of any deep sense of the sacred, of any myths, of any revealed word. It is not difficult to imagine that he is praising something like the Unitarianism that Jefferson so admired, and it is arguable that religion so understood is no longer religious. In this event, Smith's "pure and rational religion" would refer not just to the political or civic doctrine of moderation but to the doctrinal substance of all the religions in question.

---

56 It is worth recalling his praise of Hume as "approaching as nearly to the idea of a perfectly wise and virtuous man, as perhaps the nature of human frailty will permit" and in general of Hume's tranquillity in the face of death. See the letter to W. Strahan (Nov. 9, 1776), in *CAS*, p. 221. Smith's words are obviously meant to parallel Phaedo's praise of Socrates at the end of the *Phaedo*. Given Hume's reputed atheism, Smith's remarks are revealing, and they caused an uproar. Cf. Smith's brief comment about atheism in the "History of Ancient Physics" 10 (*EPS*, p. 116).

Were liberty of religious belief to lead there, and indeed from there to widespread agnosticism or atheism, Smith would be presented with an unintended consequence of his own proposals. He would no doubt appreciate the irony, having himself described the forces that led in unforeseeable ways to the dissolution of the medieval Catholic church. Although he celebrates the undoing of an institution that threatened "the liberty, reason, and happiness of mankind" (*WN* V.i.g.24), I have argued that he would find the demise of religion itself to be a matter for grave concern, especially if that demise were to occur in the context of a modern commercial society.

## 3. MORAL CAPITAL, CORRUPTION, AND COMMERCE

The problem of organizing a state, however hard it may seem, can be solved even for a race of devils, if only they are intelligent.

Immanuel Kant [57]

Having elaborated Smith's argument for the interdependence of virtue and liberty in the case of religion, let me now turn back to the problems of corruption associated with "bettering our condition." The paradigm of religion illustrates the virtues of liberty, as well as the benefits both of dispersing power and sovereignty and of allowing the intermediary institutions and arrangements of civil society to flourish. Religions may also offer a partial antidote to some of the "corruptions" in commercial society, such as the anomie of workers in urban contexts.

Quite probably the most pressing problem Smith saw in commercial society, except for the old and persistent danger of religious fanaticism, was that of the dehumanization of the workers caused by the very engine that drives the creation of wealth, namely, the division of labor. Smith's famous pronouncements on this score are so direct and powerful that taken in isolation they might seem to amount to ringing condemnations of the entire "system of natural liberty." For that system might seem to cause the most serious "corruption" of all, namely that of the human spirit.[58] The dehumanized worker cannot "judge" (to use Smith's word)

---

57  I. Kant, *Perpetual Peace* ("First Supplement"), in *On History*, p. 112.

58  To recall a passage quoted in Chapter 5, Smith writes that the worker or one of the "labouring poor" doomed to repetitive operations "generally becomes as stupid and ignorant as it is possible for a human creature to become. The torpor of his mind renders him, not only incapable of relishing or bearing a part in any rational conversation, but of conceiving any generous, noble, or tender sentiment, and consequently of forming

what is in the interest of his country, nor can he defend his country in war, since his courage and his body's vigor have been sapped. Smith follows this rhetorical explosion with a forceful statement of the paradox: "His dexterity at his own particular trade seems, in this manner, to be acquired at the expence of his intellectual, social, and martial virtues" (*WN* V.i.f.50). It is easy to see why Marx was, as one commentator says, "fond of quoting from these passages" and that they may be a source of his own notion of "alienation."[59]

Reasons of humanity temporarily to one side, does the dehumanization of the working poor matter, on Smith's view? The answer is affirmative, for the political implications of dehumanization are great, especially in free countries.[60] His political economy bears, not just on the nature and causes of prosperity but also on the conditions necessary to self-government. The latter picks up on an old "civic humanist" theme going back to Aristotle and Plato. A level of civic virtue, including intellectual virtue (note Smith's reference to " judgment" in the sentence quoted in n. 60 and recall our consideration of judgment in Chapter 5), is thus indispensable on Smith's view, and it is not outside the purview of government to be concerned with the moral character of its citizenry. How are these virtues to be fostered?

There is no single answer to this question, and the multiple answers are themselves dependent on each other for their effectiveness. First, as we have noted, religious sects provide part of the solution, as model "mediating institutions" (in our current phrase). Second, as we have also seen, the possibly deleterious consequences of religion ought be countered by the study of science and philosophy, a study that should be required of "all people of middling or more than middling rank and fortune," as well as by "publick diversions" to which the state must give "entire liberty" (*WN* V.i.g.14, 15). In another example of Smith's ap-

---

any just judgment concerning many even of the ordinary duties of private life" (*WN* V.i.f.50).

59 See R. L. Meek, *Smith, Marx, and After: Ten Essays in the Development of Economic Thought* (London: Chapman & Hall, 1977), p. 14. Passages similar to those in the *WN* may be found in *LJ*(B)333: "These are the disadvantages of a commercial spirit. The minds of men are contracted and rendered incapable of elevation, education is despised or at least neglected, and heroic spirit is almost utterly extinguished. To remedy these defects would be an object worthy of serious attention."

60 "In free countries, where the safety of government depends very much upon the favourable judgment which the people may form of its conduct, it must surely be of the highest importance that they should not be disposed to judge rashly or capriciously it" (*WN* V.i.f.61).

proving of the state's imposition on the liberties of the people for reasons of public utility, he further argues that the government should
require that the "common people" receive basic education in reading,
writing, and arithmetic, partly at public expense (*WN* V.i.f.52-54). Commerce itself, by improving the lot of the working poor and making them
less dependent on the rich than, say, feudal servants or retainers were
on their lords provides another avenue for countering the dehumanization of the workers.[61] Liberty to sell one's labor is not only just, on
Smith's view, but may be conducive to right formation of character. The
cluster of skills involved in taking responsibility for oneself and for the
improvement of one's condition are conducive to acquiring "just judgment concerning many even of the ordinary duties of private life" and
to overcoming the "torpor" that workers experience. In a commercial
setting, liberty helps to foster virtues such as self-reliance while increasing
the interdependence of citizens. That interdependence in turn leads to
competition, which embodies principles of justice that protect freedom.
Monopolies create artificial and one-way dependencies and in turn tend
to corrupt the characters of both monopolizers and monopolized. As in
the case of impartiality among religious sects, so too with respect to impartiality among competing economic ventures or among workers, it is
an overarching argument of *The Wealth of Nations* that such impartiality
is not only just, and conducive to general utility, but also supportive of
"middling" virtues, whereas the alternatives in a modern commercial
society (as well as some in premodern societies) are not.

Smith nowhere indicates that he has located all of the necessary measures that might be taken to counteract the deleterious effects of the
division of labor, and everything in his outlook encourages us to look
for further measures and to use judgment as the specific circumstances
warrant. His outlook also encourages us to develop any such schemes
with a clearheaded awareness of the power of self-interest as motivation,
and of the "law of unintended consequences."[62] Self-interest must con-

---

61 As Smith notes at *LJ*(A)vi.6, "Nothing tends so much to corrupt and enervate and debase
the mind as dependency, and nothing gives such noble and generous notions of probity
as freedom and independency. Commerce is one great preventive of this custom" (p.
333). See also *LJ*(B) 205 and 326.

62 His own suggestions in Book V of *WN* with regard to publicly required (and to some
extent publicly financed) education, for example, are filled with contrivances for ensur-
ing that teachers remain responsive to the needs of their students and that monopolies
or cartels of teachers do not arise. Similar reflections inform his discussions of fair taxation and of funding the military. See Lingren, *The Social Philosophy of Adam Smith*, pp.
126–7.

stantly be pitted against self-interest in order to help prevent the degeneration that accompanies assured power and income. Both competition and liberty to enter and leave a trade will almost always be essential. A burden-of-proof argument suffuses Smith's writing in political economy; the state may intervene in all sorts of ways, but those who would have it do so are required to show why it should in this particular instance, for how long, in precisely what fashion, and how its intervention will escape the usual dangers of creating entrenched interest groups and self-perpetuating monopolies.

Smith's discussion of these matters also communicates three other points. First, competition and liberty, protected by a spectating "night-watchman state," are in themselves insufficient to sustain a peaceful and just society, for they cannot be counted upon always to generate the requisite civic virtue. The dialectically self-negating character of human life precludes a simple laissez-faire attitude, as the problem of the dehumanization shows. If only for reasons of public utility, therefore, considerations of civic virtue are necessarily on the table as legitimate topics for discussion and possibly for the state's attention. As surprising as it might seem, Smith would not agree with Kant's view (quoted at the beginning of this section) that the problem of organizing a state can be solved by a race of rational devils, that is, by a race of intelligent, self-interested utility maximizers.[63] Intelligent self-interest *alone* will not solve the problem of social cooperation; this has been a contention of Smith's from the first sentence of *The Theory of Moral Sentiments*. Without a modicum of habituated virtue (moral and intellectual) in the citizens, the invisible hand behaves like an iron fist. Second, there is no *single* solution to the problem of civic virtue; a mix of interdependent institutions and arrangements will always be required. Third, *what* mix is appropriate will depend on the historical circumstances; there is no *a priori* Smithean dogma about that. His policy prescriptions are, just as in the case of the impartial spectator's responses to the particulars, sensitive to the context, within a general conception of virtue (including, of course, justice), human psychology, and relevant considerations of utility.[64]

---

63 *TMS* II.ii.3.2 might be cited against this, but the next paragraphs make clear that a sense of justice is required to uphold the whole "edifice" of society, and that sense amounts to more than the capacity for prudential calculation, as we have seen in Chapters 5 and 6.

64 The conjunction of the three points mentioned in this paragraph makes it impossible to see Smith as either "conservative" or "liberal," "right" or "left," in the contemporary American sense of these terms.

For example, we saw in Chapter 5 that concentric "circles of sympathy" are vital to moral education; thus the family, for example, is a crucial "civic institution," and society has a legitimate interest in its preservation. But how exactly ought the family to be defined? What precisely are the legal relationships among its members, and what steps should be taken to ensure its survival where it is threatened? There can be no simple answer. Smith analyzes polygamy, entail, and primogeniture and the (sometimes unanticipated) negative consequences as well as injustice of these institutions are drawn out.[65] Such analyses supply a negative benchmark, an indication of how things ought *not* to be arranged. We may spell out how they ought to be arranged but will have again to work from case to case, against the backdrop of the factors mentioned earlier. If we expect social philosophy to have a more rigorous structure, then all of this will seem hopelessly unsystematic and ad hoc. Here as elsewhere Smith is skeptical about just that expectation.

Two other features of the system of free commerce help to connect political economy with our earlier issues of virtue and moral education. One concerns the "civilizing" role of persuasion, and the other the question of why Smith views the opportunity to sell one's own labor as conducive not to alienation but rather to the development of moral personality. Each theme serves as a bridge between *The Theory of Moral Sentiments* and *The Wealth of Nations*. Toward the beginning of the latter book, Smith argues that the division of labor and the opulence it creates result, without anyone's intending it, from "a certain propensity in human nature . . . to truck, barter, and exchange one thing for another." Smith follows this up with an intriguing query about this uniquely human propensity: "Whether this propensity be one of those original principles in human nature, of which no further account can be given; or whether, as seems more probable, it be the necessary consequence of the faculties of reason and speech, it belongs not to our present subject to enquire"

65 For example, Smith points out with respect to primogeniture that "nothing can be more contrary to the real interest of a numerous family, than a right which, in order to enrich one, beggars all the rest of the children." Entails naturally follow primogeniture, and in spite of their function during a certain period of history, are "founded upon the most absurd of all suppositions, the supposition that every successive generation of men have not an equal right to the earth, and to all that it possesses" (*WN* III.ii.4, 6). These passages lead up to one of Smith's discussions of slavery, and his criticisms of all of these practices are structurally similar. (See my discussion of slavery in Ch. 5.) Polygamy is discussed in both sets of lecture notes on jurisprudence. Winch argues that Smith's stand on primogeniture allied him with both Paine and Price and set him against Burke. *Riches and Poverty*, pp. 151–2.

(*WN* I.ii.2). Nowhere in the extant *corpus* does he work this out explicitly. Notice that this passage leads up to the famous remark about our addressing ourselves to the self-love rather than the benevolence of the butcher, brewer, and baker.[66] Life in a market society is an ongoing exercise in rhetoric.

The necessity of developing our rhetorical skills is great in "civilized society," where, for at least two reasons, we are highly interdependent. First, with the progress of the division of labor, each person is less and less capable of providing basic necessities for himself; everything depends on exchange. Second, as Smith also points out here, in a society of "great multitudes," one's "whole life is scarce sufficient to gain the friendship of a few persons" (*WN* I.ii.2). In other words, in a "civilized" society, the arts of persuasion, communication, and noncoercive speech are essential. His typically counterintuitive claim is thus that precisely in appealing to each other's self-interest, precisely in enacting what seems to be our fundamental separateness and indifference to one another, we "civilize" ourselves and each other by binding ourselves to one another through speech. Paradoxically, in a "collection of strangers" (to quote MacIntyre's phrase once more), or what Smith calls "an assembly of strangers" (I.i.4.9) – that is, in modern society – civility is all the more important *and* likely. Although when we deal with the butcher, the baker, and brewer, we "address ourselves, not to their humanity but to their self-love," the unintended result is that their humanity and ours is enriched. Not only is our mutual dependence binding, but its accomplishment through language is civilizing.[67]

We might also term this outcome "socializing," or perhaps "humanizing." Elementary processes of exchange require that we look at the situation from each other's point of view, grasp the other's situation and

---

66 In the parallel passage in *LJ* (B) 221–2, Smith is reported as remarking: "Thus we have shewn that different genius is not the foundation of this disposition to barter, which is the cause of the division of labour. The real foundation of it is that principle to perswade which so much prevails in human nature. When any arguments are offered to perswade, it is always expected that they should have their proper effect. . . . We ought then mainly to cultivate the power of perswasion, and indeed we do so without intending it. Since a whole life is spent in the exercise of it, a ready method of bargaining with each other must undoubtedly be attained." Smith's inclusion of the "brewer" among the tradespeople to whose self-love we appeal is meant to stress, I think, that "need" or "necessity" is to be understood as "want," "perceived need," as that which custom has rendered rightfully expected (a point Smith indicates at *WN* V.ii.k.3).

67 This point is discussed by Fleischacker in his *Third Concept of Liberty*. Smith is here building on Hume's argument in "Of Refinement in the Arts" (to be found in the *Essays Moral, Political, and Literary*).

perspective, and calibrate our own demands accordingly. This is not merely analogous to the process of sympathy described in *The Theory of Moral Sentiments*; it is built upon it. Commerce and trade may contribute significantly to habits and experiences of sympathy between spectators and actors, and thus to the "harmony of society" (I.i.4.7). We ought not to be surprised, then, by Smith's claim that economic interdependence within the framework of liberty, justice, and competition, mediated by processes of persuasion, encourages the virtues of mutual accommodation and responsiveness (e.g., honesty, trustworthiness, reliability, frugality, punctuality, prudence, abstention from the use of force; *WN* II.iii.36; III.iv.3, 4; IV.vii.c.54; *LJ*(B) 326). Self-command, learned in the "great school" of the "bustle and business of the world," may also be expected (III.3.25).

By contrast, the vast inequality of power entailed by the one-sided dependence of slave on master, serf on his lord, or worker on proprietor under conditions of monopoly, and the like, lead to just the opposite (e.g., *WN* I.viii.41–8). The structure of the argument Smith made with respect to religion is in effect reiterated here. Thus commerce, when undertaken within this framework, may itself help to prevent the corruption and decay of the spirit.[68]

In Chapter 2, I discussed the following passage from the end of *The Theory of Moral Sentiments*: "The desire of being believed, the desire of persuading, of leading and directing other people, seems to be one of the strongest of all our natural desires. It is, perhaps, the instinct upon which is founded the faculty of speech, the characteristical faculty of human nature." Since "speech is the great instrument of ambition," and since the propensity to truck, barter, and exchange is the consequence of the faculties of reason and speech, it would seem that our "desire of being believed" (*TMS* VII.iv.25) shares center stage in a "civilized society" of commerce. This is, in turn, to be understood in terms of the moral psychology and views about the "self" in *The Theory of Moral Sentiments*. The desire to be trusted is the visible face of our secret consciousness that outside of human society we are nothing and that trust

---

68 J. Cropsey makes the interesting comment that "Marx insists on presenting free commerce as though its essence were conflict; Smith presents it as though its essence is a kind of sociality or collaboration." "The Invisible Hand: Moral and Political Considerations," in G. P. O'Driscoll, Jr., ed., *Adam Smith and Modern Political Economy: Bicentennial Essays on "The Wealth of Nations"* (Ames: Iowa State University Press, 1979), p. 166. Some of the points I have just been making are nicely discussed in Berry, "Adam Smith and the Virtues of Commerce."

is earned by being trustworthy. Smith implies that this virtue of trust-worthiness is a characteristic of properly structured free commercial societies. We see once again how *The Theory of Moral Sentiments* and *The Wealth of Nations* complement one another.

Let us turn to the second feature of the free market, that concerning the reasons why the opportunity to sell one's own labor may be conducive not to alienation but rather to the development of moral personality. Smith insists that "the property which every man has in his own labour, as it is the original foundation of all other property, so it is the most sacred and inviolable" (*WN* I.x.c.12). As long as the worker does not harm another person, he may sell his labor as he thinks best, and others may purchase it as they judge best. My concern at this point is with the question of why, on Smith's view, the worker who sells his labor, strength, and abilities, as well as the products of his efforts, is not harmed by doing so. Is one not reduced to the status of a mere commodity if one's own labor is viewed as "property" (even if one's own property) that can be bought and sold? Does not the emergence of commercial society bring with it the commodification of work and workers?

Smith's answer is that it is precisely when conditions emerge under which one *can* sell one's labor (or more precisely, that which it can produce) as one thinks best – that is, when one's labor has exchangeable value in a market – that one is in principle free *not* to be identified with one's work. When we do sell our labor, we are not selling ourselves, and those who command our labor do not rule us (as a master does a slave). Our labor is alienable *because* our "property" in it, that is, our right to it, is "sacred and inviolable." Under competitive conditions in a free market, when the state generally leaves deployment of one's talents to the individual, one is free – perhaps even compelled – to view one's abilities as alienable and thus to stand at a distance from them. "Every individual is continually exerting himself to find out the most advantageous employment for whatever capital he can command" by means of the "study of his own advantage" (*WN* IV.ii.4). One is led to look upon one's work and oneself in a somewhat detached way and thus as being more than just this or that worker doing just this or that task for just this or that master. This detachment affords the possibility of perspective on self and on the value one's labor and its context has, or ought to have, for oneself.

Similarly, under these conditions others may view one's labor as a commodity but cannot act as though the worker is himself a commodity that can be bought or sold. The freedom *not* to be identified with one's

work, which is the flip side of understanding one's labor to be a commodity that one can alienate as one thinks most advantageous, forms
part not only of the "system of natural liberty" and of natural justice
that Smith advocates but also of his antidote to dehumanization. For one
source of the extraordinary benumbing of the understanding of the "inferior ranks of people" in a "civilized society" is the fact that "there is
little variety in the occupations of the great part of individuals." One
performs nearly the same operation endlessly; one becomes the particular work that one does. Where a member of the "inferior ranks" is
prevented by restrictive legislation or corporate power from changing
profession or workplace or level of responsibility within his profession,
he may be condemned to "drowsy stupidity." We have seen that education provides an avenue of escape from reduction of self to the status
of a cog in the machine, an avenue to acquiring sufficient distance from
one's occupation and so some perspective upon it and one's society (*WN*
V.i.f.50, 51, 61). The successful emergence of a free market in which
individuals are in fact able to deploy their talents when, where, and how
they judge best relieves to a considerable degree the reification of the
laborer. This is part of Smith's moral case for the system of natural liberty.[69]

In sum, liberal commercial society does require civic virtue and may
in turn encourage it. The indispensable virtue of the public sphere is
commutative justice, but that virtue is not the only one, and it both
sustains and is sustained by the others. This said, questions analogous to
those raised in our consideration of religion also arise here. The free
market, including the market of religions, inevitably entails the constant
circulation of labor, capital, views about the human good, and political
opinions (especially given the flourishing of education, science, philosophy, and the arts). Yet Smith holds that sentiment, imagination, and
understanding, not philosophical reason, are the basis of sympathy, and
one of the chief points in his thinking about liberal societies concerns
the interdependence of its various institutions and social arrangements.
Were economic freedom to undermine social and political stability – and
thus the conditions that ensure it – then, ironically, the moral capital

69 My discussion in the preceding three paragraphs about alienation and liberty is much
   indebted to P. Werhane's fine analysis in chapter 5 of her *Adam Smith and His Legacy for
   Modern Capitalism* (Oxford: Oxford University Press, 1991). Werhane points out that the
   laborers should be able to look at their work in a detached way, as impartial spectators,
   this being possible under historical conditions when laborers are "free" in Smith's sense
   (p. 146).

created by liberal commercial society would consume itself. Smith's ultimate reply to such a prospect once again hinges on the solidity of the moral sentiments, including our propensity to respect "rank," to be habituated to defer to "general rules" of justice, and to be attached to our kin. But it would be out of keeping with his philosophy to dismiss these questions. It may be that economic liberty does corrode other valuable features of social life. Smith might well say that philosophers – whose leisure and specialization has been made possible by commercial society – ought to think creatively about remedies while keeping an ear attuned to the unexpectedly dialectical quality of the subject matter, and while also furnishing themselves with a knowledge both of the theory of moral sentiments and of the fundamental principles of political economy and jurisprudence.[70]

## 4. IMPERFECTION AND UTOPIANISM IN POLITICS AND POLITICAL PHILOSOPHY

That kings are the servants of the people, to be obeyed, resisted, deposed, or punished, as the public conveniency may require, is the doctrine of reason and philosophy; but it is not the doctrine of Nature.

Adam Smith, *TMS* I.iii.2.3

In this concluding section I return to the question of Smith's political philosophy. I noted in the Introduction that he did not envision an explicit place for political philosophy in his *corpus*. He does not tell us clearly what political system is best without qualification or spell out in detail the part of the system of "natural jurisprudence" that is alone always and everywhere best, nor even (in the manner of Aristotle and Montesquieu) analyze types of political regimes. One well-known thesis about his approach holds that political philosophy has here been de-

---

70 For example, with characteristic verve Smith criticizes the ancient remedy for deficient martial virtue and patriotism – namely, a militia – and proposes instead a well-regulated standing professional army, noting that the nature of modern weaponry, the division of labor in commercial society, and other social and historical factors, make the militia undesirable as a means of defense (*WN* V.i.a15–44). With a turn so typical of his dialectical approach to things, Smith concludes: "The invention of fire-arms, an invention which at first sight appears to be so pernicious, is certainly favourable both to the permanency and to the extension of civilization" (V.i.a.44). But this leaves us with the question of social cohesiveness and public-spiritedness earlier satisfied by militias, and here reflection on other "mediating institutions" would be called for.

flected or replaced by political economy.[71] There is some truth to this thesis, but that truth emerges only if we see that the deflection is itself the work of a political philosophy.

Smith remarks that implementation of the "system of natural liberty" would be a "Utopia" or "Oceana" (*WN* IV.ii.43; V.iii.68). These are striking remarks, because that utopia would merely permit the creation and distribution of wealth in a perfectly efficient and just manner. As premised on the never-ending effort to better our condition and thus as founded on the "deception" of the imagination, this utopia would be markedly imperfect as regards the noblest virtue and truest happiness of its citizens. It would be the high perfection, not of character but of the successful and successfully broad-based pursuit of "opulence" under conditions of commutative justice, and would be supportive of "middling," or "respectable," virtue. Under its regime, governments would deal "equally and impartially" with every kind of industry, for example (*WN* intro. 7); the rule of impartial spectatorship would be utopia. Yet this would be, so to speak, an imperfect utopia or, differently put, a utopia suited for imperfect creatures. We saw in *The Theory of Moral Sentiments* that, like a critic, the impartial spectator may judge according to the highest imaginable standard or according to a standard that is more commonly achievable. The standard by which *The Wealth of Nations* measures utopia is of the latter sort, that of the best *practicable* (which, as "best," may still be very difficult indeed to achieve).

The displacement of a "utopia" in the full sense (say, in the sense sought by the "city in speech" in Plato's *Republic*) by the utopia of liberty – and thus the displacement of a political philosophy oriented by a vision of that most perfected sense with a political economy and jurisprudence oriented by a vision of an imperfect utopia – is not a rejection of political philosophy altogether but an exemplification of a particular approach to the subject. At the core of this approach lies the recognition of our imperfection. To begin with, I refer to the inability of reason to determine the truth of contending "metaphysical" theses closely connected

---

71 The term "deflection" is J. Cropsey's, in "Adam Smith and Political Philosophy," in Skinner and Wilson, *Essays on Adam Smith*, p. 132; see also Minowitz, *Profits, Priests, and Princes*, esp. p. 97. (Minowitz tends to refer to the "eclipse" of politics by economics.) There is a significant body of literature on the question of Smith's politics and political philosophy, prominent in which is certainly Winch, *Adam Smith's Politics*. Winch there grants that Smith is not a "*political* philosopher in every significant sense of the term" but adds: "I do wish to maintain that Smith has a 'politics' which is far from being trivial" (p. 23). An excellent discussion of the matter will be found in D. Forbes, "Sceptical Whiggism, Commerce and Liberty."

with Platonic utopias. Smith's skepticism testifies to our imperfection at that deep level. The relative impotence of reason to guide human affairs on a grand scale, and the pivotal role of emotion or passion, reinforces the same point. The emotions are in turn, as we have seen, heavily influenced by the imagination, but the imagination often deceives us, sometimes for the better and sometimes not. In our pursuit of happiness, we are in the imagination's grip; that pursuit, as normally executed, also testifies to our imperfection. So too with our proclivity for the debased pleasure of exercising power over others (recall Smith's explanation of slavery), our easy fall into the pleasure of mutual sympathy with each other's vanity, and our willingness in some circumstances to press our sense of duty to the point of fanaticism. Our self-love and ignorance are continual themes in Smith's analysis of our lot.

Our imperfection in the sense of our inability to predict the movements of the invisible hand across the broad canvas of history, or to comprehend and direct with sufficient accuracy the industry of multitudes, or to resist the intervention of fortune in our individual and collective lives is, of course, a famous Smithean theme. The explicit reference to the invisible hand in *The Wealth of Nations* is in the context of the contribution to the public interest (understood as the creation of wealth) made by the exertions of individuals who act from self-interest rather than from a view to the social utility of their actions (*WN* IV.ii.9). To revert to our simile of the theater, they are like actors in a drama unaware that they are playing a part in an organized plot and thus also unaware that they are actors on the stage of history. This is *The Wealth of Nations* version of *The Theory of Moral Sentiments* thesis that ordinary persons need not be philosophers in order to lead productive lives.

There are many other passages in the two books where the idea of an invisible hand is present even though the term itself is not used. Sometimes this unseen force produces beneficial results, sometimes not. For example, in the historical account in Book III of *The Wealth of Nations*, Smith shows how in the feudal period the vulgar self-interest of the great proprietors of land combined with the gradual rise of foreign trade and domestic manufacturing to liberate their dependents from their influence. "For a pair of diamond buckles" the feudal lords exchanged their traditional authority (*WN* III.iv.10). As a result, "a revolution of the greatest importance to the publick happiness" was brought about by the lords and by the merchants, each of whom was acting without "the least intention to serve the publick" (*WN* III.iv.17). Smith argued in a parallel way in explaining the rise of liberty of religious belief. What Hegel would call the "cunning of Reason" governs history. As we have seen, Smith's argument against a theory of distributive justice stresses the epistemic limits of statesmanship. The very nature of justice itself testifies to the fundamental imperfection of human life in the sense of its lack of intrinsic harmony.

As the quotation at the beginning of this section indicates, Smith traces (in good Humean spirit) our acceptance of social rank to the "doctrine of Nature," in contrast to what reason and philosophy teach us. We are governed by authority, tradition, and the contingencies of birth and wealth, for reasons explained by Smith's moral psychology (*TMS* I.iii.2.3, and context; *LJ*(B) 12–13). Precisely what kind of authority and tradition we will be inclined to espouse depends to some degree on the historical circumstances (*WN* V.i.b.3–12, *LJ*(A)v.115–134). Here again, more perfect creatures, governed by reason and philosophy, would judge and act differently. Yet our proclivity to respect and admire rank may be counted as a useful "irregularity of sentiments" analogous to the one that I discussed in Chapter 6. We are not to infer that social arrangements are inaccessible to philosophical criticism or that Smith's "politics of imperfection" amounts to a "Burkean" quietism. We have seen repeatedly that this is not the case.

Both in *The Theory of Moral Sentiments* (VI.ii.2.16) and *The Wealth of Nations*, Smith refers to the saying attributed to Solon that the laws he laid down were, though not simply the best, the best that (in Smith's words) "the interests, prejudices and temper of the times would admit of" (*WN* IV.v.b.53). In the former context, Smith is criticizing the "man of system" who insists on establishing all at once his conception of the perfected and beautiful political system, treating others as pieces on a chessboard. A "general, and even systematical, idea of the perfection of policy and law" is no doubt necessary (VI.ii.2.18). But the statesman must also orient himself by the limits intrinsic, not just to the particular situation or age at hand but to human nature. This is precisely what *The Wealth of Nations* does. Consequently, any measures proffered by Smith in light of this orientation must themselves be tempered by the realization that they will be imperfect. Recall his remark: "What institution of government could tend so much to promote the happiness of mankind as the general prevalence of wisdom and virtue? All government is but an imperfect remedy for the deficiency of these" (*TMS* IV.2.1).

Granting that the remedy for the deficiency is imperfect, what *is* the remedy? Once again the answer is multilayered and involves a system of checks and balances (such as the separation of powers)[72] and of free competition (such as between religious sects or interests of all sorts; see *TMS* VI.ii.2.7); the education of the people, so that they can judge government effectively; a degree of civic virtue (such as a sense of justice); a sober acknowledgment that it is prudent to expect *less* of human beings when they act in their collective capacity and in the political theater than when they focus on their private pursuits; and finally a careful delineation of the limited duties of the sovereign and of measures for restraining the sovereign's powers within these limits.[73]

Smith's political economy and doctrine of justice are formulated against the backdrop of a picture of human finitude and its political and social consequences. The distinction between best and second-best standards of perfection is certainly familiar to us from classical political philosophy. Smith's understanding of that distinction provides the context for his view of the threefold duties of the sovereign (namely, to exercise justice and to preserve order, to provide for national defense, and to undertake certain public works; *WN* IV.ix.51). His argument that those alone are the duties of the sovereign, an argument that greatly restricts the role of the state in political and social life, is unintelligible unless seen in light of that distinction. So too with other aspects of his argument that clearly fall under the rubric of a political theory, such as his endorsement of the separation of powers, and of the separation of church and state. The combination of Smith's view of the general "deficiency" of wisdom and virtue in human life, the imperfection of the "remedy" for them, and finally the ease with which faction and fanaticism arise leaves him with a rather skeptical view of the fruitfulness of ambitiously ameliorative political engagement.

Smith's emphasis on liberty, then, reflects his conception, not just of the moral primacy of the individual but also of the serious obstructions faced by any notion of a "science" of politics. The notion of "liberty" is of course prominent in *The Wealth of Nations* and should be understood

---

72 E.g., *WN* V.i.b.25: "When the judicial is united to the executive power, it is scarce possible that justice should not frequently be sacrificed to, what is vulgarly called, politics. The persons entrusted with the great interests of the state may, even without any corrupt views, sometimes imagine it necessary to sacrifice to those interests the rights of a private man. But upon the impartial administration of justice depends the liberty of every individual, the sense which he has of his own security."

73 E.g., at *WN* V.i.b.20, 21 and V.i.i.2, Smith applies economic analysis to the courts and the fee structures involved in their operation. The same kind of analysis is applied to public works (V.i.d.4 and context).

in light of the major theses of *The Theory of Moral Sentiments*. In his narration of the "natural" stages of progress, Smith remarks that "Commerce and manufacturers gradually introduced order and good
government, and with them, the liberty and security of individuals,
among the inhabitants of the country, who had before lived almost in a
continual state of war with their neighbours, and of servile dependency
upon their superiors" (*WN* III.iv.4). This development, he says, was accompanied by the "regular execution of justice" (*WN* III.iv.15), the ability to be "secure of enjoying the fruits of their industry" and so to "exert
it to better their condition, and to acquire not only the necessaries, but
the conveniences and elegancies of life" (*WN* III.iii.12; see also IV.v.b.43,
IV.ix.51). With the removal of "villanage and slavery," the burghers "became really free in our present sense of the word Freedom," for they
could dispose of their property as they saw fit, engage in "freedom of
trade," give away their own daughters in marriage, govern their inheritance through wills, and in general conduct their affairs independently
of the king. This new freedom included their taking responsibility for
their own defense and for the administration of justice, except for "pleas
of the crown" (*WN* III.iii.5, 6). Liberty to form interest groups and to
compete for prestige and influence is part and parcel of a free society.
We have seen that it includes the liberty to sell one's labor as one sees
fit and thus to engage in and change trades as one wishes (*WN* I.x.a.1),
as well as to reside where one prefers (*WN* I.x.c.59, 41). It entails freedom of assembly, possibly including the freedom of representatives to
assemble for political deliberation about taxes and in general to manage
their own affairs (cf. *WN* IV.vii.b.51; IV.vii.c.78). Crucially, it assumes
liberty of religious belief and the impartiality of the state with regard to
religious sects. We also recall Smith's worry about any scheme of justice
that would lead to an "inquisition" into human motives or sentiments.
In a passage already quoted, finally, he makes it clear that the citizens
of a free country must be capable and willing to judge its government.[74]
These are extensive and recognizably modern liberties and will no doubt
often be specified in terms of "rights," it being the task of "natural
jurisprudence" to do so.

Because Smith leaves underdetermined just what institutional character political self-governance will take, he cannot be recruited without

---

74  *WN* V.i.f.61. Cropsey remarks that "freedom," for Smith, means "freedom to do unlimited business." *Polity and Economy*, p. 36. This is too restrictive a view of the matter.

qualification into the ranks of liberalism.[75] Whatever shape liberty, in the sense of citizen participation in governance, ought to assume must be a matter of practical wisdom such as an impartial spectator would judge best given the historical circumstances.[76] Smith did not make the mistake of holding that a free market and representative government are inseparable. All this said, it seems to me that the logic of his system of natural liberty pushes in the direction of a democratic political scheme, if only for a prudential reason – namely, that of controlling the sovereign and minimizing the abuse of power which Smith everywhere predicts (cf. *WN* V.i.e.26). I grant that he himself may have judged mixed forms of government to be superior to representative democracy. The "qualification" referred to at the beginning of this paragraph is nonetheless relatively weak.

It should be clear by now that we ought not to make the old mistake of inferring from the political open-endedness of Smith's "utopia" that his politics is merely quietist.[77] He explicitly allows that at times "political wisdom" may judge that a constitution ought to be altered (*TMS* VI.ii.2.12). His insistence on the moral defensibility of conceptions of liberty and justice – even if the latter is understood primarily as "negative" – provides him with a normative standard by which to criticize existing traditions, practices, and political arrangements. "Natural jurisprudence," which seems ultimately founded on the impartial spectator theory, provides a normative basis for social and political action. *The*

---

75 Haakonssen notes: "Smith's refusal to see the future of commercial society in any particular one of the available political systems is clearly underpinned by his scepticism toward complete systems of politics." In "What Might Properly Be Called Natural Jurisprudence?", p. 221. Haakonssen there argues that for Smith "justice is not necessarily dependent upon political liberty and, consequently, that problems of justice may be coped with by 'despotical' as well as by 'free' governments" (p. 221). This goes too far, in my opinion, at least if liberty of religious belief, for example, is included under the umbrella of "political liberty."

76 That judgment will take into account the ability of the citizenry wisely to govern themselves. Smith refers at *WN* I.x.c.59 to "The common people of England, . . . so jealous of their liberty, but like the common people of most other countries never rightly understanding wherein it consists. . . ."

77 A point also made by Winch in chapter 4 ("The Wisdom of Solon") of *Riches and Poverty*. Winch concludes the chapter by remarking that ". . . cautious and sceptical though it might be, Smith's science [of the legislator] embodies a definite form of prudential wisdom rather than a denial that practical statecraft has any part to play in the life of commercial societies" (p. 123). I am much in agreement with Winch's emphasis on Smith's anti-utopian recognition of imperfection.

*Wealth of Nations* is itself an attack on what Smith takes to be an unjust, not to mention inefficient, view of political economy.[78]

To return to a now familiar point, political economy is one branch of natural jurisprudence, and natural jurisprudence is a branch of moral philosophy. In the passages leading up to one of the references to *The Wealth of Nations* as promoting a "utopia," Smith refers to the "science of a legislator, whose deliberations ought to be governed by general principles which are always the same" (*WN* IV.ii.39), and this reminds us of the "great statesman" or "great legislator" whose possession of high prudence and virtue accords him "very nearly the character of the Academical or Peripatetic sage" (*TMS* VI.i.15). Persons of this character seek "great authority over the sentiments and opinions of mankind" and try to inaugurate "the greatest revolutions" in "the situations and opinions of mankind" (*TMS* VI.iii.28). But, as I argued in Chapter 5 (section 3), Smith is well aware of the dangers this type of legislator poses and is best understood as claiming for himself a moderated and humanized version of political prudence. There can be little doubt that *The Wealth of Nations* attempts to articulate a "science of a legislator" so understood – that is, the perfection of *human* political wisdom. It follows that as the author of the system, Adam Smith sought to claim the title "legislator," and hence the virtues of a noble prudence or wisdom.[79] And it also follows that the project of the book cannot possibly be understood as independent of the moderating moral and philosophical considerations we have been studying.

How is advocacy of a "system of natural liberty" to be reconciled with the rejection of systematic politics, or the wisdom of the "great legislator" with the insistence on imperfection? The answer is that this "system" of liberty is the other side of his skepticism about system. It is a system that liberates politics *from* system, a sort of anti-utopian utopianism. Although positive action is required to maintain the system of natural liberty, it generally takes the form of removing obstacles to liberty and then refraining from reinstituting them: "All systems either of preference or of restraint, therefore, being thus completely taken away, the obvious and simple system of natural liberty establishes itself of its own

---

78 As I noted in Chapter 1, Smith himself characterized the book as "the very violent attack I had made upon the whole commercial system of Great Britain" (letter to A. Holt of Oct. 26, 1780; *CAS*, p. 251).

79 Winch comes close to identifying Smith as the "legislator" in "Adam Smith's 'Enduring Particular Result': A Political and Cosmopolitan Perspective," in *Wealth and Virtue*, pp. 256–7.

accord" (*WN* IV.ix.51). Under such a system, the great philosophical legislators would be relieved of the burden of ruling.

The anti-utopian utopianism and the skepticism about system cut even deeper than this, however for, as I suggested in my discussion of Smith's notion of happiness, the true utopia would be not only impossible but undesirable. A republic of perfectly virtuous and philosophical Stoics would be "egalitarian barbarism."[80] As a political ideal, therefore, it is to be rejected; the "perfect" is imperfect. Smith's utopia is clearly second-best, or the best practicable, recommended not only by the improvements it would bring to extant practices but in light of the defects of an absolutely "best" utopia. To see this is to understand the limits of the rule of mere passion and force, *as well as* of the rule of perfect virtue and philosophy. Enlightenment is wisdom about the limits of the cave – to revert to a simile proposed by a certain "Academical" philosopher – *and* about the limits of transcendence. I noted Smith's repeated references, in *The Wealth of Nations*, to the limitations of "human wisdom." The most famous philosopher to claim "human wisdom" was the teacher of that "Academical" sage. In Plato's depiction of Socrates' trial, Socrates tells his fellow citizens that he possesses only an *anthropinē sophia* (human wisdom), or knowledge of ignorance (*Apology* 20d, 29b). In the *Gorgias*, Socrates claims that he alone possesses true political wisdom (*politikē technē*) and thus by implication is alone qualified to be statesman or legislator (*Gorgias* 521d6–8 and context). These claims to human wisdom and to true political wisdom come to the same thing. I suggest that, in a parallel way, Smith's "science of a legislator" is a knowledge of ignorance, or of imperfection.

The two conceptions of imperfection are only parallel, however. Socrates also announces publicly, at the end of his trial, that the "unexamined life is not worth living for a human being" (*Apology* 38a5–6), and by this he plainly means a life unexamined by philosophy. Smith never says any such thing, not because he is constrained from it by reasons of political prudence but because his comprehensive skepticism and his ethical position would not admit of it. The defense of the standpoint of the ordinary person, as disclosed in both of Smith's published works, and the subordination of theoretical to practical reason, are inconsistent with Socrates' claim.

---

80 The quoted phrase is that of Hont and Ignatieff; see their "Needs and Justice in the 'Wealth of Nations,' " in *Wealth and Virtue*, p. 10. Smith would surely have remembered Mandeville's reflections on the fate of the hive become virtuous.

It is striking that Smith refers to "philosophers" in the first chapter of *The Wealth of Nations*. The passage has the effect of debunking any claim that the philosopher escapes the principle of the division of labor that governs all of "civilized" society (*WN* I.i.9). Academic philosophers are specialized workers who produce items called "systems" and offer various services for sale.[81] This is followed in the second chapter by a similarly deflationary statement that "the difference between the most dissimilar characters, between a philosopher and a common street porter, for example, seems to arise not so much from nature, as from habit, custom, and education" (*WN* I.ii.4). To ensure that the point is driven home, Smith continues: "By nature a philosopher is not in genius and disposition half so different from a street porter, as a mastiff is from a greyhound, or a greyhound from a spaniel, or this last from a shepherd's dog." Granting that Smith has a very broad sense of "philosophy" in mind, it is difficult to avoid recalling Socrates' famous comparison of philosophers to shepherd's dogs, offered, of course, in a dialogue that led to the proposition that there will be no rest from ills until philosophers rule (*Republic* 375d–376c and 416a; 473d–e). Smith wishes to reject that sort of utopianism while preserving the Socratic insistence on finitude and knowledge of ignorance.

Smith does all this, however, in a manner that invites the Platonist to confront him with an important issue concerning the relation between philosophy and "nature." Consideration of the issue will bring us to what I take to be the true "Adam Smith problem." I shall set the stage by noting that if philosophy is one species of work devoted to the construction of comprehensive systems, then Smith's system is in some sense a construction as well, and the wisdom underlying it is, in Platonic terms, not "acquisitive" but "poietic" or productive (*Sophist* 265a4–5). Let us next turn to this topic of nature.

---

81  Smith's discussion in Book V of *WN* (i.f.26–34) of academic philosophy follows this approach. What Smith says of the "philosopher" at the start of *WN* can apply to the "philosopher" in the sense appropriate to figures such as Smith and Plato. I note that at I.i.9 he remarks on "philosophers or men of speculation, whose trade it is, not to do any thing, but to observe every thing; and who, upon that account, are often capable of combining together the powers of the most distant and dissimilar objects." This is the power that Smith connects with philosophy in the "History of Astronomy" essay.

# 8

## PHILOSOPHY, IMAGINATION, AND
## THE FRAGILITY OF BEAUTY:
## ON RECONCILIATION WITH NATURE

First, it is clear that all human affairs, like the Sileni of Alcibiades, have two aspects quite different from each other. Hence, what appears "at first blush" (as they say) to be death, will, if you examine it more closely, turn out to be life; conversely, life will turn out to be death; beauty will become ugliness; riches will turn to poverty; notoriety will become fame; learning will be ignorance; strength, weakness; noble birth will be ignoble; joy will become sadness; success, failure; friendship, enmity; what is helpful will seem harmful; in brief, you will find everything suddenly reversed if you open up the Silenus.

Desiderius Erasmus[1]

### 1. THE NATURE OF NATURE

Virtually all of the ancient schools, whether philosophical or antiphilosophical, sought to ground their ethical and political theories in "na-

---

1 *The Praise of Folly*, pp. 42–3. A strikingly similar line of thought may be found in Hume, *The Natural History of Religion*, sec. XV, p. 74. In Greek mythology, Sileni were satyrlike creatures. Little statues of them were commonly available and could be opened up to reveal a hollow cavity. Erasmus is presumably alluding to Plato's *Symposium* 215b, where Alcibiades compares Socrates to a Silenus statue – ugly and bestial on the outside but beautiful and divine on the inside.

ture." This included "human nature" (as distinguished from human beings as convention has shaped them) though often understood within a larger whole or ethically relevant framework. Book X of the *Laws* contains one of Plato's strongest statements to the effect that nature, in the sense of the whole, is governed by reason (personified by the gods) rather than by chance or any human art (i.e., convention). We are enjoined to live according to nature, that is, to subject our self-love to the perspective of reason, or "the life of the whole" (903c). In the *Gorgias* Callicles forcefully appeals to nature (as opposed to convention) in arguing that the strong should rule (483a–e). In the *Protagoras*, the sophist Hippias distinguished between a community founded on kinship that is natural and that founded on convention and "contrary to nature" (337c–d). In Aristotle's work, the appeal to nature in book 1 of the *Politics* is perhaps most striking. Stoics, Epicureans, Skeptics, and Sophists appealed to the same notion. Only some of these ancient appeals to nature amount to appeals to teleology.[2] In one form or another, the notion of nature continued to play a major role down through Cicero, Lucretius, Augustine, Boethius, and Aquinas and through Hobbes, Spinoza, and Leibniz, among many others, to the eighteenth century and beyond.[3] "Nature" is certainly one of the pivotal terms in classical Western ethical and political theory.

Already in Hume, however, the notion comes under attack. Hume wrote to Hutcheson:

> I cannot agree to your Sense of *Natural.* Tis founded on final Causes; which is a Consideration, that appears to me pretty uncertain and unphilosophical. For pray, what is the End of Man? Is he created for Happiness or for Virtue? For this Life or for the next? For himself or for his Maker? Your Definition of *Natural* depends on solving these Questions, which are endless, & quite wide of my Purpose.[4]

Hume nonetheless uses the term frequently.

With Kant the traditional usages of the term come under further attack. In a famous passage in the preface to the second edition of the

2 For an excellent discussion of this point and of the role of "nature" in ancient ethical theory, see J. Annas, *The Morality of Happiness* (Oxford: Oxford University Press, 1993), ch. 2.
3 See Basil Willey, *The Eighteenth Century Background: Studies on the Idea of Nature in the Thought of the Period* (London: Chatto & Windus, 1940).
4 Letter of Sept. 17, 1739, in vol. 1 of Hume's *Letters*, p. 33. In the *Treatise* Hume discusses the different senses of the word (*T* 474–6, 484). The problem of the relevance and sense of "nature," that is, was well established by the time Smith wrote *TMS*.

*Critique of Pure Reason*, Kant tells us that "reason has insight only into that which it produces after a plan of its own" and that reason "must not allow itself to be kept, as it were, in nature's leading-strings, but must itself show the way with principles of judgment based upon fixed laws, constraining nature to give answer to questions of reason's own determining."[5] It is only because of this injunction, Kant states, "that the study of nature has entered on the secure path of a science," whereas all traditional, metaphysical appeals to nature are dogmatic and unwarranted (Bxiv). The second *Critique* continues the attack, this time on the ethical relevance of the notion of "nature" as distinguished from the notion of "freedom." Most of Kant's successors carried on in the same vein. Mill and Sidgwick, for example, found the notion of nature incomprehensible or useless as far as ethical theory goes primarily because "nature" was understood as the factual, the nonevaluative, brute "given."[6] Today, moral and political philosophers tend either to ignore the notion – "nature" is hardly referred to in John Rawls's *Political Liberalism*, for example – or to view the notion of natural teleology as intelligible but no longer credible – as remarks by Nagel and Williams show.[7] The exceptions in moral and political philosophy are those who argue in conjunction with religious views and philosophical traditions that draw on them, and those many who argue for some version of a naturalistic ethics (in most of which "nature" is understood from the point of view of modern natural science).[8]

5 Bxiii. Trans. N. K. Smith (New York: St. Martin's, 1965).
6 H. Sidgwick, *The Methods of Ethics*, 7th ed. (Indianapolis: Hackett, 1981), bk. I, ch. VI.2. Sidgwick sees the appeal to nature as a strategy for moving from "what is" to "what ought to be" and thinks that move impossible (p. 81). He concludes: "On the whole, it appears to me that no definition that has ever been offered of the Natural exhibits this notion as really capable of furnishing an independent ethical first principle" (p. 83). Sidgwick attacks the Stoic dictum that we are to "live according to nature" on the grounds that it is both circular and vacuous (bk. III, ch. XIII.2). The reference to Mill is to his essay "Nature" (published in 1874), reprinted in *John Stuart Mill: Nature and Utility of Religion*, ed. G. Nakhnikian (Indianapolis: Bobbs-Merrill, 1958), pp. 3–44.
7 See Annas, *Morality*, pp. 137–41.
8 An example of the former may be found in J. Finnis, *Natural Law and Natural Rights* (Oxford: Oxford University Press, 1980). Naturalistic ethics takes a wide variety of shapes. For a helpful overview, see Darwall et al., "Toward *Fin de siècle* Ethics," pp. 24–30. In *Wise Choices, Apt Feelings*, Gibbard argues that "normative talk is part of nature, but it does not describe nature" (p. 7). The idea is to see the "capacity to accept norms" as "a human biological adaptation" (p. 7). Cf. S. Hampshire's remark in *Two Theories of Morality* (Oxford: Oxford University Press, 1977), p. 54: "By naturalism I here mean the habit of representing judgements about the moral strengths and defects of persons as resembling in most respects judgements about the physical strengths and defects of person, and of rep-

The result, at least in ordinary discourse, is that the term "nature" and its cognates have virtually lost all normative meaning for us in ethical and political discussions, to the point that notions such as "natural right," or "the laws of nature and of nature's god" – Jefferson's phrase in the Declaration of Independence – begin to sound like mysterious relics from a bygone era. Yet although the vocabulary may be atrophied, I suspect that many of us feel a need to articulate the place of human beings in nature, in order to ground our "values" in something other than our contingent customs or wishes.

Smith occupies a defining moment in the history of the notion of nature. As we have seen, he shared with Hume a skepticism about "metaphysical" senses of the term. Understood as the "essence" or "substance" or "form" of a thing, "nature" is already dead in Smith's philosophy. In his published works, Smith seems to say that moral norms arise not from nature but from the impartial spectator – that is, from a principle that seems closer to Kant's notion of autonomous self-legislation than to some notion of natural moral perfection. On the other hand, Smith uses the term and its cognates with great frequency throughout his work. It occurs in the title of one of his two published books, and there may even be a role for teleology in his system. Smith thus seems to be one of the last major philosophers whose work is a defense of nature, even though he has dropped some of its traditional meanings.

First among these traditional meanings is that of "essence," or "form." In a second sense, nature is distinguished from, and is the standard for, the conventional (*nomos*). It is in this sense that Smith speaks of "natural justice"; when he distinguishes it from "positive law," the context makes clear that he means conventions that are "more or less imperfect" attempts to embody what "the natural sense of justice would dictate" (VII.iv.36). The conventional is in time, and therefore nature in our second sense may be contrasted with "history." As just intimated, the natural in this second sense is determined, on Smith's view, by the impartial spectator.

A third meaning of the term distinguishes the natural from the artificial or designed (*physis* from *techne*). For example, Smith contrasts the teachings of the sentiments of natural religion to the teachings of "ar-

resenting virtue as an excellent state of the soul or mind, and vice as a diseased state of the soul or mind, manifested in action, just as health is an excellent state of the body." This is a more classical, Aristotelian view of naturalism, because of its teleological character.

tificial reasoning and philosophy" (III.5.4). And as we have seen, he consistently argues against the view that moral judgments, moral rules, and most moral sentiments are "artificial" in the sense of envisioned or designed with an eye to their utility. Yet in other contexts, he conflates the natural and the artificial – for example, when he uses the machine as a metaphor for nature, as I shall discuss shortly.

A fourth meaning of the term equates nature with what is given to us, what impresses itself upon us, or simply what appears to us. Smith frequently uses the term in this sense, as is shown by some of his references to "human nature" (e.g., I.ii.intro.2) and the many adverbial or adjectival occurrences of the word. The "natural" is easily seen here as consisting of the phenomena studied by the natural sciences, as "the empirical" understood from the scientific standpoint. It may also include the phenomena studied by moral philosophers, historians, and critics. In some cases the fourth sense of "natural" just comes down to the habitual, that to which we are accustomed.[9] A moral agent may take certain values or traditions to be natural, even though they may in fact be conventional. This somewhat blurry fourth meaning of nature ties in with the version of skepticism I have attributed to Smith, for it allows him to refer to "nature" understood as what is presented to reflective observers (e.g., sympathy, imagination, passions, pleasure and pain, and their interaction) without raising theological or metaphysical questions appropriate to an investigation of nature in our first sense.

A fifth meaning opposes the natural to the supernatural (e.g., to the miraculous, or the divine). This distinction is difficult to find in Smith in precisely those terms, though perhaps it may be detected in his contrast between "the governing principles of human nature" and those principles "regarded as the commands and laws of the Deity" (III.5.6). When he speaks of the "Author of nature" (III.5.7) he implies a distinction between Author and nature. From the standpoint of ordinary life, as Smith describes it, the "supernatural" understood as the divine certainly has an important ethical role to play. But since Smith's ethical theory does not depend on any notion of the supernatural, it is thoroughly "naturalistic" in this fifth sense.

The natural may also be understood as the teleological, as referring to that which a thing or being is as perfected or fulfilled. This is the sense Hume has in mind in his letter to Hutcheson, quoted near the

9  Cf. Hume's comment "habit is nothing but one of the principles of nature, and derives all its force from that origin" (*T* 179).

beginning of this chapter, and I shall count it as our sixth. Teleological talk is found in Smith's work. In one place, Smith speaks of the "final cause" of the "irregularity of sentiments," the "purpose of his [man's] being" which Nature intends, namely "the happiness and perfection of the species" (II.iii.3.2, 3). But teleology should there be understood in relation to the unity of the whole or universe, as purposiveness in the sense of a thing's useful place or function in an organized whole. Instead of being understood in terms of the perfection of the entity in question, teleology may also be understood in terms of the utility of a thing relative to a larger whole, and so in terms of a thing's harmony with a totality. This sense does figure prominently in Smith's thought. Yet, as we have already seen, Smith's meaning in such passages is not straightforward, for nature also structures things such that most people pursue illusory happiness (e.g., in the form of wealth and power).

"Nature" is frequently used to mean "the whole," "the world," "the universe." Let us count this as a seventh meaning of the term; of the senses just distinguished, it will be my main but not exclusive concern in this chapter. This and the fourth sense are not always easy to tell apart from one another.[10] This seventh meaning of the term has strong affinities with the way in which some Stoics thought of "nature." Focusing on this last sense of "nature" therefore provides us with an opportunity to examine further Smith's critique of Stoicism. It also allows me to investigate questions pointed to by Smith's moral philosophy that will help us to draw together several threads of the present study and that are of contemporary philosophical interest (for example, questions about the relative merits of the "impersonal" and the "subjective" standpoints). We will investigate several large-scale speculative issues concerning the sense in which nature can serve as a guide for morality, the "invisible hand" and the status of the religious dimension of Smith's thought, the role of the imagination and of beauty in rendering nature whole, philosophy's restless search for reconciliation with nature, and finally (as well as briefly) the place of history in Smith's account.

---

10 Often the various senses occur next to one another, as at III.3.11: "Among the moralists who endeavour to correct the *natural* inequality of our passive feelings by diminishing our sensibility to what peculiarly concerns ourselves, we may count all the ancient sects of philosophers, but particularly the ancient Stoics. Man, according to the Stoics, ought to regard himself, not as something separated and detached, but as a citizen of the world, a member of the vast commonwealth of *nature*" (emphasis added). "Nature" in the first sentence corresponds to my fourth sense of the term; "nature" in the second sentence, to my seventh sense.

I have argued throughout this book that Smith is a dialectical thinker. This will be particularly evident in what follows, as I seek to excavate successive layers of the discussion, going over the same ground but going deeper. Or to switch metaphors to that suggested by the passage from Erasmus quoted at the beginning of this chapter, my discussion here will resemble a series of Sileni, one nested inside the next, but all resonating with one another in a sort of *pros hen* or focal-meaning way.

Smith could not have been ignorant of the multiplicity of uses of the term "nature," a multiplicity evident enough from the history of the term and also remarked upon by Hume. No word "is more ambiguous and equivocal," Hume wrote in the *Treatise*, than "the definition of the word, Nature" (*T* 474). Yet Smith both uses the word often and slides from one sense to another without warning. Although this ought to be seen as deliberate and as in keeping with his resistance to the formation of a technical vocabulary, it complicates the task of sorting out the place of nature in his ethical theory.

## 2. LIVING IN ACCORDANCE WITH NATURE: SMITH'S CRITIQUE OF STOICISM

"According to nature" you want to *live?* O you noble Stoics, what deceptive words these are! Imagine a being like nature, wasteful beyond measure, indifferent beyond measure, without purposes and consideration, without mercy and justice, fertile and desolate and uncertain at the same time; imagine indifference itself as a power – how *could* you live according to this indifference? Living – is that not precisely wanting to be other than this nature?

Friedrich Nietzsche[11]

I have mentioned previously the importance of Stoicism in Smith's moral philosophy.[12] His emphasis on self-command, his use of the figure of the completely virtuous Stoic sage, his allusion to a Stoic maxim that each person is best qualified to care for himself – all recall Stoic themes. Of all of the philosophical schools preceding him, Smith accords Stoicism by far the most attention. He struggles with its teachings, not just in his review of the history of moral philosophy at the end of *The Theory of Moral*

---

11 *Beyond Good and Evil*, trans. W. Kaufmann (New York: Vintage, 1966), sec. 9, p. 15.
12 I will not discuss here the accuracy of Smith's interpretation of the Stoics. He focuses mainly on Epictetus and Marcus Aurelius, and to a much lesser extent Cicero and Seneca, and then rather selectively. As noted in Chapter 4, Smith ignores Stoic logic, metaphysics, and epistemology, concentrating on what he takes to be Stoic moral philosophy.

*Sentiments* but throughout the book. In his repeated revisions of this work, the passages on Stoicism were rearranged and repositioned a number of times; clearly he gave them and their placement in the volume a great deal of thought. Stoicism is the first school identified by name, and this occurs in Part I (I.ii.3.4). Smith writes:

> The ancient stoics were of opinion, that as the world was governed by the all-ruling providence of a wise, powerful, and good God, every single event ought to be regarded, as making a necessary part of the plan of the universe, and as tending to promote the general order and happiness of the whole: that the vices and follies of mankind, therefore, made as necessary a part of this plan as their wisdom or their virtue; and by that eternal art which educes good from ill, were made to tend equally to the prosperity and perfection of the great system of nature. No speculation of this kind, however, how deeply soever it might be rooted in the mind, could diminish our natural abhorrence for vice, whose immediate effects are so destructive, and whose remote ones are too distant to be traced by the imagination.

Smith criticizes this school in his first reference to it. What exactly is the criticism?

This passage is part of the chapter in which Smith explains the "unsocial passions" of hatred, anger, and resentment. We recall that these passions are useful in that they are the "guardians of justice," although as moral agents we do not normally evaluate them in light of that utility but in the specific context in which they manifest themselves or with which they are associated. Even though we seem irrational in our refusal to focus on the question of utility – that is, on their role or function within a whole – Smith argues for what one might call the "contextuality" of the moral sentiments. And it is just at this point that he makes his statement about the Stoics. The Stoics adopted what one might call the standpoint of reason, in the sense of a synoptic, comprehensive, or simply a philosophical standpoint. We must note that Smith does not deny that one can take a synoptic standpoint or that doing so would amount to a kind of philosophizing about the phenomenon in question, or that when appropriate one should do so. On the contrary, he frequently connects philosophy with such synopticism, and at times himself "speaks" in just that voice.[13] As he states in the passage on the Stoics,

---

13 E.g., at III.5.7 Smith writes: "The happiness of mankind, as well as of all other rational creatures, seems to have been the original purpose intended by the Author of nature, when he brought them into existence. No other end seems worthy of that supreme

from that standpoint it appears that even our irrational behavior (our "follies"), even our "vices," have their place in promoting the "general order and happiness of the whole." He seems to agree that from the Stoic's elevated standpoint there is no real distinction between virtue and vice; "every single event" serves "equally to the prosperity and perfection of the great system of nature."

In other words, from the standpoint of nature, or the whole, moral distinctions disappear; therefore, we cannot live in accordance with nature as a whole. In the passage quoted, Smith refers to "that eternal art which educes good from ill." His well-known metaphor, the "invisible hand," expresses just that process by which good may be educed from ill. The Stoic background of the metaphor is undeniable; correspondingly, when Smith uses it, he is adopting the standpoint of the philosopher who observes things synoptically. Both *The Theory of Moral Sentiments* and *The Wealth of Nations*, but especially the latter, are full of examples not just of unintended consequences but of good consequences arising from bad actions, emotions, or situations. That the term "nature" occurs in the title of *An Inquiry into the Nature and Causes of the Wealth of Nations* is perhaps indicative, then, of the removed "speculative" standpoint on human life that political economy often assumes.

When taken together with its context, the passage on the Stoics suggests that moral distinctions reappear when perceived in context and that moral perception requires the work of sentiment and sympathy. Moral distinctions show themselves from the standpoint of the part, not of the whole. Smith is here asserting that no philosophical "speculation" can diminish our hatred or resentment of vice or, we may infer, our appreciation of virtue. The speculative pronouncements of reason ought not to obviate the moral judgments of sentiment. Smith is here urging us to recognize the difference between the standpoint of the moral actor and that of the theorist or philosopher. He invites us to join in his harsh

---

wisdom and divine benignity which we necessarily ascribe to him; and this opinion, which we are led to by the abstract consideration of his infinite perfections, is still more confirmed by the examination of the works of nature, which seem all intended to promote happiness, and to guard against misery. But by acting according to the dictates of our moral faculties, we necessarily pursue the most effectual means for promoting the happiness of mankind, and may therefore be said, in some sense, to co-operate with the Deity, and to advance as far as in our power the plan of Providence." Shortly after this pronouncement, however, Smith observes that natural sentiments often reject the "natural course of things" and then provides us with a quotation from the bishop of Clermont (discussed shortly) that calls into question the sunny optimism of this passage.

condemnation of "stoical apathy" that results from conflating them.[14] As the book unfolds, we come to see that a person schooled in Stoicism – that is, in the view that philosophy ought to be a "philosophy of life," to use a current term – shapes his or her moral sentiments accordingly. (See VII.ii.1.47: "That the Stoical philosophy had very great influence upon the character and conduct of its followers, cannot be doubted.") And this Smith clearly thinks is generally a bad thing, for it amounts to an erosion of the basis for moral distinctions. He therefore argues not just that we ordinarily do not confuse the standpoints of part and whole but that we ought not to confuse them. The decision about the appropriate level of spectatorship is, in part, an ethical one.

The underlying issue in Smith's discussions of Stoicism concerns the relationship between philosophy and ordinary moral life, and his repeated discussions of Stoicism are a sign that this issue pervades *The Theory of Moral Sentiments*. It is precisely because he accepts the Stoic view of the kind of standpoint that a traditional sort of philosophical reason would adopt – namely that of "nature" (in our seventh sense of the term) or "the whole" – and because he accepts the Stoic view of what morality would look like if viewed solely from that standpoint, that Smith is both deeply attracted to and critical of Stoicism. He commends a limited moral imitation of philosophical synopticism, namely, the standpoint of the impartial spectator. For the Stoics had something right when they urged us to diminish our natural affection for ourselves by viewing ourselves from a detached perspective. In the second through the fifth editions of *The Theory of Moral Sentiments*, Smith wrote that "the stoical philosophy, in this respect, does little more than unfold our natural ideas of perfection" (*TMS* p. 141). But the Stoics push our natural ideas too far when they insist that "man . . . ought to regard himself, not as something separated and detached, but as a citizen of the world, a member of the vast commonwealth of nature" (III.3.11). Stoicism thus supplies Smith with a case study of how natural moral sentiments become distorted when pressed philosophically.

In the course of his long discussion of Stoicism in Part VII of the book, Smith quotes Epictetus's crucial question and answer, "In what sense are some things said to be according to nature, and others contrary

---

14 The reference is to his discussion of familial affection, in which Smith notes that "the sense of propriety," far from requiring us to approve of a person who feels nothing, say, for his own children, leads us to blame such a person's lack of that "extraordinary sensibility" (III.3.14). We reviewed this passage in Chapter 5 when examining moral education (section 4).

to it? It is in that sense in which we consider ourselves as separated and detached from all other things"; as a human being one is "a part of a whole, upon account of that whole" (VII.ii.1.19; *Discourses* 2.5.24–6). The passage quoted by Smith concludes with Epictetus's recommendation of the famous Stoic apathy and ties that stance to the Stoic sage's insistence on viewing himself from the standpoint of the whole. The sage's happiness consisted, Smith says, "in the contemplation of the happiness and perfection of the great system of the universe" and in "discharging his duty," that is in discharging with absolute propriety whatever role in the universe God had assigned him. His emotions completely under control, with indifference to what fortune might bring, and paying no attention to the consequences of his actions – these being out of his control and under the administration of the "Superintendant of the universe" – the sage was assured tranquillity. If his situation for some reason became unbearable, he could always escape it through suicide.

Although Smith paints a sympathetic and extended portrait of this doctrine, it culminates in the criticism implied by a point made much earlier in the book, where he remarks that the doctrine of Stoic equanimity was a result of "metaphysical sophisms" (III.3.15). At the end of *The Theory of Moral Sentiments*, Smith characterizes the Stoic doctrine of suicide as "altogether a refinement of philosophy" (VII.ii.34). In order to substantiate the charge, he appeals to nature, but now in a different sense: "Nature, in her sound and healthful state, seems never to prompt us to suicide," nor does nature lead us to approve of suicide even when it is performed so as to avoid some deep "melancholy" or "distress" (VII.ii.1.34). Smith claims: "No natural principle, no regard to the approbation of the supposed impartial spectator, to the judgment of the man within the breast, seems to call upon us to escape from it [distress] by destroying ourselves." On the contrary, suicide strikes "us" as moral weakness, and as evidence Smith provides one of his favorite examples of fortitude, the "American savage." He notes that the "savage" would endure torture, not merely without attempting to commit suicide but with contempt for his tormentors (VII.ii.1.34). The sense of "nature" that speaks here against the Stoics is a variation of our sense 2; it is "nature" as determined by the impartial spectator.

In sum, Smith denies that the Stoic conception of what it means to live according to nature can be entirely correct. It is correct insofar as it enjoins us to examine our motives and conduct from the standpoint of an impartial spectator – a general standpoint, in the sense that it serves as a check against egoism, unwarranted self-exemption, and selfishness. We do benefit at times from adopting a relatively synoptic, "speculative" point of view. Stoicism also rightly emphasizes the value of self-command, of disciplining self-love, of having a perspective on self (III.3.44, III.3.11; III.3.22 and context). Further, Smith cites with evident approval the notion that "every man . . . is first and principally recommended to his own care" and "is certainly, in every respect, fitter and abler to take care of himself than of any other person" (VI.ii.1.1). (Presumably he is alluding here to the Stoic doctrine of *oikeiosis*, that is, affinity, belonging, taking something as one's own.) As we saw in Chapter 5 (section 5), he also approves of the Stoic notion that true happiness "consists in tranquillity and enjoyment" (III.3.30).

But Stoic doctrine is misleading insofar as it altogether assimilates that standpoint of the impartial spectator to one that is entirely "speculative" or "objective" and that consequently requires us to see ourselves as mere cogs in "the whole machine of the world" (VII.ii.1.37). It is from exactly that confusion that all of the "paradoxes" of Stoicism, including those of *apatheia* and suicide, are derived, or so Smith explicitly argues (VII.ii.1.38–9). We act in accordance with nature, he maintains, when we impartially evaluate our *local* situation, the "little department" over which we have some management and direction, and when we are guided by the moral passions – including self-interest – that nature furnishes us. The emotions, as well as our detached perspective on them, focus on the requirements of the specific situation. The impartial spectator does not consider "propriety" with an eye to our place in the whole or the absolute standard of benevolence appropriate to God but with an eye to how we are placed in *this* part of the whole, here and now. For it is to that place that our emotions are chiefly tied, and from the emotions functioning in specific situations that ethical distinctions arise. The whole is not a "situation" or "place" with which one can empathize, and theoretical reasoning is not empathetic. Smith's critique of the Stoics is thus the flip side of his theory of the moral sentiments.[15]

Natural religion does, of course, supply us with a view of the whole as God's creation, and Smith commends this view as a natural support to

---

15 Cf. T. Nagel's comment that "The pursuit of objectivity with respect to value runs the risk of leaving value behind altogether. We may reach a standpoint so removed from the perspective of human life that all we can do is to observe: nothing seems to have value of the kind it appears to have from inside, and all we can see is human desires, human striving – human *valuing*, as an activity or condition." *The View from Nowhere* (Oxford: Oxford University Press, 1986), p. 209.

morality. This does not contradict his critique, however, for this view of the whole is really a "sense of propriety" concerning the degree of gratitude or reverence or even fear that we imagine we ought to feel toward the Deity, understood as a benevolent designer (III.5.12). The "natural principles of religion" reinforce our "natural sense of duty," and that sense is always responsive to a specific context, unless "corrupted by the factious and party zeal of some worthless cabal" (III.5.13). Hence natural religion provides us with a holistic context that increases our sympathetic attention to right character and conduct here and now and has an influence opposite to that of Stoicism. Smith explicitly protests against the metamorphosis of natural religion into a religious teaching that insists that "all affections for particular objects, ought to be extinguished in our breast, and one great affection take the place of all others, the love of the Deity, the desire of rendering ourselves agreeable to him, and of directing our conduct, in every respect, according to his will" (III.6.1).

Smith concludes that "the plan and system which Nature has sketched out for our conduct seems to be altogether different from that of the Stoical philosophy" (VII.ii.1.43). Nature does offer us Stoic philosophy in a moment of consolation of our misfortunes, but "Nature has not prescribed to us this sublime contemplation as the great business and occupation of our lives" (VII.ii.1.46). Nature, then, bids us to view the whole from the standpoint of the part; in reversing this natural order the Stoic makes a mistake characteristic of philosophers, namely that of transforming into a governing principle that which is merely one element in experience. For nature also bids us to view the part impartially, from outside itself, and this is an imitation of a philosophical stance. But the Stoics understood what is ordinarily given to us far too ambitiously.

We should live in accordance with the impartial spectator, the "Great inmate, the great demi-god within the breast" (VI.iii.18). It is not so much nature as our attitude toward it that should guide us. Perhaps Smith's deepest debt to Stoicism consists in just that point. It is a matter of emphasizing the priority of the standpoint of the spectator, a theme that runs through all of Smith's philosophy. Our view of nature is prior to nature itself. His break with Stoicism consists in his determination of what the appropriate attitude is. That is, according to him the Stoics confused levels of spectatorship. In the Moor–Hutcheson translation of Marcus Aurelius's *Meditations* (5.9) Smith would have read: "Don't return to philosophy with reluctance, as to a severe tutor. . . . Remember that philosophy requires no other things than what your nature requires."[16] He could not have accepted this proposition without qualification, both for the reasons that we have been considering and for others to which we now turn.

## 3. NATURAL CONFLICT AND HUMANIZING INTERVENTION

All Nature is but Art, unknown to thee;
All Chance, Direction, which thou canst not see;
All Discord, Harmony, not understood;
All partial Evil, universal Good:
And, spite of Pride, in erring Reason's spite,
One truth is clear, "WHATEVER IS, IS RIGHT."

Alexander Pope[17]

Let us take our consideration of this matter forward one step at a time and open up the next Silenus figure. As just discussed, we cannot or ought not to live in accordance with a view of nature as a whole, that is, with purely "theoretical" reason. We are to live in accordance with right perspective on nature as a part, that is, with moral reason. When we act in accordance with "the dictates of our moral faculties," we "co-operate with the Deity" and "advance as far as is in our power the plan of Providence." Smith immediately complicates this cheerful assessment, for we are also capable of acting against those dictates, in which case we "declare ourselves, if I may say so, in some measure the enemies of God" (III.5.7). The phenomena attest to our ability to act in both ways, yet Smith declares that a consideration of God's "infinite perfections" and an "examination of the works of nature" lead us to the belief that the "Author of nature" intended the happiness of mankind (III.5.7). Obviously, there lurks here the old theological problem of evil. And things get more complex as Smith develops his point.

16 "καὶ μὴ ὡς πρὸς παιδαγωγὸν τὴν φιλοσοφίαν ἐπανιέναι.... μέμνησο δέ, ὅτι φιλοσοφία μόνα θέλει, ἃ ἡ φύσις σου θέλει." The translation is reproduced in *The Meditations of the Emperor Marcus Aurelius Antoninus. Newly translated from the Greek: with Notes, and an Account of his Life* (Glasgow: R. Foulis, 1742). The names of the translators (referred to in the introduction to the book only as "the authors of this translation") are not printed on the title page, but a letter from Francis Hutcheson (one of Smith's teachers) indicates that Hutcheson himself and James Moor (eventually a holder of the Chair of Greek at Glasgow University) were the translators. See J. Bonar, *A Catalogue of the Library of Adam Smith*, 2nd ed. ([1894]; rpt. New York: Kelley, 1966), pp. 13–14.

17 *Essay on Man* I.289–294, ed. F. Brady ([1733–4] Indianapolis: Bobbs-Merrill, 1981), p. 15.

For human experience amply testifies that the workings of nature and of our "natural sentiments" (III.5.9) not only can but sometimes ought to be at odds with one another. Smith himself insists on the point in a passage that illuminates the connection between his political economy and the moral theory. He takes the examples of an "industrious knave" who cultivates the soil and an "indolent good man" who does not. Of these two, "Who ought to reap the harvest? who starve, and who live in plenty? The natural course of things decides it in favour of the knave; the natural sentiments of mankind in favour of the man of virtue." Non–human nature is absolutely rational and fair in her judgments (also III.3.27), yet human nature will not and ought not to accede and demands a quite different proportion between virtue and reward, vice and punishment. "Thus man is by Nature directed to correct, in some measure, that distribution of things which she herself would otherwise have made" and "like the gods of the poets, he is perpetually interposing, by extraordinary means, in favour of virtue" (III.5.9–10). It thus seems that nature is self-contradictory, and the problem is driven home by what Smith says next: "The natural course of things cannot be entirely controlled by the impotent endeavours of man." We not only fail to humanize nature, but, as Smith especially emphasizes in *The Wealth of Nations*, our efforts to do so sometimes have the perverse effect of making things even worse.

Smith assures us that "the rules which she [Nature] follows are fit for her, those which he follows for him, but both are calculated to promote the same great end, the order of the world, and the perfection and happiness of human nature" (III.5.9). Yet Smith has just shown us that this view is not credible. Indeed, with literary deftness he casts doubt on what he has just asserted by quoting, out of the blue, the "eloquent and philosophical bishop of Clermont." The lines quoted are as poignant and direct as any on the subject:

> does it suit the greatness of God, to leave the world which he has created in so universal a disorder? To see the wicked prevail almost always over the just . . . ? From the height of his greatness ought God to behold those melancholy events as a fantastical amusement, without taking any share in them? Because he is great, should he be weak, or unjust, or barbarous? . . . O God! if this is the character of your Supreme Being . . . I can no longer acknowledge you for my father. . . . You would then be no more than an indolent and fantastical tyrant. (III.5.11)

Smith neither prepares us for this outburst nor has a word to say in response to it. The paragraphs immediately preceding it suggest that we turn to God for comfort in the face of the injustices of the "natural course of things." The two paragraphs that immediately follow it simply reassert the importance, for a coherent moral life, of trust in an "All-powerful Being," even though that is precisely what the bishop's lament has just called into question. The bishop's "philosophical" words disrupt rather than confirm Smith's narrative about natural religion as the appropriate response to the opposition between our moral sentiments and the course of nature.

We could conclude from Smith's quoting this passage that we find ourselves in a hopeless situation. On the one hand, we cannot live in accordance with nature as a whole, for to do so is to abstract from moral considerations. On the other hand, we cannot live in accordance with nature as it shows itself to us in our individual lives, because our lives are so frequently dominated by a "course of nature" we are unwilling to accept and impotent to control or understand. The phenomena are conflictual. We are left with the bishop's rebuke to a God who structures things thus, but a denunciation is neither a philosophy of life nor a comfort to the afflicted.[18]

Let us backtrack for a moment. Smith has made it clear that morality protects us from nature *qua* whole, for without the moral sentiments focused on particulars and contexts, we are reduced to cogs in that "machine of the world." Our survival also depends on *techne*, from the art of agriculture, to the system of law, to the intellectual artifact of political economy. Moral reason, technical intelligence, and in some instances theoretical reason are needed to guide human affairs. Smith sometimes reassures us that these inventions are themselves natural developments and thus stresses the beneficence of nature. We have not been abandoned by nature. This is so even where the aims dictated by "human nature" are simply not defensible on their own grounds or in comparison with what human experience teaches. The most striking case that he mentions is nothing other than the pursuit of wealth, which, as we saw in Chapters 5 and 7, is fueled by a "deception" imposed on us by the imagination. A simple trick of the imagination, in combination with the passions and sympathy, is responsible for changing "the whole face of the globe" and completely shaping our individual lives, for thanks to it we force ourselves to work, create, compete, strive. The contrivances of the imagination, including deceptions, are defenses against a niggardly nature that does not sufficiently provide for us.

18 T. D. Campbell argues that for Smith "God is a utilitarian." *Adam Smith's Science of Morals*, p. 217. This would just be to underline the problem, however, for God so understood seems to do wrong in order to assist others.

It is in this passage that the one reference in *The Theory of Moral Sentiments* to the "invisible hand" occurs. The metaphor is introduced in order to explain how the unequal accumulation of wealth in fact benefits the whole of society. Thus nature, precisely in its dividedness of whole from part, seems harmonized with itself. Not just our inability to live in accordance with a view of the whole but both our inability to control the natural course of things and our illusions about how best to advance our individuals lives are themselves conducive to the improvement of nature considered as a whole. As he says when discussing the "irregularity" in our judgments of justice, "every part of nature, when attentively surveyed, equally demonstrates the providential care of its Author, and we may admire the wisdom and goodness of God even in the weakness and folly of man" (II.iii.3.2).[19] Nature's plan is being fulfilled even as we reject it. The conflict between the whole and the part is not itself to be corrected; it may be lamented at a moral level but need not be at a theoretical level. It is a natural conflict that embodies an underlying harmony. *Sympatheia* governs the orders of nature. This resembles Smith's comment that a "fallacious sense of guilt ... constitutes the whole distress of Oedipus and Jocasta upon the Greek, of Monimia and Isabella upon the English, theatre" (II.iii.3.5). The guilt is and ought to be deeply felt, but it is "fallacious" because these characters are not in fact responsible. Similarly, the "world" or "nature" resembles a tragedy, but one that does not have a tragic ending.

This is spoken from the standpoint of the philosopher and does not obviate lament from the standpoint of the actor. Smith seems to think that the lament itself becomes destructive, as it were, from the standpoint occupied by the "eloquent and philosophical" bishop and therefore ought not to be brought to that level. This is why, immediately after quoting the good bishop, Smith turns his back on him and continues, without any comment, to commend natural religion for supporting our "natural sense of duty" by reinforcing our trust that a wise Deity will reward the good and punish the wicked. Nevertheless, by quoting the bishop Smith shows that he understands the problem.[20]

---

19 Much later in the book, Smith uses the same phrase when again discussing the influence of fortune on our moral judgments: "This great disorder in our moral sentiments is by no means, however, without its utility; and we may on this, as well as on many other occasions, admire the wisdom of God even in the weakness and folly of man" (VI.iii.31).

20 Campbell asks whether, if for Smith God is good and has ordered all things well, then Smith is not "precluded from suggesting improvements." Campbell responds that Smith's scheme commits him to noninterference with the "natural" in the sense of the "normal," for the system "is on the whole good," and where it is not we must inter-

Theoretical reconciliation with nature, or the view that natural conflict embodies an underlying harmony, is possible only when we understand that we are not to live in accordance with a synoptic perspective, that the natural course of things cannot be entirely mastered, that the deceptions of the imagination are not necessarily to be corrected. History is littered with misunderstandings of these points, as Smith seeks to demonstrate not only in his treatment of Stoicism but also in his discussions of, say, systems of political economy preceding his own. It is here that one role for the philosopher shows itself. Philosophy attempts to distinguish between unnatural and natural stances and harmonies and to guide us toward the latter (by means of a book on the "wealth of nations," for example). Similarly, moral reconciliation with nature is possible only if "natural principles of religion" are not corrupted by fanatics (III.5.13). History is also littered with such corruptions. Here too the philosopher can be of use in illustrating this point (by means of a book on the moral sentiments, for example).

But things are still more complicated. For left to itself, nature seems to generate the unnatural – cabals, misplaced interventions by political utopians or misguided philosophers – and often fails in providing the antidote – namely, the Smithean philosopher. Thus, even if the latter succeeds in guiding us, we are left with a disturbing suggestion: the need for the philosopher's intervention to help to protect us either from misunderstanding nature's odd harmony or from corrupted moral sentiments testifies to the potential for a disharmony in nature that cannot itself be viewed, from *either* a theoretical or moral perspective, as good. That is, the existence of the Smithean philosopher testifies to the need for what one might call an "extranatural" human intervention in nature, like that of the "gods of the poets," to quote Smith's phrase once again. This raises the possibility that because the human good does not seem in fact to be nature's principal object, we need, as Mill remarks, not to imitate nature but to amend it.[21] Nature must be helped to be its har-

---

fere. *Adam Smith's Science of Morals*, p. 62. If God requires our cooperation, however, He is not God, and what Smith says about God's benevolent ordering of things is untrue.

21 "The scheme of Nature regarded in its whole extent cannot have had, for its sole or even principal object, the good of human or other sentient beings. What good it brings to them, is mostly the result of their own exertions. Whatsoever in nature gives indication of beneficent design proves this beneficence to be armed with limited power; and the duty of man is to co-operate with the beneficent powers, not by imitating but by perpetually striving to amend the course of nature – and bringing that part of it over which we can exercise control, more nearly into conformity with a high standard of justice and goodness." J. S. Mill, "Nature," in *John Stuart Mill: Nature and Utility of Religion*, p. 44.

monious self, which is precisely *not* to say, once again, that all corruptions or delusions or religion or self-love are to be extirpated and replaced by a Stoic "philosophy of life." Yet it *is* to say that, at the end of the day, that there does not exist some still higher-altitude perspective from which we can declare that nature is, after all, a harmonious whole. Disharmonious conflict is natural to nature. This thought reiterates our familiar point that the horizon of Smith's discussion is the phenomenon of war, dissolution, disassociation, or simply of chance. The sheer contingency of the world and the difficulty of introducing into it the harmony we so desire only seem to make that harmony all the more desirable.[22]

Therefore we need to revise our statement that philosophy will guide us toward natural stances and harmonies. Philosophy cannot be guided simply by nature if it is also to resolve nature's conflicts. We must make nature liveable and comprehensible to ourselves, that is, make nature measure up to our standards. And it follows that Smith's books, which embody his philosophical efforts, are not simply "descriptive," even when they seem to be. They are necessarily protreptic. Thus *The Wealth of Nations*, which so often speaks of "nature" and the "natural course of things," repeatedly recommends the intervention of artifice (sometimes in the form of governmental measures or programs) in social and economic life. *The Theory of Moral Sentiments* too is protreptic, or interventionist – for example, when it condemns fanaticism and corruption, praises a certain set of virtues and criticizes others, selects some examples and not others. Unreflective ordinary life is not self-sufficient, and Smith appeals to and defends an emended version of it. Likewise, he does not maintain that some miraculous "spontaneous harmony" will take care of everything, if only we let the natural course be; his notion of the nature of nature prevents any such comprehensive laissez-faire stance. Although no sentiment or passion is per se evil, human nature must be helped to be its harmonious self. It becomes clear that nature cannot ultimately be our moral standard or guide. In some sense, we must be our own guides and standard. Moral value is not natural (except perhaps

---

22  Cf. Cropsey's view that "Smith's solution [to the problem of the relation between nature and norms] implies the simultaneous naturalness and arbitrariness of the normative ranking of the virtues: man is naturally disposed to reverse the natural. Then human nature is in some sense *sui generis*, not wholly an aspect of nature simply but partly a denial or negation of it. This is the dubious position Smith occupies in order to maintain the distinction between the noble and ignoble while at the same time conceding the indifference of nature to nobility." *Polity and Economy*, p. 40.

in the lame sense of "given" to us), and moral systems are not simply articulations of nature.

## 4. SMITH'S ANTI-PLATONIC AESTHETICS: HARMONY, BEAUTY, PURPOSIVENESS

We can best pursue these issues by turning in a direction suggested by my use of the term "harmony," and by retracing our steps. For this and related notions are favorites of Smith's. Beauty is a pervasive theme in *The Theory of Moral Sentiments*. From the start, he argues that we naturally take a disinterested pleasure in the situations of others and in a correspondence of our sentiments. That "fellow feeling with any passion whatever" which Smith terms "sympathy" (I.i.1.5) is a kind of "correspondence" of sentiments (I.i.2.2). We judge the "propriety" of the affections of others by means of their "concord" or "dissonance" with our own (I.i.3.2). "Propriety" is itself defined in terms of "proportion" (I.i.3.5), the moral beauty of which is judged in terms of its "harmony" (I.i.4.5) with our own sentiments. In order that the agent's emotions may "beat time" with the spectator's, the agent must adjust the "pitch," "flatten" the "natural tone," so as to obtain the "harmony and concord" with the spectator, that being sufficient for "the harmony of society" (I.i.4.7). It is the "perfection of human nature" that "can alone produce among mankind that harmony of sentiments and passions in which consists their whole grace and propriety" (I.i.5). Toward the end of the book, he remarks that the "great pleasure of conversation and society, besides, arises from a certain correspondence of sentiments and opinions, from a certain harmony of minds, which like so many musical instruments coincide and keep time with one another" (VII.iv.28). These musical metaphors pervade the book and express Smith's conviction that life is suffused with a spontaneous love of beauty.[23] From the

23 The power of beauty is explicitly recognized in *WN* (V.i.f.25); this is another bridge between *WN* and *TMS*. Smith is of course picking up an old theme in the Scottish Enlightenment. Cf. Shaftesbury, *Advice to an Author* (pt. III, sec. III): "For harmony is harmony by nature, let men judge ever so ridiculously of music. So is symmetry and proportion founded still in nature, let men's fancy prove ever so barbarous, or their fashions ever so Gothic in the architecture, sculpture, or whatever other designing art. 'Tis the same case where life and manners are concerned. Virtue has the same fixed standard. The same numbers, harmony, and proportion will have place in morals, and are discoverable in the characters and affections of mankind; in which are laid the just foundations of an art and science superior to every other of human practice and comprehension." In volume 1 of *Characteristics*, pp. 227–8.

first sentence of the book, he attacks views that seek to interpret our praise of beauty or harmony in purely prudential terms. Ordinary life is spontaneously "theoretical" in the sense that it is given to contemplation of the beautiful without regard to utility. Correspondingly, Smith speaks of virtue as "beautiful" (I.i.5.6) and of the "natural beauty of virtue" (VII.ii.2.13), of passions as "graceful" or the contrary (I.ii.intro.2), of the beauty that self-command has over and above its utility (VI.iii.4), of the "beauty of conduct" (V.2.1). He presents moral education as a process by which we come to see, step by step, what this beauty or harmony consist in. The "wise and virtuous man" is even "more deeply enamoured" of the "exquisite and divine beauty" of a high standard for human perfection, and in perfecting himself accordingly "he imitates the work of a divine artist" (VI.iii.23).

Smith's encomium to the force of beauty in human life goes still farther. The word "beauty" appears in two chapter headings in Part IV, this being literally the center of the book. This is the context in which the reference to the invisible hand occurs. Smith first argues that it is not the utility of "any production of art" – that is, not the end for which that production is designed – that bestows beauty on our productions. Objects that are ordered or finely made or exactly crafted, regardless of whether these properties allow them better to fulfill their goal, are immensely attractive. (One of Smith's examples is a watch, but he also mentions palaces, gardens, clothes, "the retinue of the great," or even a room in which the furniture is well ordered.) As in the case of the "harmony" of moral sentiments, we take disinterested pleasure in the purposeless purposiveness of things and, naturally, want to possess them. Further, we imagine that in possessing them we will find "happiness and tranquillity," in part because we are aware that others will admire the possessor of these "trinkets of frivolous utility" (a phrase Smith uses twice here; IV.1.6, 8). The admiration of spectators is itself a result, in part, of their aesthetic appreciation of the beauty or artfulness of the objects possessed by the rich (IV.1.8). Unless one is born rich, acquiring these objects entails "unrelenting industry." All of commerce depends on the love of beauty.

This striking account of wealth getting is followed by still other observations of the influence of "the same principle, the same love of system, the same regard to the beauty of order, of art and contrivance." Smith singles out the effect of this love of beauty on public-spiritedness and argues that public benefactors (including legislatures) are often inspired not so much by sympathy with those in need of help as by the pleasing "contemplation" of so "beautiful and grand a system" of law or constitution or economic measures. Public-spiritedness can be improved by the "study of politics," that is, "works of speculation" that exhibit the beauty of ordered complexity (IV.1.11). Heroic self-sacrifice can also be inspired by the "unexpected, and on that account the great, the noble, and exalted propriety of such actions" (IV.2.11). Thus the love of beauty has not only significant moral and economic consequences but decisive political consequences, though the point in each case is that we do not espouse beauty for the sake of its utility.

Smith takes all of this yet another step, noting that we admire works in the "abstruser sciences" such as mathematics on account not of their utility but of their exactitude and orderliness (IV.2.7). In his essays on the history of astronomy and of physics, Smith develops at some length the notion that good "philosophy" (in a sense broad enough to include what we today call "science") grips us because of the elegance, conceptual fineness, systematic arrangement, and capacity to explain much on the basis of few principles. Theoretical intelligence too is attracted by the beauty of the "machine," regardless of its external purpose, and nature is one such machine or system, human nature another. The passages from Smith's posthumously published essay "Of the Nature of that Imitation which Takes Place in What are Called the Imitative Arts" (which I quoted at the end of Chapter 1) may once again be brought to bear here. Smith there describes a "well-composed concerto of instrumental Music," noting that

> in the contemplation of that immense variety of agreeable and melodious sounds, arranged and digested, both in their coincidence and in their succession, into so complete and regular a system, the mind in reality enjoys not only a very great sensual, but a very high intellectual, pleasure, not unlike that which it derives from the contemplation of a great system in any other science. (II.30, *EPS*, pp. 204–5)

In contemplating the vast system of nature as though it were a well-composed concerto, the theorist, instead of imagining its utility for some further purpose, enjoys its intricate internal order.

The much-debated issue of teleology in Smith's philosophy should be seen in the light of his account of both our drive for a picture of the whole as harmonious and of the beautiful as that which inspires human endeavor at all levels and hence as that which makes utility possible. Teleology, understood as the notion of an ordered nature or world, is here parasitic on an aesthetics, not on some independent religious faith of Smith's or on an argument from design, whose fallacies Smith had already learned from Hume. Teleology is here not a description of how the world is but a postulation of the harmony we yearn for it to have. It is therefore a regulative ideal, and in terms of the theorist's demand for system it performs work. The doctrine of nature's unity is formulated at various levels, as is appropriate to the rhetorical voice Smith wishes to adopt.[24] At times he speaks, in a relatively conventional manner, of the purposes of the "Author of Nature" or of some superior wisdom (e.g., VI.ii.2.4); at other times he speaks in a somewhat unconventional manner about an "invisible hand" and nature's conflictual harmony. All are ways of rendering experience whole, organized, harmonious, of presenting a picture of unity and beauty.

Thus, when Smith refers to the "invisible hand of Jupiter" in his "History of Astronomy," he uses the metaphor to characterize a mythological view held by the "vulgar superstition" of polytheism (III.2, EPS, p. 49). Smith has his own uses for the "invisible hand," but they are – and on his own account must be – sophisticated refinements of the same sort of exercise of the imagination. Just as the "invisible hand of Jupiter" was part of the vocabulary of ancient "superstition," the "invisible hand" is part of Smith's philosophical and protreptic rhetoric whose purpose is likewise to establish order persuasively. The many "teleological" or even, on occasion, "religious" statements in The Theory of Moral Sentiments must be understood in connection with this aestheticized speculative outlook.[25] Although Smith is adamant that we not confuse teleological characterizations of the philosophical sort with appeals to efficient causality, we must still attempt such characterizations in order to satisfy the imagination's yearning for beauty.

In sum, we seem to be presented with a prospect of one aesthetically pleasing order nested inside another, from the harmony of moral sentiments on some particular occasion all the way up to the harmony of

---

24 The rhetorical nature of some of Smith's more theological-sounding teleological statements is noted by Raphael in Adam Smith, p. 36.

25 For a recent discussion of the problem of teleology in Smith, see Kleer, "Final Causes in Adam Smith, Theory of Moral Sentiments." Kleer does not note the connection with Smith's aesthetics, the role of the aesthetics in theorizing, the multilayered character of the rhetoric about nature's purposes, or the seeming challenges to the natural order that Smith himself points out (such as the fanaticism and the "corruption" of the moral sentiments). Kleer's ultimate conclusion is this: "I maintain that Smith's references in this connection [that of the coordination between virtue and happiness] to the wisdom of Nature are far from being mere window-dressing. I am not claiming that The Theory of Moral Sentiments has an unavoidable logical dependence upon the idea of an 'invisible hand' " (p. 299).

the parts of the universe as articulated in an elegant theory of nature. The vision sounds thoroughly Platonic, with beauty serving as a continuous ladder stretching from the sensual to the most abstract and philosophical. The natural whole is perfectly ordered, and even seeming disruptions of the kind articulated by the bishop of Clermont may themselves be seen as notes in the cosmic symphony.[26]

As before, however, things are more complicated. There is, yet again, a figure hidden within the Silenus we have been examining. For Smith's aesthetics is profoundly anti-Platonic, and in a way that does not seem to support the doctrine of a perfectly ordered natural whole. Beauty is both enlightening and deceiving on Smith's account, and this is so at all levels. At the level of sympathy, the "correspondence of sentiments" may lead to a mutually reinforcing system of vanity, and this too figures into our pursuit of wealth; "it is because mankind are disposed to sympathize more entirely with our joy than with our sorrow, that we make parade of our riches, and conceal our poverty" (I.iii.2.1). Our sympathy with the "passions of the rich and the powerful" lead us to social inequality, and this is not "the doctrine of reason and philosophy" (I.iii.2.3). Although under the right conditions this "deception" is useful, Smith also terms it "the great and most universal cause of the corruption of our moral sentiments" (I.iii.3.1). Unchecked, nature seems to turn beauty into glamor and then into moral decay.

Similarly, the love of beauty that animates public-spiritedness also animates political fanaticism, and Smith concludes his discussion of public-spiritedness with a remarkable commentary on the "man of system" who is "so enamoured with the supposed beauty of his own ideal plan of government" that he is led to treat people entirely without sympathy, as though they were "pieces upon a chess-board" (VI.ii.2.17). "Intoxicated" rulers are certain "of the immense superiority of their own judgment"; drunk with beauty and sense of self, they are inhumane even without entertaining any overtly tyrannical thoughts. Although Smith does not make this explicit, we may detect the same pattern in his account of religious fanatics, whose "false notions of religion" cause a "perversion of our natural sentiments." There is beauty and authority in such a system of rigorous duties and rules – but also fanaticism, in-

---

26 Campbell argues that "utility is . . . very much *the* meta-principle for Smith. It is to be found at the basis of his whole moral outlook, but it operates most typically at the level of contemplation." *Adam Smith's Science of Morals*, p. 219. I am arguing that beauty, not utility, plays this role.

humanity, and ugliness. Like the intoxication with a system of the "political speculators," here too the love of beauty ignores the humanity of those whom we would perfect. The fanatic collapses the good into the beautiful and then loses all moral perspective on the beautiful. (See Chapter 4, section 1.)

We noted in Chapter 1, finally, that Smith thinks synoptic philosophizing to be connected with the attraction of beauty, elegance, and conceptual harmony and that in ethics this type of philosophizing tends to extinguish the moral qualities it seeks to elucidate. The propensity of philosophers to account for the phenomena from as few principles as possible rather than to be guided by the phenomena themselves (VII.ii.2.14), for example, reveals that the philosopher's love of system may have a distorting effect. Thus, there too beauty is in one sense good but in another bad; it both reveals and conceals.

Not only is beauty at each level both good and bad; either the various levels are not connected to each other by a continuous line or, where they are, the connection is frequently undesirable and conflictual. In particular, Smith presents us with no dialectical ascent from the ordinary yearning for sympathy to the philosopher's yearning for systematic explanation. He does hold that there is a natural – or is it unnatural? – development of our need to observe ourselves from an impartial standpoint to the Stoics' demand that we view ourselves as mere parts of a vast universe – but that is a development generally to be resisted. Beauty is an unreliable yet indispensable guide at any level. The notion of the noble or perfect – as a synthesis of the beautiful and the good – seems to have disintegrated.

The moral ambiguity of beauty, and the conflict among levels of beauty, recapitulate the problem of the unity of nature as a whole, though at first beauty seemed to promise a solution. The hostility of nature to human beings seems reiterated even as nature offers the beauty of harmony at all levels. But another step in this dialectic remains to be taken, and it will bring us to what is perhaps the bedrock of his view of the matter. For Smith's aesthetics is rooted in a teaching about the imagination, and this is the next figure within a figure to which we turn. The anti-Platonic dimension of Smith's teaching will become further visible as the combination of the precariousness of our mastery of nature, the fragility of moral beauty, and the ambiguity or power of the imagination crystallizes.[27]

---

27 Because the imagination creates both deceptions and harmonies, Smith is faced with Hume's quandary as to "how far we ought to yield to these illusions [of the imagina-

## 5. IMAGINATION, *POIESIS*, AND
## SELF-EMPOWERMENT

Nothing is more free than the imagination of man; and though it cannot exceed that original stock of ideas furnished by the internal and external senses, it has unlimited power of mixing, compounding, separating, and dividing these ideas, in all the varieties of fiction and vision. . . . Wherein, therefore, consists the difference between such a fiction and belief?

David Hume[28]

Some of the levels of beauty or harmony that I have mentioned define our moral lives and thus are central to "sympathy," which itself is dependent on the power of the imagination. It is sympathy that allows us "fellow feeling with any passion whatever" (I.i.1.5). Moral reflection on self is an exercise of the sympathetic imagination, thanks to which we see ourselves through the eyes of another (sometimes an imagined spectator, not any actual one). Theorizing, whether about moral philosophy or a system of religious duties or astronomy, is also heavily dependent, for Smith, on the imagination. By contrast with empathetic imagining, however, theoretical imagining does not require us to put ourselves in the situation of another human being, to grasp the emotions that move him. As we have seen, Smith argues at the beginning of the book that we have no "sympathy" with ideas; we either agree or disagree with them but are not interested in them in the way we are in the emotions and situations of our fellows. Morality is not primarily a philosophical, theological, or scientific matter, nor are these intellectual pursuits primarily ethical.[29]

Although sympathy and theoretical reason are distinct for Smith, then, both are dependent on the imagination. Philosophical views of "the whole" are not so much discoveries of preexisting harmonies as

tion]. This question is very difficult, and reduces us to a very dangerous dilemma, whichever way we answer it." For although "nothing is more dangerous to reason than the flights of the imagination," at the same time "the understanding, when it acts alone, and according to its most general principles, entirely subverts itself" (*T* 267).

28 *Enquiry Concerning Human Understanding*, p. 47.

29 Smith remarks: "It is to be observed, that so far as the sentiment of approbation arises from the perception of this beauty of utility, it has no reference of any kind to the sentiments of others." As he goes on to explain, whereas a person who grew up outside of society might perceive a beauty in traits such as prudence and temperance and so might view himself as a "well-contrived machine," they would not be *moral* virtues in his eyes, since he would not view them, via sympathy, through the eyes of a spectator (*TMS* IV.2.12).

they are creative and rational efforts to render harmonious what the appearances present to us. At a high theoretical level, as we observe the "great theatre of nature" so as to "render" it "a coherent spectacle to the imagination," we are in effect seeking to answer questions that individual phenomena, as well as our construal of the phenomena, goad us into asking.³⁰ Whether theories "really" link up with nature (in our first sense of the term, or simply in the sense of "mind-independent reality") is a question about which Smith has suspended judgment, as was discussed in Chapter 4. His skepticism goes hand in glove with the view that the mind somehow shapes "nature" and what appears to us. In my discussion of Smith's view of love and of the *theatrum mundi*, I pointed out that his theory of spectatorship is ultimately anti-Platonic: there is finally no looking outward; we are always (and are better off) mirroring ourselves (recall *TMS* III.1.3). At the moral level, the actor views himself in the mirror of the imagined impartial spectator; the skeptic recognizes that even in theorizing we are contemplating the phenomena as taken up in the "inventions of the imagination" and thus are in a certain sense contemplating ourselves. At all levels, self-knowledge is ultimately inward-looking. If Smith were given to the use of Hegelianisms, he might speak of the world as the Self's mediation of itself.

Smith makes it abundantly clear that the beauty apprehended by the imagination is not, as far as we know, a passive assimilation of preexisting form. The imagination is fundamentally creative and story-telling. To quote again from the conclusion of his essay on the history of astronomy, "we have been endeavouring to represent all philosophical systems as mere inventions of the imagination."³¹ The very notion of nature as a machine is an imaginative metaphor and led, on Smith's account, to the

---

30 For the quoted phrases, see "History of Ancient Physics" 2 (*EPS*, p. 107). In the "History of Astronomy" essay, Smith sets out to explain how each system "was fitted to sooth the imagination, and to render the theatre of nature a more coherent, and therefore a more magnificent spectacle, than otherwise it would have appeared to be" (II.12; *EPS*, p. 46). The imagination converses with itself in the context of its observation of events on the great stage of nature.

31 "History of Astronomy" IV.76, (*EPS*, p. 105). At IV.33 Smith remarks: "For, though it is the end of Philosophy, to allay that wonder, which either the unusual or seemingly disjointed appearances of nature excite, yet she never triumphs so much, as when, in order to connect together a few, in themselves, perhaps, inconsiderable objects, she has, if I may say so, created another constitution of things, more natural indeed, and such as the imagination can more easily attend to, but more new, more contrary to common opinion and expectation, than any of those appearances themselves" (*EPS* p. 75).

postulation of a Designer of the machine; thus nature imitates art.[32] That Smith should use, not some organic whole but a humanly created artifact (the machine) as the paradigm for unity, natural or otherwise, is itself indicative of the drift of his account.[33] A machine is designed to accomplish a certain end, of course, whether it is the production of pins (*WN* I.i.3) or the explanation of the movements of the celestial bodies. It is a means to *production* and thus captures the fundamentally "poietic" nature of the imagination. It is also an artificial thing invented by us for the satisfaction of our desires and, often, for the manipulation of external nature. In seeing various sorts of organization as "machines" Smith points to the fundamentally "creative" nature of the human animal, even as he observes that we naturally deploy this machinery, not for prudential reasons but because we find order and harmony immensely attractive. "Production" would seem to be the engine that drives theory and practice forward.[34]

We have also listened to Smith say that "like the gods of the poets, he [man] is perpetually interposing, by extraordinary means, in favour of virtue" (III.5.9–10), and say of the moral agent seeking perfection that "he imitates the work of a divine artist" (VI.iii.23). It is the demand of the imagination for order, harmony, and for tranquillity that drives our desire for both "correspondence of sentiments" and intellectual co-

---

32 "History of Ancient Physics" 9 (*EPS*, pp. 113–14); also "History of Astronomy" IV.19, (*EPS*, p. 66): intellectual "systems in many respects resemble machines. . . . A system is an imaginary machine."

33 Although Smith very often uses this metaphor of the machine, in one place he uses an organic metaphor. At *WN* IV.ix.28, he compares the ability of the "political body" to withstand the false prescriptions of political economists to that of the human body to withstand bad medicine. This fortunate fact is attributed to the "wisdom of nature." Cf. *TMS* VII.iii.1.2: "Human society, when we contemplate it in a certain abstract and philosophical light, appears like a great, an immense machine, whose regular and harmonious movements produce a thousand agreeable effects." At *TMS* I.i.4.2 Smith refers to "the various appearances which the great machine of the universe is perpetually exhibiting, with the secret wheels and springs which produce them."

34 For discussion of Marx's not entirely dissimilar view, see D. Lachterman, "The Ontology of Production in Marx: The Paradox of Labor and the Enigma of Praxis," *Graduate Faculty Philosophy Journal* 19 (1996): 3–23. In the "Alienated Labor" essay of the first 1844 manuscript, Marx writes (strikingly, from the perspective of Smith): "The practical construction of an *objective world*, the *manipulation* of inorganic nature, is the confirmation of man as a conscious species-being, i.e. a being who treats the species as his own being or himself as a species-being. . . . Animals construct only in accordance with the standards and needs of the species to which they belong, while man knows how to produce in accordance with the standards of every species and knows how to apply the appropriate standard to the object. Thus man constructs also in accordance with the laws of beauty." In *Early Writings*, pp. 127–8.

herence.[35] Smith remarks: "when we consider such actions as making a part of a system of behaviour which tends to promote the happiness either of the individual or of the society, they appear to derive a beauty from this utility, not unlike that which we ascribe to any well-contrived machine" (VII.iii.3.16; also IV.2.1). But we thus "consider" actions as being parts of a larger unity and system because of the imagination's restless drive for order.

The "world" (both natural and social) is, as a unified "system," constituted or given to us by our own imaginations. Thus all of the talk in *The Theory of Moral Sentiments* about nature *as a whole* is itself an "invention of the imagination." Or more bluntly put, both *The Theory of Moral Sentiments* and *The Wealth of Nations* are themselves, *qua* systems or unifying accounts, "inventions of the imagination."[36] The Stoic view of self from the standpoint of the whole is, just as in the case of the view of self from the standpoint of an imagined impartial spectator, a sort of self-characterization within an imagined frame of reference. Underlying Smith's discussion about both practice and theory is a view of the imagination as "poietic" (or unifying, productive, fashioning, shaping) and thus a view about the limits of reason; for creativity stems from the imagination. Implicit in Smith's philosophy is this decisive turn in the history of "nature."[37]

This is not to be confused with the notion that the imagination creates the world *ex nihilo*, or that objects of perception are fantasies in the mind, or that science is an arbitrarily spun "story." Rather, Smith is building on Hume's remarks about the imagination and is arguing that the world

35 "History of Astronomy" IV.13 (*EPS* p. 61): Smith seeks to show that "the repose and tranquillity of the imagination is the ultimate end of philosophy" whereas wonder and perplexity provoke philosophy (a term that here includes science). At *TMS* V.2.1 he mentions that "our sense of beauty depends" on "principles of the imagination."

36 Raphael remarks: "It follows, then, that Smith would say of his own system of economics what he says of the Newtonian system of astronomy. It is sounder than its predecessors but it is still a theoretical system, a product of the imagination, not a description of 'real chains which Nature makes use of to bind together her several operations.'" *Adam Smith*, p. 112. The notion that "nature" must itself be, on Smith's own view, a "construction" is argued by Cropsey in "The Invisible Hand," p. 172.

37 This is in confirmation of Lachterman's argument (already adverted to in the Introduction) that "the 'idea' giving significant shape to the 'constellation' of themes ingredient in modernity, *in both its revolutionary and projective modes*, is the 'idea' of construction or, more broadly, the 'idea' of the *mind* as essentially the power of making, fashioning, crafting, producing, in short, the mind as first and last *poiétic* and only secondarily or subsidiarily *practical* and *theoretical*. . . . making is *definitive* of the mind's 'nature' or better of its comportment in and toward the 'world.'" *The Ethics of Geometry*, p. 4.

as unified or coherent, as intelligible and sense possessing, as part of a connected narrative or account within which it has meaning or value, is formed by the imagination – but not formed out of thin air.[38] Perhaps one ought to speak of the imagination as "demiurgic" to bring out the implication that it resembles a worker who "produces," not from nothing but by (re)shaping what is given. The imagination works on givens, including complex "systems" previously shaped by the imagination. It systematizes, organizes, harmonizes, gives shape, establishes correspondences and coherencies. It thereby helps to render its objects intelligible and to confer value. For Hume, of course, one crucial way in which the imagination unifies the world is by attributing relations of cause and effect to events in it. Our ordinary assumption that objects continue to exist through time and are independent of the mind, our memory of particulars and of events as really having occurred, even our systems of philosophy – all are founded on the imagination.[39]

Let us avoid another possible misunderstanding by noting that just as we ought not to infer that for Smith the world is a fantasy of the imagination, we also ought not to infer that it is somehow "unreal" or "subjective" because rendered whole by the imagination. To be sure, morals, norms, customs, science, and philosophy do not on this account "correspond" to some completely mind-independent reality; no "reality" in that "Platonic" sense in fact appears to us. But as we noted earlier (Chapter 4, section 2), moral norms, for example, are fully "real" in the sense that they organize the social world; that we rely on them in making decisions, from the most inconsequential to the gravest; and that we both appeal to them and develop them in praising and blaming our fellows, which praise and blame, in turn, guide much of human life. These norms are not just "intersubjectively" real in the sense that communities may agree to them but also in the sense that people act on them and have

38 Smith's views about the imagination's role in human life and in inquiry owe so great a debt to Hume that they may be seen as an extension of Hume's views. For some discussion of that connection, see A. S. Skinner, "Science and the Role of the Imagination," in Skinner, *A System of Social Science: Papers Relating to Adam Smith* (Oxford: Clarendon Press, 1979), pp. 14–41. For a general discussion of Hume on the imagination, see G. Streminger, "Hume's Theory of Imagination," *Hume Studies* 6 (1980): 91–118.

39 "The memory, senses, and understanding are, therefore, all of them founded on the imagination, or the vivacity of our ideas" (*T* 265). Hume next remarks on the "illusion of the imagination" thanks to which such things as causality appear in ordinary life to be independent of the mind (*T* 267). For discussion see R. Fogelin, *Hume's Skepticism in the "Treatise of Human Nature"* (London: Routledge & Kegan Paul, 1985), ch. 5 ("Skepticism and the Triumph of the Imagination"). On pp. 89–90 Fogelin discusses Hume's view that "the imagination is the ultimate judge of all systems of philosophy."

warranted confidence in them.[40] As we saw in Chapter 5 (section 2), these norms can be critically evaluated. Moral and intellectual mistakes can certainly be specified and corrected, on this view. That norms are not "natural" in the sense of grounded in an independent order of moral facts does not entail that they are subjective (in the sense of "relative"). This is not all that some philosophers may want from a notion of the "real," nor all that nonphilosophers assume about the reality of what presents itself as natural. Smith's reply to the philosophers would be that it is all that we in fact have, and, to ordinary agents, that their exaggerated assumption is an "illusion of the imagination" (to repeat Hume's phrase, also used by Smith, III.2.4), albeit a beneficial one.

The standpoint of the spectator is always emphasized whenever questions of judgment or intelligibility or perspective or knowledge are at stake. Nature does not illuminate; our viewing of it does. Smith can give no definite account of what nature is unilluminated; nature does not come presorted and organized into a coherent whole, such that it can in its eidetic integrity and harmony be absorbed by the mind. For the reasons we have reviewed, the account he does provide necessarily makes the self the source of light, as it were, and in thus privileging the self, Smith is joined by many modern philosophers, especially when issues of value are at stake. Nature is insufficient for our moral and theoretical purposes.[41]

---

40  In light of Smith's remarks about our desire to be believed and thought trustworthy and our corresponding desire to persuade (see ch. 2, sec. 5), he might find congenial Baier's point (made with reference to Hume) about the connection between "truth" and "trust"; "whatever is true is trustworthy." *A Progress of Sentiments*, p. 286.

41  Toward the end of their review of the last five or so decades of moral philosophy, Darwall et al. comment that "moral realists, constructivists, and quasi-realists alike look to the responses and reasons of persons, rather than some self-subsistent realm, to ground moral practice." "Toward *Fin de siècle Ethics*," p. 34. Schneewind comments in "Natural Law, Skepticism, and Ethics" that Kant's theory of agency as freedom "enables us to understand morality, with its due weight, as a human creation" and that "the exponents of the skeptical method all approach this belief, to a lesser or greater degree" (p. 307). The exponents in question are the British moralists – Shaftesbury, Hutcheson, Hume, and Smith are mentioned – as well as figures such as Montaigne. M. Warnock traces the centrality of the notion of the imagination as creative from Hume to Kant to various post-Kantians (e.g., Fichte and Schelling) to Romantic poetry and beyond. She quotes Schelling as saying that "the objective world is only the original, still unconscious, poetry of the spirit" and glosses this as meaning that "the human imagination is at work in this poetry, as in what is usually called poetry. The conscious and unconscious workings of the imagination are a unity." *Imagination* (London: Faber & Faber, 1976), p. 66. This is not altogether dissimilar to the view I find in Smith. Warnock remarks that for both Hume and Schelling "there would be no world to be understood without a prior imag-

Smith's analysis of the synthetic role of beauty in our lives, that is, of the imagination's power to draw us to harmonies, is also an account of our potential for defining nature, even if as a system or machine. And this amounts to a potential for self-assertion in the face of an indifferent or hostile nature. This holds true at all of the levels Smith's aesthetics touches, from our capacity to form social wholes and the "correspondence of sentiments," to our love of persuasion and thus of bartering and selling, to our drive to better ourselves through the creation of wealth and the mastery of physical nature, to our ability to examine ourselves through the eyes of an imagined impartial spectator, and finally to our ability to emend nature whether through scientific systems or poems. At all these levels, our instinctual love of beauty can enlighten nature and improve it. I speculate that the pleasure of apprehending beauty at all levels is connected to the fact that beauty is an exhibition of our own power over nature and thus of our freedom. The pleasure of tranquillity is derived in part from contemplation of ourselves writ large, whether in a social or natural whole.[42]

To summarize: for Smith "nature" is made liveable and intelligible thanks to our shaping of it. In and of itself, it is obscurity and shadows to us. Light is provided by the imagination, and this light seeks the form of harmony. At the moral level, sympathetic imagination seeks the mutual composition of harmony between actor and spectator, allowing the one to transport himself into the situation of the other, to become the other in some measure. It allows selves to mirror each other, and a self to perceive itself through the eyes of an imagined spectator. The imagination in effect fashions most of the emotions that govern human life, not out of whole cloth but by continually reweaving them into the complex tapestry of conventions, norms, goals, and economic and social institutions. Norms are products of the communal imagination over time and are regulated by the impartial spectator, itself a stance of the reflective imagination. "Natural jurisprudence" is guided not by mind-independent nature but by the impartial spectator; viewed abstractly, "rights" represent the self-assertion of the imagination in appropriate contexts. The imagination provides for the "appearance" of selves on the stage. Philosopher and moral actor both seek to understand these

inative construction" (p. 71). See also Lovibond, *Realism and Imagination in Ethics*, pp. 110–17.

42 A similar point about the connection between Smith's aesthetics of inquiry and the idea of self-empowerment is made by Lindgren, *The Social Philosophy of Adam Smith*, pp. 8–15.

appearances by taking the stance of the "critic." Their imagination shapes standards for judgment of varying degrees of demandingness. At the theoretical level, the imagination stages "systems," sometimes ideal and tenseless ones, and thus presents nature or human nature to us as though it were a machine to be contemplated.

Just as we do not know what nature is in and of itself, so too we do not know what the imagination in and of itself is, but we can describe its works in all of the ways that I have specified. Since we lack a theoretical account of mind *qua* mind, we seem to be largely left with an account of mind in terms of how it comes to see nature in this or that particular way, and that is just the kind of account Smith aims to provide. If he was, as I surmise, a skeptic, Smith would not have sought to provide a theory about the nature of the imagination as such; we are limited to the appearances, including those of the imagination (the "of" being both the objective and subjective genitive).[43] In some of the essays referred to in this chapter, Smith talks about the "histories" of the imagination's works. These histories are meant to illustrate "the principles which lead and direct philosophical enquiries"; but beyond arguing that these "principles" are the various intellectual sentiments (such as wonder, admiration, and surprise), and beyond showing in detail how they work in the context of inquiry, his surviving writings provide no further account of the imagination "in itself."[44] The nature of the imagination is revealed through its products; we know it primarily by what it does – by the sentiments it engenders, by its drive for order, by its desire for holism.

We seem stretched between two poles – nature on the one side and imagination on the other. The inner constitution of each is obscure to us. We can see *that* we are positioned between these mysteries, that there

---

43 Cf. Kant's statement that the schematism of the imagination "is an art concealed in the depths of the human soul, whose real modes of activity nature is hardly likely ever to allow us to discover and to have open to our gaze" (*Critique of Pure Reason* A142 = B180–1), and Hume's reference to the imagination as "a kind of magical faculty in the soul, which, tho' it be always most perfect in the greatest geniuses, is however inexplicable by the utmost efforts of human understanding" (*T* 24). Hence Warnock's point that for Kant, as for Hume, "the activity of imagination" is in the end "inexplicable and unanalyzable." *Imagination*, p. 41. Smith's reticence about the inner constitution of the imagination is not, then, unusual.

44 This is similar to Hume's view, if we accept G. Deleuze's interpretation of Hume. *Empiricism and Subjectivity*, trans. C. V. Boundas (New York: Columbia University Press, 1991), p. 133. Deleuze there comments: "In short, as we believe and invent, we turn the given itself into a nature. . . . Philosophy must constitute itself as the theory of what we are doing, not as a theory of what there is."

is light in the space between them, and that in specifiable ways we are responsible for the light. This is the light of social and intellectual harmony, and we are powerfully attracted to it. In our enjoyment of it, we partake of that for which we are somehow responsible. We cannot help but feel self-approbation, as well as a measure of tranquillity, in contemplation of it.

## 6. PHILOSOPHY AND THE ELUSIVE TRANQUILLITY OF RECONCILIATION

The whole is a riddle, an aenigma, an inexplicable mystery. Doubt, uncertainty, suspence of judgment appear the only result of our most accurate scrutiny, concerning this subject. But such is the frailty of human reason, and such the irresistible contagion of opinion, that even this deliberate doubt could scarcely be upheld; did we not enlarge our view, and opposing one species of superstition to another, set them a quarrelling; while we ourselves, during their fury and contention, happily make our escape into the calm, though obscure, regions of philosophy.

David Hume[45]

Nature is ordered by spectatorship inspired by beauty; beauty is brought to life by imagination seeking tranquillity or equipoise; and that tranquillity embodies an ideal of freedom. As suggested in Chapter 4 (section 3), an ideal of self-sufficiency is embedded in the "ethical" vision at the heart of Smith's philosophy, and in spite of his criticisms of Stoicism one detects in his philosophy the Stoic themes of independence, freedom, and autonomy. This vision resonates with the passages in which Smith expresses his deep admiration for the well-composed concerto and helps explain why he commends pure instrumental music on the ground that it does not imitate anything. Through this music, whose "meaning, therefore, may be said to be complete in itself," we entertain ourselves with our own creation, and in so doing demonstrate our mastery.[46] Smith writes that "No action can properly be called virtuous, which is not accompanied with the sentiment of self-approbation" (III.6.13). A theorist who composes a comprehensive musical system would feel worthy of the highest self-approbation, for then "he imitates the work of a divine artist" (VI.iii.23).

---

45  *The Natural History of Religion* XV, p. 76.
46  I quote here from "Of the Imitative Arts" II.30 (*EPS*, p. 205).

Why does this not lead to a collapse of the polyphony created by a "system of natural liberty" into the monotone of a philosophical system? Do we not risk falling into the undesirable senses of "selfishness" discussed in Chapter 2? Part of the response is that not just any sense of self-sufficiency will do, not just any notion of beauty or imagining. As theorists we should not compose a system that reduces harmonies to monotones, or forces one instrument to play the sounds of another, or suppresses the demonstration of passion and the illusion of spontaneity, or pretends that the beauty can be appreciated without the music being heard and thus without the concerto being performed. The musical metaphor underlines the importance of our sensitivity to particulars, as well as the critical role of the sentiments in appreciating the production. As moral actors, we achieve harmony through mutual responsiveness and responsibility. Smith sees that the hubris implied in imitating the work of a divine artist must be appropriately moderated if we are to succeed; we must be sensitive to the particulars and the context and be accepting of each for what it can contribute. Recall his powerful criticism of the misplaced love of system or beauty that would lead us to treat our fellows as "pieces upon a chess-board," as though each lacked "a principle of motion of its own" (VI.ii.2.17). Human society, he adds, "will go on easily and harmoniously" only if this danger is avoided. Recall too the interrelationship of justice, fortune, and philosophy, discussed in Chapter 6. The subordination of theory to practice, of speculative philosophy and Stoicism to action and sentiment, is fundamental to Smith's affirmation of (in my terms) Enlightenment liberalism in the economic and political spheres. His skeptical aesthetics entails a keen awareness of the danger of confusing the levels of beauty and is thus consistent with his defense of ordinary life. Composition of a "system of natural liberty" would occasion warranted self-approbation just because, paradoxically, it acknowledges our power to prepare for reason's misleading claims to omnipotence and so our power to see the limits of reason.

Smith tells us that "nature . . . seems to abound with events which appear solitary and incoherent with all that go before them, which therefore disturb the easy movement of the imagination . . ." and that this disorganization is answered by philosophy that "endeavours to introduce order into this chaos of jarring and discordant appearances, to allay this tumult of the imagination, and to restore it, when it surveys the great revolutions of the universe, to that tone of tranquillity and composure, which is most agreeable in itself, and most suitable to its nature."[47] Ordinary life too is given to "this chaos of jarring and discordant appearances," as is shown by the long history of religious war, for example. The imagination's pleasure would be all the greater when the order contemplated is, because of its understanding of the phenomena, as seemingly unsystematic and surprising as that of a "system of natural liberty." This "system" embodies, as I put it in Chapter 7, an anti-utopian utopianism and a skepticism about system, as warranted by a clear understanding of both human imperfection and the great role of chance in human life. To see the beauty in that strange "system" would be to admire the "uncommon and unexpected acuteness and comprehensiveness" of the system and of the mind that conceptualized it. Both would deserve our "admiration and applause" (I.i.4.3).

Happiness is to be understood as tranquillity, and tranquillity is to be viewed as a sort of reflective integration over time. Are Smithean philosophers happy – that is, peaceful, at rest, and appropriately reconciled – given that they understand "nature" and system appropriately? Concertos are composed and conducted, but of course fortune or nature is not so easily coordinated with our purposes. Our moral and political compositions and efforts at conducting will be open-ended at best, and more often incomplete and open to question. Can the imagination be entirely tranquil if the world is not, even when "unity" has the polyphonic character we have described? In the lines from the "History of Astronomy" quoted in the preceding paragraph, Smith speaks of the "chaos" of nature, the imagination's consequent restlessness, and philosophy's creative attempt to order. Earlier (in Chapter 2) we saw that Smith's view entails that we have no "self" outside of society, at least no moral self, and that both our dread of solitude and our drive to persuade others arise from our sense that without sympathy we are dissolved. Not simply the prevalence of contingency and finitude but our anxiety about the reappear-

---

47 "History of Astronomy," II.12 (*EPS*, pp. 45–6). In the course of his discussion of Ptolemy's astronomical system ("History of Astronomy" IV.13), Smith offers a comment that connects with a number of the themes I have been discussing in this chapter: "Those philosophers transported themselves, in fancy, to the centres of these imaginary Circles, and took pleasure in surveying from thence, all those fantastical motions, arranged, according to that harmony and order, which it had been the end of all their researches to bestow upon them. Here, at last, they enjoyed that tranquillity and repose which they had pursued through all the mazes of this intricate hypothesis; and here they beheld this, the most beautiful and magnificent part of the great theatre of nature, so disposed and constructed, that they could attend, with ease and delight, to all the revolutions and changes that occurred in it" (*EPS*, p. 62).

ance of chaos and the pain that that would entail nip at the heels of the love of beauty. The problem of the Silenus returns.

This is especially nagging for philosophers who, like Smith, understand the force of questions directed against their own conception of their enterprise. The tranquillity of contemplating a polymorphous and polytonal "system" (even were so complex a "utopia" to come into being) is shadowed by the question of its own groundedness, its own harmony with that on which it rests. Philosophy reiterates its restlessness even in its highest level of self-apprehension. Smith's view ultimately seems to require that he detach himself from himself at various levels – not just as theorist from actor but as theorist (who accepts views on the premise that they are "agreeable to truth and reality" and knows his views are accepted on the same basis) from himself as observer of theorists (including himself). Smith will not, as meta-theorist of self, view himself in the light in which theorists commonly view themselves and are viewed, namely, as articulating what is Platonically objective. For from this metastandpoint, Smith holds that in truth he can see only the whole that the imagination paints, even as the imagination persuades him that the products of its work represent the "really real." The metastandpoint resembles that of the unmasker or ironist who cannot live or think only from that standpoint. The unavoidable oscillation between detachment and attachment would seem to jeopardize tranquillity.

Just as in the case of the lover of wealth who is deceived by the imagination into thinking he will achieve happiness, so the theorist seems driven to pursue a satisfaction that his imagination promises but can never deliver for long. The recognition that this is so can be accepted with tranquillity only by one both steeped in self-command – *the* Stoic virtue, for Smith – and absolutely committed to the inviolability of the ethical domain regardless of the paradoxes of the speculative. Although we seem fated to unending striving, whether or not we are philosophers, perhaps there is a practical remedy to the loss of tranquillity caused by philosophical perplexity, namely the "society and conversation" Smith recommends to "men of retirement and speculation" (I.i.4.10; recall also VII.iv.28 on the "musical" harmony of conversation). Rhetoric in the best sense of the term – as humanizing conversation, persuasion, and communication immersed in ordinary life – is essential to this remedy, as long as it possesses, in the ways we have explored, capacities for self-evaluation and moral criticism. Smith's rhetoric exhibits these qualities, especially in its dialectical aspects. His use of the term "nature" and its cognates may serve as a paradigm of his complex rhetorical strategy, whose aim it is to let us be both guided by philosophy and liberated from it. Highly self-reflexive philosophy must make itself be a moment in a life of activity. Perhaps Smith's recognition that *that* is so constitutes the ultimate completion of his philosophy, one that makes possible reflective integration of one's life, as long as its consequence is remembered, namely, that happiness cannot be found in philosophy alone. Philosophy's defense of the standpoint of ordinary life is thus also a defense against both itself and nature. This requires skepticism, a dialectical self-knowledge and a synoptic view that is philosophical but not Platonic in its claims and reality.

Even granted all this, however, the fit between philosophy and ordinary life is imperfect. On the one hand, for both theoretical and moral reasons Smith must appeal to ordinary life, the integrity of practice, harmonious sentiments, and the weakness of reason and the limits of philosophy, and the like, in order to make his case. Philosophy cannot ground itself independently of ordinary experience, cannot satisfy its own traditional demands for self-knowledge unless firmly rooted in common soil. Smith insists on this priority of the prephilosophical.

On the other hand, some forms of "ordinary life" are corrupt, and the difference between good and bad harmonies is generally visible to the philosopher (using the term in a sense broad enough to include the political economist) rather than the ordinary moral actor. Happiness both personal and public requires the intervention of philosophical intelligence, and this is exactly what Smith's books represent. The fact of their publication – and recall here the ambitious projected *corpus* – means that unreflective prephilosophical life cannot be left entirely to its own devices. Smith encourages one particular form of ordinary life in all of its various manifestations (moral, psychological, political, literary, economic, and religious). *The Theory of Moral Sentiments* is also a moral theory of the moral sentiments.

The tensions inherent in Smith's project go still deeper, because (as already suggested in Chapter 4, section 3), the skepticism entertained at the theoretical level might itself subvert common life. The flip side of that skepticism is the doctrine, inspired by Hume, of the "poietic" imagination – the view that, in the final analysis, unity and value stem from "us" rather than from "nature." The danger is, of course, that this view might sap the robust realism that is the spirit of ordinary life. Smith responds that at both the moral and the theoretical level the "inventions of the imagination" do not normally *appear* to be inventions, especially when those inventions succeed in their task.[48] But this is not to say that they can only appear that way.[49] I shall return to these difficulties in the Epilogue.

## 7. CONVENTION AND HISTORY

To comprehend *what is* is the task of philosophy, for *what is* is reason. As far as the individual is concerned, each individual is in any case a *child of his time;* thus philosophy, too, is *its own time comprehended in thoughts.*

G. W. F. Hegel[50]

Smith's use of the vocabulary of "nature" gives the impression that there is a timeless structure to things, for "natural" might also be contrasted to "historical," as in the second sense of the term "nature." Yet the theory of moral sentiments, implicitly if not explicitly, introduces time, convention, and culture into our conception of the given. As we have seen, the impartial spectator determines what is "natural" in the normative sense, but the impartial spectator is rooted in time and place, and

48 Recall the remarkable conclusion to the "History of Astronomy" (IV.76, *EPS*, pp. 104–5), where Smith describes the response of even "the most sceptical" to Newton's system.
49 Whether in fact any such broadly Humean (and Smithean) theory could seep into moral life and, in so doing, cause damage, continues to be contested. One contemporary follower of Hume views the worry about this seepage as a "mistake." S. Blackburn writes that D. Wiggins's critique of noncognitivism "results in the charge that projectivism cannot be true to the 'inside of lived experience.' Other writers (I would cite Nagel, Williams, and Foot) seem to illustrate similar unease. The thought is something like this: it is important that there should be some kind of accord in our thinking about ethical stances from the perspective of the theorist, and from that of the participant. Our story about ethical commitment is to explain it, not to explain it away. But projectivism threatens to do the latter. . . . It threatens to do so because it shows us that our commitments are not external demands, claiming us regardless of our wills or in direct opposition to our passions. It makes our commitments facets of our own sentimental natures; this softens them, destroying the hardness of the moral trust." "How to Be an Ethical Antirealist," rpt. in Darwall, Gibbard, and Railton, eds., *Moral Discourse and Practice*, pp. 174–5. Blackburn notes that "projectivism" (his term) is "intended indeed to be a modern version of Hume's theory of the nature of ethics, but without any commitment to particular operations of passions such as sympathy" (p. 168). Cf. C. Larmore's recent argument that such a view would "sap any confidence we may have in the objectivity of these norms [of reasoning and value]" and is at bottom identical with Nietzsche's thesis that we are the authors of all value. *The Morals of Modernity* (Cambridge: Cambridge University Press, 1996), p. 102.
50 Preface to *Elements of the Philosophy of Right*, ed. A. W. Wood, trans. H. B. Nisbet (Cambridge: Cambridge University Press, 1995), p. 21.

Smith's philosophy is agnostic about timeless structures and entities (such as the "immortal soul," for example). Must not history therefore assume a crucial role in every aspect of Smith's philosophy? One might ultimately conclude that for him all moral and intellectual views are not just expressed in but defined by the historical moment, and further that this leads inevitably to historicism (understood very roughly as the doctrine that moral evaluation and philosophy are limited to or are only expressions of their historical epoch).

The issue of custom is explicitly raised in Part V of *The Theory of Moral Sentiments*, "Of the INFLUENCE OF CUSTOM and FASHION upon the Sentiments of Moral Approbation and Disapprobation." This discussion immediately follows Smith's analysis of utility and precedes that of virtue, as though to put a question to the views about aesthetics and theory set out in the one, and about character in the other. The section on custom culminates in the example of infanticide (which we have considered in Chapter 5, section 2). However, Smith clearly assumes that custom need not interfere with our ability to grasp the truth about different societies or individuals. He assumes a basic transparency of human beings to each other, within the limits of sympathy. *In principle*, "the savages in North America," about whom he discourses without the slightest doubt of his ability to grasp their situation, are no more and no less mysterious than is one's neighbor. In the same passage, he provides the moving example of the virtues of the enslaved "negro from the coast of Africa" and the perversity of the European masters (V.2.9). These examples show his obvious ability to stand at a critical distance from the mores of his own time and of earlier periods, as well as to enter into the situation of someone who is quite differently placed.

When discussing the histories of thought, whether of moral philosophy in Part VII of *The Theory of Moral Sentiments* or of natural science in the essays collected in *Essays on Philosophical Subjects*, he never suggests that we are so fully governed by convention or history that we cannot accurately or impartially understand different or temporally distant philosophies. Instead, Smith treats moral philosophers as interlocutors in an ongoing conversation. His philosophy does not take itself to be historicist in the sense just specified, nor must it do so. There may be no escape from the *theatrum mundi*, but it does not follow that the mind is unalterably cooped up in its particular historical milieu.

We might skeptically ask how Smith would prove that historicism is untenable. It will not surprise us at this stage to learn that he has, and can have, no *systematic* answer to such a question, if that is taken to mean, an *a priori* answer or a decisive knock-down argument. He would instead deploy a number of the strategies we have observed. These would range from dialectical arguments against the person who holds that historicism is tenable to piecemeal instances of our understanding this or that person or culture or theory. He would rehearse his views of selfishness and sympathy, arguing that the human soul is not "too selfish to enclose its vision within another horizon," to borrow a phrase from Nietzsche.[51] The possibility of critical moral reflection is reiterated even in the section of *The Theory of Moral Sentiments* on custom (V.2.5); the reactions of the impartial spectator continue to serve as the standard (cf. V.2.13). Moral criticism is attentive to context, presupposes custom, and engages understanding from within a specifiable temporal context, but as we have seen at length, moral criticism is not therefore blinded by custom or bound by the actor's point of view in the sense that reduces meaningful appraisal to the mere expression of emotion and opinion.

Smith is well aware that morality and thought have relevant histories. Tradition and convention certainly play a huge (and often invisible) role in our judgments about moral and aesthetic value. For most people, most of the time, the conception of the virtues and their relative importance is shaped by convention (V.2.7), even though the role of convention will largely escape them. In a now familiar manner, Smith portrays that fact as an inevitable and beneficial effect of the self-effacing quality of the imagination's *poiesis*.[52] Notwithstanding the self-assurance typical of custom, judgments and mores are not only intelligible to educated sympathy and mind; they can be thoughtfully appraised. Conceptions of what counts as a virtue and as beautiful vary wildly throughout history. Even so, the variation in mores is not total: the "natural principles of right and wrong" are not reducible to custom or fashion (V.2.2), and indeed he remarks that "I cannot . . . be induced to believe that our sense even of external beauty is founded altogether on custom" (V.1.9).

As an example of reflective evaluation and philosophical theorizing, Smith's work is not (by its own lights) confined to a narrowly circumscribed historical period. This is not to say that Smith thinks his own philosophy could have been formulated at just any historical time, any

---

51 "History in the Service and Disservice of Life," p. 90.
52 "Few men therefore are willing to allow, that custom or fashion have much influence upon their judgments concerning what is beautiful, or otherwise, in the productions of any of those arts; but imagine, that all the rules, which they think ought to be observed in each of them, are founded upon reason and nature, not upon habit or prejudice" (V.i.4).

more than Newton's philosophy could have been written in fourth century B.C. Athens. His thought too has a relevant history. Yet the *basis* of
the explanations he provides in ethics, political economy, and indeed in
every subject about which he wrote is presented as, on the whole, unchanging. That is, he seems to assume that the principles of human
nature are constant through time.[53] The "principles" that are "illustrated" by the essays on the histories of natural science seem not themselves to be in history. This implicit claim to articulation of an unchanging "nature" is not inconsistent with what I have argued, if two
points are kept in mind. The first is that such modes of speaking are as
ingrained in the activity of theorizing as they are in the activity of moralizing, as is evident in Smith's own work. His theory addresses this quite
common feature of human life. Indeed, for ethical and protreptic purposes he may want to insist on the importance of such modes of speech,
since he is well aware of "when the historical and when the unhistorical
sense is needed."[54]

The second point is that when pushed for the "proof" of his assumption that principles of human nature are stable, he may legitimately fall
back upon his doctrine of the unifying and demiurgic activity of the
intellectual imagination. If we ask whether that activity has functioned
persuasively in the case of his own theory – including in his positing
stable principles of human nature – the answer can only consist in the
account that is the sum and substance of his writings. If the overall account convincingly shows us how the phenomena can be brought into a
satisfying explanatory system when certain stable principles are posited,
then of course we have good reason to accept those principles. This
remains faithful to his theoretical framework, just so long as it is remembered that the imagination is the origin of all such theorizing. To yearn
for more – and even Smith seemed to do so when contemplating the

---

53 Cf. Hume's comment in the *Enquiry Concerning Human Understanding*: "It is universally
   acknowledged that there is a great uniformity among the actions of men, in all nations
   and ages, and that human nature remains still the same, in its principles and operations.
   ... Mankind are so much the same, in all times and places, that history informs us of
   nothing new or strange in this particular. Its chief use is only to discover the constant
   and universal principles of human nature" (p. 83).

54 The quoted phrase is borrowed (once again) from Nietzsche, "History in the Service and
   Disservice of Life," p. 90: "Cheerfulness, good conscience, joyful action, faith in the future
   – all these depend, in an individual as in a people, upon the existence of a line that separates the bright and lucid from unilluminable darkness, upon knowing how to forget at the
   right time as well as how to remember at the right time, upon sensing, vigorously and instinctively, when the historical and when the unhistorical sense is needed."

reach of the grand system he envisioned – is to fall into perplexities we have already reviewed.

In contrast with the generally nonhistorical tenor of *The Theory of Moral Sentiments*, the historical sense is very much in evidence in the "natural jurisprudence" branch of his work. Both in the *Lectures on Jurisprudence* and in *The Wealth of Nations*, history plays a significant role. This seems perfectly natural given the project in which Smith is there principally engaged – namely, the account of the "different revolutions" undergone by "the general principles of law and government" in the "different ages and periods of society" (these words occur in the paragraph with which *TMS* concludes). Consideration of the role played by the historical context and provenance of institutions and practices points to the possibility that history may possess a larger explanatory and even justificatory function in his philosophy than I have conceded. For example, it is striking that the "system of natural liberty" is introduced in book III of *The Wealth of Nations* with an account of its historical genesis. Smith is well aware that the complex social, legal, and political practices making up this system (practices that Hegel later referred to as composing "civil society") are a modern development (*WN* III.iii.5 and context). Smith provides a genetic account that, as a compelling narrative of almost epic character, makes that outcome seem "reasonable" or "motivated" relative to the failures and follies from which it emerged. It is equally striking that Smith underlines paradoxes intrinsic to that very "system of natural liberty" (such as that of the dehumanization of the workers), thus raising the possibility that it too may succumb to the dialectic of history by depleting its resources for solving the problems it generates. Were it thus to undermine itself, would it have demonstrated a deeply entrenched irrationality?

If the self-undermining resulted from a specifiable mismatching of problems and solutions, rather as in the case of the "Platonic tradition" of civic religion, then Smith might agree that history – and perhaps only history – can in some cases teach us lessons about the "irrationality" of the given practice or institution. Yet Smith would certainly be skeptical of any straightforwardly progressivist history (excluding his histories of intellectual inquiries). Not only is history's "logic" often opaque and its upshot morally complex; its "moral" cannot be determined absent the responses of a well-informed impartial spectator. A fascinating and instructive tale may be told about the genesis of the system of natural liberty, and, perhaps, about its demise. The assessment of the virtues of that system ought to be informed by that tale but could never be exhausted by it. For that assessment, we must also call upon the resources that are available to us as persons of good judgment and character who are appropriately rooted in the relatively unhistorical "natural" outlook of common life. Smith ultimately can offer us no more than all this and, by his own lights, need offer us no more. Grasped in its totality, it is in fact a great deal. But is it enough?

# EPILOGUE

[A man] must not expose himself to the charge which Avidius Cassius is said to have brought, perhaps unjustly, against Marcus Antoninus [Marcus Aurelius]; that while he employed himself in philosophical speculations, and contemplated the prosperity of the universe, he neglected that of the Roman empire. The most sublime speculation of the contemplative philosopher can scarce compensate the neglect of the smallest active duty.

Adam Smith, *TMS* VI.ii.3.6

I began this book with a general discussion of the Enlightenment and of the widespread unease about its prospects and about its virtues. I suggested that Adam Smith is both a partisan and critic of the Enlightenment; he purposes to preserve what is best about the movement by drawing upon resources ancient and modern, while also analyzing its unintended shortcomings. I have argued throughout that the old problem of the relationship between philosophy and ordinary experience is itself fruitfully seen as a principal theme in his reflections on what it would mean for human life to be enlightened. At several junctures I queried the persuasiveness of the manner in which particular themes and arguments are treated in Smith's work – for example, the priority of the spectator over the actor in matters of ethical evaluation, the safe-guards against the possible degeneration of the pleasure of sympathy into selfishness and vanity, the circularity of ethical reasoning, and the pre-scriptions for liberty of religious belief and their implications for the survival of energetic religion. On each occasion I sought to articulate Smith's likely reply to questions that might legitimately be put to him. In this Epilogue, I review several of the merits as well as key difficulties of Smith's project and then suggest how the latter might be alleviated.

I

*The Theory of Moral Sentiments* and *The Wealth of Nations* contain many com-ments about the limits of reason and of philosophy. In keeping with the interpretive principles outlined in the Introduction, I have construed Smith's skepticism in the most favorable light available to it, as a synthesis of Pyrrhonist and Humean views. I speculated that Smith's skepticism is motivated by the view that certain timeworn philosophical arguments and debates are fruitless, by the fear of the fanaticism associated with the passion for theological and metaphysical systems, and by an appreciation of the salutary consequences of refocusing our attention on issues that are of genuine concern and about which progress can actually be made. I suggested that Smith's skeptical framework forms part of a broadly enlightened ethical vision of the self-sufficiency, dignity, and indeed lib-erty of the human being, for it holds that we have within ourselves sources of moral guidance that allow us to direct our lives and live co-operatively. His outlook is also motivated by the ethical purpose of pre-serving the stability and richness of ordinary human life.

I suggested that Smith *enacts* the view according to which the old debate about how things "really" are can largely be dropped so that the more constructive business of philosophy may proceed. Smith's theory of moral sentiments, including his Humean theory as to the pervasive-ness of the imagination in human life (both in its theorizing and ethical dimensions), is the obverse of his skepticism. This constructive business of philosophy takes place within the "appearances," within the reach of human reason, and includes accounting for the ways in which the ap-pearances or phenomena are misunderstood. Even though we are ori-ented by and within the "appearances," we may truthfully be said to make mistakes about them. For example, Smith argues that people reg-ularly misunderstand the nature of happiness. The constructive project of philosophy will also include work on aspects of language (aspects such as the "origin" or formation of language and the ways in which rhetoric is woven into daily life as well as inquiry). Smith clearly intended to explore such matters farther. On my construal Smith agrees with Hume that the life of the skeptic is not livable, thereby granting a crucial distinction between theory and practice. The distinction pertains to theory as well (to theory and its practice, so to speak), for to theorize as a self-conscious skeptic is not much more sustainable than to live as a skeptic. Especially in ethical theory, Smith remains as much as possible within the fold of ordinary life. So understood, his basic framework demonstrates his engagement with long-standing metaphilosophical issues.

Smith's moral philosophy and political economy are developed within this framework. The analyses of the emotions, sympathy, imagination, and practical reason – the moral psychology, in short – are buttressed by a skillfully drawn phenomenology of ethical experience. His sensitive portrayal and analysis of inner moral life, especially of sympathy, are impressive, as is his analysis of the problem of selfishness. The book to which I have devoted the bulk of my attention here is of course a theory of the moral emotions, and it helps to explain how they can be communicated and understood, how they can be thought of as moral, and how as moral they involve impartiality and spectatorship in ways that do not destroy the primacy of context and particularity. Smith makes the topic of virtue central to ethics and provides for a view of moral reasoning that heavily emphasizes judgment while also retaining an important place for moral rules and various forms of ethical reasoning. The impartial spectator theory shows that ordinary life possesses the capacity for substantive moral criticism: we do have nontheoretical moral knowledge and are not condemned to relativism by a skepticism or agnosticism about ancient metaphysical conundra. All of this fits with an account of happiness as tranquillity that brings together aspects of his moral psychology and virtue theory.

Moral education is a pervasive theme in Smith's work, and provides one occasion for the fruitful introduction of literature into the scope of moral philosophy. Through moral education we come to be self-determining agents. His account of agency does not rest simply at the abstract level of philosophical psychology but shows how agency might be understood as embedded in complex social and moral relations, from the family to the economic and jurisprudential conditions of modern commercial society. The account plausibly suggests that we need to consult experience in order to understand agency. This understanding requires both our educated "sympathy" and theoretical intelligence.

As a virtue theorist, Smith speaks in the vocabulary of character, judgment, happiness, sentiment, and imagination. He has much to say about friendship and love. His analyses of the individual virtues, his sketches of the character types possessing them, his recognition that the virtues are not reducible to one another, and his formulation of the differences among them – especially between justice and the others – are discerning. The distinction between judgments of propriety and merit is perceptive, as is the emphasis on the underlying notion of appropriateness and suitedness. He exploits the idea of "proportion" to surprising effect: the longing for beauty and harmony, it turns out, pervades all aspects of human life, from wealth getting to the pleasure of ethical consensus to the tranquillity we seek in creating powerful explanatory systems. This account sheds light on the satisfactions as well as the *pathos* intrinsic to the *theatrum mundi*. Further, the beautiful and the good are not perfectly matched, for some harmonies are corrupting and some are not. An appeal to nature as the standard for value and thus for the conduct of human life is not defensible philosophically. Among the other questions this prompts is whether tranquillity is available to the philosopher who contemplates the often indifferent beauty of "the whole."

Readers of Smith's work are typically struck by the elegance and power of his writing. Starting in the first chapter, I traced key elements of his rhetoric and examined how they are grounded in, and in turn serve to support, a view about the subject matter of ethics. These elements include his use of examples, of the pronoun "we" and the interplay of other literary "voices," and of the metaphors of the critic and the theater. They also encompass his intertwining of the virtue and moral psychology questions, and the structural dialectic of *The Theory of Moral Sentiments*. How one "does" ethics and what it is that ethics could concern itself with are closely connected. Many contemporary moral philosophers would agree with his general position that ethics is something one can fruitfully theorize about only insofar as one is already engaged in ethical practice and its cultivation through ethical reflection. Smith's defense of this position against the revisionist or systematizing impulses of philosophers is compelling. His approach to the doing of ethics holds that human life harbors its own moral wholeness and virtues, as well as rich resources in the form of the emotions, understanding, sympathy, and judgment. He recognizes that common life has its own rationality, or *Verstehen*, thanks in part to the way in which the emotions and understanding are interwoven. He does not force it to be answerable to the court of philosophical reason on pain of condemnation as mere prejudice. The common fund of knowledge that we do possess is generally (though not always) sufficient for the conduct of life. It is not, perhaps, capable of answering Socratic questions on their terms – but then, Socrates did not answer them either.[1]

The dialectical character of Smith's writing embodies a method of inquiry well worth continuing. It shows sensitivity to the unexpected twists and turns that the phenomena under investigation take and insists that one be guided by the subject matter rather than by methodological preconceptions about it. His method of reflection allows him to draw freely upon history, literature, rhetoric, economics, philosophy, and other disciplines, as suits the subject matter and his purpose. His method also undermines dogmatism of all sorts, including any self-assured dogma about the "autonomy of the free market." He is under no illusion that the free market somehow solves all problems in and of itself, and he does not think that it is a kind of machine that follows its own laws and infallibly produces the best outcome for all. His vivid description of the dehumanization of the workers would alone destroy any such dogma. Even when the free market is working efficiently and justly, the hard work and thrift of its laborers earn just our "cold esteem."

At the same time, he also shows that commercial society should not be understood as premised on a doctrine of monadic individualism, of greed-driven and selfish utility maximization. Modern commercial society cannot be reduced to mere economic association. Smith illuminates the interdependence of virtue and institutions (social, political, and economic). A flourishing commercial society requires, and in turn may support, "moral capital," that is, virtue. Smith's balanced arguments in favor of the free market and of liberty are supported by his critiques of long-

---

1 As mentioned in the Introduction, when referring to "Socrates" I mean only the character in Plato's dialogues and am not drawing distinctions between Plato and the Socrates of his dialogues. I realize that my assertion (to be offered shortly) of a deep continuity between Socrates' metaphysical views and the realism of common life is, as a matter of interpretation of Plato, controversial. Indeed, whether or not Socratic philosophizing preserves the relevant aspects of common life – better than might the view of a certain kind of Sophist, for example – is an issue disputed within the Platonic dialogues, as the *Protagoras* shows.

standing alternatives (such as the "Platonic tradition" concerning civic religion). His counterintuitive solution to the problem of religious strife is one such argument.

Smith's entirely credible skepticism about routine politics and the motivations of economic agents cautions us against misplaced designs and expectations. His famous emphasis on the "invisible hand" and on the ironies of human life as well as of history, and hence his emphasis on the continually unexpected and never quite controllable flow of events, restrain the desire to master fortune. Put simply, human life is not a resource to be manipulated at will, not a machine that can or should be controlled by calculative reason. But the alternative is not uncritical acceptance. Especially given the events of our century, we profit by relearning Smith's wisdom, not only about attempts at misguided "social engineering" but also about the moral limitations and periodic failings of life in an imperfect "utopia" of liberty. His outlook encompasses a passionate commitment to commutative justice and to the betterment of the lot of the ordinary person. His project is reconciliationist but not quietist or passive.

This commendation of moderation and prudence is not, then, politically motivated, nor does it arise from a conservative fear of change, or from distrust of the people, or from a historicist view that makes criticisms of the age impossible, or from the ideology of "the bourgeoisie." Rather, it arises from a complex assessment of "idealism" or "utopianism," as well as from both a view that ordinary experience does possess genuine resources for self-criticism and virtue, and an ingrained wariness of fanaticism of all stripes. The sense of balance and judgment that grows out of the careful weighing of the alternatives and of an understanding of the self-undermining potential of the phenomena – the sense that Smith's writings, in their form and content, convey – works against any such fanaticism and also supplies critical support to the commendation in question. He is a "systematic" thinker who sees that the appropriate "system" in moral and political philosophy is more like a "well-composed concerto" than a "Newtonian" arrangement.

Smith's humane vision is at the core of what I have called the virtues of enlightenment. It is arguably an outlook intrinsic to the liberal Enlightenment, and so to the promise of modernity. Taken as a whole, this humane outlook is more attractive than the aristocratic view so ingrained among the ancients, and more attractive than any view, ancient or modern, that would force social and political life into the mold of a rigid theory or system. Although my primary purpose in this book has been to offer an interpretation of principal themes of Smith's philosophy, I now reiterate the suggestion that his work is a valuable resource in our efforts to continue what is best in the Enlightenment. He provides materials for a persuasive response to well-known critiques of the Enlightenment; for example, to those who argue that the period reduces morality to emotivism (leaving no room for reasonable "moral criticism"), virtue to rules that serve to make possible the liberation of the vulgar passions, social life to the cold and self-interested exchanges of the market, the rule of the best to mass egalitarianism, reason to means-oriented calculative rationality, or finally reason to hegemonic "rationality" modeled on science.

## II

These summarizing comments by no means exhaust the richness of Smith's contributions, but are intended to capture a number of them. No doubt each of the issues summarized requires further development, and the incompleteness of his *corpus* leaves a defender of his line of thought with still other avenues to develop. Naturally, his views are not without difficulties of their own. In this section of the Epilogue I further discuss several that strike me as particularly pressing and propose certain emendations to his line of thought that develop both his appropriation of the ancients and his understanding of the relationship between the virtue and moral psychology questions.

I begin with the image of "poiesis." It is useful to remind ourselves of the background against which that idea recommends itself. Simply stated, Smith holds that neither nature nor God may in truth be relied upon to supply us with moral norms. Nature (understood as the whole, or totality) is ultimately indifferent to our purposes, and God – if such exists – is a source of personal inspiration but not of rational governance. In the well-worn phrase, nature is "disenchanted." Even were nature benevolently designed, we could not live our lives just from its impersonal or "objective" perspective, could not live "according to nature" (as Smith took the Stoics to say). What this ultimately means is that we will have to find within ourselves the source of moral enlightenment and consequently that, in some sense or other, morality is of our making. It would be difficult to find a significant modern moral philosophy that denies this general conclusion, and although "making" is construed in

widely varying ways, the reasons for the centrality of the notion are compelling.[2]

The issues here that call for extending Smith's thought occur at both
the theoretical and the practical level. At the theoretical level, the chief
difficulty pertains to the way in which part of his moral philosophy is
dependent on the phenomena it is meant to explain. I have argued that
he offers a moral psychology that is not in one crucial respect continuous
with ordinary experience. For it implies that, contrary to the agent's
perspective, moral terms ultimately do not correspond to external, mind-
independent reality but express our sentiments and judgment. (I further
noted that the drift away from ordinary experience is evident even in his
somewhat forced redefinition of the common word "sympathy.") This
looks suspiciously like a philosopher's reinterpretation of the "true basis" of moral experience. Although such reinterpretation is to some degree inevitable in any moral philosophy, in the present instance we are
left with a significant tension between his theory of moral sentiments
and the demand that theories lean heavily on experience. Ordinary
agents "Platonize" reality and assume that morality mirrors the abiding
structure of the world. Seen from Smith's theoretical standpoint, they
are exaggerating what can be known to be the case. Moral "reality" and
the objective "fabric of the world" are best understood, for Smith (as
for Hume), as decisively formed by the self, and, in particular, by the
imagination.[3] The power of the imagination is felt all the way from the

2 See Chapter 8, note 41, and D. Wiggins, "Truth, Invention, and the Meaning of Life," in
   Wiggins, *Needs, Values, Truth: Essays in the Philosophy of Value* (Oxford: Blackwell Publisher,
   1987), pp. 126–7. As R. Pippin states, in summarizing Hegel's view: "there are and can
   be no straightforwardly 'natural' or 'divine' norms, no facts about the natural world, or
   revelations about God's will, or intuition of non-natural properties, that, just by *being* such
   facts or revelations, thereby constrain or direct my conduct." See "Hegel's Ethical Rationalism," in *Idealism as Modernism* (Cambridge: Cambridge University Press, 1997), p. 428.
   Smith would agree, as long as the pronoun "my" adverts to the standpoint of a philosopher.
3 Recall once again Smith's statement at VII.iii.2.7: "But nothing can be agreeable or disagreeable for its own sake, which is not rendered such by immediate sense and feeling,"
   and III.5.5: "There is no appeal from the eye with regard to the beauty of colours, nor
   from the ear with regard to the harmony of sounds, nor from the taste with regard to the
   agreeableness of flavours. . . . The very essence of each of those qualities consists in its
   being fitted to please the sense to which it is addressed. It belongs to our moral faculties,
   in the same manner to determine when the ear ought to be soothed, when the eye ought
   to be indulged, when the taste ought to be gratified, when and how far every other principle of our nature ought either to be indulged or restrained. What is agreeable to our
   moral faculties, is fit, and right, and proper to be done; the contrary wrong, unfit, and
   improper. The sentiments which they approve of, are graceful and becoming: the contrary,

formation and guidance of the emotions to the creation of systematic conceptual syntheses. Although this view of the formative power of the imagination is the obverse of his skeptical outlook, with respect to the issue of the source of value, it does not "save the appearances" in terms that would be recognized by the actors who live within the fold of everyday life.

Where the phenomenology and the moral psychology do not entirely harmonize at a basic and pervasive level, Smith leaves himself open to the criticism he leveled against Hume (with respect to Hume's invocation of "utility"). The difficulty in determining how moral philosophy is rooted in prephilosophical life – that is, rooted in the self-understanding of moral agents – does not necessarily undermine his analysis of the imagination's work at a number of levels, such as its role in sympathy or its role in our falsely associating happiness with wealth. The relevant tension between ordinary and philosophical understandings arises when the question of the source of morals – and so the objectivity of morals altogether – is at stake.[4] I argued that for Smith the impartial spectator "defines" right and wrong; the impartial spectator is ultimately constitutive of the moral outlook. But the impartial spectator presumably interprets himself or herself as making a determination that expresses what is objectively and really so.

It is as vital not to overstate the difficulty as not to wave it away. To recall the end of Chapter 4, section 2, Smith's theory does hold that norms are "real" in that they get objectified (in the sense of "become objective") in the world (in character, institutions, traditions, practices). Norms guide action and are lived by; they are not illusions or "just in the mind." "Mind dependency" is significantly different from "subjective" (in the sense of "relative to the individual or society"). Nonetheless, in tracing the source of this objectification to "us," the theoretical perspective deprives norms of the "reality" or "objectivity" that ordinary sentiments themselves assume and indeed require for their own flourish-

---

ungraceful and unbecoming. The very words, right, wrong, fit, improper, graceful, unbecoming, mean only what pleases or displeases those faculties." Cf. the references to Hume in Chapter 4, notes 21, 31.

4 In Chapter 1 I discussed the following passage in TMS: "A system of natural philosophy may appear very plausible, and be for a long time very generally received in the world, and yet have no foundation in nature, nor any sort of resemblance to the truth. . . . But it is otherwise with systems of moral philosophy, and an author who pretends to account for the origin of our moral sentiments, cannot deceive us so grossly, nor depart so very far from all resemblance to the truth." For we are there cognizant "of what passes in our neighbourhood, and of the affairs of the very parish which we live in" (VII.ii.4.14).

ing. The sheer "presentedness" of value pushes against the view that value is intersubjectively established. All of this opens Smith to the criticism of not being entirely faithful to the methodological principles by which he judges Hume and others.

A variety of replies to this line of criticism is available to a defender of Smith's position. A first is that the fundamental features of our common situation – the unavailability of nature or the divine as the source of norms – are undeniable, from which it follows that, insofar as any philosophical account is to be given, "we" must be taken as the author of morality, however that is to be spelled out. So far as anybody can tell, there is no "moral sense," no moral instructions in the book of nature, no faculty of intuition for discerning immutable Forms, and nothing inexpressibly "out there" for us to know or fail to know. Whatever dissatisfactions we have on this score result (so the reply might continue) from our misplaced expectations, from our simply having failed to assimilate the skeptic's point that the whole demand for some more profoundly and Platonically real reality ought itself be dropped along with any idea of a sliding scale of reality. When that is done, that to which extraordinary reality was being contrasted will be as "real" as anybody could wish. This is just the reality that Smith is trying to provide a theory of, and that theory of moral sentiments includes a view of the imagination and sentiments as complexly constituting or shaping or bringing to life the moral world.

A second reply reiterates that although norms may indeed be termed "made by us" when viewed from a theoretical perspective, in all the other respects I have summarized they are rightly taken as "real" and "out there." Because they are "made," it does not follow that they are not "real." These "made" values are so thoroughly embedded in social life, individual character, tradition, that they may be termed "natural." Further, as "intersubjective," they are external, outside any one of us. The idea is not that values are made by individuals, contrary to a crude version of a Romantic view of the self. The process is a social and "sympathetic" one governed by the standpoint of the spectator. So with respect to the issue at hand, the theory is perfectly consistent after all with the usual phenomenology of ordinary life. The contrast to some *other* sense of "reality" as "Platonic" (the contrast that "made" implies) is not false, then, but lacks practical import. From the standpoint of moral agents, the philosopher's contrast between "made" and "discovered" is just beside the point.

A third reply would express puzzlement with the charge that the theory is discontinuous with ordinary experience in an unusual way. Every moral theory is, simply by virtue of being a theory, to some degree discontinuous with experience. This particular theory is exceptionally sensitive and attentive to experience, far more so than many of its major modern competitors. The intertwining of the two questions of any theory of moral sentiments (the "What is virtue" and the "moral psychology" questions) itself demonstrates this resolve to attend to experience. The analysis is not pulled out of a hat. Further, it is revisable in light of improved understanding of ordinary life. Smith's is not (to recall the discussion of the title page of *TMS* in Chapter 1) "the" theory in the sense of "the conclusive" theory. The analysis includes (the reply continues) a persuasive moral psychology explaining how morality is due to us, and the account is consistent with the theory's other plausible examples of the imagination's makings (e.g., the imagination's deception about the character of true happiness). The analysis is not undermined just by noting its discontinuity with ordinary life, unless that discontinuity amounts to an explanatory failure or a failure to remain within the limits of the evidence that experience provides.

Fourth, a defender of Smith might reply that his philosophy reconciles us with the world at both the practical and the theoretical level and also, by virtue of its skepticism as well as ethical commitments, makes possible the affirmation of the humane moral vision summarized at the beginning of this Epilogue. To recall an earlier example from Chapters 5 and 7, reconciliation can be accomplished through seeing that the universal activity of "bettering our condition" is both compatible with virtue *and* fueled by a "deception" of the imagination. Further, in showing that together we are self-sufficient in our capacity to care for ourselves and not altogether dependent on nature or the divine for the provision of value, a skeptical outlook supports a humane moral vision.

Finally, it could be replied that whatever the theoretical difficulties concerning the relation between philosophical and ethical perspectives, the difficulties are, so to speak, merely theoretical and do not disturb practice in any significant respect. This last reply points to the difficulty at the practical level that I have discussed repeatedly and that concerns the deleterious effect Smith's moral psychology and skepticism might have were they taken by ordinary agents to be true. To this worry, Smith could respond that a key feature of his skepticism has not been grasped, namely, that the relevant aspect of the moral psychology concerning the source of value is purely theoretical. No demand is being made that agents live in accordance with it, as though moral reasons could "count" for us only if "we" understood those reasons in their full philosophical dimensions. That is, systematic issues of moral psychology are of concern *to the philosopher,* but the ethical and political commitments coordinated with these issues may nonetheless be perfectly viable *for the reflective moral actor.* The separation between theory and practice comes to its own rescue, as it were, and does so just as long as the wrong kind of demands are not made of it, namely, certain philosophical demands. The moral sentiments and the norms they give rise to are as "real" and "objective" as it is necessary for them to be for the conduct of life.

The dialectic here is complex and could be pursued at length. The replies just sketched do have considerable merit and, of course, touch on issues that have been intensively discussed in contemporary moral philosophy. I do not think, however, that these replies are entirely satisfactory. Let me continue with the practical concern, and offer a suggestion for meeting it, before I return to the issue of harmonizing at the theoretical level the notions of realism and *poiesis.* The core common to both of these theoretical and practical levels constitutes the true "Adam Smith problem" and, so understood, it is a problem that remains ours.[5] Precisely because Smith insists on the primacy of the everyday and so successfully works out his views accordingly, the presence of this difficulty in his thought is especially instructive.

As I have interpreted Smith, it has been one of his "protreptic" purposes to warn philosophers against forcing certain kinds of questions on ordinary life. This protreptic attitude toward philosophy is evident throughout *The Theory of Moral Sentiments,* including in the structure of the book. Smith seeks to thwart philosophers' natural drive to produce systematic explanations that squeeze common life into the mold of elegant systems. He sometimes highlights the damage that drive may do and at other times points out the utility and beauty of even the follies of human life. His effort to curb philosophy's ambitions stems in part, as we have remarked, from a sense of humanity.

Yet his concern would be unnecessary were it not that philosophy can,

---

5 Cf. Nietzsche's pointed observation: "Have we not exposed ourselves to the suspicion of an opposition – an opposition between the world in which we were at home up to now with our reverences that perhaps made it possible for us to *endure* life, and another world *that consists of us* – an inexorable, fundamental, and deepest suspicion about ourselves that is more and more gaining worse and worse control of us Europeans and that could easily confront coming generations with the terrifying Either/Or: 'Either abolish your reverences or – *yourselves!*' The latter would be nihilism; but would not the former also be – nihilism? – This is *our* question mark." *The Gay Science,* trans. W. Kaufmann (New York: Random House, 1974), sec. 346, p. 287.

like religion, adversely affect common life. Thus, as argued in Chapter 4 (section 3), his protestations to the effect that discussions of moral psychology are "a mere matter of philosophical curiosity" of no importance "in practice" (VII.iii.intro.3) and, more generally, that differences in philosophical outlook "ought all of them to be matters of great indifference to us both" (I.i.4.5) ought themselves to be understood as part of his protreptic rhetoric. Practice is not necessarily insulated from theory, even from theory about the sources of value.

On the one hand, Smith is acutely aware of the possibility of unintended consequences unleashed by the philosopher's helping hand, including a still more destabilized, factionalized common life. He is also aware of the well-established tendency of philosophers to adopt contemptuous or reductive views of ordinary experience. Yet, on the other hand, peaceful practice, ordinary life, and reasonable custom are not self-subsistent, as for example, the problem of religious fanaticism shows. Hence the philosopher – Smith, for instance – is needed. Practice or ordinary experience calls for philosophy and philosophers. Smith understands that the world does not go on finely without the intervention and inventions of human intelligence. His humanistic and philosophical effort to enlighten without proclaiming a liberating revolution depends on the "insulation" of ordinary life from both Socratic philosophy and skepticism while simultaneously injecting philosophy into human life in both interventionist and reconciliationist modes.[6]

Smith is therefore faced with the complex problem of intervening in common life – by publishing his books, for example – without generating those undesirable consequences or misinformed followers who will themselves bring about such consequences. He must intervene, sometimes without seeming to be intervening, and do so while making a persuasive case for a conception of morality that appeals successfully to "our" ordinary moral intuitions as decent, ordinary agents. This makes for a complex solution to the old Platonic problem of how philosophers should be "in" ordinary life, a complexity reflected in the rhetoric of Smith's writings. I have therefore paid a great deal of attention to his rhetoric. It is marked by a sense of moderation, prudence, and balance, even

---

6 In Chapter 5 (sec. 3), I suggested that Smith aspires to be an appropriately prudent or wise instance of those "splendid characters . . . who have brought about the greatest revolutions, both in the situations and opinions of mankind," one of the "greatest statesmen and legislators, the eloquent founders and leaders of the most numerous and most successful sects and parties" (VI.iii.28) – in short, to be a philosophical lawgiver comparable to Solon (recall VI.ii.2.16 and our discussion in Ch. 7 [sec. 4]).

when, as in *The Wealth of Nations* especially, he denounces or unmasks. Even the strikingly polyphonic dialectic of his work is meant to encourage virtues such as moderation and to involve the reader in a deliberate – so to speak, "sympathetic" – conversation guided by a sense of humanity.[7]

To note the complexity of such a project is not to refute it. Yet it seems to me that, precisely in order to help the project succeed, an extension of Smith's notion of "conversation" in a more aggressively "Socratic" direction is warranted. The aim would be to mitigate this "practical" or ethical problem concerning the constructive role for philosophy in the guidance of human life. Despite the dialectical character of the method that leads the reader into and through *The Theory of Moral Sentiments*, genuinely Socratic dialogue, at least as represented by Plato, is systematically avoided. Instead, Smith encourages conversation, understanding, good judgment, sympathy, and moral imagination. The need for extending "conversation" beyond this is not inscribed in the stars but is given by the culture that we have inherited from, among others, Smith. In a free market of ideas, especially religious ideas, to establish a meaningful moral community – that which the pronoun "we" seeks to evoke and fortify – is considerably more of a struggle than even Smith anticipated. The fragmentation of common life, which he certainly understood to be typical of the modern age, and to which his philosophy responds, has reached a point where direct questions of the kind that Socrates asked his fellow citizens must regularly be brought to bear upon the opponents of decency, civility, common humanity, and reason. For those opponents – not so much the Critos, but the Thrasymachuses and the Callicleses – are themselves commonplace. The political, ethical, and rhetorical situation has changed and with it, Smith might himself agree were he writing today, the demands on the mode of public presentation and involvement required of philosophy. The bluntness, directness, and insistence of Socratic dialectic makes it especially valuable in the cultural conditions of late modernity.

7 It is surely one of the ironies of Smith's literary fate that not long after his death he nearly disappeared from the philosophical canon and that his political economy was read in a highly inaccurate way, albeit with the encouragement of some of his more striking epigrams about the system of natural liberty. The turn of the century "Adam Smith problem" is itself a misreading that signals his difficulty in conveying his project as a whole. For discussion of the history of misreadings, see G. Muller, "Some Unanticipated Consequences of Smith's Rhetoric," chapter 15 of *Adam Smith*, pp. 185–93. The issue of Smith's "reception" signals well-known difficulties concerning the role of philosophy in public life (of course he is neither the first nor the last philosopher to be so poorly understood).

A related reason for expanding "conversation" in a Socratic direction stems from Smith's rich view of moral criticism and education. According to that view, we exercise moral criticism at a local level, in reference to a particular context, and seek to conduct ourselves in a manner worthy of a person of virtuous character. We learn to "identify" with the "impartial spectator," and that judicious observer is not a philosopher. Yet in *The Wealth of Nations* (V.i.g.14) Smith suggests that the study of "science and philosophy" be required of "all people of middling or more than middling rank and fortune" so that religious fanaticism and superstition may successfully be resisted by the citizenry. The meaning of "philosophy" here is unclear. It seems not to consist in Socratic dialogue. Philosophy and liberal education generally assist citizens in seeing through fraudulent claims to authority but not, apparently, to evaluate the social or political system as a whole. It clearly is not an education intended to lead us to reject the authority of "rank" or "distinction" in society or to question the "doctrine of Nature" in serious political matters (I.iii.2.3). Yet Smith also acknowledges that the delicate task of judging when the system as a whole must change cannot always be avoided (VI.ii.2.12). Would "philosophy" prepare us to judge wisely at such moments, unless it were understood in a more radically Socratic mode?

Of course, Smith himself did judge when the "system as a whole" required change, and did question the authority of "rank" or "distinction," along with just about everything else. The query is not about the scope of *his* philosophizing but about that which he is, or ought to be, willing to propagate widely. By separating philosophy and ordinary life in such a way as to mute the role of Socratic dialogue in leading us from the one to the other and back, he makes it unnecessarily difficult to see how one becomes a Smithean philosopher, that is, an "impartial spectator" capable of the broad-gauged, systematic ethical assessment and philosophical conversation Smith performs so well. As already noted, the problem is exacerbated by his simultaneously muting philosophy's radically zetetic and aporetic (that is, Socratically questioning and open-ended) voice, demanding that in some form philosophy be widely promulgated, and holding that science be left free to create knowledge. It seems inevitable that philosophy will both spread (and in the process trivialize itself by becoming a popular "philosophy of life") and contract. The contraction would occur through the transformation of philosophers into intellectuals, or perhaps into laborers in some specialized corner of the academic research industry (recall *WN* I.i.9). As such it would encourage an examination of everything but also, perhaps, of little that really matters. This odd but by now familiar combination of extension and suppression would seem to risk depleting both philosophy and ordinary life of the resources each requires to contribute fruitfully to its own and the other's flourishing. Smith would be the first to remark upon and query any such phenomenon, as his own acerbic comments about academia and the division of intellectual labor suggest. In his writing, teaching, and life, he stood against that outcome.[8]

To deepen these worries about the role of philosophy in public life, one may note that the nature of some of *Smith's* own theories is cause for particular concern. Not just any "philosophical curiosity," but Smith's complex version of the "skeptic's method of ethics" and associated views about the imagination risk becoming common currency. In such a process they might well be misinterpreted and debased into vulgar skepticism, a subjectivized aesthetics, and crude expressivism. As already suggested, his moral psychology provides an explanation of moral and political judgments, as well as of theoretical inquiry, that is not entirely harmonious with the sense of moral reality those judgments and inquiry assume. One can understand why he would want to claim that debates about moral psychology – that is, about human nature – are of no practical consequence whatever. But since that is not altogether true, he is left with the attempt to make moral practice self-sufficient while also basing it, and all other human activity, on a doctrine of the emotions and the imagination whose *poiesis* must be made to conceal its own work so as to sustain the Platonic commitments habitual to ordinary moral life as well as intellectual inquiry.

---

8 Contrast this with T. Pinkard's view that for Hegel "Only in what seems to be the detached and alienated institutions of the 'absolute spirit' of late modernity – in its somewhat alienated art, in its modern religious institutions with their apparently peripheral involvement in everyday political life, and in its philosophy, nowadays safely professionalized into distinct departments with their own budget lines in universities – can the participants in modern life assume the impersonal point of view necessary for critically evaluating whether they are truly setting their own ends." The task of modern philosophy, art, and religion "will be to construct and evaluate those accounts of who we are and to continue to skeptically ask if . . . we aren't just fooling ourselves again." *Hegel's Phenomenology* (Cambridge: Cambridge University Press, 1996), pp. 342, 343. Smith would want to ask how philosophers so understood, working in institutions so understood, could possibly construct and evaluate truthful accounts of who "we" are rather than simply reflect the selves they have, thanks to their specialized and removed labors, become. I suspect Smith would infer that we need to rethink the institutional context of philosophy, and so what it means to do philosophy. In this general spirit, see A. Baier, "Doing without Moral Theory," in *Antitheory in Ethics and Moral Conservatism*, ed. S. G. Clarke and E. Simpson (New York: State University of New York Press, 1989), pp. 29–48.

The practical instability of this scheme is underlined by the facts not only that the imagination can destroy as well as create but also that the "fashioned" basis of practice risks becoming an open secret. It is by no means impossible for the residents of the "prison home" to realize that what they took to be natural in a normative sense is an artifact or construction and that there is no return or "ascent" to the natural. And should the "poetry" of the cave be recognized, along with the impossibility of any escape; should Smith's rhetoric fail to soften the character of this aspect of his theoretical project; then his principal theses risk being inverted when disseminated as the public philosophy of modern liberal commercial societies. This has been, arguably, the historical fate of the Enlightenment, whatever causal role Smith's own writings may have played.

In my examination of the crucial exercise of the imagination that Smith terms "sympathy," I argued that although much in Smith's theory depends on the priority of the spectator's standpoint in the sympathetic process, with a slight shift of epistemic emphasis one could (mistakenly) also make veridical – as many have – the standpoint of the actor. That shift destroys the notion of the impartial spectator, the argument against selfishness, the importance of virtues such as self-command and benevolence, and the whole priority of the public, the communal, the shared. Yet just that shift in perspective would be encouraged by the thought that moral judgments are founded not on the impartial spectator's superior grasp of truth and reality but on expression of the self (or so the view might be misinterpreted). Why should not the agent's imagination and passions (or those of similarly situated actors) be granted priority if the measure of right judgment lies in our "moral faculties," contrary to any edifying illusions engendered by custom and history? If practice itself is a complex kind of production, a historical and cultural artifact, then let us liberate ourselves from the constraints that suppress this skeptical truth and rejoice in our newfound freedom. Why should that license to fashion ourselves self-consciously be the preserve of the elite?

Smith would no doubt find any such outlook repulsive and dangerous, for among other things it would risk replacing sympathy and the correspondence of sentiments, all structured around the perspective of the impartial spectator, with agent-centered expressivism and narcissism. As discussed in previous chapters, he has persuasive theoretical and moral responses to any such turn. In our present circumstances, however, what is required in order to disseminate those responses effectively is a more direct attack on the irrationalities, relativisms, and vulgarized skepticisms of the day, in order to preserve the virtues of enlightenment that Smith himself develops so well. This is why the reserve Smith generally shows in his moral philosophy (though he often sheds it in the political economy) should be, as the occasion warrants, replaced with the directness of Socratic inquiry. Doing so would alleviate the difficulties in which Smith's rhetorical stance finds itself, as well as help to fulfill Smith's own ethical project. It would help relieve the tension between his words and his deed of writing, between his statements about philosophy and his activity as a philosopher.

The Socratic dialogue suitable to this task would seem best understood as a means to disabuse one of certain kinds of misleading preconceptions. That is, Socratic dialogue is best understood here primarily as clearing away obstacles, even when this is accomplished through demands that a "What is it?" question be answered. Innocuous as this may sound, it would allow such dialogue to fulfill the ethical and political roles I have sketched. This view of Socratic dialogue helps to reconcile it with the ethical reflection practiced by Smith's impartial spectator, a reflection that yields a judgment about the particular matter at hand. Judgments of propriety and merit (and so, on Smith's account, of proportion and fittingness) can be immensely complicated. Confronting prejudices and ignorance, and Socratically reviewing arguments and accounts of various types, can contribute to clearing a space for discerning judgment. Wise assessment may also require, on some occasions, a systematic appreciation of a sphere of inquiry (say, Smith's political economy) or a comprehensive view of the imperfections of human life (say, of the kind described in *The Theory of Moral Sentiments*). Such occasions on which the impartial spectator ought to philosophize may include those Smith has in mind when recommending that philosophy be required of liberally educated persons. On those occasions, judgment should not be *replaced* by the search for systematic principles but informed and sharpened by it.[9]

The appropriation of Socraticism that I am suggesting clearly amounts

---

9 Gibbard remarks that "Socrates taxed his fellow Athenians with question after question; he forced them to try to give rationales for their unreasoned convictions. He went to extraordinary lengths in pressing them for consistent, principled answers. His targets knew what they thought, and their convictions helped them make sense of the world and to live together. We are all part righteous, muddled Athenian and part Socrates – and we need both parts of this equipment. We want a moral vision that is worth having. The Socratic part adjusts moral vision, but it can subvert it as well. Ideally we would find a scheme to satisfy both parts of our natures, but we may have to settle for a partly articulate skill in balancing them." *Wise Choices, Apt Feelings*, p. 322.

to a very selective use of Plato's Socrates. Socrates may certainly be understood as aiming, through his insistent "What is it" question, at producing a "definition" of the timeless essence of the matter under discussion. I am not, however, proposing that we attempt to extend Smith's views by resurrecting the standard picture of Platonic metaphysics, with its "two-world" theory, doctrine of immortal soul, and so forth. Nor is the proposal that morality somehow be read off from the facts of nature or the will of God. And we ought undoubtedly to drop anything like Platonic social engineering, the rule of philosopher kings or of a Nocturnal Council. Perhaps it follows that there is a better label than "Socraticism" for the stance that I am suggesting, especially given the contrast frequently drawn in this book between Smith, on the one hand, and Socrates or Plato, on the other.

Yet the figure of Socrates is useful at this stage because, first, the name does stand for a method of inquiry whose directness and effectiveness are of the sort now needed. Further, to return to the problem of harmonizing at the theoretical level notions of realism and *poiesis*, Socraticism preserves our trust that "reality" is knowable in principle, and this too makes it useful here, in spite of the potential for misunderstanding. It does not subvert our ordinary assumption that moral judgments as well as theoretical inquiry would be right if ultimately founded on what is the case (not just the case "intersubjectively" or "according to received social practice"). In spite of the disruptive nature of the Socratic enterprise, which understandably provokes fears, that enterprise is in one respect less revisionist than Smith's because more continuous with ordinary life in the way just mentioned. Even the postulation of the ethical Forms (especially "the Good") may capture a quite ordinary conviction about the abidingness and surpassingness of the moral qualities that underlie, in a way notoriously hard to put into words, the harmonies of self and world.[10]

---

10 Although this is scarcely the place to develop a reading of Plato, consider J. McDowell's remark: "It seems plausible that Plato's ethical Forms are, in part at least, a response to uncodifiability: if one cannot formulate what someone has come to know when he cottons on to a practice, say one of concept-application, it is natural to say that he has seen something. . . . The remoteness of the Form of the Good is a metaphorical version of the thesis that value is not in the world, utterly distinct from the dreary literal version which has obsessed recent moral philosophy. The point of the metaphor is the colossal difficulty of attaining a capacity to cope clear-sightedly with the ethical reality which *is* part of our world. Unlike other philosophical responses to uncodifiability, this one may actually work toward moral improvement; negatively, by inducing humility, and positively, by an inspiring effect akin to that of a religious conversion." See "Virtue and Reason," in *An-*

Socrates promises nothing more than knowledge of ignorance. But precisely in order to do so, he also holds us to an "in principle" standard of truth that orients our doubts about what is really the case. This standard may be accused of propagating those doubts but may be defended as possessing the resources to respond to them constructively, by which I mean, in part, in such a way as to discourage the descent into agent-centered expressivism and to encourage the ascent to a life governed by reasoned discovery of truth and error. Even in its self-professed finitude, the Socratic stance is prepared to confront directly the worship of false idols, to hold up to it an image of transcendence through love, and to invite us to participate in a dialogue whose assumptions and purposes are continuous with what we, in practice, most often trust. Both sides of this Socratic project – the dialogical, and the promise of discovery of truth – are needed. Smith would have no objection to talk about an "in principle" standard of truth; the debate concerns how the notion is to be interpreted, and how any tension between it and the self-understanding of ordinary impartial spectators is to be resolved.

The challenge is to develop a pared-down Platonism that encompasses the pedagogic and political benefits of Socratic dialogue as well as the view that philosophy ought to give an account of objectivity and reality that preserves – *at the theoretical level* – the pervasive convictions about the meaning of these notions evident at the phenomenological level. How is any such account even to get started, from within the "moral sentiments" and "ideal judge" framework held by the likes of Smith, a framework whose general assumptions about the sources of value are difficult for us to reject?

This is a hard question, and aspects of any possible answer (issues concerning moral realism, for example) are intensively debated in contemporary ethics. Even when keeping the focus on Smith's moral philosophy, I can here do little more than suggest that one might begin with his guiding vocabulary of the beautiful, proportion, propriety, gracefulness, fittingness, appropriateness. The answer would do well to pick up on this and on his musical metaphors. The "aesthetic" terminology is pervasive in his work because the phenomenon of beauty is, as he convincingly shows, woven into human life at every level. Such notions recur even in his statement that the "essence" of moral qualities is to be understood in terms of their relation to the moral sentiments (see n.

*litheory in Ethics and Moral Conservatism*, ed. S. G. Clark and E. Simpson (New York: State University of New York Press, 1989), p. 105.

3 above). The "qualities" that the "moral faculties" find fitting *do* fit the "moral faculties." Qualities and sentiments, or values and sensibilities, may be matched or suited to each other. This is how it looks at the level of ordinary discourse and experience (including the level of the process of ethical reasoning as described by Smith) even as, by contrast, at the most abstract theoretical level the solution to the implicit "*Euthyphro* problem" tilts toward the doctrine of *poiesis* (that is, the view that things are valuable because we value them).[11] Something like the bidirectionality experienced at the practical level ought to be better preserved at the level of the theoretical account.

Smith's phenomenology faithfully and skillfully articulates the reciprocity of value and valuing that shows itself at that practical level. In order to remain true to the phenomena, we ought to attempt to work out the metaphysics of the circularity of moral quality and human sensibility implied by Smith's Platonic notions of "fittingness." His notion of conversation (with which his notion of imaginative sympathy resonates) might itself help to explain this reciprocity. The strain implicit in a theory of this general kind would perhaps be lessened by the fact that the moral "qualities" in question are for the most part "natural" only in the sense of "given." (Recall that in Chapter 8, this was our fourth sense of the term "nature.") If an account of this kind could be made consistent with the bulk of Smith's moral sentiments theory and political economy, it would contribute to "saving the phenomena" as he so insightfully describes them, in part because it would be more faithfully lodged within them. Taken as a whole, it would be an extension (perhaps one should say, a completion) of Smith's own project, designed to preserve its manifold contributions by developing its resources.[12]

A modulation of a certain kind of philosophical activity, traditionally understood (thanks to Plato) as Socratic dialogue, ought to fill out the notion of "philosophy" Smith himself means to require of educated persons. This might help not only to complete his theoretical project in the manner just described but also to promote the civilizing function

11 As stated in Plato's *Euthyphro* (10a), the problem concerns whether something is good because it is loved by the gods or whether the gods love it because it is good.

12 In pursuing this line of inquiry about the status of moral qualities, one would want to consider whether to weaken the force of *poiesis* by relying yet again on the metaphor of light, taking a clue from Wiggins's concluding remarks in "Truth, Invention, and the Meaning of Life." He there suggests a phenomenological account that sees "value properties not as created but as *lit up* by the focus that the man who lives the life brings to the world" (p. 137). Wiggins's essay is one source of inspiration for my gestures toward a metaphysics of "reciprocity" of valuing and values.

EPILOGUE

urgently required of liberal education in the late modern age. Smith tells us that sound education is partly a matter of emulating an "archetype of perfection."[13] We ought to work out further the place of the love of wisdom in this moral ideal, in the hope of understanding how the "sublime speculation of the contemplative philosopher" Smith refers to in the passage quoted at the beginning of this Epilogue may be more fully harmonized with the virtues of ordinary human life.

13 At *TMS* VI.iii.25 Smith describes the high "idea of exact propriety and perfection" and remarks that the wise man "has studied this idea more than other people, he comprehends it more distinctly, he has formed a much more correct image of it, and is much more deeply enamoured of its exquisite and divine beauty. He endeavours as well as he can, to assimilate his own character to this archetype of perfection." Cf. the reference in Plato's *Laws* (817b) to the importance of our imitating the "most beautiful and best way of life," which is the "truest tragedy."

# BIBLIOGRAPHY

The bibliography includes all the works cited in this book, as well as works bearing on Adam Smith that I have found particularly useful in preparing this study but have not cited in the notes. I have not aimed to compile a complete bibliography of works on Adam Smith or of works relevant to the study of Smith. For further bibliographical references, the reader should consult the books by Amano, Cordasco and Franklin, and Lightwood, as well as the bibliography in Ross, *The Life of Adam Smith* (cited below). For Smith's works, see "Texts and Acknowledgments" in the present volume.

Abel, G. *Stoizismus und Frühe Neuzeit.* Berlin: de Gruyter, 1978.
Addison, J., and R. Steele. *The Spectator.* 5 vols. Ed. D. F. Bond. Oxford: Clarendon Press, 1965.
Adiseshiah, M. S. *Some Thoughts on Adam Smith's Theory of Division of Labour.* Trivandrum, India: University of Kerala, 1977.
Adorno, T. W. *Negative Dialectics.* Trans. E. B. Ashton. New York: Continuum, 1973.
Agnew, J.-C. *Worlds Apart: The Market and the Theater in Anglo-American Thought, 1550–1750.* Cambridge: Cambridge University Press, 1986.
Amano, K. *Bibliography of the Classical Economics.* Science Council of Japan, Economic Series, no. 27. Tokyo: Science Council of Japan 1961.
Anderson, G. M. "Mr. Smith and the Preachers: The Economics of Religion in the *Wealth of Nations.*" *Journal of Political Economy* 96 (1988): 1066–88.
Annas, J. "Doing without Objective Values: Ancient and Modern Strategies." In

*The Norms of Nature: Studies in Hellenistic Ethics*, ed. M. Schofield and G. Striker. Cambridge: Cambridge University Press, 1986. Pp. 3–29.

*The Morality of Happiness.* Oxford: Oxford University Press, 1993.

Anscombe, G. E. M. "Modern Moral Philosophy." *Philosophy* 33 (1958): 1–19.

Anspach, R. "The Implications of the *Theory of Moral Sentiments* for Adam Smith's Economic Thought." *History of Political Economy* 4 (1972): 176–206.

Appleby, J. O. *Economic Thought and Ideology in Seventeenth-Century England.* Princeton: Princeton University Press, 1978.

Arac, J., ed. *Postmodernism and Politics.* Minneapolis: University of Minnesota Press, 1986.

Aristotle. *Nicomachean Ethics.* Trans. T. Irwin. Indianapolis: Hackett, 1985.

Audi, R. "The Separation of Church and State and the Obligations of Citizenship." *Philosophy and Public Affairs* 18 (1989): 259–96.

Bagolini, L. *David Hume e Adam Smith.* Bologna: Pàtron, 1976.

"The Topicality of Adam Smith's Notion of Sympathy and Judicial Evaluations." In *Essays on Adam Smith*, ed. A. S. Skinner and E. T. Wilson. Oxford: Clarendon Press, 1975. Pp. 100–113.

Baier, A. C. "Doing without Moral Theory." In *Anti-theory in Ethics and Moral Conservatism*, ed. S. G. Clarke and E. Simpson. New York: State University of New York Press, 1989. Pp. 29–48.

*A Progress of Sentiments: Reflections on Hume's "Treatise."* Cambridge, Mass.: Harvard University Press, 1991.

Bailiff, J. D. "Some Comments on the 'Ideal Observer.' " *Philosophy and Phenomenological Research* 24 (1963–4): 423–8.

Barish, J. A. *The Antitheatrical Prejudice.* Berkeley and Los Angeles: University of California Press, 1981.

Barnes, J. "Aristotle and the Methods of Ethics." *Revue Internationale de Philosophie* 34 (1980): 490–511.

Bayle, P. *The Dictionary Historical and Critical.* 5 vols. Ed. B. Feldman and R. Richardson, Jr. New York: Garland, 1984.

Beck, L. W. *The Actor and the Spectator.* New Haven: Yale University Press, 1977.

Becker, C. L. *The Heavenly City of the Eighteenth-Century Philosophers.* New Haven: Yale University Press, 1966.

Becker, L. C. *Reciprocity.* London: Routledge & Kegan Paul, 1986.

Berger, P. L. *Facing Up to Modernity: Excursions in Society, Politics, and Religion.* New York: Basic Books, 1977.

Berkeley, G. *Works on Vision.* Ed. C. M. Turbayne. Indianapolis: Bobbs-Merrill, 1963.

Berlin, I. *Four Essays on Liberty.* Oxford: Oxford University Press, 1969.

Berns, L. "Aristotle and Adam Smith on Justice: Cooperation between Ancients and Moderns?" *Review of Metaphysics* 48 (1994): 71–90.

Berry, C. J. "Adam Smith: Commerce, Liberty and Modernity." In *Philosophers of the Enlightenment*, ed. P. Gilmour. Edinburgh: Edinburgh University Press, 1989. Pp. 113–32.

"Adam Smith and the Virtues of Commerce." In *Virtue*, vol. 34 of *Nomos*, ed. J. W. Chapman and W. A. Galston. New York: New York University Press, 1992. Pp. 69–88.

"Adam Smith's *Considerations* on Language." *Journal of the History of Ideas* 35 (1974): 130–8.

Bevilacqua, V. M. "Adam Smith and Some Philosophical Origins of Eighteenth-Century Rhetorical Theory." *Modern Language Review* 43 (1968): 559–68.

"Adam Smith's Lectures on Rhetoric and Belles Lettres." *Studies in Scottish Literature* 3–4 (1965–67): 41–60.

Billet, L. "The Just Economy: The Moral Basis of the *Wealth of Nations*." *Review of Social Economy* 34 (1976): 295–315.

Bittermann, H. J. "Adam Smith's Empiricism and the Law of Nature." Pts. 1–2. *Journal of Political Economy* 48 (1940): 487–520, 703–34.

Black, R. D. "Smith's Contribution in Historical Perspective." In *The Market and the State: Essays in Honour of Adam Smith*, ed. T. Wilson and A. S. Skinner. Oxford: Clarendon Press, 1976. Pp. 42–71.

Blackburn, S. "Errors in the Phenomenology of Value." Rpt. in *Morality and the Good Life*, ed. T. Carson and P. Moser. Oxford: Oxford University Press, 1997. Pp. 324–337.

"How to Be an Ethical Antirealist." Rpt. in *Moral Discourse and Practice: Some Philosophical Approaches*, ed. S. Darwall, A. Gibbard, and P. Railton. New York: Oxford University Press, 1997. Pp. 167–78.

Blum, L. A. *Friendship, Altruism and Morality*. London: Routledge & Kegan Paul, 1980.

Bonar, J. *A Catalogue of the Library of Adam Smith*. 2nd ed. 1894. Rpt. New York: Kelley, 1966.

*Moral Sense*. London: New York: Macmillan, 1930.

Bowman, J. R. "Competition and the Microfoundations of the Capitalist Economy: Towards the Redefinition of *Homo economicus*." *Politics and Society* 18 (1990): 233–42.

Brague, R. *Aristote et la question du monde*. Paris: PUF, 1988.

Brandt, R. B. *Ethical Theory: The Problems of Normative and Critical Ethics*. Englewood Cliffs, N.J.: Prentice-Hall, 1959.

"Traits of Character: A Conceptual Analysis." *American Philosophical Quarterly* 7 (1970): 23–37.

Broad, C. D. "Some Reflections on Moral-Sense Theories in Ethics." *Proceedings of the Aristotelian Society* 45 (1944–5): 131–66.

Broadie, A. *The Tradition of Scottish Philosophy*. Edinburgh: Polygon, 1990.

Brown, K. L. "Dating Adam Smith's Essay 'Of the External Senses.' " *Journal of the History of Ideas* 53 (1992): 333–7.

Brown, M. *Adam Smith's Economics*. London: Croom Helm, 1988.

Brown, V. *Adam Smith's Discourse: Canonicity, Commerce and Conscience*. London: Routledge, 1994.

Brown, W. H. *The Power of Sympathy*. Columbus: Ohio State University Press, 1969.

Brühlmeier, D. *Die Rechts- und Staatslehre von Adam Smith und die Interessentheorie der Verfassung*. Berlin: Duncker & Humblot, 1988.

Bryson, G. *Man and Society: The Scottish Inquiry of the Eighteenth Century*. 1945. Rpt. New York: Kelley, 1968.

Buchanan, A. *Ethics, Efficiency, and the Market*. Totowa, N.J.: Rowman & Allanheld, 1985.

Buchanan, J. M. "Public Goods and Natural Liberty." In *The Market and the State: Essays in Honour of Adam Smith*, ed. T. Wilson and A. S. Skinner. Oxford: Clarendon Press, 1976. Pp. 272–95.

Burnyeat, M. "Can the Skeptic Live his Skepticism?" In *The Skeptical Tradition*, ed. M. Burnyeat. Berkeley and Los Angeles: University of California Press, 1983. Pp. 117–48.

"The Sceptic in His Place and Time." In *Philosophy in History*, ed. R. Rorty, J. B. Schneewind, and Q. Skinner. Cambridge: Cambridge University Press, 1990. Pp. 225–54.

Butchvarov, P. *Skepticism in Ethics*. Bloomington: Indiana University Press, 1989.

Butler, J. *Sermons*. 1726. Ed. W. E. Gladstone. Oxford: Clarendon Press, 1896.

Cairncross, A. "The Market and the State." In *The Market and the State: Essays in Honour of Adam Smith*, ed. T. Wilson and A. S. Skinner. Oxford: Clarendon Press, 1976. Pp. 113–34.

Campbell, R. H., and A. S. Skinner, eds. *The Origins and Nature of the Scottish Enlightenment*. Edinburgh: Donald, 1982.

Campbell, T. D. "Adam Smith and Natural Liberty." *Political Studies* 25 (1978): 523–34.

*Adam Smith's Science of Morals*. Totowa, N.J.: Rowman & Littlefield, 1971.

"Scientific Explanation and Ethical Justification in the *Moral Sentiments*." In *Essays on Adam Smith*, ed. A. S. Skinner and E. T. Wilson. Oxford: Clarendon Press, 1975.

Campbell, T. D., and I. Ross. "The Theory and Practice of the Wise and Virtuous Man: Reflections on Adam Smith's Response to Hume's Deathbed Wish." *Studies in Eighteenth-Century Culture* 11 (1982): 65–75.

Campbell, T. D., and A. S. Skinner. *Adam Smith*. London: Croom Helm, 1985.

Carson, T. L. "Could Ideal Observers Disagree? A Reply to Taliaferro." *Philosophy and Phenomenological Research* 50 (1989): 115–24.

*The Status of Morality*. Dordrecht: Reidel, 1984.

Casey, J. *Pagan Virtue: An Essay in Ethics*. Oxford: Clarendon Press, 1990.

Cassirer, E. *The Philosophy of the Enlightenment*. Trans. F. C. A. Koelln and J. P. Pettegrove. Princeton: Princeton University Press, 1968.

*The Platonic Renaissance in England*. Trans. J. P. Pettegrove. New York: Gordian, 1970.

Caton, H. "Adam Smith's Legacy." In *The Politics of Progress: The Origins and Development of the Commercial Republic, 1600–1835*. Gainesville: University of Florida Press, 1988. Pp. 348–56.

Cavell, S. *The Claim of Reason: Wittgenstein, Skepticism, Morality, and Tragedy*. Oxford: Oxford University Press, 1979.

Chapman, J. W., and W. A. Galston, eds. *Virtue*, vol. 34 of *Nomos*. New York: New York University Press, 1992.

Clark, H. C. "Women and Humanity in Scottish Enlightenment Social Thought: The Case of Adam Smith." *Historical Reflections* 19 (1993): 335–61.

Clarke, M. L. *Greek Studies in England, 1700–1830*. Cambridge: Cambridge University Press, 1945.

Clarke, T. "The Legacy of Skepticism." *Journal of Philosophy* 69 (1972): 754–69.

Coase, R. H. "Adam Smith's View of Man." *Journal of Law and Economics* 19 (1976): 529–46.

Coats, A. W. "Adam Smith: The Modern Re-appraisal." *Renaissance and Modern Studies* 6 (1962): 25–48.

Cole, A. H. "Puzzles of the *Wealth of Nations.*" *Canadian Journal of Economics and Political Science* 24 (1958): 1–8.

Condorcet, S. Grouchy Ve. *Théorie des sentimens moraux ou essai analytique; Sur les Principes des Jugemens que portent naturellment les Hommes, d'abord sur les Actions des autres, et ensuite sur leurs propres Actions: Suivi d'une Dissertation sur l'Origine des Langues; Par Adam Smith; Traduit de l'Anglais, sur la septième et dernière Édition, par S. Grouchy Ve. Condorcet. Elle y a joint huit Lettres sur la Sympathie. Tome Second.* Paris: F. Buisson, 1798.

Cooper, J. "Review of M. Nussbaum's *The Fragility of Goodness: Luck and Ethics in Greek Tragedy and Philosophy.*" *Philosophical Review* 97 (1988): 543–64.

Copley, S., and K. Sutherland, eds. *Adam Smith's "Wealth of Nations": New Interdisciplinary Essays.* Manchester, UK: Manchester University Press, 1995.

Cordasco, F., and B. Franklin. *Adam Smith: A Bibliographical Checklist.* New York: Franklin, 1950.

Cremaschi, S. "Adam Smith: Skeptical Newtonianism, Disenchanted Republicanism, and the Birth of Social Science." In *Knowledge and Politics: Case Studies in the Relationship between Epistemology and Political Philosophy,* ed. M. Dascal and O. Gruengard. Boulder, Col.: Westview, 1989. Pp. 83–110.

Cropsey, J. "Adam Smith and Political Philosophy." In *Essays on Adam Smith,* ed. A. S. Skinner and T. Wilson. Oxford: Clarendon Press, 1975. Pp. 132–153.

"The Invisible Hand: Moral and Political Considerations." In *Adam Smith and Modern Political Economy: Bicentennial Essays on "The Wealth of Nations,"* ed. G. P. O'Driscoll, Jr., Ames: Iowa State University Press, 1979. Pp. 165–76.

*Polity and Economy: An Interpretation of the Principles of Adam Smith.* 1957. Rpt. Westport, Conn.: Greenwood, 1977.

Cumming, R. D. *Human Nature and History: A Study of the Development of Liberal Political Thought.* 2 vols. Chicago: University of Chicago Press, 1969.

Curtius, E. R. *European Literature and the Latin Middle Ages.* Trans. W. R. Trask. New York: Harper & Row, 1953.

D'Alembert, Jean le Rond. *Essai sur les eléments de philosophie.* 1759. Vol. 2 of D'Alembert, *Oeuvres philosophiques, historiques et littéraires,* ed. R. N. Schwab. Hildesheim: Olms, 1965.

Dancy, J. *Moral Reasons.* Oxford: Blackwell Publisher, 1994.

Danner, P. L. "Sympathy and Exchangeable Value: Keys to Adam Smith's Social Philosophy." *Review of Social Economy* 34 (1976): 317–31.

Danto, A. *s.v.* "Naturalism." In *The Encyclopedia of Philosophy,* ed. P. Edwards. New York: Macmillan, 1967.

Darwall, S. L. *The British Moralists and the Internal "Ought": 1640–1740.* Cambridge: Cambridge University Press, 1995.

Darwall, S. L., A. Gibbard, and P. Railton. "Toward *Fin de siècle* Ethics: Some Trends." In *Moral Discourse and Practice,* ed. Darwall, Gibbard, and Railton. New York: Oxford University Press, 1997. Pp. 3–47.

Darwall, S. L., A. Gibbard, and P. Railton, eds. *Moral Discourse and Practice: Some Philosophical Approaches*. New York: Oxford University Press, 1997.

Darwin, C. *"The Descent of Man" and "Selection in Relation to Sex."* 2 vols. London: J. Murray, 1871.

Davenport, H. J. "The Ethics of the *Wealth of Nations*." A discussion of G. R. Morrow's *Ethical and Economic Theories of Adam Smith*, with reply. *Philosophical Review* 34 (1925): 599–609.

Davis, D. B. *The Problem of Slavery in the Age of Revolution: 1770–1823*. Ithaca: Cornell University Press, 1975.

*The Problem of Slavery in Western Culture*. Ithaca: Cornell University Press, 1967.

Dawson, D. "Is Sympathy So Surprising? Adam Smith and French Fictions of Sympathy." *Eighteenth-Century Life* 15 (1991): 147–62.

Deigh, J. "Empathy and Universalizability." *Ethics* 105 (1995): 743–63.

Deleuze, G. *Empiricism and Subjectivity: An Essay on Hume's Theory of Human Nature*. Trans. C. V. Boundas. New York: Columbia University Press, 1991.

Dent, N. J. H. *The Moral Psychology of the Virtues*. Cambridge: Cambridge University Press, 1984.

Den Uyl, D. J. "Power, Politics, and Religion in Spinoza's Political Thought." *Jewish Political Studies Review* 7 (1995): 77–106.

"Self-Love and Benevolence." *Reason Papers* 9 (1983): 57–60.

"Shaftesbury and the Modern Problem of Virtue." *Social Philosophy and Policy* 15 (1998): 275–316.

*The Virtue of Prudence*. New York: Lang, 1991.

Den Uyl, D. J., and C. L., Griswold, Jr. "Adam Smith on Friendship and Love." *Review of Metaphysics* 49 (1996): 609–37.

Descartes, R. *The Philosophical Works of Descartes*. 2 vols. Trans. E. S. Haldane and G. R. T. Ross. Cambridge: Cambridge University Press, 1972.

Dickey, L. "Historicizing the 'Adam Smith Problem': Conceptual, Historiographical, and Textual Issues." *Journal of Modern History* 58 (1986): 579–609.

Dionysius of Halicarnassus. *On Literary Composition*. Ed. and trans. W. R. Roberts. London: Macmillan, 1910.

Du Bos, M. l'Abbé. *Critical Reflections on Poetry and Painting*. Trans. T. Nugent. 1748. Rpt. New York: AMS, 1978.

Dumont, L. *From Mandeville to Marx*. Chicago: University of Chicago Press, 1977.

Dunn, J. "From Applied Theology to Social Analysis: The Break between John Locke and the Scottish Enlightenment." In *Wealth and Virtue: the Shaping of Political Economy in the Scottish Enlightenment*, ed. I. Hont and M. Ignatieff. Cambridge: Cambridge University Press, 1985. Pp. 119–35.

Dwyer, J. *Virtuous Discourse: Sensibility and Community in Late Eighteenth-Century Scotland*. Edinburgh: Donald, 1987.

Edelstein, L. *The Meaning of Stoicism*. Cambridge, Mass.: Harvard University Press, 1966.

Eisenberg, N., and J. Strayer, eds. *Empathy and Its Development*. Cambridge: Cambridge University Press, 1987.

Eliot, T. D. "The Relations between Adam Smith and Benjamin Franklin before 1776." *Political Science Quarterly* 39 (1924): 67–96.

Epictetus. *Discourses*. 2 vols. Trans. W. A. Oldfather. Cambridge, Mass.: Harvard University Press, 1979.

Erasmus, D. *The Praise of Folly*. 1511. Trans. C. H. Miller. New Haven: Yale University Press, 1979.

Evensky, J. "Adam Smith on the Human Foundation of a Successful Liberal Society." *History of Political Economy* 25 (1993): 395–412.

Evensky, J., and R. P. Malloy, eds. *Adam Smith and The Philosophy of Law and Economics*. Dordrecht: Kluwer, 1994.

Fay, C. *Adam Smith and the Scotland of His Day*. Cambridge: Cambridge University Press, 1956.

*The World of Adam Smith*. Cambridge: Heffer, 1960.

*Federalist Papers, The*. Ed. C. Rossiter. New York: New American Library, 1961.

Ferguson, A. *An Essay on the History of Civil Society*. 1767. Rpt. New York: Garland, 1971.

Ferreira, M. J. "Hume and Imagination: Sympathy and 'The Other.'" *International Philosophical Quarterly* 34 (1994): 39–57.

*Scepticism and Reasonable Doubt*. Oxford: Clarendon Press, 1986.

Finnis, J. *Natural Law and Natural Rights*. Oxford: Oxford University Press, 1980.

Firth, R. "Comments on Professor Postow's Paper." Discussion. *Philosophy and Phenomenological Research* 12 (1978): 122–3.

"Ethical Absolutism and the Ideal Observer." *Philosophy and Phenomenological Research* 12 (1951–2): 317–45.

Fleischacker, S. "Philosophy in Moral Practice: Kant and Adam Smith." *Kant-Studien* 82 (1991): 249–69.

*A Third Concept of Liberty: Judgment and Freedom in Aristotle, Adam Smith, and Kant*. Princeton: Princeton University Press, in press.

Fleischmann, W. B. "The Debt of the Enlightenment to Lucretius." *Studies on Voltaire and the Eighteenth Century* 25 (1963): 631–42.

Fogelin, R. *Hume's Skepticism in the "Treatise of Human Nature."* London: Routledge & Kegan Paul, 1985.

"The Tendency of Hume's Skepticism." In *The Skeptical Tradition*, ed. M. Burnyeat. Berkeley and Los Angeles: University of California Press, 1983. Pp. 397–412.

Foley, V. "The Division of Labor in Plato and Smith." *History of Political Economy* 6 (1974): 220–41.

"Smith and the Greeks: A Reply to Professor McNulty's Comments." *History of Political Economy* 7 (1975): 379–89.

*The Social Physics of Adam Smith*. West Lafayette, Ind.: Purdue University Press, 1976.

Forbes, D. "Sceptical Whiggism, Commerce and Liberty." In *Essays on Adam Smith*, ed. A. S. Skinner and T. Wilson. Oxford: Oxford University Press, 1976. Pp. 179–201.

Foucault, M. *The Foucault Reader*. Ed. P. Rabinow. New York: Pantheon, 1984.

*The Order of Things: An Archaeology of the Human Sciences*. London: Tavistock, 1970.

Frank, R. *Passions within Reason*. New York: Norton, 1988.

Frankfurt, H. G. "Freedom of the Will and the Concept of a Person." *Journal of Philosophy* 68 (1971): 5–20.

Franklin, R. S. "Smithian Economics and Its Pernicious Legacy." In *Adam Smith: Critical Assessments*, ed. J. C. Wood, vol. 3. London: Croon Helm, 1984. Pp. 470–8.

Frede, M. *Essays in Ancient Philosophy*. Minneapolis: University of Minnesota Press, 1987.

"The Sceptic's Two Kinds of Assent." In *Philosophy in History*, ed. R. Rorty, J. B. Schneewind, and Q. Skinner. Cambridge: Cambridge University Press, 1990. Pp. 255–278.

French, P. A., T. E. Uehling, and H. K. Wettstein, eds. *Ethical Theory: Character and Virtue*. Midwest Studies in Philosophy, no. 13. Notre Dame, Ind.: University of Notre Dame Press, 1988.

Fry, M., ed. *Adam Smith's Legacy*. New York: Routledge, Chapman, & Hall, 1992.

Gadamer, H.-G. *Truth and Method*. 2nd rev. ed. Trans. J. Weinsheimer and D. G. Marshall. New York: Continuum, 1994.

Galston, W. A. "Practical Philosophy and the Bill of Rights: Perspectives on Some Contemporary Issues." In *A Culture of Rights*, ed. M. Lacey and K. Haakonssen. Cambridge: Cambridge University Press, 1991. Pp. 215–65.

"Tocqueville on Liberalism and Religion." *Social Research* 54 (1987): 499–18.

Gerber, J. C. "Emerson and the Political Economists." *New England Quarterly* 22 (1940): 336–57.

Gibbard, A. *Wise Choices, Apt Feelings*. Cambridge, Mass.: Harvard University Press, 1990.

Gill, E. R. "Justice in Adam Smith: The Right and the Good." *Review of Social Economy* 34 (1976): 275–94.

Glahe, F. R., ed. *Adam Smith and the Wealth of Nations*. Boulder: Colorado Associated University Press, 1978.

Goffman, E. *The Presentation of Self in Everyday Life*. New York: Anchor, 1959.

Goldman, A. I. "Empathy, Mind, and Morals." *Proceedings and Addresses of the American Philosophical Association* 66 (1992): 17–41.

Goldstein, L. J. "The Two Theses of Methodological Individualism." *British Journal for the Philosophy of Science* 9 (1958): 1–11.

Gramm, W. S. "The Selective Interpretation of Adam Smith." *Journal of Economic Issues* 14 (1980): 119–42.

Grampp, W. D. "Adam Smith and the Economic Man." *Journal of Political Economy* 56 (1948): 315–36.

Grave, S. A. *The Scottish Philosophy of Common Sense*. Oxford: Clarendon Press, 1960.

Gray, A. *Adam Smith*. London: Historical Association, 1948.

Gray, J. *Enlightenment's Wake: Politics and Culture at the Close of the Modern Age*. New York: Routledge, 1995.

Griswold, C. L., Jr. "Happiness, Tranquillity, and Philosophy." In *In Pursuit of Happiness*, ed. L. Rouner. Boston University Studies in Philosophy and Religion, no. 16. Notre Dame, Ind.: University of Notre Dame Press, 1995. Pp. 13–37. Rpt. (with significant emendations) in *Critical Review* 10 (1996): 1–32.

"Nature and Philosophy: Adam Smith on Stoicism, Aesthetic Reconciliation, and Imagination." *Man and World* 29 (1996): 187–213.

"Plato's Metaphilosophy: Why Plato Wrote Dialogues." In *Platonic Writings, Platonic Readings*, ed. C. L. Griswold, Jr. New York: Routledge & Kegan Paul, 1988. Pp. 143–67.

"Religion and Community: Adam Smith on the Virtues of Liberty." *Journal of the History of Philosophy* 35 (1997): 395–419.

Review of V. Brown, *Adam Smith's Discourse: Canonicity, Commerce, and Conscience;* P. Minowitz, *Profits, Priests, and Princes: Adam Smith's Emancipation of Economics from Politics and Religion;* M. J. Shapiro, *Reading "Adam Smith": Desire, History, and Value;* and P. Werhane, *Adam Smith and His Legacy for Modern Capitalism.* All in *Times Literary Supplement,* July 14, 1995, p. 30.

Review of J. Muller, *Adam Smith in His Time and Ours;* S. Justman, *The Autonomous Male of Adam Smith;* and H. Mizuta and C. Sugiyama, eds., *Adam Smith: International Perspectives.* All in *Journal of the History of Philosophy* 35 (1997): 629–32.

"Rhetoric and Ethics: Adam Smith on Theorizing about the Moral Sentiments." *Philosophy and Rhetoric* 24 (1991): 213–37. Rpt. (with emendations) in *Science, Politics, and Social Practice* (Festschrift for Robert S. Cohen), ed. K. Gavroglu, J. Stachel, and M. W. Wartofsky (Dordrecht: Kluwer, 1995). Pp. 293–318.

*Self-knowledge in Plato's "Phaedrus."* New Haven: Yale University Press, 1986. Rpt. with new preface and bibliography. University Park: Pennsylvania State University Press, 1996.

Groenewegen, P. D. "Adam Smith and the Division of Labour: A Bicentenary Estimate." *Australian Economic Papers* 16 (1977): 161–74.

"A New Catalogue of Adam Smith's Library." In *Adam Smith: Critical Assessments,* ed. J. C. Wood, vol. 3. London: Croon Helm, 1984. Pp. 98–105.

Grotius, H. *On the Law of War and Peace.* 1625. Trans. F. W. Kelsey. Oxford: Clarendon Press, 1925.

Gutmann, A., ed. *Multiculturalism: Examining the Politics of Recognition.* Princeton: Princeton University Press, 1994.

Guttridge, G. H. "Adam Smith on the American Revolution: An Unpublished Memorial." *American Historical Review* 38 (1932–3): 714–20.

Haakonssen, K. *s.v.* "Adam Smith." *Routledge Encyclopedia of Philosophy,* ed. E. Craig. London: Routledge, in press.

"Hume: Realist and Sceptic." Review of P. Jones, D. Miller, D. F. Norton, J. P. Wright. *Australasian Journal of Philosophy* 62 (1984): 410–419.

"Jurisprudence and Politics in Adam Smith." In *Traditions of Liberalism,* ed. K. Haakonssen. St. Leonards, Australia: Centre for Independent Studies, 1988. Pp. 107–115.

"Moral Philosophy and Natural Law: From the Cambridge Platonists to the Scottish Enlightenment." *Political Science* 40 (1988): 97–110.

*Natural Law and Moral Philosophy: From Grotius to the Scottish Enlightenment.* Cambridge: Cambridge University Press, 1996.

"Natural Law and the Scottish Enlightenment." In *Man and Nature,* ed. D. H. Jory and C. Stewart-Robertson. Proceedings of the Canadian Society for Eighteenth-Century Studies, vol. 4. Edmonton: Canadian Society for Eighteenth-Century Studies, 1985. Pp. 47–79.

*The Science of a Legislator: The Natural Jurisprudence of David Hume and Adam Smith.* Cambridge: Cambridge University Press, 1981.

"What Might Properly Be Called Natural Jurisprudence?" In *The Origins and Nature of the Scottish Enlightenment,* ed. R. H. Campbell and A. S. Skinner. Edinburgh: J. Donald, 1982. Pp. 205–225.

Habermas, J. *Communication and the Evolution of Society.* Trans. T. McCarthy. Boston: Beacon, 1979.

*The Philosophical Discourse of Modernity: Twelve Lectures.* Trans. F. Lawrence. Cambridge, Mass.: MIT Press, 1995.

Halévy, E. *The Growth of Philosophic Radicalism.* Trans. M. Morris. London: Faber & Gwyer, 1928.

Hamowy, R. *The Scottish Enlightenment and the Theory of Spontaneous Order. Journal of the History of Philosophy* Monograph Series. Carbondale: Southern Illinois University Press, 1987.

Hampshire, S. *Innocence and Experience.* Cambridge, Mass.: Harvard University Press, 1989.

*Two Theories of Morality.* Oxford: Oxford University Press, 1977.

Hardie, W. F. R. "The Final Good in Aristotle's Ethics." *The Journal of the Royal Institute of Philosophy* 40 (1965): 277–95.

Hare, R. M. *Moral Thinking: Its Levels, Method, and Point.* Oxford: Clarendon Press, 1981.

Harman, G. "Moral Agent and Impartial Spectator." The 1986 Lindley Lecture, published by the Philosophy Department, University of Kansas, 1986.

"Moral Relativism Defended." *Philosophical Review* 84 (1975): 3–22.

*The Nature of Morality.* New York: Oxford University Press, 1977.

Harpham, E. J. "Liberalism, Civic Humanism, and the Case of Adam Smith." *American Political Science Review* 78 (1984): 764–74.

Harrison, J. "Some Comments on Professor Firth's Ideal Observer Theory." *Philosophy and Phenomenological Research* 17 (1956): 256–62.

Hayek, F. A. *New Studies in Philosophy, Politics, Economics and the History of Ideas.* Chicago: University of Chicago Press, 1978.

Heath, E. "The Commerce of Sympathy: Adam Smith on the Emergence of Morals." *Journal of the History of Philosophy* 33 (1995): 447–66.

Hegel, G. W. F. *Elements of the Philosophy of Right.* Ed. A. W. Wood, trans. H. B. Nisbet. Cambridge: Cambridge University Press, 1995.

*Faith and Knowledge.* Trans. W. Cerf and H. S. Harris. Albany: State University of New York Press, 1977.

Heilbroner, R. L. "The Paradox of Progress: Decline and Decay in *The Wealth of Nations.*" *Journal of the History of Ideas* 34 (1973): 243–62.

Heise, P. A. "Stoicism in the *EPS*: The Foundation of Adam Smith's Moral Philosophy." In *The Classical Tradition in Economic Thought,* ed. I. H. Rima, vol. 11 of *Perspectives on the History of Economic Thought.* Hants, UK: Elgar, 1995. Pp. 17–30.

Herman, B. *The Practice of Moral Judgment.* Cambridge, Mass.: Harvard University Press, 1993.

Hetherington, N. S. "Isaac Newton's Influence on Adam Smith's Natural Laws in Economics." *Journal of the History of Ideas* 44 (1983): 497–505.

Hildebrand, B. *Die Nationalökonomie der Gegenwart und Zukunft, und andere gesammelte Schriften*, with introduction by H. Gehrig. In vol. 22 of *Sammlung Sozialwissenschaftlicher Meister* (Jena: 1922).

Hindson, P., and T. Gray. *Burke's Dramatic Theory of Politics*. Aldershot, UK: Avebury, 1988.

Hirschman, A. O. *The Passions and the Interests: Political Arguments for Capitalism before Its Triumph*. Princeton: Princeton University Press, 1977.

Hobbes. *Leviathan*. 1651. Ed. E. Curley. Indianapolis: Hackett, 1994.

Hogan, J. M. "Historiography and Ethics in Adam Smith's Lectures on Rhetoric, 1762–1763." *Rhetorica* 2 (1984): 75–91.

Hollander, S. *The Economics of Adam Smith*. London: Heinemann, 1973.

"The Founder of a School." In J. M. Clark et al., *Adam Smith, 1776–1926*. 1928. Rpt. New York: Kelley, 1966. Pp. 22–52.

Hont, I., and M. Ignatieff, eds. *Wealth and Virtue: The Shaping of Political Economy in the Scottish Enlightenment*. Cambridge: Cambridge University Press, 1985.

Hook, A., and R. B. Sher, eds. *The Glasgow Enlightenment*. East Lothian, UK: Tuckwell, 1995.

Hope, V., ed. *Philosophers of the Scottish Enlightenment*. Edinburgh: Edinburgh University Press, 1984.

*Virtue by Consensus: The Moral Philosophy of Hutcheson, Hume, and Adam Smith*. Oxford: Oxford University Press, 1989.

Horkheimer, M., and T. W. Adorno. *Dialectic of Enlightenment*. Trans. J. Cumming. New York: Continuum, 1995.

Howell, W. S. "Adam Smith's Lectures on Rhetoric: An Historical Assessment." In *Essays on Adam Smith*, ed. A. S. Skinner and T. Wilson. Oxford: Clarendon Press, 1975. Pp. 11–43.

Hoy, D. C. "Nietzsche, Hume, and the Genealogical Method." In *Nietzsche as Affirmative Thinker*, ed. Y. Yovel. Dordrecht: Nijhoff, 1986. Pp. 20–38.

Hudson, W. D., ed. *The Is–Ought Question: A Collection of Papers on the Central Problem in Moral Philosophy*. London: Macmillan, 1969.

Hume, D. *Enquiries Concerning Human Understanding and Concerning the Principles of Morals*. Ed. L. A. Selby-Bigge; 3rd rev. ed., ed. P. H. Nidditch. Oxford: Clarendon Press, 1989.

*Essays Moral, Political, and Literary*. Rev. ed. Ed. E. F. Miller. Indianapolis: Liberty, 1987.

*The Letters of David Hume*. 2 vols. Ed. J. Y. T. Greig. Oxford: Clarendon Press, 1932.

*The Natural History of Religion*. Ed. H. E. Root. Stanford: Stanford University Press, 1957.

*A Treatise of Human Nature*. Ed. L. A. Selby-Bigge; 2nd rev. ed., ed. P. H. Nidditch. Oxford: Clarendon Press, 1978.

Hundert, E. J. *The Enlightenment's Fable: Bernard Mandeville and the Discovery of Society*. Cambridge: Cambridge University Press, 1994.

"Performing the Passions in Commercial Society: Bernard Mandeville and the Theatricality of Eighteenth-Century Thought." In *Refiguring Revolutions: British Politics and Aesthetics, 1642–1789*, ed. K. Sharpe and S. N. Zwicker. Berkeley and Los Angeles: University of California Press. 1998. Pp. 141–72.

"A Satire of Self-Disclosure: From Hegel through Rameau to the Augustans." *Journal of the History of Ideas* 47 (1986): 235–48.

Hundert, E. J., and P. Nelles. "Liberty and Theatrical Space in Montesquieu's Political Theory." *Political Theory* 17 (1989): 223–46.

Hutcheson, F. *An Essay on the Nature and Conduct of the Passions and Affections with Illustrations on the Moral Sense.* Gainesville, Fla.: Scholars' Facsimiles and Reprints, 1969. Facsimile of the third edition (1742), with an introduction by P. McReynolds.

*A System of Moral Philosophy.* 1755. Rpt. New York: Kelley, 1968.

Huxley, T. H., and J. Huxley. *Evolution and Ethics, 1893–1943.* London: Pilot, 1947.

Ignatieff, M. "Smith and Rousseau." In Ignatieff, *The Needs of Strangers.* New York: Viking Penguin, 1985. Pp. 105–31.

Jefferson, T. *Thomas Jefferson: Writings.* Ed. M. D. Peterson. New York: Viking [Library of America], 1984.

Jones, C. "Adam Smith's Library – Some Additions." *Economic History* 4 (1940): 326–8.

Jones, H. *The Epicurean Tradition.* London: Routledge, 1989.

Johnson, M. *Moral Imagination.* Chicago: University of Chicago Press, 1993.

Johnston, M. See Smith, M.

Justman, S. *The Autonomous Male of Adam Smith.* Norman: University of Oklahoma Press, 1993.

Kant, I. *Critique of Practical Reason.* Trans. L. W. Beck, 3rd ed. New York: Macmillan 1993.

*Critique of Pure Reason.* Trans. N. K. Smith. New York: St. Martin's, 1965.

*Grounding for the Metaphysics of Morals.* Trans. J. W. Ellington, 3rd ed. Indianapolis: Hackett, 1993.

*On History.* Ed. L. W. Beck, trans. Beck, R. E. Anchor, and E. L. Fackenheim. Indianapolis: Bobbs-Merrill, 1963.

Kittsteiner, H.-D. *Naturabsicht und unsichtbare Hand: Zur Kritik des geschichtsphilosophischen Denkens.* Frankfurt: Ullstein, 1980.

Kleer, R. A. "Final Causes in Adam Smith's *Theory of Moral Sentiments.*" *Journal of the History of Philosophy* 33 (1995): 275–300.

Knight, F. H. *The Ethics of Competition and Other Essays.* 1935. Rpt. Freeport, N.Y.: Books for Libraries, 1969.

Kosman, L. A. "The Naive Narrator: Meditation in Descartes' *Meditations.*" In *Essays on Descartes' Meditations,* ed. A. O. Rorty. Berkeley and Los Angeles: University of California Press, 1986. Pp. 21–43.

Kruschwitz, R. B., and R. C. Roberts, eds. *The Virtues: Contemporary Essays on Moral Character.* Belmont: Wadsworth, 1987.

Lacey, M., and K. Haakonssen, eds. *A Culture of Rights: The Bill of Rights in Philosophy, Politics, and Law – 1791–1991.* Cambridge: Cambridge University Press, 1991.

Lachterman, D. R. *The Ethics of Geometry: A Genealogy of Modernity.* New York: Routledge, 1989.

"The Ontology of Production in Marx: The Paradox of Labor and the Enigma of Praxis." *Graduate Faculty Philosophy Journal* 19 (1996): 3–23.

Lamb, R. B. "Adam Smith's Concept of Alienation." *Oxford Economic Papers* 25 (1973): 275–85.

"Adam Smith's System: Sympathy Not Self-Interest." *Journal of the History of Ideas* 35 (1974): 671–82.

Lang, B. "Descartes between Method and Style." In Lang, *The Anatomy of Philosophical Style.* Oxford: Blackwell Publisher, 1990. Pp. 45–85.

Larmore, C. E. *The Morals of Modernity.* Cambridge: Cambridge University Press, 1996.

*Patterns of Moral Complexity.* Cambridge: Cambridge University Press, 1987.

Lasch, C. *The True and Only Heaven: Progress and Its Critics.* New York: Norton, 1991.

Leacock, S. "What Is Left of Adam Smith?" *Canadian Journal of Economics and Political Science* 1 (1935): 41–51.

Lear, J. *Aristotle: The Desire to Understand.* Cambridge: Cambridge University Press, 1988.

"The Disappearing 'We.'" *Proceedings of the Aristotelian Society,* suppl. vol. 58 (1984): 219–42.

Leathers, C. G., and J. P. Raines. "Adam Smith on Competitive Religious Markets." *History of Political Economy* 24 (1992): 499–513.

Lee, A. *An Essay in Vindication of the Continental Colonies of America, from A Censure of Mr. Adam Smith, in his Theory of Moral Sentiments; with some Reflections on Slavery in general.* London: 1764.

Lefebvre, H. *Introduction à la Modernité.* Paris: Minuit, 1962.

Levy, D. "Adam Smith's 'Natural Law' and Contractual Society." *Journal of the History of Ideas* 39 (1978): 665–74.

*The Economic Ideas of Ordinary People: From Preferences to Trade.* New York: Routledge, 1992.

"The Partial Spectator Theory in the *Wealth of Nations*: A Robust Utilitarianism." *European Journal of the History of Economic Thought* 2 (1995): 229–326.

Lewis, D. See Smith, M.

Lewis, T. J. "Adam Smith: The Labor Market as the Basis of Natural Right." *Journal of Economic Issues* 11 (1977): 21–50.

Lightwood, M. B. *A Selected Bibliography of Significant Works about Adam Smith.* Philadelphia: University of Pennsylvania Press, 1984.

Lindgren, J. R. "Adam Smith's Theory of Inquiry." *Journal of Political Economy* 77 (1969): 897–915.

*The Social Philosophy of Adam Smith.* The Hague: Nijhoff, 1973.

Locke, J. *An Essay Concerning Human Understanding.* 1690. Ed. P. H. Nidditch. Oxford: Clarendon, 1990.

*A Letter Concerning Toleration.* 1689. Ed. P. Romanell. Indianapolis: Bobbs-Merrill, 1985.

*The Reasonableness of Christianity.* 1695. Ed. I. T. Ramsey. Stanford: Stanford University Press, 1958.

Long, A. A. "Aristotle and the History of Greek Scepticism." In *Studies in Aristotle,* ed. D. J. O'Meara. Washington, D.C.: Catholic University of America Press, 1981. Pp. 79–106.

Lovibond, S. *Realism and Imagination in Ethics.* Minneapolis: University of Minnesota Press, 1983.

Löwith, K. *Nature, History, and Existentialism.* Ed. A. Levison. Evanston, Ill.: Northwestern University Press, 1966.

Lucretius. *De rerum natura.* Ed. and trans. C. Bailey. 3 vols. Oxford: Clarendon Press, 1947.

Lyotard, J.-F. *The Postmodern Condition: A Report on Knowledge.* Trans. G. Bennington and B. Massumi. Minneapolis: University of Minnesota Press, 1984.

Mabbott, J. D. "Reason and Desire." *Philosophy* 28 (1953): 113–23.

Macfie, A. L. "Adam Smith's *Moral Sentiments* as Foundation for his *Wealth of Nations.*" *Oxford Economic Papers* 2 (1959): 209–28.

*The Individual in Society.* London: George Allen & Unwin, 1967.

"The Scottish Tradition in Economic Thought." *Scottish Journal of Political Economy* 2 (1955): 81–103.

MacIntyre, A. *After Virtue: A Study in Moral Theory.* 2nd ed. Notre Dame, Ind.: University of Notre Dame Press, 1984.

*Three Rival Versions of Moral Enquiry: Encyclopaedia, Genealogy, and Tradition.* Notre Dame, Ind.: University of Notre Dame Press, 1990.

*Whose Justice? Which Rationality?* Notre Dame, Ind.: University of Notre Dame Press, 1988.

Mackie, J. L. *Ethics: Inventing Right and Wrong.* London: Penguin, 1977.

Makkreel, R. A. "How Is Empathy Related to Understanding?" In *Issues in Husserl's Ideas II,* ed. T. Nenon and L. Embree. Dordrecht: Kluwer, 1996. Pp. 199–212.

Marcus Aurelius. *The Meditations of the Emperor Marcus Aurelius Antoninus. Newly translated from the Greek: with Notes, and an Account of his Life.* [Trans. by F. Hutcheson and J. Moor.] Glasgow: R. Foulis, 1742.

Marshall, D. *The Figure of Theater: Shaftesbury, Defoe, Adam Smith, and George Eliot.* New York: Columbia University Press, 1986.

*The Surprising Effects of Sympathy: Marivaux, Diderot, Rousseau, and Mary Shelley.* Chicago: The University of Chicago Press, 1988.

Martin, M. A. "Utility and Morality: Adam Smith's Critique of Hume." *Hume Studies* 16 (1990): 107–20.

Marx, K. *Karl Marx: Early Writings.* Ed. and trans. T. B. Bottomore. New York: McGraw-Hill, 1964.

McCloskey, D. *The Rhetoric of Economics.* Madison: University of Wisconsin Press, 1985.

McDowell, J. "Aesthetic Value, Objectivity, and the Fabric of the World." In *Pleasure, Preference and Value: Studies in Philosophical Aesthetics,* ed. E. Schaper. Cambridge: Cambridge University Press, 1983. Pp. 1–16.

*Mind and World.* Cambridge, Mass.: Harvard University Press, 1994.

"Virtue and Reason." In *Anti-theory in Ethics and Moral Conservatism,* ed. S. G. Clark and E. Simpson. New York: State University of New York Press, 1989. Pp. 87–109.

Meek, R. L. *Economics and Ideology and Other Essays: Studies in the Development of Economic Thought.* London: Chapman & Hall, 1967.

*Smith, Marx, and After: Ten Essays in the Development of Economic Thought.* London: Chapman & Hall, 1977.

Meek, R. L., and A. S. Skinner. "The Development of Adam Smith's Ideas on the Division of Labour." *Economic Journal* 83 (1973): 1094–1116.

Megill, A. D. "Theory and Experience in Adam Smith." *Journal of the History of Ideas* 36 (1975): 79–94.

Meikle, H. W. *Scotland and the French Revolution.* 1912. Rpt. New York: Kelley, 1969.

Mercer, P. *Sympathy and Ethics: A Study of the Relationship between Sympathy and Morality with Special Reference to Hume's "Treatise."* Oxford: Clarendon Press, 1972.

Mercier-Josa, S. "Après Aristote et Adam Smith que dit Hegel de L'agir?" *Études Philosophiques* 3 (1976): 331–50.

Mill, J. S. "Nature." In *John Stuart Mill: Nature and Utility of Religion,* ed. G. Nakhnikian. Indianapolis: Bobbs-Merrill, 1958. Pp. 3–44.

Millar, J. *The Origin of the Distinction of Ranks.* 4th ed. Edinburgh: W. Blackwood, 1806.

Miller, F. D., Jr., and J. Paul. "Communitarian and Liberal Theories of the Good." *Review of Metaphysics* 43 (1990): 803–30.

Miller, R. D. *An Interpretation of Adam Smith's "Theory of Moral Sentiments."* Harrogate, UK: Duchy, 1990.

Minowitz, P. *Profits, Priests, and Princes: Adam Smith's Emancipation of Economics from Politics and Religion.* Stanford: Stanford University Press, 1993.

Mizuta, H. *Adam Smith's Library: A Supplement to Bonar's Catalogue.* Cambridge: Cambridge University Press for Royal Economic Society, 1967.

"Moral Philosophy and Civil Society." In *Essays on Adam Smith,* ed. A. S. Skinner and T. Wilson. Oxford: Clarendon Press, 1975. Pp. 114–31.

Mizuta, H., and C. Sugiyama, eds. *Adam Smith: International Perspectives.* New York: St. Martin's, 1993.

Moor, J. *An Essay on the End of Tragedy According to Aristotle.* Glasgow: A. Foulis, 1794. *Essays, Read to a Literary Society at Their Weekly Meetings within the College at Glasgow.* 1759. Rpt. New York: Garland, 1971.

Morrow, G. R. *The Ethical and Economic Theories of Adam Smith.* 1923. Rpt. New York: Kelley, 1969.

"The Ethics of the *Wealth of Nations.*" *Philosophical Review* 34 (1925): 599–611.

"The Significance of the Doctrine of Sympathy in Hume and Adam Smith." *Philosophical Review* 32 (1923): 60–78.

Mossner, E. C. *Adam Smith: The Biographical Approach.* Glasgow: George Outram, 1969.

Muller, J. Z. *Adam Smith in His Time and Ours.* Princeton: Princeton University Press, 1993.

Musgrave, R. A. "Adam Smith on Public Finance and Distribution." In *The Market and the State: Essays in Honour of Adam Smith,* ed. T. Wilson and A. S. Skinner. Oxford: Clarendon Press, 1976. Pp. 296–329.

Myers, M. L. "Adam Smith as Critic of Ideas." *Journal of the History of Ideas* 36 (1975): 281–96.

Nagel, T. "Moral Conflict and Political Legitimacy." *Philosophy and Public Affairs* 16 (1987): 215–40.

*Mortal Questions.* Cambridge: Cambridge University Press, 1988.

*The View from Nowhere.* Oxford: Oxford University Press, 1986.

Nehamas, A. *Nietzsche: Life as Literature.* Cambridge, Mass.: Harvard University Press, 1985.

Nieli, R. "Spheres of Intimacy and the Adam Smith Problem." *Journal of the History of Ideas* 47 (1986): 611–24.

Nietzsche, F. *Beyond Good and Evil.* Trans. W. Kaufmann. New York: Vintage, 1966.

*The Gay Science.* Trans. W. Kaufmann. New York: Random House, 1974.

"History in the Service and Disservice of Life." Trans. G. Brown. In *Unmodern Observations,* ed. W. Arrowsmith. New Haven: Yale University Press, 1990. Pp. 73–145.

Norton, D. F. *David Hume: Common-Sense Moralist, Sceptical Metaphysician.* Princeton: Princeton University Press, 1982.

"How a Sceptic May Live Scepticism." In *Faith, Scepticism, and Personal Identity,* ed. J. J. MacIntosh and H. A. Meynell. Calgary: University of Calgary Press, 1994. Pp. 119–39.

Nozick, R. *Anarchy, State, and Utopia.* New York: Basic Books, 1968.

Nussbaum, M. "Compassion: The Basic Social Emotion." *Social Philosophy and Policy* 13 (1996): 27–58.

" 'Finely Aware and Richly Responsible': Literature and the Moral Imagination." In *Literature and the Question of Philosophy,* ed. A. J. Cascardi. Baltimore: Johns Hopkins University Press, 1987. Pp. 167–91.

*The Fragility of Goodness.* Cambridge: Cambridge University Press, 1986.

*Love's Knowledge: Essays on Philosophy and Literature.* Oxford: Oxford University Press, 1990.

*Poetic Justice: The Literary Imagination and Public Life.* Boston: Beacon, 1995.

O'Connor, D. K. "Aristotelian Justice as a Personal Virtue." In *Ethical Theory: Character and Virtue,* ed. P. A. French, T. E. Uehling, and H. K. Wettstein. Midwest Studies in Philosophy, no. 13. Notre Dame, Ind.: University of Notre Dame Press, 1988. Pp. 417–27.

O'Driscoll, G. P., Jr., ed. *Adam Smith and Modern Political Economy: Bicentennial Essays on "The Wealth of Nations."* Ames: Iowa State University Press, 1979.

O'Neill, O. "Duties and Virtues." In *Ethics,* ed. A. P. Griffiths. Royal Institute of Philosophy Supplements, no. 35. Cambridge: Cambridge University Press, 1993. Pp. 107–20.

Oneken, A. "The Consistency of Adam Smith." In *Adam Smith: Critical Assessments,* ed. J. C. Wood, vol. 1. London: Croon Helm, 1984. Pp. 1–6.

Oswald, D. J. "Metaphysical Beliefs and the Foundations of Smithian Political Economy." *History of Political Economy* 27 (1995): 449–76.

Pack, S. J. "Adam Smith on the Limits to Human Reason." In *Selected Papers from the History of Economics Thought Conference, 1991,* ed. R. F. Hébert, vol. 9 of *Perspectives on the History of Economic Thought.* Hants, UK: Elgar, 1993. Pp. 53–62.

"Adam Smith's Unnaturally Natural (yet Naturally Unnatural) Use of the Word 'Natura.' " In *The Classical Tradition in Economic Thought,* ed. I. H. Rima, vol. 11 of *Perspectives on the History of Economic Thought.* Hants, UK: Elgar, 1995. Pp. 31–42.

"Theological (and Hence Economic) Implications of Adam Smith's 'Principles which Lead and Direct Philosophical Enquiries.' " *History of Political Economy* 27 (1995): 27–307.

Pakaluk, M., ed. *Other Selves: Philosophers on Friendship.* Indianapolis: Hackett, 1991.

Palyi, M. "The Introduction of Adam Smith on the Continent." In J. M. Clark et al., *Adam Smith, 1776–1926*. 1928. Rpt. New York: Kelley, 1966. Pp. 180–233.

Parker, H. T. *The Cult of Antiquity and the French Revolutionaries.* New York: Octagon, 1965.

Paul, E. F. "Adam Smith: The Greater Founder." In Paul, *Moral Revolution and Economic Science.* Westport, Conn.: Greenwood, 1979. Pp. 9–44.

Peacock, A. "The Treatment of the Principles of Public Finance in the "Wealth of Nations." In *Essays on Adam Smith*, ed. A. S. Skinner and T. Wilson. Oxford: Clarendon Press, 1975. Pp. 553–67.

Petrella, F. "Individual, Group, or Government? Smith, Mill, and Sidgwick." *History of Political Economy* 1–2 (1969–70): 152–76.

Pike, E. R. *Adam Smith.* London: Weidenfeld & Nicolson, 1965.

Pincoffs, E. L. *Quandaries and Virtues: Against Reductivism in Ethics.* Lawrence: University Press of Kansas, 1986.

Pinkard, T. *Hegel's Phenomenology: The Sociality of Reason.* Cambridge: Cambridge University Press, 1996.

Piper, A. M. S. "Impartiality, Compassion and Modal Imagination." *Ethics* 101 (1991): 726–57.

Pippin, R. "Hegel's Ethical Rationalism." In Pippin, *Idealism as Modernism.* Cambridge: Cambridge University Press, 1997. Pp. 417–450.

*Modernism as a Philosophical Problem.* Oxford: Blackwell, 1991.

Plato, *Laws.* Trans. T. Pangle. New York: Basic Books, 1980.

*Republic.* Trans. A. Bloom. New York: Basic Books, 1968.

*Symposium.* Trans. A. Nehamas and P. Woodruff. Indianapolis: Hackett, 1989.

Pocock, J. G. A. "Cambridge Paradigms and Scotch Philosophers: A Study of the Relations between the Civic Humanist and the Civil Jurisprudential Interpretation of Eighteenth-Century Social Thought." In *Wealth and Virtue: The Shaping of Political Economy in the Scottish Enlightenment*, ed. I. Hont and M. Ignatieff. Cambridge: Cambridge University Press, 1985. Pp. 235–52.

Pope, A. *Essay on Man.* 1733–4. Ed. F. Brady. Indianapolis: Bobbs-Merrill, 1981.

Popkin, R. *The History of Scepticism from Erasmus to Spinoza.* Berkeley and Los Angeles: University of California Press, 1979.

Postow, B. C. "Ethical Relativism and the Ideal Observer." *Philosophy and Phenomenology Research* 12 (1978): 120–1.

Price, L. L. "Adam Smith and His Relations to Recent Economics." In *Adam Smith: Critical Assessments*, ed. J. C. Wood, vol. 2. London: Croon Helm, 1984. Pp. 9–19.

Prichard, H. A. "Does Moral Philosophy Rest on a Mistake?" In Prichard, *Moral Obligation and Duty and Interest.* Oxford: Oxford University Press, 1968. Pp. 1–17.

Prince, M. *Philosophical Dialogue in the British Enlightenment: Theology, Aesthetics, and the Novel.* Cambridge: Cambridge University Press, 1996.

Prior, A. N. *Logic and the Basis of Ethics.* Oxford: Clarendon Press, 1949.

Putnam, R. A. "Reciprocity and Virtue Ethics." *Ethics* 98 (1988): 379–89.

Quinton, A., ed. *Political Philosophy.* Oxford: Oxford University Press, 1967.

Rae, J. *Life of Adam Smith.* Bristol, UK: Thoemmes, 1990.

Raphael, D. D. *Adam Smith.* Oxford: Oxford University Press, 1985.
"Hume and Adam Smith on Justice and Utility." *Proceedings of the Aristotelian Society* 73 (1973): 87–103.
"The Impartial Spectator." In *Essays on Adam Smith,* ed. A. S. Skinner and T. Wilson. Oxford: Clarendon Press, 1975. Pp. 83–99.
*The Moral Sense.* Oxford: Clarendon Press, 1947.
" 'The True Old Humean Philosophy' and Its Influence on Adam Smith." In *David Hume: Bicentenary Papers,* ed. G. P. Morice. Edinburgh: Edinburgh University Press, 1977. Pp. 23–38.
Raphael, D. D., ed. *British Moralists, 1650–1800.* 2 vols. Oxford: Clarendon Press, 1969.
Raphael, D. D., and T. Sakamoto. "Anonymous Writings of David Hume." *Journal of the History of Philosophy* 28 (1990): 271–81.
Rashid, S. "Adam Smith's Rise to Fame: A Reexamination of the Evidence." *Eighteenth Century: Theory and Interpretation* 23 (1982): 64–85.
Rawls, J. *Political Liberalism.* New York: Columbia University Press, 1993.
*A Theory of Justice.* Cambridge, Mass.: Harvard University Press, 1980.
Raynor, D. "Hume's Abstract of Adam Smith's *Theory of Moral Sentiments.*" *Journal of the History of Philosophy* 22 (1984): 51–79.
Recktenwald, H. *Ordnungstheorie und Ökonomische Wissenschaft: Drei Beiträge.* Erlangen: Universitätsbund Erlangen-Nürnberg, 1985.
Reid, T. *Essays on the Active Powers of Man.* 1788. Rpt. New York: Garland, 1977.
Rorty, R. *Contingency, Irony, and Solidarity.* Cambridge: Cambridge University Press, 1989.
Rorty, R., J. B. Schneewind, and Q. Skinner, eds. *Philosophy in History.* Cambridge: Cambridge University Press, 1990.
Rosen, S. *Hermeneutics as Politics.* Oxford: Oxford University Press, 1987.
Rosenberg, N. "Adam Smith and the Stock of Moral Capital." *History of Political Economy* 22 (1990): 1–17.
"Adam Smith on the Division of Labour: Two Views or One?" *Economica* 32 (1965): 127–39.
"Some Institutional Aspects of the *Wealth of Nations.*" *Journal of Political Economy* 68 (1960): 361–74.
Ross, I. "Adam Smith as Rhetorician." In *Man and Nature,* ed. R. L. Emerson, W. Kinsley, and W. Moser. Proceedings of the Canadian Society for Eighteenth-Century Studies, vol. 2. Montreal: The Canadian Society for Eighteenth-Century Studies, 1984. Pp. 61–74.
*The Life of Adam Smith.* Oxford: Clarendon Press, 1995.
Rousseau, J.-J. *The Reveries of the Solitary Walker.* Trans. C. Butterworth. New York: New York University Press, 1979.
*Rousseau: "The Discourses" and Other Early Political Writings.* Trans. V. Gourevitch. Cambridge: Cambridge University Press, 1997.
Rutherford, R. B. *The Meditations of Marcus Aurelius: A Study.* Oxford: Clarendon Press, 1989.
Salkever, S. *Finding the Mean: Theory and Practice in Aristotelian Political Philosophy.* Princeton: Princeton University Press, 1990.

Samuels, W. J. "Adam Smith and the Economy as a System of Power." *Review of Social Economy* 31 (1973): 123–37.

"The Political Economy of Adam Smith." *Ethics* 87 (1977): 189–207.

Scheler, M. F. *The Nature of Sympathy.* Trans. P. Heath. New Haven: Yale University Press, 1954.

Schmidt, J., ed. *What Is Enlightenment? Eighteenth-Century Answers and Twentieth-Century Questions.* Berkeley and Los Angeles: University of California Press, 1996.

Schmitt, C. B. "The Rediscovery of Ancient Skepticism in Modern Times." In *The Skeptical Tradition,* ed. M. Burnyeat. Berkeley and Los Angeles: University of California Press, 1983. Pp. 225–51.

Schneewind, J. B. "The Misfortunes of Virtue." *Ethics* 101 (1991): 42–63.

"Modern Moral Philosophy: From Beginning to End?" In *Philosophical Imagination and Cultural Memory,* ed. P. Cook. Durham, N.C.: Duke University Press, 1993. Pp. 83–103.

"Natural Law, Skepticism, and Methods of Ethics." *Journal of the History of Ideas* 52 (1991): 289–308.

Schneider, H. W. *Adam Smith's Moral and Political Philosophy.* New York: Hafner, 1948.

Schofield, M. *The Stoic Idea of the City.* Cambridge: Cambridge University Press, 1991.

Scott, W. R. *Adam Smith as Student and Professor.* 1937. Rpt. New York: Kelley, 1965.

Scruton, R. "Emotion, Practical Knowledge, and Common Culture." In *Explaining Emotions,* ed. A. O. Rorty. Berkeley and Los Angeles: University of California Press, 1980. Pp. 519–36.

Sen, A. "Adam Smith's Prudence." In *Theory and Reality in Development: Essays in Honour of Paul Streeten,* ed. S. Lall and F. Stewart. New York: St. Martin's, 1986. Pp. 28–37.

*Sextus Empiricus.* Trans. R. G. Bury. 4 vols. Cambridge, Mass.: Harvard University Press, 1968–83.

Shaftesbury, 3rd Earl of (Anthony Ashley Cooper). *Characteristics of Men, Manners, Opinions, Times, Etc.* 1714. 2 vols. Ed. J. M. Robertson. Bristol, UK: Thoemmes, 1995.

Shapiro, M. J. *Reading "Adam Smith": Desire, History, and Value.* Newbury Park, Calif.: Sage, 1993.

Shearmur, J. "Adam Smith's Second Thoughts: Economic Liberalism and its Unintended Consequences." In *Adam Smith,* ed. K. Haakonssen. Aldershot, UK: Dartmouth, in press.

Sher, R. B. *Church and University in the Scottish Enlightenment.* Princeton: Princeton University Press, 1985.

Sher, R. B., and J. R. Smitten, eds. *Scotland and America in the Age of the Enlightenment.* Edinburgh: Edinburgh University Press, 1990.

Sherman, N. *The Fabric of Character: Aristotle's Theory of Virtue.* Oxford: Clarendon Press, 1989.

Sidgwick, H. *The Methods of Ethics.* 7th ed. Indianapolis: Hackett, 1981.

Silver, A. " 'Two Different Sorts of Commerce': Friendship and Strangership in Civil Society." In *Public and Private in Thought and Practice,* ed. J. Weintraub and K. Kumar. Chicago: University of Chicago Press, 1997. Pp. 43–74.

Simpson, P. "Contemporary Virtue Ethics and Aristotle." *Review of Metaphysics* 45 (1992): 503–24.

Skinner, A. S. "Adam Smith: Rhetoric and the Communication of Ideas." In *Methodological Controversy in Economics: Historical Essays in Honor of T. W. Hutchison*, ed. A. W. Coats. Greenwich, Conn.: Jai, 1983. Pp. 71–88.

*Adam Smith and the Role of the State.* Glasgow: University of Glasgow Press, 1974.

"Science and the Role of the Imagination." In Skinner, *A System of Social Science: Papers Relating to Adam Smith.* Pp. 14–41.

"The Shaping of Political Economy in the Enlightenment." *Scottish Journal of Political Economy* 37 (1990): 145–65.

*A System of Social Science: Papers Relating to Adam Smith.* Oxford: Clarendon Press, 1979.

Skinner, A. S., and P. Jones, eds. *Adam Smith Reviewed.* Edinburgh: Edinburgh University Press, 1992.

Skinner, A. S., and T. Wilson, eds. *Essays on Adam Smith.* Oxford: Clarendon Press, 1975.

Skinner, Q. *Reason and Rhetoric in the Philosophy of Hobbes.* Cambridge: Cambridge University Press, 1996.

Smith, M. "Dispositional Theories of Value." In *Proceedings of the Aristotelian Society*, suppl. vol. 61 (1989): 89–111. See also the further discussion of the same topic by D. Lewis and M. Johnston in the same journal. Pp. 113–37 and 139–73.

Smith, S. G. "The Ideal Observer." In Smith, *The Concept of the Spiritual: An Essay in First Philosophy.* Philadelphia: Temple University Press, 1988. Pp. 217–21.

Sobel, I. "Adam Smith: What Kind of Institutionalist Was He?" *Journal of Economic Issues* 13 (1979): 347–68.

Spence, P. "Sympathy and Propriety in Adam Smith's Rhetoric." *Quarterly Journal of Speech* 60 (1974): 92–9.

Spengler, J. J. "Smith versus Hobbes: Economy versus Polity." In *Adam Smith and the Wealth of Nations: 1776–1976, Bicentennial Essays*, ed. F. R. Glahe. Boulder: Colorado Associated University Press, 1978. Pp. 35–59.

Stack, G. J. "Self-Interest and Social Value." *Journal of Value Inquiry* 18 (1984): 123–37.

Stein, E. *On the Problem of Empathy.* Trans. W. Stein. The Hague: Nijhoff, 1964.

Stein, P. "Adam Smith's Jurisprudence: Between Morality and Economics." *Cornell Law Review* 64 (1979): 621–38.

Steuart, J. *An Inquiry into the Principles of Political Oeconomy*, 2 vols. Ed. A. S. Skinner. Chicago: University of Chicago Press, 1966.

Stevens, W. *Collected Poems.* New York: Knopf, 1989.

Stewart, D. *Biographical Memoirs of Adam Smith, William Robertson, Thomas Reid*, ed. W. Hamilton. 1858. Rpt. New York: Kelley, 1966.

"Of the Speculation Concerning Final Causes." 1814. Rpt. in *The Scottish Moralists: On Human Nature and Society*, ed. L. Schneider. Chicago: University of Chicago Press, 1967. Pp. 143–65.

Stewart, M. A. "The Stoic Legacy in the Early Scottish Enlightenment." In *Atoms, Pneuma, and Tranquillity: Epicurean and Stoic Themes in European Thought*, ed. M. J. Osler. Cambridge: Cambridge University Press, 1991. Pp. 273–96.

Stewart-Robertson, J. C., and D. F. Norton. "Thomas Reid on Adam Smith's Theory of Morals." *Journal of the History of Ideas* 41 (1980): 381–98.
"Thomas Reid on Adam Smith's Theory of Morals." *Journal of the History of Ideas* 45 (1984): 309–21.
Stocker, M. "The Schizophrenia of Modern Ethical Theories." *Journal of Philosophy* 73 (1976): 453–466.
Stokes, A. P., and L. Pfeffer. *Church and State in the United States.* New York: Harper & Row, 1950.
Strauss, L. *Philosophy and Law: Contributions to the Understanding of Maimonides and His Predecessors.* Trans. E. Adler. Albany: State University of New York Press, 1985.
"The Three Waves of Modernity." In *Political Philosophy: Six Essays by Leo Strauss,* ed. H. Gildin. Indianapolis: Bobbs Merrill, 1975. Pp. 81–98.
Streminger, G. *Adam Smith: Mit Selbstzeugnissen und Bilddokumenten.* Reinbek: Rowohlt, 1989.
"Hume's Theory of Imagination." *Hume Studies* 6 (1980): 91–118.
Stroumsa, G. G. "Le radicalisme religieux du premier christianisme: Contexte et implications." In *Les retours aux Ecritures: Fondamentalismes présents et passés,* ed. E. Patlagean and A. Le Boulluec. Louvain: Peeters, 1993. Pp. 357–82.
Swingewood, A. "Origins of Sociology: The Case of the Scottish Enlightenment." *British Journal of Sociology* 21 (1970): 164–80.
Sypher, W. "Hutcheson and the 'Classical' Theory of Slavery." *Journal of Negro History* 24 (1939): 263–80.
Taylor, C. *The Ethics of Authenticity.* Cambridge, Mass.: Harvard University Press, 1991.
*Sources of the Self: The Making of the Modern Identity.* Cambridge, Mass.: Harvard University Press, 1989.
Taylor, W. L. *Francis Hutcheson and David Hume as Predecessors of Adam Smith.* Durham, N.C.: Duke University Press, 1965.
Teichgraeber, R. F., III. *"Free Trade" and Moral Philosophy: Rethinking the Sources of Adam Smith's "Wealth of Nations."* Durham, N.C.: Duke University Press, 1986.
"Rethinking das Adam Smith Problem." *Journal of British Studies* 20 (1981): 106–23.
Thal, P., V. S. Afanasev, A. V. Anikin. *Adam Smith Gestern und Heute: 200 Jahre "Reichtum der Nationen."* Berlin: Akademie, 1976.
Theophrastus. *The Characters of Theophrastus.* Ed. J. E. Sandys, trans. R. C. Jebb. Salem: Ayer, 1992.
Thoreau, H. D. *The Portable Thoreau.* Ed. C. Bode. New York: Penguin, 1981.
Trapp, M. *Adam Smith – Politische Philosophie und politische Ökonomie.* Göttingen: Vandenhoeck & Ruprecht, 1987.
Trilling, L. *Sincerity and Authenticity.* Cambridge, Mass.: Harvard University Press, 1971.
Tucker, S. I. *Enthusiasm: A Study in Semantic Change.* Cambridge: Cambridge University Press, 1972.
Vetlesen, A. J. *Perception, Empathy, and Judgment: An Inquiry into the Preconditions of Moral Performance.* University Park: Pennsylvania State University Press, 1994.
Viner, J. s.v. "Adam Smith." *International Encyclopedia of the Social Sciences,* ed. D. L. Sills. Vol. 14. New York: Macmillan Free Press, 1968.

"Adam Smith and Laissez Faire." In J. M. Clark et al., *Adam Smith, 1776–1926*. 1928. Rpt. New York: Kelley, 1966. Pp. 116–55.

*The Role of Providence in the Social Order*. Princeton: Princeton University Press, 1972.

Vivenza, G. "Adam Smith e la fisica antica." *Economia e Storia* 1 (1982): 65–72.

*La presenza della tradizione classica nell'opera di Adam Smith*. In *Aspetti della formazione culturale di Adam Smith*. Verona: Università degli Studi di Padova, 1980.

"Platone e Adam Smith sulla divisione del lavoro." *Studi in Onore di Gino Barbieri* 3 (1983): 1573–95.

Voltaire. *Philosophical Letters*. Trans. E. Dilworth. New York: Macmillan, 1961.

Warnock, M. *Imagination*. London: Faber & Faber, 1976.

Waszek, N. "Bibliography of the Scottish Enlightenment in Germany." *Studies on Voltaire and the Eighteenth Century* 230 (1985): 283–303.

"The Division of Labor: From the Scottish Enlightenment to Hegel." *Owl of Minerva* 15 (1983): 51–75.

*Man's Social Nature: A Topic of the Scottish Enlightenment in its Historical Setting*. 2nd ed. Frankfurt: Lang, 1988.

"Miscellanea: Adam Smith and Hegel on the Pin Factory." *Owl of Minerva* 16 (1985): 229–33.

*The Scottish Enlightenment and Hegel's Account of "Civil Society."* Dordrecht: Kluwer, 1988.

"Two Concepts of Morality: A Distinction of Adam Smith's Ethics and Its Stoic Origin." *Journal of the History of Ideas* 45 (1984): 591–606.

Weber, M. *The Protestant Ethic and the Spirit of Capitalism*. New York: Scribners, 1958.

Wenley, R. M. *Stoicism and Its Influence*. Boston: Marshall Jones, 1924.

Werhane, P. H. *Adam Smith and His Legacy for Modern Capitalism*. Oxford: Oxford University Press, 1991.

West, E. G. *Adam Smith*. Indianapolis: Liberty, 1976.

"Adam Smith and Alienation: Wealth Increases, Men Decay?" In *Essays on Adam Smith*, ed. A. S. Skinner and T. Wilson. Oxford: Clarendon Press, 1975. Pp. 540–51.

"Adam Smith's Philosophy of Riches." In *Philosophy* 44 (1969): 101–15.

Westermarck, E. *Ethical Relativity*. New York: Harcourt, Brace, 1932.

Wiggins, D. "Truth, Invention, and the Meaning of Life." In Wiggins, *Needs, Values, Truth: Essays in the Philosophy of Value*. Aristotelian Society Series, no. 6. Oxford: Blackwell, 1987. Pp. 87–137.

Willey, B. *The Eighteenth Century Background: Studies on the Idea of Nature in the Thought of the Period*. London: Chatto & Windus, 1940.

*The Seventeenth Century Background: Studies in the Thought of the Age in Relation to Poetry and Religion*. New York: Columbia University Press, 1950.

Williams, B. *Ethics and the Limits of Philosophy*. Cambridge, Mass.: Harvard University Press, 1985.

*Making Sense of Humanity, and Other Philosophical Papers*. Cambridge: Cambridge University Press, 1995.

*Moral Luck*. Cambridge: Cambridge University Press, 1988.

*Problems of the Self: Philosophical Papers, 1956–1972.* Cambridge: Cambridge University Press, 1973.

Wilson, J. Q. *The Moral Sense.* New York: Free Press, 1993.

Wilson, T. "Sympathy and Self-Interest." In *The Market and the State: Essays in Honour of Adam Smith,* ed. T. Wilson and A. S. Skinner. Oxford: Clarendon Press, 1976. Pp. 74–112.

Wilson, T., and A. S. Skinner. *The Market and the State: Essays in Honour of Adam Smith.* Oxford: Clarendon Press, 1976.

Winch, D. "Adam Smith: Scottish Moral Philosopher as Political Economist." *Historical Journal* 35 (1992): 91–113.

"Adam Smith's 'Enduring Particular Result': A Political and Cosmopolitan Perspective." In *Wealth and Virtue,* ed. I. Hont and M. Ignatieff. Cambridge: Cambridge University Press, 1985. Pp. 253–69.

*Adam Smith's Politics.* Cambridge: Cambridge University Press, 1978.

*Riches and Poverty: An Intellectual History of Political Economy in Britain, 1750–1834.* Cambridge: Cambridge University Press, 1996.

Wispé, L. *The Psychology of Sympathy.* New York: Plenum, 1991.

Wittgenstein, L. *Philosophical Investigations.* Trans. G. E. M. Anscombe. New York: Macmillan, 1968.

Wood, J. C., ed. *Adam Smith: Critical Assessments.* 4 vols. London: Croon Helm, 1983–4.

Woodruff, P. "Engaging Emotion in Theater: A Brechtian Model in Theater History." *Monist* 71 (1988): 235–57.

Worland, S. T. "Mechanistic Analogy and Smith on Exchange." *Review of Social Economy* 34 (1976): 245–57.

Young, J. T. "The Impartial Spectator and Natural Jurisprudence: An Interpretation of Adam Smith's Theory of the Natural Price." *History of Political Economy* 18 (1986): 365–82.

# INDEX